STUDIES IN BUSINESS CYCLES

4

INVENTORIES AND BUSINESS CYCLES

Relation of the Directors to the Work and Publications of the National Bureau of Economic Research

1. The object of the National Bureau of Economic Research is to ascertain and to present to the public important economic facts and their interpretation in a scientific and impartial manner. The Board of Directors is charged with the responsibility of ensuring that the work of the National Bureau is carried on in strict conformity with this object.

2. To this end the Board of Directors shall appoint one or more Directors of Research.

3. The Director or Directors of Research shall submit to the members of the Board, or to its Executive Committee, for their formal adoption, all specific proposals concerning researches to be instituted.

4. No report shall be published until the Director or Directors of Research shall have submitted to the Board a summary drawing attention to the character of the data and their utilization in the report, the nature and treatment of the problems involved, the main conclusions and such other information as in their opinion would serve to determine the suitability of the report for publication in accordance with the principles of the National Bureau.

5. A copy of any manuscript proposed for publication shall also be submitted to each member of the Board. For each manuscript to be so submitted a special committee shall be appointed by the President, or at his designation by the Executive Director, consisting of three Directors selected as nearly as may be one from each general division of the Board. The names of the special manuscript committee shall be stated to each Director when the summary and report described in paragraph (4) are sent to him. It shall be the duty of each member of the committee to read the manuscript. If each member of the special committee signifies his approval within thirty days, the manuscript may be published. If each member of the special committee has not signified his approval within thirty days of the transmittal of the report and manuscript, the Director of Research shall then notify each member of the Board, requesting approval or disapproval of publication, and thirty additional days shall be granted for this purpose. The manuscript shall then not be published unless at least a majority of the entire Board and a two-thirds majority of those members of the Board who shall have voted on the proposal within the time fixed for the receipt of votes on the publication proposed shall have approved.

6. No manuscript may be published, though approved by each member of the special committee, until forty-five days have elapsed from the transmittal of the summary and report. The interval is allowed for the receipt of any memorandum of dissent or reservation, together with a brief statement of his reasons, that any member may wish to express; and such memorandum of dissent or reservation shall be published with the manuscript if he so desires. Publication does not, however, imply that each member of the Board has read the manuscript, or that either members of the Board in general, or of the special committee, have passed upon its validity in every detail.

7. A copy of this resolution shall, unless otherwise determined by the Board, be printed in each copy of every National Bureau book.

(Resolution adopted October 25, 1926 and revised
February 6, 1933 and February 24, 1941)

INVENTORIES AND

BUSINESS CYCLES

with

Special Reference to Manufacturers' Inventories

MOSES ABRAMOVITZ
Professor of Economics, Stanford University

NATIONAL BUREAU OF ECONOMIC RESEARCH, INC.

To My
Mother and Father

PREFACE

THE AIM AND METHOD OF THIS BOOK need, I think, little explanation. As nearly as I could, I have tried to discover, by studying statistical records, how inventories have moved during business cycles and what influence they have had on business activity. And as far as possible, the theories about inventory movements and their influence to which the work leads are generalizations from recorded experience. Needless to say, the qualifying phrases in these sentences are important. Hypotheses and preconceptions are necessary guides to all research and inevitably leave their traces on its results. Statistical records are never wholly adequate, and this difficulty is especially serious for inventories. The validity of my conclusions will be settled only when put to the test of later experience.

Most of the book is devoted to a study of the stocks held by one important branch of industry, manufacturing. The reasons are partly that the data for other branches are less plentiful and partly that the study of manufacturers' stocks itself is so complicated. I have tried, however, to establish the typical behavior of total stocks and to show the gross similarities and differences between inventories held by manufacturing industries and other branches of the economy. Moreover, the analysis of manufacturers' stocks has yielded many suggestions that seem useful in understanding the behavior of stocks in the other branches. Finally, a substantial part of the work on cycles in the pace of inventory accumulation and liquidation is concerned with total business inventories. The general title of the book, therefore, seems justified.

This study was undertaken at the suggestion of Wesley C. Mitchell and Arthur F. Burns, and it is hardly possible to overstate what it owes to their help and to the atmosphere of free inquiry and scientific caution they have created at the National

Bureau of Economic Research. As an introduction to the subject, I had the benefit of an unpublished chapter on stocks by Professor Mitchell, a fragment of the mass of unpublished studies on business cycles which his death has left unfinished.

A number of talented assistants contributed immeasurably to the progress of the study. My principal helpers were Evelyn Firestone and, for almost the entire period of the study, Carolyn Cahn Landau. Later Judith Moss and Helmut Frank joined in the work. I owe a special debt to Fred Lynn who, with the help of David L. Rolbein, carried through most of the laborious job of revising the price indexes used to adjust inventory data in current values for changes in prices. I am very grateful also to Regina S. Sands who checked the manuscript, to Erika Teutsch who prepared the index, and to Hanna Stern who checked and improved the accuracy of the catalogue and description of statistical series in Appendix G.

The work owes a great deal also to the members of the National Bureau's division of business cycle studies. Many of the series were compiled or checked by Karl Laubenstein, Frances Goldberg, and Hanna Stern. Sophie Sakowitz and the late Denis Volkenau were mainly responsible for the computation of seasonal and cyclical measures. In this work Julius Shiskin's advice was of great importance in solving the many technical problems that arose. The numerous charts were designed and executed by H. Irving Forman with his customary clarity and skill.

Many of the original data were supplied by the U. S. Department of Commerce, and I gratefully acknowledge the help of Louis Paradiso, Frederick C. Murphy, and Irwin Friend who put the files of the Department at my disposal, gave me many unpublished figures, and patiently answered many questions about the reliability and significance of the data. The National Industrial Conference Board also kindly consented to the use of its data. I owe a debt too to George O. May and Robert D. Gracie of Price, Waterhouse and Co. for their help with accounting questions involved in the interpretation of inventory records. The members of this firm supplied answers to an extensive questionnaire concerning inventory accounting procedures in various industries.

My work was furthered at every stage by the critical attention of my colleagues on the staff of the National Bureau: Millard Hastay, Thor Hultgren, Ruth Mack, Frederick C. Mills, Geoffrey H. Moore, and R. J. Saulnier. In my absence, Mr. Moore also undertook the heavy task of guiding the manuscript through the press. I had the benefit also of useful comments from several Directors of the National Bureau, especially Percival F. Brundage, Gottfried Haberler, and Oswald Knauth. Their suggestions made possible a substantial improvement of the substance of the book. The writer—and the reader—both owe a debt to Martha Anderson. The form of the argument was bettered and its length reduced by her persistent and ingenious editing. My wife, Carrie Glasser Abramovitz, had an intimate part in it all. She worked through most of the argument with me and is responsible for much of the preparation of the final draft. My hearty thanks go to all these helpful friends.

MOSES ABRAMOVITZ

Palo Alto, California
July, 1950

CONTENTS

Part One

Theories, Materials, and Methods of Measurement

Part Two

Cyclical Behavior of Inventories

Part Three

Cyclical Behavior of Inventory Investment

Part One

Theories, Materials,
and Methods of Measurement

Chapter I

Setting and Scope

The recurring alternations of prosperity and depression we now call business cycles have been a prominent feature of capitalist economies for at least a hundred and fifty years. Systematic thought about the causes and control of economic crises goes back over a century. For perhaps fifty years business cycle research has been pursued on a large scale, as such things go. Yet even today we know relatively little about what happens during business cycles. In whatever direction speculation about the causes of cycles turns, one comes up against hard questions of fact. Do prices fluctuate more violently than wages? Do costs rise during the last stages of business expansions? Does construction activity turn down before or after business activity at large? Do consumers save a larger or smaller portion of their incomes in prosperity than in depression? The unsettled questions are innumerable, and many must be answered before a firmly founded theory of business cycles will be possible.

To find answers to some of the many questions is the aim of the National Bureau's systematic investigation of business fluctuations. By adding to the materials from which an explanation may be constructed, we hope to provide students of cycles with more comprehensive and tested information about the phenomena they are attempting to explain.

This book, a report on a portion of the larger study, examines an almost virgin territory, manufacturers' inventories.

1 Importance of Inventory Fluctuations

Students of business cycles will not demand documentation for the assertion that fluctuations in inventories, though not utterly neglected, have, until recent years, occupied only a minor place in both descriptions of business cycles and speculation about their causes. In the minds of businessmen the accumulation and liquidation of stocks have played a larger role. With some notable exceptions, however, even professional economists who stress the instability of business investment have neglected inventories. They emphasize rather fluctuations in the production of durable capital equipment and construction. Investment in inventories, though often recognized as subject to many of the influences that determine other types of investment, is usually relegated to a secondary position.

The root cause has undoubtedly been lack of knowledge about the size of inventories and of the rate at which they are built up and liquidated. Fortunately this situation is changing. The speculative inventory boom of 1920 and the events connected with the recession of 1937-38 drew the attention of economists to inventory movements and stimulated government and business to more active collection of information. At the same time the publication of Simon Kuznets' estimates of capital formation provided the first comprehensive estimates of inventories and of inventory investment.[1] With these data it is possible to establish the role of stocks in the fluctuations of capital investment and of business at large.

Table 1 presents a composite picture of the changes in total national production during the five business cycles between the two world wars and of the portion of those changes that took the form of changes in inventory investment, that is, in the rate of production of goods that were added to or removed from stock. For business expansions the underlying figures are the differences between the standings of each element of gross national product in trough years and those in succeeding peak years; the figures for contractions are the differences between peak and succeeding trough years. The changes for each full cycle are the differences between the changes during the expansions and contractions that make up each cycle measured from trough to trough. The figures in Table 1 are averages for the five expansions, contractions, and full cycles.

---

[1] These terms follow current usage in economics. 'Inventories' are the stock held by business at a given time. 'Inventory investment', the net volume of goods added to, or removed from, stock during a given period, is synonymous with net inventory accumulation.

TABLE I

Gross National Product and Its Main Components
Average Changes, 5 Business Cycles, 1919-1938

	AV. AN. VALUE, $ BILLION, 1929 PRICES	CHANGE, $ BILLION, 1929 PRICES			CHANGE AS % OF CHANGE IN GNP		
		Exp.	Contr.	Cycle	Exp.	Contr.	Cycle
	(1)	(2)	(3)	(4)	(5)	(6)	(7)
1 Gross national product	79.8	12.1	—7.2	19.3	100.0	100.0	100.0
2 Flow of goods to consumers	66.5	7.3	—1.4	8.7	60.5	19.6	45.2
a Durables	6.3	1.6	—1.4	2.9	12.9	19.1	15.2
b Nondurables	36.2	3.3	0.1	3.2	26.9	—1.4	16.3
c Services	24.0	2.5	—0.1	2.6	20.7	1.9	13.7
3 Capital formation	13.3	4.8	—5.8	10.6	39.5	80.4	54.8
a Construction	7.1	0.7	—0.8	1.5	6.1	11.0	8.0
1) Public	2.0	—0.2	0.2	—0.4	—1.5	—3.0	—2.1
2) Business	2.5	0.5	—0.6	1.1	4.1	8.8	5.9
3) Residential	2.6	0.4	—0.3	0.7	3.3	4.7	3.8
b Prod. durable equip.	5.1	1.7	—1.9	3.6	14.4	26.0	18.7
c Net change in claims against foreign countries					—4.1	—3.6	—3.9
d Net change in inventories (inventory investment)	0.50	—0.5	0.3	—0.8			
1) Total	0.56	2.8	—3.4	6.3	23.3	47.5	32.4
2) Total, excl. farmers	0.58	2.4	—3.1	5.5	20.0	42.8	28.5
3) Mfr. inventories	0.36	1.4	—1.8	3.2	11.7	24.9	16.6

Sources: All dollar figures, except line 3d(3) are derived from estimates by Simon Kuznets, *National Product since 1869* (NBER, 1946). The table numbers refer to his book. Percentage figures are derived from estimates in dollars.

LINE

1	Table I-15
2 and 2a-c	Table I-5
3a(1)-(3)	Table I-8
3b	Table I-6
3c and d	Table I-11

Net changes in manufacturers' inventories, line 3d(3), are from Kuznets' *Commodity Flow and Capital Formation* (NBER, 1938), revised and extended by me. Differences between these figures and those included by Kuznets in the total, line 3d(1) are not substantial. For a description of the estimates underlying line 3d(3), see App. A of this volume.

Method of Computation: (see also text, note 4).

COLUMN
1 Simple average of annual values in all years 1919-38
2 Difference between standings in trough years and in succeeding peak years averaged for five expansions
3 Difference between standings in peak years and in succeeding trough years averaged for five contractions
4 Difference between standings in col. 3 and in col. 2.

Col. 1, lines 3c, 3d(1)-(3) is computed to two decimal places because original data involve values below $0.5 billion which are carried to two decimal places in the source.

Because totals and subtotals are computed from rounded values for individual cycles, they do not always equal sum of components.

The trough and peak years that bound the expansions and contractions are those selected by the National Bureau as the years in which business at large reached its highest and lowest levels in successive business cycles.[2]

Inspection quickly reveals what a large part of the cyclical changes in gross national product, that is, the total output of the country, took the form of changes in the rate of accumulation and

[2] See Arthur F. Burns and Wesley C. Mitchell, *Measuring Business Cycles* (NBER, 1946), Ch. 4.

liquidation of inventories.[3] The average change in gross national product during the five expansions was about $12 billion. The corresponding average change in inventory investment was some $2.8 billion, about 23 percent as much. Excluding investment by farmers, the change was somewhat smaller. The average increase of manufacturers' inventories alone was some $1.4 billion, nearly 12 percent of the average increase in gross national product.

[3] It may be useful to note at this point the way in which inventory changes enter into national production and its changes. National product for any year equals the value of the goods that pass into the hands of consumers plus the value of the goods added to the national stock of capital, plus or minus the net change in our claims against foreign countries. Net national product, as conventionally measured, excludes the value of the output of durable goods and construction that merely replaces goods in these classes that wear out during the year. Gross national product, the measure used here, includes it. Consequently, the value of the additional goods placed in business inventories during a year (that is, the value of *inventory investment*) must be added to goods flowing to consumers in order to get total output for the year. Or if the volume of goods in inventories declines, the value of the goods removed (that is, the value of *inventory disinvestment*) must be subtracted. The change in the rate of inventory investment between any two years is simply the difference between the rate of investment in the second year and that in the first. The change in gross national product between two years is the sum of the changes in its components.

The accompanying hypothetical figures, which assume that national product has only two components, illustrate the computations.

Gross National Product and Its Components

A Value

	1900	1901	1902
1 Flow of goods to consumers	1000	1100	900
2 Net change in inventories (inventory investment)	100	200	−100
3 Gross national product	1100	1300	800

B Changes

	1900-01 (1)	1901-02 (2)	Difference (1) − (2)
1 Flow of goods to consumers	+100	−200	300
2 Net change in inventories (inventory investment)	+100	−300	400
3 Gross national product	+200	−500	700

Part B is derived by obvious means from Part A. The figures in col. 2-7 of Table 1 correspond to those in Part B of this hypothetical table. The figures for expansion in Table 1 correspond to those in the first column, those for contraction to the figures in the second column, and those for full cycles to those in the third column. The figures for net changes in inventories in Table 1 correspond to those in line 2.

During contractions changes in inventory investment constituted an even bigger part of the average change in total output.
The average decline appears to have been nearly half, 47 percent,
the average decline in gross national product. The average cyclical
decline in investment in manufacturers' inventories alone was
about one-fourth the average decline in total output.

The results of taking expansions and contractions together are,
of course, intermediate between those obtained by taking each
phase separately. The average fluctuation in total output from
trough to peak and back again was over $19 billion. About 32 per-
cent apparently took the form of changes in the rate of investment
in inventories generally; excluding farmers, the share was over 28
percent; inventory investment by manufacturers was over 16 percent.

Cyclical changes in inventory investment are not only a large
part of changes in total output; they are comparable in size with
changes in construction and in the output of producer durable
equipment, elements that have received far more attention in business cycle research. Indeed, on the face of Kuznets' estimates, fluctuations in inventory investment appear to be much larger than in
either of the other principal components of total capital formation.
The average change in total inventory investment during expansions was 23 percent of the average change in total output, in construction, 6 percent, and in producer durable goods, 14 percent. In
contractions the figures were 47 percent for inventory investment,
11 percent for construction, and 26 percent for producer durables.
Manufacturers' inventory investment alone apparently accounted
for just about as large a portion of the average cyclical change in
total output as did changes in the output of producer durables, and
for a larger portion than construction. Similar statements might be
made about the relative size of the fluctuations in inventory investment and in the production of consumer durable goods, another
component of output whose instability has attracted attention in
analyses of cycles.

These comparisons of the size of cyclical fluctuations in the various categories of output take on even more importance when considered in connection with the average flow of goods within each
category. The absolute amount by which output in a certain cate-

gory increases between depression and prosperity depends partly on its sensitivity to changes in business activity and partly on its size. The changes in the flow of nondurable goods and of services to consumers are large: the average full cycle changes were some $3.2 and $2.6 billion, respectively. But these are the largest components; their average annual value for the entire period 1919-38 were some $36 and $24 billion, respectively. In view of their average size, the fluctuations are small; these are stable categories. Producer and consumer durable goods and construction are far less stable. Their average cyclical fluctuations, $3.6, $2.9, and $1.5 billion, are to be set against average annual rates of production of only $5.1, $6.3, and $7.1 billion. By the same criteria, the cycles in inventory investment are the most violent of all. The average full cycle change was $6.3 billion for total inventory investment and $3.2 billion for manufacturers' investment. The average annual investment in all inventories, however, was no more than $560 million, and that in manufacturers' stocks only $360 million.

These estimates are, of course, crude, but they are sufficiently accurate to establish several important propositions. One is that, on the average, a very considerable portion of the cyclical changes in total output has been in the form of a change in the volume of goods added to stocks. A second is that, during ordinary business cycles,[4] fluctuations in the rate of inventory investment as a whole have been larger, in terms of the value of goods involved, than those in construction or in the flow of durable goods to either producers or consumers. And a third proposition is that inventory investment, in terms of violence of fluctuation, is the most volatile of the main components of output. In Chapter 21 we shall see whether these statements, suggested by the average behavior of inventories, apply regularly to business cycles in case after case, and whether they are equally applicable to cycles of all types.

2   Inventories in Business Cycle Literature

These broad findings clearly establish the prime importance of inventory fluctuations in business cycles. They emphasize the need for further work to uncover the character and causes of inventory

[4] In Chapter 21 we shall find reason to distinguish between longer and shorter cycles.

cycles and to gauge their influence upon business in general. As a
first step, it will be useful to review the work of earlier writers.
Though necessarily tentative and based on a fragmentary view of
the actual behavior of stocks, their theories are still a useful introduction to this book. Their conclusions illustrate well the range of
issues to which our investigation is relevant. Implicitly or explicitly,
their theories impute a certain pattern of behavior to inventories
during business cycles; they suggest the factors that govern the
movements of inventories; and they indicate a number of the ways
in which inventory fluctuations may influence business in general.
A comprehensive review of the literature of business cycles is not
possible, but I shall attempt to summarize the leading ideas of representative students. Aside from incidental comment, such criticism
and confirmation as emerge from this study are presented at later
points.

MITCHELL ON THE ROLE OF STOCKS

Characteristically, Mitchell develops his ideas about inventories as
part of his description of how the events that occur during a contraction of business lead to revival; how revival leads to expansion,
and so through the cycle. During cyclical contractions, he writes,

"Merchants require smaller stocks and cut their orders more than
sales fall off. A similar policy is followed by other enterprises. Thus
the reduction in volume of trade is amplified stage by stage as it
travels back through wholesale dealers to manufacturers and producers of raw materials."[5]

The reduction of stocks helps to intensify contraction, but it has
its limits. When stocks have been reduced as far as they safely can
be, goods must be replaced as rapidly as they are sold. This bolsters
the demand for goods, and may actually cause merchants' orders
and manufacturers' purchases and production to increase.

"First, the accumulated stocks of goods carried over from the preceding period of prosperity are gradually disposed of. Even when
current consumption is small, manufacturers and merchants can reduce their stocks of raw materials and finished wares by filling orders
chiefly from what is on hand and confining purchases to the small
quantities needed to keep full assortments. But when the stocks have

[5] *Encyclopedia of the Social Sciences* (Macmillan, 1937), III, 104.

once been reduced to the smallest dimensions allowed by the regular filling of orders, then current purchases and current production are perforce increased, even though current consumption does not grow larger."[6]

The necessity of halting, or at least retarding, the liquidation of stocks is thus one of the factors that, in Mitchell's opinion, help to bring the depression to an end. And once output and sales begin to increase, businessmen feel the need for larger stocks to support their larger activity. Their purchases and output, therefore, tend to increase more than their sales, adding momentum to the expansion. The incentive to build up stocks, moreover, comes not only from increasing activity but also from rising prices when these are thought to be an omen of further increases.

[Businessmen] "become eager to lay in large stocks or to make long contracts while quotations are still moderate and terms are still easy. Thus the anticipation of future advances in prices not only prevents present advances from reducing demand, but actually makes demand grow in the face of a rising level of prices."[7]

As activity increases and prosperity becomes more general, the balanced growth of stocks and production is upset. For many reasons prices tend to weaken after the upward phase has proceeded for some time. Businessmen attempt to maintain prices by keeping goods off the market and permitting current output to pile up. This policy, however, meets its own special obstacles and can, in any case, be a source of merely temporary relief. When prosperity is on the wane the attempt to stave off declines in prices by stockpiling current output must eventually fail. The liquidation of the unduly large inventories during the ensuing depression intensifies the subsequent contraction.

"High discount rates also impede the efforts, often made toward the end of a prosperous period, to maintain selling prices by keeping goods off the market and allowing current output to pile up in huge stocks, which are held for sale at a more opportune moment. . . . A temporary relief from a threatened fall of prices may be obtained in this way, but the potential danger becomes more grave. The heavy interest cost of 'carrying' the unsold stocks saps the financial strength

[6] *Business Cycles and Their Causes* (University of California Press, 1941), p. 143.
[7] Ibid., p. 11.

of even the largest enterprises and makes long persistence in this course hazardous. If buyers get wind of the situation, they hold off for the drop in prices they expect will come when the stocks are finally 'sacrificed'. In short, there can be but one end to such a policy when initiated under the business conditions of waning prosperity, and that disastrous end is hastened by high discount rates."[8]

'OVERPRODUCTION' THEORIES

In Mitchell's analysis of the forces involved in business cycles, stocks are an auxiliary factor, one of many causes accounting for the cumulation of prosperity and depression and for the transition from expansion to contraction. Other explanations assign a more crucial role to inventories. One, put forward by the so-called 'overproduction' theorists, is summarized by R. G. Hawtrey:

"The classical economists argued that general overproduction was impossible, because no one produced except with a view to consuming, and therefore demand was necessarily equal to supply. Moreover, production was at its greatest during the active phase of the trade cycle, and fell off during the phase of depression, at the very time when the symptoms of overproduction appeared. These difficulties could be met if the overproduction were supposed to take the form of accumulation of excessive stocks of commodities. If production outstrips demand, it was said, a part of the products remains unsold, and traders, encumbered with unsold goods, become reluctant to produce more. Restricted production means a restricted employment. These conditions will continue so long as unsold stocks remain above normal. The redundant goods have to be sold off at a sacrifice of price. When that process is completed, traders' stocks will have been brought into relation with a reduced scale of production and consumption. The pressure on markets being then relieved, there is found to be a margin of unemployed capital and labour, anxious to start producing. When production revives, the existing stocks of commodities are found to be insufficient for the needs of markets, and the process of replenishing stocks makes for active production. Production in fact, exceeds consumption, and will continue to do so till excessive stocks have again been accumulated, and the cycle is then started afresh."[9]

To account for excessive stocks two explanations are offered.

[8] Ibid., p. 59.
[9] *Trade and Credit* (Longmans, Green, 1928), pp. 84-5. The term 'traders', as used by Mr. Hawtrey, includes manufacturers as well as merchants.

First, the attempt to replenish stocks as well as to meet current demand is said to lead to the construction of new capacity. During
this time-consuming process stocks remain inadequate; construction is, therefore, likely to be overdone. Secondly, a period of activity gives rise to optimistic expectations which induce businessmen to make larger commitments in plant and inventories than
actual markets will warrant. As Hawtrey puts it (p. 85):

"At the end, therefore, of a time of depression, the period of recovery would be prolonged during the process of extending the equipment of industry. The climax would come when the fresh capital
came into use, and the swollen output of consumable commodities
would increase stocks up to normal and thereafter would exceed demand."

It seems consistent with these views to expect that inventories
will rise and fall together with business activity but that accumulations as measured, say, by the ratio of stocks to output or sales, will
be excessive only toward the end of expansions. Similarly, deficient
inventories would be expected toward the end of contractions.

HAWTREY'S THEORY

Although this convenient summary of the overproduction theory
was taken from one of Hawtrey's books he, of course, holds quite
different views. His name is, indeed, associated primarily with the
idea that the trade cycle is a 'purely monetary phenomenon'. But
while he contends that the essential feature of business cycles is an
expansion and contraction of the money supply, the vehicle on
which the additional money is brought to the public and later
taken away is the inventory policy of businessmen.[10]

Hawtrey believes that easy credit conditions and low interest
rates are an incentive to merchants to borrow in order to hold bigger stocks. Their increased orders, financed by new credit, stimulate production and employment and lead to larger incomes and
consumer expenditures. These in turn cause businessmen to seek
still larger stocks to support their growing business. Thus the forces
making for business expansion cumulate. And while the initial impulses to augment stocks come first from easy credit terms, then
from bigger sales, they gain strength, later in the expansion, from

[10] See especially his *Currency and Credit* (Longmans, Green, 1930), Ch.
I-IV and IX-XI; also his *Trade and Credit*, Ch. V, VII, and VIII.

rising prices. The period of increasing activity is brought to an end because, as incomes rise, the banking system tends to lose cash both to foreign countries and to the domestic circulation. The depletion of reserve cash causes a rise in interest rates and a restriction in bank loans. Merchants then try to liquidate stocks, and smaller orders set in motion the mutually reinforcing processes of contraction.

This version of Hawtrey's theory is well known. Perhaps less appreciated than it ought to be is that Hawtrey's explanation of business cycles rests on a virtual, not on an actual, cycle of inventories. That is, under the impulse given by low interest rates, merchants attempt to build up stocks by placing larger orders. But since the employment and income thereby created stimulate consumer expenditures, the first effect is bigger sales of finished goods. Thus larger stocks of goods in process are offset by depleted stocks of finished goods. Hawtrey sometimes writes as if the net result were to cause total stocks to rise but by less than the desired amount, leading to a still further increase of orders and output.[11] At other times he seems to contend that the depletion of inventories of finished goods entirely offsets the growth of goods in process so that business stocks as a whole actually remain constant (pp. 156, 157) :

"Increased working capital, in the form of goods in course of production, is provided [during expansion] not by a 'windfall' conferred on producers through a rise in prices, but by supplies of money, which enable consumers to draw on the finished products in stock. . . . Goods previously idle pass into consumption, and are replaced for the time being as an item of working capital by goods in the course of manufactures. The total of working capital in the entire community remains unchanged, and therefore becomes *less* in proportion to production, but the shortage of working capital is felt only in the stocks of finished products, which can be varied within fairly wide limits without inconvenience. The shortage of finished products is a direct stimulus to increased activity. If it goes too far and threatens exhaustion of supplies in the face of a continued demand, dealers defend themselves by raising prices to the consumer above replacement value."

The significance of these passages is clear on one point. The actual change in stocks is not, in Hawtrey's view, the effective pro-

[11] *Trade and Credit,* p. 91.

pellant and may, indeed, not be very large. The operative force is the *desire* to increase or decrease inventories and the consequent larger or smaller orders.

How Hawtrey thinks stocks behave is less easily said. Dealers' stocks may rise or fall during expansions. Manufacturers' stocks of goods in process must of course rise, but their supplies of purchased raw materials or finished goods may fall. One feature implicit in Hawtrey's theory, however, seems to require total inventories, as distinct from individual categories, to rise during expansions and fall during contractions. Since Hawtrey contends that attempts to increase stocks will result in greater employment and income only if there is a net expansion of bank credit, the larger liabilities of borrowers must be balanced somewhere in their accounts by additional capital assets. These new assets may take the form of plant or equipment, but in the context of Hawtrey's argument, it is more reasonable to think of them as commodity stocks.

KEYNES' THEORY OF WORKING AND LIQUID CAPITAL

Of the inventory theories proposed by leading writers on business cycles, J. M. Keynes' are perhaps the best developed and possibly the most penetrating.[12] It may be worth while to review at least the broad features of Keynes' treatment. More details will be noted in later chapters. For purposes of analysis and exposition, Keynes divides all inventories into two categories, "working" and "liquid" capital. He defines working capital as "the aggregate of goods . . . in course of production, manufacture, transport and retailing, including such minimum stocks, whether of raw materials or of finished products, as are required to avoid risks of interruption of process or to tide over seasonal irregularities (e.g., intervals between harvests or fluctuations of individual harvests about the mean) . . . [Working capital] includes without distinction goods in process, such as food or textiles . . . the consumption of which will be spread over a short time, and goods in process . . . which will emerge as fixed capital, the consumption of which must be spread over a period, and are not immediately available."[13]

[12] *Treatise on Money,* I, Ch. 18 and II, Ch. 27-9; *General Theory of Employment, Interest and Money,* Ch. 22 (Harcourt, Brace, 1930 and 1936).
[13] *Treatise on Money,* II, 116. Keynes defines goods in process more broadly than I do; see Ch. 7 below.

Liquid capital, in contrast, is defined as surplus stocks, that is, stocks over and above the goods necessary to carry on a given volume of production and distribution.

In practice, however, working and liquid capital cannot be clearly differentiated. Goods actually passing through a specific process of fabrication (hides in the tanning vat, for example) are objectively related to the rate of production. But how large a supply of purchased raw materials does a manufacturer require to support a given output? Though Keynes was, of course, not unaware of the difficulty, he merely says (I, 129): "normal stocks required for efficient business are part of working capital and therefore in process, whilst surplus stocks are to be regarded as liquid".

With these definitions in hand, Keynes is able to draw his picture of the cyclical behavior of inventories and to show its significance. Working capital, since it represents goods in process and other inventories 'required' to support production and distribution, must, as a matter of definition, fluctuate together with output and roughly in the same proportion. More important, as Keynes later argues, it comprises the bulk of inventories, so that its movements dominate the behavior of inventories as a whole.

Keynes develops his views on liquid capital in rebutting Hawtrey's argument about the behavior of stocks. Keynes takes the position, contrary to Hawtrey, that fluctuations in liquid capital can no more than partly offset fluctuations in working capital. In support of this view, he advances three arguments.

1) During slumps production falls off much more sharply than consumption. And since the evidence does not suggest that the excess consumption is fully balanced by diminished investment in fixed capital, stocks must become somewhat depleted. Hence the liquidation of working capital must exceed any accumulation of liquid capital.

2) An investigation into the volume of stocks at different dates leads Keynes to think that the true surplus stocks of liquid capital in existence at any time are too small to offset the cyclical movements of working capital.

In addition, Keynes writes (II, 134, 135):

" . . . the figures corroborate the expectation that [in the case of a slump which has been brought about by other causes than an exces-

sive investment in fixed capital] stocks tend to attain their maximum
in an early phase of the slump and are at a low point when the improvement of trade is definitely beginning. . . . This confirms expectation because, when the slump begins, the falling off of production
does not show itself immediately at the finishing end of the machine
of process, whilst it does show itself immediately in the amount which
is being fed back into the mouth of the machine: so liquid stocks increase. Later on, however, the diminished production results in diminished available output, whilst current consumption does not fall
off so much as does production—with the result that there can be no
increase of liquid stocks, but rather the contrary."

3) The costs of carrying surplus stocks, including the risk of loss due
to price drops, are very high. Hence if such stocks come into existence, they force their own reabsorption by causing prices to fall
and production to be restricted. "Recovery—broadly speaking—
cannot begin until [surplus] stocks have been absorbed . . ." (II,
145). Consequently, the liquidation of working capital characterizing a slump must eventually be reinforced, not offset, by a liquidation of surplus stocks. Keynes therefore concludes, contrary to
Hawtrey, that surplus stocks, having been worked off during the
slump, cannot counteract the accumulation of working capital in
the ensuing recovery, except perhaps in its very earliest stages.

These various considerations lead Keynes to a general view
about the behavior of stocks as a whole, working capital and liquid
capital together (*General Theory*, p. 319):

"In the earliest phase of a typical slump there will probably be an
investment in increasing [surplus] stocks which helps to offset disinvestment in working capital; in the next phase there may be a short
period of disinvestment both in [surplus] stocks and in working capital; after the lowest point has been passed there is likely to be a further disinvestment in [surplus] stocks which partially offsets reinvest-
ment in working capital; and finally, after the recovery is well on its
way, both factors will be simultaneously favorable to investment."

A review of the statistics on manufacturers' stocks will demonstrate how discerning this passage is. Meanwhile, taking Keynes'
argument at face value, we may ask some questions. Working capital increases with output, but when does the rate of investment,
that is, the rate of growth in working capital reach its peak? At
the same time as output or earlier? Surplus stocks are supposed to

increase both before and after the peak of the cycle. When do they grow most rapidly? Before or after the peak? Similar questions remain to puzzle us about the course and mechanism of the slump.

Keynes supplements his theory about the behavior of stocks with arguments about the size and significance of inventories and their fluctuations and their relation to the length of cyclical expansions and contractions. On the basis of some rough estimates he concludes that the impairment of working capital in a severe decline such as 1920-22 was probably about 15 percent or £250 million sterling.[14] Since he takes this sum to be equal to approximately half of a year's savings in Great Britain in a normal year, and since he considers that fluctuations in liquid capital can offset those in working capital to only a small extent, Keynes is able to satisfy himself about a number of interesting points.

First, the fluctuations in working capital that inevitably accompany fluctuations in demand and output are an important intensifying if not initiating factor, tending to reinforce movements of demand in either direction. In the language of the *Treatise on Money* (II, 116): "It is evident that fluctuations in the amount of Working Capital are so large that they can, on occasion, be an *important* factor in bringing about a disequilibrium between the rates of Saving and Investment." Thus if for any reason manufacturers receive larger orders, their attempt to fill them entails additional working capital which in turn increases incomes and presumably the demand for goods even before the original orders can be filled. The effect of this process, Keynes thinks, must be a rise in prices relative to costs, thereby giving businessmen a further incentive to invest (I, Ch. 18).

So strong, indeed, does Keynes consider the impact of investment in working capital on prices that he suggests it may determine the pace and average length of cyclical expansions and contractions. For if there is an attempt to raise the rate of employment too rapidly, the necessary investment in working capital will be so large as to cause a severe inflation in the prices of consumer goods, and presumably of the materials that enter into them.

[14] The basis of Keynes' calculations is admittedly unsatisfactory, but there is better evidence now to demonstrate that cyclical changes in inventory investment are relatively large (see Table 1 above).

"When, therefore, the time comes for the replenishment of working capital, it may be *impossible* to effect this rapidly without rupturing the equilibrium of prices and incomes. Even if appropriate steps are taken in good time, two years or more may elapse before working capital can be restored; and if such steps are not taken, a longer interval may be required."[15]

Finally, just as his theory about working capital explains for Keynes the relatively moderate pace of expansion, his theory about liquid capital accounts for the relatively swift pace of contraction. The essence of his view is that the speculative risks of holding surplus inventories, added to the burdens of deterioration, warehousing, insurance, and interest, make the cost of carrying redundant stocks very high. As a consequence, when surplus stocks accumulate at the beginning of a slump, their holders will themselves curtail production, if they can, in order to liquidate the stocks promptly; if they cannot, their attempts to sell will force prices down drastically, thereby bringing a sharp reduction in output.[16] Of course, the curtailment of output will itself reduce demand and retard the rate of inventory absorption, necessitating still further restriction of output and so on cumulatively, at least for a time. Hence the violence of contraction.

Keynes is less clear concerning the length of the process. In the *Treatise on Money* he confines himself to examples covering single commodities. In the *General Theory*, however, he suggests two factors that control the length of depressions (p. 318). The first is "the average durability of capital in a given epoch".

"The second stable time-factor is due to the carrying-costs of surplus stocks which force their absorption within a certain period, neither very short nor very long. The sudden cessation of new investment after the crisis will probably lead to an accumulation of surplus stocks of unfinished goods. The carrying-costs of these stocks will seldom be less than 10 percent per annum. Thus the fall in their price

---

[15] *Treatise on Money,* II, 112-3. In this connection Keynes cites Mitchell's 1913 calculations that the mean length of an expansion is just under two years and the maximum about three years.

[16] Ibid., II, 146. "Just as the improvement in the volume of production can take place only gradually, owing to the time which it takes to build up Working Capital again; so must the falling off in the volume of production take place suddenly, when there is surplus Liquid Capital, owing to the short time within which Liquid Capital must be absorbed."

needs to be sufficient to bring about a restriction which provides for their absorption within a period of, say, three to five years at the outside. Now the process of absorbing the stocks represents negative investment, which is a further deterrent to employment; and, when it is over, a manifest relief will be experienced."

Keynes' suggestion of a three to five year period is significant. As we shall see, the record lends some support to his picture of the behavior of surplus stocks during contractions of this length. On the other hand, contractions that persist for as long as three years are rather exceptional.[17] In shorter depressions, stocks have not behaved in accordance with Keynes' hypothesis. For these shorter episodes the mechanism of contraction and recovery must be different from the one Keynes sketches.

THE ACCELERATION PRINCIPLE AND THE PATTERN OF INVENTORY INVESTMENT

The theories reviewed above have at least one thing in common. Either implicitly or explicitly all rely upon changes in the rate of inventory investment to explain at least part of the impact of inventories on business cycles. But the descriptions of the behavior of stocks run exclusively in terms of level, not of rate of growth. It is clear, however, that the peaks and troughs of inventory investment may, and in general will, precede the peaks and troughs of stocks themselves.[18] The number employed in producing goods destined for stock may, therefore, be declining while inventories themselves are still rising. If we treat inventory investment in a fashion strictly parallel with investment in durable goods, we would say that inventories are exercising a depressing influence on employment when the rate of inventory investment declines, not when inventories begin to be liquidated. It is, therefore, of first

[17] The National Bureau chronology of monthly business cycles records 16 contractions in Great Britain and 21 in the United States between 1857 and 1938. Of these, only 4 British and 3 United States contractions lasted as long as 3 years. Even contractions of 2 years are in the minority: there have been only 6 in Great Britain and 5 in the United States since 1857. See *Measuring Business Cycles*, Table 16, pp. 78-9.

[18] This, of course, is not necessary. If the rate of growth of stocks increased until the peak of an inventory cycle was reached, inventories and inventory investment would turn down simultaneously.

importance to have a well founded idea about the cyclical behavior of inventory investment as distinct from the level of stocks
themselves.

One suggestion consists in applying the well known principle
of the magnification and acceleration of derived demand to the
accumulation and liquidation of stocks. Although this principle,
derived from the hypothesis that the rate of net new investment is
controlled by the rate of change in, not the level of, demand for
consumer goods, has been studied largely in connection with investment in producer durable equipment, its application to inventories was recognized by J. M. Clark in his initial treatment in
1917.[19] Kuznets stressed this application in his study of cycles in
the merchandising trades and in a later general critique of the
acceleration principle.[20]

In its simplest form the principle assumes that manufacturers
and merchants are both desirous and able to maintain inventories
in constant ratio to their output or sales. Inventories would vary
directly and proportionately with sales or output, but the rate of
inventory investment would vary directly with the rate of change
in sales, and its magnitude would bear the same relation to the
magnitude of the change in sales as stocks themselves bear to sales.
Hence if a manufacturer kept inventories four times his monthly
sales, a $1,000 increase in his monthly sales would call for an in-
ventory investment of $4,000.

An arithmetical example will make these relations clearer. It assumes that the desired inventory-sales ratio is 4 to 1 and that if the
rate of sales changes, the firm will be able, by purchases or output,
to restore inventories to the desired ratio by the end of the month
in which the change occurs. Table 2 illustrates several leading
propositions that together may be said to constitute the principle
of the magnification and acceleration of derived demand as applied to inventory investment:

[19] Business Acceleration and the Law of Demand: A Technical Factor in
Economic Cycles, *Journal of Political Economy*, March 1917, pp. 217-35.

[20] *Cyclical Fluctuations; Retail and Wholesale Trade, United States, 1919-
1925* (Adelphi, 1926), and the Relation Between Capital Goods and Finished Products in the Business Cycle, *Economic Essays in Honor of Wesley
Clair Mitchell* (Columbia University Press, 1935). See also Gottfried Haberler, *Prosperity and Depression* (Geneva, 3d ed., 1941), pp. 85 ff.

TABLE 2

Sales, Inventories, and Business Expenditures
Hypothetical Example

	MONTHS											
	1	2	3	4	5	6	7	8	9	10	11	12
1 Stocks at beginning of month	400	400	408	432	452	460	460	452	432	408	400	400
2 Sales at cost	100	102	108	113	115	115	113	108	102	100	100	102
3 Increase in sales	0	+2	+6	+5	+2	0	−2	−5	−6	−2	0	+2
4 Stocks required at end of month (line 2 x 4)	400	408	432	452	460	460	452	432	408	400	400	408
5 Expenditures required for												
a) Replacement (line 2)	100	102	108	113	115	115	113	108	102	100	100	102
b) Inventory investment (line 4 − line 1)	0	8	24	20	8	0	−8	−20	−24	−8	0	8
6 Total expenditures (line 5a + b)	100	110	132	133	123	115	105	88	78	92	100	110

1) Inventory investment varies directly and proportionately with the rate of change in sales, not with sales proper. Although in the example sales continue to rise through the fifth month, their rate of increase and inventory investment fall after the third. After the peak, sales decline until the tenth month, but their rate of decline and inventory investment reach troughs in the ninth.

2) Inventory investment equals the absolute change in sales multiplied by the inventory-sales ratio.

3) Total business expenditures follow a pattern that is a compound of the patterns of expenditures to replace sales and those required for inventory investment. Usually they will reach their peaks and troughs later than expenditures for inventory investment but before expenditures for replacements. Thus inventory investment reaches its peak in the third month, total expenditures in the fourth, and replacement expenditures in the fifth.

4) The absolute amplitude of the fluctuation in total business expenditures is a compound also of the amplitudes of the fluctuation in sales and of the much wider fluctuation in inventory investment. As a result, its relative amplitude is wider than that in sales.

These propositions express the principle of acceleration and magnification in its simplest form. Clark, Kuznets, and other writers stress certain qualifications and extensions of the theory. In particular, they recognize that inventory-sales ratios are not rigid. On the one hand, expenditures for both replacement and inventory investment are likely to lag, creating a tendency to reduce both the lead and magnitude of investment cycles relative to sales. On the other hand, the lags create initial shortages relative to demand which cause prices to rise, with the result that inventory investments motivated by price speculation are likely to overlie those motivated by changes in sales. In addition, Clark emphasizes that the causal sequence does not run simply from final demand to demand for investment goods, but also from investment, via the consumer incomes created, to consumer expenditures. Each type of demand reinforces the others and modifies its pattern in a process of adaptation that at first magnifies the initial impulse, but is, in the end, self-limiting and self-reversing.[21]

[21] Cf. Clark's Additional Note on Business Acceleration and the Law of Demand, *Preface to Social Economics* (Farrar & Rinehart, 1936), pp. 349-54.

HANSEN'S THEORY OF THE ROLE OF INVENTORIES IN LONG AND SHORT CYCLES

An important problem with respect to the role of inventories in business cycles had been raised by Alvin H. Hansen. In his *Fiscal Policy and Business Cycles*[22] he substantially accepts Schumpeter's theory that several business cycle types may be distinguished: among them, long waves of approximately 50 years, "major" cycles of about 8 years, and "minor" fluctuations most of which last 3 or 4 years. Hansen, like Schumpeter, attributes the long waves and the major cycles to fluctuations in investment activity in durable equipment and construction work, connected with important economic innovations. He attributes the minor cycles, however, primarily to fluctuations in inventory investment.

In Hansen's view the ebb and flow of inventories not merely "dominates the so-called minor cycle"; he contends also that inventory investment is an important stimulus to revival after major depressions. In the period covered by the national product data to which he refers, there were two such depressions, 1920-21 and 1929-32. The improvement in business from 1921 to 1922 was accompanied by an increase in inventory accumulation; that from 1932 to 1933 was accompanied by a sharp decline in inventory liquidation. Both, of course, helped to raise the level of business. Hansen concludes (p. 60) that "inventory investment plays consistently an important role in the initiation of revival".

Professor Hansen's theories may prove important leads toward an understanding of business cycles. The influence of inventory investment in long and short cycles and its role in initiating revivals and recessions are studied below in the introduction to Part Three, and in Chapters 14 and 21.

METZLER'S THEORY OF SELF-GENERATING INVENTORY CYCLES

The idea that the short business cycle is to be attributed mainly to fluctuations in inventory investment has been developed further by Lloyd A. Metzler.[23] He has formulated a theory of short cycles

[22] (Norton, 1941). Professor Hansen emphasized also the importance of a cycle in building construction with an average period of 17 to 18 years.

[23] Nature and Stability of Inventory Cycles, *Review of Economic Statistics*, Aug. 1941, and Business Cycles and the Modern Theory of Employment, *American Economic Review*, June 1946.

on the simplifying assumption that the sole effects of a change in income are certain adaptive responses in inventory investment together with the secondary changes in incomes and consumer expenditures caused by business outlays to increase stocks.

Metzler bases his theory on two hypotheses:

1) The economic system is essentially stable, though subject to more or less regular oscillations. The oscillations are marked by cycles of investment, income, and expenditure induced by impulses that may originate in preceding phases or may be of independent origin (such as the commercial application of a new invention). The cycles are, however, self-limiting and self-reversing fluctuations about an equilibrium level.[24]

2) Oscillations of income about its equilibrium level may consist of several cycles reflecting the response of various activities to the same impulse or impulses. Individual cycles are attributed to induced demands for consumer or producer durable goods, to the demand for housing and for inventories. Other cyclical responses are, of course, possible. Each presumably has special features of its own that in isolation would give rise to business cycles with characteristic amplitudes and durations. In practice, of course, the several cycles impinge upon and modify one another, producing the complex business cycles of experience.[25]

Metzler's articles are directed to the theory of inventory cycles, that is, to the character of the general business cycles that would be generated by the response of inventory investment to a change in income. His general picture of events during an inventory cycle runs as follows:

1) The first effect of an increase in income and expenditures is a

[24] The equilibrium level is defined as equality between intended saving and intended 'non-induced' investment (i.e., investment not itself motivated by a cyclical change in the rate of expenditure). The tendency for oscillations to reach a peak and reverse their direction is implicit in the hypothesis that the relation of increases in income to consumers' expenditures, on the one hand, and to induced investment, on the other, eventually retards the rate of increase in income. This causes the rate of induced investment to fall, which in turn causes an absolute decline in income.

[25] This concept of the general character of business cycles is now fairly common, as Metzler points out. In particular, it has been described at length by J. M. Clark in his *Strategic Factors in Business Cycles,* and has been developed also by later writers who have based their work on Keynes' theory of employment equilibrium.

decline in inventories because producers are unable to expand output rapidly enough.

2) Thereafter production is increased both to meet the bigger demand and to replenish inventories and build them up in consonance with the larger output.

3) As output is stepped up, demand also rises and stocks remain abnormally low, despite efforts to increase them. Nevertheless, since consumers do not spend all their augmented incomes, stocks do increase to some extent.

4) Eventually incomes rise to a level consistent with the rate of non-induced investment (investment, that is, not sustained by the cyclical increase of incomes). They do not stop at this level, however, since inventories are still low relative to the rate of activity. Inventory investment, therefore, pushes incomes still higher.

5) Metzler describes the reversal of business activity as follows (*American Economic Review*, June 1946, p. 288):

"Once the level of income has risen above its new equilibrium, a subsequent decline is inevitable. The inflated level of income is sustained and increased only by investment in inventories, and such investment cannot be continued indefinitely. As income rises, inventories also rise, and this process continues until a normal relation between inventories and expected sales is established. Thereafter, business men plan no further increases in stocks; they attempt, instead, to produce only what they expect to sell. Since production plans in earlier periods included production for stocks as well as for sale, the decision to produce only for sale means an absolute decline in total output. As a result, income in the hands of consumers declines, sales are reduced, and a period of general contraction develops. The contraction is accelerated by the fact that sales fall below expectations, since this causes inventories to become abnormally large and business men therefore reduce output still further in an attempt to restore their stocks to a normal level."

From this point forward, Metzler's description of contraction and revival is symmetrical with the description of expansion and recession set forth above. In the absence of further disturbances from outside the system of business responses or adaptations, Metzler expects that developments in contraction will lead to another revival, and so on around. But he thinks subsequent cycles will be highly damped.

Metzler's model is interesting because it presents not only a modern theory of business cycles in which inventories play a leading role but also a fairly definite hypothesis about the cyclical behavior of inventories that may be tested. Metzler assumes that stocks act in the following fashion:

1) Inventories rise after the peak of business and begin to fall only some time after contraction has started; they continue to fall after business has reached its trough and begin to rise only some time after expansion is under way.

2) The rate of inventory accumulation reaches a peak near the peak of business and a trough near the trough of business. It is not clear, however, whether the intended investment just preceding the peak is larger or smaller than the unintended investment immediately following it. Nor is it clear whether a period of low investment intervenes between the intended investments of late expansion and the unintended accumulations of early contraction. Similar remarks might be made about the cyclical trough.

3) The inventory-output (or inventory-sales) ratio must fall immediately after business begins to revive. Thereafter it may continue to fall or reverse its course. Toward the end of expansion, however, it must be rising, for Metzler holds that planned inventory investment reaches a peak when a 'normal' relation between inventories and sales is established. Since the first effect of expansion is to establish an abnormally low ratio (sales increase while inventories fall), the ratio must start to rise later and continue to rise until the end of expansion. In contraction the expected development is symmetrical but opposite.

BLODGETT'S ANALYSIS OF THE EVIDENCE

To my knowledge, the only systematic empirical study of cycles in the stocks of American manufacturers is Ralph H. Blodgett's *Cyclical Fluctuations in Commodity Stocks* (University of Pennsylvania Press, 1935). In his valuable pioneer work, Blodgett examined a considerable part of the material used in this report and, indeed, analyzed his data by means of the National Bureau measures of cyclical behavior. My material, however, differs from Blodgett's in several respects. I discarded a few of the series Blodgett studied because they included inventories held by nonmanufacturers in too great a degree, because they were deemed insufficiently reliable, or because they covered too short a time span. Many of Blodgett's other series, which I too studied, are now available for a longer period than when he wrote. Finally, I had the advantage of a considerably larger body of data, in particular the estimates based on corporation balance sheets, the only comprehensive data on manufacturers' inventories as a whole.

Despite these differences in data, Blodgett anticipated the results of this study in certain notable instances. For example, he concluded that, while stocks of finished staple goods held by manufacturers normally increase during business contractions and decline during expansions, this inverted movement is reversed in the course of long and severe contractions, and stocks tend to decline together with business activity.[26] This and certain other detailed instances of agreement and disagreement between Blodgett's findings and my own are noted at various points below. Here the important thing to record is Blodgett's general conclusion about the cyclical behavior of manufacturers' stocks (p. 104):

"Some of the stocks of finished commodities and materials held at the producers' . . . are positive in their cyclical movements, while others are inverted. These two groups of stocks appear to be quite equal in so far as numbers are concerned. When it is remembered, however, that the stocks of the inverted type are very much larger than the stocks of the positive type, on the average, and are much more active cyclically, the necessary conclusion is that stocks of finished commodities and materials at the producers' of the finished products show a net tendency toward inverted cyclical behavior in relation to the reference cycles of general business."

Now this statement, by itself, is rather seriously at variance with my conclusions, which, as we shall see, are that cycles in manufacturers' stocks as a whole tend to conform positively to cycles in business activity at large, though with a lag perhaps as long as 9 months. It is well, however, not to overstress the difference between our conclusions. At least a substantial minority of business cycle phases are no longer than 18 months, so that if stocks lag

[26] Op. cit., pp. 53, 54. Blodgett does not present empirical support for the conclusion that this class of stocks acts differently in long and short phases. It is, however, essentially correct, as will be seen below; and is true for expansions as well as contractions.

as much as 9 months, they move counter to business activity for a major portion of these short phases, though not for their entire length, as Blodgett implies. Among American business cycles since 1855, 4 of 21 expansions and 13 of 21 contractions did not exceed 18 months.[27] Add to this Blodgett's belief that positive conformity may be expected in long severe contractions, and it will be seen that our findings, though different, are not wholly dissimilar.

GENERAL CHARACTERISTICS OF THE LITERATURE

This review of earlier work suffices to suggest the major ideas advanced and to illustrate the startling differences among economists' notions about inventory behavior. From Mitchell's suggestion that stocks move in rough positive conformity with business activity to Hawtrey's theory that cycles in stocks of finished goods and of goods in process are approximately offsetting, to Blodgett's finding that manufacturers' stocks as a whole normally vary inversely to business activity, one traverses almost the entire range of possible hypotheses about inventory behavior. Meanwhile, with the notable exceptions of Clark and Metzler, singularly little attempt has been made to state precisely how inventory investment acts. Yet from the standpoint of the impact of inventories on business cycles, investment counts more than the level of inventories.

There is another prominent characteristic of the literature: all the ideas about inventory behavior reviewed above except Blodgett's are exceedingly simple and general. Distinctions are few; in some cases the same behavior is implicitly attributed to the stocks of both merchants and manufacturers. In others the divisions are broad indeed: between working and liquid capital or between finished goods and goods in process. A review of the evidence on manufacturers' holdings, however, indicates that such simple theories will not do. The behavior of manufacturers' stocks is a compound of the diverse behavior of many classes of stocks.

The literature exhibits a striking variety of views in other ways. With respect to the forces controlling stocks, Hawtrey stresses the influence of interest costs. Clark and other writers who depend upon the acceleration principle hold that the level of stocks is determined by sales or output. Mitchell and many other students

[27] *Measuring Business Cycles,* p. 78.

assign some regular, significant influence to price expectations, among other causes. The 'overproduction' theorists in earlier times and Keynes more recently held that stocks are redundant at some stages in cycles, deficient at others because changes in production do not keep pace with changes in sales to ultimate consumers.

Finally, turning to the impact of inventories on business, we find a number of intriguing suggestions. There is general agreement that stocks influence business cycles chiefly through changes in the expenditures businessmen make with the purpose of increasing their inventories, that is, through changes in the amount of investment planned per time period. So if the magnitude and timing of such planned expenditures relative to other actions by businessmen and consumers can be determined, we should be in a position to state how inventories make their influence felt and how strong that influence is. On these questions, however, earlier writers are in disagreement. Clark suggests that planned inventory investment rises, generating an expansion in business, as long as sales and output grow at an increasing rate; thereafter it begins to drop, tending to depress business. In contraction the rate of planned investment falls (or liquidation increases) as long as sales drop at an increasing rate. In this stage inventory investment has a depressing influence, but when the decline in sales is retarded, the rate of liquidation also is reduced, which spurs business activity.[28]

Keynes holds that inventory policy influences the severity and duration of contractions in a special way. He begins with the idea that contractions open with an undesired accumulation of stocks because business is unable to reduce output as fast as sales fall off. The attempt to liquidate these redundant stocks causes a precipitate drop in orders and output. And since this in turn causes incomes and, therefore, sales to fall, the period of liquidation is necessarily protracted, requiring, in Keynes' opinion, from 3 to 5 years.

Hansen advances the idea that business cycles differ in the importance of fluctuations in inventory investment as causal factors. He distinguishes a relatively long cycle, of about 10 years, which he attributes to a wave of investment in durable goods and construc-

---

[28] This is an unduly simplified version of Clark's position since he allows for business forecasts of changes in sales and in prices and for the time it takes to execute decisions and translate them into actual outlays.

tion. In the course of the upswing of such equipment cycles, however, he believes that inventories from time to time become seriously out of balance with sales and output. Business contractions then develop owing to sharp reductions in inventory investment. In Hansen's view, therefore, the upswings of relatively long cycles are broken into shorter cycles during which contractions of investment in plant and equipment are small. Consequently, changes in output during short cycles largely take the form of changes in the rate of inventory investment. In the longer swings the relative importance of changes in inventory investment is smaller.

This wide variety of theories about the cyclical fluctuations of stocks, their causes, and their impact on business cycles is a good starting point for this study. Those that raise questions the data can be organized to answer are reexamined below. Others are helpful because they aid in defining the significance of the results yielded by this investigation. And still others will serve to remind us of issues raised by earlier work that this study was unable to resolve.

3   Materials for the Study of Manufacturers' Stocks

The views held in the past about the behavior of inventories during business cycles, in both their diversity and simplicity, reflect the paucity of the information available for study. Even now when records of inventories are much better, and even in the United States, for which records are more plentiful than in other countries, they are seriously inadequate.

Data on American manufacturers' stocks fall into two blocks. First, there are estimates of the value of inventories based on company balance sheets or other books of account. The most comprehensive estimates that utilize such materials are those prepared by Simon Kuznets for the period since 1918. From 1926 forward Kuznets built upon virtually complete reports for all corporations filed for tax purposes. Before 1926 he depended in part upon tax reports and in part upon smaller samples of corporations. Supplementing Kuznets' data are estimates by other investigators who rely upon somewhat different sources and methods, cover different but overlapping periods, and include both yearly and monthly reports. These series are in current values; Kuznets' data have been corrected for changes in prices and so constitute indexes of the physical volume of manufacturers' stocks.

Because of the breadth of their coverage the estimates based on corporate accounts offer the best, indeed the only fairly reliable, picture of the behavior of manufacturers' stocks as a whole. For this purpose they are invaluable. But they have serious deficiencies for an analytical study of inventory cycles. The estimates that cover a considerable number of business cycles are based on annual reports, an obvious defect in studies of business movements whose duration from peak to trough is sometimes no longer than 12 or 18 months. Of the two available sets of monthly data, one starts in 1929 and covers only two contractions and one expansion in general business before the beginning of World War II. The other begins in 1939, after the close of the last prewar cycle.

Another difficulty with the estimates based on corporate accounts is their inadequate classification. Total holdings by manufacturers are divided into a relatively few broad industrial groups each of which comprises several large industries. Our analysis, however, suggests that the classification of inventories that best illuminates the factors governing inventory behavior runs by stage of fabrication—raw materials, goods in process, finished goods—and by subdivisions of these stages, rather than by industry.

A final difficulty with this block of materials is that it necessarily reports inventories in dollar values. Changes in the reported level of stocks are, therefore, affected by changes not merely in physical quantity but also in unit value.[29] To get an index of the physical volume of inventories it is necessary to correct the reported value figures for the influence of changes in prices, an inherently treacherous and inaccurate process.

Despite all these limitations, the materials derived from corporate accounts are of prime importance. They are based either on large samples of corporations or on full reports for all corporations. And despite their defects with respect to form, subdivision, and frequency, they outline at least roughly the movements

[29] The revaluation of inventories that accompanies changes in prices is in itself a matter of great interest, for it accounts for a large proportion of the changes in the book profits of enterprises. A forthcoming National Bureau study of cyclical changes in profits will discuss this subject.

of manufacturers' stocks as a whole. A theory about the cyclical behavior of manufacturers' total holdings can be constructed also from the movements of series representing stocks of particular commodities. As we shall see, however, it is an hypothesis full of gaps that must be filled by speculation, and it gains credibility only because it can be checked against the broad pattern of manufacturers' inventory cycles traced by the nearly complete data from corporate accounts.

Supplementing the data from corporate accounts are a considerable number of series representing the holdings of specific commodities in physical units. The 38 such series used constitute all the data that seemed sufficiently trustworthy and covered a long enough period to contribute to a study of business cycles. The sources and composition of the individual series are described in Appendix G and, as far as necessary, at appropriate points in the text. Their faults and virtues are the antitheses of those of the corporate reports. The commodity materials are in no sense a large or representative collection. Aggregated in any simple fashion, they would present a misleading picture of the behavior of manufacturers' stocks as a whole. On the other hand, they are reported in physical units and at monthly or quarterly intervals and, best of all, they cover the holdings of a considerable variety of important types of stock. By classifying these series in significant ways and by close study of their similarities and differences, we can derive valuable information about the factors that account for the cyclical behavior of stocks in the aggregate.

4   Plan of the Study

Although this report is concerned primarily with manufacturers' stocks, brief notice is taken in Chapters 4, 5, 14, 15, 20, and 21 of the cyclical behavior of stocks held in the other principal divisions of the economy. The body of the report is presented in Parts Two and Three. Part Two deals with cycles in the level of inventory holdings, Part Three with cycles in inventory investment. The organization of the two parts is similar. Part Two begins with an investigation of manufacturers' total holdings. It attempts to answer two questions: first, do manufacturers' stocks typically rise during expansions of general business and fall during contractions;

secondly, do inventories typically reach their peaks and troughs before or after business activity? By studying cycles in the ratio of inventories to sales and output we attempt to discover also whether inventories 'pile up' or become unduly large during business expansions. An explanation of the typical behavior of total inventory holdings is then sought in succeeding chapters through studies of several categories of stocks: raw materials, goods in process, and finished goods, as well as various subcategories. As these classes typically behave in widely different fashion, there can be no simple theory about the cyclical behavior of manufacturers' stocks. An explanation is offered for the behavior of each category. The action of the total can be roughly accounted for in terms of the diverse behavior of the several components.

Part Three is concerned with cyclical changes in inventory investment, that is, with changes in the pace at which stocks are built up or liquidated. Dealing first with the timing of inventory investment cycles, it asks whether the peaks and troughs of such investment regularly precede, follow, or coincide with the peaks and troughs of business cycles. It takes up next the relative timing of turning points in inventory investment and those in the rate of change in output. Ensuing chapters are devoted to a study of the behavior of investment in different types of stock. These studies are the basis for an explanation of the timing of cycles in aggregate investment. A final chapter examines the magnitude of the changes in inventory investment between prosperity and depression, compares them with changes in other components of total output, and presents a theory to account for the relative importance of inventory investment fluctuations in cycles of different lengths.

Since this investigation tries to build a theory of inventory cycles from a systematic examination of the data, the exposition is necessarily long and tedious. Specialists who wish to satisfy themselves about the validity of the results will, of course, want to study the entire report. Readers with more general interests may grasp the essentials by following a more selective reading plan. For them, the following notes may be useful.

The gist of the argument may be found in Chapters 4-5, 13-14, and 20-1. Chapters 7-12 are concerned with detailed studies of cyclical fluctuations in stocks of different types: goods in process, raw materials, finished goods, and several subdivisions of these classes. Chapters 16-19 contain similarly detailed studies of fluctuations in investment in different kinds of inventory. These chapters are the foundation for the more general accounts of inventory and inventory investment cycles in Chapters 13 and 20, but the nonprofessional reader may wish to accept the details on trust. Other chapters are outside the main stream of the argument or serve an ancillary purpose. Chapter 6 is a digression on cycles in inventory-sales and inventory-output ratios. Chapter 2 compares manufacturers' stocks with holdings in other branches of the economy. Chapter 3 describes the measures and discusses their reliability. Briefer descriptions of the measures appear where they are first employed. But Chapter 3 will serve readers who want a fuller explanation or who do not read the book as a whole and so miss the explanations of measures where they appear in the body of the argument.

CHAPTER 2

Size and Relative Importance of Manufacturers' Inventories

Since this study is concerned mainly with manufacturers' inventories it is important at the outset to establish how large a portion of total inventories manufacturers hold. Table 3 presents two sets of estimates of inventories in the principal divisions of the economy. I have modified both sets and, to preserve comparability with estimates for manufacturing used elsewhere in this volume, substituted Kuznets' estimates for manufacturing for those prepared by Wendell D. Hance for the Department of Commerce.[1] Both estimates are based upon the same data, use similar methods to account for stocks held by unincorporated firms, and yield essentially similar results.

To facilitate comparison, the period 1928-33, in which the Kuznets and Commerce data overlap, is shown on both sides of the table. In two categories, Trade and Other, Kuznets' estimate is higher. The total discrepancy is $2.5 billion or about 10 percent of aggregate inventories. The lack of agreement arises from a large number of detailed differences in the procedures. For our purposes it suffices to note that since the Department of Commerce estimates of total inventories are lower the share of manufacturing is about 4 percentage points or 10 percent higher than in Kuznets' estimates in the period of overlap.

Apparently, manufacturing industries were, by a small margin,

[1] Kuznets has prepared estimates also for all industrial categories for years after 1933. These have not been published, although estimates of net annual changes in inventories derived from them, after correction for changes in prices, appear in his *National Product since 1869* as well as in this volume. With certain exceptions, however, I do not here rely on Kuznets' data after 1928 because Department of Commerce estimates are based upon more recent and complete information.

the leading holders of commodity stocks. Their value averaged somewhat less than $13 billion in 1918-27 and about $11 billion thereafter. The value of stocks held by other industrial divisions appears to have fallen further, for the share of manufacturers' inventories rises slightly over the whole period. In Kuznets' estimates the average share of manufacturing was about 38 percent of total inventories in 1918-27, and a little over 40 percent in 1928-33. In the Commerce figures it was 44.5 percent in 1928-33, and just under 46 percent in 1934-39. The changes from period to period are not large, however, in view of the rather long periods covered. The total rise from the early to the late years of the interwar period does not appear to have exceeded 4 percentage points. It seems

TABLE 3

Value of Inventories Held by Major Industrial
Divisions, 1918-1939

(Dollar figures are averages of year end figures in billions at current book values. Percentage figures represent proportion of each category in total.)

| | KUZNETS' ESTIMATES MODIFIED BY NBER[a] | | | | | | COMMERCE DEPT. ESTIMATES MODIFIED BY NBER[b] | | | | | |
| | 1918-1933 | | 1918-1927 | | 1928-1933 | | 1928-1939 | | 1928-1933 | | 1934-1939 | |
	$	%	$	%	$	%	$	%	$	%	$	%
1) Mfg.	12.1	39.0	12.7	38.0	11.0	40.4	11.0	45.3	11.0	44.5	11.0	45.8
2) Mining	.7	2.3	.8	2.4	.5	1.8	.4	1.6	.5	2.0	.4	1.7
3) Trade	11.5	37.1	12.4	37.1	10.1	37.1	8.3	34.2	8.4	34.0	8.3	34.6
4) Transp.	.9	2.9	.9	2.7	.9	3.3	.8	3.3	.9	3.6	.7	2.9
5) Agr.	3.9	12.6	4.6	13.8	2.9	10.7	3.0	12.3	2.9	11.7	3.0	12.5
6) Other	1.9	6.1	2.0	6.0	1.8	6.6	.8	3.3	1.0	4.0	.6	2.5
7) Total	31.0	100.0	33.4	100.0	27.2	100.0	24.3	100.0	24.7	100.0	24.0	100.0

Except as noted below, estimates cover total inventories in each industrial division.

Line 4, *Transportation and other public utilities*: Corporations only; unincorporated business, however, is negligible.

Line 5, *Agriculture*: Covers only wheat, corn, oats, cattle and calves (except milk cows), hogs, sheep and lambs. Principal crop omitted is cotton; principal livestock omitted is chickens. Other important livestock categories, for example milk cows and horses, are excluded because they are of the nature of durable capital equipment.

Line 6, *Other*
Construction: Kuznets' data involve duplication with other industrial divisions to the extent that building materials are held by enterprises outside the construction industry in order to carry on construction on force account.

Service: Kuznets' data cover corporations only. For 1928-39 the Department of Commerce estimates the average inventories of unincorporated firms to be $151 million.

Finance and nature not given: Both Kuznets and the Department of Commerce cover corporations only. The latter excludes stock and bond brokers and dealers.

[a] From *Commodity Flow and Capital Formation*, Table VII-6. Line 5 comprises revised estimates of the same scope as the original figures but incorporates later Department of Agriculture revisions of the underlying data. For details of the procedure see ibid., Part VII.

[b] Prepared by Wendell D. Hance and published in the *Survey of Current Business*, Sept. 1942, p. 18, except for categories noted below:

Manufacturing: Estimates by Kuznets, 1928-36, and by me, 1937-39, were substituted for those prepared by Hance. For a description of the procedures see App. A. These figures differ in only minor respects from Hance's estimates. They are used here to preserve comparability with other data in this volume.

Agriculture: Data comparable in scope with those presented in *Commodity Flow and Capital Formation* are substituted for Hance's estimates which cover only agricultural corporations.

possible to say, therefore, that on Kuznets' calculations manufacturers normally held about 40 percent of all inventories; on the Commerce estimates, about 45 percent.

These estimates are subject to several qualifications. A minor difficulty is that neither estimate of total stocks is quite comprehensive and there is some double counting (see Table 3, notes). The net sum of all the omissions and duplications, however, would hardly increase total inventories as much as 2 percent. It is safe to conclude that they would not reduce the apparent share of manufacturing more than one percentage point.

A more serious difficulty is the vague boundary of the manufacturing division. The central notion suggested by the word is the manipulation of raw materials, as opposed either to their extraction or transportation to the fabricating plant or to the sale and distribution of the fabricated commodity. Every manufacturing concern, however, engages in some activities that are not manufacturing operations thus conceived. Some operations concerned with the assembly of raw materials and supplies and with the sale and distribution of the finished product appear almost always to be connected with the performance of the manufacturing function itself, and a large part of manufacturers' inventories are held in order to facilitate these operations. On the other hand, firms commonly considered to be engaged in mining, transportation, or trade usually perform some manufacturing operations. Mining firms often clean, crush, and concentrate the materials they extract. Trading firms often perform minor manufacturing operations on at least part of the goods they handle. In some cases they own establishments engaged primarily in manufacturing. The line between manufacturing and other industrial divisions is necessarily hazy.

In practice there are two solutions to the problem. One is the device adopted by the Census of Manufactures—to use the establishment as the basic unit of classification.[2] The implicit test for admitting nonmanufacturing activities to the manufacturing

[2] The Bureau of Census describes an establishment as follows: "As a rule the term 'establishment' signifies a single plant or factory. In some cases, however, it refers to two or more plants operated under a common ownership or located in the same city, or in the same State but in different municipalities

sphere is location in the same works or small area where operations are subject to central direction.

The second solution, that used by the Bureau of Internal Revenue in compiling *Statistics of Income,* underlies the estimates of Table 3. The reporting unit is the company or corporate unit. The implicit test for the admission of nonmanufacturing activities to the manufacturing sphere is the corporate charter. Nonmanufacturing activities carried on by a company whose main activity is fabrication are classified with other manufacturing industries whether carried on in a single plant or not; manufacturing activities carried on by a company whose main activity lies outside manufacturing are excluded.

The fuzziness this practice introduces into the industrial classification was, during part of the period, even more important than this statement suggests. From 1921 to 1933 affiliated corporations were permitted to make tax returns on a consolidated basis. Companies whose accounts were consolidated with those of affiliated companies were, of course, classified according to the main activity of the group, not according to their own main activity.[3]

As it happens, the company basis of classification brings a considerably larger volume of inventories within manufacturing than does the establishment basis (see App. A). Nonmanufacturing establishments owned by manufacturing companies are far more important than manufacturing establishments owned by non-manufacturing companies. At the end of 1936, a date for which we have information on both bases, the adjusted census total of manufacturing inventories was $9.8 billion. Kuznets' estimate was $11.2 billion. A large part of the difference was due to Kuznets' inclusion of distributive establishments owned by manufacturing companies. An additional but smaller portion was accounted for by mining establishments similarly owned, while part of the remainder can be laid to shortages in census coverage.

(Continuation of footnote 2)
or unincorporated places having fewer than 10,000 inhabitants. On the other hand, separate reports are occasionally obtained for different industries carried on in the same plant, in which event a single plant is counted as two or more establishments."

[3] Problems raised by consolidated reports and their effect on the classification of companies are discussed in Appendix A, Section 1B(3).

Kuznets' total obviously includes a larger volume of inventories held to support nonmanufacturing activities strictly conceived than does the census total. It does not follow, however, that the criterion of classification underlying Kuznets' data is less useful than that underlying the census data, for the establishment criterion does not exclude from manufacturing distributive activities and the inventories that support them. It excludes them only if they are carried on in a separate establishment. The rival criterion draws the line at separate ownership, denoted by a distinct corporate charter. Both are arbitrary.

If some nonmanufacturing activities must be included, a more reasonable criterion than either would be to include any such activities as are exclusively or dominantly devoted to supporting the manufacturing activities of a given firm. This is the definition of the scope of manufacturing this study tries to apply. Thus wholesale distribution confined to the products or raw materials of a single firm might well be classified as part of manufacturing. From this point of view, the establishment criterion makes certain that few if any nonmanufacturing activities not confined exclusively to the support of a given company's manufacturing activities are included. But it will exclude many nonmanufacturing activities that on this criterion ought to be included. The ownership criterion manifestly has the opposite virtues and faults.

We are left, therefore, with the impression that the most useful measure of manufacturers' inventories is something under Kuznets' level but something above the census level. If so, we may reduce Kuznets' estimate by, say, half the difference between his and the census figure, that is, by roughly $700 million. In that event the share of manufacturing in the Commerce total would be about 43.5 percent, and the share on Kuznets' calculations about 37.5 percent. A good round number, therefore, to express the relative share of total inventories held by manufacturers in the interwar period is 40 percent. It is with this considerable block of total stocks that this study is concerned.

CHAPTER 3

National Bureau Measures of Cyclical Behavior

This study uses extensively the National Bureau technique of describing and measuring the cyclical behavior of economic data. When we wish to know, for example, how regularly inventories rise during business expansions and fall during contractions we use the Bureau's measure of 'conformity'. When we wish to know whether cycles in manufacturers' inventories generally reach their peaks before or after general business activity, or before or after manufacturing production or sales we use its measure of 'timing'. When we wish to know how wide the cyclical swings of inventories are compared with those of production or shipments we compute measures of 'amplitude' according to the Bureau's method. And so on.

The National Bureau measures of cyclical behavior, together with elaborate tests, are described in detail in *Measuring Business Cycles*. Close students of business cycles are referred to that volume. Other readers will need a brief description of the Bureau's statistical techniques if they are to understand the methods and conclusions of this study. This chapter attempts to meet that need.[1] It relies heavily on Chapter 2 of *Measuring Business Cycles*. Indeed, entire pages of that chapter and all the illustrative tables are reprinted below. Verbal alterations have been made in some sections because of the difference in context, and some material has been added.

The description in Chapter 2 of *Measuring Business Cycles* applies in detail only to the measures made from data reported by

[1] The measures used by the Bureau are not complicated, but they are numerous. The reader would probably do well to read this chapter once, then refer back to relevant sections as the results of particular measurements are set forth.

months. In the absence of monthly data, we often have to use quarterly or annual data, and this is especially true of this study. Annual data, moreover, come in various forms: as aggregates or averages for calendar or fiscal years, and as values for a certain month or day, the latter notably in financial data based on end of year balance sheets of corporations. We therefore supplement the description of the procedures applied to monthly data with an explanation of the methods followed when the figures are for calendar years or single dates. Fiscal year data are not treated, since the procedures are identical with those applied to calendar year series, except that the chronology of business cycle turns is for a fiscal instead of a calendar year. Nor are the measures applied to quarterly data described, since they closely resemble the methods used for monthly data. Readers interested in the minor differences will find them described in *Measuring Business Cycles,* pp. 197–202.

The results from annual data are not nearly as accurate as those from monthly or quarterly data. Yet annual data can yield very useful information. But if they are to be more helpful than misleading, their limitations must be known and respected. The latter part of this chapter is, therefore, devoted to a brief discussion of the differences to be expected when the figures are annual instead of monthly or quarterly.

1 Description of the Measures[2]

REFERENCE DATES, REFERENCE CYCLES, AND SPECIFIC CYCLES

To learn how different economic processes behave in respect of business cycles, their movements must be observed during the revivals, expansions, recessions, and contractions in general business activity. Before we can begin observing we must mark off these periods. To that end we constructed a table of 'reference dates', showing the months and years when business cycles reached troughs and peaks. These dates were based first upon the business annals compiled for the National Bureau by Willard L. Thorp; then we refined, tested, and at need amended the dates by studying statistical series. These turning points of the cyclical movements in

[2] This section largely, though not entirely, duplicates Chapter 2 of *Measuring Business Cycles.*

general business activity can be made more precise as the field covered by statistics expands. Hence we have more confidence in the later than in the earlier dates. Table 4 sets forth the National Bureau standard reference dates for the United States since 1853.

TABLE 4

Reference Dates, United States, 1853-1939

MONTHLY		QUARTERLY		CALENDAR YEAR		FISCAL YEAR (ENDING JUNE 30)	
Peak	Trough	Peak	Trough	Peak	Trough	Peak	Trough
	Dec. 1854		4Q 1854	1853	1855		
June 1857	Dec. 1858	2Q 1857	4Q 1858	1856	1858		
Oct. 1860	June 1861	3Q 1860	3Q 1861	1860	1861		
Apr. 1865	Dec. 1867	1Q 1865	1Q 1868	1864	1867		1868
June 1869	Dec. 1870	2Q 1869	4Q 1870	1869	1870	1869	1871
Oct. 1873	Mar. 1879	3Q 1873	1Q 1879	1873	1878	1873	1878
Mar. 1882	May 1885	1Q 1882	2Q 1885	1882	1885	1882	1885
Mar. 1887	Apr. 1888	2Q 1887	1Q 1888	1887	1888	1887	1888
July 1890	May 1891	3Q 1890	2Q 1891	1890	1891	1890	1891
Jan. 1893	June 1894	1Q 1893	2Q 1894	1892	1894	1893	1894
Dec. 1895	June 1897	4Q 1895	2Q 1897	1895	1896	1896	1897
June 1899	Dec. 1900	3Q 1899	4Q 1900	1899	1900	1900	1901
Sept. 1902	Aug. 1904	4Q 1902	3Q 1904	1903	1904	1903	1904
May 1907	June 1908	2Q 1907	2Q 1908	1907	1908	1907	1908
Jan. 1910	Jan. 1912	1Q 1910	4Q 1911	1910	1911	1910	1911
Jan. 1913	Dec. 1914	1Q 1913	4Q 1914	1913	1914	1913	1915
Aug. 1918	Apr. 1919	3Q 1918	2Q 1919	1918	1919	1918	1919
Jan. 1920	Sept. 1921a	1Q 1920	3Q 1921	1920	1921	1920	1922
May 1923	July 1924	2Q 1923	3Q 1924	1923	1924	1923	1924
Oct. 1926	Dec. 1927a	3Q 1926	4Q 1927	1926	1927	1927	1928
June 1929	Mar. 1933	2Q 1929	1Q 1933	1929	1932	1929	1933
May 1937	May 1938a	2Q 1937	2Q 1938	1937	1938	1937	1939

Source: *Measuring Business Cycles*, Table 16, p. 78.

a The following reference dates have been revised by the National Bureau since the computations in this study were completed: Sept. 1921 to July 1921; Dec. 1927 to Nov. 1927; May 1938 to June 1938.

After eliminating seasonal variations we divide the series into segments marked off by reference troughs. Since each segment spans an interval between successive reference troughs we call it a 'reference cycle segment', or 'reference cycle' for brevity.[3] Next we compute the average of the monthly values during each 'reference cycle' and convert the data into percentages of this base; these percentages are called 'reference cycle relatives'. The application of a uniform set of dates to all series, and the reduction of the original data expressed in diverse units to relatives of their average values during the periods thus marked off, put all the materials into com-

[3] We find it convenient to use the term 'reference cycle' in two senses: first, to denote the section of a time series between the dates of successive reference troughs (or peaks); second, to denote the interval between successive troughs (or peaks). The meaning should be obvious from the context.

parable form and enable us to see how different processes behave during successive business cycles.

Next, we look in every series for wavelike movements whose length is of the same order as that of business cycles. We call the cyclical movements peculiar to a series its 'specific cycles'. In most series the dates of the troughs and peaks of the specific cycles are fairly clear, but in some series they are obscured by erratic fluctuations. We mark off the specific cycles by the dates of their turning points as well as we can, compute the average value of the monthly data during each cycle, and convert the monthly data into 'specific cycle relatives' which correspond in every respect to the reference cycle relatives, except that they show movements during the cycles in the series itself.

One complication requires attention at this point. Most series studied in connection with business cycles tend to rise during expansions of general business and to fall during contractions. They have what we call 'positive' cycles. Many series, however, have 'inverted' cycles, that is, they tend to fall during business expansions and rise during contractions. Such 'inverted' series are especially numerous among manufacturers' inventories. The specific cycles in 'positive' series are treated as units running from trough to trough, those in 'inverted' series are treated as units running from peak to peak.

We distinguish between 'positive' and 'inverted' series in the following manner. If a series typically moves in the same direction as general business activity over a larger portion of a reference cycle than it moves in the opposite direction, we treat the series as 'positive'.[4] In the opposite case we treat it as 'inverted'. If a series typically rises from the middle of a reference expansion to the middle of a reference contraction, or from the middle of contraction to the middle of expansion, we call the series 'neutral', but we arbitrarily analyze the specific cycles on a 'positive' basis, that is, as units running from trough to trough. The same procedure is followed in the case of series whose movements have no regular relation to business cycles.

We illustrate our procedure for a positive series. We chose coke

[4] We measure the size of the portion in terms of the 9 'reference stages' into which each reference cycle is divided; see below.

production because it is a relatively short series and presents few
of the complications we ordinarily encounter (Table 5). The seasonally adjusted figures are plotted on Chart 1, which shows also
the turning points of business cycles and of the cycles in coke production. The average monthly production of coke during its first
complete cycle, November 1914 to May 1919, was 4,246,000 short
tons. With that figure as a base, the monthly values in Table 5 for
the months covered by this cycle are converted into specific cycle
relatives. The first reference cycle covered by this series runs from
December 1914 to April 1919. Average monthly output was
4,305,000 short tons, and on this base we compute the first set of
reference cycle relatives. During the second specific cycle, May
1919 to July 1921, average monthly output was 3,565,000 short
tons; during the second reference cycle, April 1919 to September
1921, it was 3,417,000 short tons. These figures are the bases upon
which relatives are computed for the second specific and the second reference cycle. The turning points shown on Chart 1 mark
off three more specific and three more reference cycles, for each of
which we compute cycle relatives. In annual series the cycle bases
are computed by striking averages including all the years from one

TABLE 5

Coke Production

(thousands of short tons)

Year	Jan.	Feb.	Mar.	Apr.	May	June	July	Aug.	Sept.	Oct.	Nov.	Dec.
1914	2973	3147	3476	3364	2940	2897	2991	2927	2797	2531	2193	2348
1915	2281	2555	2675	2897	2990	3410	3613	3873	3959	4320	4475	4553
1916	4381	4564	4554	4425	4581	4581	4392	4667	4684	4655	4593	4499
1917	4664	4523	4672	4720	4693	4778	4731	4611	4693	4542	4577	4452
1918	3855	3957	4415	4639	4801	4941	5228	5067	5033	5017	4844	4730
1919	4763	4126	3773	3335	2977	3173	3777	3987	3943	3157	3600	3624
1920	4329	4261	4360	3885	4031	4299	4412	4536	4520	4496	4284	3971
1921	3314	2886	2203	1855	1860	1679	1497	1637	1719	2076	2231	2338
1922	2391	2512	2658	2798	2979	3180	3038	2413	2927	3638	4145	4342
1923	4650	4695	4853	5174	5250	5216	5076	4901	4641	4362	4132	4107
1924	4278	4493	4386	4199	3581	3108	2923	2936	3132	3466	3596	4182
1925	4599	4458	4259	4204	3950	3900	3804	3838	4102	4333	4836	5087
1926	5244	5280	4746	4719	4643	4635	4721	4606	4578	4604	4665	4495
1927	4471	4426	4521	4553	4389	4320	4219	4219	4112	4027	3887	3991
1928	4249	4348	4276	4365	4450	4413	4286	4344	4332	4524	4569	4688
1929	4822	4798	4889	5005	5250	5311	5361	5295	5000	4961	4761	4502
1930	4441	4480	4387	4562	4460	4316	4041	3817	3579	3480	3280	3193
1931	3195	3193	3187	3266	3167	2870	2682	2522	2396	2403	2356	2277
1932	2150	2174	2037	1948	1761	1619	1586	1522	1598	1741	1817	1846
1933	1853	1819	1664	1720	1948	2363	2928	3029	2803	2553	2443	2523

Adjusted for seasonal variations. The original data come from *Mineral Resources of the
United States* (Bureau of Mines, 1925), Part II, p. 545, and later annual numbers (now
called *Minerals Yearbook*).

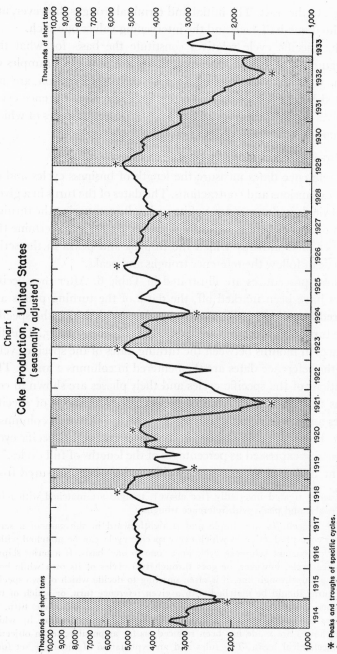

Chart 1

Coke Production, United States
(seasonally adjusted)

Logarithmic scale

* Peaks and troughs of specific cycles.
Contractions (shaded) and expansions (unshaded) are marked off by the monthly reference chronology.

trough to the next. The initial and terminal troughs, however, are
weighted one-half each and the intervening values one each.

The specific cycle relatives constitute the basis for what the
Bureau calls 'S' tables. Five such tables are prepared; samples of
them, together with explanations of their construction are reprinted here as Tables 6-10. In the same way the reference cycle
relatives are the basis for three or four 'R' tables, samples of which
are reprinted here as Tables 11-14.

TIMING AND LENGTH OF SPECIFIC CYCLES

The reference dates measure the length of business cycles and of
their expansions and contractions. The dates of the turns in a given
series yield similar measures of its cycles. By comparing the turning
dates of specific cycles with the reference dates, we determine the
number of months by which the troughs and peaks in the series
precede or follow the reference troughs and peaks.[5]

These procedures are illustrated in Table 6. After the specific
cycles have been marked off, the dates of the turning points are
entered in column 1. The reference dates with which the specific
cycle turns are compared are entered in columns 3 and 5. The differences in months between the turning dates of the specific cycles
and the reference dates are then entered in columns 2 and 4. The
durations of the specific cycles and their phases are shown in columns 6 to 8. The differences between the durations of specific
cycles and corresponding reference cycles are shown in columns 9
to 11. Finally, in columns 12 and 13 the lengths of the specific cycle
phases are expressed as percentages of the lengths of full cycles.[6]

The timing of the turns of specific cycles when measured from

[5] For series treated invertedly (see above), troughs are matched with reference peaks, and peaks with reference troughs.

[6] These procedures are simple and straightforward in the case of a series
such as coke production in which every specific cycle can be matched with a
closely concurrent reference cycle on a 'one to one' basis. If a series skips a
reference cycle, however, or goes through two cycles of its own while business is going through one, it is often puzzling to decide which of two specific
cycle turns should be matched with a given reference turn, or which of two
reference turns should be matched with a given specific cycle turn, or
whether no comparisons at all should be made. The procedure by which
these choices are made has been reduced, as far as possible, to an objective
and mechanical basis. The rules and an explanation of them are set forth
in *Measuring Business Cycles*, pp. 116 ff.

TABLE 6

Sample of Table S1 : Timing and Length of Specific Cycles
Coke Production

DATES OF SPECIFIC CYCLES			TIMING AT REFERENCE				LENGTH OF CYCLICAL MOVEMENTS (MO.)						% OF LENGTH OF SPECIFIC CYCLES	
			Peak		Trough		Specific cycles			Excess over ref. cycles				
Trough	Peak	Trough	Lead (−) or lag (+) months	Ref. peak	Lead (−) or lag (+) months	Ref. trough	Exp.	Contr.	Cycle	Exp.	Contr.	Cycle	Exp.	Contr.
(1)			(2)	(3)	(4)	(5)	(6)	(7)	(8)	(9)	(10)	(11)	(12)	(13)
11/14					−1	12/14								
11/14–7/18– 5/19			−1	8/18	+1	4/19	44	10	54	0	+2	+2	81	19
5/19–8/20– 7/21			+7	1/20	−2	9/21	15	11	26	+6	−9	−3	58	42
7/21–5/23– 7/24			0	5/23	0	7/24	22	14	36	+2	0	+2	61	39
7/24–2/26–11/27			−8	10/26	−1	12/27	19	21	40	−8	+7	−1	48	52
11/27–7/29– 8/32			+1	6/29	−7	3/33	20	37	57	+2	−8	−6	35	65
Average			−0.2		−1.7		24.0	18.6	42.6	+0.4	−1.6	−1.2	57	43
Average deviation			3.4		1.9		8.0	8.3	10.3	3.5	5.5	2.6	12	12

annual data is necessarily crude. The year of the specific cycle turn may be compared with the year of the corresponding reference cycle turn or the midpoint of the year of the specific cycle turn with the midpoint of the corresponding monthly reference cycle turn. For single-date series, the latter method involves a comparison of turns on that date with the corresponding monthly reference turns. Both theoretical expectation and experiment support the view that the second method is better (see Sec. 2 below).

It is a characteristic of timing measures made from annual data, however, that the measures for individual turns have little value in themselves. They are used only to establish an average timing relation for several cycles. The National Bureau does not make such comparisons or compute averages unless the series conforms well to business cycles and at least a dozen specific and reference turns can be compared. In one class of cases, however, we did not adhere to these rules. When preparing tables combining the timing behavior of ten groups of manufacturing industries, we noted every comparison possible in each individual series. But the results are used only to help establish the timing characteristics that are applicable to manufacturing as a whole, not the differences that may characterize the behavior of the individual groups (the validity of our procedure is discussed further in Sec. 2 below).

The length of specific cycles based on annual data is measured in the same way as of those based on monthly data. For the former, however, columns 9-11 of Table 6 are omitted.

MEASURING SPECIFIC CYCLE AMPLITUDE

Amplitude is measured by the rise of the specific cycle relatives
from the initial trough of a cycle to the peak and of the fall from
the peak to the terminal trough. To diminish the influence of random factors, we use 3-month averages centered on the troughs and
peaks. Of course, the amplitudes express the rise and fall as percentages of the average value of the series during each cycle.

Table 7 gives these amplitude measures in three forms. Columns
2-4 show the 3-month averages of the specific cycle relatives centered on the initial trough, peak, and terminal trough. Columns
5-7, obtained from columns 2-4, show the rise from trough to
peak, the fall from peak to trough, and the total rise and fall. Columns 8-10, obtained by dividing the figures in columns 5-7 of
Table 7 by the corresponding duration figures, columns 6-8 of
Table 6, show the amplitudes per month.

TABLE 7

Sample of Table S2: Amplitude of Specific Cycles
Coke Production

DATES OF SPECIFIC CYCLES	3-MO. AV. IN SPECIFIC CYCLE RELATIVES CENTERED ON			AMPLITUDE OF			PER MO. AMPLITUDE OF		
Trough-Peak-Trough	Initial trough	Peak	Ter- minal trough	Rise	Fall	Rise & fall	Rise	Fall	Rise & fall
11/14–7/18– 5/19	55.5	119.6	74.5	64.1	45.1	109.2	1.5	4.5	2.0
5/19–8/20– 7/21	88.7	125.9	45.0	37.2	80.9	118.1	2.5	7.4	4.5
7/21–5/23– 7/24	44.3	144.0	82.6	99.7	61.4	161.1	4.5	4.4	4.5
7/24–2/26–11/27	69.4	118.2	92.1	48.8	26.1	74.9	2.6	1.2	1.9
11/27–7/29– 8/32	105.5	141.6	41.7	36.1	99.9	136.0	1.8	2.7	2.4
Average	72.7	129.9	67.2	57.2	62.7	119.9	2.6	4.0	3.1
Average deviation	19.5	10.4	19.1	19.8	22.2	23.0	0.8	1.7	1.2

Amplitude measures for annual data are made in the same
fashion as for monthly data. The standings in columns 2-4 of
Table 7, however, are based on the years (or single dates) marking the cyclical turns.

MEASURING SECULAR MOVEMENTS

Our method of computing cycle relatives as percentages of the
average value during a specific or a reference cycle eliminates
from the original data what we call the 'inter-cycle' portion of the
secular trend. We do not try to eliminate the 'intra-cycle' portion,
because we wish to reproduce as faithfully as may be the 'cyclical
units' of actual economic experience.

Table 8 throws into relief the secular component of the specific cycles. Columns 2 and 3 show the average values of the seasonally adjusted data during the phases of specific cycles. Column 4 shows the average values during full specific cycles, the values on which the specific cycle relatives are based. Column 5 shows the percentage change from the average standing during a contraction to the average during the following expansion, and column 6 shows the percentage change from the average standing during an expansion to the average during the following contraction. Column 7 shows the percentage change from the average standing during one full specific cycle to that during the next. And column 8 reduces the measures in column 7 to a per month basis, the divisor being the number of months from the midpoint of one cycle to the midpoint of the next.

TABLE 8

Sample of Table S3: Secular Movements
Coke Production

DATES OF SPECIFIC CYCLES			AV. MONTHLY STANDING (000 short tons)			% CHANGE FROM PRECEDING PHASE		% CHANGE FROM PRECEDING CYCLE ON BASE OF			
								Preceding cycle		Av. of given & preceding cycle	
Trough	Peak	Trough	Exp.	Contr.	Cycle	Contr. to exp.	Exp. to contr.	Total	Per mo.	Total	Per mo.
(1)			(2)	(3)	(4)	(5)	(6)	(7)	(8)	(9)	(10)
11/14–7/18– 5/19			4193	4479	4246	...	+7	...	...	...	...
5/19–8/20– 7/21			3906	3099	3565	−13	−21	−16	−0.40	−17	−0.42
7/21–5/23– 7/24			3171	4326	3620	+2	+36	+2	+0.06	+2	+0.06
7/24–2/26–11/27			4107	4488	4307	−5	+9	+19	+0.50	+17	+0.45
11/27–7/29– 8/32			4577	3319	3760	+2	−27	−13	−0.27	−14	−0.29
Average			...	...	...	...	...	...	...	−3.0	−0.05
Average deviation			...	...	...	...	...	...	...	12.5	0.30
Weighted average			...	...	...	...	...	...	...	...	−0.08

Column 9 is the same as column 7 except that the percentages are based on the average of the two cycles being compared instead of on the first cycle. This shift of method frees the percentages from secular 'bias' and permits us to strike averages for all cycles. Column 10 bears the same relation to column 9 as column 8 bears to column 7. The weighted average at the bottom of column 10 is obtained by weighting the entries by the intervals between the midpoints of successive cycles.

In the case of annual data the average standings during expansions and contractions, columns 2 and 3, include all years from one turn to the next. The values at the turns, however, are weighted one-half each. Similarly, the average standing for the full cycle, column 4, includes all the years from trough to trough. The initial and terminal trough values, however, are weighted one-half each, intervening values one each. The other measures in Table 8 are prepared in the same way for monthly and annual data.

CYCLICAL PATTERNS

To depict the behavior of a series during the course of its cycles in more detail than in Table 7, each cycle is divided into nine stages. Stage I covers the three months centered on the initial trough, stage V the three months centered on the peak, and stage IX the three months centered on the terminal trough. Stages II-IV cover successive thirds of the expansion, and stages VI-VIII successive thirds of the contraction. By averaging the specific cycle relatives for the months included in each stage we get 'specific cycle patterns' (Table 9).

TABLE 9

Sample of Table S4: Specific Cycle Patterns
Coke Production

			I	II	III	IV	V	VI	VII	VIII	IX
							AVERAGE IN SPECIFIC CYCLE RELATIVES AT STAGE				
DATES OF SPECIFIC CYCLES			3 mo. cen- tered on initial trough	EXPANSION			3 mo. cen- tered on peak	CONTRACTION			3 mo. cen- tered on ter- minal trough
Trough	Peak	Trough		First third	Middle third	Last third		First third	Middle third	Last third	
(1)			(2)	(3)	(4)	(5)	(6)	(7)	(8)	(9)	(10)
11/14–7/18– 5/19			55.5	81.3	108.0	107.1	119.6	118.7	112.6	88.2	74.5
5/19–8/20– 7/21			88.7	101.2	110.9	117.8	125.9	124.4	86.8	50.4	45.0
7/21–5/23–11/24			44.3	58.8	78.9	124.3	144.0	137.0	118.1	105.5	82.6
7/24–2/26–11/27			69.4	84.8	95.1	106.2	118.2	108.3	105.2	99.0	92.1
11/27–7/29– 8/32			105.5	113.8	118.4	133.3	141.6	122.4	86.2	55.9	41.7
Average			72.7	88.0	102.3	117.7	129.9	122.2	101.8	79.8	67.2
Average deviation			19.5	15.6	12.2	8.9	10.4	6.9	12.2	21.3	19.1

We make 'reference cycle patterns' on a similar plan except that we mark off nine stages on the basis of the turning dates in general business. By dividing each reference cycle into nine segments, we reveal the behavior of economic processes from stage to stage of business cycles. Table 11, presenting the reference cycle patterns, differs from Table 9 in only two respects: the troughs and peaks are taken from the standard list of reference dates instead of from the turning points of specific cycles, and the entries are expressed in units of reference cycle instead of specific cycle relatives.

TABLE 10

Sample of Table S5: Rate of Change from Stage to Stage
of Specific Cycles, Coke Production

			AV. CHANGE PER MO. IN SPECIFIC CYCLE RELATIVES BETWEEN STAGES						
DATES OF			I-II	II-III	III-IV	IV-V	V-VI	VI-VII	VII-VIII	VIII-IX
SPECIFIC CYCLES			EXPANSION				CONTRACTION		
Trough	Peak	Trough	Trough to first third	First to middle third	Middle to last third	Last third to peak	Peak to first third	First to middle third	Middle to last third	Last third to trough
(1)			(2)	(3)	(4)	(5)	(6)	(7)	(8)	(9)
11/14–7/18– 5/19			+3.4	+1.8	—0.1	+1.7	—0.4	—2.0	—8.1	—6.8
5/19–8/20– 7/21			+4.2	+2.2	+1.5	+2.7	—0.8	—10.7	—10.4	—2.7
7/21–5/23– 7/24			+3.6	+2.9	+6.5	+4.9	—2.8	—4.2	—2.8	—9.2
7/24–2/26–11/27			+4.4	+1.7	+1.8	+3.4	—2.5	—0.5	—1.0	—1.7
11/27–7/29– 8/32			+2.4	+0.7	+2.3	+2.4	—3.0	—3.0	—2.5	—2.2
Average			+3.6	+1.9	+2.4	+3.0	—1.9	—4.1	—5.0	—4.5
Average deviation			0.6	0.6	1.6	0.9	1.0	2.7	3.4	2.8
Av. interval (mo.)			4.3	7.7	7.7	4.3	3.4	5.9	5.9	3.4

Additional information concerning cyclical patterns is supplied by Tables 10 and 12. Table 10, obtained by dividing the differences between successive figures on each line in Table 9 by the number of months from the middle of one specific cycle stage to the middle of the next stage, shows the rate of change from one stage of specific cycles to the next. Table 12, made from Table 11 just as Table 10 is made from Table 9, shows the rate of change from one stage of reference cycles to the next.

When compelled to use annual data our procedure is simpler. The cyclical patterns of Tables 9 and 11 are made on a five- instead of a nine-stage basis, but to avoid confusion we call these stages I, III, V, VII, and IX. The standings at stages I, V, and IX

TABLE 11

Sample of Table R1: Reference Cycle Patterns
Coke Production

			AVERAGE IN REFERENCE CYCLE RELATIVES AT STAGE							
			I	II	III	IV	V	VI	VII	VIII	IX
DATES OF REFERENCE CYCLES			3 mo. centered on initial trough		EXPANSION		3 mo. centered on peak		CONTRACTION		3 mo. centered on terminal trough
Trough	Peak	Trough		First third	Middle third	Last third		First third	Middle third	Last third	
(1)			(2)	(3)	(4)	(5)	(6)	(7)	(8)	(9)	(10)
12/14– 8/18– 4/19			52.8	83.9	106.7	106.6	118.7	116.7	111.0	91.7	78.1
4/19– 1/20– 9/21			98.4	96.9	116.1	101.3	119.2	123.2	117.1	52.3	53.0
9/21– 5/23– 7/24			48.4	63.3	80.2	124.2	139.5	132.7	114.4	102.2	80.0
7/24–10/26–12/27			69.5	90.0	98.4	111.6	107.4	105.0	102.4	94.5	94.0
12/27– 6/29– 3/33			114.4	123.1	124.8	138.9	150.2	128.2	83.3	52.3	49.1
Average			76.7	91.4	105.2	116.5	127.0	121.2	105.6	78.6	70.8
Average deviation			23.8	14.8	12.8	12.0	14.3	8.2	10.2	21.0	15.8

TABLE 12

Sample of Table R2: Rate of Change from Stage to Stage
of Reference Cycles, Coke Production

				AV. CHANGE PER MO. IN REFERENCE CYCLE RELATIVES BETWEEN STAGES							
				I-II	II-III	III-IV	IV-V	V-VI	VI-VII	VII-VIII	VIII-IX
DATES OF REFERENCE CYCLES				E X P A N S I O N				C O N T R A C T I O N			
Trough	Peak	Trough		Trough to first third	First to middle third	Middle to last third	Last third to peak	Peak to first third	First to middle third	Middle to last third	Last third to trough
(1)				(2)	(3)	(4)	(5)	(6)	(7)	(8)	(9)
12/14– 8/18– 4/19				+4.1	+1.6	0.0	+1.6	−1.3	−2.3	−7.7	−9.1
4/19– 1/20– 9/21				−0.8	+7.7	−5.9	+9.0	+1.1	−0.9	−10.0	+0.2
9/21– 5/23– 7/24				+4.3	+2.6	+6.8	+4.4	−2.7	−4.1	−2.7	−8.9
7/24–10/26–12/27				+4.1	+1.0	+1.6	−0.8	−1.0	−0.6	−1.8	−0.2
12/27– 6/29– 3/33				+2.5	+0.3	+2.6	+3.2	−2.8	−3.1	−2.1	−0.4
Average				+2.8	+2.6	+1.0	+3.5	−1.3	−2.2	−4.9	−3.7
Average deviation				1.6	2.0	3.2	2.6	1.1	1.2	3.2	4.3
Av. interval (mo.)				4.3	7.5	7.5	4.3	3.6	6.5	6.5	3.6

are, of course, the same as the standings computed for initial
trough, peak, and terminal trough in Table 7. The mid-expansion
and mid-contraction standings (stages III and VII) are approximated as closely as possible. If an expansion lasts three years, for
example, the value in the second year is taken to represent stage
III. If it lasts four years, the stage III standing is computed by averaging the two middle years. If the expansion lasts only two years,
we have to calculate a stage III standing by interpolation, that is,
by striking an average of the trough and peak values.[7]

Tables 10 and 12 are prepared in the same way for annual as for
monthly data. Applied to annual data, however, the entries are
confined to the rate of change from trough to mid-expansion (I-
III), mid-expansion to peak (III-V), peak to mid-contraction
(V-VII), and mid-contraction to terminal trough (VII-IX).

MEASURES OF CONFORMITY TO BUSINESS CYCLES: MONTHLY DATA

The comparisons in Table 6 between specific and reference cycles
show roughly how the wavelike movements in a given series conform to the movements in general business activity. Further light
is shed by the similarity or difference between the average specific
cycle and the average reference cycle patterns of Tables 9 and 11.
But it is desirable to measure explicitly the varying degrees of conformity.

Table 13 gives the measures we seek. Column 4, derived from

[7] For treatment of phases longer than four years, see *Measuring Business
Cycles,* p. 199.

TABLE 13

Sample of Table R3: Conformity to Business Cycles
Coke Production

DATES OF REFERENCE CYCLES			CHANGE IN REFERENCE CYCLE RELATIVES DURING REFERENCE						AV. CHANGE PER MO. DURING REF. CONTR. MINUS THAT DURING	
			EXPANSION			CONTRACTION				
Trough	Peak	Trough	Total change	Interval in mo.	Av. change per mo.	Total change	Interval in mo.	Av. change per mo.	Preceding ref. exp.	Succeeding ref. exp.[a]
(1)			(2)	(3)	(4)	(5)	(6)	(7)	(8)	(9)
12/14– 8/18– 4/19			+65.9	44.0	+1.50	−40.6	8.0	−5.08	−6.58	—
4/19– 1/20– 9/21			+20.8	9.0	+2.31	−66.2	20.0	−3.31	−5.62	—
9/21– 5/23– 7/24			+91.1	20.0	+4.56	−59.5	14.0	−4.25	−8.81	—
7/24–10/26–12/27			+37.9	27.0	+1.40	−13.4	14.0	−0.96	−2.36	—
12/27– 6/29– 3/33			+35.8	18.0	+1.99	−101.1	45.0	−2.25	−4.24	...
Average			+50.3	...	+2.35	−56.2	...	−3.17	−5.52	...
Average deviation			...	...	0.88	...	...	1.25	1.78	...
Index of conformity to reference										
Expansions					+100					
Contractions								+100		
Cycles, trough to trough									+100	
Cycles, peak to peak										+100
Cycles, both ways										+100

[a] Only the sign of the difference is entered.

columns 2 and 3, supplies essential information on the conformity of the series to business cycle expansions. That is, the entries in column 4 indicate the average rise or fall per month during successive reference expansions; the average near the bottom is the average rate of change during all the reference expansions covered by the series. Column 7 supplies similar information concerning the behavior of the series during reference contractions. Finally, column 8 expresses the difference between the rates of change during reference expansions and contractions; this measure is needed because some series with rapidly rising trends continue to advance even during reference contractions, and we wish to know how much, if at all, the rate is intensified during expansions in general business and diminished during contractions.

While the averages near the bottom of columns 4, 7, and 8 are useful measures of conformity, they do not indicate the regularity with which a series 'responds' to the stimuli of general business expansion and contraction. To bring out this feature of cyclical behavior we make a second set of conformity measures, 'indexes of conformity', which take account of the direction of the movements but not their magnitude. When a series rises during a reference expansion we mark it +100; when it remains unchanged we mark it o; when it falls we mark it —100. By casting up the algebraic sum of these entries for all cycles and dividing by their number, we get an index of conformity to reference expansions. This result, entered at the bottom of column 4, may vary between +100 (positive conformity to all the reference expansions covered) and —100 (inverse conformity to all the expansions). An equal number of positive and inverse movements produces an index of o.[8] To measure conformity to reference contractions we proceed similarly, but a decline in column 7 is now marked +100, and a rise —100, for a decline means positive conformity to reference contractions and a rise means inverse conformity.

Finally, we make indexes of conformity to business cycles as wholes. Here we wish to take account of the fact that some series rise or decline throughout reference cycles, but at different rates during expansions and contractions. A preliminary index is obtained by crediting each difference in column 8 with +100 when the difference is minus, with —100 when it is plus, then striking an arithmetic mean. This index shows merely the conformity to business cycles marked off by troughs; hence it is supplemented in column 9 by a similar index showing conformity to business cycles marked off by peaks. A weighted average of the two preliminary indexes gives our final index of conformity to business cycles taken as wholes. A value of +100 means that the rate of change per month during a reference contraction is without exception algebraically lower than the rate of change during the preceding and following expansions.

Table 13 illustrates these computations. The 'expansion index' is +100 because all entries in column 4 are plus. The 'contraction index' is +100 because all signs in column 7 are negative. The preliminary 'full cycle index', taken on a trough to trough basis, is +100, as is the index of conformity to full cycles on a peak to peak basis, since all signs in columns 8 and 9 are negative. The final full cycle index is obviously + 100, since it is an average of two preliminary indexes each of which is +100.

The procedure illustrated in Table 13 is adequate for a series

---

[8] An index of +50 means positive conformity in 3 and inverse conformity in 1 case out of 4; an index of +33 means positive conformity in 2 and inverse conformity in 1 case out of 3.

like coke production which typically rises from reference stage I to V and declines from reference stage V to IX. For the many series that normally lead or lag behind the turns of business activity the results furnished by Table 13 would misrepresent their relation to business cycles or the regularity with which they respond. For such series, therefore, a second conformity table, 14, is prepared.

The preparation of Table 14 begins with an attempt to determine the reference cycle phases between which a series typically rises. The usual procedure is to plot cycle by cycle the reference patterns in Table 11. Each stage interval is then inspected to see whether the series rose or fell during it. If there is no great regularity between one business cycle and the next, we dispense with Table 14. If there is considerable regularity, we determine the stages between which the series typically rises and those between which it typically falls. The division of stages between expansion and contraction need not be equal. Thus we may determine that a series typically rises between stages I and VI and falls between VI and IX, or rises between VII and II and falls between II and VII. Only in rare cases, however, do we make divisions more unequal than five stage intervals for expansion and three for contraction, or vice versa.

Once the division of reference cycles has been decided upon, the next step is to classify the series as 'positive', 'inverted', or 'neutral'. This classification determines whether the specific cycles are to be marked off from trough to trough or from peak to peak, and also plays a part in the computation of Table 14. We class a division of reference cycles as positive when the selected expansion segment contains more stages in the reference expansion than in the contraction; or, what comes to the same thing, when the selected contraction segment contains more stages in the reference contraction than in the expansion. We class the division of reference cycles as inverted when the selected expansion covers more stages in the reference contraction than in the expansion. When the selected expansion overlaps equally reference expansions and contractions, the division is classed as neutral.

Whatever the division, it is applied uniformly in subsequent operations to all the reference cycles covered by the series. When the division is positive, the expansion segments are matched with reference expansions and the contraction segments with contractions. When the division is inverted, the contraction segments are matched with reference expansions and the expansion segments with contractions. When the division is neutral, the division is treated as if it were positive; that is, the expansion segments are

TABLE 14

Sample of Table R4: Conformity to Business Cycles
Timing Differences Recognized
Railroad Bond Yields

(Expansion covers stages III-VI. Expansions are matched with reference expansions.)

DATES OF REFERENCE CYCLES			CHANGE IN REFERENCE CYCLE RELATIVES DURING STAGES MATCHED WITH REFERENCE						AV. CHANGE PER MO. DURING STAGES MATCHED WITH REF. CONTR. MINUS THAT DURING STAGES MATCHED WITH	
			EXPANSION			CONTRACTION				
Trough	Peak	Trough	Total change	Inter-val in mo.	Av. change per mo.	Total change	Inter-val in mo.	Av. change per mo.	Pre-ceding ref. exp.	Suc-ceeding ref. exp.[e]
(1)			(2)	(3)	(4)	(5)	(6)	(7)	(8)	(9)
12/54-	6/57-	12/58	...	...	...	−18.8[a]	25.5	−0.74[a]	...	−
12/58-	10/60-	6/61	+0.9	12.5	+0.07	−24.4	29.5	−0.83	−0.90	−
6/61-	4/65-	12/67	+25.4	28.5	+0.89	0.0	35.5	0.00	−0.89	−
12/67-	6/69-	12/70	+5.2	12.5	+0.42	−6.3	31.5	−0.20	−0.62	+
12/70-	10/73-	3/79	−6.4	28.0	−0.23	−25.5	72.0	−0.35	−0.12	−
3/79-	3/82-	5/85	−4.2	24.5	−0.17	−11.7	42.5	−0.28	−0.11	−
5/85-	3/87-	4/88	+0.8	13.5	+0.06	−5.4	24.0	−0.22	−0.28	−
4/88-	7/90-	5/91	+5.1	15.5	+0.33	+0.6	18.0	+0.03	−0.30	−
5/91-	1/93-	6/94	+0.6	13.0	+0.05	−5.5	23.0	−0.24	−0.29	−
6/94-	12/95-	6/97	−2.0	12.5	−0.16	−5.0	26.5	−0.19	−0.03	+
6/97-	6/99-	12/00	−4.6	15.5	−0.30	+1.7	25.0	+0.07	+0.37	−
12/00-	9/02-	8/04	+5.1	14.5	+0.35	+3.5	35.5	+0.10	−0.25	−
8/04-	5/07-	6/08	+7.9	19.0	+0.42	−4.3	20.0	−0.22	−0.64	−
6/08-	1/10-	1/12	+5.0	14.0	+0.36	+2.0	25.5	+0.08	−0.28	−
1/12-	1/13-	12/14	+4.2[b]	10.0	+0.42[b]	−0.2[b]	41.0	0.00[b]	−0.42[b]	−
12/14-	8/18-	4/19	+16.6	23.5	+0.71	+2.1	11.0	+0.19	−0.52	−
4/19-	1/20-	9/21	+8.7	8.0	+1.09	−19.2	26.5	−0.72	−1.81	−
9/21-	5/23-	7/24	+5.7	12.5	+0.46	−3.0	25.0	−0.12	−0.58	+
7/24-	10/26-	12/27	−4.1	16.0	−0.26	+1.4	20.5	+0.07	+0.33	+
12/27-	6/29-	3/33	+1.0	17.0	+0.06	−19.4	62.0	−0.31	−0.37	...
Average[c]			+3.7	...	+0.24	−6.2	...	−0.17	−0.41	...
Average deviation[d]			...	...	0.32	...	...	0.20	0.33	...

Index of conformity to reference
Expansions   +47
Contractions   +30
Cycles, trough to trough   +79
Cycles, peak to peak   +58
Cycles, both ways   +68

[a] Computed on base of inverted cycle, June 1857–Oct. 1860. Excluded from av. and av. dev.
[b] Computed on base omitting Aug.–Nov. 1914.
[c] Arithmetic mean determined separately for each column. Hence (7) — (4) may differ from (8) in the last place.
[d] Measured from the mean.   [e] Only the sign of the difference is entered.

matched arbitrarily with reference expansions and the contraction segments with contractions. For each series we indicate the procedure by writing at the top of Table 14 what stages are considered characteristic of expansions, and whether expansions are matched with reference expansions or contractions, implying that contractions are matched with the other reference phase.[9]

The other steps in preparing Table 14 are like those for Table 13 except in one respect. For any given cycle the average rate of change per month is computed uniformly for whatever stages have been matched with expansion, not uniformly for stages I-V as in Table 13. Similarly, the average rate of change per month is computed for whatever stages have been matched with contraction, not uniformly for stages V-I.

MEASURES OF CONFORMITY TO BUSINESS CYCLES: ANNUAL DATA

The procedure for preparing Table 13 from annual data is exactly the same as from monthly data. Expansions and contractions, of course, are marked off according to the calendar year, fiscal year, or, in the case of single-date year end series, according to a special end of year chronology. For Table 14, however, a choice of methods is open. If we proceed by the methods applied to monthly data, the stages matched with reference expansions are restricted by the five-stage pattern used for annual series. The stages matched with expansions may, in principle, be I-III, I-V, I-VII, III-V, III-VII, III-IX, V-VII, V-IX, V-III, VII-IX, VII-III, and VII-V. In practice, however, the alternatives are fewer. Since reference phases and, in particular, American contractions, frequently last only a year the standings at stages III and VII are often purely artificial. There is, therefore, seldom enough solid evidence to justify a division between typical expansions and contractions at stage VII. And in short series it is often impossible to use stage III. When stage VII is excluded, the choices are I-III, I-V, III-V, III-IX, V-IX, and V-III. When both III and VII are excluded, the sole choices are I-V and V-IX, that is, Table 14 becomes impossible, and we are restricted to Table 13.

To avoid these difficulties another procedure was devised and

[9] This paragraph and the one preceding are from *Measuring Business Cycles,* pp. 188-9.

is generally used in this study. Instead of attempting to determine the timing of a series in terms of cycle stages, we use the regular timing measures described above to determine its tendency to lead or lag in terms of months. Thus if a series tends to lead the reference dates by 12 months, we simply postdate it one year, then compute its conformity on the basis of a typical expansion running from stage I to V, as in Table 13. If a series tends to lag 12 months, we predate it one year and again proceed as in Table 13. If a calendar year series tends to lag 6 months, we predate it 6 months, that is, the figures for calendar years 1929, 1930, etc. are treated like figures for the fiscal years ended June 30, 1929, 1930, etc. Conformity is then computed on a typical expansion running from stage I to V of the fiscal year reference cycles. If a calendar year series tends to lead 6 months, we postdate it 6 months; that is, calendar year figures for 1928, 1929, etc. are treated like figures for the fiscal years 1929, 1930, etc. In this case again conformity indexes can be derived by matching the series synchronously with fiscal year reference dates. To give additional flexibility, special reference dates were determined for years ending March 31 and September 30. In this way we can deal with the following timing categories in months (leads are marked —, lags +) : —12, —9, —6, —3, synchronous, +3, +6, +9, and +12. The full reference chronology for these timing categories is set forth in Table 15. The timing measures are rounded to determine under which category a series falls for the purpose of measuring conformity. Series that appear to lead or lag by more than one year are treated as if their lead or lag were only 12 months.

The accuracy of this procedure obviously depends in part upon whether we can determine the timing of the series whose conformity is to be measured. As will be shown below, however, timing measures from annual data cannot be assumed to be wholly reliable. To reduce the danger of being misled we adhere to two rules. As in measuring the timing of annual data, only groups of series are measured for conformity, and conclusions are drawn only about the groups as wholes, not about individual members. And we never measure conformity on other than a synchronous basis unless the indicated lead or lag is based on at least seven comparisons between specific and reference cycle turns.

The procedure for end of year series is analogous to that for calendar year series. The conformity of synchronous series is measured by the chronology of the year ends when business reached its peaks and troughs. A year end series that tends to lag a quarter-year is predated 3 months, that is, its values are treated as if they were for September 30. Conformity is then measured on a synchronous basis in conjunction with a September 30 chronology of business cycle turns. In effect we observe our predated series to see whether it regularly rises during expansions bounded by years when the September 30 levels of business were low or high, and

TABLE 15

Reference Dates for Annual Series with Various Leads or Lags
Relative to General Business

The years in each column are the calendar years when a process
may be expected to reach its peaks and troughs under the specified assumptions regarding its timing.

LEAD (−), LAG (+), MONTHS

	−12	−9	−6	−3	0	+3	+6	+9	+12
	(1)	(2)	(3)	(4)	(5)	(6)	(7)	(8)	(9)
			CALENDAR	YEAR	SERIES				
Trough	1913	1914	1914	1914	1914	1915	1915	1915	1915
Peak	1917	1917	1917	1917	1918	1918	1918	1918	1919
Trough	1918	1918	1918	1918/19	1919	1919	1919	1919/20	1920
Peak	1919	1919	1919	1919/20	1920	1920	1920	1920/21	1921
Trough	1920	1920	1921	1921	1921	1921	1922	1922	1922
Peak	1922	1922	1922	1923	1923	1923	1923	1924	1924
Trough	1923	1923	1923	1924	1924	1924	1924	1925	1925
Peak	1925	1926	1926	1926	1926	1927	1927	1927	1927
Trough	1926	1927	1927	1927	1927	1928	1928	1928	1928
Peak	1928	1928	1928	1929	1929	1929	1929	1930	1930
Trough	1931	1931	1932	1932	1932	1932	1933	1933	1933
Peak	1936	1936	1936	1936	1937	1937	1937	1937	1938
Trough	1937	1937	1938	1938	1938	1938	1939	1939	1939
			YEAR	END	SERIES				
Peak	1911	1911	1912	1912	1912	1912	1913	1913	1913
Trough	1913	1913	1913	1914	1914	1914	1914	1915	1915
Peak	1916	1916	1917	1917	1917	1917	1918	1918	1918
Trough	1917	1917	1918	1918	1918	1918	1919	1919	1919
Peak	1918	1918	1919	1919	1919	1919	1920	1920	1920
Trough	1919	1920	1920	1920	1920	1921	1921	1921	1921
Peak	1921	1922	1922	1922	1922	1923	1923	1923	1923
Trough	1922	1923	1923	1923	1923	1924	1924	1924	1924
Peak	1925	1925	1925	1926	1926	1926	1926	1927	1927
Trough	1926	1926	1926	1927	1927	1927	1927	1928	1928
Peak	1927	1928	1928	1928	1928	1929	1929	1929	1929
Trough	1931	1931	1931	1932	1932	1932	1932	1933	1933
Peak	1935	1936	1936	1936	1936	1937	1937	1937	1937
Trough	1936	1937	1937	1937	1937	1938	1938	1938	1938

See Appendix B for notes on the derivation of this table.

whether it regularly falls during contractions bounded by these years but looking from peaks to troughs. An end of year series that lags one-half year is predated 6 months and matched with a June 30 chronology. An end of year series that leads one-half year is postdated 6 months, that is, figures for December 31, 1928 and 1929 are treated like figures for June 30, 1929 and 1930, respectively. Its conformity is then measured on a June 30 chronology. Similar procedures are applied to other timing categories ranging from 12-month leads to 12-month lags. The reference chronology used in conjunction with year end series is set forth in the lower half of Table 15.

AVERAGES AND AVERAGE DEVIATIONS

Most of the measures described above are made for every reference and for every specific cycle covered by a series, then averaged for each set of cycles. When averages are struck for all the cycles covered by a series, features peculiar to single cycles tend to fade, while features common to all or most cycles tend to stand out prominently.

In general, the more cycles a series covers, the greater is our confidence that the average discloses faithfully what cyclical behavior is typical of the economic process represented. But in analyzing price and value series, we usually exclude cycles affected by grave monetary disturbances from the averages. We make exclusions also when some exceptionally powerful random factor, such as a major strike, has warped an individual cycle out of resemblance to other cycles in the array. When a long series gives definite indications of having undergone a secular or structural change, we divide it into relatively homogeneous segments and compute an average for each segment.

Our attempt to find what cyclical behavior is characteristic of different economic processes does not end in the contemplation of averages, for a leading feature of specific and of business cycles is that they vary in length, intensity, and other respects. To keep this feature prominently before our minds, we compute average deviations from the averages. These deviations are simple measures of the degree to which the figures for individual cycles in a series are clustered about the arithmetic means which we use to represent 'central tendencies'.

CHARTS OF CYCLICAL PATTERNS

Several results of our analysis that lend themselves readily to graphic presentation are embodied in charts of cyclical patterns. The sample for coke production, Chart 2, pictures the averages and average deviations in Tables 9 and 11, and certain additional measures from Tables 6, 10, and 12. The curves trace the specific and reference cycle patterns made by averaging the standings of the individual cycles at each of the nine stages in Tables 9 and 11. Since coke production corresponds closely in timing to business cycles, the two patterns are almost identical. The more irregular the timing of a series in relation to business cycles, the smaller will be the amplitude of the reference cycle pattern relative to that of the specific cycle pattern. The representative value of the two patterns is indicated by the lengths of the vertical lines, which show the average deviations of the individual cycles from their average standings at the nine stages.

The long horizontal lines above and below the cyclical patterns represent the average lengths of the specific and reference cycles. We call them 'duration lines'. The vertical lines representing the average deviations from the average standings are dropped from or erected at the midpoints of the cycle stages. The ruler at the bottom of the chart defines the time scale; with its aid all durations can be approximated.

When, as in coke production, the specific and reference cycles correspond to each other, the two duration lines are placed so that they show average leads or lags. When specific and reference cycles do not correspond throughout, the duration lines are so placed that the peak standings of the two patterns are aligned vertically.

With a few exceptions when amplitudes are very wide, the charts of cyclical patterns presented below were drawn to a strictly uniform set of scales. However, to help the reader understand our method, the scales in Chart 2 are larger. The explanatory comments are not repeated for subsequent charts, nor are the scale numbers for average deviations of the standings in successive cycle stages.

Chart 2
Sample Chart of Cyclical Patterns

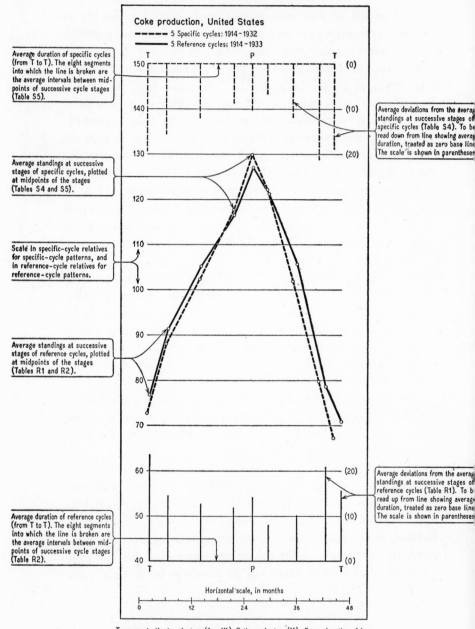

Coke production, United States
- - - - - 5 Specific cycles: 1914–1932
—————— 5 Reference cycles: 1914–1933

Average duration of specific cycles (from T to T). The eight segments into which the line is broken are the average intervals between midpoints of successive cycle stages (Table S5).

Average deviations from the average standings at successive stages of specific cycles (Table S4). To be read down from line showing average duration, treated as zero base line. The scale is shown in parentheses.

Average standings at successive stages of specific cycles, plotted at midpoints of the stages (Tables S4 and S5).

Scale in specific-cycle relatives for specific-cycle patterns, and in reference-cycle relatives for reference-cycle patterns.

Average standings at successive stages of reference cycles, plotted at midpoints of the stages (Tables R1 and R2).

Average deviations from the average standings at successive stages of reference cycles (Table R1). To be read up from line showing average duration, treated as zero base line. The scale is shown in parentheses.

Average duration of reference cycles (from T to T). The eight segments into which the line is broken are the average intervals between midpoints of successive cycle stages (Table R2).

Horizontal scale, in months

T represents the trough stage (I or IX), P the peak stage (V). For explanation of how the line representing the average duration of specific cycles is placed in relation to the line representing the average duration of reference cycles, see text.

2 Reliability of Annual Data

Most business cycles in the United States and, indeed, in other major commercial countries, are relatively brief. The National Bureau has identified 21 business cycles between 1854 and 1938 in the United States.[10] Their average length was almost exactly four years. Only 6 were longer; the others lasted 48 months or less. The brevity of most business cycles greatly restricts the number of observations that can be made on annual data. In a 4-year cycle in which expansion and contraction are equal, we might have 5 annual observations: one at the initial trough, one at the peak, one at the terminal trough, and one each at mid-expansion and mid-contraction. If expansion and contraction are not equal, the observations on the shorter phase are reduced to 2, and if the full cycle itself is shorter than 4 years, the number of observations may be no more than 2 on expansion or contraction.

In these circumstances, annual data necessarily distort, in greater or less degree, our view of the actual cyclical behavior of economic series. This happens partly because some cycles that appear in a monthly series are skipped in its annual form; more rarely because annual data inject cycles not found in the monthly series. Corresponding cycles in monthly and annual series, moreover, are likely to be of different length and shape. A monthly series may reach a cyclical peak in June of a given year, but in annual form it may reach a peak in the same year or in the year preceding or following. Thus the form of the data may affect the timing as well as the length of the cycles in a series. For closely corresponding cycles, when both monthly and annual data turn in the same year, the amplitude of the swing in the latter is necessarily less, since in monthly series the standing at the peak covers the three months centered on the highest value attained during the cycle, and the standing at the trough the three months centered on the lowest value. The same results are probable even when the cycles in the annual and monthly data do not correspond closely. Annual data not only distort results; they seriously reduce the information yielded. The year is a coarser unit of measurement than the month or the quarter, a matter of obvious importance when timing and duration are to be measured. Used with caution, how-

[10] Ibid., p. 78.

ever, and a knowledge of their limitations, annual data can be of great value.

In what ways and to what degree will our measures be affected by the use of annual data? For a detailed discussion and the results of many illuminating tests, readers are referred to *Measuring Business Cycles,* Chapter 6. The argument below is confined to the three measures we use most frequently: timing, amplitude, and conformity.

TIMING

We measure the timing of annual data by comparing the monthly reference cycle turn with the midpoint of the corresponding annual specific cycle turn. We prefer this procedure to the alternative—comparing an annual specific cycle turn with the midpoint of the corresponding annual reference turn. Test comparisons support this preference,[11] as does the logic of the case. We take as our standard the results that would be attained by comparing monthly specific cycle turns with monthly reference cycle turns. The method we prefer will produce an error whenever the monthly specific cycle turn does not occur at the midpoint of the year in which the annual series reaches a peak or trough; in the case of year end series, whenever it does not occur at the end of the year in which the annual series turns. But a procedure that depends upon comparisons of midpoints of annual specific cycle turns with midpoints of annual reference turns can be in error because it misplaces the one or the other, and these sources of error will tend to augment more often than they will tend to offset each other.[12]

---

[11] Ibid., Table 61.

[12] Call the procedure by which monthly specific cycle turns are compared with monthly reference turns Method A; that by which annual specific cycle turns are compared with monthly reference turns Method B; and that by which annual specific cycle turns are compared with annual reference turns Method C. If M stands for the monthly specific cycle turn and N for the monthly reference turn, timing by Method $A = M - N$. Timing by Method $B = M + S - N$, where S is the distortion in the timing of the specific cycle turn caused by annual data. Timing by Method $C = (M + S) - (N + R)$, where R is the distortion in the timing of the reference turn caused by annual data. The difference between Methods A and B is S; that between Methods A and C is $S - R$.

Whether Method B will yield a better approximation to Method A than Method C depends on whether $S - R$ tends to exceed S. For any group of

The elimination of distortion due to the misplacement of the date of reference cycle turns, however, still leaves important sources of error due to the misplacement of specific cycle turns. Since most of the annual data used below are end of year series, our argument is developed with reference to such series. With minor modifications, however, it is applicable to annual data generally.

Individual timing comparisons made with end of year data are usually in error since the true specific cycle turn is unlikely to occur precisely at the year end. The reliability of annual timing measures, therefore, depends upon averaging many observations. Yet the average of even many observations will yield a poor approximation to the true timing if the direction of the displacement of the specific cycle turns in the annual data is biased relative to the true dates or, in the absence of bias, if the errors do not offset one another sufficiently in a small sample.

The displacement may be biased if, in the period under review, the monthly reference cycle turns usually occur nearer the beginning than the ends of years, or the reverse. Consider a series, A, with monthly turns that are synchronous with reference turns. If the reference turns usually occur in the second half of calendar years, the specific cycle turns in the year end version of series A will tend to come at the ends of the years in which the reference turns occur rather than at their beginning, other things being equal. An average of individual timing measures would be biased in the direction of a lag. Similarly, if the reference turns usually occur in the first half of calendar years, the measure of timing from annual data would be biased in favor of a lead.

------

reference cycles R may be plus, minus, or zero on the average. If many series are analyzed for the period covered by reference cycles, the expectation is that S will be plus in as many cases as it will be minus. Now if R is zero, the results of Method B will agree with those of Method C. If S is zero on the average, S − R must exceed S, unless R too is zero, in which case Methods B and C again give the same results. If S and R are of opposite sign, then S − R once more must exceed S. And the same will be true when S and R are of the same sign whenever R > 2S. Hence there is a greater probability that (S − R) > S than that (S − R) < S. The expectation, therefore, is that Method B will give a better approximation to Method A than will Method C.

This argument is adapted from *Measuring Business Cycles*, p. 229, note 25.

This particular source of error, fortunately, is unlikely to trouble us much. In the period since 1913, with which this study is generally concerned, National Bureau reference dates are fairly evenly distributed over the calendar year.[13]

NUMBER OF PEAKS AND TROUGHS

	1913-38	*1919-38*		*1913-38*	*1919-38*
January	2	1	July	1	1
February	0	0	August	1	0
March	1	1	September	1	1
April	1	1	October	1	1
May	3	3	November	0	0
June	1	1	December	2	1

Another, more important, source of bias will exist if the shapes of specific cycles are such as to throw the peaks and troughs of a year end series back to the ends or forward to the beginnings of the years in which the turns of a corresponding monthly series occur. For example, the peaks in the year end version of a monthly series that declines more slowly immediately after passing its peaks than it rises toward its peaks will tend to come at the ends of the years in which the peaks of the monthly series occur. Indeed, they may not come until the end of the next year. A year end series of this type would tend to show lags on the average, whatever the timing of its cycles in the monthly data. The reverse, of course, would be true if the monthly data generally fell away more rapidly after their peaks than they rose toward them.

Even if these sources of bias were completely absent, in the sense that the average timing measured from annual data would be accurate when based upon a large number of observations, the errors of individual observations may not cancel in a limited number of cycles. This possibility is heightened somewhat by the fact that annual data sometimes skip cycles that occur in monthly data, thereby reducing the number of comparisons yielded by a given number of cycles. The seriousness of these sources of error can be appraised only by comparing results from monthly and annual data. To this end we prepared average timing measures for

---

[13] If we call January 0.5, February 1.5, March 2.5, December 11.5, and so on, a perfectly even distribution of reference cycle turns would yield an 'average' turn with a value of 6. But the 'average' reference turn since 1913 has a value of 5.8 and the 'average' turn since 1919 a value of 5.6. Moreover, the distribution of reference cycle turns by months is markedly even.

monthly and annual data for 6 series. In order to approximate the kind of annual data used in this study, we constructed annual series from December values, and computed average leads and lags for periods covering 5 or 6 reference cycles.

The discrepancies between the measures derived from monthly and annual data are serious but not so large as to render annual data unusable. The average difference is roughly 2.6 months, and more than 75 percent of the measures from annual data are within 4 months of the measures yielded by monthly data.

TABLE 16

Average Timing of Specific Cycles during Brief Periods, Six American Series, Monthly and Annual (December) Data

	TIMING AT REFERENCE PEAKS						TIMING AT REFERENCE TROUGHS		
PERIOD COVERED	Number of observations		Av. lead (−) or lag (+), months		Number of observations		Av. lead (−) or lag (+), months	
	M	A	M	A	M	A	M	A
			DEFLATED CLEARINGS					
1879-1897	5	3	+3.8	−1.3	5	3	−6.2	−4.7
1897-1914	5	3	+4.2	+1.7	5	3	−7.4	−8.3
1914-1933	4	2	+1.2	−3.5	5	3	−3.8	0
			PIG IRON PRODUCTION					
1879-1897	5	3	+0.8	−1.3	5	2	−3.2	−5.5
1897-1914	5	5	+3.4	+0.4	5	5	−7.2	−6.6
1914-1933	5	5	+1.4	−1.2	6	6	−0.3	+0.2
			RAILROAD STOCK PRICES					
1858-1888	5	5	−7.6	−8.4	5	5	−13.4	−14.8
1888-1908	6	5	−2.2	−4.4	6	5	−1.2	−1.0
1908-1933	6	5*	−7.3	−2.8*	7	7	−8.6	−7.7
			SHARES TRADED					
1879-1897	5	5	−11.4	−7.6	5	4*	−2.2	−2.0*
1897-1914	5	4	−12.0	−13.5	5	4	−4.8	−5.2
1914-1933	5	4	−7.8	−12.2	6	5	−6.5	−3.2
			CALL MONEY RATES					
1858-1888	6	6	−3.3	−8.0	6	6	−1.2	−2.3
1888-1908	6	6	+4.2	−2.7	6	6	+3.0	+1.2
1908-1933	7	6	−1.0	−2.0	7	6	+2.6	+4.2
			RAILROAD BOND YIELDS					
1858-1888	6	6	+9.2	+8.0	6	6	+17.8	+11.7
1888-1908	5	4	+9.2	+8.2	5	4	+14.4	+10.5
1908-1933	5	5	+4.8	+7.8	5	5	+1.8	+8.2

The sources of this and other tables of Chapter 3 are described in *Measuring Business Cycles*, p. 210, notes 6 and 7.

* In comparing monthly reference dates and the turns of year end or other single-date series, we omit leads or lags longer than 24 months in order to avoid prejudicing averages based on few comparisons. Accordingly, one lead was omitted in each case designated by an asterisk.

M: monthly date; A: annual.

In one respect the comparisons of Table 16 put the results to be expected from our inventory materials in a less favorable light than is just. The averages are usually based on 6 comparisons or fewer; in some cases on only 2 or 3. Our timing measures on annual inventory data are usually based on 7 to 10 comparisons. To do this, however, we have to lump together observations on peaks and troughs, a procedure that would increase the likelihood of error if the timing of stocks at peaks and troughs were significantly different. Since we have not found any evidence of such a difference in annual inventory data, it seems valid to combine our comparisons at peaks and troughs into single averages. We expect the results to be somewhat better than those suggested by Table 16.

For all that, annual data can obviously provide only crude indications of timing. We attempt therefore to safeguard our results by taking two precautions. First, we disregard small differences in timing relations—differences of, say, less than 3 or 4 months. Secondly, we confine attention to results that appear to be characteristic of manufacturing as a whole as judged by a consensus of nine or ten groups of industries.

AMPLITUDE

When cycles in the monthly and annual forms of a series correspond closely in time, the amplitudes of the latter will almost always be smaller. The reason, as already stated, is that in monthly series the standing at the peak covers the 3 months centered on the highest value attained during the cycle, and the standing at the trough covers the 3 months centered on the lowest value. The peaks and troughs of calendar or fiscal year data, of course, cover many more months and cannot stand as high as the peak value or as low as the trough value in monthly series. When the cyclical peaks and troughs of the monthly series occur in the same years as those in the annual series, the rule hardly admits of exception,[14] and the same relations may be expected to hold in a large majority of cases when the cyclical turns of monthly and annual data occur in different years, if the cycles correspond approximately.

[14] The rule might be upset in rare instances if a random peak or trough is disregarded in marking off specific cycles in monthly data, or if the month preceding and the month succeeding the peak (trough) month are sufficiently below (above) the calendar year average.

The same relations may be expected to hold also when single-date annual series are in question, but now two further exceptions must be noted. If the highest value in a monthly series occurs in close proximity to the day or month when the annual series reaches its peak, the monthly peak may be lower than the annual since peaks in monthly series are 3-month averages centered on the highest value. The relation may be upset also if random high or low values occur on the day or month for which the annual data are reported and if they are taken to be the annual, but not the monthly, cyclical peaks or troughs, as is likely to be the case. That annual data tend to yield smaller amplitudes than monthly data, however, is the basic rule whatever the form of the annual data, and it leaves its imprint clearly on test comparisons.

It has been established also that the reduction in amplitude produced by annual summarizing varies inversely to the length of cyclical phases, though several other factors combine to cause the degree of reduction to vary widely: the months in which the cyclical turns occur, the amplitude of the movement relative to the underlying trend, and the patterns of both the cyclical swing and of the random fluctuations that accompany it.[15]

These factors serve to make uneven the damping effect of annual data even for cycles that correspond to those in monthly data. The degree of reduction in measures of average amplitude from annual data is rendered still more uneven by the fact that annual data sometimes skip cycles that occur in monthly data and inject cycles not found in monthly data. If annual data skip a contraction in a series with a rising trend, their expansion will tend to almost equal the sum of the two monthly expansions they span. If they skip two successive contractions in these circumstances, their total rise will comprise three expansions in the monthly series. When they skip cycles, the average amplitude of the remaining cycles tends to be larger than it otherwise would be and, in some conditions, larger than the average amplitude measured from monthly data. When they inject cycles, the reverse will, of course, be true, but this happens much less frequently.

The effect of all these factors, which in the aggregate tend to reduce the amplitude of cycles in annual data but which do so un-

[15] See *Measuring Business Cycles,* pp. 230-2.

evenly, is illustrated in Table 17. To preserve the erratic effects that may be expected to characterize single-date series such as the end of year inventory data, our annual series are based on the December values of the sample series.

TABLE 17

Average Amplitude of Specific Cycles, Six American Series during Brief Periods, Monthly and Annual (December) Data

PERIOD COVERED (1)	NO. OF CYCLES M (2)	A (3)	AV. AMPLITUDE IN SPECIFIC CYCLE RELATIVES Rise M (4)	A (5)	Fall M (6)	A (7)	Rise & fall M (8)	A (9)	AN. AV. AS % OF MONTHLY Rise (10)	Fall (11)	Rise & fall (12)
			DEFLATED CLEARINGS								
1878-1893	5	3	29.6	38.8	12.5	11.7	42.1	50.5	131	94	120
1893-1910	5	3	27.3	35.9	10.0	10.1	37.3	46.0	132	101	123
1910-1933	5	3	23.7	32.1	17.6	21.9	41.3	54.0	135	124	131
			PIG IRON PRODUCTION								
1879-1896	5	2	62.3	78.2	44.4	52.2	106.7	130.5	126	118	122
1896-1914	5	5	64.4	60.2	48.3	48.1	112.8	108.4	93	100	96
1914-1933	5	6	59.5	29.4	71.5	40.0	131.0	69.3	49	56	53
			RAILROAD STOCK PRICES								
1857-1889	6	6	45.8	33.6	30.6	18.1	76.4	51.6	73	59	68
1889-1907	6	5	29.2	27.6	22.7	20.1	51.9	47.7	95	89	92
1907-1932	6	6	31.7	25.1	42.0	34.4	73.7	59.5	79	82	81
			SHARES TRADED								
1878-1897	5	5	74.5	60.1	73.1	55.9	147.6	116.0	81	76	79
1897-1914	5	4	108.0	76.4	111.5	87.6	219.5	164.1	71	79	75
1914-1933	5	4	111.7	101.3	92.6	67.7	204.3	169.0	91	73	83
			CALL MONEY RATES								
1858-1880	7	8	109.9	37.1	108.2	32.4	218.1	69.4	34	30	32
1880-1904	8	8	141.6	94.0	147.9	95.2	289.5	189.1	66	64	65
1904-1931	8	8	95.6	59.9	91.2	63.6	186.8	123.6	63	70	66
			RAILROAD BOND YIELDS								
1860-1876	6	4	12.3	9.8	14.4	18.4	26.6	28.1	80	128	106
1876-1905	7	5	7.4	4.6	12.8	8.0	20.2	12.6	62	62	62
1905-1931	7	6	13.0	12.0	10.8	8.9	23.7	20.8	92	82	88
Average of all comparisons									86.3	82.6	85.0
Average deviation									22.8	19.5	21.4

M: monthly data; A: annual. The periods cover, approximately, successive thirds of the specific cycles in monthly data.

Table 17 illustrates the strong tendency for annual data to understate amplitude. Of the 18 comparisons of total rise and fall (col. 12) 13 show smaller amplitures in the annual series than in the monthly. The average degree of understatement is nearly 15 percent. This, however, is relatively unimportant. If the degree of understatement were fairly constant we could readily allow for it.

In any case, our usual concern is not with the absolute amplitude of a series but with judgments about the relative amplitudes of two or more annual series. But the variation in the measures yielded by annual data is great. During 1910-33 cycles in annual reports of deflated clearings had an amplitude 31 percent larger than those in monthly reports. During 1858-80 the amplitude of cycles in call money rates was 68 percent lower in the annual than in the monthly data. For the 18 comparisons of total rise and fall the average deviation from the mean relative amplitude of annual data compared with monthly was 21 percentage points.

Divergences from the mean degree of understatement are widest when the annual data either skip several cycles or inject an extra cycle. Thus every comparison in which the average amplitude measured from annual data was wider than that measured from monthly data involved annual data that skip two or more cycles recognized in the monthly data. The two cases in which the annual data inject a cycle yielded the only comparisons in which the average amplitude was less than half as large as that measured from monthly data.

To render measures of amplitude from annual data useful at all, we use a combination of procedures. First, amplitudes computed from annual data are never compared with those based on monthly data. Secondly, we confine our conclusions to those supported by several series. For example, we base judgments about the relative amplitude of output and inventories for manufacturers in general on measures for nine or ten industry groups. Thirdly, we supplement averages of cyclical amplitude based on all specific cycles observed in two series with averages based only on corresponding cycles. In this way the extreme variations illustrated by Table 17 are avoided.

CONFORMITY

The erratic influences exercised by annual reporting upon the number of cycles, their timing, and their pattern combine to render conformity measures from annual data less reliable than their monthly counterparts. Since annual data sometimes skip contractions when the secular trend of a series is rising, they tend to understate conformity to reference contractions in growing activities. And since they sometimes skip expansions when the secular trend is falling, they tend to underestimate conformity to reference expansion in declining activities. The displacement of peaks and troughs, sometimes forward, sometimes backward in time, helps to conceal regular response to business cycles. Moreover, when there is evidence of a regular lead or lag it can be allowed for more flexibly in monthly or quarterly data. An additional trouble is the irregular way in which annual data alter the patterns of cycles. Finally, if a reference peak or trough is misdated by a year, this is likely to affect the conformity indexes of annual data, while the smaller errors that might be made in monthly reference dates would generally have slight influence on the indexes of monthly series. It may be expected that if an activity conforms well to business cycles annual data will yield conformity indexes that tend to understate its true conformity. If an activity conforms poorly, an-

TABLE 18

Conformity of Monthly and Annual (Calendar Year)
Data to Business Cycles, Six American Series

	NO. OF REF. CYCLES*	STAGES MATCHED WITH REF. EXP.	INDEX OF CONFORMITY TO REF.		
			Exp.	Contr.	Cycle
DEFLATED CLEARINGS					
Monthly, 1879-1933	15	VIII-V	+100	+73	+86
Annual, 1878-1932	15	I-V	+100	+7	+86
PIG IRON PRODUCTION					
Monthly, 1879-1933	15	I-V	+100	+100	+100
Annual, 1878-1932	15	I-V	+100	+73	+100
RAILROAD STOCK PRICES					
Monthly, 1858-1933	19*	VIII-IV	+79	+60	+74
Annual, 1858-1932	19*	I-V	+68	+40	+63
SHARES TRADED					
Monthly, 1879-1933	15	VIII-IV	+87	+73	+93
Annual, 1878-1932	15	I-III	+87	+47	+86
CALL MONEY RATES					
Monthly, 1858-1933	19*	I-V	+68	+100	+100
Annual, 1858-1932	19*	I-V	+79	+68	+84
RAILROAD BOND YIELDS					
Monthly, 1858-1933	19*	III-VI	+47	+30	+68
Annual, 1858-1932	19*	III-VII	+26	+35	+63

Source: *Measuring Business Cycles*, Table 82, p. 266.

* The contraction and full cycle indexes cover an additional reference contraction at the beginning of the series.

nual data will yield conformity indexes that may be either higher or lower than monthly data would yield.

The quantitative importance of these various difficulties can, of course, be judged only by comparing results from monthly and annual series (Table 18). The indexes from annual data are usually lower than those from monthly data. In only a few cases, however, are they much lower.[16] In only two comparisons, moreover, are they higher, and then by only minor amounts.

These fairly favorable indications may, however, reflect the relative stability introduced into our measures by the large number of cycles covered by the six test series. Table 19, covering five

TABLE 19

Conformity of Monthly and Annual (December)
Data to 5 Business Cycles, Six American Series

	STAGES MATCHED WITH REF. EXP.	LEAD (−) OR LAG (+), MONTHS	INDEX OF CONFORMITY TO REF.		
			Exp.	Contr.	Cycle
	DEFLATED CLEARINGS				
Monthly, 1914-1933	VIII-V		+100	+60	+56
Annual, 1914-1932		0	+100	−20	+78
	PIG IRON PRODUCTION				
Monthly, 1914-1933	I-V		+100	+100	+100
Annual, 1914-1932		0	+60	+20	+33
	RAILROAD STOCK PRICES				
Monthly, 1914-1933	VII-III		+20	+60	+33
Annual, 1913-1931		−6	+20	+20	+33
	SHARES TRADED				
Monthly, 1914-1933	VIII-III		+100	+60	+100
Annual, 1913-1931		−6	+60	+60	+56
	CALL MONEY RATES				
Monthly, 1914-1933	I-V		+60	+100	+100
Annual, 1914-1932		+3	+60	+60	+100
	RAILROAD BOND YIELDS				
Monthly, 1914-1933	I-V		+20	+80	+56
Annual, 1914-1932		+6	+60	+60	+56

[16] But bear in mind the instability of our conformity indexes! One defection in 19 cases reduces the index from 100 to 84 as in Call Money Rates; one defection in five cases reduces the index from 100 to 60, etc. See ibid., pp. 183-5, 195.

reference cycles, provides a sterner test. The annual data here employed are of the one month per year variety which resemble our end of year inventory data more closely than annual aggregates. Conformity measures of the annual data are made by the special method described in Section 1 and applied to annual data in the rest of this study.

Reducing the number of cycles does indeed widen the divergence between the indexes yielded by monthly and annual data. The results, however, are still quite good. In one series, pig iron production, the annual indexes would cause us to be doubtful about the response to business cycles when, in fact, conformity was highly regular. In the other five series the indications of conformity yielded by the annual measures are generally accurate in view of the instability of our indexes when few cycles are compared.

While these comparisons of conformity measures are fairly reassuring, the erratic action of annual data must be borne in mind. Low indexes are not necessarily inconsistent with regular association, and sometimes the index may be high when conformity is low. Our practice, therefore, is to base our findings on the showing of several indicators and to reach positive conclusions only when there is a fair consensus.

Part Two

Cyclical Behavior of Inventories

CHAPTER 4

Total Inventories during Business Cycles

This chapter and the next two are devoted to the cyclical behavior of manufacturers' inventories in the aggregate. The data are derived from accounting records and are dollar values. In the case of one important block of data, current (book) values are corrected for the influence of changes in prices to yield indexes of physical volume. This chapter deals first with inventories in current prices, then with their volume as indicated by values in constant prices.

1 Inventories in Current Prices

The materials used in this chapter are described fully in Appendix A. Brief notes will suffice here.

THE DATA
Kuznets' estimates

Kuznets' estimates show the book value of inventories held on December 31 of each year 1918-41.[1] For 1926-41 the basic figures are drawn from the balance sheets filed with the United States Treasury Department by manufacturing corporations and published in *Statistics of Income*. A small adjustment sufficed to allow for corporations that did not file balance sheets and somewhat larger adjustments for inventories held by unincorporated firms. From 1918 to 1925 the estimates are derived by applying inventory-sales ratios for samples of corporations in each manufacturing group to the

---

[1] Kuznets' estimates for 1918-33 were published in *Commodity Flow and Capital Formation*, Part VII. He generously put his figures for 1934-38 at my disposal. In making estimates for later years, I used the same sources and methods.

gross income of all corporations from *Statistics of Income*.[2] Adjustments were then made for unincorporated firms. While Kuznets' estimates constitute the most useful and extensive body of dollar value materials, other data supplement, extend and, to a certain extent, check them.

Dun and Bradstreet wartime estimates

Dun and Bradstreet compiled the accounts of 106 large manufacturing corporations that publish year end balance sheets 1913-22,[3] constituting 20-25 percent of all manufacturing activity. To construct a general index for manufacturing as a whole, data for individual companies were aggregated to yield indexes of inventories in 15 industry groups. The industry indexes were then combined in both weighted and unweighted averages.[4] The two types of average yield indexes for all manufacturing that are remarkably similar; in no year does the difference exceed 2 percent.

The Schmidt-Young estimates

In connection with their studies in business financing C. H. Schmidt and R. A. Young gathered reports of 81 large manufacturing corporations, 1914-22, holding about 18 percent of total manufacturing inventories.[5] The industrial coverage is not comprehensive.

Terborgh's estimates

George Terborgh prepared composite indexes for 8 durable and 11 nondurable goods industries for each year end, 1915-23, weighted

[2] The level of the data was corrected by computing inventory-sales ratios from sample data for 1926 and using the sample ratios for 1926 and earlier years as an index to extend inventory-gross income ratios for 1926 from *Statistics of Income* to earlier years. Minor adjustments sufficed to bring the level of the estimates into line with data from capital stock tax returns for 1923 and 1924.

[3] *Dun's Review*, Feb. 1940. A few concerns engaged in mining are included. In manufacturing apparently no leather tanning firms are included and the sample seems especially weak in lumber and textiles.

[4] The weights were based on the 1937 Census inventory figures adjusted for differences in the rates of growth of the various industries since the period to which the index applies.

[5] The Effect of War on Business Financing: Manufacturing and Trade, World War I, NBER *Occasional Paper 10*, Nov. 1943, pp. 31 ff., and App. A.

largely by Kuznets' estimates of inventory holdings by industry in 1923.[6] Stocks held by unincorporated firms are allowed for. The estimates of total inventories and of inventories in the durable and nondurable goods groups are expressed both as indexes on a 1915 base and in dollars.

The sample on which the estimate is based for each year, 1916-23 "covers nearly all of the manufacturing concerns for which both the opening and closing inventories are reported in Moody's Manuals."[7] The sample companies are estimated to have held about 25 percent of total manufacturing inventories in 1916 and about 40 percent in 1923.

Currie's estimates

Lauchlin Currie compiled balance sheet information for a still larger sample of manufacturers for year ends, 1922-28.[8] In 1928 they held more than 35 percent of total manufacturers' inventories. Mr. Currie's comment upon his results is significant:

"Although care was taken to include the available reports of all the smaller companies and also of companies in depressed industries, the series as a whole is mainly representative of the larger and more successful companies, owing to the greater availability of their financial statements."

The Dun and Bradstreet, Schmidt-Young, Terborgh, and Currie estimates all serve to check Kuznets' figures for the years before 1926 when the latter are based on small samples of corporations. Kuznets' estimates before 1926 are based on corporation samples that differ in size and composition from those used by the other four estimators, which also differ among themselves. But the latter estimated inventories directly while Kuznets estimated total stocks by constructing indexes of inventory-sales ratios in ten industry groups. From these indexes he extrapolated the inventory-sales ratios for all corporations in these groups in 1926 and applied the resulting ratios to comprehensive sales figures for all corporations.

[6] Manufacturing Inventories During and After the World War, *Federal Reserve Bulletin,* July 1941, pp. 613-7.

[7] Ibid., p. 613.

[8] The Decline of the Commercial Loan, *Quarterly Journal of Economics,* Aug. 1931, p. 699.

National Industrial Conference Board indexes

The National Industrial Conference Board presents estimates by months since January 1929 for a sample of large and small firms. Coverage was small in the earlier years of the period, but by 1940 about one-sixth of all manufacturing activity was represented. The index is so constructed that the growth of the sample does not affect the trend of the data. Companies manufacturing food products, tobacco, liquors, petroleum, and certain lumber products are not included "because these industries are so closely tied up with agriculture or with the extractive industries" and "do not represent the more active sector of industry in which the individual decisions of industrial management have greatest effect on business activity".[9]

Department of Commerce indexes

A far more extensive sample reporting by months has been organized by the Department of Commerce, giving figures since December 1938.[10] The reporting firms now number more than 1,200, representing nearly 40 percent of total manufacturing. Nevertheless, in some industries the sample is still quite inadequate (e.g., only 16 apparel manufacturers were reporting in June 1940). Moreover, the sample of companies having total assets of less than $500,000 was purposely kept small in order to lighten the task of handling the large number of reports required to cover this group properly. The Department of Commerce notes, however, that these companies hold only 12.5 percent of all manufacturing inventories. In constructing the index, data were aggregated by industries and combined by weighting inventory relatives by the value of inventories held by the various industries at the end of 1938 as indicated by the Census of Manufactures. Adjustments were made for groups not covered or incompletely covered by the census.

CONFORMITY AND TIMING

Chart 3 shows these seven series plotted in a fashion that distin-

---

[9] *Economic Record,* II, Supplement, Dec. 26, 1940: Inventories, Shipments and Orders, 1929-1940, p. 2.

[10] Monthly Industry Survey, *Survey of Current Business,* Sept. 1940, pp. 7 ff.

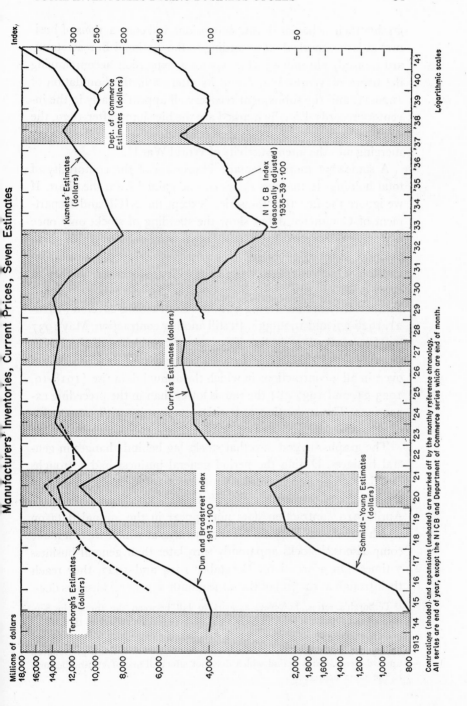

Manufacturers' Inventories, Current Prices, Seven Estimates

Contractions (shaded) and expansions (unshaded) are marked off by the monthly reference chronology.
All series are end of year, except the N I C B and Department of Commerce series which are end of month.

guishes their behavior during expansions and contractions of business at large, marked off according to the National Bureau standard monthly chronology. The vigorous expansion accompanying the boom of World War I and its aftermath, the liquidation of 1920-21, and the subsequent recovery all appear clearly in the inventory records. Equally marked are the big slump after 1929, the 1933-37 recovery, and the succeeding depression and recovery merging into the intense activity of World War II.

A somewhat more systematic impression of the conformity of total holdings to business cycles can be gained from the chart. If we ignore the fact that the series (except the NICB and Department of Commerce data) show the standing of stocks only once a year, and if we treat the lines drawn from one December 31 to the next as though they represented continuous series, several interesting observations can be made. First, stocks are higher at every peak of general business than at the preceding trough.[11] Further, they decline during 3 of the 6 contractions covered (1920-21, 1926-27, and 1929-33). In still another contraction, May 1937 to May 1938, they decline if we take the evidence of the NICB monthly series although in Kuznets' annual data they rise. Moreover, in all 3 contractions in which the annual data rise (1918-19, 1923-24, and 1937-38) the rate is lower than in the preceding expansions. The suggestion of positive conformity with movements of general business, therefore, is strong.

The graphs suggest also that stocks lag behind changes in general business. During the period general business had 7 troughs and 6 peaks—13 turns in all. A turning point in stocks is found in the vicinity of 6 troughs and 5 peaks, since the September 1918-April 1919 contraction does not appear in the annual data on which we have to depend. Of the 11 turns at which we can make comparisons,[12] stocks apparently turn later than general business 7 times. On 2 occasions, December 1914 and 1927, they reach their trough at the end of the same month as general business does.

[11] Terborgh's series, however, appears to fall between the trough in September 1921 and the peak in May 1923, although Kuznets' series rises.

[12] Currie's sample skips the 1923-24 contraction, apparently because it represents the inventories of large corporations only. It thus has a pronounced upward trend in this period which does not affect all manufacturing business to the same degree.

The evidence at the other 2 turns is mixed. At the trough in March 1933 Kuznets' annual series appears to lead, but the NICB monthly series lags. The 2 series are sufficiently similar in their movements to suggest that the lag in the latter would appear also in Kuznets' series were it available by months. At the business cycle peak of October 1926, however, the evidence suggests that stocks turned before business at large. Kuznets' series reaches a peak on December 31, 1925, the year end preceding the business cycle peak. Currie's series reaches a peak on December 31, 1926, the year end following the monthly peak in business. The apparent lag of Currie's series may, however, reflect only its upward trend, a feature consistent with the fact that his sample is supposed to represent fully only large corporations.

Inspection of a chart is suggestive, but the need for more systematic measurement of the relation between stocks and business cycles is obvious. For this purpose we use the measures of conformity and timing described in Chapter 3.[13] For both we adapt National Bureau methods to the peculiarities of year end series and apply them to Kuznets' estimates for total manufacturing and for his ten component industry groups.

Table 20 presents the timing measures. It tells whether stocks tend to lead or lag at the turns of general business as determined by the National Bureau monthly chronology. The table was prepared by calculating the number of months by which the December 31 turns of stocks preceded or followed the monthly reference dates. The average lead or lag is the simple mean of the individual comparisons. All inventory series were treated positively, that is, peaks in stocks were compared with corresponding peaks in business, and troughs in stocks with corresponding troughs in business.

These systematic timing comparisons reveal a pronounced tendency for inventories in book values to lag behind general business. The series representing the aggregate holdings of manufacturers lags in 8 comparisons out of 10. Of the 77 comparisons that could

---

[13] Conformity measures were not computed for the shorter annual series or for the monthly NICB data depicted in Chart 3. None was long enough to make such measures meaningful. As far as they go, however, their behavior is fully consistent with the calculations made from Kuznets' series, which are longer.

be made for the ten industry groups, 58 were lags, 19 leads. If we
add a few comparisons suggested by marked changes in trend,[14] the
count becomes 64 lags and 19 leads in 83 comparisons. Roughly
speaking, 3 out of 4 comparisons were lags. Leads outnumbered
lags in only one of the ten industry groups, textiles, and then only
by 5 to 3. The total and nine of the ten component groups yielded
average lags; only one group, again textiles, appeared to lead on
the average.

TABLE 20

Manufacturers' Inventories, Current Prices
Timing at Business Cycle Turns, 1918-1938

(1)	NUMBER OF Leads	NUMBER OF Lags	AV. LEAD (−) OR LAG (+), MO. Actual turns	AV. LEAD (−) OR LAG (+), MO. Actual & indicated turns[b]
	(2)	(3)	(4)	(5)
Total manufacturing	2	8	+3.8	
Food, beverages & tobacco	2	4	+3.7	
Textiles & textile products	5	3	−2.2	
Leather & leather products	3	3(2)[a]	+4.0	+4.4
Rubber & related products	1	7(2)[a]	+5.4	+6.2
Lumber & wood products	1	3	+3.8	
Paper, printing & publishing	3	7	+5.0	
Chemicals & allied products	1	9	+5.0	
Stone, clay & glass products[c]	0	8(2)[a]	+12.1	+11.2
Metals & metal products	2	6	+6.1	
Miscellaneous	1	8	+6.1	
Sum of 10 groups	19	58(6)[a]		
Av. of 10 groups weighted by no. of turns			+5.0	+5.2

[a] Figures in parentheses are the number of additional comparisons suggested
by marked acceleration or deceleration of trend.
[b] Includes turns suggested by a marked change in trend.
[c] Averages include a peak in 1930 and a trough in 1922. The standing of the
series, however, was the same in 1929 as in 1930 and virtually the same in
1921 as in 1922. Substituting these earlier dates changes column 4 to +9.1;
column 5, to +8.8.

Concerning the length of the lag, one must speak more warily.
Timing comparisons made from annual data cannot be very accurate, and it is better to think in terms of a range than of a single
figure. On the average, the aggregate holdings of manufacturers

[14] That is, the point of pronounced reduction in an upward trend (or acceleration of a downward trend) is counted as a peak; the point of pronounced acceleration of an upward trend (or reduction of a downward
trend) is counted as a trough.

appeared to lag 3.8 months behind the turns of general business. Eight of the ten industry groups yielded average lags of 3.7 to 6.1 months. There was one longer lag and one shorter lead. If we think of inventories in current prices as tending to lag 3-6 months behind business in general, we shall probably not be far wrong.

This conclusion should be applied to manufacturers' inventories as a whole, not to individual industries or commodities. In Chapter 3 I argued that timing measures made from annual data are unlikely to be reliable unless the series is very long. Our own series are shorter than the standard there laid down. I use them because I can bring to bear the evidence not of one but of ten indicators of manufacturers' stocks. It is important, however, to use the results to get a general impression about manufacturers' holdings in the aggregate and not to seek more detailed results for members of the group.

To say that stocks tend to lag 3-6 months at reference turns implies a certain regularity in their behavior. This can be tested by measures of conformity. For this purpose we adapt the National Bureau standard measure to the peculiarities of annual single-date, year end series. The reader will recall that to establish a chronology of business expansions and contractions for synchronous series we determined the December 31's when business successively reached peak and trough levels. If a series tends to lag 3 months we predate our year end stocks 3 months and use a September 30 business chronology. If a series tends to lag 6 months, we predate year end stocks 6 months and use a June 30 chronology, and so on. We choose the timing category in which a series belongs by consulting our regular timing comparisons (in this case Table 20), then round the average lead or lag to the nearest 3-month interval. We measure conformity on other than a synchronous basis only if average timing is based on at least seven comparisons and we never assume a lead or lag longer than 12 months. Seven comparisons are hardly enough to give reliable results for individual series, although this is a fairly strict standard for series that extend through only five business cycles. Once again, therefore, we apply our findings only to manufacturers' stocks as a whole and avoid conclusions about individual series.

As to the meaning of the indexes, it is only necessary to remember that in order to score +100 in conformity to expansion, a series must stand higher at the end than at the beginning of every business expansion. A score of +50 means that the series rose in three out of four expansions; +33 means it did so in two out of three (or four out of six) times, and so on. Conformity to contraction is measured in the same way, except that +100 means that the series declines in every contraction. There is one complication. A series with a rising trend is likely to have a high score in expansions and a low score in contractions. Hence our measure of conformity to full cycles is based on a comparison of the rates of growth during both contraction and expansion. Thus a series can score +100 in conformity to full cycles if it either rises in every business expansion and falls in every contraction or if it simply rises more rapidly in each expansion than in adjacent contractions. Of course if a series tends to decline in expansions and rise in contractions our indexes will have negative signs, and if a series does so invariably it will score —100. Our results for inventories in current prices are summarized in Table 21.

The lesson to which the table as a whole points is clear. Allow-

TABLE 21

Manufacturers' Inventories, Current Prices
Conformity to Business Cycles, 1918-1938

| (1) | LEAD (—) OR LAG (+) ASSUMED[a] (MO.) (2) | NO. OF PHASES[b] (3) | INDEX OF CONFORMITY TO BUSINESS | | |
			Exp. (4)	Contr. (5)	Cycle (6)
Total manufacturing	+3	10	+100	+100	+100
Food, beverages & tobacco	0[c]	10	+60	−20	+56
Textiles & textile products	−3	10	+20	−20	+33
Leather & leather products	+3	10	+20	+60	+56
Rubber & related products	+6	11	+60	+67	+60
Lumber & wood products	0[c]	10	+20	−20	−33
Paper, printing & publishing	+6	11	+20	0	+20
Chemicals & allied products	+6	11	+100	+67	+100
Stone, clay & glass products	+12	11	+100	+33	+100
Metals & metal products	+6	11	+60	+33	+80
Miscellaneous	+6	10	+60	+60	+78

[a] From Table 20, col. 4 and 5. Results are rounded to the nearest 3-month interval.

[b] That is, expansions plus contractions. The number of phases varies slightly from series to series because the business chronology of certain timing categories brings an extra phase within the period covered by our series.

[c] Inventories are matched synchronously with business cycles because timing comparisons were too few to furnish a sound basis for any other procedure.

ing for timing differences, the degree of conformity is high—strikingly so for annual data. Seven of the ten industry groups yield conformity indexes for full cycles that are higher than 50; all except one are positive. The indexes for total manufacturing indicate perfect conformity to expansions and contractions as well. Manufacturers' aggregate holdings rose in each of five expansions, fell in each of five contractions. Even the one defection from positive behavior, lumber, is a doubtful case. Conformity was measured on a synchronous basis because only four comparisons were available to establish a typical lead or lag. If we relax our rule and allow for a 3-month lag as suggested by the average timing of this series, its conformity indexes would run +60, +20, +100.

The expansion and contraction indexes point a lesson of their own. True, manufacturers' aggregate holdings conformed perfectly to individual phases, but the expansion indexes of the individual groups run somewhat lower than the full cycle indexes, and the contraction indexes are much lower, sometimes negative. Consequently, a considerable portion of the regular positive conformity evidenced by the full cycle measures must reflect the impact of business cycles on the trend of the growth of stocks rather than on the direction of their movement. Stocks often do not fall in contractions, but they almost always grow more slowly. This qualification, however, is probably less serious than our measures indicate. An annual series with a rising trend will skip more contractions than will a monthly series. We can be fairly sure that if we had monthly data, both the expansion and the contraction indexes would be higher. Subject to these qualifications, one can say: inventories in current prices tend to conform positively to business cycles if we allow for a 3-6 month lag. Judged by the interwar record, this is a regular feature of business cycles.

All these lessons can be confirmed and more learned by close inspection of Chart 4. These graphs were drawn in a way that helps bring out the regular association between inventory movements and business cycles. The years covered by expansion and contraction are not the same in all graphs because the same business chronology is not appropriate to all timing categories. The eye, therefore, can get a rough impression of the regularity with which inventories respond to the changing phases of the business cycle.

Chart 4
Manufacturers' Inventories, Current Prices
Total and Ten Groups

I   Series that Lag 3 Months
Contractions (shaded) and expansions (unshaded) are marked off
by the September 30 business chronology

II   Series that Lag 6 Months
Contractions (shaded) and expansions (unshaded) are marked off
by the June 30 business chronology

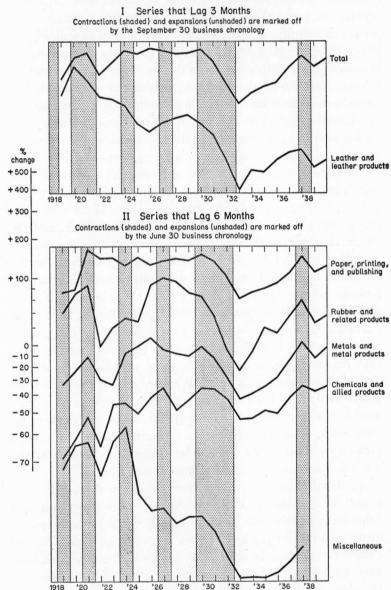

Chart 4 (concl.)

III   Series that Lag 12 Months
Contractions (shaded) and expansions (unshaded) are marked off
by the December 31 business chronology postdated one year

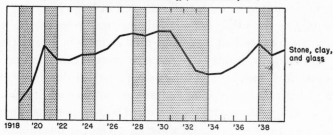

Stone, clay, and glass

1918   '20   '22   '24   '26   '28   '30   '32   '34   '36   '38

IV   Series that Lead 3 Months
Contractions (shaded) and expansions (unshaded) are marked off
by the March 31 business chronology

%
change

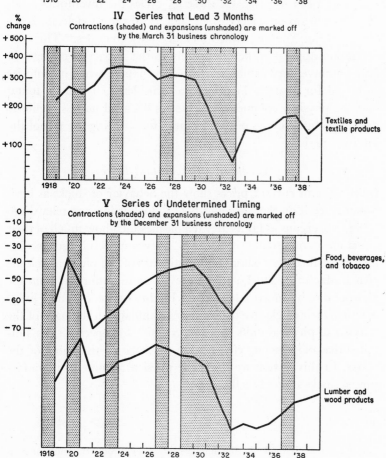

+500
+400
+300
+200
+100

1918   '20   '22   '24   '26   '28   '30   '32   '34   '36   '38

Textiles and textile products

V   Series of Undetermined Timing
Contractions (shaded) and expansions (unshaded) are marked off
by the December 31 business chronology

0
-10
-20
-30
-40
-50
-60
-70

Food, beverages, and tobacco

Lumber and wood products

1918   '20   '22   '24   '26   '28   '30   '32   '34   '36   '38

A striking feature is the difference in the response of inventories to the milder and more violent episodes of the period. The 1920-21 deflation, the great depression after 1929, and the marked recovery beginning in 1933 are all reflected in large inventory movements. On the other hand, mild business cycles in the middle 'twenties are matched by equally mild changes in inventories.

Consonant with this is the fact that most of the defections from conformity come in this short period of relative calm, 1923-29. The series that represent the ten industry groups extend, in the aggregate, over 95 business cycles, measured both from trough to trough and from peak to peak. Of these 95 cycles the inventories series do not conform on 21 occasions. But 13 of the 21 defections occurred during 1923-29 which included only 30 cycles.[15] This concentration appears to be due chiefly to the impact of changes in prices on inventory values. Later in this chapter, when inventories corrected for changes in prices are considered, it will be found that the physical volume of inventories behaved no less regularly during the mild cycles of the 'twenties than during the rest of the interwar period.

2   Inventories in Constant Prices

Inventories in current prices show the behavior of stocks as businessmen see it on their account books. Book values are relevant to business decisions as far as they tell businessmen how much of their assets are committed in this form. They are useful also because they are a first approximation to estimates of the physical volume of manufacturers' stocks, which are far more important from the viewpoint of business cycle analysis. For businessmen usually judge whether their stocks are deficient or redundant on the basis of the number of physical units they hold relative to expected sales, output, price movements, etc., not on the basis of the value of the goods. In this section we study the physical volume of manufacturers' stocks more directly.

---

[15] If allowance is made in the lumber and wood products series for a 3-month lag, defections number only 15, of which 11 occur between 1923 and 1929.

METHODS OF ESTIMATION

We can construct an index of quantities of stocks from book values provided they can be corrected for changes in prices. This is not easy, and we cannot expect to obtain anything more than crude approximations. Nevertheless, such corrections were carried through for Kuznets' estimates of inventories in his ten manufacturing groups.[16] The estimates for the individual industry groups were then aggregated to yield an estimate of manufacturers' holdings. We have at hand also Terborgh's figures corrected for changes in prices. The procedures by which the influence of changes in prices on Kuznets' estimates was eliminated are described fully in Appendix A, Part 2. Here we indicate only the major difficulties—difficulties that could not be wholly overcome.

Manufacturers usually value their inventories at cost except that they mark them down at the end of the year when replacement costs are lower than original costs. Of this more below. Valuation at cost means that a substantial portion of manufacturers' stocks—goods in process and finished goods—enter the inventory accounts at unit values made up of the purchase price of raw materials consumed plus allowances for labor costs per unit, for other direct costs, and for overhead. This in turn means that the behavior of unit values of goods in process and of finished goods cannot be represented accurately by the movements of commercial prices of purchased materials for which there are public records. We can allow for labor costs in a few cases but in no industry were we able to allow for changes in overhead costs per unit.

As a consequence, the indexes of purchased material prices that enter into the indexes used to correct inventory values for changes in prices were inevitably overweighted. I estimate that labor and overhead costs should have borne a weight of not less than 18 percent. They may have constituted as much as 30 percent of the cost of inventories though it is highly unlikely that they were so large.

[16] For 1918-25 the price indexes used in all groups were devised by Kuznets and his staff and published in *Commodity Flow and Capital Formation*, Part VII. The same is true of the indexes used in later years for metal and metal products; stone, clay and glass; and miscellaneous manufacturing. For the other seven groups, revised indexes for the years after 1925 were prepared by me with the assistance of Fred Lynn and David Rolbein.

A second element of crudity inheres in the fact that the commodity price series in our indexes are far outnumbered by the commodities included in inventories. In addition, the price series represent goods at early stages of fabrication more adequately than they do goods at later stages.

These defects in the price indexes have an identifiable bias. While different classes of prices tend to turn at about the same time, the prices of highly fabricated goods have a somewhat smaller cyclical amplitude than the prices of less highly fabricated goods, which are given undue weight in our indexes. Similarly, commodity prices probably have a larger cyclical amplitude than labor costs per unit, which are inadequately represented. In general, therefore, because of the price deflators we use, the amplitude of inventories in constant prices is probably understated to some degree.[17] Moreover, the turning points of inventories in constant prices are probably shifted somewhat in a fashion discussed below.

Finally, we must remember that while most manufacturing companies mark down inventory values at the end of the year when replacement costs are lower than original costs, not all do so. Since I could not discover the exact proportion of deviations from the common practice I assumed that all manufacturers follow the rule of 'cost or market, whichever is lower'. I do not believe, however, that this particular difficulty can cast serious doubt on my findings. The maximum degree of error that could be engendered was tested by comparing our figures with those based on the assumption that only half the manufacturers in each industry follow the cost or market rule (see App. A, Part 2).

Since the estimates of inventories in constant prices must obviously be subject to serious error I do not rely upon the detailed results for individual industries, but merely seek to determine what general characteristics are strongly supported by the bulk of the evidence for all industries. Even with this restriction, the data yield useful information.

---

[17] Indirect evidence that this is so is presented by Harold Barger in *Outlay and Income in the United States, 1921-1938* (NBER, 1942), App. C.

CONFORMITY AND TIMING

Chart 5 shows Kuznets' and Terborgh's estimates of manufacturers' total inventories in constant prices arranged so as to distinguish their behavior during business expansions and contractions. For purposes of comparison, Kuznets' estimates appear in two forms: one based on the assumption that all manufacturers value inventories at the lower of cost or market, the other on the assumption that all value inventories at cost. Once more a simple inspection of the chart yields some useful preliminary findings about the relation between inventories and business cycles.

Chart 5
Total Manufacturers' Inventories, Constant Prices

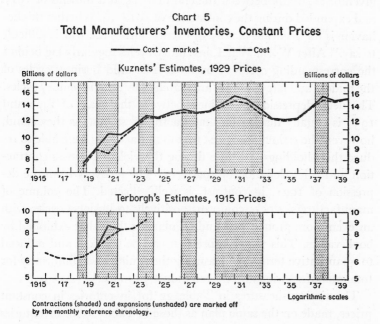

————— Cost or market   ----- Cost

Kuznets' Estimates, 1929 Prices

Terborgh's Estimates, 1915 Prices

Logarithmic scales

Contractions (shaded) and expansions (unshaded) are marked off
by the monthly reference chronology.

We note first the close similarity between the two forms of Kuznets' estimates. Both move in the same direction and at nearly the same rate in every year of the period except two, 1919-20 and 1920-21. The big drop in prices at the end of 1920 produces a high corrected value for inventories at the end of that year when we assume that markdowns were universal but a low value when we assume that they were nonexistent. Since most stocks are probably valued at the lower of cost or market, and since both series move in substantially the same way except in the two years noted, we feel justified in confining attention to the former, though the truth must lie between them.

Perhaps the most striking feature of the graph is the regularity with which the peak and trough values of inventories lag behind the monthly reference dates. Beginning with the reference peak in 1920, a peak in inventories follows every peak in business and a trough in inventories every trough in business. This regularity is broken only in the expansion of World War I and in the subsequent short contraction. As represented by Terborgh's estimates, inventories shrank between the end of 1915 and the end of 1917 and expanded during the contraction of 1918-19. Whether this behavior is an accurate picture of events during the war is difficult to say.[18] After World War I, inventory cycles regularly lag behind the corresponding cycles of business. The mild business cycles of the middle and late 'twenties are matched by mild inventory cycles. The deep depression in business between the peaks of 1929 and 1937 is equally marked in manufacturers' stocks. As they stand, however, the estimates suggest that manufacturers were able to reduce their holdings but little during the violent business contraction and price deflation of 1920-21.[19] The recovery from the depression of 1921, in contrast, is well reflected. The volume of manufacturers' stocks conforms positively to business cycles with an even more pronounced and regular lag than that exhibited by book values. This visual impression can be checked and reduced to quantitative terms by measuring the timing and conformity for total manufacturing and the ten industry groups.

The timing measures in Table 22 for inventories in constant prices, made on the same plan as those in Table 20 for inventories in current prices, strongly support our preliminary observations.

[18] Terborgh got his estimates in constant prices by computing separate price indexes for each of the 19 component industries that make up his total. He assumes that all inventories were valued at cost, except at the end of 1920 when he assumes that they were marked down if replacement costs were lower than original costs.

[19] This is only a suggestion. Price correction is especially likely to err in such an excited period of inflation and deflation, and our year end figures may well, in this case, misrepresent the true height of the peak of stocks and the true depth of their trough.

TABLE 22

Manufacturers' Inventories, Constant Prices
Timing at Business Cycle Turns, 1918-1938

(1)	NUMBER OF Leads[a]	Lags[a]	AV. LEAD (−) OR LAG (+), MO. Actual turns	Actual & indicated turns[b]
	(2)	(3)	(4)	(5)
Total manufacturing[c]	0	10	+8.6	
Food, beverages & tobacco[d]	1	4	+5.5	
Textiles & textile products	2	6	+6.0	
Leather & leather products	0	10	+9.9	
Rubber & related products[d]	0	5 (2)	+11.9	+8.9
Lumber & wood products[e]	0	7	+16.4	
Paper, printing & publishing[d]	0	1	+9.5	
Chemicals & allied products[d]	0 (2)	4	+4.0	+1.2
Stone, clay & glass products	0	8	+13.6	
Metals & metal products	2	6	+7.6	
Miscellaneous	0	8	+8.8	
Sum of 10 groups	5 (2)	59 (2)		
Av. of 10 groups weighted by no. of turns			+10.4	+9.3

[a] See Table 20, note a.

[b] See Table 20, note b.

[c] The average in col. 4 includes a turn of stocks at the end of 1934. From 1933 to 1934 stocks declined only 1 percent. Had we assumed that stocks turned at the end of 1933, the average lag would be only 7.4 months.

[d] One or more lags in 4 series were disregarded because they exceeded 24.5 months.

	DATE OF TURN	LAG (MONTHS)
Food, beverages & tobacco	1932	+42.5
Rubber & related products	1931	+30.5
	1936	+45.5
Paper, printing & publishing	1931	+30.5
Chemicals & allied products	1931	+30.5
	1935	+33.5

[e] The average in col. 4 includes a turn of stocks at the end of 1934. The standing at the end of 1933 was virtually the same as at the end of 1934. Had we assumed that stocks turned at the end of 1933, the average lag would be 14.6 months.

Based on ten comparisons, all of which are lags, manufacturers' total holdings turned on the average 8.6 months later than business. The ten industry groups also lagged consistently. Of the 64 comparisons between reference dates and turns in the inventories held by individual industry groups, inventories lagged in 59 and led at only 5.

There is evidence here of a strong tendency for inventories to lag behind business by a considerable number of months. It is not easy, however, to determine the length of the lag. Total manufacturing lagged 8.6 months. An average of all 64 comparisons yielded by the ten groups suggests a lag of 10.4 months.[20] But the dispersion about these figures is great. The average lag for the ten groups ranges from about 3 to over 16 months. In view of the deviations to be expected of measurements on annual data from the true average lag, it does not seem safe to say more than that the average lag of the physical volume of stocks behind general business is probably more than 6 and less than 12 months.

This implies that the lag of stocks in constant prices tends to be longer than that of stocks in current prices. The record clearly supports this implication. First, in the measures for the ten industry groups, inventories in current prices led the reference turns in nearly 25 percent of the comparisons. For inventories in constant prices, the leads were only some 8 percent of the comparisons. The average for all comparisons between reference dates and the turns of the ten industry groups (including the few judged from marked changes in trend) yielded a 5.2 month lag for inventories in current prices and a 9.3 month lag for inventories in constant prices. In current prices, manufacturers' total holdings lagged 3.8 months on the average; in constant prices, 8.6 months.

This characteristic difference between the timing of inventories in book values and in constant prices is easily explained in terms of the cyclical behavior of prices. We have concluded that manufacturers' inventories in constant prices tend to turn 6-12 months later than general business. If prices were actually constant near business peaks and troughs the movements of stocks in current prices would parallel the movements of stocks in constant prices at cyclical turns. But if prices begin to decline before business reaches a peak or if they lag less than stocks, the rise of stocks in current prices will be impeded, and they will tend to reach a peak and decline before stocks in constant prices. Again, stocks in current prices will tend to lead stocks in constant prices at business troughs if prices begin to rise before business reaches a trough or

[20] The average would be 9.3 months if we included the four turns indicated by the marked changes in trend.

if they lag by a shorter interval than do stocks in constant prices.

The actual behavior of prices is consistent with this explanation. Of the 11 turns of general business between April 1919 and May 1938, the period for which we have inventory data also, the Bureau of Labor Statistics wholesale price index led the National Bureau reference dates at 8. Only one of the three lags exceeded 4 months. Raw materials, moreover, have more weight in determining inventory values than do wholesale prices in general. The BLS index of prices of raw materials turned before general business on 9 of 10 occasions between 1919 and 1938.[21]

These observations help to bolster our conclusions about the timing of the physical volume of inventories. It is not clear, however, that the difference between the timing of inventories in current and constant prices is as large as our figures seem to indicate. Since the amplitude of fluctuations in the indexes used to correct inventory values for changes in prices is probably too large, the timing of inventories in constant prices is affected. If our deflators overstate the movements of the unit value of inventories immediately after the peak in business, the turning points of inventories in constant prices will tend to be postponed, relative to those of inventories in current prices. If, therefore, the data indicate that inventories in constant prices turn 6-12 months later than business activity, the true lag is probably closer to 6 than to 12 months.

Table 23, summarizing our measures of the regularity with which manufacturers' stocks respond to business cycles, is drawn up on the same plan as Table 21. In measuring conformity, the lag of stocks behind business is allowed for. The lags indicated in Table 22 were used after rounding to the nearest 3-month interval. Three

[21] The BLS index, however, is made up exclusively of unfabricated goods whereas the raw materials used by many manufacturers include partly fabricated goods purchased from other manufacturers.

The cyclical timing of prices was different before World War I. Between 1857 and 1914, peaks in the index of wholesale prices lagged behind those of business cycles on 9 of 13 occasions. On the average, prices lagged 1.5 months. At troughs prices lagged at 8 of 13 turns; the average lag was 4.5 months. These measures are based on the Warren-Pearson index before 1890 and on the BLS index since that date.

This tendency for prices to lag behind business cycle peaks and troughs before 1914 suggests that the relation between inventories in constant prices and in book values may not have been the same as that since 1919.

groups, food, paper, and chemicals, were treated on a synchronous basis because their average timing measures rested on too few comparisons to do otherwise.

TABLE 23

Manufacturers' Inventories, Constant Prices

Conformity to Business Cycles, 1918-1938

(1)	LEAD (—) OR LAG (+) ASSUMED[a] (MO.) (2)	NO. OF PHASES[b] (3)	INDEX OF CONFORMITY TO BUSINESS Exp. (4)	Contr. (5)	Cycle (6)
Total manufacturing	+9	11	+100	+33	+100
Food, beverages & tobacco	0[c]	10	+20	−20	−11
Textiles & textile products	+6	11	+60	+33	+40
Leather & leather products	+9	11	+20	+67	+80
Rubber & related products	+9	11	+100	0	+40
Lumber & wood products	+12	11	+60	+33	+60
Paper, printing & publishing	0[c]	10	+100	−60	+11
Chemicals & allied products	0[c]	10	+20	−60	+33
Stone, clay & glass products	+12	11	+100	0	+60
Metals & metal products	+9	11	+100	0	+80
Miscellaneous	+9	10	+60	+20	+33

[a] From Table 22, col. 4 and 5. Results are rounded to the nearest 3-month interval.

[b] See Table 21, note b.   [c] See Table 21, note c.

The indexes for full cycles confirm our impression that inventories conform positively to business cycles. The expansion and full cycle indexes for total manufacturing are +100. Six of the ten groups have full cycle indexes of +40 or better. The full cycle indexes of the groups are, on the whole, lower than those for inventories in current prices, but since annual data usually yield lower indexes than monthly series a fairly high degree of regularity of behavior is indicated.

The response of the volume of inventories to business cycles took the form of a variation in trend rather than of actual cycles in level even more often than did the response of inventories in current prices. The trend was strongly upward, as is evidenced by the high expansion indexes. The contraction indexes, in contrast, are low, sometimes negative, indicating a net tendency in at least some groups for inventories to continue rising during contractions. As shown by the full cycle indexes, however, the rate of rise during contractions even in these groups was generally lower than in expansions. Allowing for the long lag already indicated, inventories conformed positively during full cycles.

Chart 6 shows the stocks held by the ten industry groups as well as by all manufacturers. Again the light and dark areas differ from frame to frame according to the timing category of each series. The graphs will help the reader form his own impression of the sensitivity of inventories to general waves of prosperity and depression.

One prominent feature of inventories in current prices is not repeated when the values are corrected for changes in prices. In the former case we found that a high proportion of all defections from conformity to business cycles came in the short period of mild business cycles between 1923 and 1929. The volume of inventories, in contrast, responds as regularly, though, of course, not as vigorously, to mild as to severe fluctuations in business. The ten industry group series representing inventories in constant prices extend, in the aggregate, over 96 business cycles measured both from trough to trough and from peak to peak. Inventories did not conform in 27 cycles. Only 10 defections come between 1923 and 1929, when the ten series together extended over 30 cycles.

3 Inventories Held by Other Industrial Divisions

Though this study is devoted to manufacturers' inventories, it is interesting to compare their cyclical behavior with inventories held in other major divisions of the economy. Estimates we consider sufficiently reliable for this purpose are available in both current and constant prices for four divisions: trade, transportation and other public utilities, mining, and agriculture. They were first compiled by Simon Kuznets;[22] minor revisions and extensions were carried through by me. The four groups together with manufacturing hold about 95 percent of total inventories (Table 3).

Charts 7 and 8, depicting the movements of the five series from 1918 through 1938 or 1939, are arranged so as to distinguish behavior during business expansions and contractions marked off

[22] Kuznets presented the estimates in their original form in *Commodity Flow and Capital Formation,* Part VII, for year ends 1918-33. Subsequently he extended the estimates to later years and used results derived from them in Commodity Flow and Capital Formation in the Recent Recovery and Decline, 1932-1938, NBER, *Bulletin 74,* June 1938, and *National Product since 1869.*

Chart 6
Manufacturers' Inventories, Constant Prices
Total and Ten Groups

I   Series that Lag 9 Months
Contractions (shaded) and expansions (unshaded) are marked off
by the March 31 business chronology

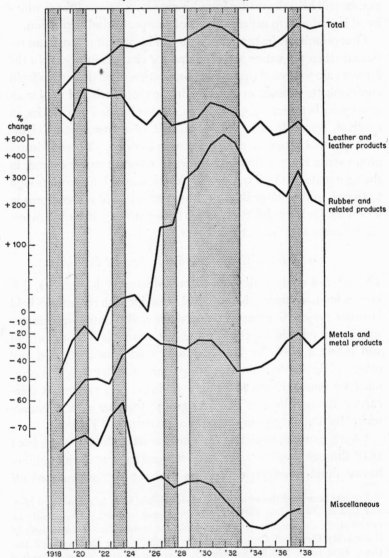

Chart 6 (concl.)

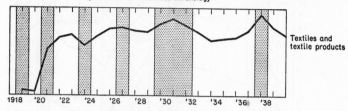

II Series that Lag 6 Months
Contractions (shaded) and expansions (unshaded) are marked off
by the June 30 business chronology

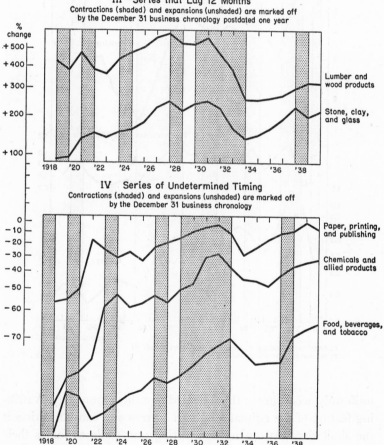

Textiles and
textile products

1918   '20   '22   '24   '26   '28   '30   '32   '34   '36   '38

III Series that Lag 12 Months
Contractions (shaded) and expansions (unshaded) are marked off
by the December 31 business chronology postdated one year

%
change
+500
+400
+300
+200
+100

Lumber and
wood products

Stone, clay,
and glass

1918   '20   '22   '24   '26   '28   '30   '32   '34   '36   '38

IV Series of Undetermined Timing
Contractions (shaded) and expansions (unshaded) are marked off
by the December 31 business chronology

0
−10
−20
−30
−40
−50
−60
−70

Paper, printing,
and publishing

Chemicals and
allied products

Food, beverages,
and tobacco

1918   '20   '22   '24   '26   '28   '30   '32   '34   '36   '38

Influence of changes in price eliminated on the assumption that inventories are
valued at the lower of cost or market.

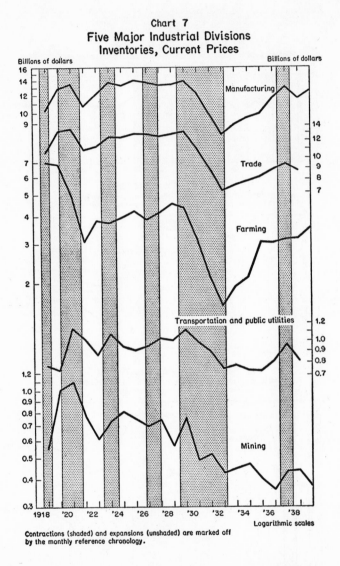

Chart 7
Five Major Industrial Divisions
Inventories, Current Prices

Contractions (shaded) and expansions (unshaded) are marked off
by the monthly reference chronology.

uniformly according to the standard monthly chronology. A striking feature of the estimates in both current and constant prices is
the similarity between manufacturing and trade as far as their
behavior can be judged from annual data. In current prices the
two series have cycles that correspond perfectly and that reach
peak and trough values at the same year ends. The estimates of

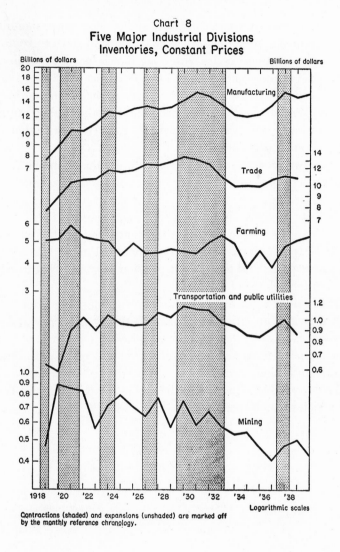

Chart 8
Five Major Industrial Divisions
Inventories, Constant Prices

Contractions (shaded) and expansions (unshaded) are marked off
by the monthly reference chronology.

physical volume, as shown by the series in constant prices, correspond almost as well. Trade skips the contraction of 1920-21,
but its growth is markedly retarded. Thereafter, its peaks and
troughs are synchronous with those of manufacturers' stocks until
the peak of 1929, when the latter turn down a year later. Both
series reach troughs in 1932, remain low until the end of 1934,

then sweep upward to a peak at the end of 1937. As in manufacturing then, the stocks held by wholesalers and retailers conform positively to business cycles with a lag that is longer for estimates of physical volume than for those in current prices.

This similarity between the inventories of the two major industrial divisions extends to transportation and other public utilities. In it, however, the lags characteristic of the two major divisions are even more pronounced.

When we turn to mining and agriculture the resemblance disappears. The peaks and troughs of the mining series are more easily matched with those of business cycles on an inverted basis, and the conformity measures indicate inverted association. These results would stand out more clearly in the charts had the big price declines of 1920-29 and 1929-32 not depressed mining inventories in current prices and the great depression after 1929 left its mark on even the volume of stocks.

The positive pattern of farm stocks in current prices is due to the violent swings in agricultural prices between prosperity and depression. The estimate in constant prices is a less regular series which appears to move inversely if there is any regular association at all with business cycles.

Table 24, which summarizes the timing comparisons, and Table 25, which presents measures of conformity, give these impressions

TABLE 24

Inventories, Five Major Industrial Divisions
Timing at Business Cycle Turns, 1918-1938

(1)	INVENTORIES, CURRENT PRICES		AV. LEAD (—) OR LAG (+), MO.	INVENTORIES, 1929 PRICES[a]		AV. LEAD (—) OR LAG (+), MO.
	NUMBER OF			NUMBER OF		
	Leads	Lags		Leads	Lags	
	(2)	(3)	(4)	(5)	(6)	(7)
Manufacturing	2	8	+3.8	0	10	+8.6
Trade	2	8	+3.8	0	8	+5.9
Transp. & other pub. ut.	1	10	+9.7	0	10[c]	+12.1[c]
Agriculture	6	1	—5.2	3	2	—1.9
Mining & quarrying[b]	4	4	—0.9	4	4	—0.2

[a] Except for agriculture, inventories are corrected for changes in price on the assumption that they are valued at the lower of cost or market. Estimates for agriculture are derived from physical quantities multiplied by end of year prices in 1929.

[b] Timing measured invertedly; see Ch. 3, note 5.

[c] One lag omitted because it exceeded 24 months.

TABLE 25

Inventories, Five Major Industrial Divisions
Conformity to Business Cycles, 1918-1938

(1)	LEAD (−) OR LAG (+) ASSUMED[a] (MO.) (2)	NO. OF PHASES[b] (3)	INDEX OF CONFORMITY TO BUSINESS		
			Exp. (4)	Contr. (5)	Cycle (6)
INVENTORIES, CURRENT PRICES					
Manufacturing	+3	10	+100	+100	+100
Trade	+3	10	+100	+100	+100
Transp. & other pub. ut.	+9	11	+100	+100	+100
Agriculture	−6	10	+20	+60	+78
Mining and quarrying	0	10	−60	−60	−56
INVENTORIES, 1929 PRICES					
Manufacturing	+9	11	+100	+33	+100
Trade	+6	11	+100	+33	+100
Transp. & other pub. ut.	+12	11	+100	+67	+80
Agriculture	0[c]	10	−20	−60	−78
Mining & quarrying	0	10	−60	−60	−78

[a] From Table 24, col. 4 and 7. Results are rounded to nearest 3-month interval.
[b] See Table 21, note b.   [c] See Table 21, note c.

objective form. The lags of inventories in manufacturing, trade, and public utilities are more consistent and longer for estimates in constant than in current prices. The transportation and public utilities series is the most serious laggard of the three, but it is doubtful that the apparent difference between trade and manufacturing (in 1929 prices) is significant. It arises partly because in these annual data trade skips the 1920-21 contraction and partly because its trough at the end of the great depression is placed at the end of 1933 instead of at the end of 1934 as is done for manufacturing. For both series the change between the two year ends is very small.

The mining and agriculture series also bear out the impression gained from the charts. The cycles in the former correspond easily to business cycles on an inverted basis and indicate an approximately synchronous association. The latter appear to lead when estimates in current prices are matched positively with business cycles. But the comparisons are fewer than for the other divisions and the irregular association is especially pronounced for estimates in constant prices.

Trade and transportation, like manufacturing, conform regularly and positively to business cycles, allowing for the indicated lag of stocks. Mining conforms inversely with fair regularity. Stocks on farms conform positively under the influence of changes in prices but inversely with fair regularity when the effect of changing prices has been eliminated.

Both the similarities and differences in inventory cycles these tables reveal are illuminating. For example, as we shall see later, the relation between business cycles and manufacturers' stocks is a composite of divers behavior traits characteristic of various categories of manufacturers' stocks. In particular we shall find that inverted behavior, or long lags verging on inverted movement, is characteristic of stocks of certain classes of staple finished goods. For such commodities, manufacturers can safely risk a certain delay in adjusting the pace of their operations fully and promptly to cycles in their sales. Inverted behavior is characteristic also of situations in which manufacturers cannot easily control the size of their stocks of purchased materials, either because they must buy them long in advance or because the conditions under which the raw materials are supplied force the rate of fabrication to adjust itself to the rate of supply rather than to the rate of demand. In the light of these findings it is significant that the stocks of both farmers and mine operators consist mainly of staple goods that are 'finished' from the standpoint of these industries; farmers, of course, cannot quickly adjust their output to demand. These facts raise the interesting possibility that the apparently different behavior of stocks in the various industrial divisions may be found to be rather readily susceptible to rationalization in terms of a single consistent hypothesis. But this is a suggestion for future investigation rather than a problem for this study.

Whether or not this possibility of reconciling differences in the action of the various divisions of the economy turns out to be a valid lead,[23] we should still notice the impressive degree to which

23 Even if it should prove possible to organize support for this theory, it seems likely that the degree of (inverted) association between business cycles and stocks on farms will turn out to be weak. For the output of crops and livestock, though subject to pronounced cycles, is either unrelated or only tenuously related to business cycles. Geoffrey H. Moore will treat this question in his forthcoming study of Harvest Cycles.

the formula earlier established for manufacturers' stocks is repeated in trade and transportation. The positive and lagged conformity of these three divisions, which together account for about 80 percent of all commodity stocks, serves to enhance the importance of the next section and of other portions of this study which appraise our findings about manufacturers' stocks.

4 Significance of the Findings

We have concluded from the interwar record that manufacturers' aggregate stocks vary positively with business cycles, lagging more than 6 but less than 12 months. It is well to realize exactly what such long lags mean. To make our ideas quite definite, assume that the true average lag is 9 months.[24] During the 21 business cycles since 1854 the National Bureau has identified, expansions lasted on the average slightly more than 26 months, contractions only 21.5 months. A 9-month lag, therefore, means that aggregate physical inventories of manufacturers would decline for slightly more than one-third of an average expansion and would continue to increase for over 40 percent of an average contraction. Moreover, 5 of the 21 expansions and 13 of the 21 contractions lasted 18 months or less. In such short phases manufacturers' inventories would move counter to business for half the phase or more. This assumes, of course, that the lag of inventories behind general business is not correlated with the length of cyclical phases.

If these observations are valid, they serve both to correct and to give precision to the suggestions put forward by earlier writers. The juxtaposition of my findings about the timing of stocks with the Bureau's measures of expansions and contractions makes it easier to see Blodgett's results in fair perspective. He concluded that manufacturers' inventories move inversely to business. In the light of my findings, this appears to be true only of the shorter movements (18 months or less) which have constituted a majority of business contractions in the United States but only a small minority of expansions. As already stated, however, Blodgett discerned a tendency for series that normally behave inversely to move with business in "long and severe" contractions. Blodgett's

[24] This figure, however, may exaggerate the true lag somewhat; see Section 2 above.

findings and our own, therefore, are more nearly consistent than
may appear at first glance.

The results of this chapter are less easily reconciled with the
views of other writers. My observations are at odds with at least
one reading of Hawtrey's theory—that cycles of stocks of finished
goods offset those of stocks of goods in process. Some such offsetting there may be during some stages of the business cycle. The
offsetting action of the two groups of stocks, as far as it exists, however, is either not continuous or incomplete. A definite cycle of inventories related to business cycles does manifest itself. Of course,
Hawtrey's theory of the trade cycle, as already stated, depends
upon a virtual cycle in the *demand* for stocks, not upon an actual
cycle of inventories physically acquired. The broad lines of his explanation of business cycles are, therefore, untouched by my observations. On the other hand, the invisible cycle in the demand for
stocks, which Hawtrey stresses, is closely related to the visible fluctuations in the amount of goods held. If businessmen desire to hold
larger inventories in the early months of expansion, their orders
and their planned output may be affected by the fact that their
stocks are shrinking in those months instead of expanding.

Both Mitchell and Keynes suggest that aggregate inventories
generally move with business, but neither appeared to expect such
a long lag as I find.[25] True, Keynes asserts that liquid stocks increase for some time after the peak of business and decline after
its trough, but he contends that their action will be outweighed by
the movements of working capital, which are (roughly) synchronous with business. If Keynes is right about the behavior patterns
of working and liquid capital, however, the fluctuations of the
latter must, in fact, be large enough to dominate the total during
the early part of business expansions and contractions. Otherwise,
we would not find the lag that appears.

Keynes' hypothesis about the interaction of fluctuations in working and in liquid capital led him to put forward a theory about the
behavior of inventory investment. He suggested that the rate of
investment is low but positive in the early months of expansion
when the increase of working capital is being offset by a decline in

[25] The same is true of Hawtrey as far as he expects to find an actual cycle
in stocks.

liquid capital and that it rises as liquid capital ceases to fall and begins to increase. Similarly, he suggests that after the peak of business, stocks will be declining but that the rate will be low as long as liquid and working capital are moving in opposite directions. When liquid capital too begins to be reduced, the rate of disinvestment accelerates. The typical cycle pattern of inventories, however, is somewhat different. Total stocks do not merely grow slowly in the early months of expansion; they actually decline. They do not merely decline slowly after the peak of business; they actually increase for some months. This suggests that the pattern of inventory investment during business cycles is unlikely to accord well with the model implicit in Keynes' views.

The above observations indicate also that the principle of acceleration as applied to inventories requires modification. This theory of inventory investment, in its simple form, holds that inventories vary directly and proportionately with output. Assuming, for the time being, that output and business at large move together, the observation that inventories lag many months behind business requires explanation. J. M. Clark, who first advanced the hypothesis, never supposed that what I have described as the theory "in its simple form" was an adequate description of reality. He stressed, from the beginning, that business decisions about investment are likely to lag behind the changes in output or sales that call for them, and that still more time is required to execute investment decisions once they are made. Both qualifications are consistent with the observed lag of inventories behind output, and I shall argue that both are involved in a complete account of inventory behavior. But other factors will also be found to be important. Moreover, the principle may have direct and simple application to some parts of total inventories.

Having found so much awry in the theories of inventory behavior even with respect to aggregate stocks, it is pleasant to end this chapter with a glance at Metzler's suggestion. His model of an inventory cycle involves the sound notion that inventories lag behind business. Whether he would expect as long as lag as I have found cannot be said, but in a broad way his theory of the dynamics of inventory cycles is consistent with the lag of inventories at cyclical turns.

CHAPTER 5

Manufacturers' Stocks during Manufacturing Activity Cycles

In Chapter 4 we found that manufacturers' stocks, in the aggregate, tended to lag behind business by a considerable number of months—a rule that appeared to operate with impressive regularity in view of our dependence upon annual data. In this chapter we shall see whether the same behavior is characteristic of stocks during cycles of activity in the various manufacturing industries.

1 Inventories in Current Prices during Manufacturers' Sales Cycles

For comparison with inventories in current prices, the most appropriate indicator of manufacturing activity seems to be manufacturers' sales in the changing prices of the period. Sales of manufacturing corporations are published by calendar years in *Statistics of Income*.[1] Adjusted for sales by unincorporated firms,[2] they can be compared with Kuznets' estimates of year end inventories (Chart 9), also based on *Statistics of Income*. To supplement these annual estimates we have the NICB monthly indexes of the value of manufacturers' shipments and inventories since 1929 (Chart 10).[3]

In both charts the suggestion that conformity is positive and that inventories lag behind sales is very strong. Kuznets' series reaches a peak at the end of every year when sales reach a peak, and the same is true for troughs. In these annual series inventories move

[1] Before 1922 the figures are for gross income alone. Since gross income and gross sales are very nearly the same, gross sales before 1922 could be estimated from gross income.

[2] The adjustment is made in the same way as for inventories; see App. A.

[3] The NICB indexes do not include manufacturers of food products, tobacco, liquors, petroleum, or certain lumber products; see Ch. 4, Sec. 1.

through one more cycle than sales, but this extra inventory cycle corresponds to a cycle in the rate of growth of sales and bears the same lagging relation to it as other inventory cycles do to actual cycles in the level of sales.

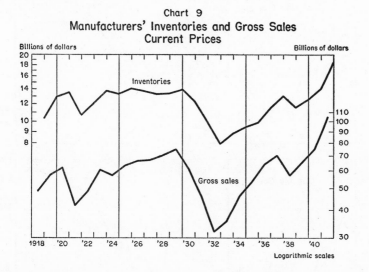

Chart 9
Manufacturers' Inventories and Gross Sales
Current Prices

These tendencies characterize the NICB monthly indexes also. Stocks lag at the two cyclical peaks and troughs that can be identified between 1929 and the beginning of the war boom. One possible exception is the behavior of stocks in nondurable goods industries at the 1929 peak of shipments. Stocks appear to lag but they may possibly have had an earlier peak, and the value of shipments of nondurable goods may have reached a peak before 1929.[4] A more definite exception occurred at the peak of the war expansion. The peak in the value of shipments is hard to date in view of the long period of high but fluctuating shipments. Inventories, how-

[4] We place the peak of the value of shipments of nondurables tentatively in January 1929 because our estimate of the value of their output (based on the Federal Reserve index of production of nondurable manufactures and F. C. Mills' index of wholesale prices of nondurable processed goods) reaches its peak in July 1929. The product of price and output indexes constructed with different weights is, no doubt, a somewhat irrational compound. But to identify the 1929 peak in this series it was necessary to discover how the value of shipments of nondurables behaved before 1929 when the NICB index begins. This procedure affords a usable approximation.

Chart 10
National Industrial Conference Board Indexes of
Value of Manufacturers' Inventories and of Shipments
(seasonally adjusted)

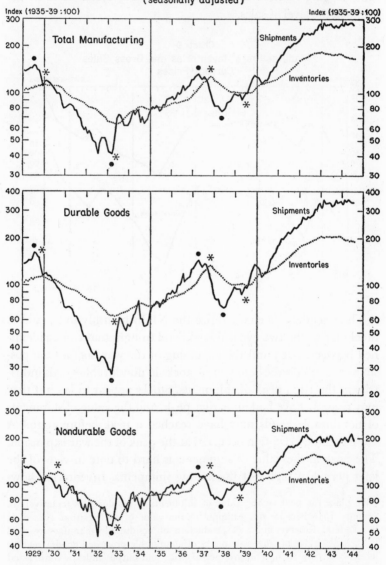

Index (1935-39 :100)

Index (1935-39 :100)

Total Manufacturing

Shipments

Inventories

Durable Goods

Shipments

Inventories

Nondurable Goods

Shipments

Inventories

1929 '30 '31 '32 '33 '34 '35 '36 '37 '38 '39 '40 '41 '42 '43 '44

✻ Peaks and troughs of cycles in inventories.
● Peaks and troughs of cycles in shipments.

Logarithmic scales

ever, apparently began to decline before shipments—which is hardly unexpected in view of the strained conditions of supply during the war.

The absence of monthly indicators of activity in current prices before 1929 makes it necessary to measure the relative timing of turns in inventories and in business activity by comparing the year end estimates of activity with calendar year estimates of sales. We assume that calendar year sales approximate the relative levels of sales on June 30. Thus if inventories reach peaks at the end of the same year as calendar year sales, we say that inventories lag 6 months behind sales. If inventories reach a peak at the end of the preceding year, we say that inventories lead sales by 6 months, and so on. In 64 comparisons Kuznets' inventory estimates lagged behind comparable estimates of manufacturers' sales at 60 turns (Table 26). This proportion is substantially larger than that found when inventory cycles were compared with monthly reference turns. Moreover, the average lag seems to have been longer. Manufacturers' total holdings lagged 6 months behind sales on the average. Indeed, according to our crude measures, they appeared to lag 6 months at every turn in sales. The comparable figure for inven-

TABLE 26

Manufacturers' Inventories, Current Prices
Timing at Turns in Sales Cycles, 1919-1938

(1)	NO. OF TIMES INVENTORIES		AV. LEAD $(-)$ OR LAG $(+)$ MONTHS
	Lead (2)	Lag (3)	(4)
Total manufacturing	0	8	+6.0
Food, beverages & tobacco	0	6	+6.0
Textiles & textile products	3	4	+0.9
Leather & leather products	0	5	+8.0
Rubber & related products	0	6	+8.0
Lumber & wood products	0	4	+6.0
Paper, printing & publishing	0	6	+6.0
Chemicals & allied products	1	7	+4.5
Stone, clay & glass products	0	8	+13.5
Metals & metals products	0	6	+8.0
Miscellaneous	0	8	+7.5
Sum of 10 groups	4	60	

tories at business cycle turns was only 3.8 months. The average timing of the ten industry groups also indicates longer lags than was true for comparisons with reference turns.

We cannot conclude with any confidence, however, that inventories in current prices actually do tend to lag behind sales by a longer interval than they do behind business at large, because in the comparisons of turns in sales and inventories there is a source of error that was not present when inventory turns were compared with reference dates. Then inventories alone were represented by annual data. Now sales as well as inventories are in annual form. The apparent difference in timing, on the order of two months, is not longer than might be accounted for by the inaccuracy with which annual data may measure the average timing of turns in sales.[5] No substantial difference, moreover, appears in the timing of the turns of the NICB monthly indexes of inventories when compared with reference dates and with the peaks and troughs of shipments. The average lag of the NICB index of manufacturers' total inventories behind the reference dates at four business cycle turns between 1929 and 1938 was 6.5 months. The average lag behind the turns in shipments was 7 months.[6] I conclude that while inventories in current prices tend to lag behind sales, the material now available is not sufficiently reliable to determine whether the length of the lag is about the same as that of inventories behind business at large—that is, 3-6 months—or somewhat longer.

The regularity of the behavior of inventories in current prices during cycles in sales is indicated by the conformity measures of Table 27. The measures are constructed on a plan identical with the National Bureau standard measure of conformity to business

[5] Assume that manufacturers' total sales turned in the same months as reference cycles, as they may well do, on the average. Assume further that the peaks and troughs of calendar year sales run synchronously with the calendar year reference dates, as they actually did from 1919 to 1938. If we now measure the timing of sales at reference turns from annual sales data by comparing the midpoint of the years of specific cycle turns with the monthly reference dates, sales appeared to lead at reference turns by 1.5 months on the average during 1919-38. This interval is about the same as the timing difference with which we are here concerned.

[6] Since 'sales' in this context represent the value of goods billed to purchasers it is scarcely conceivable that there is a significant difference between turns in sales and in the value of shipments.

TABLE 27

Manufacturers' Inventories, Current Prices
Conformity to Sales Cycles, 1919-1938*

(1)	NO. OF PHASES[a] (2)	INDEX OF CONFORMITY TO SALES[b] Exp. (3)	Contr. (4)	Cycle (5)
Total manufacturing	7	+100	+100	+100
Food, beverages & tobacco	7	+100	+50	+67
Textiles & textile products	7	+33	+50	+67
Leather & leather products	7	+33	+100	+100
Rubber & related products	7	+33	+100	+100
Lumber & wood products	9	+50	+20	+75
Paper, printing & publishing	5	+100	+100	+100
Chemicals & allied products	7	+100	+100	+100
Stone, clay & glass products	7	+100	+50	+67
Metals & metal products	7	+33	+50	+67
Miscellaneous	7	+100	+100	+100

* Except miscellaneous. Since an estimate of sales for 1938 comparable with earlier years was not available, the last specific cycle phase that could be identified for this group ends in 1932.
[a] That is, expansions plus contractions; see Table 21, note b.
[b] A 6-month lag of inventories behind sales is allowed for; that is, end of year inventories are predated 6 months and their changes measured during expansions and contractions in calendar year sales.

cycles except that the reference expansions and contractions with which the movements of inventories are matched are marked off by the turns in the sales of the various manufacturing groups. The lag of inventories behind sales is allowed for by treating end of year inventory figures as if they represented calendar year figures for the same year. This amounts to predating inventories 6 months, an interval suggested by the timing measures of Table 26.[7]

The behavior of inventories in current prices during cycles in sales seems highly regular. If we allow for a 6-month lag, the total and three of the groups conformed perfectly to both expansions and contractions. Inventories in two other groups conformed perfectly to full cycles in sales; that is, they consistently rose more rap-

[7] Since sales run by calendar years, inventories could be matched with sales only by predating them either 6 or 18 months, etc. Other combinations could be arranged only by the awkward device of averaging year end inventories to get calendar year estimates. Neglecting this device, it appeared that predating by 6 months agreed well with the timing shown in Table 26 in all groups except stone, clay and glass for which it might have been appropriate to assume a longer lag.

idly when sales were expanding than during neighboring contractions in sales. The lowest full cycle measure is +67, indicating positive conformity in five out of six cycles.[8] The relation between inventories and sales was evidently more regular than between inventories and business cycles.

This striking degree of association between cycles in inventories and in sales raises the question whether the connection already observed between business cycles and the value of inventories is not to be traced largely to the relation between inventories and manufacturing activity on the one hand, and to that between manufacturing activity and the congeries of economic fluctuations that make up business cycles on the other. Plausible arguments may be advanced to the effect that inventories are held primarily to support the activities of production and distribution rather than as objects of price speculation. Combined with the close and regular connection in time between the turns of business cycles and those of manufacturing output, these arguments suggest that the connection between inventories and manufacturing activity may be the key to the connection between inventories and business cycles. But even a tentative statement is better postponed until we have reviewed the relation between inventories and manufacturing activity free from the common influence of prices.

2   Inventories in Constant Prices during Output Cycles

The regularity with which inventories in current prices follow the movements of dollar sales is doubtless to be attributed in considerable degree to the influence of price movements on both. To discover the extent to which these relations hold when prices are stable, we examine the behavior of inventories in constant prices during cycles in manufacturers'. output.[9] The inventory data are

[8] As indicated in Table 27, most industry groups could be observed during 7 cyclical phases of sales. Seven phases, that is, expansions and contractions, make up 6 full cycles measured both from trough to trough and from peak to peak.

[9] We might have compared inventories with sales, both in constant prices. To do so, however, dollar sales would have had to be corrected for changes in prices, a procedure subject to error. In addition, we would have had to rely on annual sales data before 1929. It seemed better to substitute output data for price-corrected sales data. Physical output and sales will, of course, diverge whenever stocks of finished goods change, but output and sales un-

Kuznets' year end estimates in 1929 prices. The output data are the FRB indexes of manufacturers' output combined into comparable major industry groups.[10] Miscellaneous manufacturing was omitted because a comparable index of output was unavailable.

Inventories in constant prices lag behind turns in the output of manufactured goods just as they do behind reference cycle turns (Chart 11). Except after 1929 and 1932, when the apparent lag is longer, inventories reached a peak or trough at the end of each year in which a monthly peak or trough in output occurs. Again the impression of positive conformity allowing for a lag of inventories behind output is strong. Our measures for the individual groups tend to confirm this impression, though the results are not as nearly unequivocal as in preceding comparisons.

Table 28 summarizes our timing measures. In each industry group the measures are based on comparisons between the peaks and troughs of cycles in year end inventories and those of corresponding cycles in monthly output. Again inventories held by all manufacturers and by the individual industry groups appear to

---

questionably follow very similar paths. And as indicators of output, the standard Federal Reserve Board indexes of manufacturing production are available in monthly form for the entire period.

[10] The following groups were constructed:

Food, Beverages and Tobacco: FRB indexes of manufactured food products, alcoholic beverages, and tobacco products

Paper, Printing and Publishing: FRB indexes of paper and paper products and of printing and publishing

Chemicals and Allied Products: FRB indexes of chemical products and of petroleum and coal products

Metals and Metal Products: FRB indexes of iron and steel, machinery, transportation equipment, and of nonferrous metals and products

The remaining five indexes—textiles and textile products, lumber and wood products, leather and leather products, rubber and related products, and stone, clay and glass products—correspond to the inventory groups of similar title.

The indexes were combined according to the system of relative weights used in the FRB Bulletin for August 1940 and the *Federal Reserve Index of Industrial Production*, Oct. 1943. The data used here take into account the 1943 revision of the index.

For 1919-22 additional adjustments were necessary owing to the omission of several series. In these cases the level of the series representing a major group before 1923 was raised to the level of succeeding series by means of an overlap in 1923.

Chart 11
Manufacturers' Inventories, Constant Prices,
and Federal Reserve Board Index of Manufacturing Production

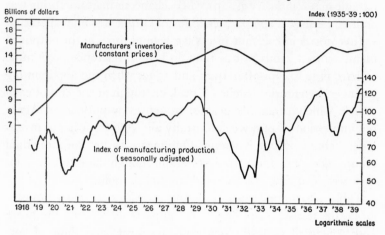

lag behind output as they did behind reference turns. When we allow for the omission of the miscellaneous manufacturing group, the number of comparisons and the proportion that were lags are about the same as in our studies of business cycle behavior. The

TABLE 28

Manufacturers' Inventories, Constant Prices
Timing at Turns in Output Cycles, 1919-1938

	NO. OF TIMES INVENTORIES		AV. LEAD $(-)$ OR LAG $(+)$
	Lead	Lag	MONTHS
(1)	(2)	(3)	(4)
Total manufacturing	0	10	+7.8
Food, beverages & tobacco[a]	1	1	+6.0
Textiles & textile products	2	6	−4.0
Leather & leather products[a]	2	9	+8.6
Rubber & related products[a]	2	2	+2.8
Lumber & wood products	0	7	+15.1
Paper, printing & publishing[a]	0	2	+5.0
Chemicals & allied products[a]	0	3	+11.2
Stone, clay & glass products	0	8	+15.4
Metals & metal products	1	7	+7.8
Sum of 9 groups	8	45	

[a] Leads or lags longer than 24.5 months were excluded. All comparisons excluded were lags: foods, leather, paper, and chemicals, each 1; rubber, 2.

length of the lag also is about the same. Manufacturers' total inventories appeared to lag 7.8 months on the average behind manufacturing output and 8.6 months behind business cycle turns. The closeness of the figures is, of course, testimony only to the virtual coincidence of peaks and troughs in total manufacturing production and in business at large. Of somewhat greater interest is the fact that the average lags of stocks behind output in the various industry groups are also of about the same length as when stocks in constant prices were compared with business cycles. This again may not argue more than that a certain degree of common association exists among business cycles, manufacturing production, and inventories. It is consistent with the hypothesis that cycles in inventories are determined by those in output and that the connection between business cycles and inventories merely reflects the underlying link between inventories and output. As far as we have yet gone, however, our findings by themselves lend little positive support to the idea.

The indexes of the conformity of inventories in constant prices to cycles in production go little further. Table 29 is prepared on exactly the same plan as Tables 21 and 23 except that the expansions and contractions with which inventories are matched are determined by cycles in the output of the various industries rather than by the National Bureau standard reference dates. In the upper portion of the table, the measures allow for the difference in the relative timing of inventory and output cycles as revealed in Table 28. Again measurements on something other than a synchronous basis were made only if average timing was based on 7 or more comparisons. Only total manufacturing and 5 of the 9 groups met this standard. Of these, all except one, textiles, appeared to lag by a long interval—almost 9 or 12 months—and all except one, again textiles, yielded indexes that imply a fairly high degree of regularity of association between inventories and full cycles in production, allowing for the indicated lag. For 4 of the 9 groups conformity was measured on a synchronous basis since average timing was based on too few comparisons to do otherwise. Two groups, paper and chemicals, yielded zero conformity indexes to full cycles in production; two others, food and rubber, appeared to vary inversely to output.

TABLE 29
Manufacturers' Inventories, Constant Prices
Conformity to Output Cycles, 1919-1938

MEASURES FOLLOWING TIMING SUGGESTED BY TABLE 28

(1)	Lead (−) or lag (+) assumed[a] (mo.) (2)	No. of phases[b] (3)	INDEX OF CONFORMITY TO OUTPUT Exp. (4)	Contr. (5)	Cycle (6)
Total manufacturing	+9	9	+100	+60	+100
Food, beverages & tob.	0[c]	7	−33	−50	−67
Textiles & textile prod.	−3	14	+14	−14	+8
Leather & leather prod.	+9	10	−20	+60	+78
Rubber & related prod.	0[c]	8	0	−100	−71
Lumber & wood prod.	+12	9	0	+20	+50
Paper, printing & pub.	0[c]	5	+100	−33	0
Chemicals & allied prod.	0[c]	7	+33	−50	0
Stone, clay & glass prod.	+12	7	+100	+50	+100
Metals & metal prod.	+9	10	+100	+20	+78

MEASURES ASSUMING A LONG LAG OF INVENTORIES BEHIND OUTPUT

	Lead (−) or lag (+) assumed (mo.) (7)	No. of phases[b] (8)	INDEX OF CONFORMITY TO OUTPUT Exp. (9)	Contr. (10)	Cycle (11)
Total manufacturing					
Food, beverages & tob.	+12	7	+100	−50	+67
Textiles & textile prod.	+12	13	0	−14	−17
Leather & leather prod.					
Rubber & related prod.	+12	8	+100	0	+100
Lumber & wood prod.					
Paper, printing & pub.	+12	5	+100	−33	0
Chemicals & allied prod.	+12	7	+100	0	+33
Stone, clay & glass prod.					
Metals & metal prod.					

[a] From Table 28, col. 4. Results are rounded to the nearest 3-month interval.
[b] That is, the number of expansions plus contractions in the output of the industrial group with which the direction of movement of inventories is matched. The number differs from group to group because the groups do not have the same number of output cycles.
[c] Inventories are matched synchronously with output because the timing comparisons were too few to do otherwise.

The irregular or negative conformity of these last four groups is less seriously at odds with the hypothesis that inventories conform positively to business activity with a long lag than may appear at first sight. As already pointed out, positive conformity with a long lag may mean inverted behavior during a major part of many cyclical phases. And though a paucity of cyclical turns makes timing measurement difficult, these series may tend to conform positively to output with a long lag. If so, low or negative indexes would be expected if conformity is measured on a synchronous basis.

In the lower portion of Table 29 this possibility is tested. Conformity indexes allowing for a 12-month lag were prepared for these four groups and for textiles, whose conformity was previously measured allowing for a 3-month lead of inventories over output. The results lend support to the general rule that manufacturers' inventories tend to follow production with a long lag. Of the five groups, three yield positive full cycle indexes, two of which are fairly high. The index for paper remains zero. Textiles yielded a very low negative index. Taking all nine groups together, and allowing for a long lag—either 9 or 12 months—the evidence of regular association with output is fairly impressive. The full cycle conformity indexes of seven groups are positive, and six indexes are +50 or higher (see Ch. 3, note 8). The indexes for the two remaining groups are of negligible size. As in the case of their relation with business cycles, therefore, I conclude that stocks tend to conform positively with a long lag—roughly 6-12 months—to cycles of manufacturers' output.

3 Some Competing Hypotheses

THE OUTPUT RATE AND MANUFACTURERS' STOCKS

Why do manufacturers' stocks conform positively to business cycles with a long lag? Primarily because of a connection between stocks and the rate of business activity? Are other factors either more significant or, at any rate, very important? If the level of manufacturing activity is a controlling factor, what is the nature of its relation to stocks?

The fact that stocks move together with output as well as with business cycles, with a long lag in both cases, does not, of course, mean that the connection between business cycles and stocks is to be traced to a connection between output and stocks. To begin with, the conformity indexes of stocks to production cycles are only moderately high. This, however, is not conclusive either way. The suggested connection would, no doubt, be more appealing if the conformity indexes were higher. But they do not differ much from those that measure the association between stocks and business cycles. Moreover, they are from annual data and, as we know, such indexes are usually lower than those computed from monthly series.

More important is the long interval by which stocks lag behind production. An hypothesis that the level of production controls the level of stocks must explain this lag and, as we shall see, the common theory that links inventories with production does not assume a lag in inventories. If this investigation concentrates on the dependence of stocks upon manufacturing activity, as it does, it is because a plausible explanation for the lag can be found.

The obvious close correlation between production, in the aggregate, and business cycles also has an important bearing on the question. This cuts two ways. Were the correlation not close, the behavior of stocks during business cycles could scarcely be attributed to fluctuations in production. On the other hand, it might be attributable wholly or substantially to other factors associated with business cycles, and the association between production and stocks may be entirely or partly incidental.

Despite the latter possibility, we concentrate upon the connection between output and stocks. Justification for this emphasis, of course, must be sought in the study as a whole, not in the findings presented so far. Some preliminary argument in support of our position may, however, prove useful. It takes two tacks. One is to state, in broad outline, a theory that rationalizes the association between output and inventories. The second is to consider the plausibility of some alternative hypotheses to account for the cyclical behavior of stocks.

A COMMON THEORY ABOUT THE RELATION BETWEEN OUTPUT AND STOCKS

Businessmen and business observers generally think that manufacturers hold inventories primarily in order to support their current and immediately prospective rate of production and sales. A corollary is that stocks will vary more or less in proportion to output. As we have seen, this is the view Keynes adopted for his theory of working capital, which in turn he took to account for the bulk of stocks. It is implicit also in the 'acceleration principle' as applied to inventories (Ch. 1, Sec. 2).

The theory has a plausible rationale, and later chapters tend to substantiate it, at least for considerable portions of manufacturers' total holdings. The argument rests in part on the fact that a portion of manufacturers' stocks consists of goods actually in process of fabrication. The volume of such stocks obviously depends more or less rigidly upon the rate of production. The quantity of goods in process must bear a relation to the rate of production per week or month, which is determined by the interval between the time goods are fed into production and the time they are finished and ready to be shipped. This interval, in turn, presumably depends upon the technique of production. It varies from industry to industry, but is probably fairly constant for any given industry during a business cycle. The average interval for manufacturing industries as a whole may, therefore, be assumed to be fairly constant during a business cycle allowing for changes in the commodity composition of output (see Ch. 8).

Other portions of manufacturers' stocks not generally considered to be 'in process' are nevertheless closely tied in volume to the level of activity; for example, raw materials and finished goods in transit to their purchasers; purchased materials and supplies that are being unpacked, sorted, cleaned, stored, and later issued to fabricating departments; and finished goods made to order and awaiting shipment. The propositions that are obviously true of goods undergoing fabrication can apparently be extended to various classes of stocks in stages preceding or following actual manipulation.

It is, of course, not clear a priori that goods in these classes make up the bulk of manufacturers' stocks. But it can be, and often is, argued that manufacturers attempt to maintain a fairly constant ratio between output or shipments and stocks even though a large part of their stocks do not consist of commodities whose volume is tied to output for technical reasons. Manufacturers are said to keep a stock of purchased materials equal to a certain number of weeks' supply at their current rate of consumption, partly to assure a smooth flow of materials into production by guarding against interruptions in deliveries, and partly to allow purchasing to proceed in an orderly fashion without immediate pressure to satisfy production requirements. Manufacturers are said to follow the same policy with respect to finished goods in order to provide a source from which delivery can be made rapidly to urgent customers. Good inventory practice is said to consist in maintaining such a relation between output or shipments and stocks as is required to support the normal functions of production and selling. Speculation is held to be a function of a specialized trader, not of a manufacturer, and descriptions of good manufacturing practice commonly call for manufacturers to hedge their inventory risks by future purchases or sales when possible and generally to manage their inventories according to the requirements of their production and selling activities.

Later chapters will suggest that this view of inventory policy contains a large element of truth for some portion of manufacturers' stocks and some element of truth for most of their holdings. But it cannot be true for all their stocks; or at least it cannot be the whole truth. If it were, inventories would fluctuate more or less synchronously with output. But they lag behind output by a considerable number of months. If, therefore, the common notion that manufacturers' stocks are held primarily to serve the convenience of the fabrication and distribution functions is to be retained, the pronounced lag of stocks must be explained. The solution is twofold. Many commodities are supplied under conditions that make it difficult for purchasers to alter promptly the rate at which they receive goods. Goods that must be brought from foreign countries over long distances or are bought on long term contract are extreme examples. But most materials destined for fabrication are purchased some time before delivery and it is difficult for manufacturers to forecast exactly, even 30 days in advance, the rate at which they will consume raw materials. Such difficulties account for part of the lag. One considerable category of manufacturers' stocks—finished staples—appears to vary inversely to the rate of output, at least in cyclical phases of short and medium length.[11] The reasons are somewhat obscure: poor forecasting perhaps or, more plausibly, a reluctance on the part of manufacturers to curtail operations until they are certain that business is falling off and a continuing reluctance even then to curtail operations as fully as would be required to prevent the accumulation of stocks and, still more, to liquidate them. When the commodities are

[11] They tend to reverse their direction of movement and to move together with output toward the end of long phases.

staples, such policies may be persisted in for many months. The lag of inventories behind output can be explained by a combination of the two factors: inability to control promptly the rate at which purchased goods are received and, in the case of staple goods, reluctance to curtail operations promptly and sufficiently.

All this, however, anticipates the argument and the evidence of later chapters. Even if strong evidence for this view is finally adduced, it will hardly be conclusive until it has been tested to reveal the influence of other factors and simultaneous measurement of their relative importance is attempted. Such simultaneous measurement is not possible, as indicated below, because of the inadequacy of the data now available. But it is useful to glance at some alternative theories to see whether any are plausible rivals for the post of working hypothesis. We consider two factors as alternatives to the rate of manufacturing activity: variations in interest rates for their bearing on the cost of carrying stocks and price speculation for its bearing on the expected return from holding inventories.

INTEREST CHARGES AND STOCKS

Though Hawtrey stressed interest charges as a factor influencing businessmen's desire to hold commodity stocks, he argued that they would be less likely to affect the calculations of manufacturers than of wholesalers. Interest charges can account for only a tiny fraction of the spread between the prices charged by manufacturers for their products and the cost of their raw materials. To wholesale merchants whose markup is small and who operate more largely on borrowed funds, the cost of credit is perhaps a bigger item. In any case, the tendency to minimize its importance to manufacturers seems justified. It may be worth while to consider the matter more closely.

Without passing judgment on their relative importance, a manufacturer's chief positive incentives to hold stocks may be said to be his desire to sustain or increase output and sales and to profit by successful price speculation. To maintain an output and rate of sales of $1,000 per month at sales prices, for example, a manufacturer may have to hold stocks of the same value for, say, three months. (The average turnover period for manufacturers between the wars was from two and one-half to three months.)

At an interest rate of 6 percent per annum—a fairly high rate for customers' loans during the 'twenties and 'thirties—the interest charge for a 3-month loan of $1,000 would be $15 or 1.5 percent. This assumes that extra business is typically financed by borrowed money—a common but not predominant practice. Since the earnings of his own funds, if not invested in his business, would probably net a manufacturer less than 6 per cent per annum, we may take 1.5 percent for three months to be the maximum interest cost required to carry stocks. The range of variation in the interest cost of customers' loans between the peaks and troughs of business cycles is perhaps 20 percent of the peak rate. The interest charge for 3-month loans, therefore, might vary between 1.2 percent at the trough and 1.5 percent at the peak, a difference altogether too small to affect a manufacturer's calculations about the profitability of carrying the additional stock necessary to do extra business.

The conclusion is similar when we consider the relation between interest charges and speculative incentives to hold stocks. In this instance we must compare the interest charge for, say, a month with the expected rate of price increase that stimulates speculative purchasing. An interest rate of 6 percent per annum is only 0.5 percent per month. The difference between a low and a high interest rate is the difference between, say, 0.4 and 0.5 percent per month. It is quite inconceivable that the monthly rate of change in prices that might stimulate speculation could be of the same order of magnitude. It seems highly unlikely, therefore, that the influence of interest rate charges could be detected in inventory records.[12]

The negligible influence of interest rates upon inventory policy was substantiated by the well known inquiry by J. E. Meade and P. W. S. Andrews (Summary of Replies to Questions on Effects of Interest Rates, *Oxford Economic Papers,* Oct. 1938). None of the managers interviewed said that the cost of borrowed funds affected his calculations about the volume of stocks he should hold.

---

[12] These arguments do not, of course, touch the more substantial point that banks may follow a more liberal loan policy in prosperity than in depression. But there is still no way to measure the influence of such changes in loan policy.

PRICE SPECULATION AND STOCKS

The influence of price speculation upon stocks stands on a quite different footing. Obviously prices often fluctuate so violently as to stimulate speculative investment in commodities. And whatever the common opinion about good practice, there can be little doubt that some manufacturers do on occasion attempt to anticipate price rises or declines by modifying their inventory policy. The ultimate problem, therefore, is to measure the specific influences of both price speculation and the rate of manufacturing activity. Unfortunately, the statistical materials at hand are not rich enough for this purpose. Preliminary consideration, however, may help to explain our neglect of price speculation in favor of the connection between output and stocks.

First, the incentives to price speculation do not have any single, clear, objective index. The most obvious indicator of the strength of the speculative motive is the rate of change in prices. The rationale of this index is that a rapid rise causes businessmen to assume a continuation of the rise, and that the rapidity of the expected rise will be proportional to the rapidity of the rise just experienced. The stocks businessmen will consider it profitable to hold would, on this argument, be expected to vary with the rate of rise in prices, with a short lag.[13]

In this simple form, the theory is not in accord with experience. Prices rise most rapidly at the beginning of expansions and reach a second maximum near the peak of business.[14] They usually fall most rapidly in the second quarter of a contraction. Manufacturers' aggregate stocks, on the contrary, approach their lowest point at the beginning of expansion and do not reach their maximum until the second quarter of contraction, just when prices are falling most rapidly.

There is, evidently, no obvious regular connection between

[13] If a businessman was absolutely sure that prices were going to rise at a rate rapid enough to cover the cost of carrying stock plus a profit, there would, of course, be no limit to the inventory he would desire to hold. The uncertainty that attaches to any forecast, however, limits the speculative investment an individual will make in any given circumstance.

[14] These observations are based on a study of the BLS index of wholesale prices, 1890-1938. The rate of change in prices during the various stages of business cycles were calculated according to the National Bureau procedure explained in Chapter 3.

stocks and the rate of change in prices. Nor is the case improved if we allow for the rate of manufacturing activity. As we shall see in Chapter 6, the ratio of inventories to sales or to output reaches its maximum at or near the end of contractions when prices are low and falling. At the beginning of expansion, just when prices are rising most rapidly, the inventory-sales ratio begins to decline, and continues to fall throughout the expansion, although prices rise slowly in the middle of expansion and more rapidly toward its close. Throughout contractions, prices fall first with increasing rapidity, then with declining rapidity; the inventory-sales ratio, however, rises throughout.

These observations suggest that price speculation is not a regular influence of great importance. But they do not settle the issue. A number of other possibilities deserve consideration.

1) Strong as the speculative motive may be when prices are rising rapidly, the attempt to accumulate stocks may not leave its mark on the statistical series now available—for two reasons. The effect of speculation may be concealed in the estimates of manufacturers' total stocks such as have been reviewed in this and preceding chapters because speculative accumulation presumably centers in stocks of purchased materials and supplies. Finished goods, that is, goods ready for sale, will be affected less, if at all, since there will be an incentive to accumulate them for speculative purposes only when the costs of fabrication, principally wage rates, are charging rapidly or when the finished product is more easily stored than the raw material. More important is the fact that a period of speculation is likely to be a period of rapidly rising production, sales, and employment consequent upon the increased orders placed with the object of anticipating a price rise.[15] As we shall see in Chapter 11, stocks of staple finished goods tend to move inversely to sales and output, perhaps offsetting any speculative accumulation of purchased materials. Unfortunately, the few examples of series representing manufacturers' holdings of purchased goods are not of a kind that might reveal the effect of speculative movements in such goods taken separately (see Ch. 9 and 10).[16]

[15] This is the course of events when expectations are bullish. When expectations are bearish, production and sales naturally tend to fall.

[16] Some of the commodities, such as crude rubber, raw sugar, and lead come from distant parts and another, newsprint at publishers, is bought on long

Even if we had adequate records on stocks of purchased materials, the effects of speculation might not be evident because manufacturers may not take sufficient account of the effect of their speculative orders upon output and employment and thus upon the demand for their products. Unless, therefore, selling prices are raised sufficiently to discourage purchasers, larger production may consume stocks of raw materials about as rapidly as they are replenished.

2) Some other stimulant to price speculation may be regularly connected with business cycles. In particular, the strength of the speculative incentive may depend less upon the rate of change in prices than upon the interval during which a rise persists. A sustained rise may give manufacturers more confidence in its continuation than a shorter period of rapidly vaulting prices. Since prices tend to rise more or less steadily from about the beginning to about the end of a business cycle, the incentive to speculation might be expected to be at a maximum at cyclical peaks. Unfortunately, from the standpoint of causal analysis, production too is ordinarily at a maximum at cyclical peaks. Thus the influence exercised by output and sales would merge with that exercised by speculative considerations.

The most obvious way to try to disentangle the influence of the two factors is to study the behavior of inventory-sales or inventory-output ratios during business cycles. The division of inventories by a comparable measure of manufacturing activity may be presumed to neutralize the influence of output and sales, and the behavior of the ratio should then reveal the influence of factors other than out-

---

term contract. These conditions preclude a prompt response of manufacturers' holdings to expected price rises. Iron ore at furnaces moves freely in response to the demand of the fabricators only during summer months. But more important, the integration of the pig iron and ore producing industries reduces the incentive of firms making pig iron to profit by speculation in iron ore.

Raw cotton, silk, and hides are situated differently. Mills can replenish their supplies easily from domestic dealers, but there is no assurance that mill stocks, which are only a portion of aggregate stocks, represent manufacturers' total holdings. They certainly do not represent the long position since mills commonly hedge their position by future sales. Almost all cottonseed stocks are held by oil mills, but the size of the cotton crop is the chief determinant of the amount.

put, of which speculation may be the strongest. As already mentioned, the ratio, computed for total inventories and sales, moves counter to the direction required by the hypothesis that the speculative incentive to inventory accumulation varies directly with the duration of a price rise.[17]

This simple test, we have noted, is rendered partly inconclusive by the fact that total inventories reflect the movements of both purchased materials and staple finished goods which are likely to offset one another to some extent during periods of rising or falling output such as characterize speculative episodes. And again the sample of stocks of purchased materials for which we have data is not such as to reveal effects of price speculation.

3) Manufacturers may not customarily speculate on commodity prices but inventory policy is undoubtedly influenced upon occasion by speculation for reasons not regularly connected with prosperity or depression. A speculative episode of this type was engendered by the devaluation of the dollar and the promulgation of NRA codes in the spring and summer of 1933. Another example is the wave stimulated by the scarcity of goods after both world wars. Although such episodes are not a regular part of business cycles, they deserve study in their own right.[18]

The foregoing considerations are inconclusive. They establish a strong presumption that variations in interest rates do not influence inventory movements greatly and they indicate that price speculation is not such an important feature of manufacturers' actions during business cycles as to leave its stamp clearly on aggregate inventories. But the matter is far from settled. Indeed, as we

[17] This assumes that price cycles conform closely to business cycles without appreciable lead or lag—an assumption consistent with experience.

[18] For what it is worth, it is interesting to notice that in the two violent speculative episodes covered by our data, 1919-21 and mid-1933, ratios of manufacturers' aggregate inventories to aggregate sales do not indicate that inventories were especially high relative to manufacturing activity (see Ch. 6, Sec. 2). The evidence, however, may misrepresent the facts, because accumulation of purchased materials is offset by liquidation of finished goods. Inventory-sales ratios for department stores clearly reflect the effects of speculation at least in the 1919-20 episode. Department stores, however, may be better able than manufacturers generally to adjust the rate at which they purchase and receive goods to the demands of a speculative inventory policy.

saw, there are reasons for thinking that the kind of evidence this study can bring to bear cannot be sufficient to settle it.

With this in mind, we proceed on the tentative assumptions that price speculation is not a major factor regularly affecting variations in manufacturers' inventories during business cycles, that it may be neglected in seeking a first approximation to an explanation of inventory movements, and that it will be illuminating to concentrate attention on the relations between stocks and production or sales. The validity of this procedure is not, of course, founded solely on the facts and arguments so far considered. It is based upon a review of all the materials available. Its soundness, therefore, can be better judged at the end of this book. But though support for this view will then be stronger, it will not be conclusive. Nor can a definite conclusion be reached until the data are sufficiently improved in detail and frequency so that something like a separate measure of the specific effects of manufacturing activity and price speculation becomes feasible.

CHAPTER 6

Inventory Turnover and the Amplitude
of Inventory Cycles

A substantial bloc of theoretical opinion has long held that down-turns of business are precipitated, if not caused, by overproduction, the mark of which is an overaccumulation of stocks. A test of these arguments naturally leads to an inspection of inventory turnover rates. True, one might interpret any accumulation of stocks above some average or trend level as dangerous, a depressant to orders and output. But common sense suggests that larger stocks are required to carry on a larger volume of business and that an undue accumulation implies that stocks are heavy, not absolutely, but relative to the volume of business. This chapter is concerned primarily with turnover rates measured in their inverse form, that is, ratios of inventories to sales or to output. As a subsidiary subject we inspect the amplitudes of cycles in inventories and sales. This information, together with the data about timing surveyed earlier, takes us a certain distance toward understanding fluctuations in inventory turnover rates. Section 5 considers the significance of our findings for the theories of cycle turns alluded to above.

1 Average Inventories Relative to Sales

To lend a certain concreteness to the cyclical measures presented later we first consider how large inventories usually are in comparison with sales (Table 30). Between World Wars I and II manufacturers kept inventories equal to about 21 percent of their annual sales on the average. In other words, their inventories were equal to about two and one-half months' sales and turned over between 4 and 5 times a year. These estimates, however, based on end of year inventories, do not take proper account of the differ-

TABLE 30

Inventory-Sales Ratios in Manufacturing, Current Prices, 1919-1938
(percentages)

	1919 -21	1921 -24	1924 -27	1927 -32	1932 -38	Av. 1919 -38
(1)	(2)	(3)	(4)	(5)	(6)	(7)
Total manufacturing	22.82	23.63	21.43	21.30	19.96	21.43
Food, beverages & tobacco	14.10	12.35	12.18	14.17	14.22	13.58
Textiles & textile products	22.02	27.20	26.45	24.09	20.38	23.57
Leather & leather products	34.78	34.08	25.83	27.61	23.35	27.76
Rubber & related products	30.78	23.57	20.90	23.61	20.92	23.08
Lumber & wood products	26.25	24.95	25.68	34.63	29.66	29.24
Paper, printing & publishing	17.30	18.92	15.10	13.94	14.00	15.28
Chemicals & allied products	26.22	27.63	24.18	21.65	20.60	23.14
Stone, clay & glass products	21.30	21.30	18.92	25.00	24.27	22.83
Metals & metal products	27.22	27.73	24.55	25.18	24.92	25.62
Miscellaneous	29.40	29.98	29.35	27.71	n.a.	28.87

n.a.: not available.

Ratios were computed from annual data on a calendar year basis. End of year inventories (Kuznets' estimates) for successive year ends were averaged and divided by calendar year sales to get inventory-sales ratios for calendar years.

For source of sales data see text, note 1. Figures in column 7 are simple averages of the calendar year ratios. Figures in other columns are averages for successive business cycles, measured from trough to trough. The average for each cycle includes all years from trough to trough; the troughs are weighted one-half each and the intervening values one each.

ence, if any, between the average for the year and stocks held on December 31. This is unquestionably serious for individual industries, but it may not be for manufacturing as a whole. Department of Commerce monthly figures, which unfortunately begin only in 1939, do not reveal any marked seasonal pattern for the holdings of all manufacturers (Chart 15).

The denominators of the ratios are the gross sales of each company aggregated by industry and for manufacturing industry as a whole. Because a large portion of the sales of manufacturing firms are made to other manufacturers, the figures tend to understate the size of stocks compared with net sales after intra-manufacturing transactions have been eliminated. The difference can be gauged roughly by comparing the value of product in manufacturing with 'value added'. For Census years 1919-39 value added by manufacturing averaged about 43 percent of the value of product. On the average, therefore, the value of inventories must have been about half of net output as measured by value added (the average inventory-sales ratio $= .21 \div .43 = .49$). Value added, again, is smaller than net sales since it excludes the value of materials purchased from other than manufacturing firms. Thus inventories must have been somewhat less than 50 percent of net sales.

This, however, is a digression. We are primarily interested in the inventory-gross sales ratios presented in Table 30. These are remarkably similar for the large industrial groups distinguished. The ratios in groups other than foods and paper, where inventories were relatively low, were between 23 and 29 percent, roughly equivalent to 2.8-3.5 months' sales and to turnover rates of 3.4-4.3.

The figures as a whole suggest a mild downward drift in inventory-sales ratios during the two decades. The trend in the total is fairly well repeated in the various industries except foods, lumber, and stone, clay and glass.

2 Cyclical Features of Inventory-Sales Ratios

The computation of inventory-sales ratios based on company accounts is complicated by an awkward fact: inventories are for December 31 while sales are for calendar years.[1] The figures were made comparable by averaging the standings of stocks at the beginning and end of each year. The effect, to dampen fluctuations in stocks somewhat, and therefore to reduce the influence of inventory fluctuations on the movement of the inventory-sales ratios, is probably an advantage for the present purpose. As argued above (Ch. 3, Sec. 2) cyclical amplitudes based on annual data tend to be smaller than those based on monthly data. But the differences between the cyclical amplitudes of monthly and calendar year series tend to be larger than those between monthly and single-date annual series.[2] Making calendar year estimates of stocks by averaging beginning and end of year figures should operate to off-

---

[1] We compute inventory-sales ratios from Kuznets' estimates of inventories in current prices and the gross sales of manufacturers in the same industry groups. Derived from data for corporations in *Statistics of Income*, they are raised to represent the sales of all corporations. The raising ratios are those used to move from corporate to total inventories. *Statistics of Income* did not publish gross sales figures until 1922. In the earlier years, therefore, gross sales are estimated from gross income after adjustment to the level of gross sales in 1922 when they constituted about 95 percent of gross income.

[2] Cf. *Measuring Business Cycles*, p. 261.

set this tendency. And it seems unlikely that the resulting series have smaller cyclical amplitudes than true calendar year inventory series.[3]

The general cyclical behavior of the inventory-sales ratios is illustrated in Chart 12 which is arranged to show the movements of the ratios for total manufacturing during business cycles and to allow comparison with sales and inventory cycles. The inverted pattern of the ratio during both business and sales cycles is apparent and so also is the approximate coincidence of turns in the ratio with those in sales and business at large. Of 7 cyclical turns in sales for which there are corresponding turns in the ratio, six coincide with an opposite turn; in 1937 the ratio turns a year earlier. It sometimes turns before, sometimes after, business activity, as might

Chart 12
Total Manufacturing: Inventory-Sales Ratio,
Sales and Inventories, Current Prices

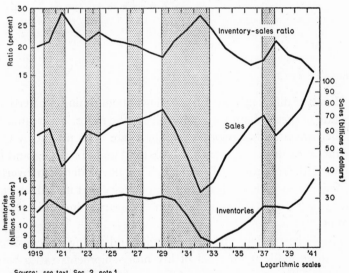

Source: see text, Sec. 2, note 1.
Contractions (shaded) and expansions (unshaded) are marked off
by the monthly reference chronology.

[3] An alternative, to estimate end of year sales (that is, the annual rates of sales at the ends of years) by averaging the sales of each pair of adjoining years, was rejected on two counts. It would have involved comparing inventories with sales as much as 12 months apart. And it would have reduced still further the cyclical amplitude of sales as compared with both monthly and single-date annual inventory figures.

be expected in an annual series whose monthly analogue tends to rise and fall synchronously with business at large.

Timing measures for total manufacturing are presented in Table 31. The small average leads are hardly significant in view of the preponderance of coincidences with the turns of sales and of the virtually even distribution of leads and lags with respect to reference dates. Additional indications of timing might perhaps be gleaned from measures for individual industry groups, but since we must depend upon annual series and since the inventory elements in our ratios are merely averages of year end figures, it would be unwise to press these data further.

TABLE 31

Inventory-Sales Ratios in Total Manufacturing, Current Prices
Timing at Turns of Cycles in Sales and Business, 1918-1938

| REFERENCE SERIES | N U M B E R   O F | | | AV. LEAD $(-)$ OR LAG $(+)$ MONTHS |
	Leads	Lags	Coin.	
Sales (annual)	1	0	6	-1.7
Business cycles (monthly reference dates)	4	3	0	-2.6

Timing measured invertedly; see Ch. 3, note 5.

However diffidently we put our views about timing, we need not hesitate to speak about the conformity of the ratios. The regularity of their inverted behavior in the aggregate is borne out by conformity measures computed for both total manufacturing and for the ten industry groups (Table 32). That the tendency to inverted conformity to cycles in both business activity and manufacturers' sales runs through all manufacturing industry is immediately apparent.

These observations about conformity and timing are consistent with those made upon a set of inventory-shipments ratios based on the NICB monthly indexes of inventories and shipments.[4] These short series, covering only four reference cycle turns, are plotted in Chart 13. Based on monthly data, they are free from the diffi-

---

[4] As indicated in Chapter 5, sales data from company accounts represent the value of goods billed to customers. The value of shipments is, therefore, the equivalent of sales in this special sense.

TABLE 32

Inventory-Sales Ratios in Manufacturing, Current Prices
Conformity to Cycles in Business and Sales

	NO. OF PHASES	INDEX OF CONFORMITY TO BUSINESS[a]			NO. OF PHASES	INDEX OF CONFORMITY TO SALES[b]		
		Exp.	Contr.	Cycle		Exp.	Contr.	Cycle
(1)	(2)	(3)	(4)	(5)	(6)	(7)	(8)	(9)
Total mfg.	10	−60	−60	−100	7	−100	−100	−100
Food, bev. & tob.	10	+20	−60	−56	7	−33	−100	−100
Textiles & textile prod.	10	−100	−60	−78	9	−100	−100	−100
Leather & leather prod.	10	−20	−60	−78	9	−100	−60	−75
Rubber & rel. prod.	10	−20	−60	−78	7	−100	−100	−100
Lumber & wood prod.	10	−60	−100	−100	9	−50	−100	−100
Paper, print. & pub.	10	−100	−40	−100	5	−100	−100	−100
Chemicals & allied prod.	10	−60	−60	−56	7	−100	−100	−100
Stone, clay & glass prod.	10	−100	−100	−100	7	−100	−100	−100
Metals & metal prod.	10	−60	−60	−56	7	−100	−100	−100
Miscellaneous	9	−60	−100	−100	7	−100	−100	−100

[a] Period covered: 1919-38 for calendar year series (except miscellaneous 1919-37). Conformity measured on a synchronous basis by reference to NBER calendar year reference dates.
[b] Period covered: 1920-38 (except food, leather, and rubber 1919-38, and miscellaneous 1920-32). Conformity measured on a synchronous basis by reference to turns in annual sales.

culties that make annual data so awkward to use. The inverted conformity of the ratio to both business cycles and shipments is apparent whether we look at the series representing all manufacturing or those representing durable and nondurable goods industries separately.

The timing measures are summarized in Table 33. Comparisons were made with the turns of both shipments and business cycles. For the total and for nondurable goods industries, alternative comparisons were made. The first set suggests that the ratio for nondurable goods industries—taken invertedly—tends to lead both shipments and business cycles, that the ratio for durable goods industries tends to move synchronously, and that when the two are combined, the total tends to lead by about three months.

The few comparisons on which these measures rest reduce our faith in the conclusion. Moreover, shipments of both nondurable goods manufacturers and of all manufacturers have a double trough near the bottom of the great depression, the first in July 1932 and the second in March 1933. The corresponding inventory-sales ratios have a double peak with identical dates. The more prominent of the two peaks in the ratios was the early one; the more prominent of the two troughs in shipments was the later one.

Chart 13
National Industrial Conference Board Indexes of
Manufacturers' Shipments and of Inventory-Shipments Ratios

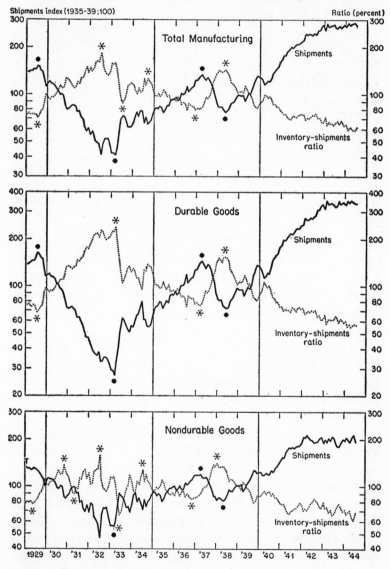

Shipments index (1935-39:100)   Ratio (percent)

Total Manufacturing

Shipments

Inventory-shipments ratio

Durable Goods

Shipments

Inventory-shipments ratio

Nondurable Goods

Shipments

Inventory-shipments ratio

1929 '30 '31 '32 '33 '34 '35 '36 '37 '38 '39 '40 '41 '42 '43 '44

✱ Peaks and troughs of cycles in inventory-shipments ratio.
● Peaks and troughs of cycles in shipments.

Logarithmic scales

Following our rules, we marked the peaks in the two ratios in July 1932 and the troughs in the two shipment series in March 1933. Our ordinary timing comparisons, therefore, indicate that the ratios lead both business cycles—the reference trough also is March 1933—and shipments. In this situation it is sensible to disregard our regular procedure and take account of the later peak of the ratios. When we do, the leads at this turning point disappear, and we have a second set of comparisons. In it the average lead of the ratio for nondurable goods industries is less pronounced, and that of the series representing all manufacturing barely apparent. The significance of such short average leads based on so few comparisons is dubious.

Whether inventory-sales ratios, taken invertedly, tend to lead or not, they plainly do not decline markedly as a rule until the

TABLE 33

Inventory-Shipments Ratios Based on National Industrial Conference Board Monthly Indexes of Inventories and Shipments
Timing at Turns of Cycles in Shipments and Business, 1929-1944

| | TIMING AT TURNS IN | | | |
| | SHIPMENTS CYCLES | | BUSINESS CYCLES (mo. ref. dates) | |
NUMBER OF	1st compar- ison	2d compar- ison	1st compar- ison	2d compar- ison
TOTAL MANUFACTURING				
Leads	2	1	2	1
Lags	0	0	1	1
Coincidences	2	3	1	2
Av. lead (−) or lag (+), mo.	−3.2	−1.0	−3.0	−1.0
DURABLE GOODS INDUSTRIES				
Leads	2		1	
Lags	0		1	
Coincidences	2		2	
Av. lead (−) or lag (+), mo.	−0.5		−0.2	
NONDURABLE GOODS INDUSTRIES				
Leads	3	2	4	3
Lags	1	1	0	0
Coincidences	0	1	0	1
Av. lead (−) or lag (+), mo.	−3.5	−1.2	−4.8	−2.8

Timing measured invertedly; see Ch. 3, note 5.
See text for an explanation of the difference between the first and second comparisons.

trough of business has been passed or rise markedly until the peak of business has been passed. In comparison with its total cyclical amplitude, increases in the inventory-sales ratio before business peaks and declines before troughs were very small (Charts 12 and 13). It seems clear that regardless of the timing of its turns, the ratio remains very low at business peaks, very high at troughs.

3   Cyclical Features of Inventory-Output Ratios

From ratios based on inventories and sales in current prices we turn to ratios based on inventory measures corrected for price changes and on indexes of output. The inventory data are indexes of Kuznets' estimates in 1929 prices; the output data are FRB indexes of manufacturing production for comparable industry groups.[5] To make the output figures comparable with the inventory data, which are for December 31, the December and January standings of the production indexes were averaged.

The inventory-output ratio for total manufacturing has the appearance of an inverted replica of the output index, and its inverted behavior during business cycles is apparent (Chart 14). These observations on the behavior of the ratio for all manufacturers are fully confirmed by conformity measures computed for the total and the various industry groups (Table 34), which, as indicated, were computed on the assumption that the ratios move synchronously with both output and business cycles.[6]

This assumption with respect to timing must now be questioned. Unfortunately the problem of measurement is again vexed by the character of our data. As in the case of all annual data that are available for only a short period, measures made on end of year inventory-output ratios may not accurately reveal the true timing of the cycles in the series. In most cases we do not know the actual degree of distortion, and we have to depend upon tests like those of Chapter 3, Section 2, as a general guide. In the present instance we can do better. We know that the timing of the turns of the inventory-output ratios is strongly influenced by that of the year end

[5] See Ch. 5, note 10, for a description of how the published FRB indexes were combined for this purpose.

[6] Only nine groups are distinguished here because it is impossible to compile a satisfactory index of output comparable with inventories held in the miscellaneous manufacturing group.

Chart 14

Total Manufacturing: Inventory-Output Ratio, Output and Inventories, Constant Prices, End of Year

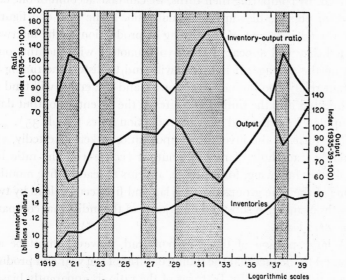

Source: see text, Sec. 3.
Contractions (shaded) and expansions (unshaded) are marked off
by the monthly reference chronology.

TABLE 34

Inventory-Output Ratios in Manufacturing, Conformity to Cycles in Business and Output

(1)	NO. OF PHASES (2)	INDEX OF CONFORMITY TO BUSINESS[a]			NO. OF PHASES	INDEX OF CONFORMITY TO OUTPUT[b]		
		Exp. (3)	Contr. (4)	Cycle (5)	(6)	Exp. (7)	Contr. (8)	Cycle (9)
Total mfg.	9	—100	—60	—100	9	—100	—60	—100
Food, bev. & tob.	9	—50	—60	—25	7	—33	—100	—100
Textiles & textile prod.	9	—100	—60	—75	13	—100	—43	—100
Leather & leather prod.	9	—50	—60	—50	9	—50	—60	—100
Rubber & rel. prod.	8	0	—50	—14	8	—50	—100	—100
Lumber & wood prod.	9	—50	—100	—75	9	—100	—60	—100
Paper, print. & pub.	9	—50	—60	—50	5	—100	—100	—100
Chemicals & allied prod.	9	—50	—20	—25	7	—33	—50	0
Stone, clay & glass prod.	9	—50	—100	—62	7	—100	—100	—100
Metals & metal prod.	9	—50	—100	—100	9	—100	—100	—100

Source: See text.
Period covered: 1919-37 for all series except rubber (1920-37).
[a] Conformity measured on a synchronous basis by reference to December 31 peaks and troughs of business.
[b] Conformity measured on a synchronous basis by reference to turns of end of year output series.

output estimates used in computing the ratios. Moreover, we have at hand the monthly indexes from which the year end data were derived. By comparing their turns, we can take account of one element of possible bias in the annual ratio. If the year end figures are a good indicator of the timing of production in the interwar period they will appear to turn synchronously with monthly output on the average. If not, they will tend to distort the timing of output relative to business cycle turns, and the errors will tend to be injected into the timing measures of the inventory-output data computed from the end of year production series (Table 35).

The turns of the inventory-output ratios, taken invertedly, apparently lead those of monthly output (col. 2-4). The ratio for total manufacturing, for example, appears to lead by five months. None of the nine groups seems to lag and five seem to lead by two months or more. A substantial majority of the individual comparisons were leads.

A large portion of this apparent lead, however, must be attributed to the fact that the timing of turns of the year end production series, which helps fix turns of the ratio, is apparently biased with respect to turns in monthly output (col. 5-7). If the shapes of the production cycles did not distort the timing of the year end series, we would expect the leads and lags in columns 5 and 6 to be about equal in number and the average timing measures in column 7 to approximate zero. Instead, the year end output series tends markedly to lead the monthly series. Except in foods and chemicals all or most of the leads in the ratios can be traced to the biased leads in the year end output series. If we subtracted the apparent lead of each year end production series from that of the ratio for the same group, we would not find any consistent tendency for the groups to lead or lag. Moreover, the residual differences from synchronous timing would be less than two months for total manufacturing and for all except three of the nine groups. Such narrow margins in annual data are not to be relied upon.

Our conclusions are much the same when we consider the timing of the ratio at business cycle turns (col. 8-10). The apparent leads are longer than at output turns. But again, after allowing for the bias injected by the year end output figures, the leads appear substantial in only a few groups. A part of the residual leads, of

TABLE 35

Inventory-Output Ratios in Manufacturing
Timing at Turns of Cycles in Output and Business, 1918-1938

TIMING AT TURNS IN OUTPUT CYCLES

	INV.-OUTPUT RATIOS[a]			OUTPUT [a]		
	NO. OF		Av. lead (—) or lag (+)	NO. OF		Av. lead (—) or lag (+)
	Leads	Lags	months	Leads	Lags	months
(1)	(2)	(3)	(4)	(5)	(6)	(7)
Total manufacturing	9	1	−4.6	8	2	−3.4
Food, beverages & tob.	4	2	−3.3	3	3	+0.2
Textiles & textile prod.	6	3	−2.8	9	3	−4.2
Leather & leather prod.	4	5	−0.1	4	4	+0.1
Rubber & related prod.	6	3	−0.1	5	4	+1.3
Lumber & wood prod.	8	0	−3.6	7	1	−4.5
Paper, printing & pub.	6	2	−2.8	5	1	−3.3
Chemicals & allied prod.	4	2	−4.3	3	3	−0.4
Stone, clay & glass prod.	7	1	−1.0	6	0	−1.5
Metals & metal prod.	6	4	−0.9	5	5	−0.9
Sum of 9 groups	51	22		47	24	

TIMING AT TURNS IN BUSINESS CYCLES

	INV.-OUTPUT RATIOS[a]			MONTHLY OUTPUT			
	NO. OF		Av. lead (—) or lag (+)	N O. O F			Av. lead (—) or lag (+)
	Leads	Lags	months	Leads	Lags	Coin.	months
	(8)	(9)	(10)	(11)	(12)	(13)	(14)
Total manufacturing	10	0	−5.8	4	3	3	−1.2
Food, beverages & tob.	7	0	−5.4	3	3	2	−0.4
Textiles & textile prod.	7	0	−4.9	5	2	3	−1.1
Leather & leather prod.	6	3	+0.5	5	4	1	+0.7
Rubber & related prod.	9	0	−7.7	8	0	1	−7.7
Lumber & wood prod.	7	1	−3.8	2	5	3	−0.4
Paper, printing & pub.	6	2	−2.9	3	4	3	−0.5
Chemicals & allied prod.	6	2	−4.1	2	5	2	+1.8
Stone, clay & glass prod.	7	1	−3.8	7	2	1	−2.6
Metals & metal prod.	6	4	−1.0	3	4	3	−0.1
Sum of 9 groups	61	13		38	29	18	

Timing measured invertedly; see Ch. 3, note 5.
[a] December 31.

course, stems from the lead of monthly output relative to business
cycles, as indicated in columns 11-14. This part is a real, not an
illusory, contribution to the timing of the ratios. It is valid for the
20 years the data cover. But one may question whether the short
average lead of output relative to business cycles during the interwar period is a persistent feature of the cyclical behavior of output.

This review, therefore, leaves us in doubt about the true timing of inventory-output ratios at the turns of output and business cycles. There may be some tendency to lead by a short interval, but we cannot trust our data to reveal it. I conclude that if inventory-output ratios lead at all, the interval is short, and the ratios remain low at business peaks and high at troughs.

4 Causes of the Inverted Pattern of the Ratios

TIMING OF INVENTORY CYCLES

This section and the next two are designed to carry us a certain distance toward understanding the reasons for the inverted behavior of inventory-sales and inventory-output ratios during cycles in business activity and in sales and output. We have already reviewed the data that point to one of the reasons. Inventories tend to lag at turns of both business activity and sales and output. Suppose now that the amplitude of inventory fluctuations, measured from troughs to peaks and back, equals the amplitudes of sales and output cycles similarly measured. Then the lag of inventories behind business cycle turns and the almost synchronous movement of sales and output with business means that stocks will rise less during business expansions and fall less during contractions than do sales and output. And stocks must also, indeed, *a fortiori,* rise less during expansions and fall less during contractions of sales and output than do sales and output themselves. Unless the amplitude of fluctuations in inventories exceeds those in sales and output, inventory-sales and inventory-output ratios must fall during expansions and rise during contractions of business, sales, and output.

The effect of the lag of inventory cycles does not depend upon any special assumption about the relative amplitudes of stocks and sales. It tends to produce ratios that conform inversely whatever the relative amplitudes of inventories, sales, and output. If inventories have narrower amplitudes than sales and output, the ratios would vary inversely even if inventories did not lag. But a lag would cause the ratios to fall further during business expansions and to rise further during contractions. If the amplitude of inventories is wider than those of sales and output, the ratios would vary positively unless inventories lagged behind (or led) the turns of business, sales, and output by a sufficient interval. The lag tends to offset the effect of wider inventory fluctuations, if they exist.

The tendency for inventories to lag is part of the explanation of the inverted pattern of the ratios. It is not the whole story, however, for the amplitude of aggregate stocks is, in fact, narrower than those of sales and output.

AMPLITUDES OF CYCLES IN INVENTORIES, SALES, AND OUTPUT

To judge the vigor of cyclical fluctuations, we use the National Bureau measure of the amplitude of specific cycles. Its computation is described in Chapter 3 where the reliability of such measures made from annual data is discussed. At this point, we need merely note that the measures are based on the same sets of annual data as those from which the annual ratios studied in Sections 2 and 3 of this chapter were computed. The amplitudes of inventory cycles, however, are computed from the original end of year data rather than from the calendar year estimates obtained by averaging data for successive year ends. Thus the smoothing effect that such averages have on cycle movements is avoided. The data we use, therefore, are end of year inventories in current and in 1929 prices, calendar year sales in current prices, and end of year (average of December and January) indexes of output. For reasons explained in Chapter 3, all these sets of annual data tend to yield lower amplitudes than corresponding monthly series. But the degree of understatement will tend to be about the same, though there is some evidence that calendar year data reduce the amplitudes that would be yielded by monthly data somewhat more than end of year figures.[7]

Table 36, presenting average amplitudes of all cycles distinguished in each series between 1919 and 1938, strongly suggests that the amplitudes of stocks are smaller than those of sales or output (col. 3 and 6; 9 and 12). For manufacturing as a whole the amplitudes are more than twice as wide. In current prices the amplitude of sales exceeds that of stocks in nine out of ten industry groups. The average amplitude of output is wider than that of inventories in constant prices in seven out of nine groups.

These observations might be thought conclusive were it not for one disturbing element: the number of cycles in stocks and in sales and output is often different. For total manufacturing in cur-

[7] See *Measuring Business Cycles*, p. 261.

TABLE 36

Inventories (Current Prices) and Gross Sales, and Inventories
(Constant Prices) and Output: Average Amplitudes of
All Specific Cycles, 1919-1938

INVENTORIES AND SALES, CURRENT PRICES

	INVENTORIES			GROSS SALES		
	No. of cycles	Total amp.ᵃ	Per mo. amp.ᵃ	No. of cycles	Total amp.ᵃ	Per mo. amp.ᵃ
(1)	(2)	(3)	(4)	(5)	(6)	(7)
Total manufacturing	4	39.0	0.7	3	79.1	1.2
Food, beverages & tob.	2	83.8	0.8	3	56.9	0.8
Textiles & textile prod.	4	46.3	0.9	3	64.0	1.0
Leather & leather prod.	3	48.1	0.9	3	53.5	0.8
Rubber & related prod.	4	65.8	1.3	3	90.5	1.4
Lumber & wood prod.	2	58.6	0.6	4	62.9	1.2
Paper, printing & pub.	5	29.1	0.6	2	106.6	1.1
Chemicals & allied prod.	5	39.6	1.0	3	68.5	1.1
Stone, clay & glass prod.	3	40.5	0.6	3	81.2	1.2
Metals & metal prod.	3	68.2	1.1	3	122.6	1.8
Miscellaneous	4	54.6	1.2	3	76.0	1.6

INVENTORIES IN 1929 PRICES, AND OUTPUT

	INVENTORIES			OUTPUT		
	No. of cycles	Total amp.ᵃ	Per mo. amp.ᵃ	No. of cycles	Total amp.ᵃ	Per mo. amp.ᵃ
	(8)	(9)	(10)	(11)	(12)	(13)
Total manufacturing	4	26.4	0.5	4	61.3	1.2
Food, beverages & tob.	2	60.8	0.8	2	52.6	0.6
Textiles & textile prod.	3	40.3	0.8	5	50.4	1.2
Leather & leather prod.	5	35.7	1.0	4	46.0	0.9
Rubber & related prod.	2	131.0	1.4	4	90.1	1.8
Lumber & wood prod.	3	54.5	1.0	3	91.4	1.4
Paper, printing & pub.	2	41.2	0.6	2	86.9	1.0
Chemicals & allied prod.	2	52.6	0.7	2	78.4	0.8
Stone, clay & glass prod.	3	47.2	0.7	2	137.5	1.6
Metals & metal prod.	3	53.8	0.8	4	101.8	2.0
Miscellaneous						

The cycles of individual series do not cover a uniform period. For each series
measures begin with the first and end with the last turn in 1919-38.
ᵃ Rise and fall, in specific cycle relatives.

rent prices, for example, stocks had four cycles, sales only three.
We know, however, that a long cycle in one series, A, that extends
over a period covering two cycles in another series, B, will tend to
have a wider amplitude than the average of the two shorter cycles.
This will be true even though the total movement of series B from
the initial trough of its first cycle to the higher of its two peaks
and down to the terminal trough of the second cycle is as large
as the total movement of series A in its single cycle. Conceivably,

therefore, part of the seeming difference in the amplitudes of inventories and sales and output may be traced to this cause.

Some reassurance can be gained from Table 36. Even if we confine attention to groups in which the comparisons are based on the same number of cycles or where the number for sales and output exceeds that for the corresponding inventory series, the amplitude of stocks is narrower than that of the corresponding sales or output series in 10 comparisons out of 13. Two of the three exceptions occur when stock cycles are fewer than sales or output cycles.

Additional confirmation can be had by inspecting the rise and fall per month instead of the total rise and fall. These measures, which represent simply the total rise and fall in each cycle divided by the length of the cycle in months, tend to avoid the difficulties due to differences in the number of cycles because the total rise and fall of a long cycle is divided by more months than are the narrower amplitudes of the two or more cycles sometimes found during the same period in a corresponding series. In current prices the monthly change in total sales is 1.2 percent of its average standing during cycles in sales; for inventories, only 0.7 percent. The average monthly change in output is again 1.2 percent of its average standing during output cycles; that of inventories in 1929 prices, only 0.5 percent. With few exceptions, differences of the same kind, though not always of the same size, are found for the various industry groups.

Finally, we turn from amplitudes based on all cycles in each series to measures based only on comparable cycles. We eliminated all cycles from the inventory series that could not be matched closely with similar cycles in the corresponding sales or output series, and vice versa. When a long cycle in, say, sales was accompanied by two or more short inventory cycles that together constituted a major inventory cycle, we ignored the smaller interruptions and compared the long sales cycle with a single long inventory cycle (Table 37).

Once again, the conclusion that sales and output have more vigorous cycles than inventories is confirmed. In current prices the total rise and fall of aggregate sales far exceeds that of total inventories: it is over 69 for sales, only 45 for stocks. All cycles in output could be matched with those in inventories in 1929 prices for total

TABLE 37

Inventories (Current Prices) and Gross Sales, and Inventories
(Constant Prices) and Output: Average Amplitudes of
Corresponding Specific Cycles, 1919-1938

	INVENTORIES AND SALES, CURRENT PRICES				
	INVENTORIES			GROSS SALES	
	No. of cycles	Total amp[a]	Per mo. amp.[a]	Total amp.[a]	Per mo. amp.[a]
(1)	(2)	(3)	(4)	(5)	(6)
Total manufacturing	2	45.0	0.8	69.4	1.2
Food, beverages & tob.	2	83.8	0.8	85.4	0.8
Textiles & textile prod.	3	60.4	0.9	64.0	1.0
Leather & leather prod.	2	69.8	0.9	71.1	1.0
Rubber & related prod.	2	124.6	1.2	131.8	1.3
Lumber & wood prod.	1	107.6	0.8	137.5	1.0
Paper, printing & pub.	1	64.4	0.9	86.7	1.2
Chemicals & allied prod.	2	46.2	1.0	53.0	1.2
Stone, clay & glass prod.	3	40.5	0.6	81.2	1.2
Metals & metal prod.	3	68.2	1.1	122.6	1.8
Miscellaneous	3	72.5	1.6	76.0	1.6

	INVENTORIES IN 1929 PRICES, AND OUTPUT				
	INVENTORIES			OUTPUT	
	No. of cycles	Total amp.[a]	Per mo. amp.[a]	Total amp.[a]	Per mo. amp.[a]
	(7)	(8)	(9)	(10)	(11)
Total manufacturing	4	26.4	0.5	61.3	1.2
Food, beverages & tob.	1	115.5	0.7	70.1	0.5
Textiles & textile prod.	3	40.3	0.8	42.3	1.0
Leather & leather prod.	0				
Rubber & related prod.	0				
Lumber & wood prod.	2	61.2	0.9	79.9	1.2
Paper, printing & pub.	0				
Chemicals & allied prod.	0				
Stone, clay & glass prod.	2	59.2	0.6	137.5	1.6
Metals & metal prod.	3	53.8	0.8	133.6	2.2
Miscellaneous					

See Table 36, note.
[a] Rise and fall, in specific cycle relatives.

manufacturing; the measures in Table 37 are, therefore, the same
as in Table 36—61 for output, 26 for inventories. In current prices
all ten industry groups showed wider amplitudes for sales than
for comparable stocks cycles. The same was true in four of the five
comparisons that could be made of indexes of physical volume.
And with one exception, foods (for which the monthly amplitudes
for sales and inventories are equal), the rates of movement per
month confirm the measures of total amplitude. We conclude,

therefore, that inventories have narrower amplitudes than sales and output. Hence the relative amplitudes of sales, output, and stocks cycles combine with the lag of inventories to account for the inverted pattern of the inventory-sales and inventory-output ratios.

OTHER FACTORS

These findings take us a certain distance, but not very far after all, toward understanding the movements of the ratios. We still want to know why inventories lag and why their amplitudes are relatively small. Later chapters will help supply answers to our questions about the timing of inventory cycles. We shall see that goods in process of fabrication in individual firms vary almost synchronously with output, that stocks of purchased goods tend to lag a few months in some cases and many months in others, that stocks of finished staples move inversely or with a very long lag, and that there is reason to think that stocks of finished nonstaples tend to lag by shorter intervals. The reasons for these differences we leave to later discussion. Here we take note of three implications of the diverse timing of different kinds of stocks relevant to the present subject.

The first is a technical point. The relatively small amplitudes of cycles in aggregate inventories held by the various industry groups are not independent of the timing differences of the various kinds of stocks making up each aggregate. The fact that inventories of different kinds reach peaks and troughs at widely different times means that the relative cyclical amplitude of the aggregate will be considerably smaller than the average cyclical amplitude of its components. It seems likely that the cycles of the components of total sales and output in each industry group will be more bunched in time than are those of inventories. Hence the amplitudes of aggregate sales and output more nearly approximate the average amplitude of their components than is the case with inventories. This helps account for the small amplitude of the cycles in aggregate stocks compared with those in sales and output.

The second point is that just as we have found that the tendency for inventories to lag is broadly characteristic of the various industry groups, so we shall see that the tendency to lag characterizes most of the various functional categories of stocks—purchased materials, finished goods, etc.—held by the various industry groups. This fact reduces the possibility that, as a general rule, any substantial category of stocks actually rises more relatively between the troughs and peaks of business or of sales and output cycles than do sales and output themselves. Hence it reduces the possibility that inventory-sales and inventory-output ratios for any substantial category of stocks will stand higher at the upper than at the lower turning points of business cycles. It does not, of course, render such a result impossible. But if inventories of a certain kind tend to lag behind sales, their amplitude must exceed that of the sales cycle in order that their ratio should rise during expansions of sales and fall during contractions. Goods in process is the only category of stocks for which the investigations reported in later chapters do not indicate a lag. As it presumably moves in cycles of about the same amplitude as output the ratio of goods in process to output probably does not vary significantly during business cycles.[8]

Third, the wide variation in the timing of the various components of aggregate stocks makes it possible that variation in timing alone accounts for the relatively small amplitude of aggregate stocks in each industry group. Conceivably, therefore, some substantial classes of stocks have cycles with a wider amplitude than output, lag only a few months, and have an inventory-output ratio that moves positively during cycles in business, output, or sales. The largest category of stocks for which this possibility arises is purchased materials which, as we shall see, accounts for about 40 percent of all manufacturers' stocks. We reason by elimination. Goods in process, by the nature of their relation with output, presumably have a fairly constant turnover rate. Since stocks of finished staples move inversely to output and shipments, their ratios to sales and output must behave inversely.

Purchased materials comprise the only other substantial category of stocks. Telling against the notion that its ratio conforms positively is evidence that it lags at turns in business activity. To dispose of the possibility that there is any large category of stocks for which the inventory-sales or inventory-output ratio conforms

---

[8] Changes in the commodity composition of output may, however, account for some change in the aggregate of goods in process relative to aggregate sales or output.

positively to business cycles would require indexes of the various categories of stocks sufficiently representative to enable us to measure the amplitude of inventory fluctuations reliably. Unfortunately out sample of stocks of purchased materials, the category especially interesting from this viewpoint, is not adequate for this purpose. The possibility that its ratio varies positively rather than inversely must, therefore, remain open—a consideration that affects the argument of the next section.

5 Significance for the Theory of Cyclical Turning Points

This chapter began with the observation that a common view about the causes of cyclical downturns holds that in the course of expansion there is, sooner or later, a piling up of stocks—presumably in relation to sales—and that the efforts of businessmen to liquidate these surpluses cause a decline of orders and output that ushers in a recession. Contraction is then a period of inventory liquidation which eventually leaves businessmen short of stock. This induces them to increase orders and output, thereby setting in motion the forces of revival.

Lloyd Metzler's explanation of cyclical turning points also depends upon the behavior of inventory-sales ratios (see Ch. 1). He argues that a revival in sales catches businessmen unawares and causes inventory-sales ratios to fall. Purchases and production are, therefore, enlarged not merely by enough to satisfy increased sales, but by additional amounts in order to raise the inventory-sales ratio to the level desired. The expansion of incomes thus engendered causes further increases in sales which again stimulate output to satisfy current demand and to rebuild stocks. As long as inventory-sales ratios remain below the levels businessmen think profitable, the force of expansion continues, for output is successively increased in order to accumulate stocks. When inventory-sales ratios have been restored to desired levels, purchases and production fall because the demand for goods to add to stocks evaporates, and the processes of contraction begin. The decline in sales again catches businessmen by surprise and causes inventory-sales ratios to rise. The attempt to liquidate stocks furnishes the motive power for further contraction, which lasts until the ratios have been reduced to the desired level.

A test of these theories is, of course, plagued by lack of an objective standard by which to judge a surplus or deficit of stocks. The most natural and obvious standard is the ratio of inventories to sales or output. To adopt this standard assumes implicitly that in the absence of special factors, businessmen try to keep some constant ratio between stocks and sales or output. A relatively high ratio means a surplus of stocks except, say, when prices are expected to rise in the near future. A relatively low ratio means a deficit unless prices are expected to fall.

By this standard the theories just mentioned are clearly not valid for manufacturing industries if they are supposed to apply to total stocks. Manufacturing inventory-sales and inventory-output ratios relating aggregate stocks to aggregate sales or output are at or near their lowest levels when business cycles reach their peaks. They are at or near their highest levels when business cycles reach their troughs. These theories, therefore, are not in accord with the facts for manufacturing industries.

The implications of our observations for Metzler's theory may be stated in another way. If businessmen wish to keep a constant ratio between inventories and sales, Metzler's theory implies that the decline in the ratio caused by the initial rise in sales must be reversed before the end of an expansion. Similarly, the rise in the ratio caused by the initial decline in sales must be reversed before the end of a contraction. His theory assumes, therefore, that if a constant level of the inventory-sales ratio is desired, the actual ratio will vary inversely to business cycles with a lead sufficient to permit it to rise (fall) to normal levels before the peak (trough). Our observation about ratios in manufacturing industries, however, suggests that while they vary inversely, we cannot be sure that they tend to lead. If they do, the lead is short, and the levels of the ratios are typically well below normal at business peaks and well above at troughs.

The inventory-sales ratios that businessmen consider profitable may, of course, vary with the volume of business. If the desired ratios decline as sales increase, actual inventory-sales ratios may become too high before the peak in business even though they also decline with sales. But there is no way now of knowing whether the desired ratios do decline with sales and, if so, whether they decline faster than the observed ratios.[9]

It may be claimed also that a change in price expectations near the peaks and troughs of business causes businessmen to regard their inventory holdings, relative to sales, as too high and too low, respectively. For example, the disappearance of bullish attitudes toward the end of expansion causes manufacturers to liquidate stocks. Similarly, the disappearance of bearish attitudes toward the end of contractions causes businessmen to desire to hold more goods. Such assertions may possibly prove valid, but they are not elements in the theories considered here, and we cannot test them.

There remains the possibility that some substantial part of manufacturers' inventories—stocks of purchased materials, for example—behaves according to the theory. As pointed out above, purchased materials may have a wider amplitude of fluctuation than sales or output. Hence, the ratios of purchased materials to output and sales may stand as high at business peaks as at troughs, or higher, even though the stocks of such goods tend to lag some months behind sales. Moreover, even if the ratio varies inversely when we consider cycles as a whole, it may rise markedly before the peaks of business and fall markedly before the troughs. We cannot exclude these possibilities, but there is no evidence now to support them.

---

[9] J. M. Clark outlines a set of considerations that lead him to opposite conclusions about the stocks businessmen like to hold per unit of sales. He expects the ratio between inventory 'required' and sales to rise during expansions and fall during contractions. His argument is directed to the situation of wholesalers and retailers, but much of it seems to be applicable to manufacturing. See *Journal of Political Economy*, March 1917.

CHAPTER 7

Relative Importance of Raw Materials, Goods in Process, and Finished Goods

Earlier chapters have given the most adequate picture we can draw of how aggregate inventories of manufacturers behave during business cycles. The materials, however, did not permit us to gain a significant understanding of this behavior. No classifications of stocks by type were available within each industry, and it seemed unwise to trust the accuracy of the data to the point of treating as significant the industrial differences that appeared.

To analyze the cyclical behavior of stocks we turn to evidence on manufacturers' holdings of various commodities. In the chapters that follow we attempt to describe and explain the behavior of three classes of inventories: finished goods, raw materials, and goods in process. This chapter is devoted to their relative size. 'Finished goods' are commodities ready for sale by the manufacturer who produces them, whether or not in the form required by their ultimate users. 'Raw materials' include all goods held by manufacturers but not yet processed by their current holders, no matter how highly fabricated by previous holders. 'Goods in process' are being fabricated by their current holders but not yet ready for sale to other manufacturers, distributors, or final consumers.

1 Census and Department of Commerce Data

The Census of Manufactures contains comprehensive annual estimates of manufacturers' stocks as of December 31 for each year 1936-39. Showing inventories classified as 'finished goods' and 'all other' stocks, these reports are the most reliable indicators of the relative importance of finished goods stocks. Since December 31, 1938 the Department of Commerce has published an additional classification into raw materials, goods in process, and finished goods (Chart 15). The original data, which are in dollar values for the ends of months, are based on a sample of manufacturing concerns (App. A). Figures for finished goods stocks are reconciled with adjusted census data for the ends of 1938 and 1939. Percentage allocations based on these two sets of reports are shown in Table 38.

Chart 15

**Raw Materials, Goods in Process, and Finished Goods
Relative Shares in Total Manufacturers' Stocks**

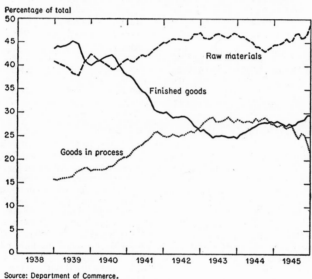

Source: Department of Commerce.

Inference from these statistics about the relative size of the three classes of stocks on the average is complicated by the fact that all do not act in the same fashion during business cycles. As we shall see, raw materials and goods in process typically vary positively with manufacturing activity, and at least a large portion of finished goods varies inversely.[1] The period covered by Table 38 includes 1941-45 when manufacturing output, under the stimulus of the defense and war programs, rose to unprecedented levels. It is not surprising that in these years the proportion of stocks repre-

[1] This is a rough statement, true for short cyclical phases; see Ch. 11.

TABLE 38

Manufacturers' Inventories, Percentage Distribution
by Stage of Fabrication

Dec. 31	RAW MATERIALS	GOODS IN PROCESS	FINISHED GOODS
1) 1936	...	...	41.6
2) 1937	...	...	43.7
3) 1938	40.8	15.7	43.5
4) 1939	42.4	17.7	40.0
ANNUAL AVERAGE OF MONTHLY STANDINGS[a]			
5) 1939	39.8	16.9	43.3
6) 1940	40.5	18.8	40.6
7) 1941	42.6	23.9	33.4
8) 1942	45.8	25.6	28.5
9) 1943	46.3	28.5	25.2
10) 1944	44.6	28.3	27.1
11) 1945	46.0	25.8	28.2
AVERAGE STANDINGS			
12) Ends of years, 1936-39	...	...	42.2
13) Ends of years, 1936-45	...	...	34.5
14) All months, Dec. 1938- Dec. 1940	40.2	17.9	41.9
15) All months, Dec. 1938- Dec. 1945	43.6	23.9	32.5

[a] Computed from original data for ends of months.

Dec. 31, 1936 and 1937: Census of Manufactures, 1937. Based on census reports for establishments representing 94.6 percent of the total value of product.

Dec. 31, 1938 and 1939: Census of Manufactures, 1939. Adjusted by Department of Commerce for underreporting (satisfactory reports were received from establishments representing 96.4 percent of total value of product) and for inadequate coverage in petroleum refining, tobacco, and printing and publishing. Census reports are classified into finished goods and all other. Relatives for raw materials and goods in process based on sample data are described below.

Monthly data, Dec. 31, 1938-May 1946: Department of Commerce data based on reports of a sample of manufacturing firms. Firms reporting finished goods separately held 28 percent of manufacturers' total stocks in June 1942; those reporting all three classes separately held 24 percent. Relatives for finished goods are adjusted to corrected census figures for Dec. 31, 1938 and 1939. See Appendix A for further description.

sented by finished goods should have sunk greatly and that the proportions of raw materials and goods in process should be correspondingly high. Consequently, lines 13 and 15, which present averages including the defense and war boom years, tend to understate the usual size of finished goods and to exaggerate that of the other two classes. For the typical importance of the three classes of stock we depend upon the averages in lines 12 and 14 which exclude the years since 1940.

Line 12 shows the average importance of finished goods at the ends of years 1936-39, which include a peak of business, a trough, and two year ends when business was recovering. This fairly balanced distribution of dates yields an average standing for finished goods of just over 42 percent of total inventories. It is, of course, necessary to remember that year end figures may not represent accurately the situation at other times in the year. Chart 15, indeed, suggests a seasonal cycle in 1939 and 1940 although there is no clear indication of a seasonal in other years. Moreover, the average of 25 months beginning with December 1938 (line 14) is almost exactly the same as that for the four year ends 1936-39.

Line 14 shows the average importance of all three classes during the months beginning December 1938 and ending December 1940. This period begins in a month when recovery was well under way and continues to a time when production was again very high. It does not include 1941 and later years when production rose to heights never reached before.[2] The average shares during the period were approximately 40 percent for raw materials, 18 percent for goods in process, and 42 percent for finished goods (line 14). These figures cannot, of course, be relied upon to represent average standings for a long period. They are, however, the best that can be extracted from the short series available.

Before leaving these materials, we note the large variations among industries with respect to the importance of inventories in two categories, finished goods and 'all other' stocks (Table 39). Similar industrial classifications for the three groups are not available.

2 Federal Trade Commission Data

Census reports for four years render our information about the relative importance of finished goods and all other inventories far more secure than our evidence about the division of all other stocks between raw materials and goods in process. *Industrial Corporation Reports, 1938* and *1939*, provide another reading on the

[2] Selected standings of the FRB index of manufacturing production help to indicate the character of the period.

Annual average, 1937	113	December 1938	100
Peak value, May 1937	123	Annual average, 1939	109
Annual average, 1938	87	Annual average, 1940	126
Trough value, June 1938	79	Annual average, 1941	168

TABLE 39
Finished Goods and All Other Manufacturers' Stocks
Average Values as Percentages of Total Stocks at
Year Ends, 1936-1939

	FINISHED GOODS	OTHER STOCKS	TOTAL STOCKS
Total manufacturing	42.6	57.4	100.0
Food, beverages & tobacco	56.1	43.9	100.0
Textiles & textile products	37.9	62.1	100.0
Leather & leather products	39.0	61.0	100.0
Rubber & related products	52.2	47.8	100.0
Lumber & wood products	53.2	46.7	100.0
Paper, printing & publishing	32.1	67.9	100.0
Chemicals & allied products	50.0	50.0	100.0
Stone, clay & glass products	55.9	44.1	100.0
Metals & metal products	35.8	64.2	100.0
Miscellaneous	33.3	66.7	100.0

Census of Manufactures, 1937 and 1939. Figures are not adjusted for the small
percentage of establishments not reporting.

significance of the latter two classes. As of the end of 1939, they
show balance sheets for 74 manufacturing industries, of which 38
classified inventories into raw materials, goods in process, and finished goods.[3]

The FTC sample was usually obtained by selecting from each
industry some "of the most important concerns in the industry
from the standpoint of investment and value of goods sold". The
sales reported in the 38 groups range from 12.5 to 97.0 percent of
the Bureau of Census value of product (excluding a few cases
where census sales were exceeded by sales of the FTC sample).[4]

[3] The information was compiled by the Federal Trade Commission from
reports submitted directly by selected corporations for their 1939 operations
and from annual reports to the Securities and Exchange Commission covering their 1938 operations. The data are compiled by corporation, not by
establishment. Most reports cover the calendar year, but some cover the
most nearly corresponding corporate fiscal year.

[4] Apparently because the FTC's unit was the corporation, whereas the
census unit was the establishment. If the census had classified a sufficiently
large number of the plants belonging to the FTC's corporations in other
industries, the result noted would be obtained. In addition, the census does
not cover establishments in foreign countries whereas the Commission includes the consolidated assets of the companies covered.

In most instances the sample accounted for over half the activity reported to the census. The sales of the FTC sample of firms reporting classified inventories amounted *in toto* to only 15 percent of the census value of product for all inventory reports in 1939. In 1938 the coverage of the sample was even less adequate.

To bolster the coverage and, in particular, to include several important groups absent from the FTC's reports, the National Bureau of Economic Research compiled additional material from SEC records (App. C). The over-all average ratio of goods in process to total stocks, was obtained by first computing this ratio for each group. A weighted average ratio was then calculated using weights proportionate to the value of inventories held in each group as reported by the Census of Manufactures, 1939 (Table 40).

TABLE 40

Ratios of Goods in Process to Manufacturers' Total Inventories
December 31, 1938 and 1939
(percentages)

	1938	*1939*
Federal Trade Commission sample	19.1	20.6
Department of Commerce sample	15.7	17.7

We cannot account for the difference in the results, and it may well be due merely to the sampling error. With such unsatisfactory materials the important thing to note is that results from the two samples do not differ by more than three or four percentage points.

3 Conclusions

We can get satisfactory estimates of the importance of finished goods on the particular dates of the census canvass. For goods in process and raw materials less reliable data are available for short periods. Finally, the specific dates and periods covered are not fully representative of conditions during the entire interwar period on which our study is centered. In these circumstances, we have to be satisfied with rough judgments about the relative size of the three categories. With these reservations, we shall assume that, on the average, raw materials account for 40 percent of manufacturers' total stocks, goods in process for 20 percent, and finished goods for 40 percent.

CHAPTER 8

Goods in Process

As we use the term, 'goods in process' refer to the inventories a
manufacturer considers to be 'in process' from the viewpoint of
his own activities. That is, they are goods the manufacturer who
owns them has processed in some fashion but has not yet put into
the form in which his goods are finally sold. They are to be distinguished, on the one hand, from materials purchased from
others but which a manufacturer has not yet manipulated and,
on the other hand, from finished goods ready for sale to other
manufacturers, distributors, or final consumers. As we have just
seen, goods in process account on the average for about 20 percent of manufacturers' total stocks.

1   Conformity to Output Cycles

It is characteristic of goods in process that the mechanics of the
production process make for a fairly close tie between their volume and the rate of production. In many industries the connection is quite rigid. In leather tanning, for example, hides must
remain in the tanning liquid for a certain fairly definite period.
Hence to sustain a certain rate of production of tanned hides, a
certain number of hides must be kept in process. The chemical
and petroleum refining industries are similar. In the steel industry, as carried on by the large integrated corporations, the economy of keeping metal hot requires that the process from pig
iron to finished rolled steel be continuous. The output of steel depends upon the quantity of metal going through this whole production process. Again, in the canning of fruits and vegetables,
the final packing must immediately follow its preparation. More
obvious illustrations are afforded by one-process industries such
as textile fiber spinning or flour milling. Only when more cotton

is being spun or more grain milled can production in these industries increase. In other industries technical considerations may be less demanding; nonetheless, there may be no convenient form in which to hold goods between the raw and finished stages. Thus, in clothing manufacture, once the cloth has been cut, there is no point in keeping the garments unassembled. Goods in process and rate of production tend to go hand in hand.

The chief exceptions occur among industries that combine the operations of making and assembling parts into a finished product. Among the nonferrous metals too there are stocks of partly refined ores which may be drawn down when the production of refined metal is to be enlarged. The same is true of cement making. In such industries a stock of parts or of semifinished goods may be kept 'between stages'. When a higher rate of production is desired, this stock may be reduced while the quantity of goods 'within' the various stages, that is, being made into parts and assembled into finished goods, increases. In such cases, therefore, it is not strictly necessary for goods in process as a whole to rise when production rises. Of course, even when it is technically possible to keep such a 'surplus' stock of semifabricated goods 'between stages' it will not always be done. Many of the goods, even at an early stage of fabrication, may not be of a sort that can be carried over from one year to the next. In manufacturing automobiles whose models change from year to year, parts that do not often change may be stocked but other parts must be made as required.[1] Again, some parts are bulky and, therefore, uneconomic to store and to handle more often than necessary.

Moreover, even when a stock of partly fabricated goods is drawn down as the rate of production rises, the total stock of goods in process may still rise. It will do so if the rate of increase in the value of the goods 'within stages' exceeds the rate of fall in the value of the 'surplus' stock 'between stages'. And even in industries in which the stock of goods in process as a whole falls in such circumstances, it will hardly do so at the same rate as it rises in industries that do not keep any 'surplus' stocks of partly

[1] Parts that change from model to model may still be carried for a long time for sale as replacements. Such inventories, however, are properly classified as 'finished' goods.

fabricated goods.[2] For in the former the drop in stocks 'between stages' will be offset by the increase in the volume of parts and other materials 'within stages'. In the latter there is no offset to the increase of goods in process.

Thus the presence of industries that can store partly fabricated stocks seems to put merely a minor qualification on the statement that stocks of goods in process rise with output. Industries in which this relation is not technically necessary are, as we shall see, probably not more than half the total. And when it is not technically necessary that goods in process move together with production, they will still do so when surplus stocks of partly finished goods 'between stages' are unimportant or, if important, when the drop in these stocks is more than offset by the increase in the volume of goods being manipulated. And finally the drop in stocks of goods 'between stages', when it occurs, is always offset in some degree by the increase in goods 'within stages'. It is reasonable to conclude, therefore, that while goods in process in some industries may move counter to production for a short interval, a sustained expansion of output in any industry will normally require an increase of goods in process.

2 Goods in Process in Continuous and Discontinuous Industries

As the preceding section indicated, the degree of probability we attach to the hypothesis that goods in process and manufacturing output move together in business cycles depends in part upon the proportion of all goods in process held in industries where it is either technically necessary or highly convenient to maintain a fairly constant relation between partly fabricated stocks and the rate of activity. We call these 'continuous' industries. Others we call 'discontinuous' industries.

The proportions of goods in process in these two categories of manufacturing can be roughly estimated. The basic data are the ratios of goods in process to total inventories for individual industries in the augmented Federal Trade Commission sample (see Ch. 7 and App. C). The industries were first classified as continuous,

2 This statement assumes that aside from surplus stocks of partly fabricated goods, the relation of goods in process to production is the same in the industries compared.

discontinuous, or mixed (App. D). They were classified as continuous if their manufacturing operations make it either technically impossible or highly inconvenient to store surplus stocks of partly
fabricated goods, or if the industry is a one-process industry. An
example of the first type is the steel works and rolling mills industry; the second type is exemplified by the rayon industry and the
dyeing and finishing of textiles. Industries were classified as discontinuous if several processes are involved and there seems no
urgent necessity for completing all without interruption; for example, the furniture industry. Finally, in some industries, such as
cotton textiles, some firms perform only a single process whereas
others combine several processes and may keep semifabricated
stocks at each stage. Such industries were classified as mixed.

For each category we computed an average ratio of goods in
process to total inventories by weighting the ratio of goods in
process to total stocks in each industry by the census value of total
stocks held. Next, each census industry was similarly classified
(App. D), and the value of total inventories held in continuous,
discontinuous, and mixed industries computed. Finally, to get an
estimate of the value of goods in process held by each category
the average ratio of goods in process to total inventories in each
was applied to the value of total inventories in its category estimated from census data. Calculations were confined to 1939, for
which the FTC sample is somewhat more satisfactory than for
1938 (Table 41).

Roughly one-half of all inventories are held by continuous
process industries. A quarter are held by mixed industries and
only a slightly higher proportion of all inventories are held by industries following predominantly discontinuous processes.

As might be expected the ratio of goods in process to total inventories in continuous industries is lower than that in mixed industries, and the ratio in the latter is lower than in discontinuous
industries. Continuous industries either cover only one stage in
fabrication or when they cover more than one stage do not hold
surplus stocks between stages. Discontinuous industries involve
two or more stages and can hold surplus stocks between stages.
Hence their goods in process tend to be more important relative
to total stocks. In consequence at the end of 1939 discontinuous

TABLE 41

Goods in Process, Continuous, Discontinuous, and
Mixed Industries, December 31, 1939

(1)	TOTAL STOCKS[a] ($ mil.) (2)	AV. RATIO: GOODS IN PROCESS TO TOTAL STOCKS[b] (%) (3)	GOODS IN PROCESS	
			Est. Value ($ mil.) (4)	% Distribution (5)
1 Continuous	4721	16.1	760	37.7
2 Discontinuous	2672	27.3	729	36.1
3 Mixed	2239	23.6	528	26.2
4 Total mfg.	9632	20.9	2017	100.0

[a] Census of Manufactures, 1939. See Table 39, note. The distribution of industries by categories is shown in App. D.
[b] Percentages estimated from augmented FTC sample (App. C). Ratios for individual industries weighted by inventories to get average for category. Average for total manufacturing computed by using weights from column 2; cf. Table 40.

industries appear to have held about the same quantity of goods in process, something over 36 percent, as continuous industries, nearly 38 percent. If inventories in the mixed industries are divided about evenly between the two main classes, we may say that about half of all goods in process is held in each.

Like so many findings in this difficult field this one too is subject to a considerable margin of error. The classification of industries is often arbitrary; the sample from which we judge the importance of goods in process is inadequate;[3] the information is for a single year. It is a calculation that should be checked as soon as better data are available.

If something like half of all goods in process belong to firms

[3] Some small degree of assurance about the representative character of the augmented FTC sample upon which these estimates are based is gained by comparing the average ratio of goods in process to total manufacturing stocks as calculated in Tables 40 and 41. The two ratios are remarkably similar, 20.6 and 20.9 percent. In the first, the ratios for each industry in the sample are weighted simply by the total stocks of the sample industries as shown by the census. In the second, weighted averages for the three categories of industries are combined in a weighted average; the weights are the census totals of stocks in the three categories. Aside from the possibility of offsetting errors, the two results would not be similar unless the relative importance of industries of the three types is about the same in the sample as in manufacturing at large. The distribution is, in fact, very similar; see App. D.

in continuous industries (and in continuous branches of mixed industries), our conclusion that stocks of goods in process as a whole vary positively with output is reenforced. Within the continuous branches, we may expect the relation between production and the volume of goods in process to be quite rigid. In other manufacturing industries, the relation need not be rigid; yet even here there is a bias in favor of a positive relation between production and goods in process. For only surplus stocks between stages can move inversely to output. The stocks within the various stages of discontinuous industries must still move together with activity in their respective stages. Since activity in these stages is closely bound together, so must output and goods in process within the various stages. Finally, it must be remembered that surplus stocks between stages need not move inversely to output; they only may do so. We may conclude, therefore, that there is, in fact, a very powerful set of forces impelling goods in process, as here defined, to move together with output in manufacturing as a whole.

3 Timing Relative to Turns in Output

In a general way it is clear that when production is relatively high, the quantity of goods in process will also be high. But when will stocks of goods in process reach their peaks as compared with production? An answer can be given for continuous industries, that is, for industries in which goods remain in a partly fabricated state for a specified interval that does not change. And our conclusions will apply as well to the relation between goods in process within any stage of a discontinuous industry and activity at that stage.

As a first step we must assign a more precise meaning to the term, goods in process. To this end we define 'output' as the number of physical units of a commodity that reach a finished state during a given period. We define 'input' as the number of units of potential output on which fabrication begins during a given period. Now let us suppose that in a certain continuous industry, c days elapse between the time goods are put into process and the time they emerge in finished form. This interval we shall call the production period. Suppose further that for each unit of potential output b_1 dollars are expended in fabricating costs (raw materials, labor, etc.) during the first day, b_2 dollars during the second day, and so on. Then if a units of input are gradually fed into the fabricating process during the first full day of processing, this batch will attain a value of $\dfrac{ab_1}{2}$ by the end of the first day, since the average unit will have received half of a full day's processing. By the end of the second day, the value of the batch will have grown to $ab_1 + \dfrac{ab_2}{2}$. Its value will be $ab_1 + ab_2 + \dfrac{ab_3}{2}$ at the end of the third day, and $ab_1 + ab_2 + ab_3 + \ldots \dfrac{ab_c}{2}$ at the end of a production period. In other words, the total stock of goods in process on a given day equals the sum of the value to which the input c days before has grown and the value to which input $c - 1$ days before has grown, and so on, the total being the sum of the values to which inputs made during an entire production period have grown by the given day.

These relations may be illustrated by an arithmetical example. Consider an industry in which $10 of costs, including costs of raw materials, are incurred for each unit of input per day and in which the production period is four days. Let input be constant at 100 units per day. The value of goods in process at the end of successive days is shown in Example 1.

EXAMPLE 1

Value of Goods in Process when Input and Output are Constant

Assumptions: Production period is 4 days
Cost of fabrication, including materials, is constant at $10 per day per unit

DAY	INPUT IN PHYSICAL UNITS	VALUE ATTAINED BY INDICATED INPUT AT END OF SPECIFIED DAYS									
		1	2	3	4	5	6	7	8	9	10
1	100	500	1500	2500	3500	4000					
2	100		500	1500	2500	3500	4000				
3	100			500	1500	2500	3500	4000			
4	100				500	1500	2500	3500	4000		
5	100					500	1500	2500	3500	4000	
6	100						500	1500	2500	3500	4000
7	100							500	1500	2500	3500
8	100								500	1500	2500
9	100									500	1500
10	100										500
Total value		500	2000	4500	8000	12000	12000	12000	12000	12000	12000
Minus finished goods	...	...	...	...	...	4000	4000	4000	4000	4000	4000
Goods in process		500	2000	4500	8000	8000	8000	8000	8000	8000	8000

When input is constant, the value of goods in process reaches a maximum at the end of one production period and thereafter remains at the same level. The values in the table are, of course, calculated according to the formula set forth above. When a and b have constant values of 100 and \$10 respectively the batch fed into process during the first day has a value of $\dfrac{ab}{2}$ or \$500 at the end of the first day. At the end of the second day, its value is $ab + \dfrac{ab}{2}$ or \$1,500; and so on. At the end of the fourth day, the value of the first batch is \$3,500; this sum plus the values attained by units fed into the process of fabrication on later days is the total value of goods in process, \$8,000.

Now provided cycles in input proceed smoothly from trough to peak, the cyclical turns of goods in process cannot lead the turns in the rate of input in industries of the type in question, although they may occur at the same time. They may lag behind the turns in input, but the lag cannot exceed one production period. Furthermore, since it is self-evident that for industries of the type in question output must reach its peaks and troughs exactly one production period after input reaches its peaks and troughs, the above statements imply that the cyclical turns of goods in process cannot lag behind those of output though they may be synchronous. Goods in process may turn before output but the lead cannot exceed one production period.

The validity of these statements may be seen from the fact that the value of goods in process on a given day depends upon the number of units fed into fabrication on each day of the production period ending with the day in question. Now if the rate of input increases steadily from its trough to its peak, the inputs made on each day from the first to the last of a production period ending with a peak of input must exceed the inputs made on the corresponding days of any production period ending before input reaches its peak. Consequently, when the rate of input reaches its peak the goods in process must have a higher value than on earlier days during the expansion. Hence the peak of goods in process cannot precede the peak of input.

Goods in process may, however, lag behind input on both the

upswing and downswing and, indeed, are likely to do so, but the lag cannot be longer than one production period. That they are likely to lag can easily be seen by considering a second arithmetical example. Example 2 is concerned with an industry in which the

EXAMPLE 2

Value of Goods in Process when Input Varies Symmetrically about a Cyclical Peak

Assumptions: Production period is 4 days
Cost of fabrication, including materials, is constant at $10 per day per unit

DAY	INPUT IN PHYSICAL UNITS	VALUE ATTAINED BY INDICATED INPUT AT END OF SPECIFIED DAYS												
		1	2	3	4	5	6	7	8	9	10	11	12	13
1	90	450	1350	2250	3150	3600								
2	100		500	1500	2500	3500	4000							
3	110			550	1650	2750	3850	4400						
4	120				600	1800	3000	4200	4800					
5	130					650	1950	3250	4550	5200				
6	120						600	1800	3000	4200	4800			
7	110							550	1650	2750	3850	4400		
8	100								500	1500	2500	3500	4000	
9	90									450	1350	2250	3150	3600
Total value						7900	12300	13400	14200	14500	14100			
Minus finished goods							3600	4000	4400	4800	5200			
Goods in process						7900	8700	9400	9800	9700	8900			

production period and the daily costs of fabrication per unit are the same as in Example 1, but input rises and falls in a symmetrical pattern about a cyclical peak. Although the pattern is symmetrical about the peak and the rate at which fabricating costs are applied is uniform throughout the production period, goods in process reach a peak two days later than input. This occurs for two reasons. The first may be illustrated by comparing goods in process at the end of the fifth day, when input reached its peak, and at the end of the eighth day. In both cases, goods in process result from previous inputs of the same number of units. But the order of the inputs is reversed. When input is at its peak, the small inputs precede the large. After the peak, the opposite is true. The difference between the two cases then lies in the fact that in the earlier it is the small inputs that have grown to their maximum values; in the later, it is the large inputs. The second reason is illustrated by comparing goods in process at the end of the fifth day, when input is at its peak, with goods in process at the end of the sixth day. Not only do the relatively large inputs come somewhat earlier in the latter case, but they are somewhat larger.[4]

The lag of goods in process behind input tends to be longer the more slowly input declines after the peak and the more rapidly input rises before the peak (Example 3, Parts A and B). In both parts production costs are applied at the same rate as in the pre-

EXAMPLE 3

Value of Goods in Process when Input Varies
Asymmetrically about a Cyclical Peak

Assumptions: Production period is 4 days
Cost of fabrication, including raw materials, is constant at $10 per day per unit

DAY	INPUT IN PHYSICAL UNITS	1	2	3	4	5	6	7	8	9
					P A R T	A				
1	90	450	1350	2250	3150	3600				
2	100		500	1500	2500	3500	4000			
3	110			550	1650	2750	3850	4400		
4	120				600	1800	3000	4200	4800	
5	130					650	1950	3250	4550	5200
6	129						645	1935	3225	4515
7	128							640	1920	3200
8	127								635	1905
9	126									630
Total value					7900	12300	13445	14425	15130	15450
Minus finished goods						3600	4000	4400	4800	5200
Goods in process					7900	8700	9445	10025	10330	10250
					P A R T	B				
1	40	200	600	1000	1400	1600				
2	50		250	750	1250	1750	2000			
3	70			350	1050	1750	2450	2800		
4	100				500	1500	2500	3500	4000	
5	130					650	1950	3250	4550	5200
6	120						600	1800	3000	4200
7	110							550	1650	2750
8	100								500	1500
9	90									450
Total value					4200	7250	9500	11900	13700	14100
Minus finished goods						1600	2000	2800	4000	5200
Goods in process					4200	5650	7500	9100	9700	8900

[4] Arthur F. Burns suggests that the same point may be made more forcefully if we consider that goods in process bear the same relation to input as a weighted moving total (plotted at the end of the moving period) does to an original series. If the original data vary in symmetrical cycles, the maxima and minima of a moving total will lag behind those in the original data even if the items in the total are unweighted. If weights of diminishing order are applied, as in our problem (that is, the latest input is given the smallest weight), the tendency to lag is even more pronounced.

ceding examples, but in Part A input declines more slowly after the peak, although it rises before the peak at the same rate as in Example 2. The peak of goods in process comes a day later than in Example 2, a difference that can be due only to the relatively slow decline of input after the peak. In Example 3, Part B, the same result emerges because input rises more rapidly before the peak than it does in Example 2, although it declines at the same rate.

The lag of goods in process behind input tends to be longer also if production costs are applied more heavily in the later stages than in the earlier stages. In Example 4, as in Example 2, it is assumed

EXAMPLE 4

Value of Goods in Process when Input Varies Symmetrically about a Cyclical Peak

Effect of Non-uniform Application of Fabricating Costs

Assumptions: Production period is 4 days
Costs per unit of input are $4 on first day; $8 on second day; $10 on third day; $18 on fourth day.

DAY	INPUT IN PHYSICAL UNITS	\multicolumn{9}{c}{VALUE ATTAINED BY INDICATED INPUT AT END OF SPECIFIED DAYS}
		1	2	3	4	5	6	7	8	9
1	90	180	720	1530	2790	3600				
2	100		200	800	1700	3100	4000			
3	110			220	880	1870	3410	4400		
4	120				240	960	2040	3720	4800	
5	130					260	1040	2210	4030	5200
6	120						240	960	2040	3720
7	110							220	880	1870
8	100								200	800
9	90									180
Total value					5610	9790	10730	11510	11950	11770
Minus finished goods						3600	4000	4400	4800	5200
Goods in process					5610	6190	6730	7110	7150	6570

that a unit of goods put into process reaches a value of $40 when it is finished; but unlike Example 2 in which a unit grows $10 each day, in Example 4 a unit grows $4 the first day, $8 the second, $10 the third, and $18 the fourth. In both examples the pattern of the input rate is the same. In Example 4 the peak of goods in process comes later than in Example 2.

The length of the lag of goods in process behind input depends then upon the pattern of the input rate and upon the pattern according to which the costs of fabrication, including raw materials costs, are incurred during the production period. But no matter what assumptions are made about these two variables, the lag cannot be longer than a single production period because, barring random fluctuations, the inputs of the production period that begins with the peak of input must exceed those of any production period beginning later.

Finally, since output must lag behind input by exactly one production period, the discussion above serves to make clear also the relation between goods in process and output. Stocks of goods in process cannot lag behind output. They are likely to lead, but the lead cannot be longer than one production period.

These conclusions, of course, apply strictly only to goods in process in continuous industries. In other industries the timing relation may well be different; in extreme cases stocks of goods in process and output may move in opposite directions. It seems justifiable, however, to think that for goods in process as a whole, the argument set forth above has a fairly high degree of relevance. Although short lags are possible, goods in process and output are likely to move together, with some tendency for the former to lead.

4   Length of the Production Period

These timing relations indicate the desirability of estimating the average length of the production period in manufacturing industries. Consider a period in which output, measured in terms of cost,[5] is steady at z dollars per day, and assume that goods in process, p, increase in value at a steady absolute rate from o to their cost as finished output during a production period of c days.

The goods put into process during any given day, then, have a value which is equal to $\dfrac{z}{2c}$ by the end of the day, that is, they will have had on the average one-half day's processing. At the end of the second day, they will, on the average, have received one and one- half days' processing and will be worth $\dfrac{3z}{2c}$. At the end of the third day, this value will be $\dfrac{5z}{2c}$, and at the end of the cth day,

---

[5] Cost in this context should include only such items as are usually entered into the accounts in establishing the cost of the inventory of finished goods.

$\dfrac{(2c-1)z}{2c}$. Now since stocks of goods in process on any day equal the sum of the values of goods at each successive stage of production, the value of goods in process on a given day equals the sum of quantities similar to those above: $p = \dfrac{c^2 z}{2c} = \dfrac{cz}{2}$

That is, on the assumption of a steady rate of production and a steady growth of value in fabrication from zero to total cost, the value of goods in process equals one-half the output (at cost) during a production period.

From this we can determine the number of days in a production period: $c = \dfrac{2p}{z}$

Under these assumptions the number of days in a production period equals the number required for daily output (at cost) to cumulate to a sum as large as twice the value of goods in process.

The factors in this equation may be roughly evaluated. Approximations to the value of goods in process were presented in Chapter 7. From the Department of Commerce estimates we compute the average value of goods in process held by all manufacturers during 1939 to be $1.69 billion. For the same year, we can find an approximate figure for the value of output at inventory cost. Inventory cost, of course, is a concept of uncertain definition (see App. A). For our purposes we may estimate its magnitude crudely by adding (1) the gross cost of raw materials, fuel and energy used by manufacturers, (2) wages and salaries, and (3) one-half the sum of overhead expenses and profits.[6] The Census of Manufactures puts this figure at $49.35 billion in 1939. The average daily rate of output at inventory cost was, consequently, $135 million. We therefore have: $p = \$1,690,000,000$ and $z = \$135,000,000$. The number of days in the average production period in manufacturing establishments $\left(\dfrac{2p}{z}\right) = 25.0$.[7]

---

[6] Wages of nonmanufacturing employees of manufacturing firms and salaries of officers are here included among overhead expenses.

[7] A minor error in this figure and in those that follow derives from the fact that output was growing during 1939. Since goods in process probably lead output by a few weeks, the average level of goods in process was probably a

This estimate of 25 days is, of course, calculated from crude figures and upon arbitrary assumptions. As regards assumptions, it should be remembered that our definition of inventory cost of output is rough. But the limits of error from this source can be stated. A maximum value for output at inventory cost would be gotten if we assumed that, while profits are never charged to the cost of goods sold, all overhead costs are. The relevant cost of output in 1939 would then be some $52.16 billion (census value of product excluding contract work, $56.25 billion, minus net profit before taxes of manufacturing firms as estimated by the Department of Commerce, $4.09 billion) instead of $49.35 billion. The value of output at cost would be a minimum if we assumed that no part of either overhead costs or of profits is charged to the cost of goods sold. The value of output at cost would then be $42.44 billion. These alternative values may be used to establish lower and upper limits for the average length of the production process in individual manufacturing establishments: lower limit, 23.6 days; upper limit, 29.1 days.

The estimate is subject to a second qualification. It is made upon the assumption that within each manufacturing establishment, the fabricating process is such that goods grow in value at an even rate per unit of time from zero to their full cost when ready for sale. Whether this is a fairly good approximation to the truth or whether fabricating processes are on the whole such that the major part of fabrication costs (including the cost of raw materials consumed) is incurred early in the process, or whether the reverse is true, we do not know. If costs are applied relatively early, the value of goods in process required to sustain a given rate of output will be relatively high; conversely, if costs are sustained relatively late, the value of goods in process required will be relatively small. *Given the cost of output and the value of goods in process,* therefore, early application of costs means a shorter production period; late application means a longer production period.

An extreme case may indicate the bounds to which varying as-

----

little higher relative to output than it would be during a year when output was constant. This would tend to make our estimates of the production period somewhat too high.

sumptions about the pattern of the application of costs can drive our estimates. Assume that all purchased raw materials are fed into process at the very beginning, then manipulated without further addition of materials during a number of days equal to a production period. This amounts to assuming a very heavy skew in the application of costs toward the beginning of the production process. The elements of the problem in this case are:

a = value of raw materials fed into process per day

b = fabricating cost per dollar of raw material input

c = number of days in the production period

p = value of goods in process.

The raw materials fed into process on a given day will on the average be worth $a + \dfrac{ab}{2c}$ at the end of the first day, $a + \dfrac{3ab}{2c}$ at the end of the second day, and $a + \dfrac{(2c-1)ab}{2c}$ at the end of the last day. The sum of these quantities for a number of days equal to the average production period is the value of goods in process. If the rate of input and fabrication is constant:

$$p = ca + \frac{c^2 ab}{2c}$$

$$= ca + \frac{cab}{2}$$

That is, the value of goods in process equals the sum of the raw material input plus one-half the value added to raw materials during a production period. The length of the production period thus indicated is: $c = \dfrac{2p}{2a + ab}$

These factors, too, may be evaluated by use of previously derived figures and additional census data:

p = \$1,690,000,000 = value of goods in process

a = \$82,900,000 = average cost of raw materials consumed per day

b = \$0.631 = fabricating cost per dollar of raw material input = (cost of fuel and energy plus wages and salaries of manufacturing employees plus one-half the sum of overhead costs and profits) ÷ cost of raw materials and supplies.

Substituting these values in the last equation, we get 15.5 days as the average production period in manufacturing establishments. This figure, of course, is only an extreme limit of the range of possible estimates. The true value is certainly higher since some raw materials or supplies are consumed at every stage in the production process.

These computations make it possible to put the argument of earlier sections in quantitative terms. In continuous industries, the stock of goods in process cannot lag behind output. Goods in process may lead output but the lead cannot be longer than one production period; it is likely to be somewhat shorter. For such industries, therefore, the lead cannot be longer than about a month at the most and is probably shorter.

As we have noted, however, in discontinuous industries, stocks of partly fabricated goods are not likely to turn as early, relative to output, as in continuous industries. In discontinuous industries, they may even lag behind output, though for reasons advanced in Section 3, the lags, if any, are likely to be short. We conclude, therefore, that aggregate stocks of goods in process tend to rise and fall almost synchronously with output. The lead that certainly characterizes goods in process in continuous industries and goods 'within stages' in other industries is no longer than a month at most, and is likely to be shorter. This diminutive lead may be further reduced by the offsetting behavior of goods 'between stages' in discontinuous industries.

5   Total Stocks of Goods in Process, Total Output, and Business Cycles

The foregoing analysis and the conclusions to which it leads apply directly to the relation between output and stocks of goods in process in individual industries. Subject to one qualification, they apply also to the relation between the total output of manufacturing industries and total stocks of goods in process.

No qualification would be necessary if total output were measured by aggregating the outputs of individual industries each weighted according to the value of goods in process held per unit of output in some base period. Total output, however, is usually measured by adding the outputs of individual industries each weighted by 'value added' per unit of output, that is, by the expenses incurred in processing a unit of goods in a given industry. This is the appropriate measure for our purposes. The nub of the problem, therefore, is whether total output, as measured by the value added method, has cycles that tend to lead or lag behind those that would be found in an output index constructed with goods in process weights.

The two methods would, of course, never yield completely identical results. But whether the differences would often be substantial for our purposes depends upon the answers to two questions: (a) Does the relative importance of value added per unit of output in various industries differ substantially from the relative importance of goods in process per unit of output? (b) Is there a marked correlation between the cyclical timing of output cycles in various industries and the relative importance of either value added or goods in process per unit? If the answer to both questions were affirmative, the virtually synchronous relation between cycles of goods in process and output, which undoubtedly exists in individual industries, would not hold for all industries taken together. Stocks of goods in process might either lead or lag behind output by a substantial interval. For example, if industries in which value added per unit is relatively high tended to turn early, and if the value of goods in process per unit in these industries were no higher than in others, total output, as usually measured, would tend to turn before total output computed by using goods in process weights. Consequently, total stocks of goods in process would tend to lag behind a standard index of total output. On the other hand, if the answer to either question were negative, the cyclical timing of total output as usually measured would be substantially the same as that exhibited by an output index computed by using goods in process weights.

These questions cannot be answered now because we do not have enough information about the value of goods in process by industry. In further argument in this book, I shall disregard the difficulty and assume that total stocks of goods in process rise and fall at about the same time as total output. It seems unlikely that aggregation will produce large differences in timing where these do not exist industry by industry. But the reader should remember that this is not certain.

Subject to the same proviso, we can describe the behavior of goods in process during business cycles. Total manufacturing output tends to reach its peaks and troughs at about the same time as business cycles.[8] If goods in process rise and fall almost synchronously with total output, they must also with business at large.

---

[8] During the cycles of the interwar period, the FRB index of manufacturing production turned before the National Bureau monthly reference dates four times; it turned later three times, and in the same month four times. The average lead was 1.1 months.

CHAPTER 9

Raw Materials: A General View

Raw materials, comprising goods purchased by manufacturers either from other fabricators or from nonmanufacturers but not yet manipulated by their owners, account for about 40 percent of the total stocks of manufacturers. We begin with some theoretical considerations bearing on the behavior of the category as a whole. In Section 2 we present evidence bearing on the conformity and timing of a small sample of raw materials inventories, and in Chapter 10 examine their behavior in more detail.

1 Conformity and Timing of Stocks

As a preliminary hypothesis there seems substantial ground for believing that stocks of raw materials generally grow and decline together with manufacturing activity. Such behavior is consistent with what seem to be the chief principles on which businessmen decide about the quantity of raw materials to hold. These principles are perhaps best described as efficiency in production and protection against loss from price fluctuations.

Efficiency in production requires a stock of raw materials that increases with the rate of consumption for two reasons. First, stocks of goods that manufacturers would classify as raw materials are, in a special sense, goods in early stages of the production process. Goods in transit to the plant at which they will be consumed, title to which has already passed to the purchaser, count as part of the raw materials stock of manufacturers. When the rate of consumption of materials increases, more raw materials are likely to be in transit to fabricators. When goods arrive at the plant they must be checked, weighed, or counted, and taken to storage rooms. If the rate of their arrival is relatively high, a relatively large quantity of goods will be going through this routine. And if the rate of consumption is high, a relatively large quantity will be going through the processes incident to feeding the raw materials into production—unpacking, perhaps cleaning, being checked out of storage and routed to the fabricating departments.

A stock of raw materials, secondly, serves to safeguard the continuity of production against delays in the arrival of essential materials. Such delays can arise for various reasons: difficulties in discovering satisfactory suppliers of precisely the kind of goods desired, delays incident to the negotiation of contracts with suppliers, interruptions in the output of suppliers due to strikes or mechanical breakdowns, delays or losses in transit, the failure of suppliers to ship goods that meet specifications. These difficulties, no doubt, increase as business expands and as suppliers and transport agencies work more nearly to capacity. Against any or all these difficulties manufacturers can guard by maintaining a stock that covers their expected requirements for a period deemed adequate. The larger their requirements, the larger the stock they will need. This relation between stocks and production is doubtless not as rigid as the first, but it constitutes a powerful incentive for adding to stocks as the level of activity rises.

Manufacturers manage their stocks of raw materials also with an eye to changes in prices. It would be fatuous, of course, to expect a high degree of foresight. Subject to interest and storage charges and the risk of depreciation, perfect foresight would involve an attempt on the part of fabricators to cover their requirements for an expansion to come at the trough of business when prices are lowest. But if such an attempt were general, it would be self-defeating. Troughs of the kind we know would not materialize. The cycle of business would be something quite different from the cycle of experience.

After the trough of business has passed and the decline of prices quite definitely ended, when recovery has been under way for some time and the near-term trend of demand seems clearly marked, however, manufacturers may begin to take some cautious steps toward protecting themselves against price rises likely to accompany active business. They may embark on a somewhat more liberal buying policy—seeking to cover their expected requirements a little further ahead than they thought wise as long as the price outlook was bearish or uncertain. Since prices in general rise and fall with business activity this policy, of course, reinforces the rise in stocks of raw materials that an increasing rate of consumption demands. Similarly, after business has begun to slump and prices turn soft, businessmen will try to reduce their commitments by covering their expected requirements for a somewhat shorter period. And this will accelerate the decline in stocks desirable in view of the decline in the rate of consumption of materials.

This picture of manufacturers' speculative activities is intended to portray the course of events that characterizes business cycles as a general rule. In periods of excited speculation, of course, the purchasing plans of businessmen are bolder and more far reaching. Then they may abandon all thought of adjusting their stocks to some expected rate of consumption in the near future. They will buy materials not merely for consumption in their own operations, but frankly against the chance of resale at a higher price. Such episodes, however, are sporadic, not typical, features of business cycles. They seem to occur when some dramatic conjuncture convinces businessmen that prices are almost sure to rise very rapidly in the near future. During our period such conjunctures seem to have occurred in 1919-20 in consequence of the universal shortages following World War I and again in 1933 when the devaluation of the dollar and the imposition of NRA Codes persuaded manufacturers that prices would leap upward. A more doubtful and certainly milder period of speculation may have occurred in late 1936 and early 1937 when several large and successful strikes threatened higher prices in the near future. Otherwise, the interwar period does not seem to have been characterized by alternating periods of bullish and bearish speculation on a wide scale. The more hesitant and limited response of stock policy to price expectations suggested by the preceding paragraph therefore seems more typical. However, taken together with inventory movements that seem desirable in view of changes in the volume of production, even this mild speculative incentive appears to imply that stocks of raw materials will rise and fall synchronously with production and that their cyclical amplitude will be about the same as that of cycles in production. If the increases in inventories motivated by changes in production alone were fully proportional to the latter, the amplitude of stock cycles, including variations due to price speculation, will be somewhat larger.

This neat outcome is hardly likely to be realized in practice. Some period, more or less long, intervenes between a decision to purchase raw materials and the actual delivery of the goods. For stocks of raw materials to begin to contract simultaneously with production, the decline in production must be foreseen far enough in advance to allow deliveries to be altered appropriately. Such accurate forecasting, however, is probably not characteristic. It seems more plausible to suppose that manufacturers do not foresee the cyclical turning point in their sales at all. Indeed, when sales and production turn down after a cyclical peak, it must typically be an open question whether the drop signals the beginning of a cyclical contraction or a temporary setback similar to several others experienced during the preceding expansion. It seems likely, therefore, that after the peak of production has passed manufacturers are likely to hesitate before deciding to cut purchases of materials below the current level of consumption.[1]

After these decisions are taken, more time still must elapse before receipts of materials at manufacturing plants begin to conform to the new rate of purchase. If the materials are bought from stock, time is required for transportation from suppliers; if they are made to order, time is required for production as well as transportation. Materials made to order are likely to be products of manufacturing industries, and here, as we have seen, production periods are likely to be short—less than a month on the average. Transportation periods, of course, vary in length. They are likely to be short, a few days or weeks, if goods are supplied from within the United States where rail transportation is the rule. If goods are procured from abroad, time is consumed in longer and slower sea voyages, customs clearance, and often transfer from ship to train for an additional rail journey.

---

[1] This hypothesis does not imply that manufacturers do not curtail orders for raw materials until production has passed its cyclical peak. They may or they may not. The hypothesis does imply that in most manufacturing industries stocks of materials are still increasing at the cyclical peaks of production. It implies also that at cyclical peaks of production in most industries, deliveries to fabricating plants and orders for materials are still running higher than the rates at which materials are being fed into the fabricating process.

If we suppose that the rate of purchases of materials does not fall below the rate of consumption prior to the peak of production, the intervals described above define a minimum lag that must intervene in a given industry between the peak of production activity and the peak of raw materials stocks. For goods procured within the United States, the interval may vary from a few weeks to 2 or 3 months depending on the promptness with which purchases are cut, whether goods are made to order or supplied from stock, and on the time required for transport from suppliers to fabricators. For goods supplied from abroad, the interval will be longer, ranging up to 5 or 6 months or more.

Whether stocks of raw materials actually begin to decline at the expiration of this minimum interval depends upon the adequacy of the initial cut in the rate of purchases. They will do so if the initial cut is large enough to bring the rate of deliveries below the rate of consumption ruling at the end of the period. The forecast that is involved is, of course, more likely to be correct if the interval is short. But whether short or long, decisions that purchases must be cut further need not wait until the period has expired. Indications that sales and production are falling more rapidly than expected will presumably be forthcoming before the initial reduction of orders is realized in the form of reduced receipts of materials. These indications may then be acted upon more or less promptly. Even so, if the initial cut is insufficient, stocks will not begin to decline until some time after the expiration of the minimum interval.

If manufacturers underestimate the pace at which their rate of production will fall during the interval between purchase and delivery, so that the initial cut in purchases turns out to be insufficient to initiate liquidation of stocks, there is no solid basis for defining the interval by which the cyclical peak of stocks will lag behind that of production. There is, however, some reason to suppose that the lag will not, in general, greatly exceed the minimum interval. For during the period of the lag stocks will pile up while production falls and the inventory-output ratio will rise rapidly. These facts can hardly be overlooked by manufacturers and they should soon precipitate drastic reductions in the rate at which raw materials are purchased. If this surmise is valid, we might expect stocks of raw materials to lag two to four months behind production. The lag in the case of goods procured from abroad is likely to be considerably longer.

This hypothesis is subject to two further qualifications. If manufacturers are bound by long-term contracts governing the rate at which they receive all or nearly all their supplies of a material, they will not be in a position to alter their rate of purchases as soon as they may desire. Such situations are presumably exceptional, but as far as they exist they will cause the cyclical turns of stocks to lag still further behind those of production.[2]

A second qualification is required to cover cases, of which agricultural crops are the chief example, in which the current output of the materials cannot be adjusted to demand in the short run. As far as manufacturers' stocks of raw materials are concerned, this does not make any difference provided the manufacturers draw their supplies from stocks held principally by dealers. But if fabricators are themselves the main holders of the stock, as in the case of cottonseed and crude rubber, the size of their stocks will be strongly influenced by the size of the crop.[3] Since most crops are not responsive to short-run demand but fluctuate markedly with weather conditions, the primary effect is to cause manufacturers' stocks to behave erractically during business cycles.[4]

These general considerations suggest that the conformity and timing of the cyclical fluctuations in raw materials inventories depend upon the character and location of the sources from which manufacturers draw their supplies. Manufacturers who procure their materials from other domestic manufacturers, or from domestic mining industries, are likely to be able to get additional

[2] Cf. Chapter 10, Section 8 on stocks of newsprint at publishers.

[3] In the case of crude rubber, by the number of rubber trees planted some years before.

[4] If we take several cycles together, supplies of such goods will tend to be about as large in expansions as in contractions. Thus if the rate of consumption moves up and down with the level of business, we may expect some tendency for stocks to vary inversely, with a lag. The lag is caused by the fact that when consumption rises, it does not immediately surpass supply. Hence stocks do not begin to fall as soon as consumption turns up. And the same thing will be true when consumption falls. In any small number of cycles, however, this tendency may be effectively smothered by the erratic fluctuations of supply in individual cycles.

supplies quickly. First, the supplying manufacturers keep on hand stocks of their finished goods which, as we shall see in Chapter 11, they allow to be drawn down when business improves. Second, the output of most manufacturers can usually be expanded fairly rapidly. Thus consumers of materials from such sources can quickly, though not immediately, get supplies in the quantities ordered. On the other hand, manufacturers who draw their supplies directly from abroad, rather than from wholesale importers in the United States, will not be able to adjust the rate at which they receive goods as promptly. Manufacturers who use agricultural raw materials are in a still different situation. If they are the principal holders of the stock, they may find their inventories fluctuating erratically with the fortunes of the growing season. If they purchase materials from dealers who themselves hold stocks large enough to absorb the variations in the size of crops, they will be in a position to adjust supplies to their requirements.

Fortunately, we can gauge the relative importance of these various sources of supply of raw materials. They were elaborately catalogued in a census monograph based upon the Census of Manufactures, 1929 (Table 42).[5] The raw materials and fuels used by manufacturers were classified in ways that make it possible for us to tell what portion was crude and what portion already processed to some degree; what portion was domestic and what foreign. The crude materials were further classified by industrial source: agriculture, mining, logging, and so on.

Most raw materials used in manufacturing in the United States are derived from sources that make possible rapid adjustment of receipts to changes in their rate of consumption. Goods from other domestic manufacturers alone account for 58 percent of the total. When the products of domestic mines, quarries, and logging, and fuels from domestic sources are added, the total percentage of products whose supply responds easily to the demand of domestic fabricators is 67.[6] Stocks of these goods, when held by manufac-

[5] Tracy E. Thompson, *Materials Used in Manufactures: 1929* (1933).

[6] There may be some question about the treatment of petroleum fuels such as crude oil. Since the total supply of petroleum is not easily controlled, crude petroleum used by refiners for processing or sold in unrefined form was placed with the items whose supply is not quickly expansible. But petroleum products used by general manufacturers for fuel can quickly be supplied in larger quan-

TABLE 42

Materials Used in Manufactures, 1929

		COST $ MIL.	% OF GROSS COST
1	Raw materials & fuels, gross cost[a]	38073	100.0
2	Domestic semimanufactures	22152	58.1
3	Imported semimanufactures	1855	4.9
4	Domestic crude materials	10472	27.5
	a) Agriculture & animal husbandry products	6763	17.8
	b) Mining & quarrying products	1562	4.1
	c) Crude petroleum, natural gas & gasoline	1717	4.5
	d) Logging products	390	1.0
	e) Fishing, hunting & trapping products	40	0.1
5	Imported crude materials	2204	5.8
	a) Agriculture & animal husbandry products	1778	4.7
	b) Mining & quarrying products	215	0.6
	c) Logging products	87	0.2
	d) Fishing, hunting & trapping products	124	0.3
6	Fuels	1390	3.7
7	Supply easily & rapidly adj.: lines 2, 4b, 4d, & 6	25494	67.0
8	Supply adj. after lag: lines 3 & 5	4059	10.7
9	Supply not responsive to demand in short run: lines 4a, c, & e	6520	22.4

Source: Tracy E. Thompson, op. cit.

[a] Excludes cost of purchased electric energy, which cannot be stored.

turers for whom they are raw materials, probably move in cycles that conform positively to their rate of consumption. Failures in forecasting, prior contractual arrangements, and the interval between purchase and delivery, however, probably combine to cause stocks to lag behind fabricating activity by a few weeks to a few months. And for similar reasons, the amplitude of inventory fluctuations measured between the troughs and peaks of manufacturing activity (as distinct from the amplitude of inventory cycles proper) seems likely to be smaller than that of fluctuations in output.

A second block of materials, small but still substantial, is derived from sources that cannot adjust their output rapidly in response to changes in demand: mainly the domestic products of

———

tity by drawing upon stocks of petroleum producers and refiners. We, therefore, count this part of the total among the items whose supply to their users can be readily expanded or contracted.

agriculture, with which we have combined crude petroleum and some minor items. In 1929 they comprised some 22 percent of the total value of materials consumed in manufacturing. The output of products from such sources tends to behave erratically during business cycles. A large part, perhaps most, of the stocks are held by dealers. To that extent the erratic fluctuations of crops will be reflected largely in dealers' stocks, and manufacturers will be free to adjust their holdings to the requirements of their operations. But when manufacturers are the main holders we expect their inventories to fluctuate irregularly and to tend to move inversely to business cycles with a lag (see above).

The group of imported products, amounting to about 11 percent of the materials consumed in manufacturing in 1929, may provide some regular offset to the behavior of the first large category. We have classified imported goods as commodities whose supply to United States manufacturers is responsive to demand, but only slowly. If this characterization is valid, it is not clear whether stocks in the hands of domestic fabricators conform positively to production with only a moderate lag or with a long lag, or even conform inversely. The evidence, as we shall see, is mixed and inadequate. Again, however, long lags or inverse behavior is probable only if domestic fabricators hold the bulk of the stock of such commodities in the United States. If they draw their supplies from wholesale importers, manufacturers will be in a position rapidly to adjust the rate at which they receive materials to changes in their requirements. Here again, we would expect stocks at manufacturers to lag behind fabrication by only a short interval.

If this analysis is substantially accurate, the bulk of the materials used by manufacturers is clearly drawn from sources that permit deliveries to be adjusted fairly rapidly to the rate of manufacturing activity. These materials include not only the products of domestic manufacturers, mines, and forests, but also such agricultural commodities and imported goods as are stocked mainly by dealers and wholesale importers. Together they probably account for over 80 percent of all materials used. The hypothesis set forth above supposes that stocks of such goods held by manufacturers conform positively to cycles of production with a short lag—perhaps two to four months—unless the manufacturers are bound by long-term contracts. Manufacturers' stocks of other imported commodities probably lag further behind production. Finally, when manufacturers are the principal holders of domestic agricultural products, stocks will tend to move erratically during cycles of manufacturing activity, with some tendency, on the average, toward inverted conformity with a lag.

2 General Indications of the Behavior of Manufacturers' Stocks

CHARACTER OF SAMPLE

Our collection of series representing raw materials held by manufacturers is, as we shall see, inadequate to be the basis for any really well-founded theory about their behavior. Certainly the above hypothesis must rest as much upon its own inherent reasonableness as upon any evidence we can present. But the materials at our disposal are not, as far as they go, inconsistent with this theory and they can serve to illuminate several factors that influence raw materials inventories. The collection comprises ten series: raw sugar at refineries, monthly, 1890-1944; raw cotton at mills, monthly, 1912-41; raw silk at manufacturers, monthly, 1921-35; raw cattle hides at tanners, monthly, 1922-41; newsprint at and in transit to publishers, monthly, 1919-44; refinable petroleum in pipelines and at tank farms and refineries, monthly, 1918-41; lead in warehouses, monthly, 1894-1918; crude rubber in and afloat for the United States, quarterly, 1923-24, and monthly, 1924-41; cottonseed at mills, monthly, 1916-41; iron ore at furnaces, monthly, 1918-39.

In comparison with the kinds of commodity that dominate the raw material holdings of manufacturers, this sample is not representative. The peculiar circumstances that control the behavior of each series are noted below and studied in some detail in Chapter 10. At this point it is useful to get a summary impression of two salient features of their cyclical fluctuations.

The relation between stocks and business activity can be judged in two ways. We can study the movements of stocks during cycles in business at large as indicated by the National Bureau chronology or we can compare stocks with manufacturing activity in a given industry. After allowing for typical timing of individual production series the two methods may be expected to yield similar results since output in most manufacturing industries rises and falls with business activity. For any small group of industries during a few cycles, however, this will not be so even for industries whose output is normally related closely to business cycles. Peculiar conditions affecting individual industries in certain periods can distort the typical cyclical conformity and timing of production. In such cases, measures of the conformity of inventories to business cycles and of the timing of inventories at business cycle turns can conceal or distort the usual relation between stocks and manufacturing activity. Since the sample of industries for which there are records of raw materials stocks is small it seems best to rely on comparisons between stocks and the rate of fabrication in the industries holding them.

The behavior of eight series can be measured by the National Bureau's methods. Difficulties encountered in correcting the data for seasonal fluctuations made special analyses necessary for cottonseed and iron ore stocks; these are presented separately in Chapter 10. The measure of conformity for each stock series was computed according to a reference chronology determined by the specific cycle peaks and troughs of the related indicator of manufacturing activity (Table 43). Timing was measured by comparing the specific cycle turns in stocks with the specific cycle turns in manufacturing activity (Table 44).

The general impression is that my hypothesis about the behavior of raw materials stocks is supported. Six of the eight measures of full cycle conformity have positive signs, five of the indexes are high. Evidence of inverted behavior is significant in only one case. The series that vary positively with manufacturing activity also tend to lag and the length of the lags are, in general, consistent with expectations.

Closer study of the tables, however, indicates that the support for my view is both weaker and stronger than first appears. I expect stocks of raw materials to vary positively with the rate of production because there is evidence that most raw materials are supplied by domestic manufacturing and mining industries or by other domestic sources that can quickly adjust their output and deliveries to changes in the requirements of the manufacturers that fabricate their products. None of the commodities in the tables is

TABLE 43
Raw Materials Stocks, Conformity to Manufacturing Activity Cycles

STOCKS	INDICATOR OF ACTIVITY	NO. OF PHASES[a]	INDEX OF CONFORMITY TO ACTIVITY[b]		
			Exp.	Contr.	Cycle
Raw cotton at mills	Cotton consumption, 1913-38	17	+50	+56	+62
Raw silk at mfr.	Raw silk deliveries to mills, 1920-33	10	+100	+20	+100
Raw cattle hides at tanners	Cattle hide wettings, 1923-42	8	+50	+50	+71
Newsprint at & in transit to pub.	Newsprint paper consumption, 1919-39	8	+50	+100	+100
Lead at warehouses	Lead imports, 1895-1918	8	+100	+100	+100
Refinable petroleum in pipelines & at tank farms & refineries	Crude petroleum consumption, 1917-38	8	0	0	+14
Raw sugar at refineries	Sugar meltings, 1891-1940	21	-20	-9	-20
Crude rubber in & afloat for U.S.	Auto. tire prod., 1923-41	8	0	-50	-71

a Determined by the number of cycles in manufacturing activity during which inventory data were available.

b Measured synchronously, except in the case of newsprint stocks, which were assumed to lag 10 months behind newsprint consumption at both peaks and troughs.

TABLE 44

Raw Materials Stocks, Timing at Turns in Manufacturing Activity

STOCKS	NUMBER OF Leads	Lags	Coin.	AV. LEAD (—) OR LAG (+) MONTHS
	AT PEAKS IN ACTIVITY			
1) Raw cotton at mills	3	5	0	+1.5
2) Raw silk at mfr.	1	3	0	+0.5
3) Raw cattle hides at tanners	2	2	1	+1.2
4) Newsprint at & in transit to pub.	0	4	0	+9.8
5) Lead at warehouses	2	2	1	+3.0
6) Refinable petroleum in pipelines & at tank farms & refineries	0	2	1	+3.7
7) Raw sugar at refineries	4	3	0	−4.4
8) Crude rubber in & afloat for U.S.[a]	1	1	0	+1.0
9) Sum of 5 series with significant positive conformity (lines 1-5)	8	16	2	
	AT TROUGHS IN ACTIVITY			
10) Raw cotton at mills	0	6	1	+5.1
11) Raw silk at mfr.	1	2	0	+1.0
12) Raw cattle hides at tanners	1	3	0	+6.2
13) Newsprint at & in transit to pub.	0	4	0	+9.2
14) Lead at warehouses	1	3	0	+3.0
15) Refinable petroleum in pipelines & at tank farms & refineries	0	3	0	+10.7
16) Raw sugar at refineries	1	6	0	+5.4
17) Crude rubber in & afloat for U.S.[a]	0	2	0	+1.5
18) Sum of 5 series with significant positive conformity (lines 10-14)	3	18	1	

For indicators of manufacturing activity and periods covered, see Table 43.
[a] Timing measured invertedly; see Ch. 3, note 5.

supplied from such sources. Newsprint may appear to fit because it comes by rail and motor transport from United States and Canadian mills. Unlike most commodities, however, it is bought on contracts that control purchases and deliveries for a year or longer. Lead stocks consist mainly of metal of foreign origin held in bond for fabrication and reexport. The output of petroleum has not, in the past, kept pace with current consumption because of the haphazard rate of discovery of new oil fields and the competition of individual producers to capture subsoil reserves. The other commodities are agricultural products whose output is not sensitive to short-run demand, and several are partly or wholly of foreign origin.

Nevertheless, the general consistency of the measures with the theory is not merely fortuitous. Materials supplied by domestic manufacturers or miners are not the only cases in which one may expect stocks to conform positively with a few months' lag. The same expectation applies to other commodities, provided large buffer stocks are held by dealers on whose inventories manufacturers can draw at need. This is the situation that characterizes raw cotton, silk, and hides. Their behavior, therefore, conforms to the rule.

The output of newsprint and lead can be readily adjusted to demand, but the former is purchased on long-term contract and the latter comes by sea from Mexico and South America. In such cases we expect adjustments to be longer delayed and the lag of stocks to be longer. The average lag of newsprint stocks at publishers behind consumption of newsprint paper was indeed long— between 9 and 10 months. The average lag of lead stocks was shorter than might have been expected, but this is a lag behind imports. If imports lag behind fabrication, as seems plausible, the lag of stocks behind their rate of utilization would have been longer than our figures show.

The output of petroleum, sugar, and natural rubber does not respond to short-run demand. But in contrast to the situation in cotton, silk, and hides, there are no dealers with large stocks to absorb cyclical discrepancies between output and consumption. American manufacturers are themselves the chief holders of the stock. Since the output of petroleum and sugar has fluctuated erratically during business cycles, the stocks held by United States manufacturers have not varied regularly during business cycles. The annual variations in rubber output, however, have been fairly small compared with the cyclical fluctuations in consumption. Hence stocks of rubber move inversely during cycles in the rate at which it has been fabricated.

These remarks suffice for a brief review of the data. Chapter 10 subjects these materials to closer study and introduces additional data bearing on stocks of cottonseed and iron ore.

CHAPTER 10

Ten Examples of Raw Materials Stocks

The sample of stocks of raw materials examined in Chapter 9 is so small and in some ways unrepresentative that interpretation and generalization was difficult. The commodities in the sample are, however, of diverse types. Much can be gained, therefore, from detailed commodity studies. This approach permits consideration also of two commodities not included in the tables of Chapter 9 because they could not be treated by the National Bureau's usual methods. We can in this way learn a good deal about how different kinds of stocks of raw materials behave and so put ourselves in a better position to speculate about the general characteristics of the class.

1   Raw Cotton at Mills

As argued in Chapter 9, the supply of raw materials to the manufacturers who use them can usually be quickly adjusted to the rate at which they are consumed provided one of two conditions is met. One possibility is that the materials are produced by other manufacturers or by mining industries in this country, the other that dealers or importers in this country hold a large stock. Our collection of series does not contain a single good example of the first possibility, but it does contain several cases that illustrate the second. Raw cotton is one. The essential point is to distinguish the factors governing total stocks from those governing manufacturers' stocks.

CROPS, CONSUMPTION, AND TOTAL STOCKS

The year to year changes in the crop of raw cotton are due mainly to weather conditions. Consequently, the behavior of the output of cotton is largely unrelated to business cycles. On the other hand, since the consumption of cotton in this country depends chiefly on consumers' incomes and the level of industrial activity, it tends to fluctuate together with business activity but to be relatively independent of the size of the cotton crop. The conformity indexes of the cotton crop to 18 business cycles 1867-1938 run $+11$, -33, -20. For 6 cycles 1914-38, the comparable indexes for cotton consumption are $+67$, $+71$, $+67$.[1] The relation of output and consumption may be judged from the correlation between the year to year directions of change in the two series.[2] The coefficient calculated from data extending from 1894, when the annual consumption series starts, to 1943 is negligible, less than $+0.12$ on a scale running from -1 to $+1$.

Of the two processes, production and consumption of cotton in the United States, fluctuations in the former are by far the larger. The average annual change in consumption (regardless of direction) between 1894 and 1944 was about 640 thousand bales. The average annual change in the crop was over three times as big, about 2.1 million bales. In these circumstances, one might expect

---

[1] This is the measure yielded when stages VIII-V are matched with business expansion. When stages I-V are used, the indexes run $+100$, $+71$, $+100$.

[2] This measure, which I use frequently, involves the computation of the number of instances in which (a) both series rise, (b) the first rises and the second falls, (c) the first falls and the second rises, and (d) both fall. The correlation coefficient is then given by the term

$$(ad - bc) \div \sqrt{(a + b)\ (c + d)\ (a + c)\ (b + d)}$$

This modification of the usual measure of correlation was devised by G. H. Moore and W. A. Wallis. Significance tests for this measure are described in Time Series Significance Tests Based on Signs of Differences, *Journal of the American Statistical Association*, June 1943, pp. 160 ff., and by Moore in his forthcoming book on Harvest Cycles.

The coefficient, of course, expresses the proportionate excess of the number of agreements or disagreements over the number expected on the basis of chance alone. It takes account of trend by making the number of agreements expected depend upon the proportionate distribution of rises and declines in the series studied. Compared with the National Bureau index of full cycle conformity, which is also based on directions of change, the Moore-Wallis coefficient is, in some ways, a more sensitive measure of association, in some ways, less sensitive. It is more sensitive in that it uses every change in the data whereas the National Bureau index takes account only of the change between peaks and troughs and troughs and peaks. It is less sensitive in that it counts every decline in one series matched by a rise in the other as a disagreement. The National Bureau index counts a decline in the rate of growth of one series during a contraction of the other as an agreement and the same with declines in the rate of fall of one series during expansions in the other.

movements of the total stock of cotton to be dominated by the shifting size of the crop and to behave during business cycles in much the same irregular fashion as the crop itself.

This might well be so were it not for exports. Foreign sales have usually taken well over half the United States cotton crop. Moreover, exports have tended to vary directly with the size of the crop. The correlation between the directions of change in the crop and exports, 1866-1942, is +.60. Apparently when the United States crop is large, the price of cotton tends to be depressed and more American cotton tends to be sold abroad for consumption and stock piling, reducing fluctuations in the supply of cotton remaining in this country. Annual fluctuations in the addition to United States supply after allowing for exports was only some 1.5 million bales, 1894-1944. The residual supply is subject to more violent changes than is consumption but the difference is not as large as that between the crop and consumption.

These considerations enable us to define certain expectations concerning the behavior of the total stocks of cotton during crop cycles on the one hand and during consumption and business cycles on the other. If consumption did not fluctuate during crop cycles, we would expect a year of good crops to be a year of large stocks. Although exports would take some of the surplus, a larger part would still remain to be absorbed into the United States stock pile. There should, however, be some tendency for the peaks and troughs of stocks to lag behind the turns of crop cycles and sometimes to skip cycles. For when crops decline after the peak year of a crop cycle, the new supply of cotton, after allowing for exports, may or may not fall below consumption. If it does, stocks will decline synchronously with the crop. If not, stocks will rise during the first year of smaller crops. If the crop declines a second year, the residual supply is likely to be deficient compared with consumption and stocks will decline; but the peak of the stock cycle will have come a year after the peak of the crop cycle. If favorable weather brings a larger instead of a smaller crop the second year, then—still on the assumption that consumption remains constant— stocks will not fall at all during that crop cycle. The decline of the crop would be matched by a decrease in the rate of growth but not by an absolute reduction of stocks.

These expectations, however, represent only a general tendency. Consumption does not remain constant during crop cycles; it fluctuates irregularly. In addition, changes in exports may sometimes completely offset changes in crops. True, changes in domestic supply, even after allowing for exports, are typically larger than those in consumption. Nevertheless, one would not expect aggregate stocks to conform perfectly to crop cycles.

Our expectations about the relation between total cotton stocks and consumption are symmetrical with, but opposite to, those we hold about stocks and crops. Thus if harvests were of constant size, we would expect stocks to vary inversely to consumption (and to business cycles, too, since consumption rises and falls with business activity). We would expect the peaks of stock cycles, however, to lag behind the troughs of consumption cycles since consumption will not begin to outrun production until consumption has recovered to a certain extent.[3] Similarly, we would expect the troughs of stocks to lag behind the peaks of consumption. This expectation, however, would hardly be fulfilled in every cycle since harvests vary widely and erratically.

The cyclical movements of total stocks accord in general with these hypotheses. Statistical confirmation, however, rests on data that are not wholly satisfactory. Estimates of total stocks of cotton in this country begin in 1913, but they are only for ends of crop years. Fortunately, two monthly series that are fair indicators of the total are available: stocks at public warehouses and compresses, compiled by the Bureau of the Census since 1912, and 'visible supplies' reported by leading financial journals and organized by the National Bureau into a continuous series running back to 1870 (Chart 16).[4]

At least at the ends of crop years, when the crop has been almost entirely marketed, stocks at public warehouses are apparently good indicators of the movements of total stocks, and visible

[3] These statements imply seasonally corrected observations at monthly intervals such as are available for consumption and stocks.

[4] Visible supplies are the stocks held at principal warehouses. The cotton in question is, therefore, in the same position as that reported by the census for stocks at warehouses, but the coverage of the visible supplies series is smaller. Monthly estimates of total stocks are provided by the New York Cotton Exchange only since 1926.

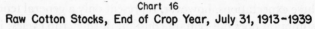

Chart 16
Raw Cotton Stocks, End of Crop Year, July 31, 1913-1939

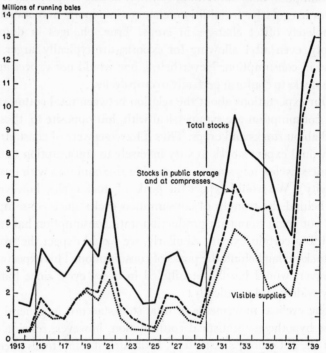

supplies are good indicators of both. The situation must obviously
be less satisfactory as one moves back from the end of the crop
year to its beginning when a larger portion of the stock is still held
on farms, but the difference can hardly be large. The cotton crop,
which begins to be picked heavily in August, is almost entirely
harvested by the end of December. By that time over 75 percent
of it has usually been sold and moved from farms to warehouses.
By the end of February the marketed portion usually exceeds 85
percent. Not all the stock owned by farmers, moreover, remains
on the farm until it is sold. Hence the portion of the stock trans-
ferred to public warehouses is probably larger on any given date
than the portion marketed by farmers. I therefore accept data for
visible supplies or stocks at warehouses as fair indicators of the
movements of total stocks. Crop year averages indicate the general
similarity of the three series since 1925 (Chart 17).[5]

[5] Comparisons based on annual averages are not available earlier since total

Chart 17
Raw Cotton Stocks
Average Monthly Standings during Crop Years

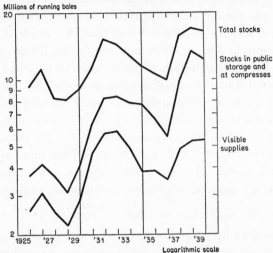

For comparisons with crop fluctuations, I use the visible supplies series because it extends back to 1870. Stocks tend to conform positively to crop cycles. The conformity indexes for crop year averages of stocks for 20 crop cycles 1870-1939 run +60, +33, +45. Some tendency for stocks to lag behind crops is indicated by the higher indexes yielded by observation of averages of stocks for calendar years beginning six months after the beginning of each crop year: +70, +80, +69.

During cotton consumption cycles our expectation is that stocks will vary inversely with a lag. Monthly consumption data since 1912 make it possible to mark the boundaries of consumption cycles by months rather than years. Since that date, too, census records of stocks in public warehouses and at compresses are available. I calculate the conformity of total cotton stocks to consumption cycles by measuring the movements of stocks in public storage during cycles bounded by monthly troughs and peaks in consumption. Evidence that stocks tend to vary inversely is provided by con-

stocks are not estimated before the middle of 1925 except for ends of crop years. These figures overstate the differences between total stocks and the other two series, since they credit the unpicked portion of the crop to stocks on farms and, therefore, to the total as of the beginning of the harvest season.

formity indexes that run —25, —33, —50 when stages V-II are
matched with expansion. This pattern, which indicates that stocks
typically do not begin to decline until one stage after consumption
has begun to rise, gives some hint that, in accordance with expectations, the turns of stocks come later than the (opposite) turns of
consumption, at least at consumption troughs. Better evidence is
afforded by direct comparison between the peaks and troughs of
consumption and the opposite turns of stocks. Six comparisons
could be made at both upper and lower turning points. The
trough of stocks lagged behind the peak of consumption on three
occasions: it fell in the same month once and led twice. At consumption troughs, the peak of stocks lagged five times and turned
in the same month once. The average lag of stocks at consumption
peaks was 0.7 months; at consumption troughs, 11.8 months.

TOTAL STOCKS AND MANUFACTURERS' STOCKS

The large and irregular fluctuations of the cotton crop during
cycles of business and cotton consumption cause warehouse stocks
of cotton—and I think total stocks as well—to vary inversely to cotton consumption. The behavior of stocks of raw cotton at textile
mills is in striking contrast (Chart 18). Mill stocks move up and
down together with consumption. The conformity indexes of mill
stocks during 8 consumption cycles 1913-38 were +50, +56, +62.
Mill stocks tend to lag behind consumption, but by only a short
interval. Of eight comparisons at peaks, stocks lagged five times;
the average lag was 1.5 months. Of seven comparisons at troughs,
stocks lagged six times and turned synchronously with consumption once; the average lag was 5.1 months.

The reason for the contrasting behavior of mill and warehouse
stocks is readily found. If manufacturers held the bulk of the cotton stock, their holdings would necessarily reflect the uncoordi-
nated fluctuations of crops and consumption. Allowing for a lag,
their stocks would tend to rise and fall with the crop during crop
cycles and to trace inverted patterns during consumption cycles.
But manufacturers are not the chief holders of cotton. Average
stocks at mills were only 11 percent of total stocks between 1926
and 1939.[6] Between manufacturers' consumption and the current

[6] This estimate, computed for the period during which monthly figures for

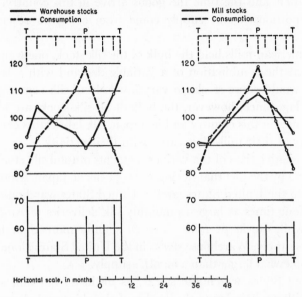

Chart 18
Raw Cotton Stocks and Consumption
Average Patterns during 8 Consumption Cycles, 1914-1938

crop stand the large buffer stocks in warehouses which afford the mills an ample and flexible source of supply. Cotton textile manufacturers, therefore, are in a position to obtain raw materials and to keep stocks at their mills in quantities appropriate to the rate at which they are converting cotton into yarn. Consequently, they keep larger quantities at mills when business is good and reduce their holdings when business contracts.

2 Raw Silk at Manufacturers

Raw silk at American silk mills presents a situation not unlike raw cotton. The output of silk, depending as it does upon the breeding of silkworms, responds slowly to changes in current demand.[7]

---

total stocks are available, probably understates the importance of mill stocks before 1926. With the onset of the great depression cotton stocks rose to very high levels and the surplus naturally remained in public warehouses. But it is unlikely that mill stocks were more than 20 percent of the total for any long period in earlier decades.

[7] In this respect, the supply of silk is like that of other animal products rather than like crops, which vary in response to weather conditions.

Moreover, the necessity of transporting the silk from Japan injects several more months between the time American importers place their orders and the time the goods arrive in this country. Only minor portions of the supply come from countries other than Japan.

If American mills held the bulk of the silk stock, one would expect that the combination of a variable demand with a laggard supply would cause stocks to vary inversely to silk consumption, with a lag. Since, however, the bulk of all silk stocks are held at warehouses in this country and in Japan, silk fabricators can keep a supply at their mills that varies with their activity.

The relative sizes of the various segments of total silk stocks are suggested by the fact that during 1925-33 silk at Japanese ports, in transit to the United States, and in United States warehouses ran about four times as large as monthly silk deliveries to American mills, while stocks at mills came to slightly more than half a month's supply. Warehouse stocks in the United States alone averaged somewhat larger than a month's supply.

United States warehouse stocks, as distinct from mill stocks, share with stocks in Japan the burden of absorbing maladjustments between supply and demand, and they may be affected also significantly by price speculation. In any case, they do not appear to fluctuate regularly either with imports of silk or with deliveries of silk to mills. The conformity indexes of warehouse stocks to cycles of imports during two cycles 1921-34 were +33, 0, 0. During 8 cycles 1920-40 the conformity indexes of warehouse stocks to cycles of deliveries to mills were +25, —25, —7.

In contrast, the relation between stocks at mills and the rate of consumption of raw silk, as measured by deliveries to mills, is apparently fairly close. For 5 cycles in deliveries 1920-33, conformity measures of stocks to deliveries run +100, +20, +78 when stages II-VI are matched with expansions in deliveries (Chart 19). When stages I-V are matched with expansions, the indexes become +100, +20, +100.

3   Raw Cattle Hides in Tanners' Hands

Like other commodities reviewed in this chapter, cattle hides are supplied under conditions that make difficult a prompt adjust-

Chart 19
Raw Silk Stocks and Deliveries to Mills
Average Patterns during Deliveries Cycles

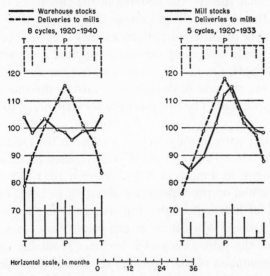

ment of supply to demand in an over-all sense. As in the cases of cotton and silk, however, stocks held by dealers make it possible for processors to get their raw materials as they require them and to maintain a stock fairly well adjusted to their rate of activity.[8]

Raw hides are a byproduct of cattle slaughtering. Since only some 10 percent of the value of an animal is derived from its hide, the rate of slaughtering is dominated by the supply of cattle and the demand for meat rather than by the supply of cattle and the demand for hides. Nevertheless, the rate of cattle slaughter (as represented by the number of cattle slaughtered under federal inspection) is not uncorrelated with the rate at which cattle hides are processed (represented by cattle hide 'wettings'). For 4 cycles 1923-42 conformity indexes of cattle slaughter to wettings cycles run +50, 0, +43.

This degree of correlation probably arises from the fact that the demand for shoes, which controls the rate at which hides are processed, and the demand for beef, which strongly influences the rate

---

[8] In her forthcoming book, *Consumption and Business Cycles—A Case Study: Footwear*, Ruth P. Mack will examine in detail the relations between hide supply and leather production, including the behavior of hide stocks.

of cattle slaughter, are both affected by fluctuations in consumers' incomes. In view of the indirect nature of the relation, it is not surprising that the cyclical patterns of the two series do not resemble each other closely (Chart 20).[9] Although these patterns show relatives on different cycle bases they suggest that at peaks in cycles of hide processing, the consumption of hides outruns the domestic supply. On the other hand, at troughs in cycles of hide consumption, the rate of slaughtering outruns the rate at which hides are processed. The two processes are responding to different stimuli.

The major parts of the differences between the rates at which hides are produced and consumed in the United States are offset by fluctuations in imports of hides. Between 1921 and 1939 imports accounted on the average for about 15 percent of the total movement of hides into sight. Imports, however, are subject to wide fluctuations. When hides in this country are scarce relative to demand, the price rises and it becomes profitable to import. When consumption of hides declines relative to domestic supply, the price falls, and importing becomes unprofitable (Chart 21).

Among the 19 year to year movements in Chart 21 there are only two disagreements between the directions of change in the two series. For one, that from 1933 to 1934, the explanation is obvious. The 1934 drought forced the slaughter of an extraordinarily large number of animals. Imports, of course, in the volume of 1933 were unnecessary, but the domestic price was maintained by the government's drought relief program.

As a result of the counterweight provided by imports, cattle hides move into sight at a rate fairly similar to that at which cattle hides are processed.[10] The conformity indexes measuring the fluctuations of movement into sight during 3 cycles of wettings 1923-37 run +33, +100, +33 (Chart 22). The patterns of the two series resemble each other far more closely than did domestic slaughter and wettings (Chart 20). The flow of imports helps make up for the insensitivity of domestic cattle slaughter to cycles in cattle hide

[9] The chart shows the movement during an initial contraction and a terminal expansion as well as the three full cycles between 1926 and 1937.

[10] Movement into sight includes hides from federally inspected slaughter, tanners' receipts of hides from uninspected slaughter, and imports.

Chart 20
Cattle Slaughter and Hide Wettings Patterns during Wettings Cycles

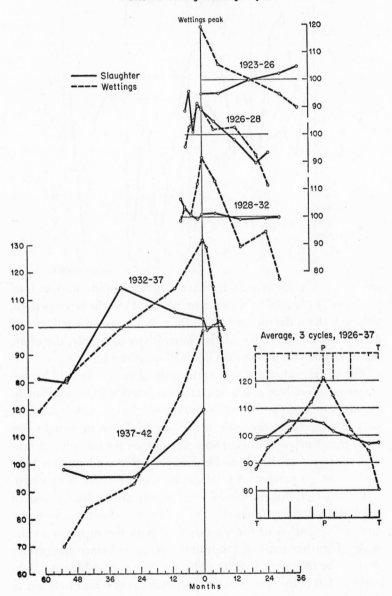

Chart 21
Cattle Hides: Net Imports and Wholesale Prices

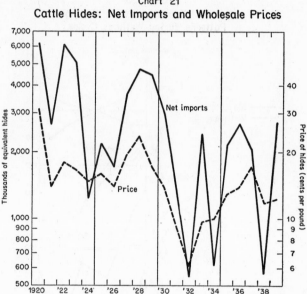

Logarithmic scales

processing. Cycles in wettings have a wider amplitude than total hide supply (judged by movement into sight) in the same periods, although the difference is far less than that between wettings and domestic slaughter. The relative insensitivity of supply, therefore, leaves its mark on the cyclical fluctuations in stocks.

The data on stocks of raw cattle hides show stocks held by two major groups of businessmen: on the one hand, packers and butchers who produce the raw hides and dealers and importers who import and assemble domestic hides (especially from slaughterers other than the large packing houses), and, on the other hand, tanners who process the hides. Dealers, importers and packers have held about 40 percent of total stocks, tanners about 60 percent.

The relative sluggishness of total supply affects total stocks of raw hides much as supply affected total stocks of cotton. Since the rate of fabrication of hides tends to outrun the supply near the peaks of leather tanning (wettings) cycles, and since the reverse tends to be true near their troughs, we may expect hide stocks to begin to fall before the peak in the wettings cycle and to begin to rise before the trough. This is, in fact, what the figures show. When we match stages VII-III with expansions, that is, if we assume a

Chart 22
Cattle Hides: Movement into Sight and Wettings Patterns during Wettings Cycles

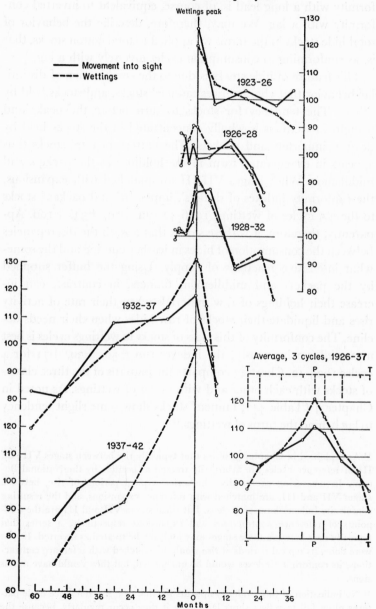

long lead, the conformity of hide stocks in all hands to wettings cycles is +50, +33, +67 for 3.5 cycles 1926-42. Such positive conformity with a long lead is, of course, equivalent to inverted conformity with a lag. We may, therefore, describe the behavior of total hide stocks in the terms we applied to total cotton stocks, that is, as conforming to consumption cycles inversely with a lag.[11]

This feature of hide stocks is due to the combination of dissimilar behavior that characterizes tanners' stocks, and stocks held by others. The tendency for stocks to turn before the peaks and troughs in wettings is wholly concentrated in the stocks held by dealers, importers and packers. The pattern of total stocks thus appears in exaggerated form in the holdings of the packers and middlemen. When stages VII-III are matched with expansions, the conformity indexes of dealers', importers' and packers' stocks to the 3.5 cycles of wettings 1926-42 run +50, +33, +100. Apparently, therefore, it is these stocks that absorb the discrepancies between the consumption of hides in leather tanning and the somewhat insensitive reactions of supply. Using the buffer supplied by the packers and middlemen, tanners, in contrast, can increase their holdings of raw materials when their rate of activity rises and liquidate their stocks of raw hides when their needs decline. The conformity of this class of stocks to wettings cycles is best measured synchronously; the indexes run +50, +50, +71 for 4 cycles 1923-42. Chart 23 compares the patterns of the three classes of stocks with each other and with cycles of wettings. As noted in Chapter 9 (Table 44), tanners' stocks show some slight tendency to lag behind the turns of wettings.[12]

[11] As explained in Chapter 3, series that typically rise between stages VII and III of reference cycles are arbitrarily treated as positive by the National Bureau. In measuring conformity, the series' typical periods of rise, between stages VII and III, are matched with reference expansions, and the resulting conformity indexes have plus signs. But since stages VII and III are the midpoints of reference contractions and expansions respectively, a series that typically rises between these stages may logically be treated as inverted. If that were done, its typical periods of rise would be matched with reference contractions, its conformity indexes would be unchanged, but they would have minus signs.

[12] No indication of this tendency appears in Chart 23. But reference cycle patterns often fail to reflect short lags, even if they occur regularly, because the stage interval is a rough unit covering several months.

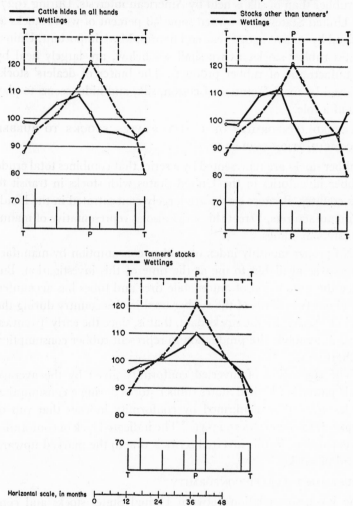

Chart 23
Cattle Hide Stocks and Wettings
Average Patterns during 3 Wettings Cycles, 1926-1937

—— Cattle hides in all hands
---- Wettings

—— Stocks other than tanners'
---- Wettings

—— Tanners' stocks
---- Wettings

Horizontal scale, in months

4   Crude Rubber Stocks

United States stocks of crude rubber have several interesting features in common with the commodities reviewed above, especially
with silk, and one crucial difference. Like silk, rubber is the product of tree culture, is produced largely in the Far East, and must

travel a long way to reach this country. The salient difference lies
in the distribution of stocks. A much larger portion of world stocks
of rubber than of silk is held by American interests. During 1927-
37 United States firms owned some 58 percent of world stocks as
judged by an average of year end figures. More important, United
States rubber stocks, as we shall see below, are largely held by
manufacturers of rubber products. The buffer of dealers' stocks
enjoyed by manufacturers of cotton, silk, and hides seems to play
less of a role.

INVERTED CONFORMITY OF UNITED STATES STOCKS TO RUBBER
CONSUMPTION CYCLES

Rubber stocks are represented by a series that combines total crude
rubber inventories in the United States with stocks in transit to
this country. Because stocks are largely concentrated in the hands
of manufacturers, I treat this series also as representative of manufacturers' holdings.

No proper monthly index of rubber consumption by manufacturers was available to me at the time of this investigation. But
since the production of automobile tires and tubes has accounted
for about two-thirds of the rubber used in this country during the
period covered by the stocks data, that is, since the early 'twenties,
I use automobile tire production to represent rubber consumption
(Chart 24).

The suggestion of inverted conformity given by the average
cycle pattern of United States rubber stocks during 3 consumption
cycles 1923-38 is confirmed by conformity indexes that run 0,
—50, —71 for 4 cycles 1923-41.[13] The indicated lack of conformity
to expansions in this inverted series is due to the marked upward
trend of stocks.

CAUSES OF INVERTED CONFORMITY

The inverse correlation between United States stocks and consumption is due to a combination of several factors inherent in the
market in which rubber is sold and conditions affecting its production. As already indicated, the consumption of rubber in this country has been dominated, since the use of automobiles became wide-

13 The conformity measure includes an extra half cycle at both the beginning
and the end of the series.

Chart 24
**Crude Rubber Stocks in and afloat for
the United States and Automobile Tire Production
Average Patterns during 3 Production Cycles, 1923-1938**

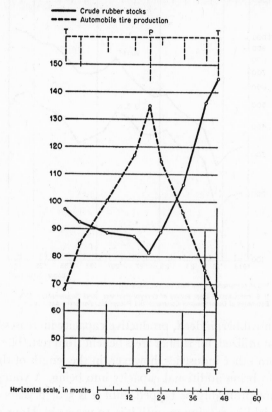

spread, by the production of rubber tires and tubes. As automobile production has fluctuated violently in response to changes in general business conditions and in consumer incomes, so, too, has the consumption of rubber in the United States. And as these changes in United States consumption were large relative to the world use of rubber, fluctuations in American consumption have tended to control changes in world consumption (Chart 25).

Were it not for governmental regulation or cooperative action among producers the industry's ability to adjust output to changes in demand would be extremely limited. The rubber industry shares with most others an inability to reduce productive capacity

Chart 25
Crude Rubber Consumption
World and United States

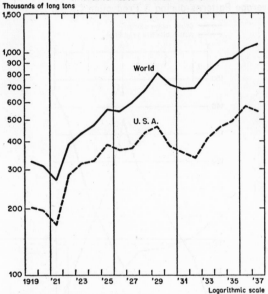

Thousands of long tons

World consumption from Rae, op. cit., Table VII.
U. S. consumption from *Survey of Current Business*, 1942 Supplement, p. 160.
Estimates of Department of Commerce and Rubber Manufacturers Association.

rapidly. In rubber, indeed, productive capacity increases for some years if not utilized, for rubber trees benefit from rest. The industry differs from other industries, however, in the length of the period required to bring additional capacity into being. A young rubber tree cannot profitably be tapped until it is 5 or 6 years old, and does not yield its maximum until it is 10 years old. However, once a tree is planted, the cost of bringing it to the age of profitable yield is very low. Thus, increments to productive capacity may be large in years when demand is low and falling, as they were in 1920-22 and again in 1929-32.[14]

The acreage planted in rubber in a given year varies with the price of rubber, apparently with some lag (Chart 26). Thus the price of rubber reached a peak in 1925, while the annual increment to acreage reached a maximum in 1927 and remained high

[14] Cf. George Rae, Statistics of the Rubber Industry, *Journal of the Royal Statistical Society*, New Series, CI, Part II, 1938. Much of the information in this section is drawn from this excellent source.

Chart 26
Capacity of Rubber Industry and Price of Crude Rubber

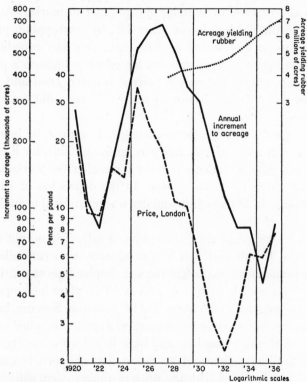

Logarithmic scales

Annual increment to acreage and prices from Rae, op. cit., Table II. To estimate acreage yielding rubber, 1927-36, annual increments to planted acreage were added to the acreage yielding in 1927 allowing for an 8-year lag between planting and maturity.

for some years. Since five years must pass before trees begin yielding and ten years for the yields to reach their peak, the additions to effective productive capacity were considerable in 1929-32 when demand fell sharply. If we assume that new trees produce an average yield in eight years, it may be estimated that between 1929 and 1931, when consumption of rubber fell 14 percent, productive capacity increased some 6 percent. Hence to reduce output by an amount equal to the decline of consumption would have required a reduction of perhaps 20 percent in the intensity with which the acreage available was worked.

There are great difficulties, however, to reducing the output from mature acreage. Direct expense is low relative to total cost and the industry is competitive. For native producers, who contribute about 40 percent of the total supply, direct costs hardly exceed the expense of bringing the product to market. And by sacrificing the yield of future years, i.e., by overtapping, present output can be augmented at little extra cost—an expedient to which hard-pressed companies are forced when business is poor.[15] As a result, output fell only 6 percent between 1929 and 1931. Even by 1932 the cut in output relative to 1929 did not exceed 14 percent.

Once production has been curtailed, it cannot be increased rapidly, even when mature tree acreage is available, for it is difficult to assemble an adequate labor force after the workers have scattered, often to distant places. In the depression of 1929-32 surplus labor in Malaya and Sumatra was repatriated to India and Java.

To help overcome these difficulties of adjusting output to demand, the British and Dutch governments, who controlled the rubber producing areas before the war, imposed quota restrictions on the exports of individual producers. Two plans have operated with some degree of effectiveness. The Stevenson Scheme, in force from November 1, 1922 to October 31, 1928, controlled exports only from British possessions and from British estates in the Netherlands Indies by means of an export duty. Exports in excess of quotas, which varied with the price of rubber, were subject to a prohibitive tax. The International Rubber Regulation Scheme, in force from May 1934 until the outbreak of the war, regulated exports of both British and Netherlands possessions. Under it export quotas were assigned directly to individual producers, except native producers in the Netherlands East Indies whose output was controlled by an export tax until January 1, 1937.

Both schemes influenced output by regulating the quantity growers might export. Both probably kept exports from increasing as rapidly as they might otherwise have done during the dominantly prosperous periods in which they were effective. Under the International Rubber Regulation Scheme, world stocks fell some 37 percent from 1934 to 1936. It is doubtful, however, that such devices can operate with sufficient flexibility and speed to prevent

15 Ibid., pp. 324-6.

a substantial increase of stocks when consumption drops rapidly. When American consumption declined in the 1937-38 contraction, world stocks rose 42 percent (between May 1937 and April 1938).[16]

We have now seen that cycles in American consumption cause marked fluctuations in the total absorption of rubber, and that rapid adjustments of output to demand are prevented by the conditions under which the product is grown and sold. Since rubber deteriorates if stored for a considerable period in the East, only stocks in transit to ports and awaiting shipment are held in producing countries. Exports, in consequence, vary with output, and stocks outside the producing areas absorb the discrepancies between consumption and an output not easily controlled. The tendency for total stocks to move inversely to world consumption, after allowing for the marked upward trend in both series, is illustrated in Chart 27.

Chart 27

Crude Rubber: World Consumption and Stocks outside Regulated Areas

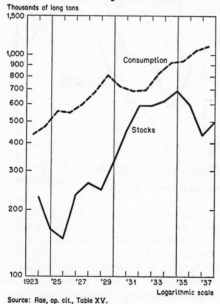

Source: Rae, op. cit., Table XV.

[16] Cf. Rae's description of the administrative problems involved in the operation of the scheme, op. cit., p. 355.

Finally, just as there is a close relation between United States and total consumption (the causal chain running from the former to the latter) so there is a close relation between United States stocks and world stocks (the causal chain running from the latter to the former) (Chart 28). The large rubber manufacturers of the United States are such big factors in the total market for rubber, and more especially in that for surplus rubber, that the absorption of unconsumed output would probably cause precipitous declines in price unless they were willing to take large portions of the excess supply.[17] Their ability to finance such holdings and their interest in the market makes such action natural.

Chart 28
Crude Rubber: World Stocks and Stocks in and afloat for the United States
End of Year, 1923-1937

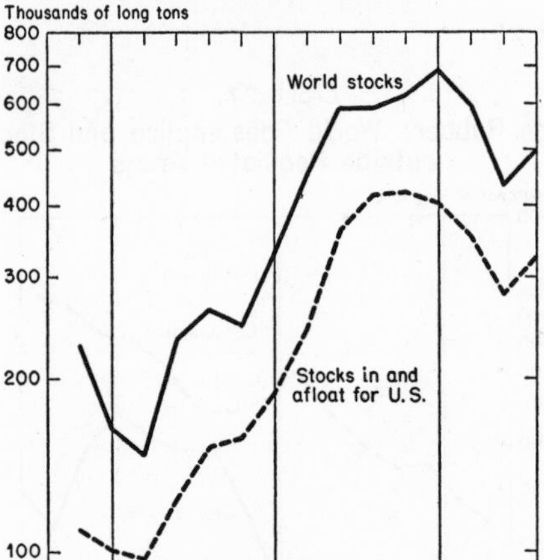

Thousands of long tons

World stocks from Rae, op. cit., Table XV.

[17] Rae writes (op. cit., p. 331) : "It seems likely that the majority of small and medium sized factories do not carry much more than their necessary working stocks. The large manufacturers, probably because of their greater commitments, must look further ahead and carry considerable stocks in addition to varying quantities of forward purchases. It would seem, therefore, that a great part of the rubber surplus to the necessary manufacturing requirements is in the hands of the larger manufacturers. The four big American manufacturers and one big British manufacturer are believed to account, between them, for nearly half the world absorption, although the buying of crude rubber by these five companies is competitive."

In short, the inverse correlation between manufacturers' stocks and consumption in the United States stems from the fact that the principal American manufacturers must themselves largely absorb the discrepancies between consumption and output that arise because of the sharp fluctuations in consumption and the sluggish response of production.

5 Cottonseed at Oil Mills

In the above examples, we found that raw materials stocks held by manufacturers tended to move together with the consumption of materials when there was a buffer stock to absorb the difference between supply and consumption. We would expect the same result when the output of the material can be adjusted rapidly to changes in demand. Cottonseed held by crushing mills is a case of a somewhat different sort. Again stocks held by fabricators move together with manufacturing activity, but this time for different reasons. Manufacturers keep a stock of raw materials that rises and falls with their output not because the supply of raw materials can be adjusted to the rate at which it is consumed, but because fluctuations in the rate of fabrication are dominated by conditions of raw material supply.

The movements in the size of the cotton crop closely resemble those in the production of crude cottonseed oil (Chart 29). Since short-term fluctuations in the cotton crop are influenced largely by the weather, this close resemblance must be due to the stimulus given by a large and cheap supply of seed.

Cottonseed, cheap and bulky, is less expensive to store after being pressed into oil. When the cotton crop is big, farmers and ginners sell large quantities of seed to avoid the cost of storage, and the crushers promptly convert the seed to oil. A larger than normal crop means that crushers hold a larger than normal stock of seed during the harvesting season and produce a larger than normal quantity of oil during the ensuing year.[18] These observations are

[18] "The bulk of a cottonseed crop is marketed within the months of September, October and November, when two-thirds of a season's crush is normally bought by the mills. From the beginning of the season, August, to the end of December, the mills must buy and receive from 80 to 85 percent of the crop, for generally neither the farmers nor the ginners are properly equipped to store and care for the seed. The cost of warehousing is a necessary and sizable expense

Chart 29
Cotton Crop, Crude Cottonseed Oil Production,
and Stocks of Cottonseed at Mills, Crop Years

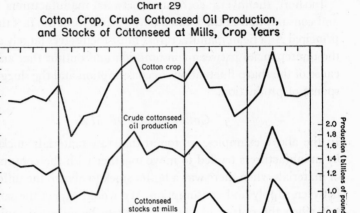

Logarithmic scales

illustrated in Chart 29 by annual data and confirmed by measures
made from monthly data. The National Bureau index of cottonseed stocks conformed perfectly to 5 cycles in oil production 1920-
40. The high degree of similarity in the average cycle patterns in
Chart 30 are consistent with the explanation given above.

A word about the probable relation of this stock to business
cycles is now in order. In the cases of the other commodities studied in this chapter, the rate of consumption of the raw material is
governed largely by influences from the side of demand. Cotton
consumption, for example, depends largely upon the demand for
cotton goods, and fluctuates with business activity. Thus to state
the relation between raw cotton stocks at mills and cotton consumption is also to state, at least approximately, their relation to
business cycles. In the present instance, however, this is not true.
Cottonseed oil production, as we have just seen, rises and falls with
the availability of its raw material rather than with demand. And

connected with handling cottonseed, and this tends to force the products on
the markets regardless of current demand." *Cottonseed and Its Products,* National Cottonseed Products Association, Feb. 1937, pp. 20-1.

Chart 30
Cottonseed Stocks at Mills and Crude Cottonseed Oil Production
Average Patterns during 5 Production Cycles, 1920-1940

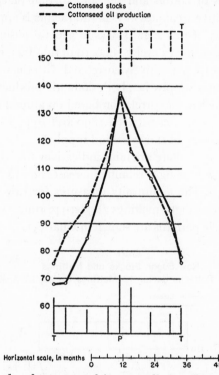

—— Cottonseed stocks
---- Cottonseed oil production

Horizontal scale, in months

since the supply of cottonseed is controlled entirely by the size of crops, it can hardly have regular relation to business cycles.[19]

6 Raw Sugar Stocks at Refineries

Raw sugar resembles the commodities already reviewed in that it is a farm product whose output is not readily adjusted to demand in the short-run. However, it need not be refined immediately. In consequence, though United States refineries absorb a major part of the sugar crops of this country, Cuba, Hawaii, Puerto Rico, and the Philippines, the size of the crops in these areas does not control the rate of sugar refining to the degree that the crop of cottonseed controls the production of cottonseed oil.

[19] The conformity measures for cottonseed stocks at mills run −20, −33, −60, but this apparent indication of inverse correlation can reflect only the accidental course of cotton crops during 1918-38, the period to which the figures apply.

In these circumstances, the behavior of stocks of raw sugar at United States refineries bears a certain similarity to that of total, not mill, stocks of cotton and silk and to that of crude rubber stocks. The relative weakness of demand factors is apparent in the slight conformity of raw sugar stocks to general business activity: conformity indexes for 13 cycles 1890-1938 run +23, 0, —8. Sugar stocks, in contrast, are positively correlated with the movements of total United States supply, i.e., both domestic production and imports. The coefficient of correlation based on annual directions of change in these two series between 1890 and 1939 is +.38, allowing for a 6-month lag of stocks behind supply.[20]

At the same time, there are faint indications that stocks tend to be drawn down when sugar refining increases and to pile up when refining declines. The conformity measures for raw sugar stocks during 10 cycles of sugar meltings 1891-1940 run —20, —9, —20. The average cycle patterns are shown in Chart 31.

Chart 31
Raw Sugar Stocks and Meltings
Average Patterns during 10 Meltings Cycles, 1893-1940

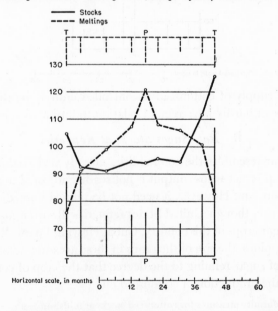

———— Stocks
— — — Meltings

20 The index would be somewhat higher if we omitted the years of World War I and its aftermath when stocks were virtually exhausted, then rebuilt.

7 Crude Petroleum

From commodities that are products of agriculture we turn to materials that have their source in mining or manufacturing operations. The supply of the first of these, crude oil, has in the past been marked by circumstances of the same inflexible and fortuitous character as makes the adjustment of agricultural output to demand so difficult and sluggish. The direct cost of producing crude oil, once a successful well has been sunk, is very low and under certain conditions may be negative, for the pools of oil underlying the wells of different firms are connected. Hence unless an entire field curtails production, individual firms who do curtail are, in effect, despoiled of their assets. Deliberate downward adjustments of supply to demand are, therefore, dependent upon cooperative action, which did not assume effective form until the 'thirties. Fluctuations in supply, in addition, have been seriously influenced by the more or less accidental discoveries of new oil fields and their exploitation. As we shall see, a good part of the movements of stocks can be traced to the sudden increases in output when new areas are opened.

Other salient characteristics of the industry are that stocks held on petroleum producing properties are very small and that the oil commonly passes into the ownership of the refining companies when it leaves the producing property. A considerable portion of the oil wells, of course, are owned by the refining companies. Stocks held on producing properties east of California, for example, have typically accounted for about 3 percent of the total stock in that area. It seems valid, therefore, to treat the total stock of petroleum as a stock owned by the refineries.

The relation between stocks and petroleum consumption in refineries reflects the accidental timing of oil field discoveries and the sluggish, even perverse, response of the rate of exploitation to changes in demand. Chart 32 shows the cycle patterns of crude petroleum consumption between 1917 and 1938 and the patterns of petroleum stocks during consumption cycles. The absence of a close relation between stocks and consumption, confirmed by conformity indexes of 0, 0, and $+14$ during 4 consumption cycles 1917-38, can be explained by developments during the various consumption cycles.

Chart 32
Petroleum Stocks at Refineries and Crude Petroleum Consumption
Patterns during Consumption Cycles

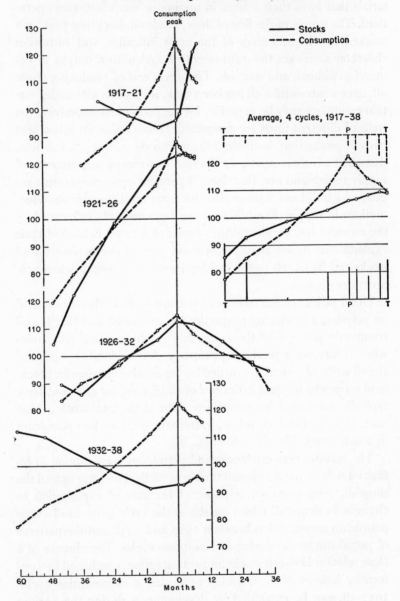

The first cycle, from December 1917 to August 1921, is the only one of the four for which we have records that was free not only from the effects of the discovery and exploitation of large new fields but also from the influence of industry or governmental attempts to regulate competition in the production of crude oil. The pattern of stocks is clearly inverse to that of consumption.

The second cycle, August 1921 to February 1926, was dominated by the output of new fields. Of the 260 million barrel increase in the output of crude oil in the United States between 1921 and 1923, almost all came from new areas. Discoveries in the Los Angeles Basin raised the output in that region 170 million barrels, from 35 million in 1921 to 205 million in 1923; 30 million barrels more came from the new Smackover area of Arkansas. After reaching a high point in 1923, production in the Los Angeles area declined and in 1925, the peak of the consumption cycle, was some 50 million barrels lower. Total production was maintained, however, by further exploitation of the Smackover area, which produced 42 million barrels more in 1925 than in 1923, and by the opening of the West Texas field, which produced nothing in 1923 but yielded 10 million barrels in 1925. Thus the rise of stocks during the expansion of consumption from 1921 to 1925 may be laid to new fields. In the short contraction that followed, July 1925 to February 1926, consumption declined little. It is to this fact, together with the absence of striking new discoveries, that we may attribute the leveling off of stocks in this period.

The growth of stocks during the following expansion in consumption, February 1926 to October 1929, again reflects the influence of discoveries. Both the West Texas field and the newly discovered Seminole Field in Oklahoma began to produce large quantities in 1927. The Los Angeles Basin, which had been producing approximately 150 million barrels per year from 1924 through 1928, suddenly jumped to 208 million barrels in 1929. The production of these three fields together was some 278 million barrels higher in 1929 than in 1925; total United States production increased only 208 million barrels.

It is difficult to say to what extent the decrease in stocks during the contraction in consumption from 1929 to 1932 reflects a normal contraction of supply in response to a decline in demand.

In part, the smaller output is due to a natural decline after the flush production in the new fields which ended in 1929. Exploration and investment in new areas also were probably curtailed. In part, the control of production enforced by martial law in Oklahoma and Texas, and applied as well in Kansas, was effective.

In the subsequent expansion of consumption stocks declined. Again it is not clear whether output could not be increased as fast as consumption or whether the control of output, effective since 1934 under the federal conservation program, was a more inportant influence. That the control did not operate swiftly enough to prevent stocks from rising during the 1937-38 contraction is probably significant.

To extract lessons of general significance from the record of crude petroleum stocks is obviously difficult. Accidental changes in the supply situation and voluntary and governmental control of production influenced the course of events too markedly in the period under review to permit much insight into the forces that would rule the industry in the absence of these factors, or into those that may rule if cooperative or governmental regulation of output becomes more effective.

8 Newsprint at Publishers

Newsprint held by publishers is our only clear case of a raw material supplied from relatively nearby sources and produced by manufacturers who can expand or contract their rate of output readily. Since manufacturers also keep stocks of paper which they draw down or allow to accumulate to meet changes in demand, and since the price of newsprint is exceptionally stable, stocks held by consumers of newsprint would seem to be susceptible of management in accord with publishers' views of the requirements of manufacturing convenience. We would expect to find stocks rising and falling in close company with newsprint consumption.

Such, however, is not the case. Publishers' stocks of newsprint do move up and down with newsprint consumption, but only with an extraordinarily long lag. Stocks lagged behind consumption at each of four peaks and four troughs of consumption; the average lag at peaks was 10.5 months, and the average lag at troughs, 9.5 months. If a 10-month lag at both peaks and troughs is allowed for, the conformity of stocks to cycles of consumption is indicated by indexes that run +50, +100, +100. Chart 33 shows the average pattern of stocks during consumption cycles with stocks advanced 10 months. Parallel with it is the average pattern of stocks during consumption cycles without allowance for lag. Apparently the lag of stocks is so long as to produce almost completely inverted behavior. That the true relation of stocks to consumption, however, is that of a laggard reaction in the same direction rather than an inverse relation is suggested by the lower conformity yielded by synchronous analysis: 0, —50, —43, and this belief is strengthened when we consider the marketing arrangements in the industry.

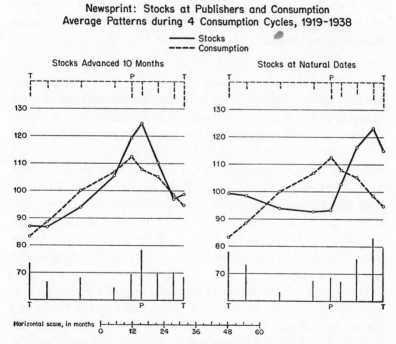

Chart 33
Newsprint: Stocks at Publishers and Consumption
Average Patterns during 4 Consumption Cycles, 1919-1938

The long lag of stocks behind consumption has a simple explanation. Newsprint is purchased on long-term contract. Cranston Williams, General Manager of the Newspaper Publishers Association writes, May 24, 1942:

". . . The general practise is that newsprint contracts are made for a certain annual amount of tonnage, the shipments to be made in equal monthly installments to the publisher.

As a rule, newsprint contracts are made in the fall of the year and run on a calendar-year basis.

Any deviations from the general practises . . . are a matter between purchaser and seller."[21]

The contracts are not an absolute bar to changes in the rate of newsprint shipments within a given year. Presumably, mills will accept orders for additional supplies, within their capacity, thus affording some flexibility to supply in an upward direction. And there is probably some margin of expected current demand not covered by annual contract which may afford some flexibility in either direction. But since annual contracts are the rule and since they generally begin, and therefore end, at the same time, the rapidity with which publishers' receipts of newsprint can respond to changes in consumption must be seriously reduced. The result is the long lag of stocks.

9   *Iron Ore Stocks at Blast Furnaces and at Lower Lake Ports*

Iron ore stocks are, in some ways, the most interesting of the commodities in our sample. They have the singular and paradoxical virtue of illustrating the effect on raw material stocks of a supply that can be readily adjusted to changes in demand and of one that can hardly be adjusted at all. The explanation lies in the fact that ore is transported principally over the Great Lakes. Additional quantities can, therefore, be brought to the furnaces in the quantities desired during the months when the Lakes are open to navigation. During the winter months, however, the Lakes are blocked with ice, and supply to the furnaces is almost completely inflexible. This fact is the key to an inventory behavior otherwise peculiar and puzzling.

Iron ore is mined mainly in the Lake Superior region and, as said above, brought by freighter through the Great Lakes and thence by railroad to furnaces in Ohio, Pennsylvania, and Illinois.[22] Ore mined in this area is stocked chiefly at three points—at

---

[21] The Federal Trade Commission, Report on the Newsprint Paper Industry, 1930, found that the contracts of the larger newsprint manufacturers ran even longer. About half were for five years or longer, but it is not clear—and it seems improbable—that the longer contracts call for deliveries at constant monthly rates during their entire life.

[22] The states comprising this iron-mining region—Minnesota, Michigan, and Wisconsin—produce about 85 percent of all the iron ore mined in the United

the mine, on the Lake Erie and Lake Michigan receiving docks, and at the blast furnaces (Table 45).

TABLE 45

Consumption and Stocks of Lake Superior Iron Ore
(thousands of long tons)

	1920	1921	1929	1932	1937
Consumption, mo. av.[a]	4531	2029	5304	857	
Stocks					
At furnaces, mo. av.[a]	21211	24512	24577	27744	
On Lake Erie docks, mo. av.[a]	8542	8818	3033	5425	
At mines, Dec. 31[b]	10367	12574	6108	16408	5261

[a] From Lake Superior Iron Ore Association as reported in *Survey of Current Business,* annual supplements.
[b] From Bureau of Mines as reported in *Mineral Resources* and *Minerals Yearbook.*

Stocks are evidently large in comparison with consumption. At the furnaces they constituted about 5 months' supply on the average in the two good years, 1920 and 1929. In the poor year, 1921, the furnaces held a supply equal to twelve times their monthly consumption, and in the worst year, 1932, stocks covered monthly consumption 30 times. On the docks, stocks are lower, varying between 1 and 2 months' supply in good years to 5 months' supply in bad years. Stocks at the mines cannot be compared as easily with consumption since we have figures only for December 31, but apparently they are in an intermediate position between holdings at furnaces and at docks.

The total holdings of Lake Superior ore relative to its rate of consumption are probably understated somewhat. Some ore is landed at Lake Michigan ports and a supply of ore is kept at these points. If the average size of this supply is in the same proportion to receipts of ore at Lake Michigan ports as the holdings on Lake Erie docks are to receipts at Erie ports, the holdings at docks should be raised about 25 percent. And some ore, finally, is in transit by land and, in summer, by water from the mines to the furnaces.

These figures do not cover all the iron ore held in the United

States, and almost 95 percent of the ore mined outside Alabama. Since most of the Alabama ore is used in the South, the Lake Superior region is the only supplying region of importance for the major pig-iron producing region— Pennsylvania, Ohio, and Illinois. Imports from abroad have been negligible.

States. About 15 percent is produced outside the Lake Superior region. In 1937 other mines held 265 thousand tons; Lake Superior mines 5.5 million tons; pig iron produced in the South, made largely from iron ore mined in Alabama, was some 15 percent of the national total. Ore held at the southern furnaces may, therefore, be substantial. Unfortunately, data on these holdings are not available. But the figures at hand cover most American iron ore holdings. Our discussion is confined to stocks at lower lake ports and at furnaces, categories of ore that presumably have passed into the ownership of pig iron manufacturers.

IRON ORE CONSUMPTION AND STOCKS

Iron ore is moved from the mines by railroad to Lake Superior ports, thence by freighter to ports on the southern shores of Lake Erie, and, in smaller quantity, to those of Lake Michigan. From these docks, where relatively small but still substantial stocks are kept, the ore goes to the furnaces where the accumulation is largest. These piles at furnaces and on the docks are the stocks from which the furnaces directly draw their supplies.

Chart 34 shows the standing of these stocks in the form of monthly averages for calendar years,[23] and the average monthly consumption of iron ore. The inverse relation between stocks and consumption is marked. Total stocks and stocks at furnaces, which dominate the total, were lower at the end than at the beginning of every expansion in consumption (white areas); they were higher at the end than at the beginning of every contraction (shaded areas). In only 4 of the 20 years did consumption and stocks at furnaces change in the same direction. For total stocks there were only three similar movements.

The tendency to inverse conformity is hardly less strong in the movements of stocks on Lake Erie docks. In only 3 of the 20 years did consumption and stocks move in the same direction. But since stocks were higher at the end of one expansion, 1919-20, and lower at the end of one contraction, 1923-24, than they were at the beginning, the National Bureau standard conformity measure could not indicate perfect inverse conformity.

While the tendency to inverse conformity is clear in the an-

[23] Figures for stocks on Lake Michigan docks are not available.

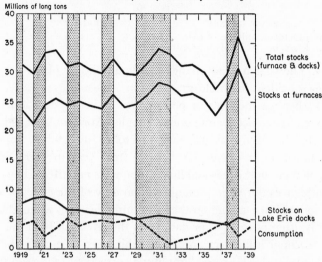

Chart 34
Iron Ore: Stocks at Furnaces and on Lake Erie Docks
and Consumption, Monthly Averages

Shaded areas indicate periods of contraction in consumption; white areas, expansion.

nual data, the reasons are more complex than usual, and to understand them we must study the monthly figures.

A peculiar method of studying monthly iron ore stocks is dictated by the character of the seasonal fluctuations in furnace and dock stocks. At blast furnaces stocks regularly reach a seasonal peak in October or November just before navigation on the Great Lakes closes for the winter and further shipments from Minnesota and Michigan are blocked. During the winter the stock pile is reduced by consumption and reaches a seasonal low in April or May depending upon the date when Lake shipments again become feasible. Stocks on Lake Erie docks follow a closely similar pattern. Only in 1932 was this pattern not followed with fidelity in either series. The movements from April to October are large both absolutely and as a proportion of the average stocks carried, and the movements of stocks at furnaces are substantially larger than those on docks by either method of measurement (Table 46).

The crucial peculiarity of these intra-annual fluctuations is that they are subject to changes in the amplitude of their swings and that these changes are themselves closely correlated with business

TABLE 46

Iron Ore Stocks, Average Seasonal Fluctuations, 1918-1939

AVERAGE CHANGE	AT FURNACES	ON DOCKS
1) April-October, millions of tons	+14.9	+2.1
2) April-October, as % of av. monthly stocks	+58.9	+34.5

cycles. The year to year change in the amplitude of the seasonal swings is evident in Table 47.

Whether we measure in percentages or in physical units, the average change between seasonal troughs, April to April, is larger than that between seasonal peaks, October to October, implying that the seasonal swings vary in size from year to year. Now if these changes in the seasonal fluctuation were not affected by cyclical influences but were a manifestation only of the effect of some noncyclical force acting on the intra-annual swing, we might reasonably attempt to free our data from the effects of both the ordinary seasonal influences and those which act to modify the seasonal amplitude. Kuznets' 'amplitude correction' factor—a measure of the degree to which the amplitude of the seasonal swing in a given year differs from the normal amplitude—is a well known device for accomplishing this and was used in an early analysis of the series.[24]

TABLE 47

Iron Ore Stocks, Average Annual Changes, 1918-1939

	AT FURNACES	AT FURNACES & ON DOCKS
April-April		
Millions of tons	3.9	4.6
As % of preceding year	22.3	22.6
October-October		
Millions of tons	2.0	2.1
As % of preceding year	6.2	3.4

In this instance, however, the amplitudes of the intra-annual movements are not uncorrelated with cyclical influences. Chart

[24] To calculate the factor for a given year, one computes the regression coefficient of the relative deviations of the original data from their annual average on the deviations of the ordinary seasonal index from 100. The deviations of the seasonal indexes from 100 are then multiplied by the coefficient to provide corrected indexes that take account of the abnormal character of the seasonal swing.

35 shows the amplitude correction factors for stocks at furnaces plotted against the consumption of iron ore, 1919-34. The two series agree almost perfectly in direction of movement, and there is even considerable similarity in the relative size of the fluctuations.

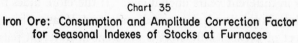

Chart 35
Iron Ore: Consumption and Amplitude Correction Factor
for Seasonal Indexes of Stocks at Furnaces

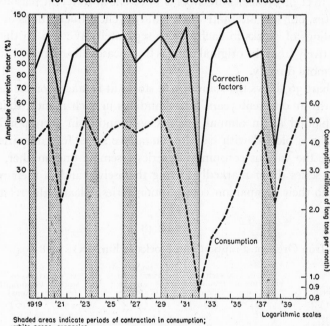

Shaded areas indicate periods of contraction in consumption; white areas, expansion.

If the seasonal amplitude changes cyclically, as Chart 35 indicates, the effect of cyclical influences upon the standing of stocks must be different at different seasons (or in different months). This must be true with respect to either the amplitude or the direction of the seasonal movement; for clearly a wider intra-annual swing in years of good than of bad business must mean one of two things: (a) the standings of stocks at the seasonal troughs and those at seasonal peaks have moved in different directions from prosperity to depression or (b) they have moved in the same direction but by different amounts.

The elimination of seasonal influences, when changes in seasonal amplitude are allowed for, must, in such a case, hide certain essential features of the cyclical fluctuations, for it would remove or distort the effect of cyclical influences on seasonal changes. The application of a constant seasonal index, on the other hand, leaves the relation between the standings of our series in the same months in different years unchanged.[25] It therefore hides nothing we wish to study; but it does not do any good. If, as we now know, the effect of cyclical influences is different in different seasons or months, our sole alternative is to study cyclical fluctuations in the standings of stocks in each month separately. We can do this as effectively from the original data as from seasonally corrected data, and more directly.

Chart 36 shows the standings of stocks at furnaces for the same months in different years. The standings in each month, that is, are plotted as an annual series. Consumption in corresponding months is plotted with each of the above series for comparison. While the various consumption series resemble one another, the stock series differ markedly among themselves and in their relation to their companion consumption series. Clearly the relation

TABLE 48

Iron Ore Consumption and Stocks at Furnaces, 1918-1940

MONTH	NO. OF YEARS WHEN DIRECTION OF CHANGE WAS The same	Different	NO. OF YEARS WITH NO CHANGE IN STOCKS[a]	AV. DEVIATIONS OF Stocks (millions of tons)	Consumption
(1)	(2)	(3)	(4)	(5)	(6)
November	16	5	1	2.1	1.2
December	13	9		1.7	1.3
January	6	15		1.9	1.3
February	2	19		2.4	1.2
March	3	18		3.3	1.4
April	7	15		3.9	1.3
May	3	18	1	3.1	1.3
June	2	19	1	2.1	1.2
July	4	18		1.6	1.3
August	6	16		1.7	1.3
September	10	12		1.8	1.3
October	12	7	3	2.0	1.3

[a] Consumption changed in every year.

[25] That is, the relative differences are unchanged if the seasonal correction is accomplished by multiplying or dividing the original data for the same months in different years by the same factor. The absolute differences are unchanged if the correction involves the addition or subtraction of a constant number.

Chart 36

Iron Ore: Stocks at Furnaces and Consumption, Annual Data by Months

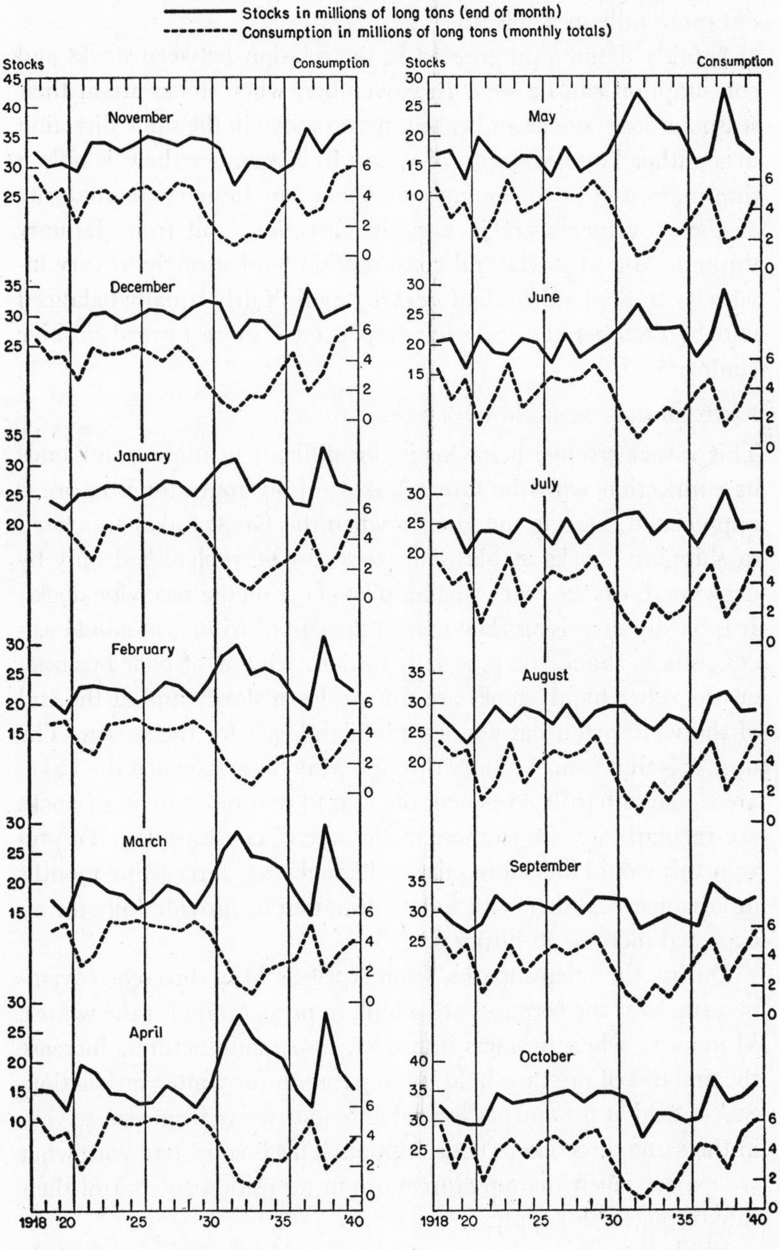

————— Stocks in millions of long tons (end of month)
---------- Consumption in millions of long tons (monthly totals)

between stocks of iron ore at furnaces and the cyclical fluctuations in consumption depends upon the season of the year, as is brought out more fully in Table 48.

A fairly definite progression in the relation between stocks and consumption can be seen. In November, when stocks are at their seasonal peak, stocks and consumption move in the same direction in a rather large majority of years. In December there is only a slim majority of conforming movements, in January the majority of the movements are in opposite direction, and from January through August stocks and consumption tend strongly to vary inversely. In September the forces are again fairly equally balanced and by October the scale has tipped once more toward positive conformity.

FACTORS INFLUENCING CYCLES IN STOCKS

This rather strange behavior is not difficult to understand once its connection with the Great Lakes supply route for iron ore is appreciated. During the months when the Great Lakes are closed to shipping, stocks at blast furnaces can be replenished only by drawing down the much smaller piles of ore on the receiving docks. It is hardly surprising then that at the end of winters of good business, stocks should be especially low. In winters of poor business, on the other hand, stocks are drawn down slowly and at the end of the winter stand at abnormally high levels for the season. The upshot is that from January through May, months when the Lakes are closed or hardly reopened, the year to year movements of stocks are regularly inverse to those of the rate of consumption. To prevent this would indeed require rather accurate forecasting months in advance, together with a determination to provide fully for an expected increase in business.

During the open months, from April or May through November, stocks at the furnaces are rebuilt in preparation for the winter. Moreover, when business improves, iron manufacturers increase the amount of ore they hold in preparation for winter production. Stocks held at the end of November tend to move from year to year in the same direction as consumption. This is consistent with what we expect when manufacturers are in a position to control their rate of materials supply.

While these inventory preparations during the open season help manufacturers to carry on their business from the close of navigation until the ice goes out, the extent of the preparation is not sufficient to prevent the annual changes of stocks between one closed season and the next from being inversely related to consumption changes. Indeed, the annual change in stocks between the same spring months of different years—after navigation has been closed for some months—is typically larger than that from November to November (Table 48). The average deviation of stocks in November from the mean level for that month is 2.1 million tons. It is somewhat lower, though not very different, from December through February. In March, however, the average deviation is 3.3 million tons, in April, 3.9, and in May, 3.1. It is these relatively large fluctuations of stocks in months when the relation between stocks and consumption is normally inverse that dominates the annual stocks figures and causes them also to move inversely (Chart 34).

This suggests that to meet the difficulty caused by ice on the Lakes, the manufacturers depend only partly on their ability to anticipate business changes during the winter by varying the level of stocks accumulated by the close of navigation. Their main reliance is on the large reserve they accumulate by November every year. We have already seen what large stocks are normally kept at the furnaces (Chart 36). The adequacy of these stocks may be judged from the fact that in April 1920 when, after a winter of high consumption, stocks were lower than in any month covered by our data, furnaces still held a supply equal to 2.5 months' consumption at the rate then current. In addition, there remained as a last resort the stocks on Lake Erie and Lake Michigan docks, a substantial supply in itself. Since iron ore users can keep such large stocks, it is little wonder that they are content to allow them to be drawn down in winters of good business.

At first sight it is somewhat surprising that even in June, after the Lakes have been opened for some weeks, the relation between stocks and consumption is still inverse. And still more surprising that this should remain true through August. Not until September does this inverse relation disappear, and in October the evidence for positive conformity is still very weak.

Again the reason seems clear. Immediately following a winter of good business stocks are abnormally low. During the ensuing months they are gradually rebuilt. If stocks are low in May when the Lakes open, they will not be rebuilt in the next four weeks to normal June levels, though some progress will be made. If stocks are still low in June they will not be rebuilt in the next four weeks to normal July levels, and so on. It is, therefore, quite consistent with the relatively large fluctuations in stocks during the winter and early spring months that the effects of these large variations are not overcome until early autumn.

If this explanation is correct, one would expect to find that the variation in stocks between the same months in different years becomes smaller as the year proceeds through spring and summer, and larger again in the autumn as the influence of the current and expected rate of consumption makes itself felt. This is, in fact, what we find. The average deviation of stocks is highest in April, 3.9 million tons; by May it has fallen to 3.1 million tons; in June it is 2.1, in July 1.6, in August 1.7. From this point, it rises to a second peak, 2.1 million tons, in November.

For similar reasons it is not surprising that, at the end of December after the Lakes have been closed for four weeks, stocks at furnaces still move in the same direction as consumption in a majority of years. But their amplitude in this month (the average deviation is 1.7 million tons), is lower than at the seasonal peak in November (2.1 million tons). This argument is completed in a formal sense by noting that in column 6 of Table 48 there are no comparable changes in the amplitude of consumption cycles, each month taken separately.

For a longer period, since 1887, figures for stocks held on Lake Erie docks at the opening and closing of navigation (that is, approximately on April 30 and November 30) confirm the findings for furnace stocks. Stocks held at the opening of navigation, about April 30, moved in the same direction as consumption in only 15 of 57 years. This represents a somewhat stronger tendency to inverse conformity than may be apparent at first sight since both stocks and consumption were subject to a strong upward trend from the beginning of the period until about 1918. On the other hand, the tendency for stocks held at the close of navigation to vary in the same direction as consumption is undoubtedly weaker in the case of stocks held on docks than in the case of furnace stocks. Despite the similarity of trend, stocks and consumption moved in the same direction in only 32 years. There can be little doubt, however, about the significance of the difference in behavior between stocks held at the opening and closing of navigation.

As in the case of furnace stocks, the difference in the amplitude of fluctuations in stocks held on docks at the opening and closing of navigation is striking. The average deviation was .46 million tons at the close of navigation and .74 million tons at the opening.[26]

Since 1918 similar figures were computed for the sum of stocks at furnaces and on Lake Erie docks for four months: April and May to represent the position at the opening of navigation, and October and November to represent the position at the close of navigation. The results are similar to those for furnace stocks alone. In 13 of the 22 years stocks in October moved in the same direction as consumption while in 2 additional years stocks did not change though consumption did. Between Novembers, stocks moved in the same direction as consumption in 17 of the 22 years. For April and May our findings were quite different. Between Aprils, stocks moved in the same direction as consumption in only 7 years; between Mays, in only 3 years.

The behavior of iron ore stocks is a striking illustration of how manufacturers' capacity to adjust the rate at which they receive raw materials affects the relation between cycles in inventories and in business. Cycles in the level of ore stocks held in months when the Lakes are closed to navigation, and for some months thereafter, move inversely to ore consumption. Stock cycles for months at the end of the open season, however, tend to vary directly with consumption. Thus iron ore stocks show the effects of both kinds of supply conditions which otherwise separately influence the behavior of individual commodities. Commodities whose rate of receipt cannot be adjusted readily to changes in requirements tend to vary inversely to consumption. Most commodities, however, appear to be supplied under conditions that do permit rapid change

[26] Because stocks on docks were influenced by a substantial trend factor, the average deviations were computed from the standings of a 9-point moving average, smoothed by a free hand curve.

in the rate of delivery to manufacturers. These, I think, will tend to vary directly with consumption.

10 Lead Stocks at Bonded Warehouses

During 1895-1918 the lead held at warehouses was imported largely from Mexico. Only a minor quantity was destined for consumption in this country; most of it came for processing in bond and re-export. Consequently, the series has a mixed character showing some of the attributes of a raw material, as we use the term, and some of the attributes of goods in process.

Although no direct evidence on the rate of consumption of these materials is available, withdrawals from bond have been estimated on the basis of imports and changes in stocks. Imports and withdrawals move in close conformity and with no significant difference in timing. I have, therefore, used directly recorded imports rather than withdrawals to measure activity. The latter are not only based on estimates, but measure a stage later than the processing of raw materials, just as imports record an earlier stage. The fact that imports and withdrawals from bond reach cyclical peaks and troughs at about the same time is presumptive evidence that the same is true of the rate of refining in bond, which would be a better measure of consumption.

The conformity of stocks to cycles of imports was high. Conformity indexes for 3 cycles 1896-1916 run +100, +100, +100. Stocks, moreover, give evidence of a tendency to lag behind turns in manufacturing activity, as far as the latter can be judged from imports. (This is, of course, consistent with our expectation about the behavior of the stock of an imported material produced by mining or manufacturing.) Including incomplete cycles at the beginning and end of the series, turns of stocks can be observed at nine turns in imports. According to the cycle patterns, stocks reached a trough or peak later than imports on five occasions and turned in the same stage four times. Stocks never led. This tendency to lag is confirmed by the average patterns in Chart 37 which shows stocks reaching a trough in stage II of imports cycles and a peak in stage VI.

Timing comparisons made in the National Bureau's usual fashion, that is, by comparing the months when stocks and imports

Chart 37
Lead: Stocks at Warehouses and Imports
Average Patterns during 3 Import Cycles, 1896-1916

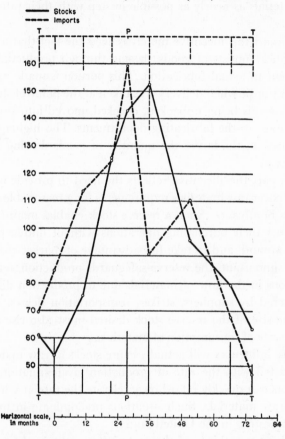

reach peaks or troughs, also suggest a tendency for stocks to lag. Of 5 comparisons at peaks, stocks lagged twice, led twice, and turned synchronously once. At troughs, they lagged in 3 of 4 comparisons and led once. The average lag at both peaks and troughs was 3 months.

11 Recapitulation

The analysis of these cases is a far less adequate basis for generalization than one could wish. But a more adequate basis does not exist today. The description and explanation of the cyclical behavior of stocks of raw materials that seems to me most consistent

with the evidence may be summarized in the following fashion:
1) Manufacturers have a strong incentive to keep their stock of
raw materials as nearly as possible in step with their rate of production.

a) In part this incentive merely reflects the fact that a portion
of the stock consists of goods passing through production stages
antecedent to actual fabrication. This portion is made up of (i)
goods in transit when delivery was taken at the point of shipment,
and (ii) goods being unpacked, checked, moved into storage, or
from storage to the fabricating departments. The higher the rate
of production, the larger the quantity of goods flowing through
these stages.

b) In part the incentive reflects the need to provide a reserve
stock to cover raw materials requirements for a reasonable number
of weeks in advance. Such a reserve stock enables manufacturers
to conduct their purchasing operations without undue pressure,
to shop around, and to take full advantage of market conditions.
Equally important, the reserve safeguards production against interruptions in the flow of materials due to production difficulties
encountered by suppliers, strikes, transportation delays, and the
like. The size of the reserve stock desired must also rise and fall
with the rate of consumption of materials.

2) These influences will actually cause stocks of raw materials to
rise and fall with the rate of production in all situations where
processors can quickly retard or accelerate the rate at which they
receive raw materials. Such situations predominate in manufacturing industries in the United States.

a) About two-thirds of the materials are obtained from other
domestic manufacturing or mining industries. Such industries can
usually increase output rapidly, they usually keep a stock of finished goods ready for shipment, and unless transport is by water,
they can deliver goods to suppliers within a few days or a few
weeks.

b) The ultimate supply of other commodities—those of agricultural or foreign origin—is less flexible. But in many cases, dealers'
stocks are adequate to make up for deficiencies and to absorb surpluses.

3) Even when manufacturers can easily control their receipts of

materials, stocks are unlikely to rise and fall synchronously with production. A firm will not immediately alter its level of purchases with each dip in requirements, and time is required for a reduction in purchases to be reflected in smaller arrivals of merchandise. Stocks of raw materials are, therefore, likely to lag behind production in the firms holding the stocks. I have estimated the length of such lags to be two or three months.

4) When commodities are imported or procured under long-term contract, the lag of stocks will be much longer. This tends to lengthen the lag of total stocks of materials.

5) When commodities are of agricultural origin and no buffer stock held by dealers is available, manufacturers' stocks must absorb the haphazard fluctuations in supply caused by weather and pests. Such stocks will fluctuate irregularly during business cycles and introduce a minor random element into the movements of manufacturers' total stocks of raw materials.

CHAPTER 11

Finished Goods Made from Nonagricultural Materials

Manufacturers' stocks ready for delivery to customers, which I call 'finished goods', are the third of the three main classes of inventories. Between World Wars I and II, they probably constituted about 40 percent of manufacturers' total stocks. Goods in process, it will be recalled, made up about 20 percent and raw materials the remaining 40 percent.

From the viewpoint of their characteristic behavior during business cycles, the finished goods category is composed of several distinct classes of stocks. One obvious distinction is between goods made to order and 'to stock' or 'for the market' that is, goods not produced against specific orders. Goods made to order, it will be seen, are likely to rise and fall in close company with production and shipments. The behavior of goods made to stock is less simply described. Our data are largely for staples that can be stored for long periods without serious physical deterioration or loss of value because of style changes. Even among staples, there are at least two subclasses. The distinction turns upon the character of the forces that govern production cycles. The production of most goods moves largely in response to cycles in demand. Production, though following demand closely, is allowed to run behind shipments during most of the upswing and to outrun shipments during most of the downswing. Stocks, consequently, tend to move inversely to the rate of manufacturing activity and to business cycles.

For a less important group of commodities the rate of fabrication is more largely influenced, at least in the short-run, by impulses from the side of raw material supply which originate independently of demand. This may happen in the processing of farm products that cannot be stored in unfabricated form. The timing of cycles in the stocks of such processed goods tends to be governed by that of cycles in the output of the raw material. But since crop cycles are usually independent of business cycles, either no regular relation can be discerned between stocks and business cycles or stocks show some tendency toward inverse conformity overlaid by many irregular movements. The outcome depends partly upon whether the fabricated product is perishable and partly upon other factors.

While these distinctions can be shown to be consistent with the evidence, they do not comprise all the main classes that need to be recognized. As said above, production cycles in most manufacturing industries are dominated by influences from the side of demand. Stocks of finished goods held by such industries are likely to vary inversely to business cycles, provided the goods are staples and provided they are made to stock. It seems unlikely, however, that manufacturers will allow perishable goods, even if made to stock, to pile up for long when demand is slumping. Manufacturers of items the demand for which depends upon style and fashion probably take drastic steps to liquidate stocks when demand begins to fall. Without excluding the possibility of a moderate lag, stocks of such goods are likely to move up and down with business, being expanded when demand is brisk and quickly cut to avoid loss when demand falls.

We have distinguished the following classes among stocks of finished goods:

1 Goods made to order
2 Goods made to stock
  a Production cycles governed by demand
    i Perishables
    ii Durable staples
  b Production cycles governed by the supply of raw materials
    i Perishables
    ii Durable staples

Of these classes evidence of a sort is available about all except 2, a, i: perishable goods made to stock whose production cycles are governed by demand. Goods made to order and other goods whose production cycles are governed by demand are discussed in this chapter. Commodities in which the supply of raw materials is an important determinant of production cycles are treated in Chapter 12.

1   Goods Made to Order

Goods are made to order in at least three kinds of situation. One arises when the varying specifications of different customers have to be met precisely. Machine tools (except for certain standard varieties) are an obvious example. Metal products whose dimensions and chemical composition must be exact are another. Goods are made to order also when the raw materials are durable but the fabricated product is perishable. Thus textiles may be stored economically for long periods in the form of fiber, yarn, or even cloth. Made up into women's dresses, however, the product must be sold before the rapid changes of fashion strip it of most of its value. A manufacturer of women's clothing will therefore make samples and perhaps a small stock to meet early orders. He will also venture to produce a certain stock against expected sales for items that are selling especially well. For the most part, however, he operates by producing rapidly against customers' orders. Finally, even quite standardized types of goods are made to order if they are very expensive and sold infrequently. Locomotives, for example, are produced only upon order.

Unfortunately, there is no evidence whereby the importance of the stocks of goods made to order can be accurately estimated. Very rough estimates suggest that only a small part of manufacturers' stocks is in this category. A large part of all manufacturing output, perhaps as much as half, is made to order. The inventory of finished goods held against this business, however, must be smaller. Generally speaking, once such goods are produced they are shipped promptly. Such stock as one finds may be attributed to early orders produced in a slack season for shipment later, to the time required to accumulate economical shipment units (say, freight car loads), to short delays in the availability of cars or other transportation facilities, and to the time required for transit when title passes at the purchaser's plant or locality. In terms of the number of weeks' supply on hand, stocks of goods made to order must be very small. These considerations, in conjunction with those determining the kinds of goods made to order, persuade me that stocks in this category constitute 15 to 25 percent of all finished goods inventories, or roughly 5 to 10 percent of manufacturers' total stocks. I guess the figure is nearer 5 than 10 percent.[1]

Stocks of finished goods made to order are likely to rise and fall with production and shipments; for, seasonal variations aside, production will not be undertaken long before the goods are due to be shipped.[2] Consequently, the higher the rate of production the larger will be the quantity of goods completed and awaiting shipment. In some cases, moreover, title to the goods will pass only upon delivery to the purchaser's establishment or city, not upon shipment from the maker's plant. In such circumstances, finished goods include goods in transit, and the higher the rate of manufacturing activity the larger the quantity of goods in transit.

Our records contain only one example of a stock of a commodity made to order, steel sheets. But it is instructive, for we can compare stocks of steel sheets made to order with those produced in anticipation of sale. Steel sheets, like many other finished rolled steel products, are made principally to customers' specifications. Purchasers prescribe the chemical composition of the steel and the physical dimensions of the goods they want. Production is, therefore, largely to order. The part that is made to stock consists presumably of sheets of standard sizes and grades.

We compare stocks of steel sheets made to order and for the market with each other and with the rates of shipment and production. The production and shipments series are composites combining goods made to order with those made to stock. As stated above, goods made to order predominate, but since sales of standard sheets probably parallel those of sheets made to order closely, it seems valid to compare stocks of sheets made for the market, as well as those made to order, with the production and shipments of steel sheets in general.

The conformity indexes for sheets made to order during 4 cycles

[1] The calculation on which this estimate is based is too rough to be worth presenting in detail. It involved a guess about the proportion of the value of product in each census industry that is made to order and an assumption that, on the average, goods made to order remain in stock two weeks between completion and delivery. It suggested that some 16 percent of all stocks of finished goods represented products made to order—equivalent to about 6 percent of manufacturers' total stocks.

[2] Production here and later is taken to be measured by output. Commodities do not form part of the stock of finished goods until they are in a form ready for shipment.

of shipments 1919-32 were +100, +100, +100; for sheets made
to stock, —50, —100, —100. Since output virtually parallels shipments, stocks clearly have the same relation to production as to
shipments. Cycles of stocks made to order conform positively to the
rate of manufacturing activity. Inventories of sheets made to stock,
however, like other examples of fabricated staples made for the
market, move inversely to the rate of activity (Chart 38).

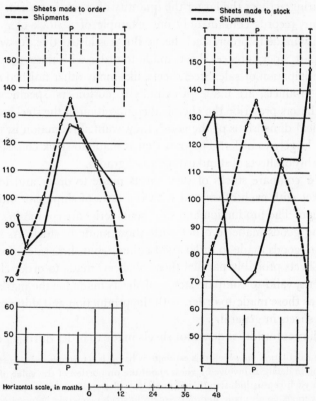

Chart 38
Steel Sheet Stocks and Shipments
Average Patterns during 4 Shipments Cycles, 1919-1932

2 *Staples Produced for the Market*

As stated above, stocks of staple goods made for the market tend
to move inversely to manufacturing activity when production
cycles are themselves largely governed by cycles in the demand for

goods. Moreover, since cycles in demand generally conform closely to business cycles, such stocks tend to move inversely to business cycles. These conditions probably hold good for a large majority of all manufactured staples. For commodities whose production cycles are controlled largely by supply conditions, however, stocks of finished goods tend to vary with cycles in production, which in turn may or may not bear some relation to cycles in demand. The relation of stocks to business cycles in the second case, therefore, depends partly upon the relation between business cycles and the underlying conditions of supply and partly upon the relative amplitudes of the supply-stimulated cycles in production and those in demand.

The distinction between goods with output cycles largely induced by demand conditions, on the one hand, and supply conditions, on the other, is doubtless the true general ground for differentiating between them. But as a practical matter, the distinction I draw initially is between goods made from farm and from nonfarm materials. Broadly speaking, short-run fluctuations in the fabrication of nonfarm products turn on the demand for them. The derived demand for the raw materials brings out the requisite supply. Raw materials grown on the farm, however, do not respond quickly to demand. On the contrary, supplies of materials tend to fluctuate independently of demand and, when they are perishable, greatly influence the rate at which they are processed.

That this is not a completely adequate approximation to the distinction required will become clear when the evidence on fabricated farm products is reviewed. Cycles in the supply of the underlying farm product do not always dominate the rate of fabrication. The distinction between farm and nonfarm products, however, serves fairly well to bring out the more important elements of the situation. In this chapter and the next I describe and analyze the behavior of stocks of these two kinds of goods.

SIZE OF THE CATEGORY

Since this is the largest category of finished products held by manufacturers, a notion of its size is essential. When industries whose products are made from agricultural materials and a few whose products are perishable though made from nonagricultural materials are excluded, the remainder comprises finished inventories, durable and staple and made from nonagricultural materials. At the end of 1939 these stocks were worth some $2.5 billion or about 63 percent of the value of stocks of finished goods.[3]

This percentage is on one count too small and on another too large to represent the broad class in which we are really interested—finished staples whose production cycles are dominated by changes in demand. It is too small because it excludes the products derived from agricultural materials whose production cycles nevertheless respond primarily to changes in demand.[4] The figure excludes products made from cotton, wool, silk, leather, and rubber. The value of finished inventories of staples fabricated from these materials was over $500 million in 1939.[5] Adding this to the previous figure raises the class to $3.0 billion or over 75 percent of finished goods—about 30 percent of manufacturers' total stocks.

The percentage is too high in that it includes finished goods made to order which, as indicated above, constitute 5 to 10 percent of total stocks. Thus I take it that the figure we are after lies between 20 and 25 percent of manufacturers' total stocks.

CONFORMITY TO CYCLES IN MANUFACTURING ACTIVITY AND BUSINESS

Table 49 shows the conformity indexes of stocks of 18 commodities to cycles in manufacturing activity. In most cases, activity is measured by shipments, in a few cases by production, in one case by manufacturers' receipts of the raw material. Fifteen commodities appear to conform inversely, as judged by the sign of the full cycle index. Rubber tires and tubes, however, are not completely qualified members of the class, for they include stocks on consignment to dealers in addition to finished goods in the hands of manufacturers. Of the remaining 16 series, 14 have negative full cycle in-

---

[3] See App. E. Most goods subject to the risk of changes in style are made from agricultural materials—cotton, wool, silk, leather, etc.

[4] They respond to demand because the raw materials from which they are made can be stored economically when demand slumps or crops are very large. Similarly, large stocks of raw materials make it possible for production to expand when demand increases.

[5] An estimate of perishable, that is, style items, has been excluded.

TABLE 49
Finished Nonagricultural Products Stocks, Conformity to Manufacturing Activity Cycles

STOCKS	INDICATOR OF ACTIVITY	NO. OF PHASES	INDEX OF CONFORMITY TO ACTIVITY[a]		
			Exp.	Contr.	Cycle
Paper, all grades	Paper prod., all grades, 1919-33	9	-20	-75	-25
Newsprint at mills, U.S. & Canada	Newsprint ship., U.S. & Canada, 1919-37	7	0	-100	-100
Southern pine lumber	South. pine lumber ship., 1919-38	12	-67	-33	-45
Oak flooring	Oak flooring shipments, 1913-41	14	-14	-71	-69
Portland cement	Portland cement shipments, 1912-38	12	-67	-67	-82
Bath tubs	Bath tub shipments, 1918-25	5	-33	-100	-100
Lavatories	Lavatory shipments, 1919-25	5	+33	0	0
Kitchen sinks	Kitchen sink shipments, 1919-25	5	+33	0	-50
Misc. enameled sanitary ware	Misc. enameled sanitary ware ship., 1919-24	2	+100	+100	+100
Gasoline at refineries	Gasoline output, 1918-38	13	+67	-43	-67
Lubricants at refineries	Lubricants output, 1918-40	15	-43	-75	-71
Pig iron at merchant furnaces	Pig iron ship. from merchant furnaces, 1919-24	4	-100	-100	-100
Steel sheets made to stock	Steel sheet ship., total, 1919-32	8	-50	-100	-100
Refined copper, N. & S. Am.	Refined copper ship., N. & S. Am., 1919-38	6	-33	-100	-60
Lead at smelteries & refineries	Lead ore receipts, 1923-38	6	+33	-100	-20
Slab zinc at refineries	Slab zinc shipments, 1921-38	10	-100	-60	-100
Auto. tires	Auto. tire shipments, 1921-38	8	0	0	-14
Auto. inner tubes	Auto. inner tube shipments, 1921-38	6	+100	+33	+20

Except as noted, all stocks series are finished goods in the hands of United States manufacturers. Stocks of automobile tires and inner tubes include stocks on consignment to dealers.

[a] Stages I-V matched with expansions in all cases.

dexes, and of these, 11 stand 50 or higher, indicating inverse conformity in three cycles out of four, or better.

These results suggest a strong tendency for this class of stocks to conform inversely to cycles in manufacturing activity. One possible area of obscurity may seem to lie in the fact that the indicator of activity was in most instances shipments and only in some instances production. There may be some question whether stocks bear the same relation to production as to shipments. The answer, however, is not really difficult. In most manufacturing industries we are accustomed to assume that the rate of production increases when the rate of shipments rises. For goods made from nonagricultural materials, the assumption is well in accord with the facts. There is evidence, it is true, that turns in production lag behind turns in shipments (Table 54), but the lag is usually very short and not significant for the present purpose.

Chart 39 depicts the average reference cycle patterns of the production and shipments of commodities for which we have comparable indicators of these two processes. The very close connection between the rates of production and shipment of manufactured staples is obvious.

The relation between stocks and manufacturing activity is reflected in a similar relation between stocks and business cycles (Table 50). One series, stocks of hardwoods, which could not be included in Table 49 for lack of a measure of activity in the industry, is added. Of the 19 series, 13 appear to conform inversely. Again, however, the exclusion of rubber tires and tubes raises the ratio of negative indexes to the total, this time to 13 out of 17. It should be noticed, moreover, that in computing the indexes for oak flooring stocks, stages III-VII were matched with reference expansions. The positive indexes for this series suggest inverted conformity with a long lead as validly as they do positive conformity with a long lag. When stages I-V are matched with expansions, the indexes run +43, −43, −23. On the whole, the conformity of stocks to business cycles is somewhat lower than to manufacturing activity, because production and shipments of individual commodities did not conform perfectly to cycles of business at large. Nevertheless, the general tendency of the class to vary inversely to general business is clear.

TABLE 50
Finished Nonagricultural Products Stocks
Conformity to Business Cycles

STOCKS[a]	NO. OF PHASES	INDEX OF CONFORMITY TO BUSINESS[a]		
		Exp.	Contr.	Cycle
Paper, all grades, 1918-33	9	−100	−100	−100
Newsprint, U.S. & Canada, 1918-37	10	−60	−100	−100
Southern pine lumber, 1918-38	11	−100	−33	−60
Hardwoods, 1926-38	4	−100	−33	0
Oak flooring, 1912-37	13	+100	+33	+67
Portland cement, 1912-38	14	−14	−14	−23
Bath tubs, 1919-29	7	0	−33	0
Lavatories, 1919-29	7	0	−33	−33
Kitchen sinks, 1919-29	7	0	−33	−33
Misc. enameled sanitary ware, 1919-29	7	0	−33	−33
Gasoline at refineries, 1918-38	11	+100	−33	0
Lubricants at refineries, 1918-38	11	−20	−100	−20
Pig iron at merchant furnaces, 1919-26	5	−100	−100	−100
Steel sheets made to stock, 1919-37	9	+20	−50	−50
Refined copper, N. & S. Am., 1919-38	10	−60	−60	−78
Lead at smelteries & refineries, 1924-38	6	−33	−100	−100
Slab zinc at refineries, 1920-38	9	−100	−100	−100
Auto. tires, 1921-38	8	+100	+100	+100
Auto. inner tubes, 1921-38	8	+100	+100	+100

See Table 49, note.

[a] Stages I-V matched with expansion in all cases except oak flooring, III-VII; lead at smelteries and refineries, II-VI; automobile tires, I-VI.

TIMING OF TURNS IN STOCKS

While cycles in stocks of finished nonfarm products generally conform inversely to cycles in manufacturing activity, this is not the whole story. When we compare the timing of their respective turns the cyclical behavior of stocks seems to depend upon the length of the cycle. The first step in establishing this characteristic was to measure the timing of the troughs and peaks of stocks at the matching turns of the corresponding indicators of manufacturing activity.[6] Since stocks conform inversely, peaks in stocks were compared with troughs in activity, and vice versa. Next, the leads and lags thus calculated were classified according to the length of the preceding expansion or contraction of the activity series, that is, according to the length of the phase ending with the turn of the activity involved in the particular comparison. Shipments of south-

[6] The indicator of activity used for each inventory series is that shown in Table 49.

Chart 39
Fabricated Nonfarm Staples, Production and Shipments
Average Reference Cycle Patterns

---- Production
—— Shipments

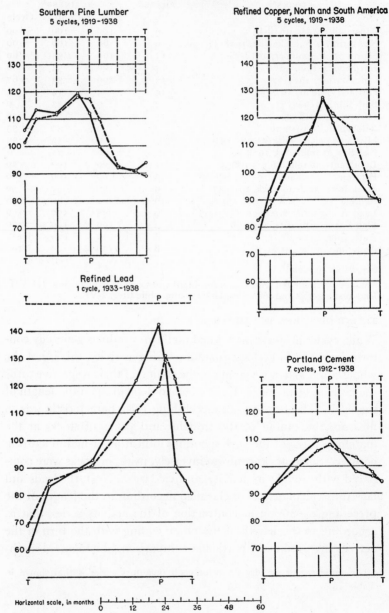

Southern Pine Lumber
5 cycles, 1919-1938

Refined Copper, North and South America
5 cycles, 1919-1938

Refined Lead
1 cycle, 1933-1938

Portland Cement
7 cycles, 1912-1938

Horizontal scale, in months

Chart 39 (concl.)

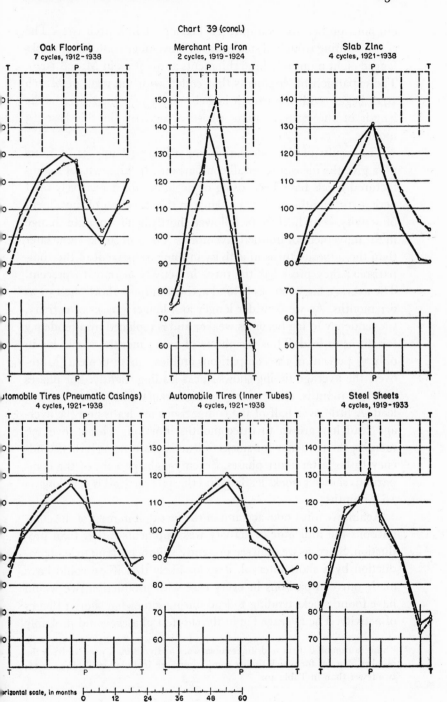

Oak Flooring
7 cycles, 1912-1938

Merchant Pig Iron
2 cycles, 1919-1924

Slab Zinc
4 cycles, 1921-1938

Automobile Tires (Pneumatic Casings)
4 cycles, 1921-1938

Automobile Tires (Inner Tubes)
4 cycles, 1921-1938

Steel Sheets
4 cycles, 1919-1933

Horizontal scale, in months   0   12   24   36   48   60

ern pine lumber, for example, reached a peak in March 1928. The corresponding trough of stocks was in November 1928. Thus stocks lagged eight months behind shipments at the peak in March 1928. The expansion of shipments that ended with the peak of March 1928 began with the trough in February 1927. This gives us the length of the corresponding phase of activity, in this case 13 months.

The results of the calculation are striking (Table 51).[7] Lines 9-12 give the measures for all comparisons. If shipments of manufactured goods have been rising or declining for a relatively brief period, 12 months or less, a change in the direction of movement of activity seems likely to be followed shortly by an opposite change in the movement of finished inventories. Turns of stocks came later than the opposite turns in activity in some 81 percent of the comparisons; they preceded the turns in activity in only 19 percent. The average lag of stocks behind activity in these short phases was 6.1 months. As we consider longer and longer phases of activity, the tendency to lag becomes weaker and is replaced by a tendency for stocks to lead. Thus for phases of 13-24 months, stocks lag in only 57 percent of the comparisons and lead in 43 percent. Moreover, the average timing shows stocks leading slightly. For phases of 25-36 months, the tendency to lag is replaced by a tendency to lead. A little over half of the comparisons are leads and the average lead has grown to three months. For long phases, over 36 months, the tendency for stocks to lead is as strong as is their tendency to lag after short phases. Seventy-eight percent of the comparisons showed stocks leading and the average lead is very long— 16.4 months.

Again, we must take account of the fact that in most of the comparisons the indicator of activity was shipments rather than production. Since, as we shall see presently, shipments tend to lead production by a short interval, it seems likely that if we could have made our comparisons in every case with production, we would have found stocks tending to lead during somewhat shorter phases of activity. The average lag in the shortest phases would probably

[7] Since automobile tires and inner tubes were analyzed on a positive basis the number of series for which timing comparisons are included in Table 51 is 16, two fewer than in Table 49.

have been shorter, and the average leads in the longer phases, longer.

TABLE 51

Finished Nonagricultural Products Stocks
Timing Comparisons at Turns in Manufacturing Activity
Classified by Length of Preceding Phase of Activity

LENGTH OF PREC. PHASE OF ACTIVITY, MONTHS	N U M B E R Leads	O F Lags	Coin.	Com- parisons	LEADS AS % OF TOTAL	AV. LEAD (−) OR LAG (+) MONTHS
	AT TURNS IN MANUFACTURING ACTIVITY THROUGH DECEMBER 31, 1929					
1) 12 & under	5	23	1	29	17.2	+8.2
2) 13-24	7	10	2	19	36.8	0
3) 25-36	5	4	1	10	50.0	−1.4
4) Over 36	10	0	1	11	90.9	−18.5
	AT TURNS IN MANUFACTURING ACTIVITY AFTER DECEMBER 31, 1929					
5) 12 & under	3	9	1	13	23.1	+1.8
6) 13-24	5	3	1	9	55.6	−2.1
7) 25-36	3	2	0	5	60.0	−6.2
8) Over 36	8	4	0	12	66.7	−14.4
	AT ALL TURNS IN MANUFACTURING ACTIVITY					
9) 12 & under	8	32	2	42	19.0	+6.1
10) 13-24	12	13	3	28	42.9	−0.7
11) 25-36	8	6	1	15	53.3	−3.0
12) Over 36	18	4	1	23	78.3	−16.4

Timing measured invertedly; see Ch. 3, note 5.

Since the business contraction beginning in 1929 and the expansion beginning in 1933 were two of the longest phases so far recorded, and since most of our series reflected these two long business movements, some question arises whether the observed difference in timing between long and short phases is not, in fact, a feature of the 1929-37 cycle alone. This question was tested by making separate calculations for timing comparisons before and after the end of 1929 (Table 51, lines 1-8). We found that the tendency operated fully as strongly in the early as in the later period. Whether we look at figures before or after the end of 1929, the lags of stocks at opposite turns of manufacturing activity grow shorter and less numerous as the length of the preceding phase of activity increases; and leads grow more numerous and longer.

The relation between the timing of turns in stocks and the length of business movements may be shown to be a characteristic also of both expansions and contractions (Table 52). Cyclical turns in stocks tend to lag behind the opposite turns in manufacturing activity when the expansion or contraction is 12 months or less. But as longer cyclical movements are considered, the lags gradually give way to leads, and in long expansions or contractions stocks turn before manufacturing activity in a large majority of all the comparisons. The results at peaks are, of course, not identical with those at troughs, but the differences are too small to warrant attention in view of the few observations on which they are based.

TABLE 52

Finished Nonagricultural Products Stocks
Timing Comparisons at Peaks and Troughs of Manufacturing
Activity Classified by Length of Preceding Phase of Activity

LENGTH OF PREC. PHASE OF ACTIVITY, MONTHS	N U M B E R O F				LEADS AS % OF TOTAL	AV. LEAD (−) OR LAG (+) MONTHS
	Leads	Lags	Coin.	Com-parisons		
	AT PEAKS IN MANUFACTURING ACTIVITY					
1) 12 & under	2	8	1	11	18.2	+3.0
2) 13-24	6	8	2	16	37.5	+0.3
3) 25-36	7	5	1	13	53.8	−2.9
4) Over 36	11	3	1	15	73.3	−15.4
	AT TROUGHS IN MANUFACTURING ACTIVITY					
5) 12 & under	6	24	1	31	19.4	+7.2
6) 13-24	6	5	1	12	50.0	−2.0
7) 25-36	1	1	0	2	50.0	−3.5
8) Over 36	7	1	0	8	87.5	−18.2

The meaning of these results may be put in this fashion. When business turns down after a short expansion, shipments tend to turn first and to drop below production after a short interval. Stocks, in consequence, turn up soon after shipments turn down. If the ensuing contraction of activity is short, stocks continue to rise during the entire phase. If the business recession is protracted, however, there is a growing tendency for stocks of finished goods to reverse their direction and to begin to move down with manufacturing activity. By the end of very long contractions, most manufacturers' inventories of finished goods will be moving in the same direction as manufacturing activity rather than in the opposite direction. When shipments finally turn up after a long downswing of business, therefore, stocks of finished goods are likely to be falling. The upturn of shipments then causes stocks to fall even more rapidly. This explanation has run in terms of events during business contractions. Expansions have the same sort of influence on finished goods inventories, but in the opposite direction.

CONFORMITY OF INVENTORIES RECONSIDERED

The significance of these results may be developed by turning our attention once more to the conformity of stocks of finished non-farm products. If they act in the fashion just described, the measure of full cycle conformity of stocks to cycles in manufacturing activity is more likely to indicate inverted conformity during short than during long cycles. Defections from the general rule of inverted behavior should be found more often during long than during short cycles. The figures bear this out.

In the 18 indicators of manufacturing activity with which the stock series of Table 49 are matched, 126 cycles, measuring both from trough to trough and from peak to peak, have been identified.[8] Stocks conformed inversely in 100 cycles, according to the National Bureau's full cycle measure,[9] and positively in 26. We classified the 126 activity cycles and the cycles in which stocks conformed positively by their length in months (Table 53). The results suggest that the chance of finding stocks moving together with activity increases with the length of activity cycles. True, the percentage that positively conforming stocks cycles are of total cycles does not, in Table 53, grow steadily with the length of the cycle. But this is due to the size of the class intervals chosen. If the class intervals are widened, a steady progression appears. If we divide cycles into those lasting less than 30 months, 30-49 months, 50-69 months, and 70 months and over, the percentages of all cycles in which inventories conformed positively are respectively 10, 13, 33, and 47. The effect of the length of cycles upon the conformity of stocks can be appreciated also by considering cumulative totals. Thus about 43 percent of all cycles were shorter than 40 months, but only some 31 percent of the positively conforming stocks cycles occurred during these short cycles of activity. Moreover, while more than half of the positive cycles of stocks occurred in activity

[8] That is, during the periods covered also by the corresponding stock series.

[9] Any one of three types of movement of stocks during a given cycle of activity constitutes inverse conformity: stocks fall during expansion and rise during contraction; stocks decline throughout the cycle but more rapidly in expansion than in contraction; stocks increase throughout the cycle but less rapidly in expansion than in contraction. Similarly, three types of movement may constitute positive conformity.

TABLE 53

Finished Nonagricultural Products Stocks
Inventory Cycles Conforming Positively to Cycles in
Manufacturing Activity Classified by Length of Activity Cycles

LENGTH OF ACTIVITY CYCLES, MO.	NO. OF ACTIVITY CYCLES OF INDICATED LENGTH, MO.	CYCLES IN WHICH INVENTORIES CONFORMED POSITIVELY No.	%
Under 20	9	1	11.1
20-29	22	2	9.1
30-39	24	5	20.8
40-49	30	2	6.7
50-59	10	3	30.0
60-69	14	5	35.7
70-79	7	5	71.4
80 & over	10	3	30.0
All cycles	126	26	20.6

cycles longer than 50 months, only 33 percent of all cycles were so long. Stocks conformed positively to activity in less than 12 percent of all cycles shorter than 50 months. They conformed positively in 39 percent of all cycles that exceeded 50 months.

It is noteworthy that even in long cycles—those over 60 months, for example—stocks still conform inversely in a majority of the cases observed. Consequently, despite the strong tendency for stocks to move in the same direction as activity toward the close of long cycles, the whole movement of stocks from the beginning to the end of even long cycles usually remains inverse to activity.

FACTORS INFLUENCING THE BEHAVIOR OF FINISHED NONAGRICUL-
TURAL STAPLES

The characteristics of the behavior of stocks of finished nonfarm staples seem fairly clear. It is not easy, however, to settle upon a well founded explanation for their behavior, especially of their tendency to inverted conformity, their major trait.

At least two lines of explanation suggest themselves. Manufacturers may fail to foresee the turning points in demand and fail equally to forecast the rate of rise of demand during expansions and the rate of decline during contractions. As they respond tardily to changes in demand, shipments tend to outrun production during the rise, and production tends to outrun shipments during the decline. Lack of foresight, of course, need not be absolute. Some time, in some cases considerable time, is required to bring additional capacity into production on the rise and to take it out of production on the decline. This amounts to saying that even if changes in demand are expected, they are not foreseen sufficiently far in advance, or early forecasts are not held with sufficient confidence to induce the required action before the change in demand takes place.

This possibility almost certainly has some force. Even at the trough of a cycle when there is idle equipment ready for operation in most plants and when additional output from employed workers can be attained by increasing hours and the pace of work, some time is required to increase output. As we have already seen (Ch. 8), the average interval between input of materials and output of completely fabricated goods is about three weeks. In some cases additional labor must be hired or facilities repaired before the rate of fabrication can increase; and these obstacles become more serious as expansion proceeds.

Forecasts even a few weeks in advance are, of course, subject to some degree of uncertainty. Indeed, the actual turning points of demand are hard to recognize when they occur. The normal course of sales during a cycle is far from smooth. It alternately advances and retreats, tracing a jagged pattern. Consequently, the advance that signals the beginning of an expansion or the decline that initiates contraction is impossible to identify immediately. It seems natural, therefore, that manufacturers will not begin to reduce their rate of operations until after sales and shipments have been declining for some time, and, as far as operations are curtailed, the reductions may for some time be inadequate. This hesitancy, of course, seems more likely at the beginning of a phase when the future is especially uncertain than later when the trend of business, up or down, is more clearly marked.

Manufacturers have other cogent reasons to allow their operations to follow, rather than to keep step with, sales and shipments. To change the rate of operations is an act of managerial judgment, and decisions once made tend to remain unaltered for some time, especially when a change in output entails a change in the labor force. Quite aside from obvious nonpecuniary reasons, it cannot be good personnel policy to hire workers who may soon have to be laid off or to lay off workers who may be needed again in a few weeks.

Businessmen will therefore probably hesitate to act upon intimations of future demand unless the volume of sales is foreseen with confidence. And this is hardly likely far in advance of the event. Of course, even if preparations for a change in demand are not made sufficiently far in advance, a gap between production and shipments is not inevitable. Sales can be held in check or encouraged, as the case may be, by changes in prices. For many reasons inherent in the character of competition in industrial markets, however, businessmen are reluctant to initiate cuts in prices to stimulate sales or to risk the loss of business that may accompany a rise in prices. Competition rather encourages manufacturers to avoid precipitating price declines when demand falls off and to try to fill an unexpected increase in orders from stock if necessary rather than to chance the loss of business by requiring purchasers to wait several weeks until additional goods can be produced.

An important question still remains. If production outruns shipments in the early months of a recession, stocks of finished goods begin to accumulate. Once this has occurred, why do manufacturers not curtail production enough to liquidate stocks? If demand falls even more than they expected, they will have moved in the right direction; if less, they will still have stocks from which to meet sales for some weeks. It is just such action that I postulate in explaining the tendency for raw materials inventories to turn in the same direction as production within a few months after the turn of business.

To this question there are two answers. The first stems from the physical character of the goods and the fact that they are finished products, not purchased supplies. The commodities under consideration are staples. They will not deteriorate physically and they are the basic materials of production, useful whatever the particular form demand for completely fabricated goods takes. Consequently, this category of stocks must be distinguished from finished nonstaples. As stated, I do not suppose that manufacturers of goods that are perishable, for whatever reason, can afford to allow stocks to accumulate for a long period. Within a short time after sales fall off, they will curtail output sufficiently to reduce their stocks. Producers of staples, however, can afford to tolerate at least a modest accumulation of stocks for a considerable period.

Stocks of finished staples must be distinguished also from stocks of purchased materials, whether durable or perishable. Inventories of purchased materials are subject to the risks of adverse changes in market prices to their full value. Consequently, except when there is good reason to think prices are firm or rising, manufacturers have a strong incentive to keep such stocks at the lowest levels consistent with the smooth operation of their plants. During business recessions, therefore, manufacturers will try to reduce their raw material stocks as quickly as possible. And having done so, the requirements of a larger volume of business will compel them to rebuild stocks in the ensuing recovery.

Stocks of finished staples too are, of course, subject to the risk of changes in prices. But the risk is smaller. Only some 60 percent of the total inventory cost of finished goods consists of the cost of raw materials.[10] The remainder comprises labor cost and the various elements of manufacturing overhead. This makes a difference in several ways. First, labor is less subject to rapid and unexpected changes in price than purchased materials. Second, against the risks of adverse changes in prices manufacturers are likely to set the economies they see in steady operation. Some of these economies, as noted below, are real, some may be illusory; but real or fancied, they probably make manufacturers more reluctant to liquidate stocks of finished goods by a radical reduction of output than stocks of raw materials by a drastic cut in purchases.

If the first part of the answer to the puzzle of manufacturers' tolerance for the perverse pattern of finished goods stocks lies in the character of the goods, the second part is that their tolerance is not unlimited. As already shown, the longer a phase lasts, the greater is the tendency for finished stocks to reverse their ordinary direction and begin to move with business activity. Apparently, if

[10] As indicated in Appendix A, raw materials account for about 53 percent of the value of product in manufacturing. Not all the elements of value added in manufacturing, however, enter into the inventory value of finished goods. In particular, profits, interest, selling costs, and general administrative expenses are excluded. If we allow 10 percent for these elements, raw materials do not make up more than 60 percent of the residual elements of value we assume are included in the inventory cost of finished goods.

a phase lasts long enough, stocks do accumulate to such uncomfortably high levels in recessions and run down to such inconveniently low levels in expansions that manufacturers are eventually compelled to alter production radically. I shall have more to say about this below.

The first line of explanation of the inverse pattern turned on uncertainty about the future of business. A second possible line, more likely to supplement than supplant the first, is that manufacturers, although they foresee the trend of sales, allow shipments to outrun production on the rise and allow production to outrun shipments on the decline as a matter of deliberate policy. To keep a certain number of people working for stock when business falls off is to avoid the dispersion of staff and the expense of preparing equipment for a spell of idleness. And having built up a surplus stock in this fashion, there are obvious reasons for liquidating the stock when business improves. Moreover, as a matter of long-run economy, if production can be kept more stable than shipments, the size of plant necessary to meet the peak load of business need not be quite as large as would otherwise be necessary. These are real advantages to using inventories to stabilize output. There are also spurious advantages. When overhead costs must be divided among fewer units of output, average total costs of production tend to rise. To avoid this increase in book costs, manufacturers may sometimes resort to production for stock even though the out-of-pocket cost of the extra output is greater, or no less, than it will be later.

The evidence is consistent with both lines of explanation. If businessmen fail to foresee changes in demand far enough in advance, we would expect production to lag behind shipments. Comparisons of the timing of peaks and troughs in the shipments and production of 7 commodities indicate a strong tendency for shipments to lead (Table 54).[11]

To this extent the evidence supports the hypothesis of imperfect forecasting. It bears also, though in minor degree, on the possi-

[11] Automobile tires and tubes, for which comparisons were made in Chart 39, are excluded because their stocks were among the few exceptions to the rule of inverted behavior. The relation of their production and shipments does not, therefore, seem relevant to an explanation of the behavior of other commodity stocks that conform inversely.

TABLE 54

Seven Fabricated Nonagricultural Staples
Timing of Turns in Shipments at Turns in Production

	NUMBER OF			AV. LEAD (−) OR LAG (+)
	Leads	Lags	Coin.	MONTHS
	AT PEAKS IN PRODUCTION			
Southern pine lumber, 1916-40	2	2	1	+1.2
Oak flooring, 1912-42	1	1	3	−1.2
Portland cement, 1911-41	6			−4.0
Merchant pig iron, 1919-26	1		1	−1.5
Refined copper, 1919-38	3			−3.0
Refined lead, 1929-41	2			−3.5
Slab zinc, 1920-39	3		1	−1.5
Total	18	3	6	
	AT TROUGHS IN PRODUCTION			
Southern pine lumber, 1916-40	3	1	2	−1.3
Oak flooring, 1912-42	4	1		−2.4
Portland cement, 1911-41	3	2	2	−0.4
Merchant pig iron, 1919-26	3			−1.3
Refined copper, 1919-38	3			−6.0
Refined lead, 1929-41	1	1		+0.5
Slab zinc, 1920-39	4	1		−3.6
Total	21	6	4	

bility that the inverse conformity of stocks reflects a deliberate attempt to stabilize production. If manufacturers could foresee peaks in sales, they would achieve a flatter production curve, other things being equal, if they began to cut output simultaneously with the decline in sales, or even before; and the same at troughs. To allow production to rise for some time after the peak of sales and to fall for some time after the trough makes the amplitude of the swings in output wider than it would otherwise be. The possibility that attempts to stabilize production may play some part in explaining our observations, however, is far from excluded by this consideration. Although manufacturers may not foresee the actual cyclical turns of sales, they must be more or less aware of the declining trend during contraction. Their willingness to accumulate stocks of finished goods might then reflect an attempt to cushion the impact of the decline of sales on output. Some such motive may in fact be present even if the future course of expansion and contraction is nebulous. Uncertain whether sales will continue to decline in recession or to increase in expansion, they prefer to keep their output steady until the pressure of events forces a change, accumulating stock in contraction and liquidating it in expansion as a necessary consequence. Thus the two lines of explanation, poor forecasting and desire to keep output as steady as possible, merge in a way that our present evidence cannot disentangle.[12]

This is as much as I can say about the general tendency toward inverted conformity. To rationalize the tendency of stocks to reverse their direction and begin to move with manufacturing activity when demand expands or contracts long enough is not too difficult. Let us consider long expansions. As an expansion proceeds, the rate of production and shipments increases and stocks fall. The longer this continues, the nearer does the relation between shipments and stocks approach the point at which it becomes inconvenient for a manufacturer to attempt to serve his customers from so small a stock. He runs the risk that he will be unable to fill a sudden accumulation of orders. It seems reasonable also to suppose that when business has been growing fairly steadily for many months, manufacturers tend to count on it, and some at least will adopt a less cautious production policy.

During contractions much the same set of influences operates in reverse. The expanded stocks weigh ever more heavily as demand contracts; a substantial time will then be required to liquidate the surplus inventory. Hence the risk of holding it increases. As the contraction proceeds, businessmen become even gloomier, and the risk of holding a given stock compounds. An increasing number will then curtail output drastically enough to reduce it below current shipments.

3 Note on Blodgett's Treatment of Finished Goods

As indicated in Chapter 1, Ralph H. Blodgett studied some of the materials used in this book. His treatment of finished goods in particular resembles mine and it is interesting to examine the similarities and differences. Since his sample was smaller, and his series were available for shorter periods, I omit differences of detail.

To begin with, Blodgett divides his commodities into two groups: those that conform inversely and positively to business

---

[12] A considerable degree of stabilization of output relative to shipments is often achieved, whether deliberately or not. The average amplitudes of production for six of the seven commodities included in Table 54 are smaller than those of shipments, by amounts ranging from 3 to 29 percent.

cycles. This grouping, of course, makes the major behavior trait of Blodgett's categories a matter of classification rather than a finding. Chief interest is, therefore, directed to his explanation of the contrasting behavior of the two classes and to certain exceptions he notices.

Blodgett considers the stocks that behave inversely to be, in general, 'disparity' stocks. "Such stocks tend to accumulate in periods of general business contraction because it seems economically unwise to curtail production as fast as, or to the same extent as, shipments of the finished products fall off. In periods of general business expansion, on the other hand, these stocks tend to be reduced because it is impossible or economically unwise to have production expand as fast as, or to the same extent as, shipments increase."[13] To explain the behavior of these stocks Blodgett notes first, that the industries holding them are, in general, industries that have developed large excess capacity. He therefore supposes that the chief reason for the inverted stock cycles is the desire of manufacturers to minimize fluctuations in production.[14] He does not mention the other explanation on which I have laid stress—that the discrepancies between shipments and production during business cycles may be attributed to the failure of manufacturers to foresee changes in demand soon enough to adjust their rate of production.

For its bearing on the ability of manufacturers to accumulate stocks when shipments are falling, Blodgett notes that his inverted series are durable and staple commodities and hence may be stored for considerable periods without fear of loss because of physical deterioration or shifts in the character of demand. Finally, Blodgett takes special note of three series specifically labeled 'unsold' stocks (p. 59).

---

[13] Op. cit., p. 50.

[14] In strict logic, excess capacity reduces the need to accumulate stocks in depression since equipment to meet the larger demands of expansion is relatively adequate. Blodgett's position, however, appears more plausible if we suppose that manufacturers base their production policy on considerations of average total cost as distinct from average variable costs or marginal costs. The larger overhead costs are, of course, the more rapidly will average total cost rise when production falls off. Manufacturers' desires to stabilize output may then be attributed to the natural, though mistaken, notion that it is in their interest to avoid increases in average total costs during recession.

"The unsold stocks represent the disparity element in stocks, and would be expected to show inverted conformity with respect to the cycles in general business whenever they could be separated out of any stock series, whether the total series was itself inverted or positive.

Indeed, it seems feasible to interpret the positive and inverted stock series in terms of unsold stocks, and to say that the inverted stock series for finished products tend to be those which are largely made up of unsold stocks, so that the behavior of the unsold stocks comes to be that of the entire series. Positive series, on the other hand, tend to be those in which the unsold stocks are small, relative to the total, so that the behavior of the series as a whole can be positive even though the unsold stocks included in them behave in an inverted fashion."

Thus Blodgett drew attention to two of the three features by which I define the category of stocks studied above: their durable and staple character and the fact that they are made to stock rather than to order. As indicated in Chapter 12, the third feature, which Blodgett omits, is that cycles in the production of these commodities are governed by changes in conditions of demand rather than in the supply of raw materials.

Another notable suggestion is Blodgett's allusion to a difference between the behavior of inverted stock series during ordinary cycles and during long and severe contractions. Observing that maintenance of relatively stable production induces large inverted fluctuations in stocks, he writes (pp. 56-7):

"It should be remembered, however, that when a business contraction is of long duration and is very severe, an end may eventually come to the financial, physical, and psychological ability of the industries to hold larger and still larger stocks, in which case a very drastic drop in the rate of operation in these industries may occur and stocks will also decline."

This prescient sentence may be taken to anticipate my finding that in long phases of manufacturing activity the inverted movement of stocks tends to reverse itself, and that the timing of turns in stocks of finished goods at opposite turns of shipments varies with the length of the cyclical phase.

Blodgett calls the positively conforming series 'convenience' stocks—small inventories whose function is to take care of minor and passing discrepancies between production and shipments. He believes stocks of commodities that are perishable or ready for the final consumer will tend to be managed in such fashion that inventories will be small and vary positively with business activity. This corresponds with my own expectations for goods in this class, as does Blodgett's observation that such stocks tend to lag behind business activity by a moderate interval. Possibly because of the mixed character of the commodities in his sample of positively conforming series, Blodgett does not follow up his distinction between goods made to order and to stock. This is an unfortunate omission since one of his positive series, total stocks of steel sheets, is composed predominantly of goods made to order. As already noted, moreover, while nonstaples made for the market are likely to conform positively, goods made to order virtually must do so, and there is probably a certain amount of overlapping between the two categories.

Blodgett's review of the behavior of stocks of finished goods brings to light many of the influences affecting this class that are mentioned here. But though Blodgett notices the important distinction between goods made to order and to stock, he does not clearly state its significance. According to the sentences quoted above, Blodgett seems to believe that goods made to order conform positively to cycles in demand, and unsold stocks inversely. The first portion of this proposition is true; the second is not. If the production of a commodity made for the market responds largely to changes in demand, it will conform inversely if the commodity is durable, but positively if it is perishable. On the other hand, if the production of the commodity is governed principally by changes in the supply of raw materials, the characteristic conformity of stocks during business cycles may be inverse, positive, or irregular (see Ch. 12). But whatever the behavior, the influences affecting commodities whose output responds chiefly to raw material supply are radically different from those affecting commodities whose output in the short-run is governed chiefly by demand. Blodgett largely ignores these distinctions. He lumps cottonseed oil, leather, and condensed milk with other inverted series, explaining their behavior in the same way as he does other 'disparity' stocks made from nonagricultural materials. On the other hand, he classifies refined sugar, wheat flour, and cold storage holdings of pork with other positive series.[15]

4 Cycles in Finished Staples Stocks and Keynes' Inventory Theory

Since the findings of this chapter are relevant to Keynes' theory of the cyclical behavior and significance of inventories we revert to it now. As explained in Chapter 1, Keynes divides stocks into two analytical categories: "working" and "liquid" capital. The first he defines as "the aggregate of goods . . . in course of production, manufacture, transport and retailing, including such minimum stocks, whether of raw materials or finished products, as are required to avoid risks of interruption of process or to tide over seasonal irregularities. . . ."[16] Liquid stocks are any surplus over and above these requirements. Again, "normal stocks required for efficient business are part of working capital and therefore in process, whilst surplus stocks are to be regarded as liquid."[17]

Hence working capital must increase and decline together with the volume of manufacturing activity.[18] Keynes expects liquid stocks, on the contrary, to grow larger during the early stages of a recession and to be liquidated in its later stages. In recovery, liquid stocks, he thinks, will first decline, then begin to accumulate.

" . . . when the slump begins, the falling off of production does not show itself immediately at the finishing end of the machine of process, whilst it does show itself immediately in the amount which is being fed back into the mouth of the machine: so liquid stocks increase. Later on, however, the diminished production results in diminished available output, whilst current consumption does not fall off so much

[15] Blodgett comes close to observing the distinction when he explains that pork is more or less fortuitously classified as positive, although it is much more influenced by the large and irregular cycles in hog slaughter than by general business conditions.

[16] *Treatise on Money*, p. 116.

[17] Ibid., p. 129.

[18] This is not a precise statement. If activity, measured by employment, expanded and contracted synchronously at every stage of fabrication, working capital in manufacturing would tend to lead output, by an interval not exceeding, say, four weeks (see Ch. 8). If we define output as the production of completely fabricated goods ready for consumers and suppose production is increased by feeding an additional batch of raw materials into the earliest stage of fabrication and passing the batch through successive stages, the lead would be much longer.

as does production—with the result that there can be no increase of liquid stocks, but rather the contrary."[19]

As suggested in Chapter 1, this picture of the behavior of liquid and working capital is a crucial part of Keynes' theory of the course and mechanism of business cycles. To the accumulation of liquid stocks at the beginning of recession he attributes the sudden and rapid development of depression, the effort quickly to unload stock intensifying the deflationary forces of contraction. With the eventual disposal of liquid stocks he connects the timing of recovery, asserting that it cannot begin until they have been absorbed. And to the inadequacy of liquid stocks during recovery he attributes the relatively moderate pace of expansion, since stocks of goods in process can then be rebuilt only by the slow method of extraction and fabrication.

It is clearly of first importance, then, to know whether Keynes' picture of the behavior of liquid stocks is accurate.[20] In this connection, the big—strictly speaking, insuperable—difficulty is that Keynes' distinctions do not correspond to any existing, or even potentially compilable, statistical categories. A distinction between 'normal' and 'surplus' stocks is not the kind that lends itself to measurement. Still, the behavior Keynes attributes to liquid stocks bears enough resemblance to that which characterizes the stocks of finished staples reviewed above to make it tempting to identify the two, at least as far as liquid stocks in the manufacturing sphere are concerned. The temptation is stronger since the United States data Keynes used are for the same or similar staple commodities.[21] In the end, of course, this temptation will have to be put aside. Appraising Keynes' theory in the light of the evidence of this chapter, however, is still useful. Manufacturers' stocks of finished staples, as far as one can judge by their behavior, are a leading example of liquid stocks in the Keynesian sense. There can be little question, in

[19] Ibid., pp. 134-5; see also the passage from his *General Theory*, quoted in Chapter 1.

[20] It is a moot point, of course, whether the rapidity of contraction is significantly greater than that of expansion, as Keynes asserts. This question, however, is too large to be faced here.

[21] Keynes refers to the total stocks of goods rather than to finished goods held by manufacturers, but in many cases the only data available cover manufacturers' stocks alone.

particular, that the major part of these stocks accumulated in recessions are surplus in the sense that they are unnecessary to the efficient conduct of current business. As far as these stocks do not behave as Keynes expected, we may come to one of two conclusions. Either Keynes' hypothesis requires modification or one must look to other categories of inventories to find the liquid stocks that do meet his specifications.

Keynes expects liquid stocks to rise in the first part of recession and to decline in later stages. It is not clear how long after the peak of business the decline of stocks is supposed to start, but by the time recovery begins, we may assume that the stocks have largely been liquidated, for Keynes makes the absorption of the stocks a condition of recovery. In the early stages of recovery, in his view, liquid stocks decline somewhat further and are subsequently built up.

Roughly speaking, this hypothesis corresponds to the recorded behavior of finished staples held by manufacturers, but only during long cycles. It is inconsistent with the evidence for this class of stocks in cycles of short or moderate length. Stocks of finished staples usually move inversely to business activity (Tables 49 and 50). Moreover, in contractions of short or moderate length, they tend to reach their peak levels after the trough of business (Table 51). True, they tend more and more to reverse direction the longer the expansion or contraction. But only in phases longer than three years did a majority of the timing comparisons indicate a reversal before the turn of business. As already indicated, however, contractions that persist for as long as three years are quite exceptional in both the United States and Great Britain.[22] Only in these especially long contractions does Keynes' hypothesis fit the behavior of finished staples.

Even in long phases, however, this category of stocks may not meet the full requirements of Keynes' theory. For it demands that as a condition of business expansion liquid stocks be largely absorbed before recovery begins. But even if a contraction lasts so

[22] See Ch. 4, Sec. 4. The same is true of United States expansions: only 4 expansions out of 21 identified by the National Bureau lasted as long as 36 months. For Great Britain the count is 9 out of 16. Behavior of surplus stocks during expansion, however, is not nearly as important for Keynes' theory as their behavior during contraction since it is the pace and duration of contractions that he connects with the behavior of liquid stocks.

long (say, three years) that finished staples in the aggregate begin to decline, the depression must be still further protracted to bring liquid stocks down to something like normal levels. This may have happened upon occasion, but whether it is a characteristic feature even of long contractions is questionable.

An additional consideration reinforces the apparent discrepancy between Keynes' hypothesis about the behavior of liquid stocks and the observed behavior of finished staples. Not all inventories of finished goods are surplus. Some part of this, and any other, category of stocks constitutes 'working' capital required for the efficient performance of the current volume of business. But if the working capital component rises and falls with the rate of manufacturing activity, as, on Keynes' definition, it must, a decline of finished goods stocks toward the end of contraction will not necessarily reflect a decline of surplus stocks. The decline may be due in full, and must be due in part, to the decline in the working capital component.

We may conclude, then, that observations of manufacturers' stocks of finished staples do not support Keynes' theory of the behavior of liquid stocks. As already noted, however, this is far from conclusive with respect to Keynes' theory in general. Other categories of stocks contain surplus components that may act as Keynes' hypothesis requires. I have suggested, for example, that manufacturers' stocks of raw materials rise for a short time after the peak of business. If they do, surplus stocks, in Keynes' sense, may well be accumulated during the early months of contraction. And since the decline in inventories of raw materials begins early in contraction, surplus stocks may be fully absorbed before the end of contraction, as Keynes supposes. Again, a considerable portion of aggregate surplus stocks may be, and presumably is, carried by dealers, and these inventories may bear out Keynes' expectations. However, such inspection of dealers' stocks of staples as we have made does not suggest that they conform to business cycles in any very regular fashion. And as far as they do, my impression is that they conform inversely with a lag, rather than inversely with a lead, as Keynes suggests. Inverse conformity with a lag means, of course, that stocks are rising, not falling, toward the end of contraction.

One cannot bring Keynes' hypothesis to a conclusive test because it is not framed in statistical categories. As far as the manufacturing sphere is concerned, however, Keynes' picture of the mechanism of contraction and of the connection between recovery and the absorption of surplus stocks can be valid at best only for very long contractions. In recessions of short or moderate length, the possibility seems strong that recovery starts while surplus stocks are high and that they are absorbed only in the course of the ensuing expansion. This possibility is supported not merely by the evidence of this chapter but also by our observation that the inventory-sales ratio for manufacturers' aggregate stocks is at its peak near business cycle troughs (see Ch. 6).

Keynes' theory, though not supported by our data, does point to a real distinction between surplus stocks (as represented, say, by finished staples) and other inventories. As will become apparent in Part Three, had Keynes stated his theory in terms of the rate of accumulation of surplus stocks rather than in terms of their level, it would have constituted a valid generalization of the evidence. It does seem to be true that surplus stocks accumulate more rapidly during the first part of contraction than during the latter part; and that their rate of liquidation is high in the first part of expansion and declines as business approaches its peak.

CHAPTER 12

Finished Goods Made from Agricultural Materials

Finished goods made from nonfarm raw materials are a fairly homogeneous group. Stocks move inversely during business cycles of ordinary length because production, while sensitive to changes in demand, responds only after a certain interval and at a certain rate. The group of products now to be reviewed—products fabricated from agricultural raw materials—does not present such a uniform picture. At bottom, the reason for their diverse behavior is that they approximate only loosely the group we wish to distinguish, namely, products whose production cycles are influenced more largely by fluctuations in conditions of supply than by those in conditions of demand. However, since many fabricated farm products do, in fact, meet this specification while others do not for identifiable reasons, a review of the group will go far toward clarifying the situation.

1   Conformity to Cycles in Business and Production
The relation of manufacturers' stocks of finished goods made from agricultural raw materials to business cycles is diverse. Of the ten full cycle indexes in Table 55, three have fairly substantial values with a negative sign, one indicates regular positive conformity; six indexes are low, and of these, three are negative, one is positive, and two are zero. But even among the group that apparently responds inversely to changes in business activity, reasons differ.

In marked contrast to the diverse behavior of this collection of inventories to business cycles is their response to production in their own industries (Table 56). Seven of the ten stock series seem to conform positively to production cycles as judged by the sign of the full cycle index, and six of the seven do so regularly, as evidenced

TABLE 55

Manufacturers' Stocks of Fabricated Agricultural Products
Conformity to Business Cycles

	NO. OF CYCLES	STAGES MATCHED WITH EXP.	INDEX OF CONFORMITY TO BUSINESS		
			Exp.	Contr.	Cycle
Evaporated milk, case goods, 1921-38	4	I-V	+50	0	—14
Shortenings, 1924-38*	3	VIII-V	+100	0	0
Cottonseed oil, crude, 1919-38*	5	I-IV	—100	—67	—100
Cottonseed oil, refined, 1919-38*	5	I-IV	—20	—33	—60
Linseed oil, 1919-38	5	I-V	—20	—60	—33
Inedible tallow, 1919-38	5	I-IV	—20	—20	—56
Beef & veal in cold storage, 1919-38*	5	I-V	—20	+67	+60
Pork in cold storage, 1919-38*	5	I-V	+20	+33	0
Lard in cold storage, 1919-38*	5	I-V	+60	0	+20
Finished cattle hide leather, 1924-38	3	I-V	—33	—33	—20

The period is that covered by the number of full cycles in the series measured from trough to trough. Asterisks indicate that the contraction and full cycle indexes cover an additional reference phase at the beginning or end.

by high indexes. It is interesting, moreover, that the stock series that conform positively to production cycles include the three that yielded high negative indexes of conformity to business cycles.

We can, therefore, say two things. First, the diverse responses of stocks of fabricated farm products to business cycles are found in association with similar response to cycles in production. Secondly, of the commodities that move inversely during business cycles some do so for reasons quite different from those that control the behavior of nonfarm products. In the latter group, stocks moved inversely to cycles in both business and production. Among farm products, however, some that behave inversely during business cycles still conform positively to cycles in production. To gain some understanding of this behavior, we consider these commodities in separate groups.

2 Crude and Refined Cottonseed Oil

Stocks of cottonseed oil may be said to be a classic example of the inventory category studied in this chapter. They represent an extreme case of a commodity whose rate of production is governed by changes in the supply of raw materials; and since the oil, whether crude or refined, is durable and staple, the behavior of cottonseed oil stocks is in striking contrast to that of the other durable commodities reviewed in the preceding chapter. It is convenient, therefore, to study cottonseed oil stocks first, then treat the other fabricated farm products as variants.

TABLE 56

Manufacturers' Stocks of Fabricated Agricultural Products Conformity to Production Cycles

STOCKS	INDICATOR OF PRODUCTION	NO. OF CYCLES	STAGES MATCHED WITH EXP.	INDEX OF CONFORMITY TO PRODUCTION		
				Exp.	Contr.	Cycle
Evaporated milk, case goods	Evaporated milk output, 1920-37	5	I-V	0	−20	+20
Shortenings	Shortenings output, 1923-40	3	I-V	+50	−100	0
Cottonseed oil, crude	Crude cottonseed oil output, 1920-40	5	I-V	+60	+100	+100
Cottonseed oil, refined	Refined cottonseed oil output, 1920-40	5	II-VI	+60	+100	+78
Linseed oil	Linseed oil output, 1922-38*	7	VIII-IV	−71	−75	−100
Inedible tallow	Inedible tallow output, 1919-37	5	I-V	+60	+20	+78
Beef & veal in cold storage	Beef, frozen & placed in cure, 1921-35	3	I-V	+100	+100	+100
Pork in cold storage	Pork, frozen & placed in cure, 1921-35	3	I-V	+100	+100	+100
Lard in cold storage	Lard output, 1925-37*	3	I-V	+100	0	+100
Finished cattle hide leather	Cattle hide leather output, 1921-40	7	I-V	−100	−14	−100

* 12-month moving average.

Stocks of crude and refined oil are not completely on a par. Refined oil stocks are larger and more surplus oil is stocked in refined than in crude form. Indeed, since a large part of refined oil output is made from crude oil produced by the same firms, and since the crude oil is usually refined promptly, stocks of crude oil have some characteristics of goods in process. Nor is refined oil a pure example of a 'finished' good in my definition, for it includes some oil held by industrial consumers, principally by manufacturers of vegetable shortenings. The latter difficulty, however, does not seem to have been sufficiently serious to obscure the essential facts of the case.

Chart 40
Cottonseed Oil Stocks and Production
Average Patterns during 5 Production Cycles, 1920-1940

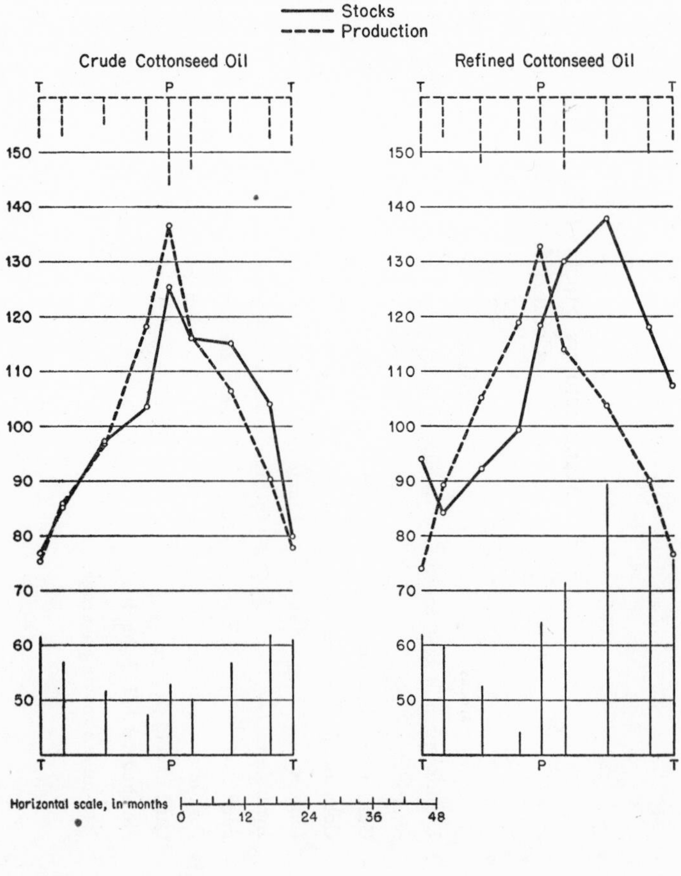

———— Stocks
———— Production

Crude Cottonseed Oil   Refined Cottonseed Oil

Stocks of both commodities appear to move inversely to business cycles. The full cycle index of conformity for crude oil during five cycles is —100, that for refined oil, —60. In this respect the behavior of these commodities resembles the nonfarm products surveyed in the preceding chapter. Unlike the latter, however, stocks of crude and refined cottonseed oil respond positively to fluctuations in production (Table 56 and Chart 40).

To understand the tendency for stocks to conform positively to production cycles, we must consider the conditions influencing output. The output of cottonseed oil, both crude and refined, is controlled largely by the supply of cottonseed. Cottonseed, being cheap and bulky, can be stored much more economically after it has been reduced to oil. The production of crude oil, therefore, tends to rise and fall with the supply of seed. And since the oil, once compressed into its crude form, is usually promptly refined, the stock of crude oil acts, to a considerable degree, as an inventory of goods in process, rising and falling in close conformity with output (Chart 41).

Chart 41

Cotton Crop and Production of Crude and Refined Cottonseed Oil
Crop Years

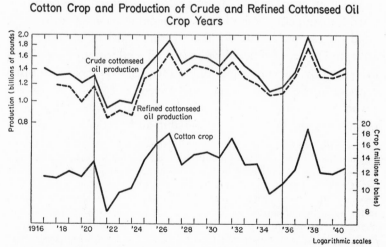

The relation between the stocks and output of refined oil is based on a different principle. The supply of cottonseed and, therefore, the output of refined oil is governed by the size of the cotton crop (Chart 41); and the latter, in turn, is governed, in the short-run, mainly by weather conditions. Hence the output of refined oil rises and falls independently of movements in the demand for oil. Stocks of refined oil will tend to increase when output rises and to decline when output falls. They do not, however, typically rise as soon as output turns up, for usually some time will elapse before the rising trend of production outruns the rate of utilization of oil. Similarly, when output falls, some time will elapse before production drops below the rate of utilization. The peaks and troughs of stocks, therefore, tend to lag behind those of output (Chart 40). Moreover, if we assume that stocks and production fluctuate synchronously, the conformity indexes of refined stocks during 5 output cycles 1920-40 are +20, +20, +11. But if we assume that stocks typically rise between stages II and VI of output cycles, the indexes run +60, +100, +78.

This is not to say that the utilization of cottonseed oil is independent of its supply even in the short-run.[1] Refined cottonseed oil has many uses in common with lard, the other principal edible fat, and with other animal fats and vegetable oils. Other things being equal, when the supply of cottonseed oil rises in consequence of a large cotton crop, its price tends to drop and it tends to be substituted for competing fats and oils in the production of shortenings, salad oils, soaps, and many other commodities. That utilization and production of refined cottonseed oil tend to move together is evidenced by the conformity indexes for refined oil output during 7 cycles in the 'disappearance' of refined oil 1920-41 which run +100, +71, +100.[2] But as might be expected, when the price of oil declines, the oil tends to be stored in anticipation of a period of

[1] Some additional explanation of the distinction between *demand* and *utilization* may be helpful. Demand for cottonseed oil can rise because, say, national income increases, stimulating activity in industries using oil. Or it can rise because the supply of substitute oils and fats declines, compelling heavier dependence on cottonseed oil. Changes in demand are accompanied by changes in the utilization of cottonseed oil, but they are not regularly accompanied by changes in the output, since that is governed by the size of the cotton crop. As indicated in the text, however, utilization is correlated also with output, since a larger supply of cottonseed oil tends to reduce its price and to encourage substitution for competing fats and oils. Economists will recognize that demand means demand in the schedule sense, while utilization means the amount removed from the market for further fabrication or consumption.

[2] 'Disappearance' is a measure of the utilization of oil in further fabrication, computed by adjusting refined oil output for changes in stocks.

lower output and higher prices. Consequently, cotton crops, cottonseed oil production, the utilization of oil, and after an interval, stocks of oil, all move together and inversely to oil prices.

The production of cottonseed oil (and ultimately the size of the cotton crop) is probably the chief influence controlling cyclical changes in the volume of oil utilization. If it were the only significant factor we would expect the cycles in production and utilization to be so closely parallel that the conformity of stocks to both would be approximately the same.[3]

It is instructive to consider another simple case. If the utilization of cottonseed oil moved in cycles unrelated to its output, that is, if utilization were influenced only from the side of demand, an increase in utilization would tend to draw down stocks, at least after an interval in which utilization overtook and ran ahead of production. A decline in utilization would cause stocks to accumulate—again, after an interval. In short, under these simple assumptions stocks would tend to vary inversely to utilization, with a lag.

Neither model fits the case. The utilization of cottonseed oil is strongly influenced by its rate of production because of the competitive relation of cottonseed oil with other fats and oils. But utilization is influenced also by two factors on the side of demand: the supply of competing fats and oils, and the level of business or national income. I do not attempt to measure their importance directly, but it may be inferred by comparing the behavior of prices of cottonseed oil and its main competitor, lard, during business cycles (Chart 42).

The similarity in the price movements of the two commodities indicates that they are close substitutes. When the supply of lard is large, it is substituted for cottonseed oil which causes the price of oil to decline in about the same degree as the price of lard. The positive conformity of both price series with business cycles indicates that the demand for fats and oils rises and falls with the level of income.[4] No other inference is open since the output of neither

[3] Cases of this sort were typical among nonagricultural commodities. There the cyclical fluctuation in demand was the dominating influence on both shipments and production, and stocks tended to vary inversely to both.

[4] Conformity indexes for the wholesale price of refined cottonseed oil at New York (11 business cycles, 1891-1938) are +45, +45, +60; those for the wholesale price of lard (5 business cycles, 1912-38) are +100, +60, +100. The war cycles, 1914-21, are omitted from both measures.

Chart 42
Refined Cottonseed Oil and Lard
Wholesale Prices, Annual Averages

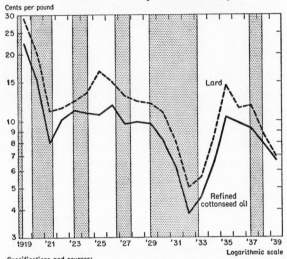

Cents per pound

Lard

Refined
cottonseed oil

1919 '21   '23   '25   '27   '29   '31   '33   '35   '37   '39

Logarithmic scale

Specifications and sources:
   Refined cottonseed oil: cents per pound, N.Y., prime, summer, yellow.
   1919-33, Department of Agriculture; 1933-39, Bureau of Labor Statistics.
   Lard: cents per pound, prime contract; Bureau of Labor Statistics.
Contractions (shaded) and expansions (unshaded) are marked off by the monthly
   reference chronology.

commodity is closely related to business at large.[5] The behavior of shortenings production, the principal consumer of cottonseed oil during the interwar period, supports our inference. The output of shortenings conformed positively to business cycles; its conformity indexes were +100, +50, +67 for 3 cycles, 1924-38. Moreover, its cyclical swings were substantial. The amplitude of shortenings production was 93.8 for 3 cycles, 1923-40; of cottonseed oil production itself, 114.8 for 4 cycles, 1922-40.

The variety of factors affecting the utilization of cottonseed oil causes the relation between stocks and utilization to be irregular. The factors influencing 'disappearance' from the side of demand, that is, the level of income and the supply of other fats and oils, would tend to produce an inverted relation, with stocks lagging. But disappearance also tends to rise and fall with cottonseed oil production. And the relation between production and stocks is

[5] The conformity indexes for lard production from federally inspected slaughter (5 cycles, 1919-38) are +20, −20, +11; those for refined cottonseed oil production (5 cycles, 1913-38) are −20, 0, −20.

Chart 43
Cottonseed Oil Stocks and Production
Average Patterns during 5 Business Cycles, 1919-1938

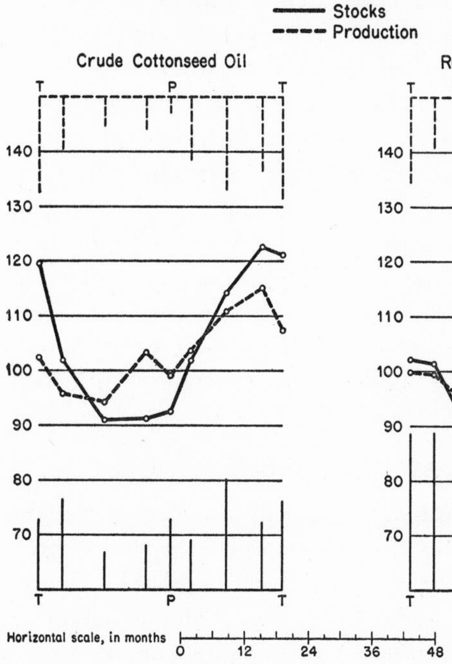

———— Stocks
———— Production

Crude Cottonseed Oil   Refined Cottonseed Oil

Horizontal scale, in months

positive, with stocks lagging. This, of course, has its effect on the relation between oil utilization and stocks. The net result is a draw. Stocks do not exhibit any regular relation to cycles in utilization. Conformity indexes for stocks during 7 cycles in the disappearance of refined cottonseed oil, 1920-38, are 0, —14, 0. This, of course, does not prove that stocks are not systematically affected by fluctuations in the demand for oil. That could be true only if the demand for oil were always constant, an assumption contrary to fact, for the demand for cottonseed oil varies with both the level of business and the supply of competing fats. The difficulty is that demand acts on stocks only through its influence on the utilization of oil, and utilization is influenced strongly also by the supply of oil. The influence of demand is therefore obscured.

This analysis enables us to understand the behavior of production and stocks during business cycles. As might be expected, the patterns of production of both crude and refined oil are very similar (Chart 43). Neither responds markedly to business cycles, although during the five interwar cycles, production rose more during contractions, on the average, than during expansions. This, in turn, reflects similar movements in the cotton crop.

The patterns of stocks are again similar to those of production, but an inverted relation to business cycles is more distinct. For the 5 business cycles 1919-38, the indexes for crude oil were —100, —67, —100; for refined oil, —20, —33, —60. The utilization of oil was, then, regularly larger than output during business expansions and regularly lower during contractions due to the influence of the level of income on the use of oil. While utilization cycles resemble production cycles closely, for reasons already stated, changes in income must have been sufficient to keep use greater than output when income was rising and lower than output when income was declining.[6]

3   Cold Storage Holdings of Pork, Lard, and Beef

Inventories of pork, lard, and beef held in storage at slaughtering plants differ from those of cottonseed oil in a vital respect: the stocks of animal products are relatively perishable. Hence their primary function is to smooth out seasonal fluctuations in the marketing of hogs and cattle. Only necessary working inventory is carried over from seasons of slack to those of heavy marketings.[7] Cottonseed oil inventories also have a seasonal function, but, in ad-

---

[6] In ideal circumstances, the correlation of utilization with business activity should tend to produce reference cycles in stocks that are related to business inversely and with a lag, rather than with a lead, as seems to have been the case. This departure from expectations is probably partly due to the pattern of cottonseed oil production itself during the cycles covered by the data (Chart 43). It may be due in part also to the influence of changes in the supply of competing goods on the demand for cottonseed oil.

[7] In response to an inquiry about the character of cold storage stocks of meat, H. B. Arthur, Manager of the Commercial Research Department of Swift and Company, writes (June 24, 1942):
"Your inquiry as to what proportion of frozen meats are surplus and what proportion are in process of distribution: In one sense none of these meats are surplus and all of them are in process of distribution. That is, meats are put in frozen storage almost entirely for the purpose of carrying surplus supplies which result from the flush marketing periods over into the season when smaller livestock marketings would otherwise result in shortages. The answer to the inquiry is, therefore, that practically all of the frozen meats are 'surplus'

dition, they serve to carry over supplies from years of relatively heavy production or light demand to years when these conditions are reversed.

Cold storage holdings of meat and lard must consequently move together with production (Table 56 and Chart 44), not because production outruns consumption when output is high but rather because the seasonal carryover is large in years of heavy animal slaughter.

To understand the behavior of these three kinds of inventory during business cycles, we must know how their output behaves. The production of all three products moves in close conformity to the rate of animal slaughter (Table 57 and Chart 45). The similarity between the three products, however, ends here. There is no firm evidence of a regular relation between pork and lard produc-

———

only in the seasonal sense and that they are 'in process of distribution' in the annual sense. The amount of frozen meats carried over from one year to the next is extremely small, although the 'out of stock' condition may come at one date for one particular cut and at a little later date for another.

Beef is frozen in very small amounts compared with pork items. Frozen beef consists almost entirely of meat to be used in the manufacture of sausage, beef specialties and leaner types of certain cuts used in lower-priced restaurants and small institutions. Beef is frozen principally in the fall months when the so-called 'grass' cattle are marketed in large numbers. The only reason why this meat is frozen is that the cattle that produce this particular type of beef are marketed in the fall of the year in such numbers as to produce a surplus. In some other seasons this grade of beef is not produced currently in sufficient quantities to take care of the demand.

Beef is not placed in cure as a result of such market factors as a decline in the demand for beef, since the amount of beef that is cured is an insignificant part of the supply and consists principally of certain cuts, such as briskets and beef hams and rump butts. The briskets are put into cure throughout the year, depending on an anticipated demand for corned beef. The beef hams and rump butts come from lean cattle which are marketed in largest numbers in the fall. The rump butts make corned beef and the beef hams are usually cured to produce dried beef. There is, of course, a very considerable demand for all of these cuts in the frozen state, and the curing is not a matter of storing surpluses but rather of preparing the product to meet a particular demand for beef that has been cured in this way.

In the case of pork there is a large surplus produced during the winter and a comparatively small supply in the summer. As stated above there is very little pork held over from one year to the next. Storage is a matter of smoothing the seasonal flow to market. In the case of smoked meats such as hams and bacon, the season of large supply is in the winter, whereas the season of large demand is in the summer."

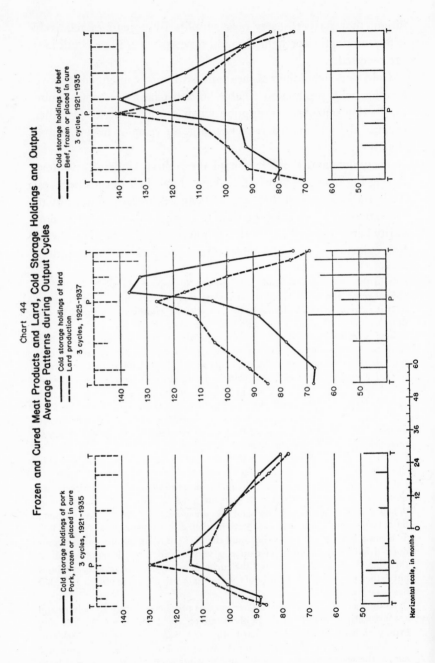

Chart 44

Frozen and Cured Meat Products and Lard, Cold Storage Holdings and Output
Average Patterns during Output Cycles

Cold storage holdings of pork
Pork, frozen or placed in cure
3 cycles, 1921-1935

Cold storage holdings of lard
Lard production
3 cycles, 1925-1937

Cold storage holdings of beef
Beef, frozen or placed in cure
3 cycles, 1921-1935

Horizontal scale, in months

Chart 45

Frozen and Cured Meat Products and Lard
Average Patterns of Output during Slaughter Cycles

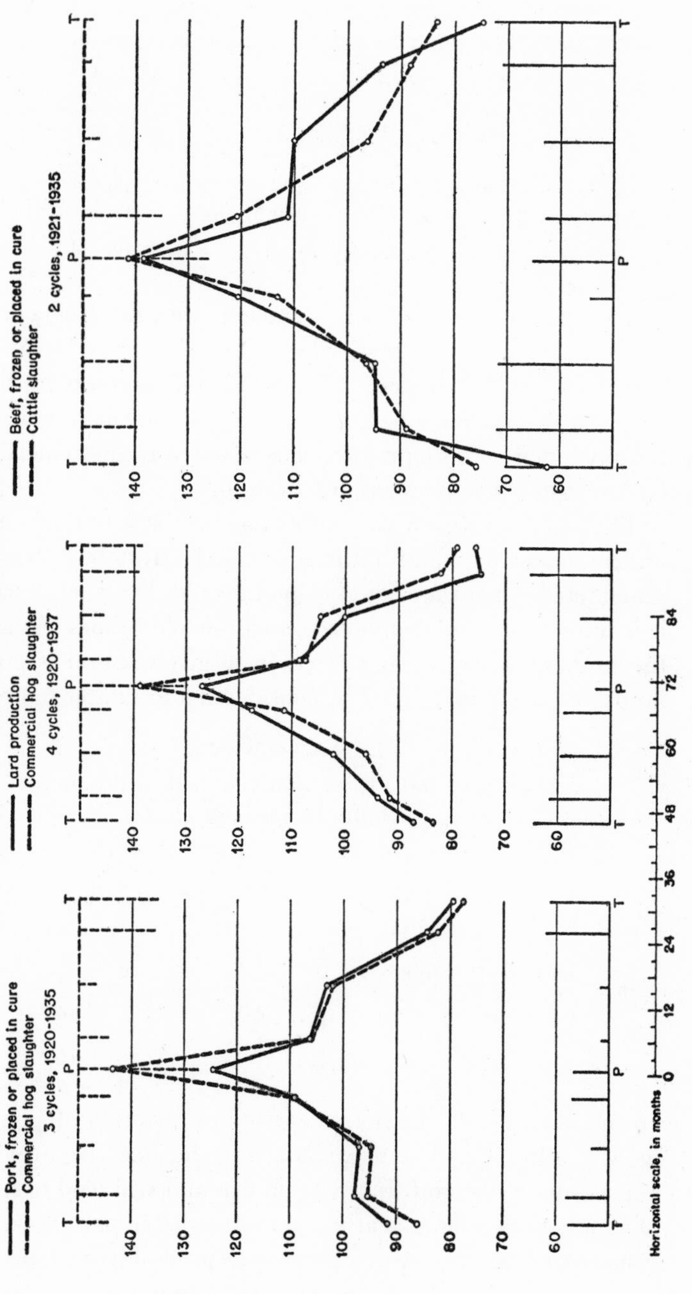
Pork, frozen or placed in cure
Commercial hog slaughter
3 cycles, 1920-1935
Lard production
Commercial hog slaughter
4 cycles, 1920-1937
Beef, frozen or placed in cure
Cattle slaughter
2 cycles, 1921-1935
T
P
140
130
120
110
100
90
80
70
60
Horizontal scale, in months
0
12
24
36
48
60
72
84

TABLE 57

Lard, Pork, and Frozen and Cured Beef Production
Conformity to Cycles in Animal Slaughter

	INDICATOR OF ANIMAL SLAUGHTER	NO. OF CYCLES	INDEX OF CONFORMITY TO SLAUGHTER		
			Exp.	Contr.	Cycle
Pork, frozen or placed in cure	Commercial hog, 1920-35	3	+100	+100	+100
Lard production	Commercial hog, 1920-37	4	+100	+60	+100
Beef, frozen or placed in cure	Cattle under fed. inspection, 1921-35	2	+100	+100	+100

tion and business cycles. Beef production, though moving in longer
cycles than general business, appears to be influenced to a marked
degree by the fluctuations in demand that accompany business
cycles (Table 58 and Chart 46). The apparently high positive conformity index for pork production is belied by the extremely irregular reference cycle patterns in Chart 46.

The causes of this disparate behavior go back to the conditions
under which hogs and cattle are raised. Most hogs by far are
slaughtered when they are 8-10 months old. With few exceptions
it is unprofitable to slaughter younger or older hogs. As a result,
the number of hogs slaughtered in a given season is governed
largely by the number farmers considered it profitable to breed 12-

TABLE 58

Lard, Pork, and Frozen and Cured Beef Production
Conformity to Business Cycles

	NO. OF CYCLES	STAGES MATCHED WITH EXP.	INDEX OF CONFORMITY TO BUSINESS		
			Exp.	Contr.	Cycle
Pork, frozen or placed in cure, 1919-33	4	I-V	0	+50	+71
Lard production, 1919-38	5	I-V	+20	−20	+11
Beef, frozen or placed in cure, 1919-33	4	I-V	0	+100	+43
Beef, frozen or placed in cure, 1919-33	4	I-IV	0	+100	+100

16 months earlier (the normal period of gestation of pigs is four
months). In part, of course, changes in the incentive to raise hogs
depend upon demand. Increases in demand will tend to stimulate
hog marketings, but only after 12-16 months. In part, however, the
incentive to raise pigs depends upon the price of feed, in the United
States chiefly corn. Since the price of corn moves inversely to the

crop and since the size of the corn crop is largely independent of
business conditions, a large element of irregularity relative to business cycles is injected into the fluctuations of pig breeding and in
turn into hog slaughter. As a first approximation, therefore, it
seems valid to say that short-term fluctuations in hog slaughter are
related only distantly to fluctuations in demand.

Chart 46

Frozen and Cured Meats and Lard
Average Patterns of Output during Business Cycles

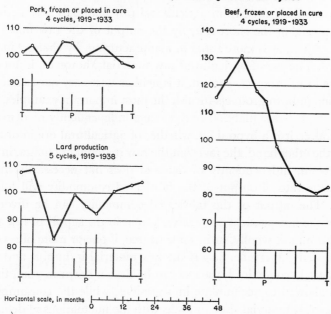

The rate at which cattle are bred also depends partly on the demand for meat and partly on the cost of raising cattle. Except
calves sold for veal, however, cattle are not marketed until they are
several years old. The number of cattle on farms is, therefore, much
larger relative to the annual rate of slaughter than is the number
of hogs, and there is more flexibility in the age at which cattle can
profitably be slaughtered. Hence cattle breeders can increase their
marketings significantly when demand and price rise by selling their
animals somewhat earlier and follow the opposite course when demand and price fall. In consequence, cattle slaughter tends to conform positively to business cycles.

The fluctuations of pork, lard, and beef inventories are consistent with these conditions in the animal breeding industry. As Table 55 indicated, cold storage holdings of pork and lard do not appear to be related to business cycles, while stocks of beef and veal conform positively. The full cycle indexes for the two hog products were 0 and +20; for beef and veal, the full cycle index was +60.

4   Inedible Tallow

The commodities reviewed above illustrated how the production of goods fabricated from agricultural raw materials is sometimes controlled, in the short-run, by the output of the raw materials rather than, as is more usual in manufacturing, by changes in demand. The use of agricultural raw materials, however, is not decisive in this respect. Indeed, it is neither necessary nor sufficient. Although farm products furnish the most important examples, the supply of a raw material may change independently of demand whenever it is a byproduct, whether of agricultural origin or not. On the other hand, the fact that the raw material fluctuates, in the short-run, independently of demand does not necessarily mean that the rate of output of the fabricated commodity will follow suit. The output of the fabricated commodity can be divorced from the independent cyclical variations in the supply of raw materials almost wholly, or in some degree, if one or more of several conditions supervene. (a) If the raw material is durable and can be stored economically, stocks can be drawn down in good times and allowed to accumulate in recessions, while the consumption of the raw material rises and falls with the fluctuations in demand for fabricated products. Cotton and rubber, reviewed in Chapter 10, are good examples. (b) If the material is a byproduct whose output, relative to the major product, is not invariant, its supply can be enlarged at special expense. Tallow, the next commodity to be studied, is an example. (c) If a considerable portion of the raw material supply comes from abroad, imports are likely to rise and fall in response to the demand for the fabricated commodity and to offset, at least in part, fluctuations in the domestic portion of the supply of materials. Linseed oil and leather production are examples we shall review below. As stated, the freedom from fluctuations in raw material supply that these conditions gain for manufacturing operations may be great or small, but when the conditions are present, the situation is worth separate notice and study.

Inedible tallow is a puzzling case in point.[8] Produced largely from the fatty wastes of slaughtered cattle and, to a much smaller extent, from those of sheep and lambs, it is a byproduct of meat production. Not all tallow, however, is produced by meat packers under true byproduct conditions. In large part it is manufactured by rendering plants which purchase fatty wastes from local slaughterers and convert them into tallow and grease. The production of the two divisions of the industry has been estimated by L. B. Zapoleon (Table 59).

TABLE 59

Inedible Tallow Produced by Meat Packers and Others

(millions of pounds)

	1914	1919	1921	1923	1925	1927
Packers	164	175	152	177	165	171
Others	34	77	175	207	214	234
Total	197	252	327	384	378	404

Inedible Animal Fats in the U. S., *Fats and Oils Studies, 3,* Stanford University, Food Research Institute, Dec. 1929, p. 107.

The United States Tariff Commission writes (*Report to the Congress on Certain Vegetable Oils, Whale Oil and Copra,* No. 41, 1932, pp. 222-4):

"Inedible tallow is derived principally from such fat of cattle and sheep as can not be utilized for food purposes. . . . Since 1914 the recovery [of tallow] has increased more than the total production of meat, evidencing a greater utilization of waste animal fats . . . the increase in production of inedible tallow was mainly by producers other than the packers . . . local rendering plants distributed in urban centers. . . . The bulk of the increase has come from the local renderers. . . .

The two principal divisions of the industry stand on a different footing as far as expansion is concerned. Speaking broadly, the packers recover now about the maximum amount of inedible fats and will probably continue to do so irrespective of price so long as it covers the cost of recovery. Production by renderers, however, must be affected largely by price, for they are not in the position of utilizing a by-prod-

[8] The chief use of tallow is in the manufacture of soap, of which it is the principal raw material.

uct of their principal manufacture but of purchasing fatty wastes and converting them into tallow and grease as major products, along with their joint products, tankage and crackling. Manifestly, the price of tallow and grease will influence the volume of production, in particular the rate of erection of new rendering plants."

It is not, of course, surprising to discover some correlation between the rate of cattle slaughter and the output of tallow. When slaughter increases, the output of tallow in the large meat-packing plants must increase as a byproduct. And the more plentiful supply of animal wastes stimulates production in the specialized rendering plants. Although the patterns of tallow output and cattle slaughter exhibit many differences (Chart 47) they conform positively to each other if we allow for the marked secular growth in the former. Conformity indexes for tallow production during 3 slaughter cycles, 1921-39, that run +100, −50, +67 constitute further evidence of this relation.

Chart 47
Inedible Tallow Production and Cattle Slaughter
Average Patterns during 3 Slaughter Cycles, 1921-1939

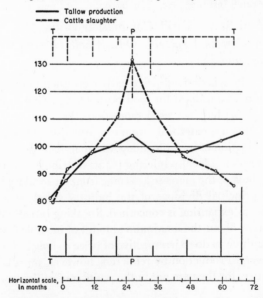

Note: Reference framework for tallow production derived from turns in quarterly series of cattle slaughtered under federal inspection. Specific cycle pattern for cattle slaughter based on monthly data.

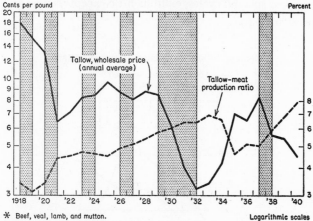

Chart 48
Wholesale Prices of Inedible Tallow and
Tallow-Meat Production Ratio*

Cents per pound

Tallow, wholesale price
(annual average)

Tallow-meat
production ratio

1918 '20 '22 '24 '26 '28 '30 '32 '34 '36 '38 '40

Percent

Logarithmic scales

* Beef, veal, lamb, and mutton.
Contractions (shaded) and expansions (unshaded) are marked off
by the yearly reference chronology.

What is surprising is that the recovery of tallow does not seem to have been sensitive to changes in its price, certainly not to inter-annual movements (Chart 48). The sharp decline in prices between 1928 and 1932, for example, did not prevent a concomitant increase in the rate of tallow recovery. Indeed, the dominant impression of Chart 48 is that the rate of tallow recovery per pound of meat has moved inversely to tallow prices. Though prices vary positively with business cycles the tallow-meat production ratio does not respond in any regular fashion to prosperity and depression. In the cycles of 1918-20, 1921-24, and 1923-26 it moves positively with business, but in the cycles of 1919-20, 1920-23, 1929-37, and 1932-38 it moves inversely. The effect of the violent cycle of 1927-32 is hardly noticeable.

I cannot explain this perverse behavior, but it is consistent with other characteristics of tallow output and stocks. For example, in the interwar period the rate of cattle slaughter tended to vary with business cycles.[9] The influence of the irregular movements of the rate of tallow recovery per pound of meat, however, was sufficient to make the output of tallow during business cycles irregular as

[9] See above, Sec. 3. The conformity indexes of cattle slaughter to the 5 interwar business cycles were +60, +100, +78.

well. The full cycle index of the conformity of tallow output was +11, and the average reference cycle pattern of tallow output, despite marked specific cycles, exhibits little except secular growth of output (Chart 49).

Chart 49
Inedible Tallow Production, Average Patterns

---- 5 specific cycles, 1919-1937
—— 5 reference cycles, 1919-1938

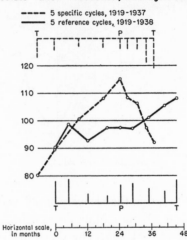

It appears, therefore, that despite a local rendering industry presumably able to increase output in response to demand, production of tallow was not, in the interwar period, sensitive to short-run changes in demand as indicated by prices. Instead, it fluctuated in cycles of its own, influenced partly by the rate of animal slaughter and partly by other factors. As a result, the relation of tallow stocks to production and business cycles is similar to that of cottonseed oil and other commodities with the same characteristics. Stocks conform positively to production cycles and inversely to business cycles, with some tendency to lead the latter (Chart 50). The conformity indexes of stocks during 5 production cycles 1919-37 were +60, +20, +78; during 5 business cycles 1919-38, —20, —20, —56 when stages I-IV were matched with expansions.

5 Linseed Oil

The behavior of linseed oil stocks permits a somewhat fuller development of the idea first encountered in the review of tallow inventories. Variations in the supply of domestic raw materials, in this

Chart 50
Inedible Tallow Stocks and Production, Average Patterns
——— Stocks
- - - - Production

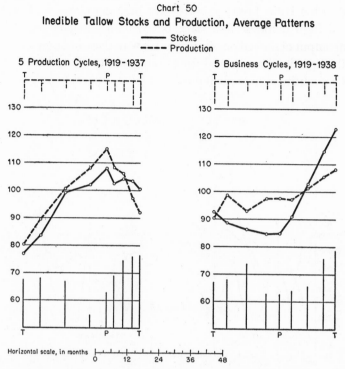

5 Production Cycles, 1919-1937   5 Business Cycles, 1919-1938

Horizontal scale, in months

case flaxseed, influence the output of linseed oil, but again another factor intervenes to enable production to proceed with some degree of independence of raw material supply and thus to be adjusted more closely to demand than in the cases of cottonseed oil and hog products.

The fact that both are vegetable oils invites comparison between cottonseed oil and linseed oil. With respect to the former, we found that output cycles were dominated by cycles in the cotton crop, since the cottonseed itself could not be stored economically; hence the production of oil was not correlated significantly with business cycles. The domestic crop of flaxseed does not impose its own pattern upon the production of linseed oil nearly as strictly. The difference reflects the different degree to which operations in the two industries depend upon the size of the domestic seed crop. While cottonseed oil is made almost exclusively from American cottonseed, approximately half of our linseed oil in recent years has been pressed from imported flaxseed. The production of flax-

seed in the United States controls the quantity of linseed oil produced from domestic materials, but year to year changes in the
total output of linseed oil often disagree with those of domestic flaxseed output in direction and size (Chart 51). The balancing factor
is the quantity of linseed oil produced from imported seed.[10]

Chart 51
Flaxseed and Linseed Oil Production

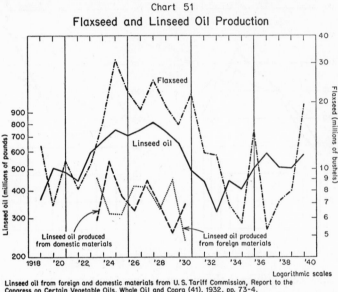

Logarithmic scales

Linseed oil from foreign and domestic materials from U. S. Tariff Commission, Report to the
Congress on Certain Vegetable Oils, Whale Oil and Copra (41), 1932, pp. 73-4.

The possibility of offsetting fluctuations in the domestic crop of
flaxseed by varying the rate of imports makes the production of
linseed oil responsive to changes in demand. To establish this relation, we estimated linseed oil shipments from output and changes
in stocks.[11] Cycles in the output of linseed oil vary positively with
shipments as evidenced by conformity indexes of +100, +100,
+100 during 2 cycles of shipments 1921-38 (actually five phases—

10 There is some suggestion in the chart that longer-run developments in domestic flaxseed production follow the trend of linseed oil production. If so,
this would aid in adjusting linseed oil production to demand by gradually re-
moving the pressure of excess supplies of raw materials when demand is falling and by gradually reducing dependence on imports during expansions.

11 Stocks of linseed oil are largely held by manufacturers, but they include
some stocks in public storage owned by others. The computed shipments series,
therefore, is strictly an index of the 'disappearance' of linseed oil from the inventories in manufacturing plants and in public warehouses.

three contractions and two expansions). The same relation is revealed by the cycle patterns in Chart 52. Output as well as shipments also conformed positively to business cycles. The average patterns are confirmed by conformity indexes of +100, +20, +78 for shipments and +60, +60, +78 for production during the 5 business cycles 1919-38.

The low conformity of shipments to business contractions reflects the fact that shipments continued to rise during the two mild recessions of the mid-'twenties. This is, of course, characteristic of commodities used in building construction during the tremendous upswing of construction that marked the period. Production, in contrast, did not rise during one of the five expansions and declined during one of the two mild contractions skipped by the shipments series. Both the rise and decline indicate that while production can be adjusted to changes in demand, other important factors help to guide its course.

Confirmation comes from a fact hidden in the average patterns and other information of Chart 52. While there were 5 business cycles during the period, and only two and one-half cycles in linseed oil shipments, the National Bureau has identified 8 cycles in linseed oil production. The situation may be clarified by inspecting the complete series of seasonally corrected production and shipments data in Chart 53. The circles and asterisks indicate the specific cycle turns identified by the National Bureau. Beginning with a peak tentatively placed in the third quarter of 1919, shipments decline until the end of 1921. They then begin a long cycle which reaches a peak at the end of 1928 and a trough in 1933. Another long cycle corresponding to the long business cycle of 1933-37-38 follows. Production has an initial expansion in 1918-19 before our shipments series begins. It has a contraction corresponding to that of shipments in 1919-22, then moves through the two long cycles found also in shipments. In addition, production moved through several shorter cycles: two during the major expansion from 1922 to 1929, one during the major contraction from 1929 to 1932, and two during the major expansion of the 'thirties.

Most of the 'extra' cycles in production may reasonably be attributed to the fact that variations in imports cannot offset immediately and completely the effects of fluctuations in the domestic

Chart 52

Linseed Oil Production and Shipments, Average Patterns

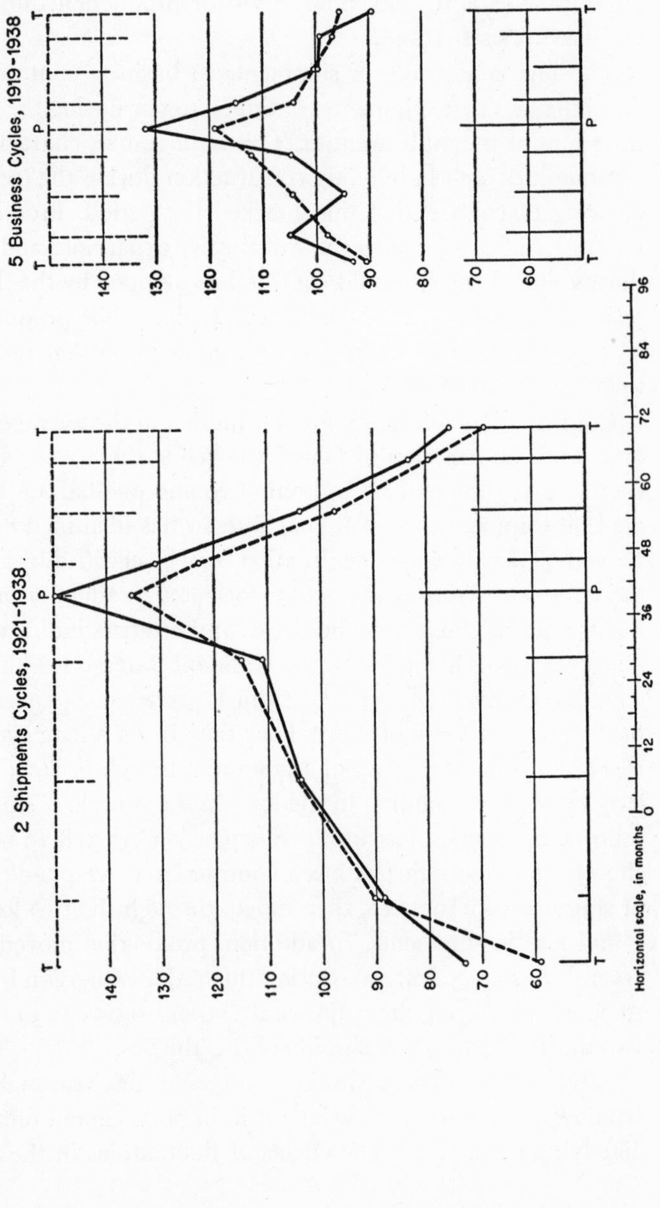
Production
Shipments
2 Shipments Cycles, 1921-1938
5 Business Cycles, 1919-1938
T
P
T
140
130
120
110
100
90
80
70
60
Horizontal scale, in months
0
12
24
36
48
60
72
84
96

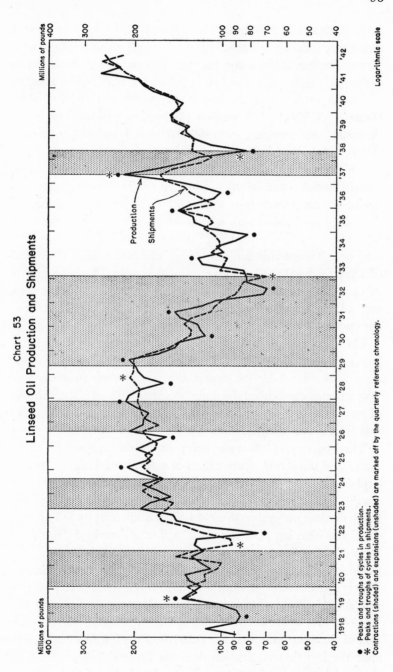

Chart 53
Linseed Oil Production and Shipments

Millions of pounds

Logarithmic scale

● Peaks and troughs of cycles in production.
✳ Peaks and troughs of cycles in shipments.
Contractions (shaded) and expansions (unshaded) are marked off by the quarterly reference chronology.

crop of flaxseed. A bumper crop, therefore, is likely to cause a temporary increase in linseed oil production; a short crop, a temporary decline. After some months, indeed, larger imports can make good deficiencies, and smaller imports remove the pressure of surplus seed. Hence the larger movements of linseed oil shipments are faithfully followed by production. Fluctuations in the domestic crop, however, seem still able to activate smaller production cycles that are independent of demand.

A glance back at Chart 51 lends support to this view. If we neglect the initial expansion of production before the shipments data begin, we can match four of the other five extra movements of linseed oil production with a pronounced fluctuation in the crop. The output peak in early 1925 then corresponds to the large flaxseed crop harvested in autumn 1924. The output peak at the end of 1927 followed the large harvest of that year. The large output of 1931 can be matched with the big crop of 1930, and in the same way a large harvest was followed by a peak in linseed oil output at the end of 1935.

The fifth extra movement in output, in 1933-34, presumably has a different explanation. It represents, I think, the additional output stimulated by the expectation of increases in prices and wages that accompanied the dollar devaluation and NRA episodes of 1933. Once these influences had spent themselves, production was cut and stocks liquidated.

These two sets of influences upon output, the longer cycles of demand and the shorter fluctuations of raw material supply, help to explain the behavior of linseed oil stocks. As already shown in connection with cottonseed oil stocks, during the shorter, supply-stimulated production cycles, stocks of linseed oil tend to follow production with a lag (Chart 54). The fluctuations in the supply of flaxseed carry linseed oil output now above, now below, the rate of shipments. When output turns up, however, it does not immediately rise above shipments, and until it does, stocks continue to fall. And similarly when it turns down. Note particularly the pattern of stocks in the first full cycle of output, 1922-26, the contraction of the next cycle, and the patterns of the last four cycles. Despite the fact that production does not proceed independently of demand but, as we have seen, is correlated also with the rate of

Chart 54

Linseed Oil Stocks and Production, Patterns during Production Cycles

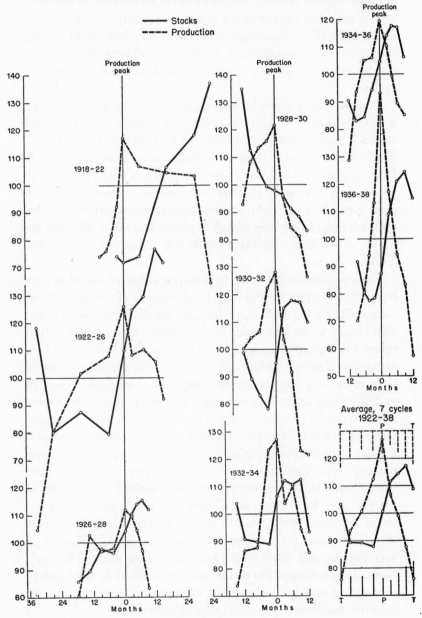

shipments, the influence of production cycles has made itself felt in fairly regular fashion. Stages IV-VIII seemed to be the most typical period of expansion for stocks during output cycles, which accounts for the negative sign of the conformity indexes. Matching the typical expansion stages of stocks with contractions of production yielded indexes of —71, —75, —100 for the seven and one-half cycles.

The movement of stocks during cycles in shipments (Chart 55) is roughly consistent with the findings of Chapter 11 for finished staples whose output can be adjusted to movements of demand. Stocks move inversely during the short contraction of shipments from 1919 to 1921 but during the exceptionally long phases 1921-28, 1928-33, and 1933-37, they move with shipments. During the short contraction of 1937-38, they again respond inversely. This even mixture of very long and short phases and of the differing behavior of stocks during them yields low indexes of conformity: +100, —33, 0.

The resemblance between the behavior of linseed oil stocks during cycles in shipments and the typical behavior of nonagricultural commodities is not, indeed, perfect, but the differences seem traceable largely to the influences of the shorter, independent output cycles. For example, stocks turn up unexpectedly early in the long expansion of shipments beginning in 1921. The explanation seems to lie in the very large increases of the flaxseed crop between 1922 and 1923 and again between 1923 and 1924. We would expect stocks to rise for a time after the peak of shipments in the last quarter of 1928 but instead they reached a peak earlier, in the second quarter of 1928, then declined. The explanation again is the movement of crops. The large flaxseed crop harvested in autumn 1927 was followed by an upsurge of production in the fourth quarter of the year and the first quarter of 1928 (see Chart 53) which lifted stocks to a peak some months later. The early decline of stocks therefore seems to reflect liquidation of excess stocks of linseed oil accumulated as a result of the bumper crop of flaxseed in 1927. Similarly, the choppiness of the pattern of stocks in the 1928-33 contraction and in the 1933-38 expansion (Chart 55) can be traced to the extra production cycles already noted.

The relation of linseed oil stocks to business cycles is fixed by

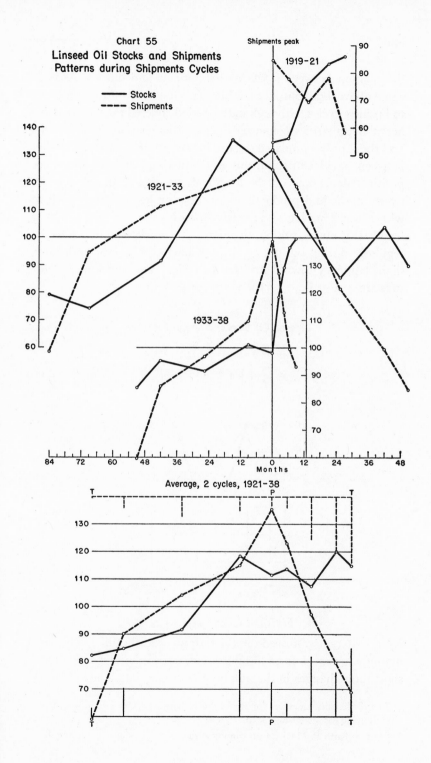

Chart 55
Linseed Oil Stocks and Shipments
Patterns during Shipments Cycles

Stocks
Shipments

1919–21
Shipments peak

1921–33

1933–38

Months

Average, 2 cycles, 1921–38

the relation between stocks and shipments and output. As indicated above, both output and shipments tend to conform positively to business cycles, although in the period covered there were significant irregularities connected with the long cycles in shipments and the supply-stimulated fluctuations in production. The relation between stocks and shipments was sometimes inverse, sometimes positive, depending on the length of the phase; the relation between stocks and production was more or less regularly positive with a very long lag—equivalent to an inverse correlation with a lead.[12] It is not surprising, therefore, that stocks should behave irregularly during busines cycles, as Chart 56 suggests, with some slight tendency toward inverted behavior: the conformity measures are —20, —60, —33 for 5 business cycles 1919-38.

Chart 56

Linseed Oil Stocks, Average Patterns

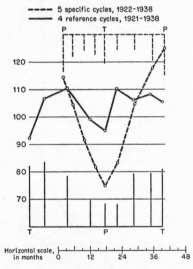

6   *Finished Cattle Hide Leather*[13]

Even better than linseed oil, the output of leather illustrates how manufacturers of farm products can proceed independently of short-term changes in the supply of raw materials. The independ-

[12] The conformity measures for stocks during output cycles are, indeed, negative allowing for a one-stage lead.

[13] See also Ruth P. Mack's forthcoming study referred to in Ch. 10, note 8.

ence, of course, is not absolute, but it is marked, and the behavior of tanners' stocks of finished leather reflects the kinship between leather and other commodities whose output in the short-run is controlled largely by demand.

The principal source of cattle hide leather in the United States is domestic slaughter. The supply of domestic hides in a given period is, therefore, influenced both by the current demand for meat and the breeding decisions made several years earlier. The current demand for leather is of little consequence since hides do not account for more than 10 percent of the value of slaughtered cattle. Despite these conditions, as we saw in Chapter 10, tanners can, in most cases, obtain enough hides to meet their current needs. First, cattle slaughter and leather output are at least indirectly related. Cattle slaughter tends to increase when consumer incomes rise. And since the demand for shoes and industrial leather too is stimulated by better business and rising incomes, the output of leather and the domestic supply of hides both conform positively to business cycles. The increase in cattle slaughter is not nearly as large as in leather output, however (Chart 20). The discrepancy between the consumption and output of hides is covered largely by imports. When demand for hides outruns supply, the price tends to rise, and with rising prices, imports increase (Chart 21). Hence, the total movement into sight of cattle hides is more nearly adjusted to the demands of leather production than is domestic cattle slaughter (Chart 22). Finally, since hides can be stored economically for long periods, a buffer stock is kept by dealers, importers, and packers on which manufacturers can draw when the current supply, whether from domestic slaughter or imports, is inadequate.

This argument, of course, is not exhaustive. When demand for hides tends to outrun supply, the rising price can and, to some degree presumably does, check leather output. To this degree the cycles in leather output are influenced by the supply of raw materials. To some degree the same is presumably true of all manufactured goods, whether from agricultural or nonagricultural materials. But here, as in the case of most nonfarm products, the influence of raw materials is not decisive. By increasing imports and drawing on stocks of hides, leather output can outrun the supply of hides from domestic slaughter, and by reducing imports and allowing excess stocks to accumulate in the hands of dealers and importers, it can be curtailed when demand falls off. One indication that tanners can adjust receipts to current needs is that their inventories of raw hides increase and decline with leather output, leaving to dealers' and importers' stocks the function of ironing out disparities between supply and demand (Chart 23). Additional confirmation is afforded by the relation between leather and shoe production. Cycles in leather output conform positively to those in shoe output, and their patterns are generally similar (Chart 57). Conformity indexes for leather output during 7 cycles in shoe output 1924-40 were +100, +75, +100.

Chart 57
Leather and Shoe Production
Average Patterns during 7 Shoe Production Cycles
1924 -1940

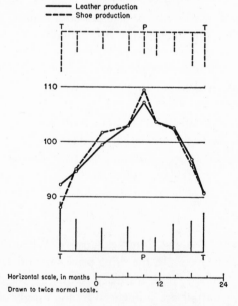

In this situation, stocks of finished leather at tanners act like the commodities derived from nonagricultural materials reviewed in Chapter 11: they move inversely to both leather and shoe output. The conformity indexes of leather stocks during 7 cycles in leather output 1921-40 were —100, —14, —100. Similarly, the conformity

indexes of leather stocks during 7 cycles in shoe output 1924-40
were —100, —50, —100 (Chart 58).

Chart 58
Finished Leather Stocks at Tanners and Leather and Shoe Production
Average Patterns during Production Cycles

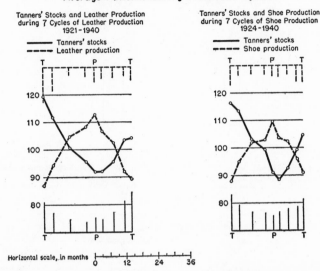

Tanners' Stocks and Leather Production
during 7 Cycles of Leather Production
1921-1940

———— Tanners' stocks
– – – – Leather production

Tanners' Stocks and Shoe Production
during 7 Cycles of Shoe Production
1924-1940

———— Tanners' stocks
– – – – Shoe production

Horizontal scale, in months

Leather stocks also tended to move inversely during business
cycles, although less regularly because of the imperfect conformity
of leather and shoe output to business cycles. The conformity indexes were —33, —33, —20 for 3 business cycles 1924-38 (Chart
59).

This behavior contrasts markedly with that of commodities
whose production is governed by the supply of raw materials. Cottonseed oil and hog products, for example, tend to move irregularly, or inversely with a lag, during cycles in demand but to conform positively to cycles in output. Leather stocks, like stocks of
other commodities whose production is dominated by demand,
tend to move inversely to output, to demand (as represented by
shoe output), and to business at large.

7   Other Fabricated Agricultural Products

Unfortunately, I cannot yet explain even tentatively the behavior
of stocks of evaporated milk and shortenings. I can merely record
some of the relevant measures of their movements.

Chart 59
Finished Leather Stocks at Tanners and Leather and Shoe Production
Average Patterns during Business Cycles

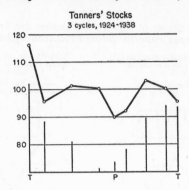

Tanners' Stocks
3 cycles, 1924-1938

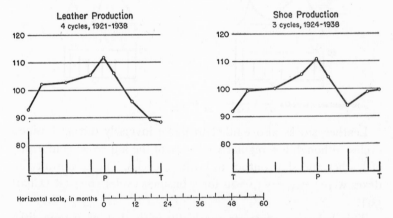

EVAPORATED MILK (CASE GOODS) AT MANUFACTURERS

During the business cycles for which we have data inventories moved irregularly. Conformity indexes for 4 cycles 1921-38 were +50, 0, —14. There does seem to be some evidence, however, of a tendency for stocks to conform positively to cycles in evaporated milk output with a lag of approximately two stages (Chart 60). Conformity indexes are +60, +33, +40 for 5 output cycles 1920-37 when the expansion of stocks was measured between stages III and VII; measured synchronously, the indexes are 0, —20, +20.

Unlike several other fabricated farm products reviewed above, cycles in the output of evaporated milk are not controlled by cycles in the supply of its raw material. The output of fluid milk is very steady compared with that of evaporated milk (Chart 61). Fluctuations in the latter must, therefore, be regarded as responses to changes on the side of demand. But these changes themselves are likely to be very complex; for evaporated milk is merely one of a fairly large number of products derived from whole milk. Hence its production would tend to be stimulated when the demand for evaporated milk is high relative to the demands for other milk products rather than when the demand for evaporated milk by itself is high. Moreover, since canning milk is one means of storing an otherwise perishable product, the demand for evaporated milk, including the demand for storage purposes, might be expected to be high when the demand for milk products in general is low. This in turn leads one at first to expect evaporated milk output to be high during depression, low during prosperity. The evidence, however, shows that it has not fluctuated in any regular fashion during business cycles. Conformity indexes for 5 cycles 1919-38 were +60, —50, 0.

I suspect that stocks tend to respond positively with some lag to cycles in evaporated milk output because the latter is influenced by the relative profitability of storing milk in this form. This hypothesis, however, should be tested by studying the cost of producing evaporated milk and its price relative to costs and prices of numerous other milk products. Apparently, too, the complex factors that control the relative profitability of producing evaporated milk as against other milk products do not make evaporated milk output respond in any regular fashion to business cycles. Hence the irregular behavior of its stocks during business cycles.

SHORTENINGS

The meager evidence we have on stocks of shortenings does not suggest behavior consistent with any of the standard patterns so far defined. Since shortenings are made from various vegetable oils and animal fats, both domestic and imported, output cycles are not likely to be strongly influenced by cycles in the output of raw materials. This, indeed, is suggested too by the conformity measures for shortenings output which run +100, +50, +67 for 3 cycles 1923-38 when expansion is calculated from stages I to V.

Stocks of shortenings do not, however, act like stocks of other fabricated goods whose output cycles are dominated by demand

Chart 60
Evaporated Milk Stocks and Production
Patterns during Production Cycles

—— Stocks
---- Production

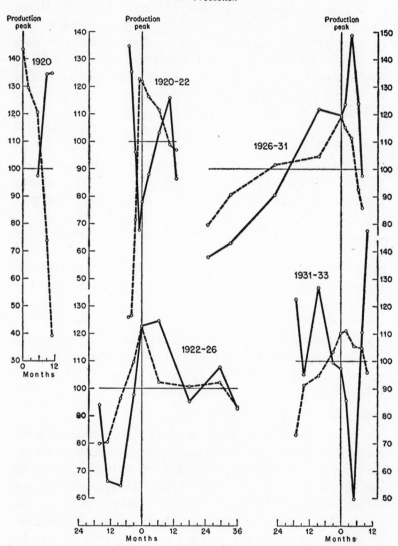

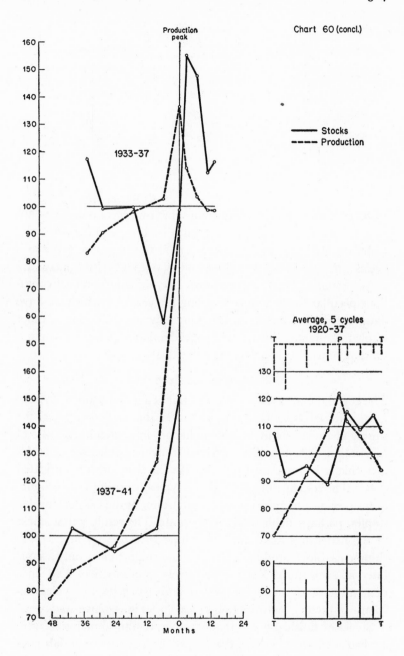

Production
peak

Chart 60 (concl.)

—— Stocks
----- Production

1933-37

Average, 5 cycles
1920-37

1937-41

Months

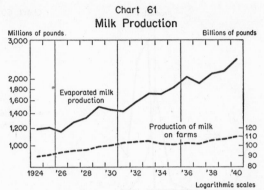

Chart 61
Milk Production

(Ch. 11). For the short period for which we have data, they appear to move irregularly during both business and output cycles (Chart 62). Conformity indexes are +100, 0, 0 for 3 business cycles 1923-38. Conformity indexes to 3 output cycles 1923-40 are +50, —100, 0. The low conformity may, of course, reflect conditions peculiar to the industry during the years for which we have data, and in the future its behavior may resemble that of other staple manufactured items whose production responds to demand. Of that, however, there is as yet no evidence.

8 A General Account

The key to the behavior of stocks of finished goods made from non-farm materials is, as Chapter 11 showed, the ready response of the supply of these raw materials to changes in demand. The rate of fabrication of commodities derived from them, therefore, fluctuates chiefly in response to changes in the demand for fabricated goods. The response of production is typically tardy (since production decisions are guided by demand) and, in the case of durable staples, perhaps deliberately inadequate. The result is that stocks of finished goods made for the market tend to vary inversely to shipments. Since production lags behind shipments by only a short interval, such stocks also vary inversely to production. And since demand and shipments conform to business cycles, the typical response of these inventories to business cycles is also inverse.[14]

Stocks of finished goods made from agricultural materials were studied separately because the supply of these raw materials generally does not respond in elastic fashion to short-run changes in

[14] Stocks of perishable goods are probably an exception; see Ch. 11.

Chart 62

Shortenings Stocks and Production, Average Patterns

—— Stocks
---- Production

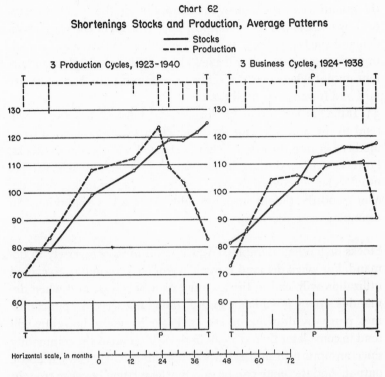

3 Production Cycles, 1923-1940   3 Business Cycles, 1924-1938

Horizontal scale, in months

demand. The current supply, as determined by weather and other natural causes, may, therefore, largely determine the rate of fabrication independently of the influence of the demand for the fabricated products. The effect of supply conditions on cycles in the stocks of finished goods, however, is not uniform. The conclusions to which the analysis of this chapter leads may be summarized in a series of statements.

1) If a fabricated commodity's principal raw material is agricultural, and if a current deficiency in supply cannot be supplemented by imports or drafts from stocks or a current surplus removed by accumulating stocks, then the level of fabrication is determined by the output of raw materials. Examples are cottonseed oil, lard, frozen and cured pork.[15]

2) If the finished product is perishable, it must be marketed fairly quickly at whatever price it will bring. Stocks, representing only

15 Frozen and cured beef is not a good example since the stock of cattle is sufficiently large to allow slaughter to respond to current changes in demand.

the quantities in the course of distribution or the seasonal carry-over, will rise and fall with output. They will not be correlated with demand since supplies cannot be carried over when supply tends to outrun demand, nor will stocks be available to supplement current output when demand tends to outrun supply. Examples are lard and frozen and cured pork.

3) If the finished product is durable, (a) finished stocks again will tend to rise and fall with the production of the fabricated commodity because the latter is not correlated with demand. Stocks, however, will tend to lag behind production since an interval will usually elapse between the time production begins to increase (decline) and the time it surpasses (drops below) consumption. An example is cottonseed oil.

Stocks of finished durables (b) will tend to vary inversely to demand. For when demand is weak, a tendency for output to exceed utilization will lead to the accumulation of stocks; and when demand is strong, a tendency for utilization to exceed output can be met partly by drawing on stocks. Peaks in stocks, however, will tend to come later than troughs in the utilization of the commodity since an upturn in utilization will not immediately carry it above output. And the same can be said for the relation between troughs in stocks and peaks in utilization. The correlation between stocks and utilization will be disturbed by the irregular fluctuations in stocks caused by irregular movements in output during cycles in utilization. The strength of the correlation will, therefore, depend upon the relative amplitudes of output and utilization. If demand and utilization are positively correlated with business cycles, stocks will tend to conform inversely to business cycles with a lag. And again this pattern will be disturbed by the irregular fluctuations of output and concomitant movements in stocks. Again an example is cottonseed oil.

4) For the above relations to hold, it is neither a necessary nor a sufficient condition that the goods be fabricated from agricultural materials. (a) It is not a necessary condition because the output of a raw material may fluctuate independently of demand for reasons other than the hazards of farming. It will do so, for example, if it is a byproduct of another commodity. (b) It is not a sufficient

condition because short-run movements in the production of the fabricated commodity can be rendered independent of current raw material supply if: (i) the material can be stored economically, (ii) supplies can be supplemented from abroad, (iii) in the case of byproducts, more can be obtained at special expense.

5) If fabrication is not controlled by current domestic supply because one or more of these conditions is present, its movements tend to follow demand. The behavior of stocks of finished goods will then resemble that of goods produced from nonagricultural materials. Examples are leather, linseed oil and, less clearly, tallow.

It would, of course, be of great interest to measure accurately the stocks held by various industries that fit each case described above. This is not possible, but rough figures indicate that manufactured commodities whose rate of output is dominated by variations in the supply of raw materials are probably of minor importance (App. E, Table 106). Apart from byproducts, a very small group, the class is confined at the outset to products that are made from agricultural raw materials. These accounted for some $1,368 million worth of stocks of finished goods on December 31, 1939, or approximately 35 percent of total finished goods stocks. Of this quantity, however, some $560 million represents goods made from cotton, wool, silk, hides, and rubber which can be economically stored in crude form. The possibility of holding large quantities of such goods for long periods undoubtedly accounts for the fact that cycles in the output of commodities made from these materials are influenced principally by changes in demand, as common knowledge assures us they are. Eliminating these goods reduces the class virtually to manufactured food and tobacco products which amounted to $808 million, or 20 percent of all finished goods.

But not all of this remainder clearly meets the specifications of the class. Products made from grains can be better stored raw than in the form of flour, and better as flour than in the form of bakery products. It is uncertain how much to allow for these exceptions. Roughly, we may say that stocks of finished foods whose output cycles are governed by raw materials supply constitute perhaps 15 to 20 percent of all finished goods inventories, or 6 to 8 percent of manufacturers' total inventories.

CHAPTER 13

A Preliminary Theory of the Cyclical Behavior
of Manufacturers' Stocks

This chapter attempts to draw together the many suggestions advanced in earlier parts of the book to explain the behavior of manufacturers' stocks during business cycles. This account, however, cannot be more than a preliminary explanation. The data so far analyzed disclose some of the significant behavior traits of inventories; but they reveal also that for many aspects of inventory behavior we cannot now obtain reliable information, and for some none is available.

1 Total Stocks

The physical volume of manufacturers' inventories, as a whole, tends to conform to business cycles with a long lag. This is the solid characteristic of inventory behavior that can be established with presently available evidence and that requires explanation.

Timing measurements point to the conclusion that the length of the lag is 6 to 12 months. As argued in Chapter 4, the true lag is probably closer to the former figure than it is to the latter, but the crudity of our estimates of inventories in constant prices makes it difficult to express the lag more precisely. In any event, the lag of the physical volume of inventories is one of the longest departures yet found among important series from the modal behavior by which cyclical turns in business are dated. Indeed it is so long that during very short expansions or contractions, inventories must typically move counter to the business tide for half a phase or more.

2 Major Classes of Stocks

The inventory holdings of manufacturers are not a homogeneous mass of goods subject to similar influences and behaving in similar fashion. Substantial differences can be discerned, and an explanation of manufacturers' total holdings must be a compound of separate hypotheses about distinct categories. This study has distinguished three major classes—goods in process, raw materials, and finished goods—and several minor classes.

GOODS IN PROCESS

To understand the behavior of goods in process, which account for about 20 percent of all manufacturers' holdings, we divided industries into two groups. In one, 'continuous' industries, the quantity of goods in process is fairly rigidly tied to the rate of manufacturing activity for any one of several reasons. There may be only one stage of fabrication or the technical conditions may be such as to enforce or make highly profitable the uninterrupted processing of raw materials. In the second group, the quantity of goods in process is not rigidly tied to the rate of manufacturing activity. Here the process is divided into stages and opportunity exists for inventories to pile up 'between stages' when activity slumps or to be drawn down when activity picks up. The two groups appear to hold about the same quantity of goods in process.

In continuous industries the behavior of goods in process can be deduced from the character of the process (Ch. 8). Stocks of goods in process rise and fall with the rate of output. They cannot lag behind output and, in fact, are likely to lead. The lead, however, must be short, for it cannot exceed the period necessary to process goods—less than one month on the average in manufacturing industries, according to my rough estimates.

As far as goods in process held by other than continuous industries are concerned, we are on less firm ground. It seems likely, however, that they too conform positively to manufacturing activity; for it is only the portion of goods in process held by such industries 'between stages' that is not rigidly tied to the rate of activity. Goods held 'within stages' must move with the rate of activity in these stages just as goods in process held in continuous industries. Moreover, there is no necessity for goods held 'between stages' to behave inversely during all or part of a cycle; there is only a possibility that they will do so if the incentive thus provided to stabilize the operations of preceding stages is sufficient.

It seems safe to conclude that goods in process move in close conformity with cycles of manufacturing activity. But it is not possible to say whether they tend to lead a few weeks, move synchronously, or lag by a short period.

RAW MATERIALS

Stocks of raw materials account for about 40 percent of manufacturers' inventories. Unfortunately we do not have an extensive sample from which we might obtain a well founded idea of how they behave. The hypothesis I have advanced was suggested by studying a small but varied collection of series.

The over-all conclusion is that stocks of raw materials tend to conform positively to business cycles with a lag of about three months, or perhaps somewhat longer. To understand why, one must distinguish the classes of commodities comprising the total stock of raw materials and the forces that control each (Ch. 9-10).

For purposes of analysis, stocks of raw materials are divided into three main groups according to source. The first and most significant includes commodities purchased from suppliers who can quickly respond to a change in the demand for their goods by increasing deliveries to customers—in broad terms, commodities purchased by manufacturers from other manufacturers or mines in this country. Such sources usually maintain stocks of finished goods from which sudden increases in orders can be filled, and they can quickly expand their output to meet a lasting increase in demand. When sales fall off, they tend to allow their stocks of finished goods to pile up and to curtail output rather than to force their goods on the market by drastic reductions in price. Finally, the time consumed in transit from suppliers to industrial consumers is usually short. In 1929 commodities supplied from such sources accounted for approximately two-thirds of all raw materials used by American manufacturers (Ch. 9).

Manufacturers who draw their raw materials from these sources can manage their purchases with a view to satisfying the requirements of economy and efficiency in production. These objectives make for a larger inventory of raw materials when the rate of manufacturing activity is high than when it is low—for three reasons. First, the raw materials must be prepared for fabrication. If delivery is accepted at the point of shipment, the goods must be transported to the point of manufacture where they are weighed, inspected, taken to storage rooms, and finally issued for fabrication. If the rate of arrival and consumption is relatively high, a relatively large quantity will be passing through the operations preparatory to actual fabrication.

Stocks, secondly, serve to protect manufacturers against delays in the arrival of the materials required to maintain production at the desired rate. They make it possible for manufacturers to seek the best sources, to negotiate contracts without the pressure of a dwindling stock upon their rate of operations, and to hold a certain insurance against failure of shipments to meet specifications and against interruptions in the receipt of goods due to strikes or mechanical breakdowns at the plants of their suppliers, or to delays or losses in transit. To guard adequately against these contingencies a manufacturer will want to hold supplies sufficient to meet his needs for some weeks or even months in advance. This, in turn, implies that he will need a larger quantity of goods for such purposes when his rate of activity is high than when it is low.

These considerations are reinforced by the precautions manufacturers take to safeguard the value of their stocks against changes in price. It seems unlikely that during ordinary business cycles manufacturers 'speculate' on price changes in the sense in which this word is appropriate to the operations of commodity traders. They are likely, however, to satisfy their routine desires for holding stocks somewhat more generously when the market for their raw materials is firm and rising, somewhat less generously when it is weak and tending to drop. Consequently, during an upswing of business they are likely to keep something more than their usual number of weeks' supply and during a downswing, somewhat less.

There are good reasons then to think that manufacturers try to manage their stocks of raw materials so that they rise and fall together with their volume of operations. And those who draw their supplies from sources able to deliver on short notice and at steady prices probably find their efforts fairly successful. It is unlikely, however, that they foresee adequately the sharp changes in the demand for their goods and in their own rate of fabrication that often take place during a business cycle. In particular, they are unlikely to become aware of the changes from contraction to expansion and expansion to contraction until after they have occurred. It is plausible, therefore, though our evidence is scanty, that stocks of raw materials do not begin to rise, even for the sensitive group of commodities now under consideration, until some time after expansion begins, and that they do not begin to fall until some time after contraction begins. The little evidence we have suggests a lag of perhaps 2-3 months, but, as will be indicated below, the lag may be somewhat longer.

A second group of commodities, comprising about 10 percent of the raw materials purchased by manufacturers, is composed of imports. Obviously, to bring goods from abroad by sea takes considerable time. This lag of receipts behind orders tends to cause the total stocks of the commodity kept in this country to fall for a considerable time after consumption has begun to increase. Similarly, when business begins to slump, the rate of imports cannot be immediately adjusted to the new rate of consumption, and total stocks tend to rise for some time. The few indications we have suggest that these lags may be so protracted as to produce inverted movements over the entire course of a business cycle. This, however, refers to total stocks of such commodities. Whether the same behavior characterizes inventories held by manufacturers themselves depends upon how large a proportion of the total they hold. If they tend to keep only a minor portion, leaving the rest in the hands of importers and dealers, wholesalers' stocks are likely to absorb the disparities between imports and consumption, and manufacturers' stocks of raw materials will rise and fall with their rate of activity.

Commodities of domestic origin whose rate of supply is subject to short-term movements that are independent of current demand form the third class of raw material inventories, accounting for approximately a quarter of manufacturers' raw materials. Cycles in the total stocks of these goods, of which agricultural crops are leading examples, tend to be controlled by fluctuations in supply and to be only remotely connected with cycles in general business. Again, however, manufacturers' stocks alone will not share these irregular traits unless they constitute a large proportion of the total stock. If dealers hold the major portion, manufacturers can get the supplies they require despite random fluctuations in the underlying supply of the commodity and thus keep an inventory of raw materials consonant with their own rate of activity.

It appears then that most raw material stocks held by manufacturers are likely to vary positively with business cycles with a short lag. This would include virtually all goods purchased from other United States manufacturing and mining industries, accounting for nearly two-thirds of total stocks of raw materials,[1] as well as commodities of foreign or agricultural origin that are imported or assembled by dealers who hold the major portion of the stock. The only important exceptions appear to be commodities of foreign or agricultural origin, most of whose stock is held by the industrial consumers themselves. In such cases, the chief effect of importation would be to lengthen the lag, and the chief influence of agricultural origin would be to inject an element of irregular or random variation into the behavior of the stocks.

We cannot, unfortunately, say how significant these exceptional cases are. They can hardly account for more than one-fourth of all raw materials stocks and they are probably much smaller. It is, indeed, hard to think of any outstanding domestic farm product for which a class of dealers does not intervene between the farmer and the manufacturer. Certainly this is true of the grain crops and of cotton. It is true also of the markets for hides. Thus I take it that the behavior characteristic of products supplied by domestic mining and manufacturing industries typifies also a large part of manufacturers' other supplies of raw materials. As already stated, therefore, total stocks of raw materials tend to rise and fall with business activity, lagging 3 months or somewhat more at turning points.

FINISHED GOODS

Several distinctions must be made in order to understand the behavior of stocks of finished goods—about 40 percent of all manufacturers' inventories. One division is that between goods made to order and those made to stock or for the market. The stock of finished goods made to order, like goods in process in continuous industries, is fairly rigidly tied to the rate of manufacturing activity. By definition, such goods are made against specific orders and, except for seasonal influences, their shipment will not be delayed

---

[1] There is a minor qualification for goods purchased on long-term contract and another for goods transported over long distances by water rather than rail. Either condition would tend to lengthen the lag.

long after fabrication has been completed. But for the same reason that goods in process tend to lead production, finished goods made to order—5 to 10 percent of manufacturers' total stocks—must lag behind production, if by only a very short interval.

Goods made to stock, on the other hand, are not mechanically related to the volume of activity; instead their behavior exhibits a variety of characteristics depending upon the nature of the commodities and the factors influencing production. The most important group, for which our materials provide a fairly adequate sample, comprises staples whose rate of output, like that of most manufactured goods, varies largely in response to changes in demand. They include 20-25 percent of manufacturers' total stocks. The evidence indicates that stocks in this group tend to vary inversely to the rate at which they are shipped from the manufacturing plant. If an expansion or contraction is of moderate length the stocks are likely to move inversely during an entire cyclical phase. But if a phase is relatively long, they are likely to reverse their course before the end of the phase, and thereafter proceed in the same direction as general business.

The tendency we observe for stocks to move sharply counter to the rate of shipments immediately after a cyclical turn is probably due to the inability of manufacturers to foresee the turn of business soon enough to adjust their rate of production to the change in sales. The continued decline of these stocks during expansion and their continued rise during contraction probably reflects a combination of several factors. On the one side are factors that tend to retard the rate and reduce the degree of adjustment of production to changes in the volume of shipments. One is the interval between input and output in manufacturing establishments (about 3 weeks, on the average), together with continuing uncertainty about the course of sales so far ahead. Another is the reluctance from the viewpoint of personnel policy to hire workers who may have to be laid off within a short time or to lay off workers who may be rehired soon. A third is the desire to gain other real or supposed benefits from stabilizing output. These combine to make manufacturers hesitate to change their rate of production until they are forced to, and thus to make adjustments late and inadequately.

On the other side there is the character of the commodities. The goods are durable and staple; they will not deteriorate physically or lose their usefulness before demand revives again; consequently an accumulation of stocks in times of declining activity can be tolerated.

So much for the inverse conformity of these stocks. That the timing of the turns of finished goods inventories of this class should vary with the length of expansions or contractions is hardly surprising. The first effect of an upturn in business is a rapid drop in stocks. As the expansion proceeds, stocks continue to fall, but the longer the expansion the closer do inventories approach the point at which it becomes inconvenient for a firm to attempt to handle its expanded business from so small a stock. The company runs the risk that a sudden accumulation of orders will find it unable to make rapid delivery and it will have to forego attractive orders. Therefore the incentive to bring the contraction of stocks to an end grows stronger as expansion proceeds. It is not difficult, therefore, to account for our finding that while stocks of finished staples tend to move inversely during short and moderately long expansions, stocks are likely to expand before the end of prosperity if the upswing is protracted. Similarly in contraction. The first result of a downturn in business is a rapid accumulation of stocks. To some extent this is not unwelcome since it allows inventories depleted in the preceding boom to be rebuilt. And to some extent even larger accumulations can be tolerated in order to cushion the rate of operations against the impact of declining sales. But after a point stocks become intolerably large and firms are forced to cut output enough to facilitate inventory liquidation. The longer the decline in business the more likely is it that this point will be reached (Ch. 11).

These findings apply only to stocks of finished staples whose output cycles are activated largely by changes in demand. In some cases, however, output cycles are determined largely by forces from the side of supply. This occurs when two conditions are found in combination: (a) when short-run fluctuations in the supply of raw materials do not respond to changes in demand; for example, when the materials are of agricultural origin, and (b) when there are no sources of raw material supply other than current domestic output, for example, stocks or imports. Under these conditions, the production of fabricated goods is governed chiefly by changes in the supply of raw materials, and these in turn, are not influenced in the short-run by changes in demand.

Stocks of finished goods produced under such conditions tend to rise and fall with the rate of fabrication. They tend to lag behind the cyclical turns in production since some time usually intervenes between an upturn in production and the day production exceeds shipments. And similarly at downturns (Ch. 12).

The behavior of stocks during business cycles depends upon the durability of the commodity after fabrication. If the commodity is perishable, the finished stock represents no more than the goods in process of distribution or the seasonal carryover. It will rise and fall with output, and since output fluctuations are irregular during business cycles, so are inventory fluctuations (see Ch. 12, Sec. 3 on pork and lard).

When the finished good is durable, however, the surplus tends to be carried over when demand is low relative to output. And when demand is relatively high it can be satisfied in part by liquidating stocks carried over from earlier years. There is some tendency, therefore, for stocks to vary inversely to business cycles. Again the peaks and troughs of stocks should lag behind the opposite turns in business because when sales turn up (down), they will not immediately outrun (fall below) output. This tendency to inverse conformity, however, will usually be more or less obscured by the effect of the irregular fluctuations of output. And the irregularity of behavior will be more pronounced the more the amplitude of fluctuations in output exceeds that in demand (see Ch. 12, Sec. 2 on cottonseed oil).

The broad conclusion is that, in the case of commodities whose production cycles are governed chiefly by fluctuations in the supply of raw materials, stocks of finished goods will tend to behave irregularly during business cycles. When the finished product is durable, there may also be some significant tendency toward inverted conformity with a lag. It is unlikely, however, that commodities whose output is determined by raw material supply constitute an important class. For even when raw material supply is not itself governed by the demand for finished products, the connection between material supply and rate of fabrication can often be broken by accumulation or liquidation of stocks of raw materials and by variations in imports. When allowance has been made for these methods of adjusting raw materials supply to demand, it seems unlikely that finished stocks of commodities whose output cycles are governed by materials supply account for more than 6-8 percent of total stocks (Ch. 12). Our finding that finished stocks of staple goods made for the market move inversely to business activity in short cycles and positively with a very long lag in long phases is, therefore, not subject to major qualification.

This finding applies to staple commodities alone. Though I do not have any way of checking my belief, it seems improbable that manufacturers would manage stocks of perishable goods or style and fashion items in the same way as they do stocks of staples. While the first effect of a decline in sales may, as in the case of staples, be a rise in stocks, manufacturers of perishable goods are likely to make strenuous efforts, through cuts in prices and production, quickly to bring their stocks of finished goods down in order to prevent serious loss through holding the goods too long. These considerations will be especially important when production and sales are seasonal, and surplus stocks must be carried over many months. It is plausible that movements of stocks of fashion goods and other perishables conform to changes in sales with only a short lag.

But stocks of this type are relatively small. Even if made for stock, the inventories are likely to be kept quite small, and a heavy reliance placed upon current production to fill current orders. The difficulty of managing business under such conditions, moreover, will tend to encourage the practice of producing to order rather than to stock.

This judgment is confirmed by some rough estimates. The value of the total stock of finished perishable goods at the end of 1939 was less than $300 million (App. E), only 7.5 percent of all finished goods held by manufacturers and hence no more than 3 percent of their total stocks. This amount, moreover, must have consisted in part of goods made to order and in part of products made from agricultural materials whose output in the short-run is dominated by supply. Even allowing for the crudity of my estimates, it seems reasonable that stocks of finished perishables made for the market in industries whose output is dominated by demand constitute a very small group—less than 3 percent of manufacturers' total stocks.

TIMING OF THE MAJOR CATEGORIES AND THE LAG IN TOTAL STOCKS

Having accounted as well as I can for the behavior of the various components, I can best complete the story by indicating how they fit together to explain the tendency of manufacturers' total stocks to vary positively during business cycles with a long lag. To begin with, it appears that none of the three major groups of stocks tends to lead the turns of business at large by a significant interval. Goods in process in continuous industries do, indeed, tend to lead production, but the lead cannot be longer than a few weeks on the average. When we consider these stocks together with goods in process in other industries, it is no longer certain whether the entire group tends to lead or to lag. But in any event, the interval is short. Goods in process tend to turn at about the same time as output and, therefore, business in general.

Another category closely tied to the rate of output is the stock of finished goods made to order. These too must rise and fall almost as soon as the output of the goods in question itself does. Whether they tend to turn before the peaks and troughs of business cycles, however, depends upon the cyclical habits of the kinds of goods that are made to order. If their output tends to lead aggregate manufacturing output, so will their finished stocks. If it tends to lag, so will their stocks. I do not know of any evidence, however, that supports the hypothesis of either a lead or a lag. Orders for manufactured goods tend to turn early, but before production declines, backlogs must be reduced and the interval between input and output bridged. Pending the accumulation of data, therefore, it is reasonable to assume that finished stocks made to order, like goods in process, turn almost synchronously with output and business in general.

These two categories of stocks account for a substantial, though minor fraction, of all manufacturers' holdings. Goods in process included about one-fifth of manufacturers' stocks in the interwar period and goods made to order 5-10 percent. Thus no more than 30 percent, probably less, of manufacturers' total stocks begin to decline or rise almost simultaneously with business. The remainder continues to rise after business begins to recede and continues to fall after the onset of expansion.

The next category to reach its cyclical turn is probably the part of raw material stocks whose size manufacturers can adjust fairly promptly to the level of business. I estimate that it includes three-quarters or more of raw materials stocks and, therefore, about 30 percent of total stocks. General considerations suggest a lag of only a few months, no more than 3 or 4, and the data indicate that it may be less than 3 months. The evidence on this point is poor, however, and these figures may underestimate the lag somewhat.

Another group of stocks that should turn at or about the same time (though no evidence is available) is finished perishable goods made in industries whose output cycles are dominated by changes in demand. As indicated above, however, this is a small group accounting for no more than 3 percent of all manufacturers' stocks. If we assume that it too turns about 3 months after business, inventory groups comprising 60-65 percent of manufacturers' total stocks have either begun to fall or just reached their peak at the end of, say, the third month after the peak in business. And the same statement might be made about the relation between stocks and business at large at business cycle troughs.

Two other notable groups conform regularly to business cycles: finished staples made for the market and raw materials imported by manufacturers. The first, as we have seen, tends to move inversely when business falls off and does not show any tendency to fall, as a class, until many months, probably more than two years, have passed. Imported raw materials also tend to lag by a long interval, though how long is difficult to say. Finished staples made for the market are a large class, perhaps 20-25 percent of manufacturers' total stocks. Allowing a few percentage points to cover imported raw materials, we get a total of 22-27 percent of all stocks that move inversely or with a very long lag. If we add these figures to the 60-65 percent of stocks mentioned above, the total thus far taken into account covers about 85-90 percent of all manufacturers' stocks. The remainder behave irregularly during business cycles and can be neglected in this discussion.

This recapitulation brings into sharp focus a certain gap in the argument. About 60 percent of total stocks reach their cyclical turning points either together with or some 3 months after the turns in business. But the lag of aggregate stocks is 6-12 months. How can this apparent gap of 3-9 months be explained?

The solution can take one or more of several forms. As we shall see in Part Three, stocks of finished staples rise rapidly in the first part of contraction and decline rapidly in the first part of expansion. This is understandable when we consider that output lags behind shipments at business turns and that the uncertainties retarding the adjustment of production to a decline of sales are at their height early in contractions and expansions. For the same reasons raw material stocks might be expected to decline slowly at first and to act similarly on the rise. At the beginning of a contraction, manufacturers are still receiving the goods ordered when the outlook was brighter. And they are still uncertain about the future course of business and less likely to reduce their purchases as drastically, say, in the first three months of recession as they will in the next three. The scant evidence we have about raw materials stocks is consistent with this view, but it is flimsy indeed. As far as it goes it seems possible, in fact plausible, to suppose that the rapid rise of finished goods stocks should, for a time, offset the decline of the remainder and so lengthen the lag of total stocks.

These considerations may possibly explain the entire gap between a lag of 3 months and one of 6-12 months, but there are two other possibilities. I may have underestimated the lag in most raw materials stocks. Three months is a judgment based on a very small and, as emphasized repeatedly, unrepresentative collection of series. The lag may well be longer and, on the reasoning of Chapter 9, probably is.

On the other hand, I may have overestimated the lag in aggregate inventories. I argued in Chapter 4 that the imperfect indexes used to adjust inventory values for changes in price probably cause the lag in physical inventories to be overstated. If the true lag is nearer 6 than 12 months, say, 7 or 8, and the lag in raw materials is as long as 4 or 5 months, the gap becomes narrow enough to be easily explicable in terms of the inverse behavior of finished staples. If the lag in aggregate inventories is as short as 6 months, the action of finished goods might bridge the gap even if the lag in raw materials is no longer than 3 months. I must end, therefore, with a largely qualitative statement: the lag in manufacturers' aggregate stocks behind business is long, 6 months or more. It is to be explained as a compound of the behavior of several groups of inventories: goods in process and finished goods made to order, which, roughly speaking, move synchronously with business; the major part of raw materials stocks, which follow business with a short lag; and imported raw materials and finished staples made for the market, which follow business activity with a very long lag or move inversely.

3 Unsettled Questions

The preceding section not only presented a tentative hypothesis about cyclical fluctuations in manufacturers' stocks but also indicated how extensive are the areas in which the theory rests upon guesses or inadequate evidence. These areas and some others deserve stress by way of conclusion.

As stated at many points above, the major question to which a more precise answer is necessary concerns the length of the lag in aggregate inventories behind manufacturing activity and business at large. We shall be able to reach such an answer only when the monthly estimates of the Department of Commerce, which begin in 1939, have extended over several peacetime cycles. Even then difficult problems of correcting inventory values for changes in prices will remain.

Following this basic question are several subsidiary problems. One concerns the relative size of the major categories of stocks. We now have a fair idea of the relative size of the three largest divisions: goods in process, raw materials, and finished goods. The separation between goods in process and raw materials, however, would be better if it rested on census data. I have calculated crudely the relative size of goods in process in continuous process industries. We need a more firmly founded estimate than my crude calculation, though if the Department of Commerce can improve its estimates of goods in process as a whole, we shall be less interested in knowing how large a part of goods in process is fairly rigidly determined by the rate of output.

Analysis of the behavior of raw materials rests on knowledge of the importance of different industries—manufacturing, mining, and agriculture—and of different geographical areas as sources of supply to industrial consumers. An estimate based on more recent materials than the 1929 Census would be valuable. Better understanding in this area depends also on knowing how large a share of stocks of imported and agricultural commodities is held by manufacturers, as distinct from dealers.

Among finished goods the most significant distinction is between goods made for the market and to order. My estimates of the size of these classes are only guesses, and the same can be said about my estimates for the various classes of finished goods made for the market: perishable goods, staples whose output cycles are dominated by changes in demand, and staples whose output cycles are governed by changes in raw material supply.

As to the behavior of the stocks in these various classes, the major question concerns the vital category, raw materials. My analysis rests on a very small sample. Some years hence the Department of Commerce series will be a valuable index to the behavior of aggregate raw materials stocks, and we shall know more about the length of their lag. The aggregate is composed of various components with different characteristics, however, and further analysis requires a more comprehensive collection of data by commodities.

These questions go far to indicate how tentative my explanation of inventory behavior is. But they do not exhaust the areas to be investigated when more adequate evidence is available. The data at hand conceal significant differences between the behavior of inventories classified by durability or by industry. Nor finally, did I consider the data sufficiently extensive to clarify the very complicated problem of the relation between price speculation and inventories during business cycles. As the data now available are reviewed by others and as records improve we hope that many of these questions will be settled and my tentative account of the behavior of manufacturers' inventories substantiated or modified.

Part Three

Cyclical Behavior of Inventory Investment

Significance of Inventory Investment

1 Inventory Investment and Production Cycles

Most commodities and services are purchased by two classes of users: consumers and business firms. This, at least, was the case before World War II, the period with which we are concerned. Since then, of course, the federal government has become a major purchaser. The quantity of goods produced depends upon the demands of these customers as anticipated by producers. An understanding of cyclical fluctuations in production, employment, and business in general, therefore, entails an analysis of cyclical fluctuations in the demand for goods and services by consumers on the one hand and businessmen on the other.

The division of output into goods made to satisfy consumer and business demand is of primary importance, for it reflects the different motives controlling purchases. Consumers buy goods to satisfy some physical or psychological need. Businessmen buy goods in order to increase the profits of their companies. The second are aptly called investment goods, the first, consumer goods.

Investment goods, in turn, are of two sorts. One consists of durable equipment, plant, and other buildings. The other, with which this study is concerned, covers goods business firms buy or produce and which, for brief or long periods, enter into their inventories. The value of business construction and purchases of durable goods during a period is usually called investment in plant and equipment. Similarly, the value of goods added to inventory is usually called inventory investment. Both represent the value of goods produced during a period and added to the stock of capital; hence each represents part of the total demand for the current output of goods and for labor and other resources to make the goods.

The task of Part Three is to study the cyclical fluctuations in the rate of inventory investment. But first, two conceptual questions must be clarified if cycles in inventory investment are to be seen in their proper light.

POSITIVE AND NEGATIVE INVENTORY INVESTMENT

Since inventories may be liquidated as well as accumulated, it might be thought that there is a qualitative difference between a change in the rate at which they grow and at which they decline. From the viewpoint of the impact upon production and employment, a reduction in the rate at which inventory is accumulated has the same effect as an acceleration in the rate at which inventory is liquidated. A reduction in the rate at which inventory is liquidated has the same effect on production as an increase in the rate at which it is accumulated.

These facts will be quickly appreciated by considering an hypothetical illustration of total output or gross national product during several periods (Table 60). Let us suppose that the part of total output in each period that takes the form of goods sold to consumers or to business firms to add to their plant and equipment remains constant. Changes in total output can then be charged entirely to changes in the rate at which goods are added to inventory.

TABLE 60

Sales, Stocks, and Total Output
Hypothetical Illustration

PERIOD	SALES TO CONSUMERS & TO BUSINESS FOR PLANT & EQUIPMENT	INVENTORIES End of period	Invest-ment	TOTAL OUTPUT Col. (2) + (4)	Change
(1)	(2)	(3)	(4)	(5)	(6)
1		500			
2	1000	510	+10	1010	
3	1000	530	+20	1020	+10
4	1000	540	+10	1010	−10
5	1000	540	0	1000	−10
6	1000	530	−10	990	−10
7	1000	510	−20	980	−10
8	1000	500	−10	990	+10
9	1000	490	−10	990	0

If we think of increases in the rate of investment and decreases in the rate of disinvestment as changes in the same direction, it is immediately apparent that each has exactly the same effect upon production, provided they are of the same size. Thus between periods 2 and 3 the rate of investment grows from +10 to +20; production increases by the same amount, from 1,010 to 1,020. In the same way the rate of disinvestment of inventories declines between periods 7 and 8 from −20 to −10; production increases by the same amount, from 980 to 990. Throughout the table the change in production equals the change in the rate of investment in inventory. Evidently from the viewpoint of their effects on production, there is no qualitative difference between investment and disinvestment,[1] and a cycle that runs from a peak of inventory accumulation to a peak of inventory disinvestment (trough of accumulation) back to a peak of accumulation is a continuous whole.

The relations between production and stock illustrated in Table 60 are true without qualification only for the economy as a whole. If we consider one sector—manufacturing industries, for example, or some single industry—then obviously among goods held in stock some will have been purchased from other sectors. To say that in this situation an addition to stock requires production in the same quantity involves a tacit assumption that there is no compensating reduction of stock elsewhere. Of course, special circumstances aside, this assumption, that other things remain equal, is necessary and valid for analytical purposes.

PLANNED VS. UNPLANNED INVENTORY INVESTMENT

Goods added to stock must have been produced—barring offsetting reductions in stock elsewhere; and the desire to add goods to stock stimulates businessmen to produce or purchase more goods. Thus the demand for goods for inventory investment is part of the total demand for goods. The converse, however, need not be true. The goods added to stock may not have been made in response to a desire to invest in inventory.

This well known paradox is easily resolved. Unless a manufacturer, for example, produces exclusively to order, he must base his decisions about the quantity of goods to purchase and to produce in large part on a guess about the quantity he will sell. If his guess is wrong, he has various alternatives. If he has overestimated demand, he may add more goods to stock than he had planned. Or by reducing prices or offering other inducements to customers, or by advertising, he may achieve his anticipated rate of sales. But price reductions may not stimulate sales sufficiently. Competitors

---

[1] Strictly speaking, this is true only as long as production is some positive quantity. If production is zero, as may sometimes happen in small sectors of the economy, there may be disinvestment in stocks at a changing rate without affecting the (zero) rate of output. But stocks cannot, of course, accumulate when production is zero.

may meet his prices, which will lessen the efficacy of a cut of any given size, and his customers may be encouraged to expect further cuts, which may cause them to curtail purchases temporarily. In any event, the quantity of goods a manufacturer sells during a given period is unlikely to be identical with the quantity he expected to sell at the beginning of the period. And since he will not be able immediately to make a full adjustment in his receipts of purchased goods and in his own rate of production, the amount of goods he holds in stock at the end of any period is unlikely to be identical with the quantity he had planned to hold. This difference between the actual stock in a businessman's possession at the end of a period and the planned stock represents unplanned accumulation or liquidation of inventories.

The fact that part of the inventory investment of any period is unplanned is significant in two ways. First, if one billion dollars of goods are added to stock during a certain period, then, strictly speaking, it is valid to say only (what is tautologically true) that output worth one billion dollars took the form of inventory investment. We cannot validly say that production worth one billion dollars was stimulated by a desire to add such a quantity of goods to stock. For the production of part of these goods may have been due to the expectation that they would be sold or used up in the fabrication of other goods. Similarly, the output stimulated by the desire to invest in inventories may exceed one billion dollars if sales were underestimated and if manufacturers were unwilling or unable to restrict sales to the quantities they had originally expected.

The distinction between planned and unplanned inventory investment is important in another way. An increase in the output of goods, whatever its cause, entails a larger outlay of funds to hire labor and to purchase the additional goods and other supplies required. This additional outlay stimulates purchases of consumer goods and the production of raw materials, thereby setting in train a series of secondary consequences that tend to increase the total output and income of the community. If the additional production takes the form of unplanned accumulation of inventories, however, there is an offsetting factor. The holders of the excess stocks are likely in future periods to attempt to curtail their output or purchases or at least to keep them below the levels at which they would otherwise have been set. Thus the secondary consequences of unplanned inventory investment are in part depressing to business. Similarly, if stocks are reduced below planned levels or if inventory investment turns out to have been smaller than businessmen desired, the secondary consequences upon orders and output decisions in subsequent periods are likely to be expansionary.

Inventory statistics are, of course, distressingly silent about the size of planned and unplanned investments. They tell us only what actually happened. But unplanned investments may sometimes be very important. The amount added to stocks is always small compared with total production and sales. Hence a small percentage error in producers' expectations of sales may cause a large unplanned investment or disinvestment in inventories, at least during any short period. Over long periods, no doubt, such mistakes are corrected and large unplanned holdings are eliminated from business inventories. The unplanned portion of the inventory investment during a year is, therefore, likely to be a relatively small part of the total annual investment. The analysis of business cycles, however, is often concerned with events that take place within one, two, or three months, and for such short periods unplanned investment may be a large part of the total, a fact that serves to becloud the interpretation of the data.

2 Plan of Part Three

Two major questions are studied in the succeeding chapters. The first concerns the cyclical timing of inventory investment. Chapters 14 and 15 compare the behavior of investment by manufacturers as a whole with inventory investment in other industrial divisions. They try to establish the timing of the turning points of inventory investment relative to the turning points of business cycles and to those in the rate of change in output. The general conclusion is that the peaks and troughs of inventory investment are near those of business and considerably later than those of the rate of change in output. These observations lead to a discussion of the influence of inventory investment in initiating business cycle turns and in determining the pace and length of expansions and contractions. The next four chapters, 16-19, examine the behavior of investment in the major types of stocks held by manufacturers in an attempt to discover the causes of inventory investment cycles in this branch of the economy. Chapter 20 draws together the results of these detailed studies.

The second major question concerns the relation between the amplitude of cycles in inventory investment and in total output. In Chapter 21, we confirm the fact (noted in Ch. 1) that a very large part of the total changes in gross national product during business cycles takes the form of changes in inventory investment. In addition, the data strongly suggest that the share of inventory investment varies inversely with the length of business cycles. A general explanation of these relations is attempted. Finally we examine the theory, advanced by Hansen and others, that minor cycles, attributable to a periodic need for inventory readjustment, regularly interrupt the course of major upswings in business.

CHAPTER 14

Timing and Conformity of Inventory Investment Cycles

1 Problems of Measurement

The rate of investment by manufacturers in their commodity stocks may be estimated in two ways. If series showing the number of units of each commodity held in stock at the end of each period were available, we could value the change in the number of units of each commodity between the end of one period and the next either by its cost in the period in question, or if we wished to eliminate the influence of price changes, by its cost in some standard period. The aggregate value of the changes in stock for all commodities would be the figure needed.

Alternatively, if one has the values of the inventories held by manufacturers at the end of stated intervals, corrected to eliminate the effects of price changes, the difference between the corrected values held at the end of successive intervals gives the number of dollars spent by manufacturers to add goods to their stocks, the commodities so added being uniformly valued at their cost in some standard period. One may then revalue the investment in each interval to take account of changes in prices between the base period and each given period.

KUZNETS' ESTIMATES

The method we follow is dictated by the material. Estimates of the value of inventories held by manufacturers at the end of each year 1918-38, based on Kuznets' original work, were corrected for changes in the value of inventory units.[1] The difference in these values, corrected for price changes, is our fundamental measure of the rate of inventory investment. Since the corrected values of

[1] The construction of these estimates and the methods used in correcting for price changes are described in Chapter 4 and in greater detail in Appendix A.

inventory at the end of each year show the amount the stock would have cost if purchased in 1929, the change in value between year ends is the cost of the current investment in inventory when the goods added to stock are valued at their 1929 prices.

While the estimates in book values and their correction for changes in price have been described in other chapters, one matter deserves repetition. Some manufacturers value inventories at original cost, others at the lower of original cost or the cost of replacement. In correcting for changes in prices some assumption must be made about the prevalence of these practices. Since I believe that the 'cost or market' method is more common, my figures for inventory investment are based upon price corrections that assume that all manufacturers used this method. As a check against this extreme assumption, I used a second set of figures based upon another extreme assumption: that as much as half the total stock is valued at cost alone and never revalued when the market price is below cost (App. A, Sec. 2D). Except in the years of violent price disturbance 1919-22, they do not differ materially. Indeed, my observations about the tendency of the rate of inventory investment to move up and down with business in general would not be altered even if inventories were universally valued at original cost (see Chart 63). This was, to be sure, not the case in the years of large price movements following World War I. In that period, however, the assumption that inventories are always valued at cost yields implausible results. It suggests that there was a net liquidation of stocks during 1920, the peak year of the postwar boom, and a rapid accumulation during 1921 when businessmen were struggling to rid their shelves of goods. The data I use, therefore, are calculated on the assumption that all stocks are valued at the lower of cost or market price.

The difficulties inherent in correcting inventory values for changes in prices are, of course, magnified when we turn from the level of inventories in different years to the rate of growth and decline in stocks, for small errors in the value of stocks at the ends of successive years can produce a large error in the inventory change during the intervening period. Add to this the errors that arise from measuring cyclical behavior with annual data and it will readily be seen that the problems are formidable. It is especially important, in using these data, to confine oneself to conclusions that apply to manufacturing as a whole based upon a clear consensus of the behavior of the various industry groups, and even then to avoid observations about details.

2 Manufacturers' Inventory Investment

Does inventory investment typically help to initiate the revivals and recessions of business? We can cast some light on this question if we know whether inventory investment reaches its peaks and troughs before or after business activity and whether it does so regularly. To discover this is the purpose of the timing and conformity measures presented in this section. Of course, the reference cycle turning dates are only benchmarks. But against these benchmarks, the timing relations of inventory investment to other crucial series may be judged.

Using the Kuznets estimates for ten large industry groups and for manufacturing as a whole, we compare the timing of the turns in inventory investment with those in business cycles and measure their conformity. To measure the timing of cyclical turns we use the National Bureau standard method for annual series. The midpoints of the years when the specific cycle turns in inventory investment occur are compared with the months in which the corresponding reference turns occur. The lead or lag is measured in months and averaged for all the turns at which comparisons can be made. Since the midpoint of the year in which a series reaches a specific cycle peak or trough is, of course, highly unlikely to be a good approximation to the actual date at which the series turns, any individual observation of relative timing will be in error by a larger or smaller number of months. The validity of the method, therefore, depends upon whether an average can eliminate a considerable part of this inaccuracy by offsetting the errors of single observations. As explained in Chapter 3, the method yields crude but useful results if based on many observations and confined to the broad features of the measures.

The timing measures do not provide a valid basis for supposing that inventory investment by manufacturers tends either to lead or to lag behind business cycle turns. The average lag for total manufacturing is only 0.2 months. An average based on all 86 timing comparisons also yields a negligible lag. There are only 10 more lags than leads, an excess of only twelve percent. In only 4 of the 10 groups was the average lead or lag longer than 3 months. Of these, 2 were leads and 2 lags. I conclude that if inventory investment tends either to lead or to lag at business cycle turns, the average lead or lag is short, probably no longer than 3 months, an interval too short to be measured reliably by annual data.

A second observation is based on the number of timing comparisons in Table 61. Our data, running from 1919 to 1939 (except for miscellaneous manufacturing which ends in 1937), cover 11 business cycle turns. But since we do not have any way of knowing whether the rate of investment in 1919 was higher or lower than in 1918, comparisons are not made at the initial business cycle trough. For the ten industry groups 99 timing comparisons were possible, and of these, 86 comparisons could actually be made— evidence of the regularity with which the rate of inventory investment by manufacturers rises and falls with general business. For if a series skips a cycle, two possible comparisons are eliminated, and if it moves through an extra cycle, a comparison must often be discarded because of uncertainty in determining which of two spe-

TABLE 61

Investment in Manufacturers' Inventories, Constant Prices
Timing at Business Cycle Turns, 1919-1938

| | NUMBER OF | | AV. LEAD (−) OR LAG (+) |
| | LEADS | LAGS | MONTHS |
(1)	(2)	(3)	(4) ·
Total manufacturing	4	6	+0.2
Food, beverages & tobacco	3	5	+3.9
Textiles & textile products*	2	5	−0.8
Leather & leather products	3	7	+2.6
Rubber & related products	4	4	−0.5
Lumber & wood products	2	7	+4.1
Paper, printing & publishing	3	7	+2.6
Chemicals & allied products	7	0	−7.6
Stone, clay & glass products	3	7	+1.4
Metals & metal products	3	6	+0.6
Miscellaneous	8	0	−8.1
Sum of 10 groups	38	48	
Av. of 10 groups weighted by no. of turns			+0.14

* One lead was excluded because it exceeded 24.5 months.

cific cycle turns should be matched with a given reference cycle turn. And the same sort of uncertainty arises in heightened degree if the series merely behaves irregularly. The large number of actual comparisons relative to the number possible provides a first indication of the conformity of inventory investment to business cycles. Moreover, it increases the reliance that can be put on our timing measures.

That inventory investment by manufacturers tends to conform positively to business cycles can be seen also from Chart 63. Two estimates of the rate of investment are shown: one based on the assumption that inventories are valued at the lower of cost or market price more nearly corresponds to reality; the other on the assumption that inventories are never marked down when prices fall. Under the first assumption, the rate of inventory investment by manufacturers was higher in every peak year of business than in adjacent trough years, and lower in every trough year than in adjacent peak years. In short, inventory investment rose during every expansion and declined during every contraction of business. Not only that, but its amplitude is roughly of the same size as that of business swings. The violent contraction of 1920-21 and the vigorous recovery of 1921-23 stand out plainly. The rate of investment dropped precipitously during the mild business contraction of

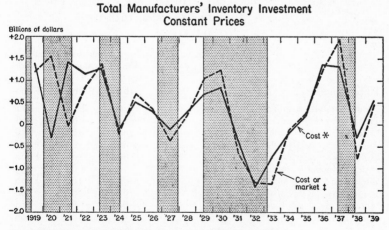

Chart 63
Total Manufacturers' Inventory Investment
Constant Prices

‡ Estimated on the assumption that inventories are valued at the lower of cost or market.
* Estimated on the assumption that inventories are always valued at cost.
Contractions (shaded) and expansions (unshaded) are marked off by the monthly reference chronology.

1923-24, but its movements were small during the mild cycle of 1924-27 and large again during the two violent business cycles that followed.

These intimations of systematic response to business cycles are fully confirmed by measures of conformity, made on the same plan as those used in Chapters 4 and 5 in connection with the level of stocks. There are, however, minor differences of procedure arising from the fact that our data are now calendar year, rather than end of year, series. Instead of comparing the movements of the investment data with a chronology based on the ends of years when business reached peaks and troughs, we use the National Bureau regular chronology of the calendar years when business was at peaks and troughs. This is our practice for series that move more or less synchronously. If a series has a pronounced lag, about six months, its movements are compared with the National Bureau fiscal year chronology. We say, in effect, that if an annual series tends to lag six months, it ought to rise and fall in conjunction with an annual chronology of business for years ending six months earlier. If a series leads by about six months, we still use the National Bureau fiscal year chronology, but predate it one year. Special business chronologies were prepared for series leading or lagging by three

TABLE 62

Investment in Manufacturers' Inventories, Constant Prices
Conformity to Business Cycles, 1918-1938

(1)	LEAD (−) OR LAG (+) ASSUMED[a] (MO.) (2)	NO. OF PHASES[b] (3)	INDEX OF CONFORMITY TO BUSINESS		
			Exp. (4)	Contr. (5)	Cycle (6)
Total manufacturing	0	10	+100	+100	+100
Food, beverages & tobacco	+3	10	+20	+20	+11
Textiles & textile products	0	10	+20	+60	+56
Leather & leather products	+3	10	+100	+60	+56
Rubber & related products	0	10	+60	+100	+100
Lumber & wood products	+3	10	+60	+100	+100
Paper, printing & publishing	+3	10	+20	−60	−33
Chemicals & allied products	−9	9	+50	+100	+100
Stone, clay & glass products	0	10	+60	+100	+100
Metals & metal products	0	10	+60	+60	+56
Miscellaneous	−9	9	+50	+100	+100

[a] From Table 61, col. 4. Figures are rounded to the nearest 3-month interval.
[b] See Table 21, note b.

or nine months.[2] By following the average timing measures of Table 61, rounding the figures to the nearest 3-month interval, I distinguish between series that run synchronously with business cycles and those that tend to lead or lag. The measure itself is simple and has been fully explained in Chapters 3 and 4.

The movements of manufacturers' inventory investment coincide with the movements of business far more regularly than do stocks themselves (Table 62). The conformity of the total is perfect and five of the ten groups have full cycle indexes of +100. Only two fall below +50, and one of these is the only negative index in this column. We may conclude that inventory investment by manufacturers as a whole responds to business cycles in a highly systematic fashion, as far as the direction of its movement is concerned. When business gets better, the rate of investment rises; when the tide of business recedes, the rate of investment declines.

There is little difference between the behavior of manufacturers' inventory investment measured in constant prices and in current prices (Chart 64).

Chart 64
Total Manufacturers' Inventory Investment
Current and Constant Prices

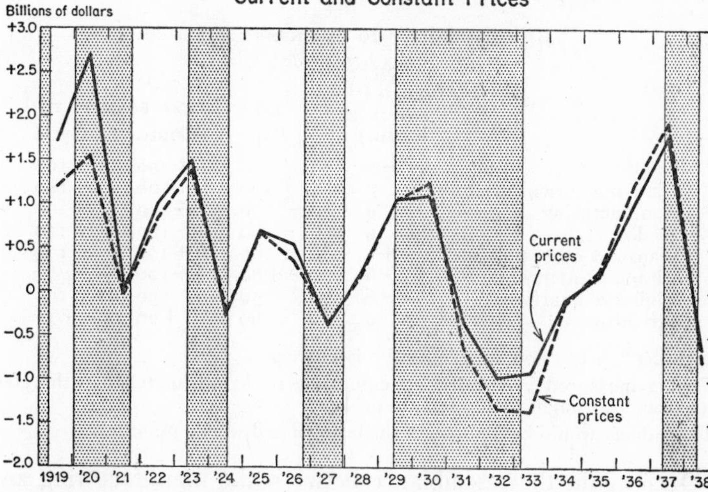

Billions of dollars

Contractions (shaded) and expansions (unshaded) are marked off by the monthly reference chronology.

[2] See Ch. 3 for a fuller description of the Bureau's conformity measures and App. B for a description of the special business chronologies.

3 Inventory Investment in Manufacturing and Other Industrial Divisions

As in our study of stock levels, I digress at this point to compare the timing and conformity of manufacturers' inventory investments with those in mining, transportation and other public utilities, trade, and farming (Table 63 and Chart 65). Some 95 percent of all commercial stocks are held by these five groups.

TABLE 63

Total Inventory Investment and Its Major Components,
Constant Prices
Timing and Conformity, 1919-1939

A TIMING AT BUSINESS CYCLE TURNS

	NUMBER OF		AV. LEAD $(-)$ OR LAG $(+)$
	Leads	Lags	MONTHS
Total[a]	5	5	−2.2
Total nonagricultural[a]	4	6	+0.2
Manufacturing	4	6	+0.2
Trade	5	5	−1.0
Transp. & other pub. ut.	1	6	+4.5
Mining & quarrying	0	6	+6.5
Mining & quarrying (inverted)[b]	8	2	−8.3
Agriculture	2	3	+1.1

B CONFORMITY TO BUSINESS CYCLES

	LEAD $(-)$ OR LAG $(+)$ ASSUMED (MO.)	INDEX OF CONFORMITY TO		
		Exp.	Contr.	Cycle
Total[a]	−3	+100	+100	+100
Total nonagricultural[a]	0	+100	+100	+100
Manufacturing	0	+100	+100	+100
Trade	0	+100	+100	+100
Transp. & other pub. ut.[c]	+6	+100	+100	+100
Mining & quarrying	+6	+50	+100	+71
Mining & quarrying	−6[b]	−50	−50	−100
Agriculture	0	+60	+20	+11

[a] Includes construction, finance, and miscellaneous.
[b] Timing measured invertedly: specific cycle peaks are matched with reference troughs, troughs with reference peaks.
[c] The indexes would be the same if the lag assumed were 3 months.

Once again the resemblance between the manufacturing and trade divisions is marked. Both tend to move up and down with general business, and neither leads or lags consistently. At some turns in business, investment by manufacturers turns before invest-

Chart 65
Five Major Industrial Divisions
Inventory Investment during Business Cycles

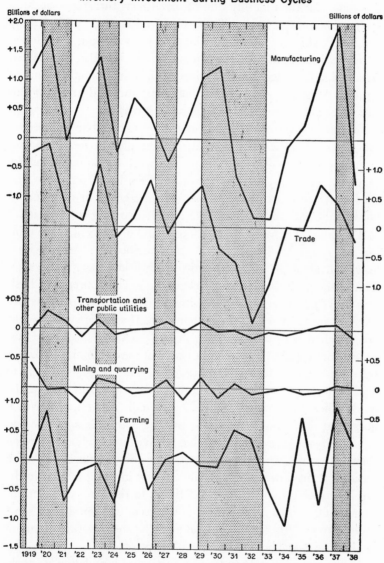

Contractions (shaded) and expansions (unshaded) are marked off by the monthly reference chronology.

ment by distributors; at other turns the reverse is true. In both cases, however, the behavior of these annual data is consistent with the view that the monthly rate of investment turns near business cycle peaks and troughs. These observations are confirmed by Table 63 which indicates that inventory investment in trade led at five business cycle turns, lagged at the same number, and yielded an average lead that is not significant since it is based on annual figures. Assuming synchronous behavior, the conformity of this category of investment to business cycles is perfect.

Inventory investment in transportation and public utilities, on the contrary, apparently lags behind business cycles. Lags predominate 6 to 1 over leads, and the average timing measures suggest a lag of 4.5 months. If we assume a lag of 6 months, the conformity measure indicates perfect agreement in direction of movement between business cycles and inventory investment.

The relation between business cycles and investment in the mining and quarrying industries may be described as inverted with a long lead about as well as positive with a long lag (Table 63). Thus if the peaks in inventory investment are compared with business cycle peaks, and troughs with troughs, six comparisons are possible, in all of which investment lags. If specific cycle troughs are matched with business cycle peaks, ten comparisons are possible: stocks lead in eight, lag in two. On the one basis, stocks appear to lag 6 months on the average; on the other, they appear to lead by 8 months. The larger number of comparisons that can be made when the series is analyzed invertedly suggest, as far as it goes, that this is the better basis. But the margin is not large and conformity measures on the two bases leave little to choose between them. However we express the relation, one thing is clear: when business turns down, inventory investment in this group, as in the public utility group, typically continues to rise for a considerable number of months. It begins to fall while contraction still has some months to run. It continues to fall after business has turned up but begins to rise well before the onset of recession.

Not unexpectedly, the rate of growth and liquidation of stocks in farming behaves irregularly during business cycles. Since short run supply is governed by harvests, it cannot be any surprise that farmers' stocks sometimes rise and sometimes fall in good years.

The behavior of total inventory investment, both including and excluding farm stocks, is dominated by the movements of manufacturing and trade. The totals, therefore, rise and fall with business and do not show any tendency to lead or lag that can be considered significant in view of the fact that the data are annual. And again, there is little difference, as far as timing and conformity go, between total investment measured in constant and in current prices (Chart 66).

Chart 66
Total Inventory Investment, Current and Constant Prices

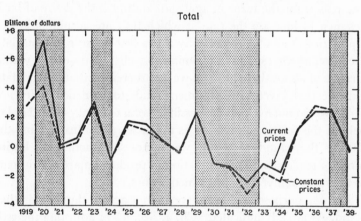

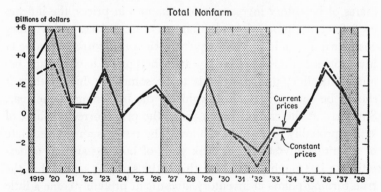

Contractions (shaded) and expansions (unshaded) are marked off by the monthly reference chronology.

4 Significance of the Timing of Inventory Investment Cycles
This review of the data clearly establishes one facet of the role of inventory investment in business cycles. Increases in inventory in-

vestment regularly act to augment the forces of expansion from about the very beginning of the upward swing of business until approximately its very end. And declines in inventory investment augment the forces of contraction in the same way. The extent to which such investment intensifies the cyclical movements of the economy is, of course, another matter. This is a question of the magnitude of the fluctuations in inventory investment, studied in Chapter 21.

What the data leave obscure is the precise influence of inventory investment near the turning points of business cycles. Is it true that one reason for the turns in aggregate output is the desire of businessmen to increase the rate at which they are accumulating or liquidating stocks? The difficulty arises first because annual data are too coarse to establish the timing of cyclical turns except within a range of about six months. If we say, therefore, that annual data indicate that inventory investment tends to turn near reference turns, we do not exclude the possibility of a tendency to lead or lag behind the reference turns by as much as 3 months. Taking the data as they stand, therefore, we cannot say whether the beginnings of expansion and contraction in production are due in part to the turns in inventory investment or not.

For our purposes, however, we cannot accept the data as they stand. As already indicated (Ch. 4, Sec. 3) in adjusting the estimates of inventory investment for changes in prices, the indexes used fluctuate more violently than accurate indexes of inventory cost per unit would do. Consequently, the price-corrected value of inventories at the end of peak years, when prices have already begun to decline, probably tends to be somewhat higher than it should be compared with its value at the beginning of the year. Similarly at the end of trough years, the price-corrected value of stocks probably tends to be too low. The result is an overestimate of inventory investment in peak years of business and an underestimate in trough years. And this is the same as saying that the true turning points in inventory investment probably come a little earlier than our estimates indicate.

A final element of ambiguity is that the observed levels of inventory investment include some quantities of unplanned accumulation or liquidation of stocks. This is especially important at the peaks and troughs of business. The analysis in Part Two has shown that the bulk of inventories (as distinct from inventory investment) tend to lag behind the turns of business by varying intervals. For the most part, the explanation appears to lie in a failure of businessmen to anticipate cyclical turns in demand far enough in advance to make sufficiently prompt and adequate adjustments in their purchases and production. In other words, immediately following a peak in business there occurs an unplanned accumulation of stocks, and immediately after a trough an unplanned liquidation. This, in turn, means that annual data on inventory investment in peak years of business are somewhat higher than they would be if they measured planned investment; in trough years they are lower. Planned investment in inventories probably turns somewhat earlier than actual investment, and actual investment a little earlier than our estimates indicate. On the basis of this analysis it seems reasonable to take the provisional position that the beginnings of recession and recovery in production are, as a rule, due in part to changes in planned inventory investment. But not until accurate monthly or quarterly data have been available for a considerable period can this provisional position be confirmed.

CHAPTER 15

Inventory Investment and Rates of Change in Output

1 Significance of the Relation

It is a common theory that businessmen attempt to maintain their inventories in a certain ratio to sales (or, in the case of manufacturers' raw materials and goods in process, in a certain ratio to production). If this were true without qualification and if the attempt were wholly successful, inventories would rise and fall synchronously with sales (or production) and inventory investment would vary synchronously and proportionately with changes in sales and production. This idea is the basis for the simplest and most mechanical application of the acceleration principle to inventory investment (see Ch. 1).

As we have seen in Part Two, however, inventories tend to lag 6-12 months behind sales and output. And Chapter 14 showed that inventory investment tends to reach its peaks and troughs at approximately the peak and trough dates of business cycles, which are also the turning points of sales and output. This suggests that inventory investment lags behind changes in output and sales. For it is plausible that the rate of growth and decline in a series of data should reach its turning points before the data themselves do. This, however, is not inevitable. Output may grow most rapidly just before it begins to decline and decline most rapidly just before it begins to rise. The cyclical pattern of the rates of change in output and sales needs to be established.

If inventory investment does tend to lag behind the rates of change in output and sales, this does not mean that businessmen do not attempt to maintain an approximately constant relation between sales and inventories, nor that the acceleration principle is not part of a valid theory of fluctuations in inventory investment. J. M. Clark, in his formulation of the acceleration principle, expected a lag and allowed for it. If inventory investment is found to lag behind changes in output, we should try to establish the length of the lag, consider its significance, and determine its causes.

The data presented in Sections 2 and 3, below, lead to the conclusion that the rate of increase in output is usually at a maximum long before the peak in business, often before half the expansion has run its course. Similarly, the rate of decline in output is usually at a maximum long before the trough in business. Occasionally—often in expansions, less often in contractions—the rate of change in output has picked up after the peak rate has been passed and retardation in growth, or decline, has begun. But typically the later peaks in the rate of growth or decline do not reach levels as high as the earlier ones.

These intra-phase (i.e., intra-expansion or intra-contraction) oscillations in the rate of change in output may themselves at times be associated with similar intra-phase fluctuations in inventory investment. It is quite possible, for example, that after an initial rise in inventory investment at the beginning of an expansion, there is a decline. This, in turn, causes the rate of growth in output to fall. Later, inventory investment picks up again and causes a renewed spurt in output.[1] Such intra-phase fluctuations in inventory investment cannot be excluded, although they do not appear in the annual data reviewed in Chapter 14. What we can say confidently on the basis of the annual data is that if there is more than one peak in inventory investment during expansions, the highest comes at the end of the phase. Similarly, the lowest of the troughs, if there is more than one, comes at the end of contraction. Typically, therefore, there is a long interval between the highest rate of increase in output and the highest level of inventory investment and between the highest rate of decline in output and the lowest level of inventory investment. The lag of inventory investment behind the

[1] An important fact that does not seem consistent with this notion is that in the initial stages of expansion, inventory investment is still negative (inventories continue to decline after output revives), though not as low as at the trough in output. In addition, inventory-sales and inventory-output ratios are declining rapidly (Ch. 6). There seems little reason to expect a widespread attempt at inventory liquidation in the first stages of expansion. Similarly, at the beginning of contraction, inventory investment is still very high—though falling —and inventory-sales ratios are rising rapidly. There seems little reason to expect inventory accumulation to become larger.

rate of change in output can be seen in another way. At the beginning of expansions the rate of increase in output is usually very high, but inventory investment is still negative. In contractions, the reverse is true: the rate of decline in output is very high, but inventories are still increasing, though at a slower pace than at the peak in business.

The lag of inventory investment affects the character of business cycles significantly, for if inventory investment leaped promptly at the beginning of business expansions and collapsed promptly at the beginning of contractions, the changes in output at these stages would be even larger than those we observe. The changes in inventory investment would then augment the changes in output due to other causes. And if inventory investment tended to fall off after the peak rates of growth in output had been reached—instead of rising to still higher levels—the peaks of output and of business cycles would occur sooner than has been true in the cycles of experience. The decline in inventory investment would tend to bring on a decline in business at large, instead of sustaining a further increase. Similarly in contractions: if inventory investment rose with the rate of decline in output after the latter had reached its lowest point, business would tend to recover sooner than it actually has. In other words, in comparison with a situation in which inventory investment varied synchronously with the rate of change in output, the lag of inventory investment tends to moderate the pace and extend the length of expansions and contractions.

This argument has anticipated the results of our study of rates of change in output, to which we now turn. Section 2 is concerned with the cyclical behavior of the rates of change in aggregate output and business activity. Section 3 is a more detailed study of rates of change in manufacturing production.

2 Rates of Change in Total Output

We use four indexes in examining the behavior of rates of change in total output or business activity: Barger's quarterly estimates of income and outlay 1921-38, the series of bank clearings outside New York City 1919-38, and the FRB index of industrial production 1919-38. Barger's estimates are indexes of total output in current prices. The bank clearings measure the volume of business transactions, also in current prices.[2] The index of industrial production measures the physical volume of production in mining and manufacturing industries.

From the viewpoint of this study, each series suffers from certain defects. Barger's series were derived by making quarterly interpolations of Kuznets' well known annual estimates of national income and output. In many sectors, however, the interpolators are of dubious accuracy, and in some sections, Barger had to resort to formal mathematical graduations.[3] The latter practice is of special significance for our problem since it necessarily produces a rounded contour at the turning points of the original data. This, in turn, makes for retardation in the rates of growth or decline of the series in the immediate neighborhood of their peaks and troughs.

The bank clearings series has two significant defects. Although it excludes New York clearings, it reflects financial as well as commercial and industrial transactions. In addition, it records transactions, not at the time when the sales took place, but later when payments were actually made. The index of industrial production, finally, is faulty in that it does not reflect activity in the extractive industries (other than mining), or in distribution, services, or government. Despite these defects, the four indexes taken together constitute a fairly satisfactory basis for judging changes in total output, if conclusions are confined to broad features of their behavior.

The quarter to quarter or month to month changes in the series are plotted in Chart 67. Five-month moving averages of the changes in the monthly data are also shown in order to help the reader follow the trend of these choppy series. Asterisks at peaks mark the dates during business cycle expansions when, in the writer's judgment, serious retardation in the rate of change begins. Asterisks at troughs mark similar dates in contractions.

[2] This series is available also in deflated form, but its rate of change fluctuates within so narrow a range that to separate cyclical movements from irregular oscillations is difficult. Whether this is due to imperfections in the price indexes used to adjust the series is not clear. As far as cyclical movements can be identified, they do not differ substantially in timing from those in the undeflated data.

[3] Including depreciation in both series, about 25 percent of outlay in 1929 was subject to graduation, about 40 percent of income. Prior to 1929 a somewhat larger fraction of both series, but especially of income, was subject to graduation. See *Outlay and Income in the United States, 1921-1938*, pp. 213-4.

Chart 67

Total Output and Business Activity, Quarterly or Monthly Changes

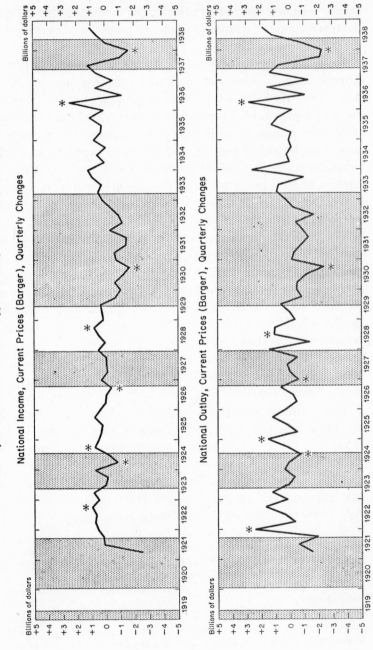

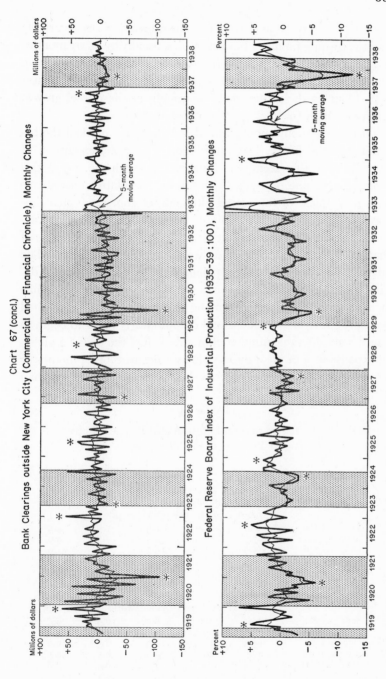

Chart 67 (concl.)

Bank Clearings outside New York City (Commercial and Financial Chronicle), Monthly Changes

Federal Reserve Board Index of Industrial Production (1935–39 : 100), Monthly Changes

✳ Peaks and troughs of cycles in quarterly or monthly changes.
Contractions (shaded) and expansions (unshaded) are marked off by the monthly reference chronology in the four panels.

The marked peaks and troughs in the rates of growth invariably lead the turning points of business cycles, usually by many months. As already said, in many expansions and in some contractions there are one or more periods of accelerated change later in the phase; but seldom do these later peaks or troughs in the rate of growth reach such high (or low) points as those marked.

The reader should notice also that I have not marked the beginning of the first serious retardation during the expansion of 1933-37 since that seemed to be associated with the speculative boom and decline of 1933. Such intense speculative movements were not typical of the period although, of course, of great importance in 1919-21. Had the 1933 episode been taken into account, the interval between the first important peak in the rate of change and the peak in business would appear to be longer. The intervals between the turning points of the rates of growth or decline and those of business cycles are shown in Table 64. While there is some disagreement among the four series in individual cycles, the rate of change in total output clearly tends to begin to retard a considerable number of months before the end of a phase. In expansions 3 of the 4 series yield average leads of 13 months or more. In contractions, all 4 series show average leads longer than

TABLE 64

Rates of Change in Total Output and Business Activity
Timing at Business Cycle Turns, 1920-1938

Reference date	Nat. income	Nat. outlay	Bank clear- ings	Indus- trial produc- tion	Av. 2 or 4 series
	LEAD AT BUSINESS CYCLE PEAKS (MONTHS)				
Jan. 1920	n.a.	n.a.	1.5	7.5	4.5
May 1923	7.5	16.5	4.5	7.5	9.0
Oct. 1926	24.5	21.5	15.5	22.5	21.0
June 1929	8.5	11.5	8.5	0.5	7.2
May 1937	13.5	13.5	2.5	28.5	14.5
Av. 4 or 5 cycles	13.5	15.8	6.5	13.3	
	LEAD AT BUSINESS CYCLE TROUGHS (MONTHS)				
Sept. 1921	n.a.	n.a.	8.5	10.5	9.5
July 1924	3.5	0.5	13.5	1.5	4.8
Dec. 1927	14.5	11.5	11.5	2.5	10.0
March 1933	29.5	29.5	39.5	39.5	34.5
May 1938	4.5	4.5	7.5	6.5	5.8
Av. 4 or 5 cycles	13.0	11.5	16.1	12.1	

12 months. In expansions at least two-thirds of all the comparisons were leads longer than 7 months; one-half were longer than 11 months. In contractions the comparable figures were 6 and 11.

There is considerable variation among cycles in the length of the leads. In terms of the average for all series, the leads ranged from 4.5 to 21 months in expansions, from 4.8 to 34.5 months in contractions. The variability, however, is far less pronounced when the leads are expressed as percentages of the length of expansion and contraction. The average leads are then all long, ranging between 29 and 78 percent of expansions and between 33 and 69 percent of contractions. It seems valid to conclude that total output and business activity tend to begin a period of serious retardation in growth or decline before the turning point in business. The interval is usually many months before the end of the phase and is always a considerable fraction of the phase.

3 Rates of Change in Manufacturing Output

The rest of this chapter has the twofold objective of testing the conclusions of the preceding section by studying many commodities and establishing the cyclical patterns of the rates of change in manufacturing. The latter aim is especially important because, as will appear in Chapter 16, the cyclical movements of investment in stocks of goods in process can be gauged from those in the rate of change in output.

OUTPUT SERIES SAMPLE

For the special purpose of gauging the changes in stocks of goods in process from output data it would be desirable to construct indexes in which series representing the output of individual industries or commodities are weighted according to the relative values of the goods in process normally held to support such output. Unfortunately no estimates of the value of goods in process by industry or commodity I could now make would be sufficiently accurate to justify the construction of specially weighted indexes. We must, therefore, remain content with the standard indexes of output weighted by value added in manufacturing. To measure the output of manufacturing as a whole and of the major industry groups I used the standard FRB indexes, supplemented by indexes compiled by Y. S. Leong and by the Federal Reserve Bank of New

York. The metals series was computed by the National Bureau from several appropriate FRB output indexes; measures for two other industry groups, printing and transportation equipment, are averages of measures of several Bureau series, the original data for which are mainly in physical units. For petroleum and rubber, consumption series in physical units, compiled by the Bureau, are used.

To help overcome the difficulties that may arise from value-added weights I compiled also measures of the rates of change in a large sample of individual production series, 57 in number, distributed throughout the main groups of manufacturing industries. A study of the cyclical patterns of numerous individual series serves a twofold purpose. It tests the consistency with which the patterns that appear to characterize the multi-industry aggregates are repeated in the individual indexes. And incidentally it indicates whether a change in the weighting scheme might make a significant difference in the behavior of the aggregates.

In selecting, from the National Bureau's much larger collection, the series to be included in the sample of individual commodities and industries, I was guided by several criteria. I sought, first, to include series for the main kinds of product or the main branches of an industry at a level of detail immediately above that represented by the major industry groups distinguished by the Federal Reserve Board. For example, I included series of cattle hide leather production and of shoe production to represent the main branches of the leather and leather products industry, but not the production of men's and women's shoes separately. I included an index of the number of animals slaughtered under federal inspection to represent activity in the meat packing branch of the foods and beverages industry, but not series representing the slaughter of cattle, hogs, or sheep separately. I gave preference, secondly, to series representing the actual output of commodities or the rate of consumption of the raw materials from which they are made and admitted series based on manhours or employment only when reliable output figures were unavailable. Finally, I included only monthly or quarterly series, since annual data are plainly too coarse to reveal the changing rates of growth and decline in output during business cycles.

MEASURE OF THE RATE OF CHANGE

Because numerous commodities are studied, it was impractical to compute month to month changes in output for this special purpose and to study the cyclical patterns of these changes directly. Instead, we use the National Bureau standard measure of the rate of change per month from stage to stage of reference cycles. The construction of this measure was described and illustrated in Chapter 3. A short restatement may, nevertheless, be useful here.

First, the seasonally corrected data of a series are divided into segments bounded by the successive troughs of business cycles as identified by the monthly chronology of business cycle turning points. The average level of the data within a given business (reference) cycle is calculated and the monthly values of the series converted to percentages of this base. These percentages are called 'reference cycle relatives'. The average standing of the relatives is then computed at each of the 9 stages into which each business cycle is divided. Stage I covers the 3 months centered on the initial trough, stage V, the 3 months centered on the peak, and stage IX, the 3 months centered on the terminal trough. The averages at stages II-IV are averages of data falling within successive thirds of the expansion; the averages at stages VI-VIII give the mean standings of the data for periods representing successive thirds of the contraction.

The rates of change in output from stage to stage of a business cycle are calculated from these figures. The rate of change between stages I and II is the difference in reference cycle relatives between the average levels of output in these stages, divided by the number of months between the midpoint of stage I and of stage II. This procedure applied to stages II and III yields the rate of change in output per month between these stages, and so on. The end result is a cyclical pattern of the rate of change in output per month from stage to stage of a single reference cycle. These rates of change between stages are averaged for as many cycles as a series covers to yield an average reference cycle pattern of the rate of change in output.

It is important to inspect one feature to establish its relevance to the present problem. Inventory investment consists of the absolute change in stocks during a period. As far as investment is connected with changes in output, the connection is presumably with such changes measured in absolute terms. We should notice, therefore, that the National Bureau measure of the rate of change per month from stage to stage of a cycle is, in fact, a measure of the absolute rate of change in a series. Within any individual cycle, differences between the level of a series at various stages measured in reference cycle relatives are exactly proportionate to the absolute differences in the original data. Thus the rate of change in reference cycle relatives validly depicts the absolute rate of change. In comparisons between cycles, the transformation of the original data into reference cycle relatives is an advantage in that the pattern of change during cycles when the level of output was relatively high is not given any more weight in our averages than the pattern of change during cycles when the level of output was relatively low.

CYCLICAL PATTERNS IN THE RATE OF CHANGE IN MANUFACTURING
OUTPUT

The need to test the consistency with which the patterns in the average behavior of multi-industry indexes are repeated in the reported activity of individual industries and commodities as well as in successive business cycles makes the presentation of the evidence awkward. It is complicated the more by the striking and significant fact that, with respect to the rate of change in output, contractions and expansions are not symmetrical.

To focus attention certain broad conclusions may be stated at the outset. First, during the early part of contractions manufacturing output tends to decline at an increasing rate; it reaches a maximum about the middle of contraction, then slackens. This simple, sine-curvelike pattern does not appear without exception. There are numerous defections, but it does appear sufficiently often to justify its identification as a tendency. Not only that: even when the balanced picture of increase, then decrease, in the rate of decline in output does not appear, the rate of decline in output almost always retards toward the end of contraction. In short, the maximum rate of decline in output is reached considerably before the trough of business cycles, and is generally falling in the latter part of contractions.

No such simple observations can be made about expansions. Indeed the most striking feature of the behavior of the rate of growth of output during expansions is its variability. The pattern of growth of total output has differed from cycle to cycle, and within any given cycle it has varied markedly from industry to industry. Business expansions are, in this respect, heterogeneous, and it will require additional work to reveal the regularities that presumably underlie the observed differences. Meanwhile, it is important to remember that, since a large part of the dynamics of business expansion—the role of investment in inventories, among other things —depends upon the pattern of the rate of output growth, explanations of these phenomena must grapple with the fact that the pattern shows little tendency to repeat itself. Our notions of how business expansions cumulate, breed obstacles, and finally destroy themselves must include several variants corresponding to the ways in which the rate of change of output behaves.

As quite different generalizations seem appropriate to contractions and expansions it is convenient to review the evidence for these phases separately. I shall begin with the more regular patterns of contractions.

RATE OF DECLINE IN OUTPUT DURING BUSINESS CONTRACTIONS

As measured by the FRB index (Table 65 and Chart 68), the rate of decline in total manufacturing production increases, reaches a maximum between stages VI and VII, then falls. The pattern characteristic of the total is repeated for durable and nondurable manufactures except that the maximum rate of decline for durables appeared to come between stages VII and VIII instead of between VI and VII.

The FRB does not divide its series into producer and consumer goods,[4] but somewhat less satisfactory indexes have been calculated by Y. S. Leong and by the Federal Reserve Bank of New York. Since their coverage and methods of computation differ, both are presented. The similarity of the measures they yield bolsters confidence in them. The two indexes of total output of producer goods have patterns similar to that for all manufacturing,

[4] Consumer goods consist of finished goods of types used principally by consumers. Producer goods include finished goods used by business as well as all goods requiring further fabrication whether destined finally for consumers or producers.

TABLE 65

General Indexes of Manufacturing Production: Average Patterns of
Rates of Change per Month, 5 Business Contractions, 1920-1938

	AV. CHANGE PER MO. IN REF. CYCLE RELATIVES BETWEEN STAGES			
PRODUCTION INDEXES	V-VI	VI-VII	VII-VIII	VIII-IX
Total manufacturing, FRB	−1.1	−2.8	−1.9	−0.5
Durables, FRB	−0.9	−3.8	−4.0	−1.1
Nondurables, FRB	−1.2	−1.9	−0.2	−0.1
Producer goods, Leong	−1.5	−3.7	−2.8	−0.7
Producer goods, FRB of N.Y.	−0.9	−1.7	−2.1	−1.0
Durable, FRB of N.Y.	−0.7	−4.3	−3.7	−1.1
Nondurable, FRB of N.Y.	−1.1	−2.1	−0.6	−0.9
Consumer goods, Leong	−1.9	−0.3	−1.2	−0.2
Consumer goods, FRB of N.Y.	−1.7	−0.8	−1.0	−0.4
Durable, FRB of N.Y.	−3.2	−3.1	−3.4	−0.7
Nondurable, FRB of N.Y.	−1.3	−0.2	−0.5	−0.3

The sources and character of the indexes are described in App. G.

again with the difference that the maximum rate of decline in
Leong's index comes between stages VI and VII, that in the Bank's
index between stages VII and VIII. And the Bank's index of durables repeats this pattern. The first apparent departure is in the
Bank's index of producer nondurable goods which attains a maximum rate of decline between stages VI and VII, begins to fall
much more slowly, then picks up speed slightly toward the end of
the phase, between stages VIII and IX.

A more serious departure from the regular pattern first discerned
in the total is found in the various consumer goods indexes. These
resemble the total and the other groups in that the rate of decline
in output falls toward the end of the phase. Both Leong's and the
Bank's indexes of total output of consumer goods, however, place
the maximum rate of decline in the first part of contraction, followed by more moderate drops, then by a more rapid decline before the pace of contraction moderates at the end of the phase. The
Bank's index of consumer nondurables behaves similarly, but the
average pattern of its index of consumer durables more nearly resembles that of total manufacturing output.

These average patterns suggest that the most general attribute
of output during contractions is that its rate of decline falls off toward the end of the phase. Somewhat less strong is a tendency for

Chart 68
General Indexes of Manufacturing Production
Average Patterns of Rates of Change per Month from Stage to Stage
of 5 Business Contractions, 1920-1938

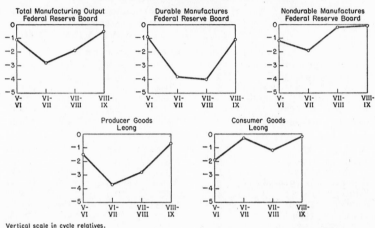

Vertical scale in cycle relatives.

the rate of decline to pick up speed in the first part of contraction and to reach a maximum about the middle. This pattern appears in all except the consumer goods segment and even there it is repeated, at least roughly, in the consumer durables category.

How consistently do these characteristics appear in measures for smaller subdivisions of manufacturing and for individual cycles? I begin with average patterns for 14 industry groups. Table 66 lends strong support to the notion that output tends to decline most rapidly about the middle of contraction and less rapidly toward the end. In these average patterns the rate of decline is regularly highest in either the interstage interval VI-VII or VII-VIII. In only one group, petroleum products, is it at its maximum in the last interstage interval of contraction; and only in leather and leather products is there an indication that the pace of contraction accelerates at the end of the phase after having moderated earlier.

The impressive uniformity of these measures is not fully maintained by the calculations made on the sample of 57 series representing individual industries and commodities some of which begin before 1919, the earliest year covered by the industry indexes. Actual measures of average rates of change are shown in Table 67.

TABLE 66

Fourteen Industry Groups: Average Patterns of Rates of Change
per Month in Production during Business Contractions

	NO. OF CONTR.	AV. CHANGE PER MO. IN REF. CYCLE RELATIVES BETWEEN STAGES			
		V-VI	VI-VII	VII-VIII	VIII-IX
DURABLE GOODS INDUSTRIES					
Lumber, 1919-38	5	−1.1	−3.3	−0.9	−0.9
Furniture, 1924-38	3	−1.6	−3.2	−2.7	−0.9
Stone, clay & glass, 1919-38	5	−1.4	−1.9	−1.3	+0.9
Metals, 1919-24, 1924-38	5	−0.9	−5.8	−4.6	−1.1
Transp. equipment, 1919-38	5	−2.7	−2.9	−5.7	−2.0
Machinery, 1924-38	3	−0.6	−3.3	−4.2	−1.5
NONDURABLE GOODS INDUSTRIES					
Food, 1919-38	5	−0.02	−0.3	−0.3	+0.2
Textiles, 1919-38	5	−3.0	−3.4	−0.1	0
Leather, 1919-38	5	−1.5	−3.1	+0.8	−0.2
Paper & pulp, 1919-38	5	−0.7	−2.5	−0.8	+0.2
Printing, 1919-33	4	−0.2	−0.9	−0.4	−0.2
Rubber, 1924-38	3	−2.3	−2.8	−1.9	+0.6
Petroleum, 1919-38	5	+0.9	+0.4	−0.2	−0.3
Chemicals, 1924-38	3	+0.1	−1.1	−1.4	−0.5

Source: App. G. The industrial classification used here and in Table 72 follows
that of the FRB. It shows data separately for 5 industries which are usually
combined with larger groups in the classification used elsewhere in this study.
The additional industries here distinguished are petroleum (otherwise included in chemicals and allied products), furniture (lumber and wood products), printing (paper, printing and publishing), machinery and transportation equipment (metals and metal products).
  The series are combined indexes of the physical output of commodities in
each industry group except that rubber and petroleum are consumption series
in physical units. The rates of change for printing are a simple average of
such measures for book paper production and newsprint paper consumption.
The rates of change for transportation equipment are a weighted average of
the rates of change for 7 series representing the output or shipments of transportation equipment items.

Table 68 shows how many and what percentage of the series had
rates of change which, on the average, rose, fell, or remained constant between the interstage intervals of contraction. The rate of
change is said to rise if, when the series is rising, its rate of rise accelerates or, when the series is falling, its rate of decline retards or
the series begins to rise. Its rate of change is said to fall if, when the
series is rising, its rate of rise retards, it reverses direction or, when
the series is falling, its rate of decline accelerates.

  Table 68 suggests that the only solid tendency of manufacturing
output during contraction is for its rate of decline to retard between stages VIII and IX, the last interstage interval of the phase.
The average rates of decline rose and fell in about the same num-

ber of series between stages VI and VII as between V and VI. And the same is true when one compares the rates of decline between stages VII and VIII with those between VI and VII. Between stages VIII and IX, however, the number of series with rates of decline lower than between stages VII and VIII exceeded those with higher rates more than 2 to 1. Thus an unweighted count of the 57 output series suggests that the rate of decline in total manufacturing remains approximately constant until near the end of contraction, then retards. The series in the important metal and metal products group do tend to decline most rapidly around the middle of contraction and their amplitude of fluctuation is wider than that of series in the other groups.[5]

But this is not the whole story. The average rates of decline in 23 series—slightly over 40 percent of the total—conform to a sine-curvelike pattern, accelerating in the first part of contraction, then retarding (Table 67). Though the sine-curve pattern does not characterize a majority of the series, it is the most common type. Seventeen other series declined most rapidly in the first interstage interval of contraction, V-VI, less rapidly thereafter. The average rates of decline in 40 of the 57 series, about 70 percent, reached maxima well before the trough of business, that is, between stages VII and VIII or earlier.

These results are based upon averages covering all the business cycles over which each individual series extends. Additional information may be had by considering measures for individual cycles. Measures made on the index of total output (Table 69 and Chart 69) show that the average pattern, in which the rate of decline first increases, then decreases, appears clearly in only two of the five individual cycles: the first and last contractions of the period, the violent downswings of 1920-21 and 1937-38. In the 1926-27 contraction the maximum rate of decline also came about the middle of the phase—between stages VII and VIII—but between stages VI and VII output increased. During the great depression of 1929-32 the rate of decline reached a maximum early, then fell at an

[5] These facts are especially relevant to the analysis of goods in process in Chapter 6. The share of the metals and metal products industries as holders of goods in process is larger than their relative contribution to value added in manufacturing.

TABLE 67

Fifty-seven Production Series: Average Patterns of Rates of Change
per Month during Business Contractions

	NO. OF CONTR.	AV. CHANGE PER MO. IN REF. CYCLE RELATIVES BETWEEN STAGES			
		V-VI	VI-VII	VII-VIII	VIII-IX
FOOD, BEVERAGES AND TOBACCO					
Animals slaughtered, 1908-38	8	−0.3	+0.3	−1.2	+0.5
Milk used in factory prod., 1919-38	5	+0.1	+0.3	+0.4	+1.9
Wheat flour, 1914-24, 1924-38	6	−0.9	0	+0.8	+2.7
Sugar meltings, 1891-21, 1921-38	13	−1.1	+0.7	+0.02	+2.4
Shortening, 1924-38	3	+2.1	+0.4	+1.3	−6.4
Tob. consumption in cigarettes, 1914-38	6	−1.8	+1.0	+1.3	−1.4
TEXTILES AND TEXTILE PRODUCTS					
Cotton consumption, 1914-38	6	−2.6	−2.1	−2.0	+0.1
Wool consumption, 1919-38	5	−5.4	−4.5	−0.04	−0.9
Raw silk deliveries, 1921-38	4	−2.9	−1.6	+0.4	+1.5
Rayon deliveries, 1924-38	3	−1.1	−1.9	−0.1	+3.0
Fabrics, factory employment, 1919-38	5	−0.7	−2.0	−0.4	−0.3
Wearing apparel, factory emp., 1919-38	5	−0.2	−1.3	−0.3	−0.3
LEATHER AND LEATHER PRODUCTS					
Cattle hide & kip leather, 1921-38	4	−2.2	−2.0	−1.2	−0.4
Shoes, 1924-38	3	−1.8	−2.4	+1.2	+0.3
RUBBER AND RELATED PRODUCTS					
Auto. inner tubes, 1921-38	4	−6.2	−0.8	−2.2	+0.8
Auto. pneumatic casings, 1921-38	4	−6.2	−0.4	−2.0	+0.05
LUMBER AND WOOD PRODUCTS					
Douglas fir lumber, 1919-33	4	−1.2	−1.4	−1.2	−0.4
Southern pine lumber, 1919-38	5	−1.1	−2.0	+0.1	−0.5
Oak flooring, 1912-38	7	−4.1	−1.3	+2.8	+1.4
Furniture, 1924-38	3	−1.6	−3.2	−2.7	−0.9
PAPER, PRINTING AND PUBLISHING					
Fine paper, 1919-33, 1933-38	5	−0.9	−2.5	−1.0	+0.6
Wrapping paper, 1924-38	3	−0.6	−4.4	+0.4	+1.1
Newsprint shipments, 1919-38	5	0	−0.7	−2.4	+0.3
Book paper, 1919-33	4	+0.1	−1.7	−0.8	−0.5
Paper boxes, factory emp., 1919-38	5	+0.04	−0.9	−1.1	−0.4
Newsprint consumption, 1919-38	5	−0.5	−0.3	−0.5	−0.2

TABLE 67 (Concl.)

		AV. CHANGE PER MO. IN REF. CYCLE RELATIVES BETWEEN STAGES			
	NO. OF CONTR.	V-VI	VI-VII	VII-VIII	VIII-IX
CHEMICALS AND ALLIED PRODUCTS					
Chemical products					
Ethyl alcohol, 1921-38	4	−3.3	+1.1	−2.1	−1.5
Fertilizer consumption, 1924-38	3	−2.5	−1.7	+1.1	−0.6
Inedible tallow, 1919-38	5	−0.4	+0.7	+1.4	+0.3
Explosives shipments, 1921-38	4	−3.5	−1.3	−1.4	−0.5
Linseed oil, 1919-38	5	−4.5	−3.5	+0.5	−3.0
Refined cottonseed oil, 1919-38	5	+1.3	+1.7	+1.8	−2.5
Petroleum products					
Gasoline, 1919-38	5	+1.6	+0.8	+0.2	−0.02
Lubricants, 1919-38	5	+0.1	+0.1	−1.6	−1.4
STONE, CLAY AND GLASS PRODUCTS					
Portland cement, 1912-38	7	−1.5	+0.1	+0.1	−1.0
Polished plate glass, 1924-38	3	−3.8	−3.8	−9.0	+0.7
Face brick, 1919-24, 1924-33	4	−1.5	−3.3	−0.4	+0.2
Prepared roofing shipments, 1919-27, 1927-33, 1933-38	5	−4.5	+0.9	+0.8	+0.2
Asphalt, 1919-38	5	+0.4	+0.3	−0.7	+2.3
METALS AND METAL PRODUCTS					
Metals					
Pig iron, 1879-1938	16	−0.6	−3.8	−3.5	−1.6
Steel ingots, 1900-38	10	−0.9	−4.6	−4.3	−1.7
Refined copper, N. & S. Am., 1919-38	5	−0.6	−0.6	−2.9	−1.9
Steel sheets, 1919-33, 1933-38	5	−4.7	−4.8	−5.2	+1.4
Lead ore shipments, 1897-1924, 1924-38	11	−3.5	−1.4	−1.2	+1.9
Slab zinc, 1921-38	4	−1.9	−1.5	−1.8	−1.7
Tin & terne plate, 1924-33, 1933-38	3	+1.5	−3.9	−5.7	−1.2
Enameled sanitary ware ship., 1919-27	3	−0.6	+2.0	−0.6	−0.7
Transportation equipment					
Passenger auto., 1914-38	6	−6.3	−0.4	−1.6	−0.03
Trucks, 1914-38	6	−5.6	−2.9	−3.4	−1.8
Auto. parts & accessories ship., 1927-38	2	−3.3	−5.0	−6.4	−0.9
Vessels under construction, 1919-38	5	+2.9	−0.5	−5.0	−6.3
Freight car shipments, 1919-38	5	+0.7	−6.7	−16.0	−1.7
R.R. passenger car. ship., 1919-38	5	+19.0	−12.4	+6.1	−20.3
R.R. locomotive ship., 1919-38	5	−0.1	−4.7	−8.4	−6.9
Machinery shipments, value					
Machine tool, 1927-33	1	−6.9	−6.2	−2.1	−1.4
Industrial pumps, 1919-33	4	+0.02	−2.7	−3.6	−3.2
Woodworking mach., 1919-38	5	−4.7	−4.0	−3.9	−2.7

Unless otherwise specified, each series represents the physical output of a commodity or is an index of the physical output of a group of commodities. Full titles and brief descriptions of the sources and character of these series are given in App. G.

ever slower pace. All these four contractions share the single characteristic that the decline in output began to fall off some time before the last part of the phase, between stages VII and VIII or earlier. Only in the mild contraction of 1923-24 did output decline most rapidly between stages VIII and IX, the last part of the phase.[6]

TABLE 68

Fifty-seven Production Series: Direction of Movement of Average Rates of Change per Month between Interstage Intervals of Business Contractions

Interstage Intervals	Rising	Constant	Falling
		NUMBER	
V-VI & VI-VII	28	3	26
VI-VII & VII-VIII	30	1	26
VII-VIII & VIII-IX	39	2	16
		PERCENTAGE	
V-VI & VI-VII	49.1	5.3	45.6
VI-VII & VII-VIII	52.6	1.8	45.6
VII-VIII & VIII-IX	68.4	3.5	28.1

By and large the measures made on the industry groups and individual industries confirm these results (Table 70). At the beginning of all three major contractions of the period (1920-21, 1929-32, and 1937-38), a majority of the industry groups declined at an accelerating rate and at the end a majority fell at a diminishing rate. In the two minor contractions of the mid-'twenties the reverse was true. In one, however, the indicated acceleration of the pace of the decline at the end of the phase is fairly weak. As in the measures of total output, in the 1923-24 contraction alone is there a clear indication that output was falling at an accelerating pace during the last part of the phase.

I conclude from these numerous observations that the rate of decline in output tends markedly to diminish well before the end of cyclical contractions. It tends to accelerate in the early part of contractions, but this tendency is weaker and its validity less assured.

---

[6] This agrees with the showing of the aggregate indexes in Section 2. The interval between the upturn in the rate of change of these indexes and the business cycle trough in July 1924 was shorter than at other troughs of business.

TABLE 69

Federal Reserve Board Index of Manufacturing Production
Patterns of Rates of Change per Month, 5 Business Contractions
1920-1938

	CHANGE PER MO. IN REF. CYCLE RELATIVES BETWEEN STAGES			
BUSINESS CONTRACTION	V-VI	VI-VII	VII-VIII	VIII-IX
Jan. 1920 - Sept. 1921	−0.6	−3.2	−2.1	+1.7
May 1923 - July 1924	−1.0	−0.9	−1.1	−2.7
Oct. 1926 - Dec. 1927	−0.6	+0.2	−0.8	0
June 1929 - March 1933	−2.1	−2.0	−1.5	−0.4
May 1937 - May 1938	−1.1	−7.9	−4.1	−1.0

Chart 69
Federal Reserve Board Index of Manufacturing Production
Patterns of Rates of Change per Month from Stage to Stage
of 5 Business Contractions

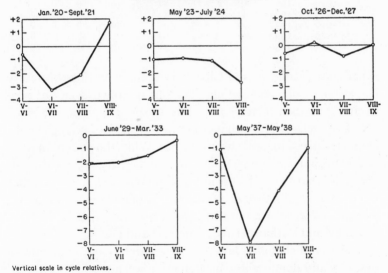

Vertical scale in cycle relatives.

RATE OF GROWTH IN OUTPUT DURING BUSINESS EXPANSIONS

To define the tendencies of the rate of change in output during expansions is far more difficult. The average patterns of the general indexes of production do indeed suggest some interesting conclusions. But these are supported only in part by the average behavior of the subgroups or of the aggregate in individual cycles.

The average pattern of the index for all manufacturing during

TABLE 70

Manufacturing Production: Direction of Movement of Rates of
Change per Month between Interstage Intervals, 5 Business
Contractions, 1920-1938

BUSINESS CONTRACTION	V-VI to VI-VII			VI-VII to VII-VIII			VII-VIII to VIII-IX		
NO. OF SERIES WITH INDICATED MOVEMENT BETWEEN INTERSTAGE INTERVALS	+	o	−	+	o	−	+	o	−
FOURTEEN INDUSTRY GROUP INDEXES									
1/1920– 9/1921	2		8	6		4	8		2
5/1923– 6/1924	7		3	5		5	2		8
10/1926–12/1927	10		4	5		9	6		8
6/1929– 3/1933	5		9	9	1	4	13		1
5/1937– 5/1938			13	9		4	11		2
FIFTY-SEVEN PRODUCTION SERIES									
1/1920– 9/1921	19		21	21		19	29		11
5/1923– 6/1924	34		13	21		26	16		31
10/1926–12/1927	40		15	22	3	30	28	1	26
6/1929– 3/1933	29	3	24	31	2	23	47	1	8
5/1937– 5/1938	15		36	32		19	31		20

expansions (Table 71 and Chart 70) is an interesting contrast to
its pattern during contractions. The rate of growth is at first relatively rapid, then retards, and picks up speed again as the phase
draws to a close. This behavior, however, has not been generally
characteristic of manufacturing output. While the pattern marked
out by the index of total output is repeated by the index of durable
goods, it is not shared by the index of nondurables. The latter, like
the total, first falls, then rises, but the rate of growth of nondurable
output is lower toward the end of expansion, that is, between
stages IV and V, than between stages III and IV.

The true dichotomy, however, is apparently not one between
durables and nondurables, but rather between producer and consumer goods. Whether we look at Leong's index or the Federal Reserve Bank's, the output of producer and durable goods seems to
act similarly, rising toward the end of expansion. The rate of
growth of consumer goods is like that of nondurables, declining toward the end of the phase. So much is only to be expected from the
degree to which these classifications overlap. With the Federal Reserve Bank indexes (Table 71) we can be more discriminating,
for they divide both producer and consumer goods into durables

TABLE 71

General Indexes of Manufacturing Production: Average Patterns
of Rates of Change per Month, 5 Business Expansions, 1919-1937

	AV. CHANGE PER MO. IN REF. CYCLE RELATIVES BETWEEN STAGES			
PRODUCTION INDEXES	I-II	II-III	III-IV	IV-V
Total mfg., FRB	+2.2	+1.6	+0.9	+1.8
Durables, FRB	+2.6	+2.5	+0.9	+2.9
Nondurables, FRB	+1.8	+0.9	+1.1	+0.9
Producer goods, Leong	+2.8	+2.1	+0.7	+1.6
Producer goods, FRB of N.Y.	+2.3	+1.4	+0.4	+1.4
Durable, FRB of N.Y.	+2.5	+2.5	+0.7	+2.1
Nondurable, FRB of N.Y.	+2.4	+0.4	+0.1	+0.7
Consumer goods, Leong	+1.5	+1.0	+1.9	+0.1
Consumer goods, FRB of N.Y.	+1.0	+0.9	+1.2	−0.5
Durable, FRB of N.Y.	+3.5	+3.9	+2.7	−1.7
Nondurable, FRB of N.Y.	+0.4	+0.1	+0.8	−0.2

See Table 65.

Chart 70

General Indexes of Manufacturing Production
Average Patterns of Rates of Change per Month from Stage to Stage
of 5 Business Expansions, 1919-1937

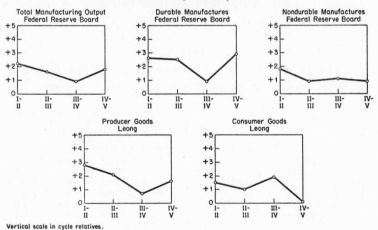

Vertical scale in cycle relatives.

and nondurables. Producer goods, whether durable or nondurable,
grew more rapidly in the last interstage interval of expansion than
in the third interval. Consumer goods, durable and nondurable,
on the contrary, grew less rapidly in the last interval than in the
third.

The tendency, if there is one, for the pace of output to accelerate toward the end of expansion is confined to producer goods. Producer goods, however, do not cover merely items of finished equipment to be sold to business. They include also goods requiring further fabrication whatever their ultimate destination. They therefore cover a much larger volume of commodities than do consumer goods which are limited to commodities ready for sale to ultimate consumers.

One final aspect of Table 71 deserves notice. Whatever the differences among the various categories of manufacturing with respect to the rate of increase in output at the end of expansion, there is virtually unanimous agreement about events during the first half of the phase. As far as these averages may be trusted, it appears to have been characteristic of manufacturing that the rate of expansion, after starting at a relatively rapid pace between stages I and II, retarded between stages II and III. This is the showing of the total and of all the component indexes except two. The rate of growth of the Federal Reserve Bank index of producer durables does not change between these two intervals; its index of consumer durables rises.

TABLE 72

Fourteen Industry Groups: Average Patterns of Rates of Change per Month in Production during Business Expansions

	NO. OF EXP.	AV. CHANGE PER MO. IN REF. CYCLE RELATIVES BETWEEN STAGES			
		I-II	II-III	III-IV	IV-V
DURABLE GOODS INDUSTRIES					
Lumber, 1919-38	5	+1.6	+0.8	+1.1	+0.8
Furniture, 1924-38	3	+0.8	+1.1	+1.2	+1.5
Stone, clay & glass, 1919-38	5	+2.0	+2.3	+0.5	+2.2
Metals, 1919-24, 1924-38	5	+3.6	+3.0	+0.6	+4.1
Transp. equipment, 1919-38	5	+0.8	+4.8	+2.3	+1.9
Machinery, 1924-38	3	+1.9	+1.6	+2.1	+2.1
NONDURABLE GOODS INDUSTRIES					
Food, 1919-38	5	+0.1	+0.3	+0.7	+0.5
Textiles, 1919-38	5	+2.6	+0.6	+1.5	+0.9
Leather, 1919-38	5	+0.9	+0.3	+0.7	+1.0
Paper & pulp, 1919-38	5	+2.2	+1.2	+1.3	+1.6
Printing, 1919-33	4	+1.7	+1.0	+0.9	+1.5
Rubber, 1924-38	3	+3.1	+2.0	+0.2	−0.1
Petroleum, 1919-38	5	+1.2	+1.0	+0.9	+0.8
Chemicals, 1924-38	3	+1.0	+1.0	+1.0	+1.1

See Table 66, notes.

How consistent are these behavior traits in series representing industry groups and individual commodities (Table 72)? The 14 industry groups cannot be divided between consumer and producer goods, but the industries have been grouped according to the durability of their products. The tendencies that appeared in the general indexes are no longer visible. Half the durable goods industries grow at a higher rate between stages II and III than between stages I and II; half at a lower rate. Virtually the same even division appears in later intervals. The latter point is true also for the nondurable goods industries, but in this category most industries advanced less rapidly in the second interval than in the first.[7]

This apparently constant rate of growth of aggregate manufacturing output during expansions is belied by the measures for individual industries and commodities. These suggest again that the aggregate conceals differences in its components. The average cycle measures in Tables 73 and 74 are strikingly similar to the results suggested by the general indexes (Table 71) in certain interesting and important respects.[8] The average rates of growth of a considerable majority of the 57 series declined from interstage interval I-II to II-III. Again the sole exception was consumer durables. Another striking similarity is the apparent change between the third and last intervals of expansion. Again the rate of growth of the output of producer goods apparently rose toward the end of expansion and that of consumer goods declined.

If these observations were true for all cycles, they would be of great significance. But cycle by cycle examination confirms the suggestions of the averages only in part. I confine the presentation

[7] The character of the durable goods index in Table 71 seems to have been determined chiefly by the weight assigned to the metals group; the character of the nondurable goods index is attributable to the weights assigned to the foods and textiles groups.

[8] In some respects the two bodies of data yield different results. For example, the rate of growth of the index of all manufacturing was lower between stages III and IV than between II and III; the growth of the Reserve Bank index of producer goods was also slower, but that of the Bank index of consumer goods was higher. A small majority of all 57 series, on the contrary, rose at a more rapid rate between stages III and IV, most of the producer goods rose at a less rapid rate and most of the consumer goods at a more rapid rate.

TABLE 73

Fifty-seven Production Series: Average Patterns of Rates of Change
per Month during Business Expansions

(1)	NO. OF EXP. (2)	TYPE OF GOODS* (3)	AV. CHANGE PER MO. IN REF. CYCLE RELATIVES BETWEEN STAGES			
			I-II (4)	II-III (5)	III-IV (6)	IV-V (7)
FOOD, BEVERAGES AND TOBACCO						
Animals slaughtered, 1908-38	8	CN	+0.6	−0.6	+0.7	−0.2
Milk used in factory prod., 1919-38	5	CN	−0.3	+0.3	+0.2	−0.4
Wheat flour, 1914-24, 1924-38	6	CN	−2.3	+0.8	+0.2	+0.1
Sugar meltings, 1891-21, 1921-38	13	CN	−0.1	+0.1	+0.2	−0.1
Shortening, 1924-38	3	CN	+2.7	+1.8	−0.1	−0.5
Tob. consumption in cigarettes, 1914-38	6	CN	−0.3	+2.5	+3.2	+0.3
TEXTILES AND TEXTILE PRODUCTS						
Cotton consumption, 1914-38	6	PN	+1.7	+0.4	+1.5	+0.9
Wool consumption, 1919-38	5	PN	+5.2	−0.7	+1.9	+2.2
Raw silk deliveries, 1921-38	4	PN	+0.2	+1.2	+0.5	+0.4
Rayon deliveries, 1924-38	3	PN	+1.8	+0.9	+1.2	+2.8
Fabrics, factory emp., 1919-38	5	PN	+1.6	+0.4	+0.5	+0.7
Wearing apparel, factory emp., 1919-38	5	CN	+0.8	+0.7	+0.9	+0.2
LEATHER AND LEATHER PRODUCTS						
Cattle hide & kip leather, 1921-38	4	PN	+1.8	−0.2	+0.2	+1.3
Shoes, 1924-38	3	CN	+1.2	0	+0.4	+1.1
RUBBER AND RELATED PRODUCTS						
Auto. inner tubes, 1921-38	4	CN	+1.6	+1.5	+0.6	−1.4
Auto. pneumatic casings, 1921-38	4	CN	+2.5	+2.2	+0.4	−0.8
LUMBER AND WOOD PRODUCTS						
Douglas fir lumber, 1919-33	4	PD	+1.6	−1.2	−0.6	+1.0
Southern pine lumber, 1919-38	5	PD	+1.2	+0.4	+0.3	−0.7
Oak flooring, 1912-38	7	PD	+4.1	+3.0	+0.7	+1.4
Furniture, 1924-38	3	CD	+0.8	+1.1	+1.2	+1.5
PAPER, PRINTING AND PUBLISHING						
Fine paper, 1919-33, 1933-38	5	CN	+3.4	+2.2	+0.9	+0.5
Wrapping paper, 1924-38	3	PN	+1.8	+0.5	+0.7	+1.1
Newsprint shipments, 1919-38	5	PN	+1.1	+1.5	+0.9	+0.5
Book paper, 1919-33	4	PN	+2.2	+1.0	+1.2	+2.8
Paper boxes, factory emp., 1919-38	5	PN	+0.6	−0.1	+0.9	+1.0
Newsprint consumption, 1919-38	5	CN	+1.2	+1.0	+0.6	+0.3
CHEMICALS AND ALLIED PRODUCTS						
Chemical products						
Ethyl alcohol, 1921-38	4	PN	+2.3	+2.1	+1.8	0
Fertilizer consumption, 1924-38	3	PN	+0.8	+0.1	+0.5	+1.2
Inedible tallow, 1919-38	5	PN	+2.0	−0.1	+0.7	+0.1
Explosives shipments, 1921-38	4	PN	+1.1	+0.2	+2.0	+0.8
Linseed oil, 1919-38	5	PN	+3.0	−2.1	+1.5	+4.0
Refined cottonseed oil, 1919-38	5	PN	+0.4	−2.0	+1.5	−1.5

TABLE 73 (Concl.)

(1)	NO. OF EXP. (2)	TYPE OF GOODS* (3)	AV. CHANGE PER MO. IN REF. CYCLE RELATIVES BETWEEN STAGES			
			I-II (4)	II-III (5)	III-IV (6)	IV-V (7)
Petroleum products						
Gasoline, 1919-38	5	CN	+1.0	+0.9	+1.5	+0.5
Lubricants, 1919-38	5	PN	+1.5	+0.8	+0.9	+0.9
STONE, CLAY AND GLASS PRODUCTS						
Portland cement, 1912-38	7	PD	+1.1	+1.2	+0.5	+1.3
Polished plate glass, 1924-38	3	PD	+3.3	+2.0	+1.7	+1.7
Face brick, 1919-24, 1924-33	4	PD	+3.4	+2.9	+0.02	+3.0
Prepared roofing shipments, 1919-27, 1927-33, 1933-38	5	PD	+0.9	−0.6	+3.2	+1.5
Asphalt, 1919-38	5	PD	+1.4	+1.5	+3.2	+0.9
METALS AND METAL PRODUCTS						
Metals						
Pig iron, 1879-1938	16	PD	+3.8	+2.0	+1.3	+2.9
Steel ingot, 1900-38	10	PD	+4.2	+2.4	+1.1	+3.3
Refined copper, N. & S. Am., 1919-38	5	PD	+0.3	+2.4	+0.9	+2.0
Steel sheets, 1919-33, 1933-38	5	PD	+4.6	+2.8	+1.3	+4.5
Lead ore shipments, 1897-1924, 1924-38	11	PD	+1.3	+0.9	+0.3	+1.4
Slab zinc, 1921-38	4	PD	+2.2	+1.6	+1.6	+2.5
Tin & terne plate, 1924-33, 1933-38	3	PD	+3.5	+1.5	+0.6	+0.6
Enameled sanitary ware ship., 1919-27	3	CD	+8.3	+2.1	+1.2	−2.8
Transportation equipment						
Passenger automobiles, 1914-38	6	CD	+3.7	+4.1	+3.2	−0.7
Trucks, 1914-38	6	PD	+2.9	+3.8	+3.9	+6.8
Auto. parts & accessories ship., 1927-38	2	CD	+3.2	+3.4	+0.8	+0.1
Vessels under construction, 1919-38	5	PD	−12.6	−2.8	+0.4	+3.0
Freight car shipments, 1919-38	5	PD	−1.1	+28.0	−13.7	+0.1
R.R. passenger car. ship., 1919-38	5	PD	−11.5	+3.9	+6.7	−9.3
R.R. locomotive ship., 1919-38	5	PD	−8.3	−3.3	+1.9	+7.8
Machinery shipments, value						
Machine tool, 1927-33	1	PD	+4.7	+4.2	+8.0	+2.7
Industrial pumps, 1919-33	4	PD	+2.3	+2.0	+4.0	+3.7
Woodworking mach., 1919-38	5	PD	+4.1	+2.8	+2.9	+2.4

See Table 67, note.

* The symbols in col. 3 indicate the classification of the industry or commodity according to durability and user, the basis for the calculations of Table 74, as follows:

CD Consumer durables   PD Producer durables
CN Consumer nondurables   PN Producer nondurables

TABLE 74

Fifty-seven Production Series Classified by User and Durability
Direction of Movement of Average Rates of Change per Month
between Interstage Intervals of Business Expansions

	DIRECTION OF MOVEMENT BETWEEN INTERSTAGE INTERVALS								
	I-II to II-III			II-III to III-IV			III-IV to IV-V		
	+	o	−	+	o	−	+	o	−
	NUMBER OF SERIES								
Consumer goods	7	10		7		10	2		15
Durable	3	1		1		3	1		3
Nondurable	4	9		6		7	1		12
Producer goods	9	31		24	1	15	23	3	14
Durable	8	15		10	1	12	14	2	7
Nondurable	1	16		14		3	9	1	7
Total durable	11	16		11	1	15	15	2	10
Total nondurable	5	25		20		10	10	1	19
All series	16	41		31	1	25	25	3	29
	PERCENTAGE OF SERIES								
Consumer goods	41	59		41		59	12		88
Durable	75	25		25		75	25		75
Nondurable	31	69		46		54	8		92
Producer goods	22	78		60	2	38	57	8	35
Durable	35	65		43	4	53	61	9	30
Nondurable	6	94		82		18	53	6	41
Total durable	41	59		41	4	55	56	7	37
Total nondurable	17	83		67		33	33	3	64
All series	28	72		54	2	44	44	5	51

See Table 73, col. 3, for industries included in each class.

of data to the general indexes and individual commodities grouped
into producer and consumer goods categories. Chart 71 depicts
the patterns of the rate of growth of total manufacturing output,
as measured by the FRB index, and of the output of producer and
consumer goods, as measured by Leong's indexes.[9] Table 75 shows,
cycle by cycle, the number and percentage of all individual commodity series whose rate of growth rises or falls between interstage
intervals. This information is furnished for all the series for which

[9] Leong's indexes are presented in preference to those of the Federal Reserve
Bank of New York because the latter are adjusted for trend and contain some
indexes of output in industries other than manufacturing. They are, therefore, less easily compared with the FRB index of total manufacturing production.

data are available in a given cycle and for these series grouped into producer and consumer goods categories.

Within the consumer goods group, certain tendencies may be identified, at least tentatively. According to the measures made from Leong's index (Chart 71), the advance in the first part of expan-

Chart 71
General Indexes of Manufacturing Production
Patterns of Rates of Change per Month from Stage to Stage
of 5 Business Expansions

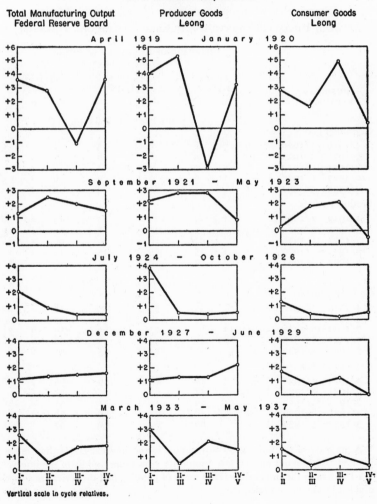

Total Manufacturing Output
Federal Reserve Board

Producer Goods
Leong

Consumer Goods
Leong

Vertical scale in cycle relatives.

sion was relatively rapid in 4 out of 5 cycles. In the second inter-stage interval, the pace moderated—again in 4 out of 5 cycles. In the third interval, the advance quickened, then slackened decisively in the fourth. The summary of the movements of individual series (Table 75) confirms the behavior of the index, at least as far as the deceleration at the end of the phase is concerned. And it does not contradict the behavior of the index in earlier intervals.[10]

TABLE 75

Fifty-seven Production Series Classified by User
Direction of Movement of Rates of Change per Month
between Interstage Intervals, 5 Business Expansions, 1919-1937

BUSINESS EXPANSION	I-II to II-III +	o	−	II-III to III-IV +	o	−	III-IV to IV-V +	o	−
	NUMBER OF SERIES								
Consumer goods									
4/1919– 1/1920	5		6	6		5	2		9
9/1921– 5/1923	10		3	6	1	6	3	1	9
7/1924–10/1926	5	2	9	4	1	11	8	3	5
12/1927– 6/1929	9	1	6	7		9	6	1	9
3/1933– 5/1937	4		12	12		4	5	1	10
Producer goods									
4/1919– 1/1920	14	1	14	12		17	19	2	8
9/1921– 5/1923	19		15	21	1	12	11	1	22
7/1924–10/1926	8		31	16		20	20	1	18
12/1927– 6/1929	24	1	15	25		15	15	1	24
3/1933– 5/1937	4		31	28		7	20		15
	PERCENTAGE OF SERIES								
Consumer goods									
4/1919– 1/1920	45		55	55		45	18		82
9/1921– 5/1923	77		23	46	8	46	23	8	69
7/1924–10/1926	31	12	57	25	6	69	50	19	31
12/1927– 6/1929	56	6	38	44		56	38	6	56
3/1933– 5/1937	25		75	75		25	31	6	63
Producer goods									
4/1919– 1/1920	49	3	48	41		59	65	7	28
9/1921– 5/1923	56		44	62	3	35	32	3	65
7/1924–10/1926	21		79	41	8	51	51	3	46
12/1927– 6/1929	60	2	38	62		38	38	2	60
3/1933– 5/1937	11		89	80		20	57		43

[10] A majority of the series grow less rapidly in the interval II-III than in the interval I-II in 3 out of 5 cycles. A majority grow more rapidly in the interval III-IV than in the interval II-III in 2 out of 5 cycles, and the series are evenly divided in one more cycle.

There is little regularity, however, in the rate of growth of producer goods industries from one cycle to the next. According to Leong's index, the pace was faster in the interval II-III than in the interval I-II in three cycles, slower in two. Between intervals II-III and III-IV it was constant in two cycles, almost unchanged in a third, faster in a fourth, and slower in a fifth. Between intervals III-IV and IV-V it accelerated in two cycles, declined in two, and remained almost constant in a fifth. Summaries of the movements of individual series indicate similar irregularity. With the exception of one cycle in Leong's data, however, there is evidence of a decisive retardation in growth in some interval before expansion ends. In this respect the measures made on manufacturing output confirm those made on the indexes of aggregate output.

As explained above, the producer goods category, which covers the output not only of finished capital goods but also of unfinished goods destined to be used by both business and consumers, is much more important than the consumer goods category. As a result, aggregate manufacturing output followed the varying pattern of producer goods production rather than the relatively stable pattern of consumer goods production.

CONCLUSION

For the readers' convenience, I shall here state categorically the chief conclusions to which I think the measures examined above lead.

1) During contractions manufacturing production tends to decline at its most rapid rate well before the trough of business is reached. There is some indication that it tends to reach its maximum rate about the middle of the phase, but it has sometimes achieved its maximum near the very beginning. In any event, the rate of decline has usually been decelerating near the trough of business. These observations are consistent with the general trend of the data, but many industries have not acted in this way in every cycle observed, and in one cycle the rule did not hold at all.

2) During expansions the rate of growth in consumer goods production appears to have shared one important characteristic of all manufacturing output in contraction: the maximum rate has usually occurred well before the peak of business. But while the rate of growth in this category has typically been much lower near the

end of expansion than earlier, no clear rule emerges about the stage when it tends to be at a maximum.

3) The pattern of the rate of growth of producer goods has been highly variable from cycle to cycle. The rate of growth near the end of expansion has sometimes been relatively high, sometimes relatively low. The same may be said for the earlier stages of expansion, except the first when it has usually been fairly high. Almost always, however, a period of serious retardation has been experienced before the end of expansion.

4) The behavior of producer goods has generally overshadowed that of consumer goods, and the rate of growth of total manufacturing output during expansions has usually been dominated by the irregular behavior of the rate of growth of producer goods output.

These detailed characteristics of the pattern of the rate of change in manufacturing production are significant for the analysis of investment in goods in process set forth in the next chapter. Here we revert to the broad finding confirmed by the indexes of both aggregate output and manufacturing production. The rate of growth in output reaches a high point considerably before the end of expansion, a trough considerably before the end of contraction. The turning points occur sometimes at the very beginning of a phase, often during its first half. A period of retarded change follows, which may last throughout the remainder of a phase or, especially in expansions, may be succeeded by a period of accelerated movement. In the latter case, the succeeding peaks in the rate of change in output are usually lower than the initial peak, and the same with the troughs.

The movements of inventory investment are quite different. The rate of accumulation of inventories is typically low—usually negative—at the beginning of expansion. And whatever oscillations it may experience during the course of the phase—annual data do not give any indication of serious intra-phase fluctuations—it normally reaches its peak near the peak of the business cycle. Similarly in contractions: the phase opens with inventories still growing; liquidation begins gradually and is normally most rapid near the trough of the business cycle.

The significance of this behavior has already been described. The lag of inventory investment behind the rate of change in output acts to moderate the pace and extend the duration of expansions and contractions. We must now try to understand the causes of the lag. The next four chapters attempt to provide an explanation as far as manufacturers' inventories are concerned. As in Part Two, we find that there are significant differences between the behavior of investment in goods in process, raw materials, and finished goods. An explanation of the behavior of total inventory investment by manufacturers must be sought in the forces that control investment in the several categories.

CHAPTER 16

Investment in Goods in Process

Goods in process comprise the commodities individual manufacturers have begun to fabricate but that are not yet ready for delivery—about 20 percent of manufacturers' holdings (Ch. 7). As argued in Chapter 8, as far as they are held in continuous process industries, that is, in industries in which it is impossible or inconvenient to keep surplus stocks of semifabricated goods over and above the quantity necessary to sustain a certain rate of activity, stocks of goods in process move up and down with the rate of production. And I presented estimates that make it seem likely that these conditions, or a reasonably close approximation to them, characterize a substantial proportion of all goods in process. In such industries stocks of goods in process cannot lag behind production. On the contrary, they are likely to lead. The lead, however, cannot exceed an interval equal to a production period; that is, it cannot exceed the time elapsing between the moment work is begun upon a prospective unit of output in a manufacturing establishment and the time it is ready for delivery. Finally, I estimated that the average length of the production period in manufacturing establishments is unlikely to be less than 15 days and is probably from 20 to 25 days.

Concerning the action of goods in process held in other industries I am less certain. However, since in establishments that combine several stages of production each stage is, so to speak, a 'continuous' industry, at least part of the goods in process must behave like the stocks of continuous industries. Moreover, it is not necessary for the stocks 'between stages' to move inversely during any part of a production cycle. There is only a possibility that they may do so. Hence it seems likely that the behavior of goods in process sketched above is characteristic of a wider range of manufacturing than 'continuous' establishments alone.

Our present concern, however, is with investment in goods in process, that is, with the absolute rate of change in such stocks per time unit, and their relation to business cycles. Now it turns out that the relations between the rate of production and goods in process in continuous industries exist also between the absolute rates of growth in production and in goods in process. The rate of investment in goods in process, we shall find, moves up and down with the rate of increase in output. It will not lag behind the rate of output, and if it leads, as it is likely to do, the lead will not be longer than a production period. If these relations can be established, we can use the pattern of the rate of change in manufacturing production (Ch. 15, Sec. 3) to determine the cyclical pattern of investment in goods in process.

1 Theoretical Relations between Rates of Increase in Output and Investment in Goods in Process

Although we are interested in the relation between output and goods in process, it is more convenient to present the argument in terms of the relation between goods in process and input. Since output must lag behind input by a production period, the relation between stocks and output can be stated by a verbal alteration of the conclusions.

To simplify the argument we assume that a unit of prospective output grows in value at the same absolute rate in dollars from the time work is begun until it is ready for delivery, that is, from the time the unit becomes a part of the stock of goods in process until it becomes a part of the stock of finished goods. Let us denote the number of units put into work continuously on successive days by the symbols a_1, a_2, a_3, and so on; and let us assume that a unit of input is worth x dollars after one day of processing, $2x$ after two days, and so on; finally let us assume that the production period is four days. Let p = the value of goods in process.

Since the value of goods in process on any given day equals the sum of the values attained by the units of input on which work began on the given day and the three preceding days, we may write the value of goods in process at the end of the fourth day after input begins as:

1) $p_4 = \dfrac{a_4 x}{2} + \dfrac{a_3 x}{2} + a_3 x + \dfrac{a_2 x}{2} + 2 a_2 x + \dfrac{a_1 x}{2} + 3 a_1 x$

This expression tells us that the units put into process on the first day, a_1, have, on the average, received three and one-half days' processing by the end of the fourth day, $\dfrac{a_1 x}{2} + 3 a_1 x$. Goods put into process on the second day have acquired two and one-half days' processing on the average, $\dfrac{a_2 x}{2} + 2 a_2 x$, by the end of the fourth day, and so on. The total value of goods in process at the end of the fourth day or, in general, any day, is the sum of values acquired by goods put into process during the given day and the number of preceding days that together make up a production period.

Equating x to unity, this expression simplifies to:

2) $p_4 = \dfrac{a_4}{2} + \dfrac{a_3}{2} + a_3 + \dfrac{a_2}{2} + 2 a_2 + \dfrac{a_1}{2} + 3 a_1$

In the same way, the value of goods in process at the end of the following day is:

3) $p_5 = \dfrac{a_5}{2} + \dfrac{a_4}{2} + a_4 + \dfrac{a_3}{2} + 2 a_3 + \dfrac{a_2}{2} + 3 a_2$

During the fifth day goods in process have grown by the difference between p_5 and p_4:

4) $p_5 - p_4 = \dfrac{a_5}{2} + a_4 + a_3 + a_2 - \left(3 a_1 + \dfrac{a_1}{2}\right)$

This expression tells us that between the fourth and fifth days (or any two days) goods in process decline by an amount proportionate to 3.5 times the number of units put into process on the first day of the sequence of five. These are the units that were put into work earliest and in our setup have 3.5 days' processing at the end of the fourth day. At the end of the fifth day all these units have moved into the finished goods category and disappeared from goods in process. On the other hand, goods in process grow by an amount proportionate to the sum of the number of units of goods put into process on the second, third, and fourth days plus half the number put into process on the fifth day. That is, the batches put into process on the second, third, and fourth days have each been given one more day's processing and the goods put into process on the fifth day have, on the average, been given one-half day's processing. The difference between the goods in process at the end of any two days is, of course, simply the difference between the amounts by which goods in process grow and decline in the course of one day.

The fourth equation may be rewritten in more convenient form:

5) $\quad p_5 - p_4 = a_4 + a_3 + a_2 - 3a_1 + \dfrac{a_5 - a_1}{2}$

As long as input increases at an accelerating rate, goods in process also will continue to increase at an accelerating rate. Consider the growth of goods in process on any two successive days during a period when input has been growing at an increasing rate. Let us call these two days, Day 5 and Day 6. The growth of goods in process during these two days may be expressed as:

6) $\quad$ Day 5: $p_5 - p_4 = a_4 + a_3 + a_2 - 3a_1 + \dfrac{a_5 - a_1}{2}$

7) $\quad$ Day 6: $p_6 - p_5 = a_5 + a_4 + a_3 - 3a_2 + \dfrac{a_6 - a_2}{2}$

The rate of growth of goods in process is increasing if the difference between these two expressions, $p_6 + p_4 - 2p_5$, is positive. If the rate of growth of input is increasing this must be so. First, the sum (in equation 7) of $a_5 + a_4 + a_3$ must, in that case, exceed $3a_2$ by more than the sum (in equation 6) of $a_4 + a_3 + a_2$ exceeds $3a_1$. The difference between the two is $(a_5 - a_2) - 3(a_2 - a_1)$. The difference between a_5 and a_2 is the sum of the following differences: $(a_5 - a_4) + (a_4 - a_3) + (a_3 - a_2)$. And as long as input grows at an increasing rate, each of these three differences is larger than the difference, $a_2 - a_1$. Hence the sum of the three exceeds $3(a_2 - a_1)$. Under the same conditions, secondly, input on Day 6 exceeds input on Day 2 more than input on Day 5 exceeds input on Day 1. That is, $(a_6 - a_2) > (a_5 - a_1)$. This must be true since a_6 exceeds a_5 by more than a_2 exceeds a_1. Therefore $(p_6 - p_5)$ $> (p_5 - p_4)$ and, in general, the rate of investment in goods in process will increase as long as the rate of input is accelerating.[1]

Since this is true, cyclical turns in the rate of investment in goods in process cannot lead turns in the rate of increase in input. Indeed, unless the rate of increase in input falls sufficiently rapidly after it reaches a peak, investment in goods in process will continue to rise for some time longer. This may be seen if we suppose that the rate of increase in input reaches a peak on Day 6. Now compare the growth of goods in process during Day 6 and Day 7. The equations are written in the manner of equation 4.

8)   Day 6: $p_6 - p_5 = \dfrac{a_6}{2} + a_5 + a_4 + a_3 - \dfrac{7a_2}{2}$

9)   Day 7: $p_7 - p_6 = \dfrac{a_7}{2} + a_6 + a_5 + a_4 - \dfrac{7a_3}{2}$

The rate of investment in goods in process will be rising if the difference between equations 8 and 9 is positive.

10) $p_7 + p_5 - 2p_6 =$
$$\dfrac{a_7 - a_6}{2} + (a_6 - a_5) + (a_5 - a_4) + (a_4 - a_3) - \dfrac{7a_3 - 7a_2}{2}$$

If input has been growing at an increasing rate through Day 6, as we assume, this expression is likely to be positive. For in that event, each of the three differences $(a_6 - a_5)$, $(a_5 - a_4)$, and $(a_4 - a_3)$, is larger than the difference $a_3 - a_2$. Hence the sum of the three larger differences is likely to be larger (it is not necessarily larger) than three and one-half times the smaller difference $a_3 - a_2$. In addition, the increase of investment in goods in process between the two days is bolstered by half the difference of input on Days 6 and 7, which will be positive, except in the unusual case in which input begins to fall immediately after it has reached a peak in its rate of growth. Equation 10 makes it clear also that the less rapid the rate of acceleration of input before the peak in the rate of growth and the more rapid the deceleration after the peak, the

[1] Since investment in goods in process tends to lag behind the peaks and troughs of the rate of growth of input (see the following text), this statement should bear the qualifying clause: *except in the immediate vicinity of a trough in the rate of increase in input.*

shorter will be the lag of investment in goods in process behind the rate of growth of input. On the other hand, the more rapid the acceleration before the peak in the rate of growth and the slower the deceleration after it, the longer will be the lag.

Example 5 illustrates these points. In Part A the rate of acceleration of input before the peak in its rate of growth is exactly the same absolutely as the rate of deceleration after the peak. The peak of growth of goods in process, which comes on Day 8, lags two days behind the peak of growth of input, which comes on Day 6. Part B shows the effect of an acceleration of the growth of input before the peak in the rate of growth that is less rapid than the rate of deceleration after the peak. Goods in process grow most rapidly on Day 7, this time only one day after the peak in the growth of input. Part C reverses these conditions; as a result, the peak in the growth of goods in process lags three days behind the peak in the growth of output.

The cyclical turns in the rate of investment in goods in process, therefore, tend to lag behind those in the rate of growth of input, and the length of the lag varies with the rate of acceleration of input growth before its peak and the rate of deceleration after its peak. Whatever the conditions, however, the lag of investment by any single manufacturing establishment cannot be longer than one production period. We may be assured of this by comparing the factors on which the growth of goods in process depends as they appear three and four days after the peak in the growth of input. As will be remembered, I assume that the production period is four days. If we assume that the peak of input growth was reached on Day 6, we need to examine the growth of goods in process on Days 9 and 10.

11) $\quad$ Day 9: $p_9 - p_8 = a_8 + a_7 + a_6 - 3a_5 + \dfrac{a_9 - a_5}{2}$

12) $\quad$ Day 10: $p_{10} - p_9 = a_9 + a_8 + a_7 - 3a_6 + \dfrac{a_{10} - a_6}{2}$

Investment on Day 10 cannot exceed that on Day 9 unless one of two conditions is met: either $a_9 + a_8 + a_7$ must exceed $3a_6$ by more than $a_8 + a_7 + a_6$ exceeds $3a_5$ or else $a_{10} - a_6$ must exceed $a_9 - a_5$. The first condition, however, will be satisfied only if

EXAMPLE 5
Rates of Increase in Input and in Goods in Process

DAY (1)	INPUT (2)	INCREASE OF INPUT (3)	GOODS IN PROCESS[a] (4)	INCREASE OF GOODS IN PROCESS[b] (5)
		PART A		
1	900			
2	910	10		
3	930	20		
4	960	30	7300	
5	1000	40	7450	150
6	1050	50	7680	230
7	1090	40	7980	300
8	1120	30	8320	340
9	1140	20	8650	330
10	1150	10	8900	250
		PART B		
1	815			
2	860	45		
3	906	46		
4	953	47	6838	
5	1001	48	7205	367
6	1050	49	7580	375
7	1090	40	7958	378
8	1120	30	8323.5	365.5
9	1140	20	8650	326.5
10	1150	10	8900	250
		PART C		
1	900			
2	910	10		
3	930	20		
4	960	30	7300	
5	1000	40	7450	150
6	1050	50	7680	230
7	1099	49	7984.5	304.5
8	1147	48	8347	362.5
9	1194	47	8740	393
10	1240	46	9125	385

[a] Calculated by equation 2.
[b] Calculated from col. 4, or by equation 9.

$(a_9 - a_6) > 3(a_6 - a_5)$. But $(a_9 - a_6) = (a_9 - a_8) + (a_8 - a_7) + (a_7 - a_6)$. No one of these differences can exceed $a_6 - a_5$ since input had reached a maximum rate of growth between Days 5 and 6 (by hypothesis). Hence $a_9 - a_6$ cannot exceed $3(a_6 - a_5)$. For the same reason $a_{10} - a_6$ cannot exceed $a_9 - a_5$.

We may conclude, therefore, that investment in goods in process will not lag behind turns in the rate of increase in input by more than one production period. These results are easily transformed into statements about the relation between investment in goods in process and increases in the rate of production. Since the rate of production lags behind the rate of input by one production period, investment in goods in process will not lag behind the rate of increase in output; it is likely to lead, but not by more than one production period.[2] Since the average production period in manufacturing establishments is about three weeks, or perhaps a little longer (Ch. 8), this period defines the maximum lead of investment in goods in process relative to the rate of growth of production.

This conclusion is subject to two qualifications. First, it applies strictly only to goods in process in continuous industries and to goods 'within stages' in other industries. These categories of stocks account for most, but not all, goods in process. Goods 'between stages' in discontinuous industries may or may not act in the fashion described above. When they do not, the effect is probably to cause goods in process in the aggregate to respond to changes in activity somewhat more tardily than they otherwise would. Hence investment in goods in process as a whole is likely to lead the rate of growth of production by less than investment in continuous industries does. It may even lag by a short interval. It seems best, therefore, to say merely that investment in goods in process and the rate of growth of output turn at nearly the same time.

The second qualification is that the relation described above applies directly only to the connection between goods in process and production in individual establishments. It will be strictly true for manufacturing as a whole only if total output weighted by value added in manufacturing turns at the same time as output weighted by the value of goods in process. This is, no doubt, approximately true, but is unlikely to be exactly true (Ch. 8).

2   Pattern of Investment

If the conclusions of the preceding section are valid, we may gauge the cyclical timing of investment in goods in process from the be-

---

[2] These conclusions are independent of the rate at which goods in process grow in value during the production period. The equations and examples in the text make the simplifying assumption that the growth in value is 1 per unit of input per day. As may be seen from the symmetry of the expressions compared in the argument above, however, any figure may be substituted, and may differ from day to day during the production period without affecting the conclusions.

havior of the rates of change in manufacturing production studied in Chapter 15, Section 3. On this basis we may conclude that the rate of liquidation of goods in process increases during the first part of business contractions. The maximum rate of liquidation occurs near the middle of contractions, sometimes earlier, sometimes later, but usually well before the end of the phase.

For expansions there is no simple rule. The rates of change in output suggest that investment in goods in process is usually high at the beginning of expansions. Thereafter the rate of growth of output falls. In some cycles the decline continues to the end of the phase; in others there is a renewed spurt. In some expansions, therefore, investment in goods in process reaches its maximum long before the peak in business and falls toward the end of the phase. In others, after a period of decline, investment turns up again and rises until very near the peak of business.[3]

From these inferences about the timing of investment in goods in process, we may judge its influence on business cycles. In the early stages of expansion and contraction, investment in goods in process intensifies the cyclical movement. But later in contractions it moves against the cyclical tide and the declining rate of liquidation helps revive output and income. In some expansions the second part of the phase is characterized by a lower rate of accumulation which helps bring on recession. In other expansions, however, investment in goods in process revives in the second half of the phase and thus helps sustain the expansion until near the peak in business.

[3] I say 'very near' because the cycle stage used above in measuring the rate of change in output does not permit one to determine timing precisely in the immediate neighborhood of the business cycle reference dates.

CHAPTER 17

Investment in Raw Materials Stocks

The essential features of my tentative account of the cyclical behavior of raw materials stocks can be stated briefly. There are two main categories of stocks of raw materials. One consists of goods moving through the pipeline between the point of delivery to the consuming manufacturer and the point at which fabrication in his plant begins. For some supplies this requires transportation, and for all goods it involves processes incident to receipt and issue: unpacking, checking, storage, and hauling to the processing shops. Another part consists of a reserve to ensure continuity of operations against irregularities in delivery of materials and to cover any likely expansion of sales in the near future. The size of both the pipeline stock and the reserve must, of course, be consonant with the rate of output, that is, with the rate at which materials are being consumed.

Were manufacturers able to control the size of their stock perfectly, they would increase it when output rose and reduce it when output fell. The cyclical peaks and troughs of stocks would coincide with those of output. Whether manufacturers would like to maintain a constant ratio between their stock of raw materials and their output we do not know. Of course, one would not expect a constant ratio to be maintained during periods of excited price speculation. But even during more typical cycles, when price speculation plays a minor role, the point is obscure. When output is high, it seems likely that there will be relatively few dead, or moribund, elements in the stock. There will be a call for a larger portion of the full line of each manufacturer, and a larger portion of all the kinds of materials carried will, therefore, be moving smoothly into production. On the other hand, when output is high there are more likely to be fears that deliveries may be delayed or that prices may rise, hopes for further expansion of production are likely to be relatively bright, and businessmen are likely to be more venturesome in meeting these contingencies. Neither the statistical record nor general reasoning provides persuasive grounds for either accepting or rejecting the hypothesis that, if manufacturers could control their stocks of raw materials perfectly, they would typically try to maintain a roughly constant ratio between stocks and output.

Whatever a manufacturer might do if his control over inventories were perfect, however, his control is far from complete. The reason is that an interval, more or less long, necessarily elapses between the time materials are ordered and the time they are delivered. Unless a businessman has second sight, a decline in output will not immediately be followed by a decline in deliveries of materials. Moreover, since stocks may be presumed to be increasing during the later stages of an expansion, raw materials will continue to rise for some time after output begins to decline. The length of this lag depends, first of all, upon the interval between order and delivery; but the lag will be extended by whatever time is required for a decline in output to be reflected in a decline in orders for materials. It will be still further extended if the initial cut in orders is insufficient to bring deliveries below the level to which consumption of materials may have fallen by the time deliveries start at the reduced rate. As suggested in preceding chapters, the lag of total stocks of raw materials at cycle turns is three or four months, and very much longer in the case of commodities whose rate of delivery the purchasing manufacturers find it difficult to control.

This information about cycles in the level of raw materials inventories is of some limited use in connection with the present problem: the cyclical behavior of the rate of change in inventories. If raw materials stocks tend to reach their cyclical turning points three or four months after manufacturing output, we can infer that inventory investment (or disinvestment) will turn somewhat earlier. For it seems very unlikely, although it is not impossible, that stocks will continue to increase at an accelerating pace until the very moment they begin to fall. It seems more likely that the rate of accumulation will slacken some time before it becomes zero and finally negative. If this surmise is valid, the rate of inventory accumulation cannot reach its cyclical peak much later than manufacturing output does, that is, in close proximity to the peak of business. And the same would be true of the timing of the maximum rate of disinvestment at the trough of business.

Useful as they are, these inferences do not take us very far. For while they enable us to fix extreme limits after which it is improbable that the maximum rates of investment and disinvestment in stocks of raw materials will occur, they do not tell us how much earlier in expansions and contractions these maxima may be reached. The crucial question is whether the peak rate of investment in raw materials coincides with, or perhaps occurs even slightly later than, the peak of business or whether it typically precedes the peak and so helps to explain the downturn. Similarly, at troughs the question is whether the rate of disinvestment in stocks drops off before the trough of business is reached.

For this purpose, it would be highly convenient if we could assume some constant relation between movements in output and stocks of raw materials during expansions and contractions. If the relation were constant, the times when the rates of change in stocks reached peaks and troughs could be gauged by studying the rates of change in output, as was done in the preceding chapter for investment in goods in process.

No such convenient assumption, unfortunately, is valid. For the raw materials required in any given month must be purchased in advance, and the period by which manufacturers must anticipate requirements may be a few days or several months. As a result, the degree of similarity between the movements in stocks of raw materials and in output from one month to the next depends upon the accuracy with which manufacturers forecast changes in their rate of operations. The accuracy of forecasts is, of course, limited and it must be expected that individual manufacturers will usually either over- or underestimate the changes in the rate at which they will consume raw materials in the months to come. In consequence, changes in their stocks will be larger or smaller than expected, and in subsequent months efforts must be made to fill up deficits or dispose of surpluses. These efforts may take the form of a more or less rapid change in stocks than in output, though both are moving in the same direction, or even of a temporary rise in stocks when output is falling or a reduction in stocks when output is rising.

For individual manufacturers, then, it seems reasonable to suppose that the relation between the size of the month to month movements in stocks and in output is very loose. On the whole, as already indicated, their stocks will be rising when output is increasing and falling when output is declining. Even small errors in forecasting, however, can make the size of stock changes in any short period quite different from that of output changes. And subsequent efforts at correction will have the same effect.

The mistakes of individuals may, of course, largely offset one another in figures that combine the records of all the members of an industry. The probability is even greater when all industries are combined. In that event some constant relation between changes in stocks and in output would probably emerge. No doubt such offsetting sometimes happens; indeed, it may happen typically, but its incidence cannot be determined by pure speculation. If the mistakes of most individuals are large, they are seldom likely to balance out even roughly. Moreover, manufacturers' forecasts may often be biased in one way or another so that most are either overoptimistic or overpessimistic at the same time.

The cyclical behavior of the rate of investment in stocks of raw materials, therefore, remains to be determined. Maximum investment is not likely to follow the peak of business but it may precede it, and maximum disinvestment is not likely to follow the trough of business but it may precede it. The rate at which stocks of raw materials are accumulated and liquidated may, because of errors in forecasting and subsequent attempts at correction, be quite irregular. This seems likely for individual concerns, and it may be true even for the mass of stocks. Finally, if investments in stocks of raw materials held by individual industries and by manufacturing at large behave in regular fashion, their timing and their relation to the behavior of the rates of change in manufacturing production are still in doubt.

These questions can be settled only by direct study of records. Although our sample is far from adequate, it is worth examination, partly for what it suggests about the pattern of aggregate investment in stocks of raw materials and partly for what it reveals about differences between commodities of diverse types.

1 The Showing of the Records

As indicated in Chapters 9 and 10, the series on manufacturers' stocks of raw materials are few and, in many ways, unrepresentative. For only 8 commodities can we analyze monthly or quarterly data. Of these, cotton, silk, and hides alone appear to be supplied to manufacturers under conditions that afford the degree of responsiveness of supply to changes in demand that characterizes most raw materials purchased by manufacturers—not, indeed, because they are supplied by other manufacturers, as most raw materials are, but because their fabricators can draw upon buffer stocks held by dealers.

The other commodities are supplied under conditions that characterize only minor fractions of the raw materials consumed by manufacturers. In some cases receipts of raw materials respond to needs so tardily that stocks either lag behind manufacturing activity by longer intervals than are typical or even move inversely; for example, lead at warehouses, because it must be imported; publishers' stocks of newsprint, because adjustments are hampered by long-term contracts; and manufacturers' stocks of crude rubber, because rubber output cannot quickly be expanded or contracted. The production of still other commodities has fluctuated haphazardly during business cycles with the result that manufacturers' stocks have moved irregularly; for example, refiners' stocks of raw sugar and of petroleum.

In analyzing fluctuations in inventories, as distinct from their rate of change, I tried to overcome the problems raised by the paucity of data by studying closely the various commodities for which statistics are available. For each commodity I tried to explain the cyclical pattern of stocks by the conditions affecting its supply and consumption. In this way, I was able to describe several characteristic situations, estimate the importance of each, and construct a general theory about the behavior of raw materials in the aggregate.

Whatever its difficulties, this was easy in comparison with the present task. Suppose that an industry's stock of raw materials rises and falls with the rate at which materials are consumed but lags behind consumption at the cyclical turns. To account for this behavior one need only explain why manufacturers desire raw materials stocks to vary directly with activity and why they cannot reduce the rate at which they receive raw materials below the rate at which they consume them until a few months after the peak of production. To account for the behavior of the rate of investment in stocks is far more difficult. One must explain not only why receipts exceed consumption at certain times, and vice versa, but why the difference between receipts and consumption rises to a maximum at one stage of the cycle and falls to a minimum at another. An explanation of the size of these differences is, I believe, beyond the reach of case studies confined to a few commodities. To yield reliable results empirical generalizations must be based on a large collection of materials; only then can an explanation be attempted. For this reason the observations drawn from our small sample should be regarded simply as a survey of the data that are now available rather than as a firm basis for generalization.

The measures of rates of change shown below are calculated on the same plan as those presented in Chapter 16, Section 3, with one exception. Cycles are marked off by the peaks and troughs in manufacturing activity in the industry holding the stocks rather than by the turning points in general business. For while manufacturing activity as a whole conforms closely to business cycles, activity in any particular industry during a few cycles may exhibit a significant degree of independence. If stocks of raw materials are strongly influenced by the rate of manufacturing activity, as apparently they are, individual stocks are likely to exhibit a fairly close relation to activity in the industry holding them, but their behavior during business cycles will depend upon the degree to which output in the industry conforms to business cycles in the period for which observations are available. In these circumstances, as stated, it seems better to observe the behavior of the few available series during cycles of manufacturing activity in the industries holding the stocks. One can then form a judgment about the typical behavior of the class during business cycles by considering these observations in conjunction with the fact that manufacturing activity as a whole moves in close conformity with business cycles.

In consonance with this view, the measures used in this chapter represent the rate of change in stocks per month from stage to stage of cycles marked off by turning points in indicators of the rate of manufacturing activity in the industries holding the stocks. As in preceding chapters, these indicators measure the consumption of the raw materials in question or are closely related to such consumption.

I begin with manufacturers' stocks of three commodities—cotton, silk, and hides—whose supplies can be adjusted rapidly to manufacturers' requirements. Charts 72-4 show the patterns of the rates of change in stocks and in raw material consumption of these commodities during individual cycles of consumption.[1] Despite

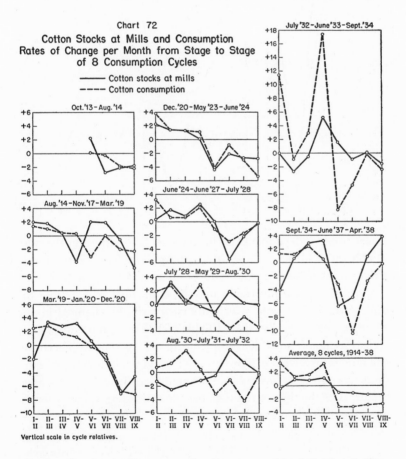

Chart 72

Cotton Stocks at Mills and Consumption
Rates of Change per Month from Stage to Stage
of 8 Consumption Cycles

——— Cotton stocks at mills
– – – Cotton consumption

Vertical scale in cycle relatives.

[1] In the case of raw silk, consumption is represented by deliveries of silk to mills.

Chart 73
Raw Silk Stocks at Manufacturers and Deliveries to Mills
Rates of Change per Month from Stage to Stage of 5 Deliveries Cycles

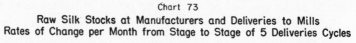

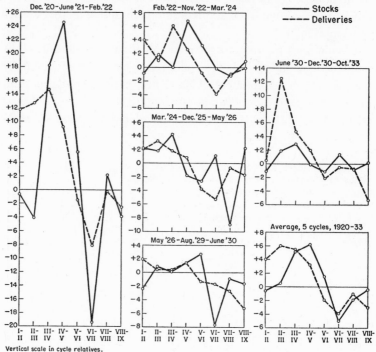

Vertical scale in cycle relatives.

considerable independence of movement, fluctuations in the rates of change in stocks of these three commodities have been remarkably similar to those in the rates of change in manufacturing activity. This visual impression may be confirmed by counting the number of instances in which the two variables changed in the same and opposite directions (Table 76). Two commodities show a clear preponderance of agreements over disagreements: in cotton the ratio is somewhat better than 2:1; in hides it is somewhat better than 3:1. In silk, however, agreements hardly exceed disagreements.[2] For the three series together the ratio of agreements to disagreements is almost exactly 2:1.

[2] This negative result may be due to the fact that the comparisons were made on a synchronous basis. But that inventory cycles lag behind activity cycles, as argued in Chapter 10, suggests that the rates of change in the two series may stand in a similar time relation. This view is supported by silk. If we post-

Chart 74
Cattle Hide Stocks at Tanners and Wettings
Rates of Change per Month from Stage to Stage of 3 Wettings Cycles

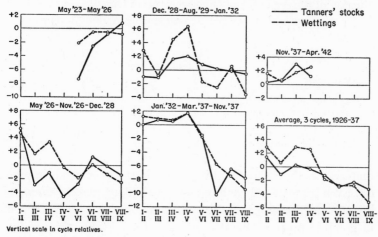

Vertical scale in cycle relatives.

These measures are consistent with the idea that investment in raw materials inventories tends to conform to cycles in the rate of change in manufacturing activity. The many disagreements between the changes in the two processes presumably reflect the mistakes of individual manufacturers in forecasting short-term fluctuations in production. The preponderance of agreements reflects the degree to which errors compensate when sufficiently large aggregates are studied. If this hypothesis is valid, we should expect the relation between total investment in raw materials by all manufacturers and the rate of change in activity to be closer than it is in individual industries. In that event, the patterns of the rates of change in manufacturing output identified in Chapter 15 could be used as guides to the cyclical timing of investments in stocks of raw

date the changes in activity by one stage interval, the direction of movement in the rates of change in the two series agree 27 times, disagree 10 times. The suggestion of a lag is not confirmed, however, by the behavior of cotton and hides. Part of the difficulty may be due to the fact that the cycle stage is an awkward interval for measuring leads or lags if these tend to be uniform for a given commodity in terms of some small number of months. Because of the inadequate data, it was not worth while to recalculate our measures to meet this difficulty.

TABLE 76

Cotton, Silk, and Hides Stocks and Manufacturing Activity
Number of Agreements and Disagreements in Direction of Movement
of Rates of Change per Month during Activity Cycles

	COTTON 8 Cycles *1914-38*	SILK 5 Cycles *1920-33*	HIDES 3 Cycles *1926-37*	ALL 3 COMMODI- TIES
Agreements	45	21	23	89
Disagreements	20	17	7	44
Interstage intervals when the rate of change in stocks or activity remained constant	2	1	1	4
Total no. of comparisons	67	39	31	137

materials as they were for investments in stocks of goods in process. Even so, there are good reasons for thinking that the timing of investment in raw materials would not coincide with investment in goods in process. One reason is that the mistakes of individual manufacturers may not consist entirely of chance errors randomly distributed throughout all industries. Some may be typical mistakes characteristic of all or most manufacturers. In the analysis of cycles in stocks (Ch. 9) it was argued that manufacturers typically fail to foresee cyclical turns in their production. Since they are therefore unable to adjust orders of raw materials soon enough, their stocks continue to rise for a few months after the peak of business and to fall for some months after the trough. It is reasonable to suppose that something similar is true of the relation between investment in raw materials and the rate of change in activity.

Another reason to think that investment in raw materials may lag behind the rate of change in activity is that not all commodities share with cotton, silk, and hides the characteristic that their rate of supply to manufacturers can be altered rapidly. We have already seen what striking contrasts in the cyclical behavior of stocks can be caused by differences in the capacity of manufacturers to change the rate at which raw materials are received (Ch. 10). The cyclical behavior of the rate of investment in raw materials affords similar contrasts (Chart 75).

In cotton, silk, and hides the peak rate of investment typically occurs either in the last stage of expansion or earlier; the trough of

Chart 75
Five Examples of Stocks of Raw Materials and Associated Indicators
of Manufacturing Activity, Average Rates of Change per Month
from Stage to Stage of Manufacturing Activity Cycles

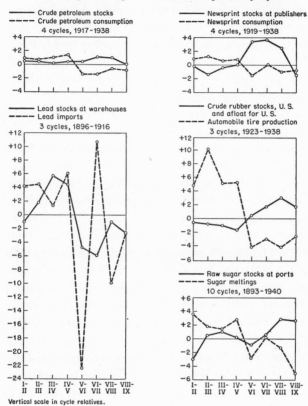

Vertical scale in cycle relatives.

investment (or highest rate of disinvestment), in the last stage of contraction or earlier. The five patterns in Chart 75 represent commodities whose rates of supply to manufacturers are less easily adjusted than are those of cotton, silk, or hides. The rates of change in lead stocks at warehouses alone display a cyclical pattern similar to those of cotton, silk, and hides. As explained in Chapter 10, lead may resemble the cotton-silk-hides group because warehouse stocks consist in part of metal being refined in bond for re-export. They are, therefore, more closely tied to the current rate of processing than are inventories that consist only of raw materials as defined here.[3]

Investment in stocks of crude rubber and in newsprint stocks at publishers follows a roughly opposite course. Accumulation is at a peak after the rate of activity begins to fall off, that is, during the contraction in consumption; liquidation is most rapid after activity has turned up, that is, during the expansion in consumption. Rubber stocks are liquidated most rapidly, indeed, near the peak of crude rubber consumption.

The lag of inventory investment in newsprint and crude rubber reflects the same conditions that make cycles in their stocks move inversely to the rate of consumption of materials. In the case of newsprint, the lag is due to the long-term contracts governing the purchase of this commodity, which prevent publishers from quickly adjusting their receipts to requirements. In rubber the lag is due to a combination of causes: (a) output tends to be stable in the short term, being insensitive to demand and largely unaffected by weather; (b) climate makes it impracticable to keep more than pipeline stocks in the Far East; (c) the big manufacturers are such large factors in the market that they must themselves hold a large proportion of the stock. These conditions cause the receipts of rubber by United States manufacturers to remain fairly steady in the short run. As a result, their stocks rise soon after their rate of fabrication falls off and fall soon after activity starts to recover.

These considerations do not, indeed, suffice to explain why inventory investment turns just when it does. But they do explain why the peak rate of accumulation is reached after the peak of fabrication and the peak of liquidation after the trough of fabrication. And as stated above, this lag of investment behind the turning points in manufacturing activity contrasts sharply with that observed when supply can be rapidly adjusted to requirements.

Crude petroleum is another commodity whose supply responds only sluggishly to short-term changes in demand. The pattern of inventory investment in crude oil stocks resembles those of newsprint and rubber, although the amplitude of the swings is very

---

[3] In the absence of direct information about the rate of lead refining, lead imports are used as an indicator. Changes in stocks are not sufficiently large, absolutely, to cause sizable divergences in movements of imports and refining.

small. But since, during the period covered, the movements of petroleum production and stocks were strongly influenced at irregular intervals by the opening of new oil fields, we do not know what persistent tendencies characterize changes in petroleum stocks.

The average pattern of investment in stocks of raw sugar at refineries is irregular, as is the movement in the rate of inventory accumulation in most cycles. In preceding chapters we have traced this irregular behavior to haphazard fluctuations in sugar crops.

Although the data are too meager to support strongly any general theory about the cyclical behavior of investment in stocks of raw materials, they have been useful in two ways. First, they suggest the possibility that, for the major portion of raw materials whose rates of supply are easily controlled by manufacturers, the rate of investment in stocks may conform positively to movements in the rate of change in manufacturing activity. Apparently, the tendency in this direction was sufficiently strong to leave its mark on data that combine the experience of all manufacturers holding a given commodity despite difficulties which, it is reasonable to think, prevent individual manufacturers from keeping stocks continuously in line with their rate of fabrication. This, in any event, is the showing of the three commodities in this class for which we have figures: cotton, silk, and hides. If additional data confirm these results, we may expect a still closer relation to emerge from the experience of all manufacturers. However, the positive conformity of investment in stocks of raw materials to movements in the rate of change in activity does not necessarily imply synchronous timing. For reasons developed above, inventory investment may well lag behind the rate of change in activity even when the supply of materials is easily controlled.

There is another reason to suspect that inventory investment in raw materials tends to lag behind the rate of change in output. Not all commodities held as raw materials are supplied under conditions that allow manufacturers quickly to adjust their rate of receipt. When manufacturers operate under such difficulties, investment in raw materials tends to lag far behind rates of change in activity, so far indeed that accumulation is highest during business contraction and liquidation highest during expansion.

CHAPTER 18

Investment in Stocks of Finished Goods
Made from Nonagricultural Materials

The analysis of inventories of finished goods in Chapters 11 and 12 showed that this general category comprises several classes whose behavior during business cycles differs. One distinction is between goods made to order and to stock. A manufacturer's inventory of made-to-order goods consists of products already sold; production has been completed and the goods merely await shipment. The volume of such goods in the hands of sellers depends principally on the volume of production and shipments. The larger the volume of orders the larger will be the volume of made-to-order goods awaiting delivery to customers.

Goods made to stock, on the contrary, are not related to the rate of manufacturing activity in the same simple fashion but differ among themselves in at least two respects: the production of some is responsive chiefly to changes in demand; that of others to changes in the supply of raw materials. Stocks of goods in the first class, provided they are staples, tend to move inversely to the rate of manufacturing activity during expansions and contractions of short or moderate duration. In long phases they vary inversely only during the first part of the phase. Before the end of a long expansion stocks tend to reverse direction and to move together with production and shipments. The same applies to long contractions. During the first part of the phase stocks accumulate when production falls off, but before the trough is reached they begin to be liquidated. Moreover, since the production cycles of these commodities are governed principally by cycles of demand, they conform closely to business cycles. The relation between stocks and business cycles is, therefore, similar to that between stocks and output or shipments.

As stated, these generalizations probably apply only to durable and staple commodities. If the goods are subject to deterioration, either physically or in style-worth, manufacturers obviously cannot afford to let stocks accumulate for long when business is declining. When a manufacturer of perishables finds sales falling and stocks increasing, he will curtail output drastically enough to liquidate his inventory. This qualification, however, is probably of only minor importance. Because such goods are risky to hold, they tend to be produced to order and unsold stocks are kept at a minimum.

The other important category of finished goods, whose output cycles are influenced chiefly by changes in the supply of crude materials, are fabricated farm products.[1] Stocks of finished goods in this category tend to conform positively, with a lag, to output cycles. Since the latter are strongly influenced by cycles in the output of agricultural materials, stocks of finished goods either behave irregularly during business cycles or show some tendency to inverted conformity, again with a lag.

These distinctions are obviously relevant to an understanding of fluctuations in investment in stocks of finished goods. The data permit me to develop the behavior characteristics of goods made to order and of two of the three categories of goods made to stock: demand-dominated staples, which I identify initially with staple goods made from nonfarm materials; and supply-dominated goods, which I identify initially with goods made from materials of agricultural origin. Investment in goods made to order and to stock from nonagricultural materials are studied in this chapter; Chapter 19 deals with goods made from agricultural materials.

1 Finished Goods Made to Order

The output of goods made to order is undoubtedly very large. It includes goods that must be fabricated to the purchaser's specifications, expensive commodities of which few of a kind are made, and many types of fashion goods that cannot safely be produced for stock in any considerable quantity. But since goods made to

---

[1] It will be recalled, however, that not all fabricated farm products have output cycles governed principally by the supply of raw materials.

order are typically delivered promptly upon completion, stocks are usually small relative to their rate of production. I have estimated very roughly that they comprise 15-25 percent of all finished goods and 6-10 percent of all manufacturers' stocks.

Stocks of finished goods made to order are a sort of goods 'in process'—in process of delivery. Their volume is presumably controlled by technical factors such as the time required for packing, for the accumulation of economical units of shipment, e.g., carload lots, and by the time required for transportation if title passes at the customer's location rather than at that of the shipper. Cancellations may affect the volume of such stocks when business drops sharply or purchasers may request delay in deliveries. The latter consideration would operate to make stocks larger relative to output and sales during contractions than during expansions. Its importance, however, cannot be measured with the few data at our disposal. For the time being, it seems best to assume, as a first approximation, that the interval between production and shipments remains fairly constant and that stocks of finished goods remain in roughly constant ratio to production and shipments over the cycle.

The implications of such an assumption for inventory investment were explored in Chapter 16 for goods in process. If the interval between the production and shipment of a unit of output is short, as it undoubtedly is in most manufacturing industries, investment in stocks of finished goods made to order will vary positively with the rate of change in production and shipments without a significant lead or lag. In the absence of direct evidence, the movements of the rate of change in output serve to indicate the cyclical movements of investment in finished goods made to order, as they do also for goods in process. The results of the study of the cyclical timing of the rate of change in manufacturing output in Chapter 15 may be applied to investment in finished goods if it is valid to assume that the cyclical behavior of the output of goods made to order is, at least in the aggregate, the same as that of manufactured goods in general. The assumption is plausible, but at present there is no way of confirming its validity.

Our collection of inventory data contains one example of a stock of finished goods made to order: steel sheets. It is especially interesting because we can compare the inventories of goods made to order and to stock. Chart 76 shows that there is a general similarity between the patterns of rates of change in shipments and in stocks of goods made to order. This is true in both the patterns taken cycle by cycle and in the average. In the four-cycle averages both stocks and shipments reach their peak rates of growth in the third quarter of expansion and their peak rates of decline in the fourth quarter of contraction. This similarity is consistent with the theory just set forth. On the other hand, there are some noticeable, though slight, dissimilarities. In neither the individual cycles nor the averages are the minor movements in the rate of change in shipments matched by stocks, nor do the peak and trough values come in the same stage in every cycle. I cannot account for these dissimilarities satisfactorily. The theory I have advanced may neglect at least secondary aspects of the behavior of investment in goods made to order. Or the discrepancies may be traceable to inaccuracies in the original data, to the correction for seasonal influences, or to intermingling of small differences between the patterns of shipments of sheets made to order and to stock in the total figures for shipments.

Whatever the truth of this matter, stocks of sheets made to order and to stock behave differently. Investment in the former traces a cyclical pattern generally similar to the rate of change in shipments; investment in the latter is markedly inverse to the rate of change in shipments. This contrast leads naturally to a general analysis of investment in finished goods made to stock.

2   Finished Goods Made to Stock

Steel sheets made to stock are an example of a larger class of finished goods—a class that accounts for half or more of all finished goods, and, therefore, for 20-25 percent of manufacturers' total stocks. The class has three significant characteristics. Output cycles are controlled principally by impulses from the side of demand, the commodities are durable and staple, and they are sold from stock. As explained in Chapters 11 and 12, this combination of qualities causes stocks to move inversely during cycles in business and in manufacturing activity. This tendency is subject to an important qualification: if an expansion or contraction is long, say, over two

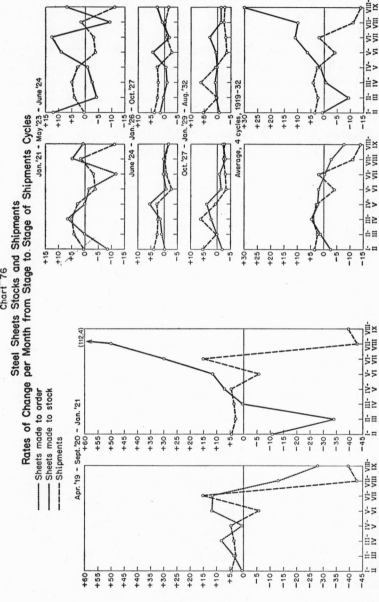

Chart 76
Steel Sheets Stocks and Shipments
Rates of Change per Month from Stage to Stage of Shipments Cycles

Sheets made to order
Sheets made to stock
Shipments

Vertical scale in cycle relatives.

years, stocks tend to reverse direction and to move together with production and shipments during the latter portion of the phase. How do cycles in the rate of accumulation of these stocks behave? Let us examine, first, the behavior of the rate of change in stocks during cycles of shipments (or some equivalent indicator of manufacturing activity) in the industries holding the goods. As a second step, we shall study the movements of the rate of change in stocks during business cycles and trace the connections between these two aspects of cyclical behavior.

RATES OF CHANGE DURING MANUFACTURING ACTIVITY CYCLES

Table 77 presents the average patterns of the rates of change per month in the finished goods inventories of 18 commodities during cycles marked off by the turning points of cycles in manufacturing activity. A composite measure of the behavior of this sample, the median rates of change, is plotted in Chart 77, together with the median rates of change in the associated series representing manufacturing activity.

Chart 77 is, of course, a highly summarized version of the joint behavior of the 18 commodities. It must be checked by other measures, but on its face it suggests the following. Between the last quarter of contraction in manufacturing activity (stages VIII-IX) and the first quarter of expansion (stages I-II), the rate of accumulation slumps sharply.[2] This decline in the rate of growth continues during the first part of expansion until accumulation gives way to

[2] This is suggested, although not accurately measured, by the difference in the rates of change shown on the chart. The inaccuracy arises in part from the fact that the National Bureau standard measures are computed from trough to trough. Hence the calculated difference between the rates of change in the first quarter of expansion and those in the last quarter of contraction represents the difference between the first and last quarters of the same cycles, not the difference between the last quarter of one cycle and the first quarter of the next. To compare accurately the rate of change between stages VIII-IX and I-II of succeeding cycles it is necessary to compute measures for cycles marked off from peak to peak. The true difference may be either larger or smaller than the apparent difference in Chart 77. In this case, the true difference (based on medians) was slightly smaller. It indicates a 2.4 drop in the rate of accumulation in reference cycle relatives between stages VIII-IX and I-II, whereas the apparent difference shown in the chart was −2.7.

Whenever, in this chapter, the rate of change between stages VIII-IX and I-II is compared, the necessary recalculation was made to measure the true difference. Comparisons between other stages are free from this difficulty.

TABLE 77

Stocks of Eighteen Finished Nonagricultural Products
Average Rates of Change per Month from Stage to Stage of Manufacturing Activity Cycles

	NO. OF CYCLES	AVERAGE CHANGE PER MONTH IN CYCLE RELATIVES BETWEEN STAGES							
		I-II	II-III	III-IV	IV-V	V-VI	VI-VII	VII-VIII	VIII-IX
Paper, all grades, 1919-33	4	+1.0	−0.6	−1.5	−2.0	−1.7	+0.9	+3.0	+0.8
Newsprint at mills, U. S. & Canada, 1919-33	3	+0.9	+0.9	−0.2	−0.8	+0.7	+1.2	+5.7	+3.1
Southern pine lumber, 1919-38	6	−0.02	−0.8	−1.6	−1.4	−0.6	+0.8	+0.4	+2.3
Oak flooring, 1913-37	6	−1.1	−2.5	−0.1	−1.2	+1.8	+5.7	+5.6	+4.9
Portland cement, 1912-38	6	+0.7	+0.1	−2.4	−3.1	+2.8	+0.2	−1.1	+2.4
Bath tubs, 1918-24	2	+3.8	−4.6	−10.0	+1.6	+8.7	+3.3	+14.5	+34.2
Lavatories, 1919-24	2	+1.2	+1.0	+1.1	−3.8	−0.2	−5.2	+3.8	+5.0
Kitchen sinks, 1919-24	2	+2.1	+0.9	−7.1	−3.2	−5.4	+9.8	+4.4	+15.8
Misc. enameled sanitary ware, 1919-24	1	+2.3	+1.8	−2.5	+2.4	−6.4	−7.4	−9.4	−1.6
Gasoline at refineries, 1918-38	6	−1.1	+0.4	+0.5	+1.4	+3.3	+2.3	+2.1	+0.7
Lubricants at refineries, 1919-40	7	−0.7	−1.0	−0.6	+0.4	+1.2	+1.8	+3.0	+1.7
Pig iron at merchant furnaces, 1919-24	2	−4.9	−9.1	−2.6	−0.4	+11.0	+20.6	+0.4	+0.4
Steel sheets made to stock, 1919-32	4	+0.6	−9.4	−0.6	+1.4	+6.4	+11.0	+10.0	+30.2
Refined copper, N. & S. Am., 1919-38	3	+0.8	−1.3	−0.03	−2.8	−0.4	+3.7	+7.4	+6.2
Lead at smelteries & refineries, 1923-38	3	−0.2	+0.1	+0.3	+0.9	+0.1	+0.9	+2.1	+0.1
Slab zinc at refineries, 1921-38	5	+1.7	−3.1	−2.8	−5.1	+2.8	+8.6	+9.0	+8.6
Auto. tires, 1921-38	4	−1.7	+0.3	+0.9	+1.2	−1.2	+1.8	+1.6	+3.9
Auto. inner tubes, 1921-38	3	+0.9	+0.6	+0.2	+1.2	−1.6	+1.8	−1.9	+8.1
Median for all commodities		+0.8	−0.7	−0.6	−0.6	+0.4	+1.8	+3.0	+3.5

For series used as indicators of manufacturing activity see Table 49.

Chart 77
Eighteen Finished Nonfarm Products
Medians of Average Rates of Change per Month in Stocks and in
Manufacturing Activity from Stage to Stage of Manufacturing Activity Cycles

——— Stocks of finished goods
––––– Manufacturing activity

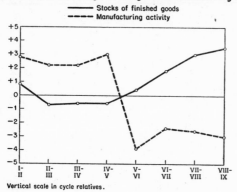

Vertical scale in cycle relatives.

liquidation. In the second half liquidation continues at a fairly constant rate. With the beginning of contraction, liquidation is soon replaced by accumulation. The rate of growth rises in the second and third quarters of contraction, but again at the end of the phase there is evidence that it begins to moderate.

The medians of the average patterns are suggestive, but they do not tell us anything about the consistency with which the composite pattern is followed by the average patterns of the individual commodities or about the regularity with which the composite pattern is repeated in the individual cycles upon which the averages are based. Table 78 attempts to make good these deficiencies, at least in part. It shows the number and percentage of all the series in the sample whose average rates of change rose, declined, or remained constant between successive interstage intervals. This bears on the first question: the consistency with which the composite pattern is followed by the average patterns of the individual commodities. The same information for all cycles covered by the series in the sample bears on the second question: the regularity with which the composite pattern is found in the individual cycles upon which the commodity averages are based. In interpreting the table the reader must remember that an increase in the rate of change may mean either of two things: when stocks are increasing, the rate of growth is rising; when stocks are falling, the rate of decline

TABLE 78

Stocks of Eighteen Finished Nonagricultural Products

Direction of Movement of Rates of Change per Month between Interstage Intervals of Manufacturing Activity Cycles

DIRECTION OF MOVEMENT BETWEEN INTERSTAGE INTERVALS

	I-II to II-III			II-III to III-IV			III-IV to IV-V			IV-V to V-VI			V-VI to VI-VII			VI-VII to VII-VIII			VII-VIII to VIII-IX			VIII-IX to I-II		
	+	0	-	+	0	-	+	0	-	+	0	-	+	0	-	+	0	-	+	0	-	+	0	-
BASED ON AVERAGE PATTERNS OF 18 COMMODITIES																								
No. of series	3		15	11		7	11		7	13		5	13		5	8		10	9	1	8	2		16
Percentage	17		83	61		39	61		39	72		28	72		28	44		56	50	6	44	11		89
BASED ON ALL CYCLES COVERED BY 18 COMMODITIES																								
No. of cases	35		40	38		37	34	2	39	45	1	24	43	2	27	31		41	32	2	38	19	1	41
Percentage	47		53	51		49	45	3	52	65	1	34	59	3	38	43		57	44	3	53	31	2	67

is diminishing. Similarly, a decline in the rate of change may mean either of two things: when stocks are falling, the rate of decline is accelerating; when stocks are rising, the rate of growth is diminishing.

Both sets of calculations bear out the general impressions gained from the composite patterns of Chart 77. In the measures based on the average patterns, for example, the rate of growth of a large preponderance of the series declined between intervals VIII-IX and I-II, that is, between the end of contraction and the beginning of expansion in manufacturing activity. The same is true as we move from the first to the second quarter of expansion. Thereafter, the situation changes. The average patterns of at least small majorities of the series show increases in the rate of growth between the second and third and the third and fourth quarters of expansions. This suggests that disinvestment is near its peak about the middle of expansion and that, in the second half, the pace of liquidation changes little or actually declines. With the transition from expansion to contraction, the proportion of series with rising rates of growth increases further and becomes a considerable majority. This change, of course, represents the end of inventory liquidation and the beginning of the accumulation that accompanies the downturn in manufacturing activity. Acceleration in the rate of accumulation is widely characteristic of the next quarter of expansion. In the last two quarters of contraction, however, the rates of growth of about as many series decline as rise. This may be taken to indicate that the rate of accumulation in this class of stocks in the aggregate does not change notably in the second half of contractions.

Similar measures based on all cycles of manufacturing activity taken individually constitute a final check. The general picture is the same: a marked increase in the proportion of series with declining rates of growth when manufacturing activity in individual industries passes from contraction to expansion; thereafter in expansions, about equal proportions of cases of increasing and declining rates of growth; as contraction begins, the proportion of series with accelerating rates of growth rises sharply; and finally in the second half of contraction, investment becomes relatively stable again.

In general, we may say that when the shipments of a staple manufactured commodity begin to decline or rise, the rate of growth in its finished stock tends to turn sharply in the opposite direction. The rate of accumulation or liquidation tends to accelerate for a time, but in the second half of expansions and contractions of activity it levels off. There is some evidence that toward the end of a phase it begins to decline, but the indications are too faint to be trusted.

There is an important qualification to this rule. The behavior of the rate of change seems to vary with the length of the expansion or contraction in manufacturing activity. To examine this question, we divided the data into four classes according to the length of the cyclical phases in the indicators of manufacturing activity: cycles of 12 months or less, 13-24 months, 25-36 months, and over 36 months. Two measures were then made. First, medians were calculated of the rates of change in stocks and in the associated indicators of activity during phases within a given duration class (Charts 78 and 79). Next, the number of instances in which the rate of growth rose, declined, or remained constant between the interstage intervals of phases in a given class was tallied (Table 79).

A rather sharp contrast is apparent between the behavior of the rate of change in stocks during relatively short and long phases. During expansions (Chart 78) the rate of liquidation proceeds at an ever faster pace during phases of 12 months or less. During longer expansions the rate of decline (or growth) remains fairly constant throughout the phase. This 'fairly constant' level, of course, is considerably lower than the rate of accumulation during the preceding contraction. (The decline is not represented on the chart, but we may be confident of the fact on the basis of the calculations set forth in Chart 77 and Table 78). Once the drop that accompanies the transition from contraction to expansion has occurred, however, it appears that, except in the shortest expansions, the pace of liquidation accelerates only slightly, then retards in the last quarter of the phase.

The same contrast between the behavior of inventory investment in shorter and longer phases of manufacturing activity can be discerned in contractions of activity (Chart 79). In contrac-

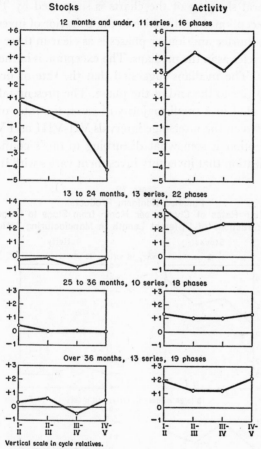

Chart 78
Finished Nonfarm Products
Median Rates of Change per Month from Stage to Stage
of Expansions of Different Length in Manufacturing Activity

Vertical scale in cycle relatives.

tions of less than a year, the pace of investment accelerates sharply from the beginning to the end of the phase. In phases of 13-24 months the rise is more moderate and interrupted by a decline. In contractions exceeding three years the picture is quite different.[3] The median rates of change indicate that the relatively high

[3] Measures for contractions of 25-36 months are not presented because only two series in our sample had contractions of that length and then only once each.

rate of growth with which such phases open is maintained into the second quarter, but that in the third and fourth quarters the rate of accumulation falls, even becomes negative.

The general showing of the charts is supported by Table 79. With one exception the difference in the behavior of inventory investment in shorter and longer phases is as clear in these data for individual cycles as in the medians. The exception is in the shortest contractions. The medians suggested that the rate of investment continues to rise to the end of the phase. The present tally, however, shows that in a small majority of cases, the rates of growth declined between the interstage intervals VII-VIII and VIII-IX.

This exception is somewhat disturbing to one's confidence in the generalization that inventory investment varies with the length

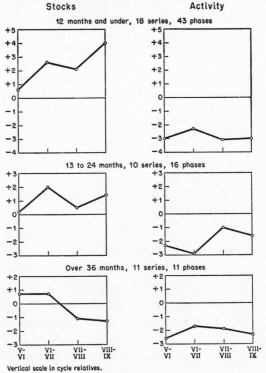

Chart 79
Finished Nonfarm Products
Median Rates of Change per Month from Stage to Stage
of Contractions of Different Length in Manufacturing Activity

Vertical scale in cycle relatives.

TABLE 79

Stocks of Eighteen Finished Nonagricultural Products

Cases in Which Rates of Change per Month between Interstage Intervals of Manufacturing Activity Cycles Rise (+), Remain Constant (o), or Fall (−), Classified by Length of Phase of Activity Cycles

LENGTH OF PHASE OF ACTIVITY, MONTHS	EXPANSION									CONTRACTION								
	I-II to II-III			II-III to III-IV			III-IV to IV-V			V-VI to VI-VII			VI-VII to VII-VIII			VII-VIII to VIII-IX		
	+	o	−	+	o	−	+	o	−	+	o	−	+	o	−	+	o	−
NUMBER OF CASES																		
12 & under	4	12	8	8			3	1	12	28	1	14	22		21	18	1	24
13-24	8	14	11	11			12	1	9	11		5	6		10	9		7
25-36	10	8	10	8			9		9			2			2	2		
Over 36	13	6	9	10			10		9	4	1	6	3		8	3	1	7
No. of cases	35	40	38	37			34	2	39	43	2	27	31		41	32	2	38
PERCENTAGE OF CASES																		
12 & under	25	75	50	50			19	6	75	65	2	33	51		49	42	2	56
13-24	36	64	50	50			54	5	41	69		31	38		62	56		44
25-36	56	44	56	44			50		50			100			100	100		
Over 36	68	32	47	53			53		47	36	9	55	27		73	27	9	64
% of all cases	47	53	51	49			45	3	52	59	3	38	43		57	44	3	53

of the phase. Another disturbing consideration is that all the observations on contractions longer than 36 months are associated with a single business contraction, the slump of 1929-32. Was the contrast between the movement of investment in this long contraction and in shorter contractions perhaps due not to the length of the phase but to other characteristics of the 1929-32 episode? In expansions, however, the contrast between the behavior of investment in short and long phases is not confined to any one period.

Still another source of doubt, this time affecting the behavior of investment during expansions, is the associated behavior of the rate of change in manufacturing activity. Turning back to Chart 78, we see that during expansions of 12 months or less, the rate of increase in output was considerably higher than during longer expansions. Moreover, it tended to rise sharply. During longer expansions the tendency for the rate of increase in output to rise, if there was one, was much less marked. Is it not the behavior of the rate of increase in output that accounts for the difference between the behavior of inventory investment in long and short expansions rather than the difference in the length of the phase? Of course, if a high and accelerating rate of increase in output is regularly associated with short expansions—and it may be—the problem would lose something in importance. But if it is not, the difference in the behavior of stocks in our sample would be fortuitous.

Were additional data available, these questions could be settled by suitable cross-classification. This cannot now be done, and our conclusions must remain subject to these patent uncertainties. Meanwhile, it is important to notice that if we abandon the generalization that the behavior of inventory investment is related to the length of the phase, the alternative appears to be to accept several special explanations to account for the observed differences between the patterns of rates of change in stocks in different cycles. The length of phase hypothesis, on the other hand, provides a unified explanation. It is, moreover, an explanation consistent with our earlier finding that the timing of finished goods stocks during cycles in manufacturing activity varies with the length of the phase. As shown in Chapter 11, after short contractions in manufacturing activity, stocks of finished goods tend to turn down only after shipments turn up. The longer the contraction, however, the earlier the downturn in stocks relative to the upturn in shipments, and in contractions longer than three years, stocks tended to turn down long before shipments turned up. Exactly the same tendencies were apparent in expansions of different lengths. The hypothesis now being considered—that the time the rate of investment in stocks is at a peak during contractions (or the rate of disinvestment is at a peak during expansions) depends upon the length of the phase and that it comes earlier (relative to the turning point in manufacturing activity) the longer the phase—is, of course, closely related to our hypothesis concerning the cyclical turning points of stocks themselves. For if stocks tend to reach a peak relatively early in long contractions, the rate of accumulation cannot reach a peak later and is likely to do so still earlier. If our previous hypothesis is valid—and the empirical support for it is strong—it tends, as far as it goes, to support our present hypothesis about rates of change in stocks of finished goods and the length of contractions and expansions in manufacturing activity.

Another supporting argument is that the considerations that served to explain why stocks should reach peaks (or troughs) together with or slightly after troughs (or peaks) of manufacturing activity when cycles are short, but should tend to lead activity during longer cycles, serve to explain also differences in the timing of the rate of accumulation of stocks (Ch. 11). The longer a contraction, the greater the burden of accumulating stocks. Manufacturers are, therefore, first moved to bring production more closely into line with shipments (thereby reducing the rate of accumulation) and eventually to cut production below shipments (thereby initiating the liquidation of stocks). Other things being equal, both steps will be taken many months before the end of contraction if the decline lasts long enough, while if it is sufficiently short, not even the first will be taken.

These considerations argue for accepting tentatively the hypothesis that the rate of accumulation of stocks of staple and durable finished goods tends to reach a peak during contractions of manufacturing activity and a trough (peak of disinvestment) during expansions. In an extremely short contraction the peak may not come until the very end of the phase, but in longer contractions it will tend to come earlier. And similarly with troughs of investment during expansions.

The evidence presented above suggests that the pattern of investment in stocks of individual commodities during cycles in manufacturing activity has the following characteristics: (a) when manufacturing activity turns down, inventory investment turns up sharply; (b) by the middle of contraction the rate of inventory investment reaches a level close to the peak for the cycle; thereafter it may continue to rise at a greatly reduced pace, or even tend to fall; (c) in relatively long contractions the tendency for inventory investment to begin to decline before the revival in business is stronger than in short contractions; (d) these generalizations are statements of tendencies characteristic of most commodities in their average behavior during cycles in manufacturing activity and also of most individual cyles, but many a commodity does not behave in this fashion in some cycles; (e) in expansions of manufacturing activity, the behavior pattern of investment is similar but opposite in direction.

RATES OF CHANGE DURING BUSINESS CYCLES

The crucial questions about investment in finished staples are whether it tends to rise (or whether disinvestment tends to decline) before the peak in business and whether it tends to fall before the trough in business. The significance of these questions will be appreciated when we recall some conclusions of preceding chapters. Aggregate investment apparently rises and falls with business activity and does not give any evidence of a tendency to lead or lag. But since our measures of aggregate investment are annual, a short lead or lag, not longer than, say, three months, cannot be excluded. This behavior, of course, is the resultant of diverse patterns in the components of the total. We have seen that investment in goods in process and finished goods made to order usually, though not always, turns down early in expansion and turns up early in contraction. And meager evidence, combined with *a priori* speculation, suggests a shorter lead for investment in raw materials. Since these three classes account for 65-70 percent of all manufacturers' stocks, we should expect aggregate investment also to display a significant lead relative to business cycles, unless there is still another class of stocks whose behavior offsets the leads in the first three. Finished staples might play such a role if investment in such stocks normally rises (or disinvestment declines) toward the end of expansions and falls toward the end of contractions.

In view of its behavior during cycles in activity in individual industries, how should we expect investment in finished goods to behave during business cycles? Since cycles of shipments and production in industries making goods from nonagricultural materials conform generally to the rise and fall of the business tide, inventory investment in stocks of finished goods held by these industries may reasonably be expected to display much the same movements during cycles in business as during cycles in manufacturing activity. But not quite the same. Cycles in the production and shipments of particular commodities in this class sometimes run counter to the business tide, sometimes skip a business cycle, and often have peaks and troughs that do not coincide closely with the turning points in business at large. The irregularities already discerned in the behavior of inventory investment during cycles in manufacturing activity may, therefore, be expected to be even more prominent in its behavior during business cycles. And they should manifest themselves especially strongly in the behavior of a small sample of series during individual business cycles, as contrasted with the group's average behavior in several cycles.

These expectations are borne out, in general, by the data; but as we shall see, this is not the whole story. Table 80 presents the average patterns of the rates of change per month in the finished goods inventories of 18 commodities during business cycles as well as a summary measure of the behavior of all the commodities in the collection. As in Table 77, this composite pattern is gotten from the medians of the average rates of change of the individual commodities. It is shown in Chart 80 along with the composite behavior of the same series during cycles of manufacturing activity.

Comparison of the two composite patterns of Chart 80 suggests two tentative conclusions. First, investment acts during business cycles much as it does during cycles in manufacturing activity. Second, it seems to act quite differently in the last quarter of both expansions and contractions. During cycles in manufacturing activity the rate of inventory investment tends to reach a level close to a peak for the cycle by the middle of contraction and a level close to a trough for the cycle by the middle of expansion. Thereafter it continued to increase at a slower rate during contractions and to decline at a slower rate during expansions. More doubtfully, I thought that investment might tend to fall toward the end of contractions and to rise toward the end of expansions. An indication of this tendency for the investment curve to level off near the end of expansions and contractions of manufacturing activity appears in the composite pattern, and other evidence was cited above. Chart 80 suggests that this feature is even stronger during business cycles. The composite pattern shows investment rising between the third and fourth quarters of expansion and falling between the third and fourth quarters of contraction. If these indications could be confirmed, we could conclude that finished staples do play the balancing role described above; that their tendency to rise toward the end of expansion helps to overcome the tendency for investment in other categories to fall at this stage of the cycle. Similarly, we could say that the tendency for investment in finished staples to fall toward the end of contraction helps to

TABLE 80

Stocks of Eighteen Finished Nonagricultural Products
Average Rates of Change per Month from Stage to Stage of Business Cycles

	NO. OF CYCLES	AV. CHANGE PER MO. IN REF. CYCLE RELATIVES BETWEEN STAGES							
		I-II	II-III	III-IV	IV-V	V-VI	VI-VII	VII-VIII	VIII-IX
Paper, all grades, 1919-33	4	+0.2	−0.8	−1.7	−2.7	+1.5	+1.8	+1.6	−0.2
Newsprint at mills, U.S. & Canada, 1919-33	4	−1.0	−0.6	−5.1	−1.6	+3.9	+3.8	+3.4	+0.6
Southern pine lumber, 1919-38	5	−1.3	−1.0	+0.7	−0.7	+2.3	+1.4	−0.1	−0.5
Oak flooring, 1912-38	7	−1.5	−0.5	+1.0	−0.4	+4.7	+3.6	−0.3	−1.4
Portland cement, 1912-38	7	+0.1	−0.2	−2.6	+0.1	+0.9	+0.8	+1.4	+1.7
Bath tubs, 1919-27	3	−2.3	−4.1	−4.7	−4.0	+1.0	+3.6	+7.8	−0.03
Lavatories, 1919-27	3	−0.4	−7.2	−8.2	−8.2	+0.7	+2.3	+6.6	+7.3
Kitchen sinks, 1919-27	3	+1.0	−5.9	−5.5	−3.8	+0.8	+1.4	+3.8	+8.9
Misc. enameled sanitary ware, 1919-27	3	+2.6	−3.5	−2.9	−5.6	−1.7	+1.1	+5.6	+7.0
Gasoline at refineries, 1919-38	5	+0.8	+0.7	+1.3	+1.2	+0.7	+0.6	+1.2	+0.2
Lubricants at refineries, 1919-38	5	+0.3	+0.1	−0.8	−1.0	+0.4	+1.0	+2.2	+0.6
Pig iron at merchant furnaces, 1919-24	2	+3.2	−8.3	−5.3	−4.2	+8.2	+9.6	+4.2	+0.1
Steel sheets made to stock, 1919-33	4	−2.0	−6.2	+5.8	−2.4	+2.9	+5.5	+5.8	+2.3
Refined copper, N. & S. Am., 1919-38	5	−1.4	−4.0	−0.9	−1.3	+1.8	+4.2	+2.2	+0.6
Lead at smelteries & refineries, 1924-38	3	+0.03	0	+0.3	−0.6	+0.7	+3.4	+1.5	+1.5
Slab zinc at refineries, 1921-38	4	−7.4	−5.4	−2.3	−3.6	+6.4	+8.4	+5.4	+9.1
Auto. tires, 1921-38	4	+1.6	+0.7	+2.2	+1.7	+2.0	−2.7	−1.0	−1.4
Auto. inner tubes, 1921-38	4	+2.4	+0.7	+1.8	+1.3	+1.3	−2.4	−1.8	−1.8
Median for all commodities		+0.1	−0.9	−2.0	−1.4	+1.4	+2.0	+2.2	+0.6

Chart 80

Stocks of Eighteen Finished Nonfarm Products
Medians of Average Rates of Change per Month from Stage to Stage of Cycles in Business and in Manufacturing Activity

——— Measures based on business cycles
— — — Measures based on cycles in manufacturing activity

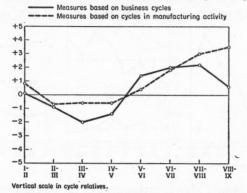

Vertical scale in cycle relatives.

overcome the tendency for other categories to rise at that time. The behavior of this class of goods would help explain the absence of a substantial lead of total inventory investment at cyclical turning points. Unfortunately, the facts are not so simple. The evidence now available suggests merely that this description of aggregate investment in finished goods would often have been valid, and nearly as often invalid. In addition, questions about the inferences to be drawn from the behavior of the sample remain.

Evidence of irregular behavior is provided by Chart 81 which shows the median rates of change in inventories during each of the five business cycles of the interwar period.[4] It is immediately apparent that the pattern of median measures based on the average rate of change in the various series (Chart 80) is largely shaped by the behavior of inventory investment in the cycle immediately following World War I, that is, 1919-21. Only in this cycle does the pattern of investment display both the timing and the amplitude characteristic of the pattern for all cycles. Nevertheless, other salient features of the average pattern do repeat themselves. For example, if we ask simply whether investment was rising toward the end of expansion and falling toward the end of contraction, we find that this was true in two expansions, 1919-20 and 1933-37, and in four contractions, 1920-21, 1926-27, 1929-33, and 1937-

[4] Too few of our series cover earlier periods to make the inclusion of cycles before 1919 possible.

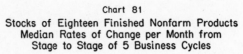

Chart 81
Stocks of Eighteen Finished Nonfarm Products
Median Rates of Change per Month from
Stage to Stage of 5 Business Cycles

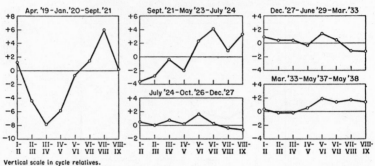

Vertical scale in cycle relatives.

38. Thus, as said above, investment in the stocks in our sample, as revealed by median rates of change, has often risen toward the end of expansion and declined toward the end of contraction. And nearly as often the reverse has been true.

The reliability of these median measures, however, may be questioned. Comparison of Table 81 with Chart 81 shows two things. First, the movement of the composite patterns from stage to stage is, in a majority of instances, consistent with the movements of the component series in Table 81. That is, in most cases, when the composite pattern rises (or declines) the rates of change in a considerable majority of the individual series also rise (or decline). When the movement of the composite pattern is very small, the number of series whose rates of change increase or decline is usually evenly divided. To this extent, the composite patterns appear to be reliable indicators of the behavior of the sample. Moreover, the similar action of many individual series adds to our confidence in the behavior of the sample as an indicator of the behavior of the class. Second, in many instances a decided movement in the composite pattern (that is, in the median rate of change in the component series) was the result of a fairly even division in the direction of movement of the rates of change in individual series. In a few cases the component pattern moved in one direction when a majority of the individual series moved in the opposite direction.

From these measures I conclude that the sample does not clearly indicate that investment in this class of finished stocks acts in a

TABLE 81

Stocks of Eighteen Finished Nonagricultural Products

Direction of Movement of Rates of Change per Month between Interstage Intervals

5 Business Cycles, 1919-1938

DIRECTION OF MOVEMENT BETWEEN INTERSTAGE INTERVALS

BUSINESS CYCLE	I-II to II-III +	o	-	II-III to III-IV +	o	-	III-IV to IV-V +	o	-	IV-V to V-VI +	o	-	V-VI to VI-VII +	o	-	VI-VII to VII-VIII +	o	-	VII-VIII to VIII-IX +	o	-	VIII-IX to I-II +	o	-
NUMBER OF CASES																								
4/1919– 9/1921	2		12	3		11	7		7	12		2	12		2	12		2	1		13	4		10
9/1921– 7/1924	10		7	14		3	6		11	16		1	8		9	8		9	12		5	6		11
7/1924–12/1927	6		11	8		9	6	1	10	9	1	7	8	1	8	10		7	8		9	9		8
12/1927– 3/1933	1	1	11	8		5	5		8	9		4	4		9	3		10	6	1	6	9		4
3/1933– 5/1938	5	1	4	4	1	5	6		4	8		2	6		4	5		5	3		7	4		6
Av. cycle measures[a]	4	1	13	12		6	6	1	11	16	1	1	11		7	10		8	5	1	12	5		13
PERCENTAGE OF CASES																								
4/1919– 9/1921	14		86	21		79	50		50	86		14	86		14	86		14	7		93	29		71
9/1921– 7/1924	59		41	82		18	35		65	94		6	47		53	47		53	71		29	35		65
7/1924–12/1927	35		65	47		53	35	6	59	53	6	41	47	6	47	59		41	47		53	53		47
12/1927– 3/1933	8	8	84	62		38	38		62	69		31	31		69	23		77	46	8	46	69		31
3/1933– 5/1938	50	10	40	40	10	50	60		40	80		20	60		40	50		50	30		70	40		60
Av. cycle measures[a]	22	6	72	67		33	33	6	61	89	6	6	61		39	56		44	28	6	66	28		72

[a] The data in this line show the distribution of series whose average rates of change move in the direction specified when averages are based on all cycles covered by a given series.

significantly different fashion during cycles in business and in the activity of individual commodities. In particular, it is not clearly established that investment typically turns up toward the end of business expansions and down toward the end of contractions. Such differences as we do observe should be attributed, I think, largely to the irregularities in the behavior of investment during cycles in manufacturing activity together with departures in the latter from perfectly synchronous conformity with business cycles.

At the same time, another feature of our observations during cycles in both manufacturing activity and business should not be overlooked. There is evidence that investment often rose toward the end of expansions and declined toward the end of contractions. In a larger sample the tendency might well emerge clearly above the irregular movements of individual commodities. Moreover, as far as it exists, the tendency would be stronger during cycles in business than during cycles in manufacturing activity, owing to a combination of two causes. The first has to do with the behavior of the rate of change in stocks just before and just after the turns of activity. It will be recalled that the first part of the expansion was marked by liquidation at an increasing rate. As the phase proceeded, however, the increase in the rate of liquidation tended to fall off. There was even some indication that the rate retards toward the end of the phase. When activity begins to decline, the rate of liquidation falls sharply and accumulation begins. The rate of accumulation increases for a time, but toward the end of the phase levels off, and finally drops sharply when activity turns up again.

The second factor is the behavior of manufacturing production during business cycles. During expansions the number of industries whose output is expanding tends to decline before business at large (or total output) reaches a peak. Similarly, during contractions the number of industries whose output is falling tends to decline before business reaches its low point. This tendency emerges clearly from a study of the 57 production series described in Chapter 15. Table 82 shows the excess of the number of series rising between successive stages of business cycles over the number falling as a percentage of the total. During contractions, of course, the number rising is typically a minority of the series, as the negative signs preceding the figures indicate. Figures with negative sign, in effect,

TABLE 82

Fifty-seven Production Series: Excess of Series Rising
between Stages of Business Cycles as Percentage of All Series
5 Cycles, 1919-1938

BUSINESS CYCLE	EXCESS OF SERIES RISING BETWEEN STAGES							
	I-II	II-III	III-IV	IV-V	V-VI	VI-VII	VII-VIII	VIII-IX
4/1919– 9/1921	50	56	24	28	−19	−36	−11	30
9/1921– 7/1924	32	66	88	40	−36	−6	−26	−36
7/1924–12/1927	76	50	23	40	−28	6	−20	−10
12/1927– 3/1933	18	32	66	37	−56	−82	−90	−53
3/1933– 5/1938	84	62	86	74	−38	−64	−46	−30
Av. for 5 cycles	53	52	57	43	−35	−36	−39	−19

show the percentage excess of series falling over series rising. If
we judge by the average behavior of this sample in the five interwar cycles, the preponderance of rising series is largest between
stages III and IV of business expansions. Between stages IV and V
the proportion of rising series begins to fall. Again during contractions the proportion of falling series is largest between stages VII
and VIII, and begins to fall between VIII and IX. Except in two
expansions, one of which, 1919-20, is a borderline case, and in one
contraction, the rule holds that the proportion of rising series falls
in the last stage of expansion and rises in the last stage of contraction (Chart 82). From Table 83 we can see that the same pattern
characterized the 18 commodities in our inventory sample.

Now it will readily be apparent that the movement of investment during cycles in manufacturing activity and of production
during business cycles should, in combination, produce a tendency
for inventory investment in finished goods stocks to rise toward the
end of business expansions and to fall toward the end of contractions. For toward the end of each phase, investment is the resultant
of two forces. In the commodities whose production and shipments
continue to rise toward the end of an expansion, the acceleration in
the rate of inventory liquidation should be leveling off, or even falling. At the same time, the production and shipments of some commodities begin to fall. Inventory liquidation in these commodities
should drop sharply, perhaps even be transformed into inventory
accumulation. The rate of liquidation in all finished goods should
decline. Near the end of contractions the reverse should be true.

As we have already seen, the effect of this influence was not
clearly apparent in the investment patterns of the 18 inventory

Chart 82
Fifty-seven Production Series
Excess of Series Rising between Stages
of 5 Business Cycles as Percentage of All Series, 1919-1938

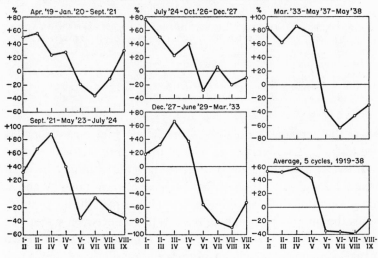

TABLE 83

Manufacturing Activity: Eighteen Nonagricultural Products
Excess of Series Rising between Stages of Business Cycles as
Percentage of All Series, 5 Cycles, 1919-1938

BUSINESS CYCLE	EXCESS OF SERIES RISING BETWEEN STAGES							
	I-II	II-III	III-IV	IV-V	V-VI	VI-VII	VII-VIII	VIII-IX
4/1919– 9/1921	86	58	58	42	0	−14	−42	86
9/1921– 7/1924	52	100	100	12	−42	64	−12	−30
7/1924–12/1927	100	88	−6	46	−30	−42	36	30
12/1927– 3/1933	38	54	24	0	−54	−100	−100	−92
3/1933– 5/1938	100	100	100	60	−40	−60	−40	−20
Av. for 5 cycles	75	80	55	32	−33	−30	−32	−5

series. The patterns were sometimes consistent with the expectations just set forth, sometimes not. The difficulty may be due to irregularities in the behavior of a small sample. Hence, although the only possible verdict on the basis of the data is 'not proven', I think it useful not to discard the hypothesis that the timing of inventory investment in finished staples made from nonagricultural materials acts to offset the tendency of other categories of inventory investment to lead at business cycle turns. The data are not inconsistent with the theory; there are good reasons to suppose that it may be valid, and additional data may lend it empirical support.

CHAPTER 19

Investment in Stocks of Finished Goods
Made from Agricultural Materials

We turn now to the last of the groups for which some empirical evidence is available. The behavior of the volume of finished goods inventories made from agricultural materials (as distinct from the rate of change in such inventories) was examined in detail in Chapter 12. I estimated that the total stock of such goods had a value of about $1.4 billion, or approximately 35 percent of the total inventories of finished goods held by manufacturers at the end of 1939 (see App. E). From the viewpoint of their cyclical behavior and of the forces determining that behavior, however, they are not a homogeneous class. Indeed, as we shall see, a large portion belong with finished goods made from nonagricultural materials. To establish the distinctions that are necessary is the objective of this chapter.

The distinction between finished goods made from nonagricultural and from agricultural materials represents an attempt to give objective expression to quite another principle of classification. As explained earlier, the difference I am really after is between goods whose production cycles are predominantly influenced by cycles in demand and goods whose production cycles are predominantly influenced by cycles in the supply of raw materials which are themselves independent of short-term fluctuations in demand. Dividing goods into those made from materials of agricultural and nonagricultural origin is only a partly satisfactory approximation, but it is the sole convenient objective criterion I can use.

Classification according to origin of materials is satisfactory in one sense. Commodities made from nonagricultural materials do have production cycles dominated largely by cycles in demand.

Thus this group, as indicated in Chapters 11 and 18, is fairly homogeneous. The distinction is unsatisfactory, however, in that commodities made from agricultural materials do not necessarily have production cycles that respond predominantly to impulses from the side of supply. A decline in the current output of materials, for example, will not impinge seriously on the output of goods manufactured from such materials if additional supplies (a) can be obtained from stock carried over from earlier periods or (b) can be fairly promptly imported.[1] If such alternative sources exist in requisite degree, cycles in the production of the fabricated good will be more heavily influenced by demand, and stocks of finished goods will, if durable and staple, tend to behave in the manner described in Chapter 18.

A second complication is that, just as in the case of goods made from nonagricultural materials, we must differentiate between perishable and durable finished goods. The latter can be allowed to accumulate when output rises or demand falls off; the former must be disposed of fairly promptly. This suggests that finished goods made from agricultural materials can be divided into two main classes, each with two subdivisions:

1 Perishable
   a) Goods whose output cycles are controlled largely by factors independent of demand (I shall call these 'supply-dominated')
   b) Goods whose output cycles are strongly influenced by fluctuations in demand (I shall call these 'demand-dominated')

2 Durable
   a) Goods with 'supply-dominated' output cycles
   b) Goods with 'demand-dominated' output cycles

---

[1] In the usual case the supply of materials is independent of the demand for the manufactured product because it is influenced by the effects of weather on the crop. In some cases, however, the difficulty of matching supply and requirements can arise if the material is a minor byproduct of the output of some other commodity. In that case, the difficulty can be overcome in whole or in part if additional supplies can be obtained by special effort or expense. A case in point is inedible tallow; see Ch. 12.

1 *Perishables*

Our collection contains three examples of commodity stocks that are perishable after fabrication: cold storage holdings of pork, lard, and beef. As explained in Chapter 12, stocks of these commodities serve to iron out seasonal disparities between supply and demand. Because they are perishable, little attempt is made to carry over stocks in frozen or cured form from years of large supply (or small demand) to years of small supply (or large demand). Postponing for a moment questions about what determines the supply of frozen and cured meats and lard, we can say that stocks tend to be large in years when supply is large primarily because the carryover between the season of heavy animal slaughter and the season of light slaughter is large. Between the slack season of one year and the flood season of the next, however, only very small stocks will be carried regardless of the rate of supply during the preceding year.

These facts do not, of course, determine a precise relation between the annual output of a year and the average stocks carried during the year because the size of the carryover depends not alone upon the output during the heavy season, but also upon expectations concerning prices in the ensuing slack season. However, if I am right in thinking that only minimum stocks are carried over from slack to flood seasons, it will also be true that stocks in the slack season will be largely unaffected by output during that period. For the stock with which the slack season opens will have been determined by output in the preceding season of large supply, together with price expectations then held. Beginning stocks will therefore be gradually liquidated almost regardless of ouput during the slack season. Consequently, if the seasonally corrected rate of production begins to rise (or fall) during the season when supply is ordinarily light, the effect may not register on stocks until the next season of heavy marketings. Some irregular tendency for cold storage stocks of meat and lard to lag behind production may, therefore, be a concomitant of conditions in the industry.

If this theory is valid, the rate of change in stocks would tend to rise and fall with (or soon after) the rate of change in output. Experience seems to be generally consistent with this expectation for we find that the rates of change in stocks and output trace similar patterns in all three commodities (Charts 83-5). There is also some evidence of a tendency for the rate of change in stocks to lag behind that in production. At the same time, instances of disagreement between the direction of change in production and in stocks of each commodity are numerous. As indicated above, these may be attributed in part to the fact that inventory accumulation to meet the sales of the season of slack production depends somewhat on price expectations which may alter independently of the rate of output.[2]

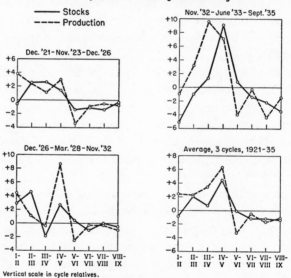

Chart 83

Pork: Cold Storage Holdings and Quantity Frozen or Placed in Cure
Rates of Change per Month from Stage to Stage
of Cycles in Freezing and Curing

Turning to the behavior of this group during business cycles, it is well to recall a distinction made in Chapter 12. There also we discovered that the stocks of all three commodities conformed to cycles of output in their own industry (that is, pork stocks to pork output, lard stocks to lard output, etc.). During business cycles,

[2] There is also the possibility, indeed certainty, of errors in the original data on production or stocks or in the seasonal correction, which are, of course, magnified when we calculate rates of change.

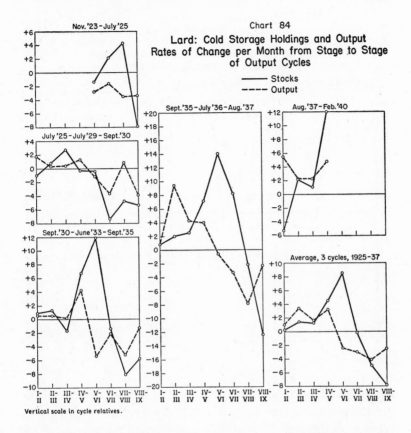

Chart 84

Lard: Cold Storage Holdings and Output
Rates of Change per Month from Stage to Stage
of Output Cycles

—————— Stocks
- - - - Output

Vertical scale in cycle relatives.

however, pork and lard stocks fluctuated irregularly, but beef stocks tended to rise and fall with general business. This difference was easily explained. The stocks of all three commodities were influenced primarily by their rate of output. The output of all three commodities, in turn, depended upon the rate of slaughter: of hogs (in the cases of cured and frozen pork and of lard) and of cattle (in the case of cured and frozen beef). Hog slaughter, however, tends to fluctuate irregularly during business cycles because the rate of slaughter is closely tied to the rate of breeding 12 to 15 months earlier. Breeding decisions in turn are heavily influenced (inversely) by the price of corn, which in turn moves irregularly during business cycles in response to the haphazard effects of the weather on the corn supply. Cattle breeding too is influenced by the supply of feed, but the rate of slaughter is less closely tied to

Chart 85
Beef and Veal: Cold Storage Holdings and Quantity Frozen or Placed in Cure
Rates of Change per Month from Stage to Stage
of Cycles in Freezing and Curing

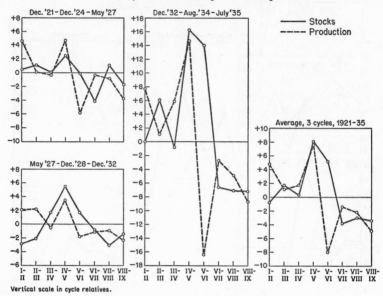

Vertical scale in cycle relatives.

earlier breeding decisions than in the case of hogs. Because cattle are slaughtered when they are older, the stock of cattle is large relative to the rate of slaughter and the age range over which cattle may profitably be marketed is wider. It is possible, therefore, for an increase in the demand for beef to cause the rate of slaughter to rise, and for a decline in demand to cause the rate to fall. In the first case, cattle are slaughtered when they are younger, and herds tend to diminish; in the second case, herds tend to increase, the slaughter of many cattle being postponed.

The animal population may, of course, be likened to a stock of materials. Hog stocks bear the same relation to breeding and slaughter as a stock of goods in process does to the input of raw materials and the output of finished goods because the age at which hogs are marketed cannot be altered much without serious loss.[3] Thus the number of hogs slaughtered can rise, in normal

[3] Beyond a point, close to the normal age when hogs are slaughtered, feeding for a longer period will rarely repay the cost.

circumstances, only if more hogs have been bred 12 to 15 months before. In the case of cattle, however, the stock of animals on the hoof can be drawn down when demand increases and allowed to rise when demand declines. Here the output of an agricultural commodity (fresh or frozen beef) is responsive to short term changes in demand because current requirements can be met by drawing on a stock.

Do these differences influence the movements of the rates of change in production and stocks during business cycles as they did the movements of production and stocks themselves? It is immediately apparent from Charts 86 and 87 that the rates of change in pork and lard stocks do not behave in any regular fashion during business cycles. This, of course, is only to be expected since production, being strongly influenced by earlier crop conditions, behaves irregularly relative to waves of general prosperity and depression.

Beef, however, is different. The rate of change in beef stocks during business cycles (Chart 88) has elements of regularity. In general during the interwar period, it tended to reach a peak dur-

Chart 86

Pork: Cold Storage Holdings and Quantity Frozen or Placed in Cure
Rates of Change per Month from Stage to Stage of Business Cycles

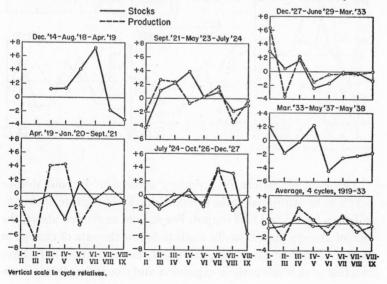

Vertical scale in cycle relatives.

ing expansions and to turn down before business reached it peak. Similarly, it tended to reach a trough during business contractions and to turn up before business reached its low point. There were exceptions, but it seems fair to say that this pattern, which may be described as positive conformity to business cycles with the rate of change in stocks leading, was characteristic of the period.

Chart 87

Lard: Cold Storage Holdings and Output
Rates of Change per Month from Stage to Stage of Business Cycles

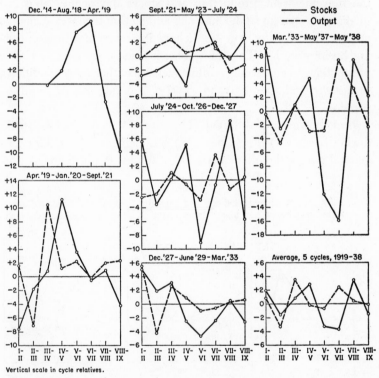

Vertical scale in cycle relatives.

The cyclical pattern of inventory investment in cold storage beef is to be attributed to the similar behavior of the rate of change in frozen and cured beef output. For reasons explained above, the rate of change in beef stocks tends to follow the rate of change in output. The rate of change in output, in turn, appears to have reached peak levels early in expansion and trough levels late in expansion or early in contraction. It therefore resembles the business cycle pattern in the rate of change in the output of consumer goods in general, which also tends to conform to business cycles with a considerable lead. All this, of course, is consistent with our notion that beef output, like that of most consumer goods, is responsive to demand. And given the perishable nature of beef, the pattern of the rate of change in output is transmitted to the rate of change in stocks.

Chart 88

Beef and Veal: Cold Storage Holdings and Quantity Frozen or Placed in Cure
Rates of Change per Month from Stage to Stage of Business Cycles

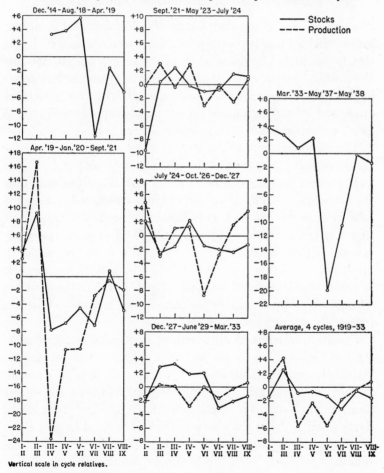

Vertical scale in cycle relatives.

The difference between the irregular behavior of investment in pork and lard stocks and the more regular pattern in beef stocks depends, therefore, on the differences in the forces that control their output. The availability of feed exercises a predominent influence on short term changes in hog slaughter and, therefore, on the supply of meat for curing and of fat for conversion into lard. The presence of a relatively large cattle population, which can be increased or drawn on by altering the age at which cattle are marketed, on the contrary, makes cattle slaughter and, therefore, the supply of beef for freezing and curing, responsive to demand.

2 Durables: Supply-dominated Output Cycles

The examples of goods that are durable in fabricated form may also be divided into two categories: those whose output cycles are clearly dominated by fluctuations in the supply of materials and those whose output cycles are influenced in greater or less degree by fluctuations in demand. Two commodities in our collection, crude and refined cottonseed oil, are clearly supply-dominated. A third, evaporated milk, is also best considered in this class.

The major relevant characteristics of production cycles in the cottonseed oil industry have already been discussed (Ch. 10 and 12). Because cottonseed is more bulky and difficult to store than the oil pressed from it, the output of crude cottonseed oil rises and falls in close relation to fluctuations in the supply of cottonseed, that is, to the size of the cotton crop. Crude oil, in turn, is promptly refined so that the three series—the cotton crop, the output of crude oil, and the output of refined oil—rise and fall together and in nearly the same proportion (Chart 41). But since the output of oil is governed by the size of the cotton crop, it tends to fluctuate irregularly during business cycles.

Despite similarities in their output fluctuations, the stocks of the two commodities do not behave in the same way because the relation between the output and utilization of crude oil is not the same as that between the output and utilization of refined oil. Crude oil, as stated, is promptly refined. The stock of crude is relatively small and has the characteristics of a good in process, or pipeline stock, flowing from the crude oil pressing operation to the refining operation. From this it may be inferred that the rate of

change in crude oil stocks varies directly and almost synchronously
with the rate of change in crude oil output (Chart 89).

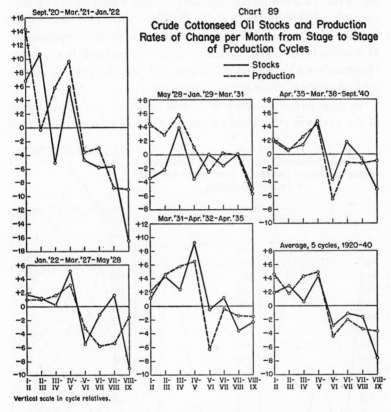

Chart 89
**Crude Cottonseed Oil Stocks and Production
Rates of Change per Month from Stage to Stage
of Production Cycles**

—— Stocks
---- Production

Vertical scale in cycle relatives.

As in the case of crude, the utilization of refined oil is also
strongly influenced by output. For when output is large, the price
falls and cottonseed oil tends to be substituted for other fats and
oils. The relation between refined output and its use, however, is
not as close as that between crude output and its use. When the
supply of refined cottonseed oil is large, it need not all be consumed
at once. It can be stored; and if the low prices that accompany
large supply promise better prices in the future, as is likely, stocks
will accumulate. Additions to the stock of surplus oil are usually
made in refined form and are reflected in disparities between refined oil output and use.

A large supply of oil is not the only factor making for low prices and large stocks. Another factor is a large supply of competing products, which tends to reduce the utilization of cottonseed oil, and a third is a low level of national income, which tends to reduce the utilization of all fats and oils. But these three influences affecting the price and use of cottonseed oil tend to move independently. It remains true, therefore, that utilization of oil tends to move synchronously with cycles in oil output and that the price of cottonseed oil tends to move inversely to output.

In these circumstances it is difficult to say *a priori* at what stage of the cycles in cottonseed oil output the rate of accumulation of

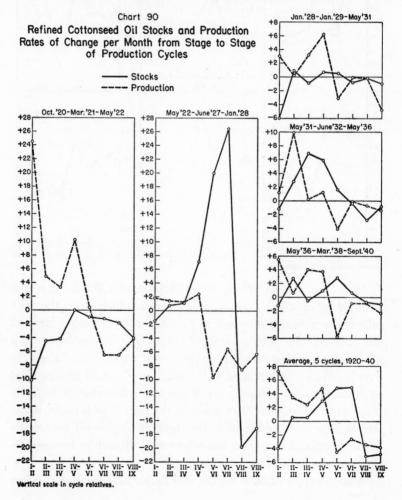

Chart 90
Refined Cottonseed Oil Stocks and Production
Rates of Change per Month from Stage to Stage
of Production Cycles

——— Stocks
----- Production

Vertical scale in cycle relatives.

refined oil stocks will tend to reach its peak. At any stage it will be affected by the quantity of stocks already in storage, by the level and movement of prices, and by other signs that seem to foretell future prices. According to Chart 90, the stage of most rapid accumulation tends to be when the level of production is highest, not when the rate of rise in output is most rapid. Similarly, the rate of inventory liquidation is usually most rapid near the troughs of output cycles. The peak rates of change in stocks cluster about stage V of output cycles, and the trough rates about stage I (or IX) regardless of the pattern of the rates of change in output.

During business cycles the rate of change in crude oil output and stocks should move in the same fashion. Since the former, controlled by movements in the cotton crop, moves irregularly during business cycles, so should the latter (Chart 91).

To understand the behavior of the pace of refined oil accumulation during business cycles is again more difficult. We must take account of the relation between inventory accumulation and both utilization and production, and of the behavior of these latter processes during business cycles. We may best begin by noting that if utilization tended to fluctuate independently of output (responding only to the level of income and to the supply of competing products), we would expect the use of cottonseed oil typically to exceed output most at the peak of cycles in utilization. If it did, the rate of the accumulation of stocks would tend to vary inversely to the level of utilization. As shown above, however, the production of cottonseed oil is itself a major influence affecting utilization. And the rate of change in stocks tends to vary positively with the level of production. These offsetting influences prevent any regular relation between utilization and inventory accumulation. The wide fluctuations in the rate of change in stocks during individual cycles in utilization all but cancel out in the averages (Chart 92).

We are left, therefore, with production as the sole influence regularly affecting the pace of inventory accumulation. We should, therefore, expect that the rate of change in stocks will tend to move like the level of production. This tendency is disturbed in individual business cycles by the haphazard impact of other factors, but the similarity between the two series stands out fairly clearly when their behavior over five cycles is averaged (Chart 93).

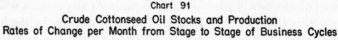

Chart 91
Crude Cottonseed Oil Stocks and Production
Rates of Change per Month from Stage to Stage of Business Cycles

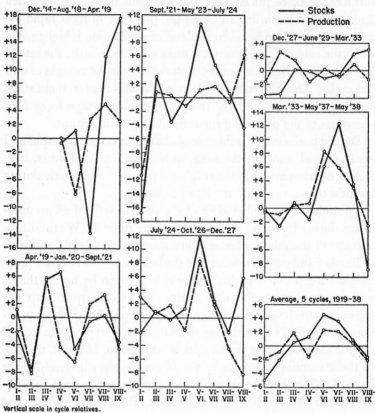

Vertical scale in cycle relatives.

Another commodity to be explained perhaps on lines analogous to refined cottonseed oil is evaporated milk. As indicated in Chapter 12, the output of fluid milk is remarkably stable. The output of evaporated milk, on the contrary, is subject to fairly wide fluctuations due to a combination of influences. Production presumably increases when consumer demand for evaporated milk rises relative to that for other milk products; for then a larger portion of the total output of fluid milk is condensed and canned. Production of evaporated milk should increase also when the demand for milk products in general falls; for canning is one of the principal ways in which surplus milk can be stored until demand revives.

If this analysis is correct, we must expect fluctuations in production often to occur independently of changes in consumer demand for evaporated milk. When they do, stocks of evaporated milk should rise and fall with output. And again stocks will tend to lag behind output because some time passes, after output begins to rise or fall, before it exceeds or drops below consumption. Whether this positive relation between output and stocks is a dominant characteristic of these series depends, of course, on whether the output of evaporated milk typically responds to changes in consumer demand for evaporated milk relative to demand for other milk products, or, inversely, to fluctuations in the demand for milk products in general. Again the patterns reviewed in Chapter 12 suggest that the latter response is more typical. Stocks do tend to conform positively, with a lag, to cycles in output.

Chart 92

Refined Cottonseed Oil Stocks
Rates of Change per Month from Stage to Stage of Cycles
in the Disappearance of Refined Cottonseed Oil

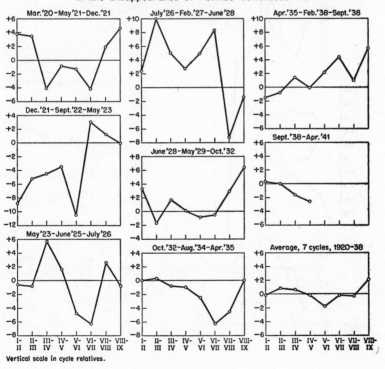

Vertical scale in cycle relatives.

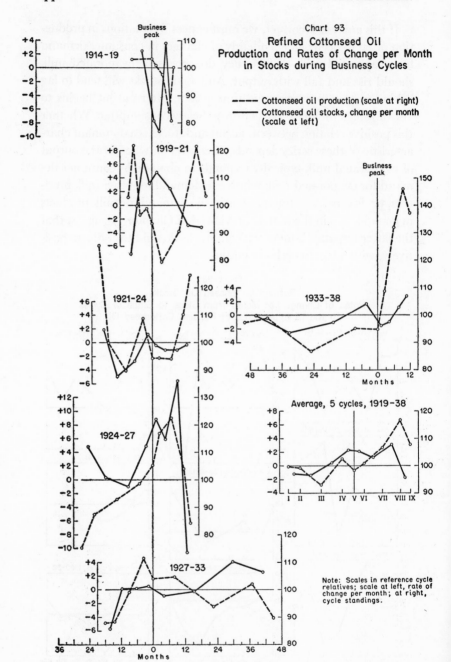

Chart 93
Refined Cottonseed Oil
Production and Rates of Change per Month
in Stocks during Business Cycles

----- Cottonseed oil production (scale at right)
——— Cottonseed oil stocks, change per month
(scale at left)

Note: Scales in reference cycle
relatives; scale at left, rate of
change per month; at right,
cycle standings.

If fluctuations in production were completely independent of consumption, we could say that the rate of increase in stocks would tend to be highest at the peak of production cycles, for production is then likely to be most in excess of consumption. Similarly, the rate of increase would tend to be lowest at the trough of production cycles. When demand for milk products declines, however, prices will drop and the consumption of evaporated milk will be encouraged. And production of evaporated milk will sometimes increase because consumer demand expands. These disturbing factors have apparently not been determining. The rate of change in stocks has usually attained its peak near the peak in production cycles and its trough near the trough in production cycles (Chart 94).

The influence of this tendency is reflected in the behavior of the rate of change in stocks during business cycles. With few exceptions, it has risen and declined with output (Chart 95). And since the production of evaporated milk has acted irregularly during business cycles, the same has been true of the pace of the accumulation of its stocks.

3 Durables: Demand-dominated Output Cycles

Two commodities in our collection, linseed oil and leather, are in this category. Linseed oil may be said to represent a transitional case between commodities whose output cycles are determined mainly by the supply of raw materials and those whose output cycles respond chiefly to impulses from the side of demand (see Ch. 12). Its output can be increased, at least tardily, when demand increases because a considerable portion of the output depends upon imports of flaxseed. By increasing imports, production of linseed oil can, after a time, be raised above the level that could be supported by the current domestic crop of flaxseed and current imports. Similarly, when demand falls, output can be cut, at least after the rate of receipts of foreign seed has been reduced. This sluggish adjustment of output to changes in demand is, of course, similar to that characterizing the output of goods made from nonagricultural materials. As a result, the behavior of stocks of linseed oil during cycles in shipments and in business tends to resemble that of finished goods made from nonagricultural materials. Dur-

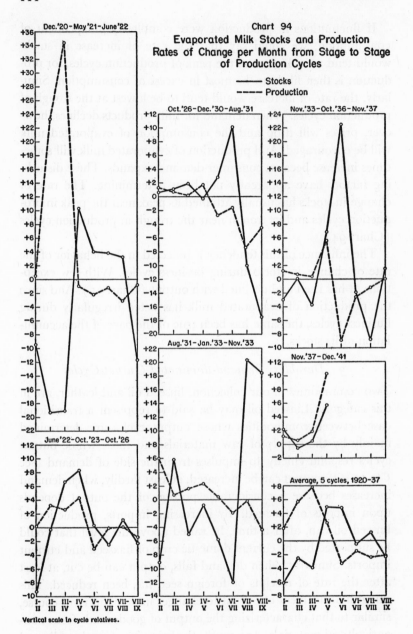

Chart 94
Evaporated Milk Stocks and Production
Rates of Change per Month from Stage to Stage
of Production Cycles

——— Stocks
- - - - Production

Vertical scale in cycle relatives.

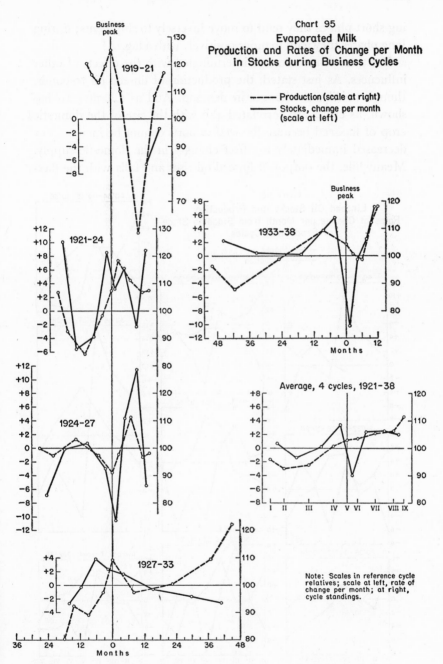

Chart 95
Evaporated Milk
Production and Rates of Change per Month
in Stocks during Business Cycles

----- Production (scale at right)
——— Stocks, change per month
(scale at left)

Note: Scales in reference cycle
relatives; scale at left, rate of
change per month; at right,
cycle standings.

ing short phases they tend to move inversely to shipments; during long phases they tend to move positively with a lag.

But these tendencies are intermingled with the effects of other influences. As just stated, the production of linseed oil responds, though tardily, to changes in demand. And as Chapter 12 has shown, its cycles are correlated also with the size of the domestic crop of flaxseed because flaxseed imports cannot be increased or decreased immediately to offset changes in the domestic supply. Meanwhile, the output of linseed oil rises and falls with the flax-

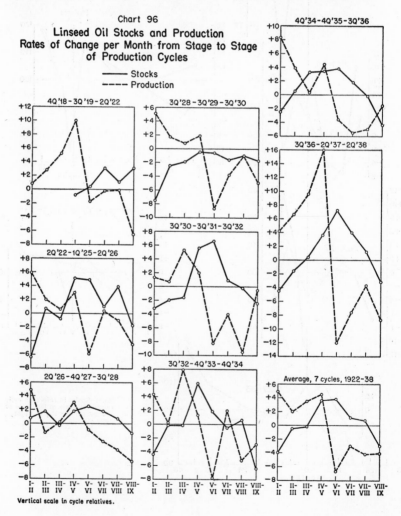

Chart 96
Linseed Oil Stocks and Production
Rates of Change per Month from Stage to Stage
of Production Cycles

——— Stocks
----- Production

Vertical scale in cycle relatives.

seed crop. The result is that the production of linseed oil fluctuates in a double cycle: it expands and contracts in response to changes in the demand for linseed oil; and around these movements winds a shorter cycle of production that is governed by the size of the domestic flaxseed crop (Chart 53). Since the cycles of production identified by the National Bureau are chiefly of the second type, stocks of linseed conform positively to production cycles with a lag. The reason, of course, is that a contraction in oil production in response to a short flaxseed crop usually leaves output below shipments; stocks therefore fall. When production begins to recover (either because imports have been stimulated or a large crop has been harvested), some time passes before it rises above shipments. Stocks, therefore, do not begin to rise until some time after production has begun to increase. Similarly on the downturn: when production begins to fall, some time intervenes before it passes below the level of shipments.

So much for the relations among stocks, output, and shipments. The cyclical fluctuations in inventory investment are consistent with these conditions. Let us begin with investment during production cycles. Since these cycles, as identified by the National Bureau, are almost all engendered by changes in the supply of raw materials, output will tend to be most in excess of shipments when it is at a peak. The deficiency of output relative to shipments will tend to be largest when output is at a trough. Consequently, stocks will tend to increase most rapidly (or decline least rapidly) near the peak of a production cycle, and to decline most rapidly (or increase least rapidly) near the trough. These expectations are, of course, the same as those advanced in connection with the supply-dominated cycles of cottonseed oil output.

The behavior of the rates of change in linseed oil stocks during production cycles confirms these expectations (Chart 96). The rate of change in stocks reached a peak in the stage immediately preceding or immediately following the peak of the production cycle in 7 of the 8 cycles covered. It reached a trough also immediately before or after the trough of production in 7 cycles. The rate of change in output was much less regular—it reached peaks at various stages of expansion, and troughs at various stages of contraction. Generally speaking, however, as long as output was increasing (that is, as long as the rate of change in output was positive), the rate of change in stocks continued to rise. As long as output was declining, the rate of change in stocks continued to decline.

Since production does respond, though slowly, to fluctuations in demand, our theory calls for inventory investment to behave during shipments cycles like investment in stocks of goods made from nonagricultural materials: for such goods we found that when shipments rise, stocks begin to be liquidated. The rate of liquidation is usually high in the first part of expansions, sometimes increasing. Before the end of expansions, however, the increase in the rate of liquidation tends to level off. There was even evidence that toward the end of expansions, especially long expansions, it tended to diminish. With the onset of contraction, inventories began to be accumulated rapidly, but as contraction proceeded, the rate of accumulation tended to fall off, especially in long contractions.

If we allow for irregular movements in stocks connected with supply-dominated cycles in production, the behavior of investment in linseed oil stocks is consistent with these expectations (Chart 97). In the two relatively short contractions, 1919-21 and 1937-38, stocks at first accumulated rapidly but as the contraction in shipments proceeded, the accumulation became less rapid. At the beginning of the long expansion of 1921-28 stocks were being liquidated, but after 3 years production caught up with shipments, allowing stocks to begin to grow with the trend of activity in the industry. The ensuing long contraction of shipments opened with stocks declining instead of rising as they would ordinarily do when shipments decline, because the domestic flaxseed harvest fell sharply between the crop years 1929 and 1930. The output of linseed oil was, therefore, drastically curtailed. This fortuitous circumstance permitted the liquidation of stocks to begin early rather than late in this contraction. Finally, the long expansion starting in 1933 opened with stocks growing instead of declining. I attribute this to the speculative episode of 1933. Subsequently stocks moved irregulary because of fluctuations in the supply of flaxseed, but the general trend of inventory investment is fairly flat, which is more nearly in accord with our expectations in a long expansion than would have been a rapid and sustained liquidation of inventories.

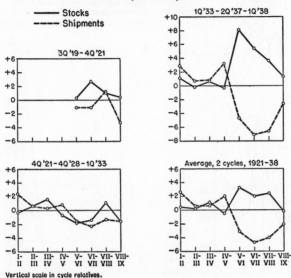

Chart 97
Linseed Oil Stocks and Shipments
Rates of Change per Month from Stage to Stage
of Shipments Cycles

Vertical scale in cycle relatives.

The behavior of inventory investment during business cycles reflects these various influences from the side of demand for oil and the supply of basic materials. Shipments of linseed oil conformed to business cycles with fair regularity. They rose during all 5 expansions between 1919 and 1938; they fell in 3 out of 5 contractions; the rate of increase during expansions was uniformly higher than during neighboring contractions and lower during contractions than during neighboring expansions in three out of four instances. (The National Bureau conformity measure is +100, +20, +78.) In view of the tardy response of production to changes in shipments, it is not surprising to find the rate of change in stocks falling during at least the first part of expansions.[4] Chart 98 shows that this was true on the average and in 4 out of 5 individual expansions. With the onset of contraction, the rate of accumulation rose sharply partly because of the decline in shipments and partly because of the delayed reaction of production to the earlier rise of shipments during expansion. The rate of change in stocks rose at

[4] Either because the rate of accumulation is falling or the rate of liquidation rising.

Chart 98

**Linseed Oil: Production, Shipments, and Rates of Change
per Month in Stocks during Business Cycles**

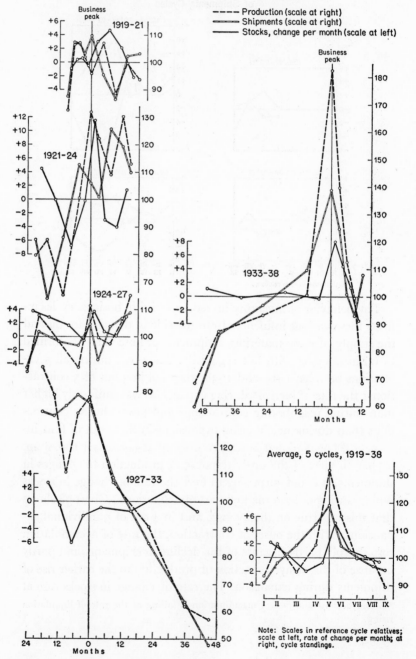

Note: Scales in reference cycle relatives;
scale at left, rate of change per month; at
right, cycle standings.

the beginning of contraction in all 5 cycles. It increased toward the end of expansion in 2 cycles and declined toward the end of contraction in 3 cycles.

All this is behavior similar to that characteristic of commodities made from nonagricultural materials. It bears out the argument with which this chapter began: a division of stocks of finished goods into those made from agricultural and nonagricultural materials does not satisfactorily separate goods whose production cycles are dominated by changes in the supply of materials from those whose production cycles respond chiefly to influences from the side of the demand for the finished commodity.

Tanners' stocks of finished cattle hide leather are an even better example of the same tendencies. Although the domestic supply of hides is only a minor byproduct of cattle slaughter, and consequently is insensitive to changes in the demand for leather, cycles in the production of leather are rather closely correlated with cycles in its use (Ch. 10 and 12). Discrepancies between the domestic supply of, and the requirements for, hides are largely offset by changes in imports and by drafts on, or additions to, stocks held by dealers and importers.

The connection between the output and use of leather is much closer than that between the output and shipments of linseed oil, as is indicated by comparing cycles in the production of leather and of shoes, which we take to represent the consumption of leather. For example, between 1923 and 1940 the National Bureau identified seven and one-half cycles in shoe output. It identified corresponding cycles in leather output in all except two cases. Even in these two there was a mild response of leather output, although the movements were not vigorous enough for cycle turns to be marked.[5] Another indication of the rather close connection between the two processes is the National Bureau index of the conformity of cycles in leather and shoe production: +100, +75, +100; and a third is the resemblance of their average cycle patterns (Chart 57). Since leather manufacturers can conduct their business on the same lines as fabricators using nonagricultural ma-

[5] This contrasts with the case of linseed oil. Between 1919 and 1938 there were only two and one-half cycles in shipments but seven and one-half cycles in production.

terials, we may expect cyclical movements of investment in leather stocks to resemble the behavior of investment in stocks of durable finished goods made from nonagricultural materials. The data bear out this expectation.

In earlier examples of durables made from agricultural materials—cottonseed oil, evaporated milk, even linseed oil—the difference between the behavior of inventory investment during cycles in production and in some index representing the utilization of the commodity was sharp. The relation between cycles in leather and in shoe production is so close that this difference is no longer found (Charts 99 and 100). As we have seen, cycles in the output of goods made from nonagricultural materials follow so closely on cycles in shipments that it seemed unnecessary to measure separately the behavior of stocks during cycles in these two types of process.[6]

The pattern of investment in leather stocks resembles also the pattern of investment in stocks of finished durables made from nonagricultural materials. Whether we look at the rate of change in leather stocks during cycles in leather or in shoe production, stocks are either being liquidated at the beginning of expansion or, if they are being accumulated, the rate is low. The rate of liquidation tends to increase during the early part of expansion; later it tends either to level off or actually decline. With the onset of contraction, the rate first rises markedly, then tapers off as the contraction proceeds,[7] and when the next expansion begins it drops. All

[6] This is not to say that production and shipments cycles in this type of commodity are virtually identical. However, the peaks and troughs of production and shipments so nearly coincide that the cyclical pattern of stocks will look much the same whether we mark off cycles by turning points in shipments or in production.

[7] The tendency for the rate of liquidation of leather stocks to decline before the end of expansion and the rate of accumulation to decline before the end of contraction seems more pronounced during cycles in leather production than during cycles in shoe production. This may be a significant characteristic of investment in this commodity and perhaps generally. If, as we suppose, manufacturers at first adjust output tardily and incompletely to declines in demand and only later, under the pressure of accumulating stocks, reduce output more drastically, the gap between output and shipments would naturally be more nearly closed by the time output reaches a trough than it is when shipments do. In the present instance, taking shoe production as an index of leather shipments, this seems to be the case.

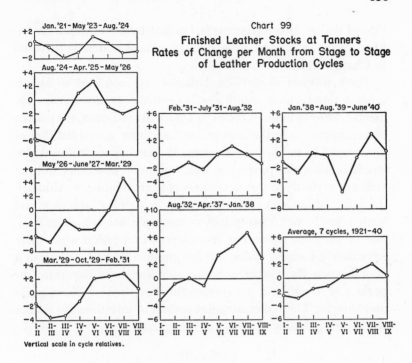

Chart 99

Finished Leather Stocks at Tanners
Rates of Change per Month from Stage to Stage
of Leather Production Cycles

Vertical scale in cycle relatives.

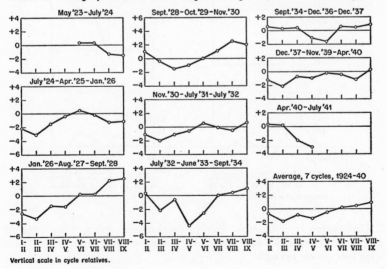

Chart 100

Finished Leather Stocks at Tanners
Rates of Change per Month from Stage to Stage of Shoe Production Cycles

Vertical scale in cycle relatives.

this, of course, is behavior made familiar by the evidence on finished durables derived from nonagricultural materials surveyed in Chapter 18.

These marked similarities, however, are confined to investment during cycles in manufacturing activity (production or shipments). During business cycles, as Chart 101 indicates, the pattern of investment in leather stocks has not closely resembled that of investment in finished durables made from nonagricultural materials because the production and utilization of leather did not conform perfectly to the movements of general business. Although the index of business cycle conformity is high for both shoe and leather production,[8] many movements were not related to business cycles. Shoe production had 6 cycles in a period when there were only 3 business cycles. Leather production had 5 cycles in a period when there were 4 business cycles; more important, its peaks and troughs did not correspond closely with business peaks and troughs. The rather irregular pattern of investment in leather stocks during business cycles is a consequence.

Chart 101
Finished Leather Stocks at Tanners
Rates of Change per Month from Stage to Stage
of Business Cycles

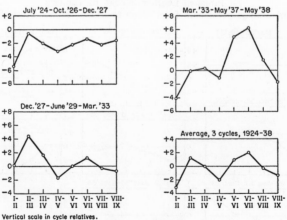

Vertical scale in cycle relatives.

[8] The conformity indexes for shoe production were +100, +50, +100 for three cycles, 1924-38; those for leather production were +50, +100, +100 for four cycles, 1921-38.

4   Conclusion

This analysis enables us to define the classes of finished goods made from agricultural materials that are significant for the cyclical behavior of inventory investment. The few commodities available for study precludes wholly persuasive empirical support for the conclusions below, but I think that the foregoing argument and review of evidence points to the following theory:

1) Stocks of finished goods made from agricultural materials do not constitute a homogeneous class of inventories. The crucial distinction turns on whether cycles in the production of a commodity are wholly, or almost wholly, governed by changes in the supply of materials. Three major conditions are required to bring about this result. One is that the output of materials fluctuates, at least in the short run, independently of the demand for fabricated goods. A second is that the materials should be drawn almost entirely from domestic sources. For if shortages or surpluses in domestic supplies can be counteracted by a fairly prompt variation in the rate of imports, the production of the fabricated product can be freed in large degree from the influence of domestic crop conditions. The third prerequisite is that the materials be difficult to store in crude form. When they are, the current supply must be promptly processed. On the other hand, if the crude materials can be stored, shortages in the current supply can be offset by drawing on stocks, and surpluses can be allowed to accumulate. If neither imports nor changes in stocks are available to offset shortages or surpluses in the domestic supply of crude materials, the rate of processing will necessarily be dominated by the domestic supply. But if either imports or stocks are available in requisite degree, fabrication can be substantially divorced from the vagaries of crops in this country and will tend to follow cycles in demand. Strictly speaking, only commodities that meet these conditions have supply-dominated production cycles and are the proper subject of this chapter. Others are better classed with the commodities studied in Chapter 18.

2) If cycles in the production of a fabricated commodity are supply-dominated, in the sense of this analysis, another distinction is important: is the product perishable or durable and staple? If perishable, it must be promptly marketed, that is, sales will be forced

to keep pace with production by appropriate changes in prices. Manufacturers will try to hold stocks at levels roughly proportionate to the current rate of output and sales, and inventory investment will tend to rise and fall with the rate of change in output. And since output under these conditions will tend to fluctuate in response to crop conditions, inventory investment during business cycles will tend to be irregular. The cold storage holdings of pork and lard are good examples.

3) If the finished product is durable and staple the outcome is different. Since production is supply-dominated, it will rise and fall with the supply of raw materials. But when it tends to outrun use, the goods need not be dumped on the market regardless of price, for they can be stored. If cycles in use are relatively independent of those in output—as they may be if use is not stimulated much by a low price or restricted by a high one—the result is simple. During cycles in the output of the finished good, the rate of inventory accumulation will tend to be highest at peaks in production, and the rate of liquidation highest at troughs in production. For if production and shipments are relatively independent, the excess of output over shipments will tend to be largest when output is at a peak. Hence the rate of growth of inventories will be highest at that time. Similarly, output will tend to be most deficient relative to shipments when it is at a trough. At such times, therefore, the rate of disinvestment in inventory will tend to be at a maximum. During cycles in use, on the contrary, the rate of inventory investment will tend to be highest at cyclical troughs and lowest at cyclical peaks. In short, inventory investment will tend to conform inversely to cycles in shipments. The reasons are parallel. If cycles in shipments proceed independently of those in production, shipments will tend to be most in excess of production when they are at a peak; they will run short of production most when they are at a trough. Moreover, if shipments conform to business cycles, as they should do generally since they are determined by demand, inventory investment too will tend to conform inversely to cycles in business at large. This, however, will be only a tendency. Since the rate of accumulation of stocks is strongly influenced also by fluctuations in production, which itself is dominated by the supply of materials, the behavior of inventory invest-

ment during any given business cycle will depend in large part on the vagaries of crops.

If the use of a commodity is sensitive to price, it will tend to rise and fall with output as well as in response to influences from the side of demand. For the price of a commodity whose output is supply-dominated will tend to vary inversely to output; e.g., cottonseed oil. Under such conditions, inventory investment presumably depends in part upon speculative considerations. Inventory holders need not absorb any difference between current output and use. They may accept lower prices and dispose of a bigger volume. Businessmen will, no doubt, be encouraged to hold larger stocks the lower the price; for other things being equal, the lower the price the better the chance that future prices will be higher. But even if one could validly assume that the price level determined the level of stocks, we would still not know when stocks would be accumulated most rapidly. The cyclical behavior of the rate of accumulation can be established only by observation.

In this connection, refined cottonseed oil and evaporated milk are instructive. The pace of accumulation tended to be highest at the peak of output cycles, lowest at output troughs. During business cycles inventory accumulation also tended to vary with the level of output, and since output acted irregularly, inventory investment did too.

4) So much for supply-dominated commodities. The fabrication of agricultural materials may, however, be so divorced from the current domestic supply that it will respond primarily to changes in demand. In the terminology of this chapter, production may be demand-dominated. Inventory investment may then be expected to behave in the fashion described in Chapter 19. If the product is durable and staple, inventories normally begin to be liquidated soon after the upturn of business. The rate of liquidation tends to accelerate in the first part of expansion, then be constant or retard in the second half. With the beginning of contraction, liquidation falls sharply and accumulation soon begins. At first stocks pile up at an increasing rate, but in the second half of contraction, the rate of accumulation tends to level off, even to decline. As might be expected, the tendency for the rate of liquidation to decline in the second half of expansion and for the rate of accumulation to de-

cline in the second half of contraction is more pronounced in long than in short phases, because after liquidation has proceeded for some time, stocks become inconveniently low and the pressure to halt the liquidation becomes more intense. If the expansion continues long enough, production is finally raised above the level of shipments and stocks begin to accumulate. Similarly during contractions: when the accumulation of stocks has proceeded for some time stocks become intolerably large, the pressure to halt accumulation becomes more intense, and if the process continues long enough, production is drastically cut and the liquidation of stocks begins. Finished leather is a good example of a commodity made of an agricultural material in which inventory investment acts in this way. To a lesser degree the same conditions seem to have controlled investment in linseed oil stocks.

5) Demand-dominated commodities will act in this fashion only if the finished product is durable. If the product is perishable, it is hardly plausible that manufacturers would tolerate the accumulation of surplus stocks for a long period when business is declining. In that event, though short lags are probably inevitable, we must expect firms to try to keep stocks of finished goods in close alignment with sales. Inventory investment would then tend to vary with the rate of change in output and sales, though probably with a short lag. The behavior of the rate of change in manufacturing production in general was described in Chapter 15. If we may attribute to perishable manufactures of agricultural origin the behavior found characteristic of manufactured goods in general, we may conclude that the rate of change in their output will usually reach a peak before the peak in business and a trough before the trough of business (Ch. 15). The length of the lead, however, appears to have been irregular. A similar uncertainty, therefore, affects the timing of inventory investment in this class of stocks. And if, as may be true, stocks tend to lag behind output by some brief, but so far unknown, interval, the timing of turns in inventory investment will be affected by another element of uncertainty. Perhaps the most definite statement that can be made now is that inventory investment in this category will tend to reach its peaks during business expansions and its troughs during business contractions and that the lead of its peaks and troughs relative to

business cycle turns will not be longer, and will probably be shorter, than that of the rate of change in output. This rule is, of course, similar to that proposed in Chapter 17 for investment in raw materials. Our collection includes only one example of a commodity whose output responds to short-run changes in demand and that is perishable in finished form: cured and frozen beef.

The size of all these classes of inventories is not exactly determinable. Something can, however, be said about the quantity of finished goods held by industries whose production cycles are demand- and supply-dominated, respectively. As pointed out in Chapter 12 and Appendix E, it seems highly likely that products made from cotton, silk, hides, and rubber, all of which can be and are stored in large quantities in crude form, have production cycles of the type we have called demand-dominated. The output of products made from these materials generally rises and falls with business activity. Stocks of finished goods made from these materials were estimated (App. E) to have had a value of about $560 million at the end of 1939, accounting for 14 percent of all finished goods. Moreover, the majority are undoubtedly durable and staple. Thus the major fraction of this portion of finished goods should, as far as its behavior characteristics go, be added to the durable staples made from nonagricultural materials treated in Chapter 18.

Other finished goods made from agricultural materials had a value at the end of 1939 of about $800 million, accounting for about 20 percent of all finished goods. Not all, however, have supply-dominated production cycles. Grains, for example, may be economically stored for long periods and it seems likely, therefore, that cycles in the production of food products made from grains are not controlled principally by grain crops. As we have seen, the same is true of cattle slaughter and the output of cured and frozen beef. It appears, therefore, that the stocks of finished goods with supply-dominated production cycles may amount to no more than 20 percent of all finished goods and perhaps to as little as 15 percent. Only 6-8 percent of manufacturers' stocks, therefore, may be presumed to exhibit the irregular cycles of inventory investment that seem to be characteristic of commodities whose production cycles are controlled by the supply of materials.

CHAPTER 20

Summary Account of the Timing of Inventory
Investment Cycles

We can now draw together the essential elements regarding the timing of turning points in inventory investment, its explanation, and interpretation.

The first question is how total inventory investment behaves. For an answer one has to depend upon the unsatisfactory indications of annual data. These tell as clear a story as such data can. In both current and constant prices total investment reached its peaks and troughs in the same years as general business at 7 of the 10 turns between the two world wars. Investment by manufacturers did the same, and investment by retailers and wholesalers did so at 8 out of 10 turns. The few investment turns that did not coincide with those in business were evenly divided between leads and lags.

As they stand these figures suggest that inventory investment tends neither to lead nor to lag behind the turning points of business cycles. The possibility that there is a regular tendency to lead or to lag by a short interval is not precluded. But our tests indicate that when annual data covering 5 cycles fail to indicate a lead or lag, the actual lead or lag, if any, will rarely be longer than, say, 3 months. If we take into consideration a certain bias due to the process of price correction on which the estimates are based, a short lead seems more likely than a short lag, but we cannot be sure.

This finding, though necessarily imprecise, is of great interest. It suggests that the common assumption that stocks are kept at a constant ratio to output and sales may be invalid. Were inventory-output and inventory-sales ratios constant, cycles in inventory investment would coincide with cycles in the rate of change in sales and output. It seems plausible to suppose, however, that the rate of change in output reaches its maxima and minima before the peaks and troughs of business. If, as it seems, inventory investment turns within a very short interval of the turns in business, it probably lags behind the rate of change in output.

This probability was confirmed by a study of rates of change in both aggregate and manufacturing output. The rate of growth or decline in aggregate output seems to have retarded markedly and regularly long before the peaks and troughs of business—often during the first half of expansions or contractions. These retardations have sometimes been followed by periods of renewed acceleration, but the subsequent peaks in the rate of growth or decline have rarely been as pronounced as the original. Inventory investment, in contrast, is near its trough when expansion begins and, at least in annual series, sweeps up smoothly to a peak near a business peak, then smoothly down to a trough near a business trough.

Further study of the rate of change in manufacturing production confirmed these general conclusions and added some interesting detail. During contractions output tends to decline at an increasingly rapid pace until about the middle of the phase, after which a period of retardation sets in. During expansions the rate of growth behaves less regularly. At the beginning of the phase output has usually been growing rapidly, then more slowly. Retardation has sometimes characterized the remainder of the phase but often it has been followed by a renewed spurt that sometimes brought the rate of growth in output to levels as high as or higher than those at the beginning of expansion.

These observations about the timing of inventory investment have an important bearing on the course and character of business cycles. If inventory-output ratios remained constant and inventory investment moved synchronously with, and in proportion to, the rate of change in output, inventory investment would rise more rapidly at the beginning of expansions and fall more rapidly at the beginning of contractions than it does. This would make the curves of output and income in the opening stages of cyclical recoveries and recessions more precipitous than they are. When the retardation of output growth sets in, inventory investment would drop and tend to bring the business expansion to an end. Similarly, when the retardation of output decline sets in during contraction, inventory liquidation would drop and tend to bring on a revival of business. Continued growth in inventory investment during expansions and continued decline during contractions after output growth or decline begins to retard means that it acts to prolong the upward and downward swings of business. It may be said, therefore, that the lag of inventory investment behind the rate of change in output serves to moderate and to lengthen business expansions and contractions. These, of course, are tendencies. How influential the behavior of inventories is depends upon the magnitude of inventory investment changes compared with those in other categories of expenditure—the subject of Chapter 21.

Study of the behavior of total inventory investment and its major components leaves us with two solid findings: first, inventory investment turns near business cycle turns; secondly, it tends to lag behind the peaks and troughs in the rate of change in output. Several problems remain. One concerns the precise timing of investment. Is it actually synchronous with business cycle turns or does it tend to lead or to lag by a short interval? Secondly, does planned investment move in the same way as observed investment? A third problem arises with respect to the causes of fluctuations in investment. Why does it lag behind the rate of change in output and turn near the turns in business? To help answer these questions, we examine the evidence on the movements of investment in manufacturers' stocks.

From the viewpoint of cyclical behavior, inventories held by manufacturers are not homogeneous. The study of inventory cycles in Part Two indicated the necessity for distinguishing four major classes: goods in process, raw materials, finished goods made to order, and finished goods sold from stock. Their behavior differs because the motives that control inventory policy vary. Within two, raw materials and finished goods sold from stock, still further distinctions are required. These stem from the fact that among manufacturers of different types of commodity the ability to control the rate at which materials are received or produced varies. Moreover, not all commodities can be stored in the same degree. These differences are reflected in the cyclical behavior of stocks.

They led us to distinguish raw materials purchased from other domestic manufacturers or dealers from agricultural products purchased from producers or any type of imports that must be purchased long before they are to be used. Manufacturers' receipts of goods in the former class can be rapidly adjusted to changes in current requirements. Their receipts in the latter class cannot be adjusted promptly. Again, among finished goods sold from stock we have to distinguish goods made from agricultural materials that cannot well be stored in crude form from goods made from other materials. Fabrication of the former is heavily influenced, if not controlled, by haphazard changes in supply, which in turn affects stocks of finished goods. Production of goods made from other materials follows changes in demand. Finally, there is a distinction to be made between finished durables and nondurables. The first may be stored for long periods; and the inventory-sales ratio may be allowed to vary widely. The second must be sold promptly; and the inventory-sales ratio must be kept fairly stable.

These distinctions are as essential to an understanding of inventory investment cycles as they are for inventory cycles. As we have seen, the cyclical behavior of inventory investment differs significantly from class to class. However, the characteristic features of investment in each class were more difficult to establish than were those of inventory cycles because cycles in the rate of change in inventories are more variable. This, of course, was only to be expected. The first differences in any series that does not move continuously are bound to follow a less steady course than their cumulative counterpart. To illustrate: small fluctuations in the amount by which, say, receipts exceed the consumption of a raw material cause the rate of inventory investment to turn although inventories continue upward. This additional element of volatility aggravates the difficulties of using small samples of series covering short periods. The significant tendencies in the data, which would doubtless be revealed if the records were comprehensive, are often masked by random movements in the few commodities for which we have records. Generalization has, therefore, been more difficult with respect to cycles in investment than in inventories. I shall, however, summarize the main suggestions I believe the study yields. For this purpose, I neglect certain minor groups of stocks which appear to behave irregularly during business cycles, and confine attention to classes whose action seems to shape the regular pattern of manufacturers' total investment.

1 Goods in Process and Finished Goods Made to Order

These two groups, which together account for 25 to 30 percent of manufacturers' stocks, may conveniently be considered together. For neither is any useful amount of data available. But both are closely tied to manufacturing production. If more goods are to be produced, more must flow through the fabricating process. And when goods are made to order, they are generally delivered promptly. They remain in stock during the time required for packing and to arrange transportation and, if delivery is to the purchaser's location, during the time required for shipment. If we ignore seasonal factors and changes in the composition of output, the inventory-output ratio should remain approximately constant. If it does, the absolute changes in inventories should be approximately proportional to those in production. As explained in Chapter 15, investment in goods in process should tend to lead the rate of change in output. By the same token, investment in goods made to order should tend to lag behind the rate of change in output. In both instances, however, the differences in timing between changes in investment and in output, at least on the average for all manufacturing, are so small that they may safely be neglected for present purposes.

With the information now available, we can best judge the movements of inventory investment in these categories from the cyclical pattern of the rate of change in output. From the viewpoint of cyclical timing, the problem was to determine the behavior of the rate of change in output, and one purpose of the detailed study of rates of change in manufacturing was to ascertain the cyclical pattern of investment in stocks of goods in process and in finished goods made to order.

Translated into terms of inventory investment, our observations about the cyclical pattern of changes in output imply that investment in goods in process and in finished goods made to order usually reach peaks and troughs long before business activity. Not infrequently, however, inventory investment in these categories turns up again just before the peak of business. Before business troughs, a reversal of this sort is not characteristic of investment.

2 Raw Materials

For reasons explained in Chapters 9, 10, and 16, manufacturers try to maintain a fairly constant ratio between their stocks of raw materials and the rate at which they are consumed in production. If we could assume that they are completely successful, we could use the rate of change in output as an indicator of investment, just as we did in the case of goods in process and finished goods made to order. But such an assumption is obviously invalid. Because a period, more or less long, elapses between an order for supplies and delivery, manufacturers must foresee their requirements for raw materials some time ahead. The order-delivery interval is indeed short for most raw materials. Even so, errors are inevitable. And whether the errors of manufacturers offset one another is uncertain. Much depends upon the size of the individual errors and, even more, on whether all or most manufacturers make errors of the same sort at the same time. Such points can hardly be settled by general reasoning. It appeared, therefore, that in the absence of direct observation, no useful statement could be made about the relation between output and inventory investment.

In this situation, it is especially unfortunate that records on stocks of raw materials are so scarce. The results they yield are badly in need of more empirical support. But as far as they go, they suggest the following conclusions.

1) For commodities supplied under conditions allowing manufacturers quickly to adjust receipts to requirements, the rate of change in stocks of raw materials is positively correlated with the rate of change in output in the industry using the materials. Despite errors that presumably affect the individual firm's decisions about purchases, this relation emerged clearly from comparisons between the stocks and rates of fabrication of three raw materials of this character—cotton, silk, and hides. Since about 75 percent of the raw materials used by manufacturers are procured under conditions similar to those that characterize our small sample, it is arguable that inventory investment in raw materials is positively correlated with the rate of change in output in most American in-

dustry. Indeed, among manufacturers as a whole, this tendency should stand forth all the more sharply. The chance errors of prediction by individual manufacturers are more likely to offset one another. And the forces making for manufacturers' errors are less likely to operate in the same direction in different industries than in a single industry.

A positive relation between investment and the rate of change in output for this major fraction of raw materials is not the same as a synchronous relation between investment and the rate of change in output for all raw materials. It is, indeed, two steps removed. First, inventory investment probably lags behind the rate of change in output even in the case of materials for which manufacturers can quickly adjust receipts to requirements. This is plausible if we assume that manufacturers judge their future requirements by recent experience. An upturn in the rate of increase in output would not then be matched immediately by an upturn in the rate of increase in receipts of materials, and inventories would not immediately grow proportionately. But manufacturers would attempt to eliminate the discrepancy in subsequent periods. Such a tendency for investment to lag was apparent in the case of silk stocks, though not in those of cotton and hides. As pointed out in Chapter 17, however, lags might well have been discovered even for cotton and hides were we in a position to make timing measurements on a finer scale. Moreover, since our three materials are all procured from dealers who hold stocks ready for delivery, the interval between order and receipt is especially short. It would be longer and the tendency to lag presumably more marked if we had data for materials purchased from other manufacturers, particularly from manufacturers whose goods are usually made to order rather than sold from stock.

There is reason, therefore, to expect investment to lag behind the rate of change in output even when materials are procured under conditions that permit a fairly rapid adjustment of receipts to requirements. As pointed out above, however, not all materials are obtained under such favorable conditions. Examples of materials whose supply cannot promptly be adjusted to requirements indicate that the lag of investment behind the rate of change in output in the industries using the materials is very long. Peak rates of accumulation, indeed, usually lag behind the peak in output itself as well as in the rate of change in output. They come, that is, during contractions in output. Peak rates of inventory liquidation generally follow revivals of output. For such materials, therefore, inventory investment tends to be rising in the period just before output reaches its peak and to be falling just before output reaches its low point. Such behavior by this minor fraction of raw materials reinforces the shorter lag in the major fraction.

All this leaves us uncertain, within a considerable range, about the timing of investment in raw materials relative to the turns in general business. If investment kept pace with the change in output, it would tend to lead business turns by a long interval, perhaps as much as half a phase on the average. In the past a lead of this length has been a fairly regular characteristic of the rate of change in output relative to business cycle troughs. In expansions the rate of increase in output has usually reached a maximum long before the business peak, but it has sometimes gone to a second peak in the last quarter of expansion. As stated, however, investment in stocks of raw materials probably tends to lag behind the rate of change in output. To this degree, of course, the lead of investment in raw materials relative to business turns must be shorter than the lead of the rate of change in output. How much shorter it is impossible now to estimate and almost futile to guess. Meanwhile, let us recall that a lead of half a phase, that is, two 'stages' in National Bureau terminology, amounts to about 13 months in the average expansion and about 10 months in the average contraction. A lag of investment in raw materials behind the rate of change in output of even 6 months would still leave this class of investment leading business turns by several months. This, of course, is presumably subject to considerable irregularity, especially near business peaks, corresponding to the irregularity in the timing of turns in the rate of change in output.

3 Finished Goods

Of the 40 percent of all manufacturers' finished goods stocks, between an eighth and a quarter are made to order. Investment in them, as we have seen, fluctuates like that in goods in process.

Another small class are finished goods sold from stock whose production cycles are influenced mainly from the side of supply. The chief cyclical characteristic of investment in this class is its irregularity. It cannot be important in explaining the typical cyclical pattern of aggregate investment in manufacturers' stocks.

Still a third small category consists of goods sold from stock whose production cycles are governed principally by changes in demand but which, for one reason or another, are perishable. Evidence about the behavior of this group is almost wholly lacking, but general reasoning suggests that since the goods are perishable they must be disposed of promptly; wide variations in the inventory-sales ratio could not be long tolerated. If so, the rate of change in output is again a good guide to the cyclical behavior of investment. But once more it seems plausible that manufacturers will not be able to predict sales accurately enough to modify their holdings of stocks simultaneously with changes in sales. On the contrary, changes in the rate of increase in sales will probably be followed by changes in the rate of increase in output only after an interval, and appropriate changes in stocks will occur somewhat later still. Thus it seems reasonable to think that investment in this class of finished goods lags behind the rate of change in output by a short period, much in the same way as in the case of investment in raw materials.

Whatever the value of this suggestion, it applies to only a small class of stocks—in all likelihood less than 5 percent of all manufacturers' inventories. Because of the nature of the goods, only small stocks can be kept relative to sales. And to reduce still further the risk of inventory losses, many perishable goods industries produce to order rather than to stock.

There remains a last important class of finished goods sold from stock—durable staples whose production cycles are governed by changes in demand—constituting between 20 and 25 percent of manufacturers' stocks. According to the rather good sample of such goods for which records are available, it appears that when shipments turn down after the peak of business, investment leaps up sharply. (I am writing here in the relative sense in which a decline in the rate of liquidation is equivalent to an increase in accumulation.) Manufacturers, presumably caught off guard by an unexpected cyclical decline in sales, were unable to reduce their rate of fabrication soon enough. During at least the early months of most contractions, the rate of accumulation of stocks increases, then levels off. A point in doubt is whether a downturn in investment begins before the trough in business. The marked indications of such a downturn in long contractions, those of three years or longer, are consistent with the finding that in long contractions the peak in stocks of this type is reached well before the upturn in business (Ch. 11). There are good reasons, moreover, for expecting such a downturn in the last part of shorter phases. The stocks that continue to accumulate during contraction, first because the downturn of shipments is not expected, later because manufacturers choose to keep their production from falling as far and fast as their sales, must become an increasing burden on the companies holding them. The motive to reduce the rate at which stocks pile up, if not to begin liquidation, must become stronger and stronger. Finally, there is evidence that toward the end of a business contraction but before the trough, the number of industries whose production is falling diminishes, the number whose production is rising increases. This undoubtedly reflects an increase in the sales of some industries. And when sales increase, the rate of accumulation of finished goods drops sharply. The fact that the number of industries in which this may be presumed to occur grows in the last stage of contraction bolsters the presumption that during this period the aggregate rate of accumulation of these stocks by manufacturers tends to fall.

There are then good reasons for expecting such a decline. But however good the argument, the fact is that our sample does not clearly support such an hypothesis. As far as contractions of short and moderate length are concerned, the matter remains in doubt.

All these observations may be repeated for business expansions. The upturn is accompanied by a sharp reduction in inventory investment. The downward movement continues for some months, then levels off. In long expansions the rate of liquidation falls before the peak in business, then accumulation begins. But in short or moderately long expansions, the evidence that investment turns up before the peak of business is passed is doubtful.

4   Pattern of Total Investment

We are now in a position to offer a partial explanation of the cyclical behavior of manufacturers' inventory investment—its tendency to lag behind the rate of change in output and reach turning points in the neighborhood of the turning points of business cycles. For we can see, at least roughly, the diverse behavior of the major components of total investment, establish their approximate size, and identify the motives and technical conditions that account for their cyclical movement. There are serious gaps, but the account takes us a considerable distance. I shall attempt a highly summarized statement in terms of movements during a business contraction. With some exceptions the account for expansions would follow the same lines except that the direction of inventory movement would be reversed.

1) In the opening stage of a contraction, investment in goods in process and in finished goods made to order, together accounting for 25-30 percent of all manufacturers' holdings, falls rapidly. This rapid drop is a simple concomitant of the sharp reduction in output to which stocks are technically bound.

Investment in raw materials, about 40 percent of the total, falls less rapidly. Manufacturers in general would like to decrease their stocks of raw materials in rough proportion to the decline in the volume of business, but for many reasons cannot. A cyclical downturn in sales seems to catch businessmen unawares. Even if they begin to reduce their orders for supplies immediately, a period of varying length intervenes between order and delivery. The interval may vary from a few days to many months depending upon the distance a manufacturer is from his source of supplies, on the mode of transportation, and on the speed with which suppliers fill orders. In addition, manufacturers are likely to hesitate at first about altering the volume of their purchases, since they are uncertain, at the moment of recession, about the course of business. Some manufacturers, finally, are bound by long term commitments made when the outlook was brighter. These will be canceled if possible, but often they will prevent a reduction in receipts of materials for a long time. As a result, stocks of raw materials continue to rise during the first 3 or 4 months of contraction, though at a declining rate, and then are reduced only gradually.

Offsetting these declines in investment in the first stage of contraction is a rapid increase in investment in finished durables sold from stock. Most such goods are produced in industries in which output is governed principally by changes in demand. (Finished goods of this sort are perhaps 20-25 percent of manufacturers' total stocks.) Again, a decline in business finds manufacturers unprepared. Their sales and shipments drop before they can reduce their output. And when they do reduce it, they do so less rapidly than shipments are falling. Manufacturers apparently prefer to see their stocks of finished goods, which have been largely liquidated in the preceding expansion, pile up rather than curtail their operations more drastically. As the goods in question are durable staples, an accumulation of stocks for the sake of cushioning production somewhat from the impact of declining sales can be tolerated.

The movement of these four categories of investment presumably causes a relatively small decline in total investment. I say presumably because it is a weakness of this account that, with respect to one important matter, it necessarily proceeds in qualitative terms. It is impossible, on the basis of the sample data now available, to measure precisely the relative rates of change in the different categories of stocks. One can say that 25-30 percent of the total fall rapidly, that 40 percent fall slowly, and that another 20-25 percent rise rapidly. I presume that this means a relatively slow rise in total stocks. And this is consistent with the general showing of the comprehensive annual data. But we cannot be certain until adequate monthly data are available for all the significant inventory classes. This is an unavoidable difficulty which qualifies the account of the early part of contraction and restricts equally the significance of the remainder of this hypothesis.

2) Liquidation of goods in process and of finished goods made to order usually increases until about the middle of contraction. Judging by the rate of decline in output, the trough in these categories of investment sometimes precedes, sometimes follows the midpoint, but the rate has usually been higher in the second quarter than in the first and sometimes even higher in the third quarter.

At the same time, the liquidation of raw materials, which lagged in the early months of contraction, begins to proceed more rapidly.

The accumulation or slow liquidation in the first quarter gives rise to redundant inventories relative to the smaller volume of business, and manufacturers are driven to curtail their orders more drastically. Finally, the rate of accumulation of finished goods, if it does not fall off, at least does not continue to increase much. There is, consequently, clear indication that the pace of inventory liquidation accelerates in the middle quarters of contraction, at least until output begins to decline less rapidly.

3) At some point in the last half of contraction output begins to fall at a slower pace. This may sometimes happen even before the midpoint, but, in any event, rarely later than the end of the third or the beginning of the fourth quarter. When it occurs, liquidation of goods in process and of finished goods made to order also begins to fall. Investment in these goods, in the relative sense in which we use the term, rises, but is countered by investment in the other two major groups. Because manufacturers do not foresee changes in the pace of business far enough in advance, investment in raw materials, the largest single group, probably continues to fall for a few months after the rate of decline in output begins to moderate. And because the stocks of finished goods, which have been piling up since the beginning of the phase, become increasingly heavy, manufacturers at least check the increase in their rate of accumulation. If the phase is long enough and prior accumulations heavy enough, liquidation may even start. Thus for a few months after the rate of decline in output begins to diminish, inventory investment in the aggregate probably continues to fall.

4) The preceding analysis explains in brief why inventory investment declines from the beginning of contraction until near the end; also why it tends to lag behind the rate of change in output. But it fails to settle a final question. Does aggregate investment turn up shortly before the revival of business and so help account for the upturn? Annual estimates cannot provide the answer and when we turn to monthly data, we are left equally uncertain. Investment in goods in process and in finished goods made to order certainly tends to rise in the later months of contraction because the peak in the rate of decline in output is usually passed still earlier. More doubtful is the case of raw materials. Since investment in raw materials probably lags behind the rate of change

in output, it may still be declining at the end of contraction. This is the more likely the later the rate of change in output turns up. It is less likely if the rate of change in output turns up early in contraction, as it sometimes does. But even if investment in raw materials begins to rise, the behavior of investment in finished goods is open to question. In long contractions stocks finally become so heavy that either liquidation begins or the rate of accumulation falls before the end of the phase. The same may be true of the somewhat shorter contractions than the 3-year phases I have been calling 'long'. These declines in investment, when they occur, act to offset the increases in the other categories.

I conclude, therefore, that the behavior of investment toward the very end of contraction is highly uncertain. It is determined partly by the lead in the rate of change in output, which varies from cycle to cycle, and partly by the movement of investment in finished goods, which depends upon the length of the phase.

5) The above analysis assumes implicitly that aggregate investment falls in a smooth curve to its trough, then rises. This assumption cannot be confirmed by annual data, and, if it is invalid, another hypothesis is open to us. Let us suppose that the tendency, such as it is, for investment in finished goods to fall before business reaches a trough is not sufficient to offset the increase in investment (decline in the rate of liquidation) in stocks of goods in process, finished goods made to order, and raw materials. Aggregate investment in inventories would then begin to rise before business reached a trough. This tendency may nevertheless be concealed in annual data by events immediately following the business trough. When sales start to rise, there is always a sharp drop in the rate of accumulation of finished goods and a beginning of rapid liquidation. It seems likely also that stocks of raw materials drop rapidly for a short time. In both cases, the reduction in investment may be due to the failure of manufacturers to foresee the rise in sales and to prepare for it by increasing production of finished goods and purchases of raw materials. The result is that aggregate inventory investment in the year of the business cycle trough is reduced by involuntary disinvestment after the (monthly) trough has passed, though it may have been rising due to a planned decline in liquidation before the trough. If this pos-

sibility should be confirmed, and it is not inconsistent with the present evidence, planned inventory investment may be one cause of cyclical revival, though the process is concealed in annual data. 6) During expansions there is a further element of uncertainty. Although the rate of change in output usually reaches a high point in the early part of the phase, then recedes, it has sometimes tended to rise again in the last quarter of expansion. Other things being equal, this should reduce the occasions when investment in manufacturers' inventories leads a downturn compared with the occasions on which it leads upturns.

Despite its many gaps and inadequacies, this account helps to establish and explain two significant aspects of the dynamics of business cycles: the approximate synchronism between business cycles and inventory investment and the lag of inventory investment behind the rate of change in output. For the latter, two general factors are responsible: One is the varying interval required for decision, for liquidation of past commitments, and for purchase, production, and transportation before a change in the rate of output and sales is reflected in the volume of investment in raw materials inventories. The other is the attempt of manufacturers to cushion the impact of changes in sales on production by tolerating large counter-cyclical changes in the stock of finished goods. With more adequate data, these qualitative conclusions may be given more precision, and the moot question settled whether inventory investment regularly operates to initiate revivals and recessions of business at large.

CHAPTER 21

Size of Cyclical Fluctuations in Inventory Investment

*1   Share of Inventory Investment in Movements of Gross
National Product*

The timing of inventory investment indicates the direction in
which it acts on business activity at different stages in the cycle.
The importance of the role of inventory investment depends upon
the size of its fluctuations. Some summary indication was given in
Chapter 1 on the basis of average experience in the interwar period
(Table 1). This preliminary discussion ended with the following
paragraph:

"These estimates are, of course, crude, but they are sufficiently accurate to establish several important propositions. One is that, on the
average, a very considerable portion of the cyclical change in total
output has taken the form of an alteration in the volume of goods
added to stocks. A second is that, during ordinary business cycles,
fluctuations in the rate of inventory investment as a whole have been
larger, in terms of the value of goods involved, than those in construction or in the flow of durable goods to either producers or consumers. And a third proposition is that inventory investment, in terms
of the violence of fluctuation, is the most volatile of the main components of output."

Table 84 subjects these conclusions to more detailed examination to see whether the observations based on averages are equally
valid for individual cycles and are not peculiar to only one or two.
If they are generally valid, fluctuations in inventory investment
will obviously have a very great effect on the movements of gross
national product. For each expansion of general business Table
84 shows the difference between gross national product in the year
of depression with which the expansion starts and that in the year

TABLE 84

Gross National Product and Its Main Components
Changes during 5 Business Cycles, 1919-1938

	AV. AN. VALUE, $ BILLION, 1929 PRICES (1)	CHANGE, $ BILLION, 1929 PRICES Exp. (2)	Contr. (3)	Cycle (4)	CHANGE AS % OF CHANGE IN GNP Exp. (5)	Contr. (6)	Cycle (7)
		FIRST CYCLE: 1919-20-21					
1 Gross national product	66.6	1.4	—3.6	5.0	100.0	100.0	100.0
2 Flow of goods to consumers	52.1	2.0	1.6	0.4	142.9	—44.4	8.0
a Durables	4.7	—0.1	—0.9	0.8	—7.1	25.0	16.0
b Nondurables	28.0	0.1	2.1	—2.0	7.1	—58.3	—40.0
c Services	19.4	2.0	0.3	1.7	142.9	—8.3	34.0
3 Capital formation	14.5	—0.6	—5.1	4.5	—42.9	141.7	90.0
a Construction	5.2	—1.2	0.9	—2.1	—85.7	—25.0	—42.0
1) Public	1.4	—1.1	0.5	—1.6	—78.6	—13.9	—32.0
2) Business	2.2	0.3	—0.1	0.4	21.4	2.8	8.0
3) Residential	1.6	—0.4	0.5	—0.9	—28.6	—13.9	—18.0
b Prod. durable equip.	4.9	—0.1	—1.7	1.6	—7.1	47.2	32.0
c Net change in claims against foreign countries	1.55	—0.7	—0.1	—0.6	—50.0	2.8	—12.0
d Net change in inventories (inventory investment)							
1) Total	2.79	1.4	—4.2	5.6	100.0	116.7	112.0
2) Total, excl. farmers	2.53	0.6	—2.8	3.4	42.9	77.8	68.0
3) Mfr. inventories	1.09	0.4	—1.6	2.0	28.6	44.4	40.0
		SECOND CYCLE: 1921-23-24					
1 Gross national product	73.3	14.6	1.5	13.1	100.0	100.0	100.0
2 Flow of goods to consumers	59.4	8.1	4.1	4.0	55.5	273.3	30.5
a Durables	5.7	2.6	0.3	2.3	17.8	20.0	17.6
b Nondurables	32.2	3.7	1.0	2.7	25.3	66.7	20.6
c Services	21.5	1.9	2.8	—0.9	13.0	186.7	—6.9
3 Capital formation	13.9	6.4	—2.7	9.1	43.8	—180.0	69.5
a Construction	7.6	2.5	1.0	1.5	17.1	66.7	11.5
1) Public	1.6	—0.1	0.3	—0.4	—0.7	20.0	—3.1
2) Business	2.7	0.7	0.1	0.6	4.8	6.7	4.6
3) Residential	3.4	1.9	0.6	1.3	13.0	40.0	9.9
b Prod. durable equip.	4.8	2.2	—0.4	2.6	15.1	—26.7	19.8
c Net change in claims against foreign countries	0.54	—1.1	0.4	—1.5	—7.5	26.7	—11.5
d Net change in inventories (inventory investment)							
1) Total	0.88	2.8	—3.7	6.5	19.2	—246.7	49.6
2) Total, excl. farmers	1.17	2.3	—2.9	5.2	15.8	—193.3	39.7
3) Mfr. inventories	0.69	1.4	—1.6	3.0	9.6	—106.7	22.9
		THIRD CYCLE: 1924-26-27					
1 Gross national product	85.4	8.2	1.0	7.2	100.0	100.0	100.0
2 Flow of goods to consumers	67.9	4.0	1.7	2.3	48.8	170.0	31.9
a Durables	8.0	1.7	—0.4	2.1	20.7	—40.0	29.2
b Nondurables	35.8	2.0	1.7	0.3	24.4	170.0	4.2
c Services	24.1	0.3	0.4	—0.1	3.7	40.0	—1.4
3 Capital formation	17.5	4.3	—0.7	5.0	52.4	—70.0	69.4
a Construction	10.3	1.6	0.1	1.5	19.5	10.0	20.8
1) Public	2.0	0.3	0.3	0	3.7	30.0	0
2) Business	3.6	1.0	0.1	0.9	12.2	10.0	12.5
3) Residential	4.7	0.4	—0.3	0.7	4.9	—30.0	9.7
b Prod. durable equip.	6.1	1.1	—0.4	1.5	13.4	—40.0	20.8
c Net change in claims against foreign countries	0.31	—0.5	0.3	—0.8	—6.1	30.0	—11.1
d Net change in inventories (inventory investment)							
1) Total	0.85	2.1	—0.8	2.9	25.6	—80.0	40.3
2) Total, excl. farmers	0.99	2.1	—1.3	3.1	22.0	—130.0	43.1
3) Mfr. inventories	0.27	0.6	—0.8	1.4	7.3	—80.0	19.4

TABLE 84 (Concl.)

	AV. AN. VALUE, $ BILLION, 1929 PRICES (1)	CHANGE, $ BILLION, 1929 PRICES			CHANGE AS % OF CHANGE IN GNP		
		Exp. (2)	Contr. (3)	Cycle (4)	Exp. (5)	Contr. (6)	Cycle (7)
		FOURTH CYCLE: 1927-29-32					
1 Gross national product	86.7	7.6	—32.0	39.6	100.0	100.0	100.0
2 Flow of goods to consumers	72.1	4.7	—15.2	19.9	61.8	47.5	50.3
a Durables	7.2	0.6	—4.5	5.1	7.9	14.1	12.9
b Nondurables	37.8	1.8	—4.4	6.2	23.7	13.8	15.7
c Services	27.0	2.3	—6.2	8.5	30.3	19.4	21.5
3 Capital formation	14.6	2.8	—16.7	19.5	36.8	52.2	49.2
a Construction	8.9	—0.5	—5.8	5.3	—6.6	18.1	13.4
1) Public	2.6	0.1	—0.2	0.3	1.3	0.6	0.8
2) Business	3.4	0.1	—2.9	3.0	1.3	9.1	7.6
3) Residential	2.9	—0.8	—2.7	1.9	—10.5	8.4	4.8
b Prod. durable equip.	5.7	1.4	—5.0	6.4	18.4	15.6	16.2
c Net change in claims against foreign countries	0.47	0	—0.4	0.4	0	1.2	1.0
d Net change in inventories (inventory investment)							
1) Total	—0.37	2.0	—5.6	7.6	26.3	17.5	19.2
2) Total, excl. farmers	—0.48	2.0	—6.1	8.1	26.3	19.1	20.5
3) Mfr. inventories	0.21	1.5	—2.4	3.9	19.7	7.5	9.8
		FIFTH CYCLE: 1932-37-38					
1 Gross national product	79.0	28.7	—3.1	31.8	100.0	100.0	100.0
2 Flow of goods to consumers	69.8	17.8	0.7	17.1	62.0	—22.6	53.8
a Durables	5.7	3.0	—1.4	4.4	10.5	45.2	13.8
b Nondurables	39.8	8.7	0.1	8.6	30.3	—3.2	27.0
c Services	24.3	6.0	2.0	4.0	20.9	—64.5	12.6
3 Capital formation	9.2	11.0	—3.9	14.9	38.3	125.8	46.9
a Construction	4.5	1.3	—0.2	1.5	4.5	6.5	4.7
1) Public	1.9	—0.1	0.2	—0.3	—0.3	—6.5	—0.9
2) Business	1.2	0.4	—0.4	0.8	1.4	12.9	2.5
3) Residential	1.4	0.9	0.2	0.7	3.1	—6.5	2.2
b Prod. durable equip.	4.4	4.1	—1.9	6.0	14.3	61.3	18.9
c Net change in claims against foreign countries	0.08	—0.2	1.1	—1.3	—0.7	—35.5	—4.1
d Net change in inventories (inventory investment)							
1) Total	0.18	5.8	—2.9	8.7	20.2	93.5	27.4
2) Total, excl. farmers	0.26	5.4	—2.4	7.8	18.8	77.4	24.5
3) Mfr. inventories	0.13	3.2	—2.6	5.8	11.1	83.9	18.2
		AVERAGE OF FIVE CYCLES					
1 Gross national product	79.8	12.1	—7.2	19.3	100.0	100.0	100.0
2 Flow of goods to consumers	66.5	7.3	—1.4	8.7	60.5	19.6	45.2
a Durables	6.3	1.6	—1.4	2.9	12.9	19.1	15.2
b Nondurables	36.2	3.3	0.1	3.2	26.9	—1.4	16.3
c Services	24.0	2.5	—0.1	2.6	20.7	1.9	13.7
3 Capital formation	13.3	4.8	—5.8	10.6	39.3	80.4	54.8
a Construction	7.1	0.7	—0.8	1.5	6.1	11.0	8.0
1) Public	2.0	—0.2	0.2	—0.4	—1.5	—3.0	—2.1
2) Business	2.5	0.5	—0.6	1.1	4.1	8.8	5.9
3) Residential	2.6	0.4	—0.3	0.7	3.3	4.7	3.8
b Prod. durable equip.	5.1	1.7	—1.9	3.6	14.4	26.0	18.7
c Net change in claims against foreign countries	0.50	—0.5	0.3	—0.8	—4.1	—3.6	—3.9
d Net change in inventories (inventory investment)							
1) Total	0.56	2.8	—3.4	6.3	23.3	47.5	32.4
2) Total, excl. farmers	0.58	2.4	—3.1	5.5	20.0	42.8	28.5
3) Mfr. inventories	0.36	1.4	—1.8	3.2	11.7	24.9	16.6

Sources and method of computation are described in notes to Table 1 except for the average cycle values shown in col. 1. To avoid downward bias the average value for each cycle is computed by weighting the years of initial and terminal trough one-half, and the other years included in a cycle one.

of prosperity with which the expansion ends. For each contraction it shows the difference between gross national product in the year of prosperity with which the contraction begins and that in the year of depression with which the contraction ends. The total change in gross national product during the expansion and contraction that make up a full cycle (measured from trough to trough) is computed by adding the change in gross national product during expansion to its change during contraction (signs disregarded).[1] Table 84 shows also the same sort of calculation for each of the principal components of total output. And each absolute change in a component is expressed also as a percentage of the change in total product during the same period. For easy reference the averages of Table 1 are repeated.[2]

The preliminary conclusions of Chapter 1 are well supported by the data for individual cycles. No less than 17.5 percent of the change in gross national product took the form of a change in inventory investment in any single phase (expansion or contraction). For full cycles the minimum figure, which occurred in 1927-32, was 19 percent. At the other extreme the change in inventory investment in one contraction, 1923-24, was nearly two and one-half times as big as the change in gross national product. Inventory investment moved down during this business recession but gross national product measured by annual data increased slightly. The maximum figure for a full cycle, that of 1919-21, was 112 percent. Excluding investment by farmers, the figures are only slightly smaller. Investment in manufacturing industries alone accounted for a large share, ranging from 28 to 100 percent of the change in all inventories and averaging almost exactly one-half.

Cycle by cycle fluctuations in the rate of inventory investment as a whole have also involved larger changes in the value of goods

---

[1] The mild business contractions of 1923-24 and 1926-27 appear in the annual gross product estimates only as virtual cessations of growth, not as actual declines. In these cases we *subtracted* the change during contraction from that during expansion to get the change over the full cycle. In effect, we treated the growth during contraction as a negative response to the business cycle.

[2] Similar computations were presented in NBER *Bulletin 74*. The importance of fluctuations in inventory investment in changes in gross national product has been emphasized also by Alvin H. Hansen, *Fiscal Policy and Business Cycles*, Ch. 1; see below, Sec. 3.

produced than in producer durables, consumer durables, or total construction. Indeed, the difference in total inventory investment between prosperity and depression was usually about twice as large as that in the first two categories, and more than twice as large as that in the third. The change in manufacturers' inventory investment alone was usually about as large as that in the output of producer and consumer durables and larger than that in construction.

Volatility is a vexed question on two counts. It suggests some measure of relative amplitude, that is, a comparison between the absolute size of the swing in a series and its normal level. However, some of the present series have negative values, notably the inventory investment series themselves. In consequence, their average level for the entire period approaches zero and in some cycles is negative.[3] Percentage computations in such cases give absurd results. True computations of volatility, in the sense stated above, are therefore impossible. But speaking loosely, there can be little question that inventory investment is extremely unstable. Imagine, for example, that manufacturers' inventory investment were $2 billion higher each year and that total inventory investment was $4 billion higher, thus eliminating all negative values. The average level of total inventory investment (either including or excluding farming) would still not exceed the average level of the output of consumer or producer durables or of total construction. And the average level of manufacturers' inventory investment would be about half as high. The relative amplitude of inventory investment in toto or by manufacturers alone would still be larger than the relative amplitudes of these other volatile series.

This, however, raises a second problem. While inventory investment is, of course, measured net, the output of producer durables and of construction is measured gross, that is, before depreciation is deducted. Since depreciation varies little during business cycles, the total cyclical swing of these activities would be little, if at all, reduced on a net basis; but their average levels would be markedly lower. Net output of producer durables is, of course, far more volatile than gross output. But for the analysis of business

[3] The same is true of 'net changes in claims against foreign countries'.

cycles the comparison between net additions to inventories and gross additions to other capital is the correct one. Decisions to purchase or produce plant and durable equipment over and above the quantity required to replace plant and equipment retired depend upon the same set of considerations as influence purchases to offset retirements. Both depend upon estimates of the profitability of the capital in the future, not simply on the operations of the current period. And since replacements rarely have the same technical capacity as the equipment retired, it is doubtful that a clear line can be drawn between production or purchase for replacement and that for additions to durable equipment. There can be little question, however, that businessmen do distinguish between purchase or production of goods for sale or consumption in the current period and that for addition to inventory, and base their decisions about each on different considerations. Subject to what has already been said about unplanned inventory investment it is this fact that makes it useful to study inventory investment in analyzing business cycles.

These questions aside, there are still qualifications to be borne in mind when studying Table 84. They do not, I think, affect the major showing of the data, but they are important. Annual estimates typically understate the size of cyclical fluctuations and do so in different degree in different cycles and in different series.[4] Monthly data would undoubtedly change the size of the cyclical swings in inventory investment compared with those in other elements of capital formation, but I would not expect my general observations about relative magnitudes to be modified.

Another consideration is that Table 84 shows the size of cyclical changes during fixed periods, namely, those bounded by the business cycle peaks and troughs identified by the National Bureau. It does not show the magnitude of the cycles in individual series. In annual data this has little effect upon the cyclical amplitude of the two inventory investment series or upon that of the output of producer durables. It does, however, reduce significantly the am-

---

[4] While quarterly estimates of gross national product are available (notably in Barger's *Outlay and Income in the United States, 1921-1938*) I do not regard quarterly estimates of aggregate or manufacturers' inventories to be sufficiently reliable for these purposes.

plitude of the fluctuations in consumer durables and construction. The reason is that the first three series responded regularly, and almost synchronously, to the ups and downs of business in the interwar period.[5] The last two, however, not only declined during the business expansion of 1919-20 but skipped the mild contraction of 1923-24; construction also skipped that of 1926-27. Nevertheless, the relations previously discerned among the cyclical magnitudes of the series still hold good if we confine our observations to the last cycle when all five series conformed closely to the movements of business at large. And the same is true if we extend our observations to 1926-38 when all except construction conformed closely to the calendar year reference dates.

We must repeat the cautionary note sounded above. The figures show how much of the change in total output between the trough and peak of business took the form of a change in the rate of inventory investment. They do not tell how much of the change in output was caused by a change in the rate of inventory investment, because the inventory investment figures include some unplanned investment or disinvestment and hence either overstate or understate the actual quantity of output that can be traced to some businessman's desire to increase his stock. Such unplanned changes in stock are, no doubt, less important in annual than in monthly data, but they are always present in some degree.

Finally, although a large portion of the cyclical changes in gross national product typically takes the form of a change in inventory investment, the share of inventory investment has varied a great deal from cycle to cycle. These variations are not entirely haphazard. If we classify our data by the length of expansion and contraction, an inverse relation is apparent between the length of the phase and the share of changes in inventory investment in changes in gross national product (Table 85). Despite some variation, the trend of the figures in each column is clearly downward the longer the phase, and the inverse relation stands out still more boldly if we average the figures for phases that lasted about a year, those that lasted about 2 years, and those that lasted about 4 years.

---

[5] Producer durables declined slightly from 1919 to 1920 when business was rising.

TABLE 85

Cyclical Changes in Inventory Investment as Percentage of Changes
in Gross National Product, by Length of Phase, 1919-1938

| LENGTH OF PHASE, YEARS* | CHANGE AS % OF CHANGE IN GNP | | |
	Total	Total, excl. farmers	Mfg.
.67	100	43	29
1.00	93	77	84
1.17	−247	−193	−107
1.17	−80	−130	−80
1.50	26	26	20
1.67	117	78	44
1.67	19	16	10
2.25	26	22	7
3.75	17	19	7
4.17	20	19	11
AVERAGES FOR PHASES OF STATED LENGTH[a]			
.67 & 1.00	96	60	56
1.50-2.25	47	36	20
3.75 & 4.17	19	19	9

* Derived from the National Bureau monthly reference cycle chronology.
[a] Phases with negative figures omitted.

2   *Factors Determining the Relative Size of Fluctuations in
Inventory Investment and in Gross National Product*

This section attempts to identify the causes of the two chief characteristics of the size of fluctuations in inventory investment: the
relatively large fraction they typically constitute of the cyclical
fluctuations in gross national product and the tendency of the
fraction to diminish the longer the expansion or contraction. We
consider first an oversimplified and, in many ways, unrealistic system, whose operation can be expressed in easy formulas. Later we
allow for the main differences between the imaginary economy described by our formulas and the more intricate economy of the real
world.

Our imaginary economy has two features important for present
purposes. First, the inventory-output ratio remains constant. This
has its elements of reality, for most businessmen try to maintain an
approximately constant ratio for most of their inventories, and
wide departures from the desired ratio will not be tolerated indefinitely. But we know also that there are often large divergences

which may persist for months. We shall have to allow for them later. The second feature concerns the pattern of cyclical fluctuations. We assume that the absolute increase in output per unit of time is constant during expansions, that the absolute decline in output is constant during contractions, and that the rates of increase and decline are equal. These assumptions taken together imply that the increase in inventories per unit of time will be constant and proportionate to the rate of increase in output.

We may now write the following equation for inventory investment in a peak year of business (I_1):

1) $I_1 = Ptr$, where

$P =$ the average value of gross national product during the preceding cycle, measured from peak to peak

$t =$ the inventory-gross national product ratio

$r =$ the annual rate of increase in gross national product during expansion

The decline in inventories during the preceding trough year of business (I_2) would be:

2) $I_2 = Pt \ (-r)$

For the whole expansion the increase in output that takes the form of an increase in inventory investment is the difference between the amount added to stock in the peak year and the amount liquidated in the preceding trough year. Writing ΔI for $I_1 - I_2$, we have:

3) $\Delta I = Ptr - Pt \ (-r) = 2 \ Ptr$

The total increase in output during expansion (ΔO) may be written:

4) $\Delta O = Pra$, where

$a =$ the length of expansion in years, and P and r are defined as in (1).

Finally, the ratio of the change in inventory investment to the total change in output $\left(\dfrac{\Delta I}{\Delta O} \right)$ is:

5) $\dfrac{\Delta I}{\Delta O} = \dfrac{2 \ Ptr}{Pra} = \dfrac{2 \ t}{a}$

We may say, then, that the share of the change in inventory investment in the total change in gross national product during an expansion depends directly upon the size of t, the inventory-output ratio, and that it varies inversely with a, the length of the phase. Of course, exactly the same thing would be true of contractions.

Given the assumptions, the bases and implications of the formula can be grasped intuitively by considering the following facts:

a)   The proportion that a given annual increase in output bears to the accompanying increase in inventories depends upon the inventory-output ratio. If the ratio is $1:4$, when output increases $100 inventories will increase $25.

b)   The change in inventory investment between a trough and a peak equals the difference in the amount of stocks accumulated in the last year of expansion and the amount liquidated in the last year of contraction. Hence the proportionate relation between a given annual increase in output and the change in inventory investment between a cyclical trough and peak must be some multiple of the inventory-output ratio. If the annual increase in output and inventories in expansion equals the decline in contraction, the multiple is, of course, 2.

c)   The change in inventory investment between a trough and a peak is, however, not to be compared with a single year's increase in output, but rather with the cumulative increase during all the years of an expansion. Given a constant absolute annual increase in output, the total change between trough and peak equals the annual increase multiplied by the number of years the expansion lasts. Hence the length of the expansion in years is the denominator of the fraction.

This summary formulation draws attention to two important and valid aspects of a true explanation of the contribution of inventory investment to general business fluctuations. One is the size of the inventory-sales ratio in the United States. The technique and organization of our economy are such that the inventories carried to facilitate production and sales are large relative to the output or sales of a year. Excluding farm stocks, which behave erratically and to which the theory does not apply, the ratio during the interwar period was about .34. Thus a given increase in output should be accompanied by inventory accumulation about

34 percent as large. And the change in inventory investment between the beginning and end of expansions or contractions should, on our preliminary assumptions, be 68 percent of the change in output during one-year phases and proportionately less during longer phases. The second point is that business cycles in the United States have typically been short. Four of the five contractions in the interwar period lasted 20 months or less, and four of the five expansions lasted 27 months or less. The simple theory outlined above suggests that the combination of a large inventory-output ratio and short cycle phases will usually produce high ratios of changes in inventory investment to changes in gross national product, and this is what we find (Table 85).

We must now make a closer comparison between the theoretical values that may be derived from our formula with the observed shares of inventory investment. Since the argument on which the formula is based clearly does not apply to farm stocks, the calculations are confined to total investment excluding farming and to investment by manufacturers. As stated, the inventory-output ratio, t, was about .34 during 1919-38; the corresponding ratio for manufacturers was about .16.[6] Theoretical values for the share of changes in inventory investment were calculated from these ratios and from the actual length of expansions and contractions as shown in the National Bureau monthly chronology of business cycles (Table 86).

Despite the wide differences in individual phases between the actual and theoretical values of inventory investment the values tend to be roughly similar, since averaging the figures for phases of about the same length greatly reduces the differences. The largest divergences are in the shortest phases, for which, as will be seen, there is a good reason. Moreover, the extreme differences appear in the two phases lasting 1.17 years—the mild contractions of 1923-24 and 1926-27, when inventory investment dropped markedly but the annual estimates of gross national product rose slightly. This made the changes in inventory investment very large compared with the (inverse) change in gross national product.

[6] The average value of nonfarm stocks in current prices was about $26 billion, that of manufacturers' stocks about $12 billion. Gross national product was about $76 billion on the average. These figures are based on Kuznets' estimates from which the inventory investment figures were derived.

TABLE 86

Cyclical Changes in Inventory Investment: Theoretical and Actual
Shares in Changes in Gross National Product, 1919-1938

	CHANGE AS % OF CHANGE IN GNP			
	TOTAL, EXCL. FARMERS		MANUFACTURING	
LENGTH OF PHASE, YEARS (a)	Theoretical values $\left(\dfrac{2t}{a}\right)$	Actual values	Theoretical values $\left(\dfrac{2t}{a}\right)$	Actual values
.67	91	43	43	29
1.00	68	77	32	84
1.17	58	−193	27	−107
1.17	58	−130	27	−80
1.50	45	26	21	20
1.67	41	78	19	44
1.67	41	16	19	10
2.25	30	22	14	7
3.75	18	19	9	7
4.17	16	19	8	11
	AVERAGES FOR PHASES OF STATED LENGTH*			
.67 & 1.00	69	60	32	56
1.50-2.25	39	36	18	20
3.75 & 4.17	17	19	8	9

* Phases with negative figures omitted.

The observed discrepancies are no less than might be expected
in view of the unreal elements in the theory on which the formula
is based. The essential requirement of the theory is that inventory
investment in the last time-unit of an expansion or contraction—
in this case the last year—be proportionate to the average absolute
increase in output per time unit during the phase. This in turn
would occur if (a) the absolute rate of change in output were constant during a phase, (b) the rate of growth in output during
(say) expansion were equal to the rate of decline during the preceding contraction, and (c) the inventory-output ratio remained
constant so that changes in inventory were always proportionate to
changes in output.

None of these requirements is wholly satisfied by the output and
inventory cycles we observe. The rate of change in output is not
constant over an entire phase. As we have seen, it usually increases
to a maximum, often early in a phase, then tends to grow or decline
at a lower rate. Irregular movements are common, and especially
in expansions output often tends to spurt toward the end of the
phase. Rarely, therefore, will the rate of change in output at the

end of the phase just equal the average rate during the phase. On the other hand, the irregularities characterizing the rate of change in output make it unlikely that the differences between the average and end of phase movements will be systematic.

Next, the rate of change in output during a given phase will rarely equal that during the preceding phase. While there is no evidence that expansions and contractions usually have different paces, the rate of change does vary from one phase of the business cycle to the next. Therefore, even if we could assume that the inventory-output ratio is always constant, the change in inventory investment per annum would seldom be exactly proportionate during any given phase to twice the rate of change in output per annum.

Finally, the inventory-output ratio is not constant because changes in inventory are not proportionate to changes in output during the same period. During the first 6-12 months of expansion of output, stocks continue the decline begun during the preceding contraction, although at a slower pace. Thereafter they grow, first slowly, then more rapidly, attaining a maximum at or near the peak of the business cycle. During contractions of output, similarly, stocks usually continue to grow, though at a slower pace, during most of the first year; thereafter they decline at an increasing pace, being most rapidly liquidated near the trough in business.

In these circumstances, it is easy to see why there are so many large discrepancies in individual cycles between the actual change in inventory investment relative to the change in gross national product and the relation indicated by the formula. But why does the formula yield results that are satisfactory in a general way? Why do the average shares for inventory investment approach the theoretical shares, attaining large values in short phases and varying inversely to the length of the phase? An answer can be formulated in general terms.

The relation between output and most categories of inventories is such that one cannot long increase or decline substantially faster than the other. If they did, stocks would become either intolerably large or inconveniently small compared with output, and businessmen would take corrective measures. For the function of most classes of stocks is precisely to facilitate output or sales. This is obvious for the bulk of stocks held by retailers and wholesalers. Most manufacturers' stocks are in one of four classes: goods in process, materials or finished goods in transit, reserves held against delays in delivery, or finished goods ordered and awaiting delivery. For all these purposes, the amount of stocks required is controlled by the rate of output or sales. The inventory-output ratio may vary, but it cannot increase or decline indefinitely without setting off a corrective reaction.

As far as can now be judged from our studies of manufacturers' stocks, when the rate of change in output leaps upward at the beginning of expansion—or downward at the beginning of contraction—businessmen are unable, and, with respect to some classes of stocks, unwilling to effectuate a simultaneous and comparable movement of inventories. Not until the better part of a year has passed are the inertial forces derived from the preceding phase so far overcome that stocks begin to move in the same direction as output. As the first year of a phase proceeds, more and more businessmen accept the fact that the cycle has definitely turned, and more are able to free themselves from old commitments. At the same time, a growing disproportion between output and stocks emphasizes the necessity for energetic measures to bring the latter into line.

In the first year of a phase, then, the net change in inventories will be small—either the preceding movement will continue at a slower pace or a small movement in the opposite direction will start. The difference between the change in output and in inventories is large in this stage. Not until the second year of a phase does accumulation or liquidation of stocks pick up speed. From that time forth, inventories may change more slowly or faster than output,[7] but their pace, though it may lag, cannot continue to differ widely from that of output without producing an intolerable departure of inventory-output ratios from the levels businessmen consider efficient. The rate of change in output in the later stages of a phase may, and in most individual instances will, differ from the average rate during the phase, but there is no general rule

[7] The indications are that the movement of inventories continues, on the whole, somewhat more slowly than that of output since inventory-output ratios vary inversely to output until near the end of phases.

about the difference between them. The average rate will some-times be higher, sometimes lower. We may, therefore, conclude that the rates of change in stocks in the latter part of a phase will, on the average, be similar to the average rate of change in output during a phase. In the same way, if there is no large systematic difference between the pace of expansions and of contractions, the difference between inventory investment at the end of any given phase and at the end of the preceding phase will, on the average, be about twice the size of either.

This argument applies to phases long enough for inventories to overcome their initial lag behind output, that is, phases of two years or more—the usual duration. But what about shorter phases? Does our argument imply that the change in inventory investment is unlikely to absorb a large part of the change in national product? On the contrary, it suggests merely that inventory investment or disinvestment in the given phase is unlikely to be large. The change from the rate of investment at the end of the preceding phase may well be large, as it was in each of the four short contractions of the interwar period. Three followed expansions of two years or longer, which ended with high rates of inventory accumulation. The fourth, 1920-21, followed the great speculative accumulation of 1919-20. Therefore, while liquidation was large in only one of these short contractions, the reduction in the rate of accumulation from that ruling at the end of the preceding expansion accounted for large reductions in output and income. In general, it would take a short contraction following a short expansion to create a presumption that a cyclical change in inventory investment would not be large relative to a change in gross national product.

The large share of the cyclical changes in gross national product that typically takes the form of a change in inventory investment is founded on a particular combination of time factors: the length of the usual cycle phase and the lag of changes in inventories behind those in output. Given the lag, changes in inventories would be a less aggravating agent in business cycles were it not that cyclical phases exceed a year. For in a phase that lasted only a year, the rate of change in stocks at the end of the phase would probably be small. It might even operate in a counter-cyclical direction as often as not. And given the duration of phases, the course and characteristics of the cycle would be different did inventory investment not lag behind the rate of change in output. For if output and stocks moved together, the swings of output would be strongly reinforced early in each phase by parallel movements in inventory investment. And inventory investment in turn would tend to fall off later in the phase as the rate of change in output often does in expansion and usually does in contraction. It would not sweep up smoothly until the end, or near the end, of expansion and down until near the end of contraction.

This formulation, however, is in an important sense unreal. The combination of phase length and inventory lag is not fortuitous. As we have seen, in contractions the rate of decline in output has usually reached a maximum well before the end of the phase, oftener than not in the first half. Thereafter it slackened. If we now suppose that inventory investment and the rate of change in output move synchronously, the rapid decline in output in the first half of contraction would be aggravated by an equally rapid decline in stocks. When the rate of decline in output falls, however, inventory liquidation also would decline. This would constitute a powerful force for revival. These considerations suggest, therefore, that if inventories changed synchronously and proportionately with sales, business cycles would be shorter and more violent than they are. The lag of inventory investment tempers the effect of the early decline in sales on output. But when the rate of decline (or growth) of sales begins to fall off, more rapid inventory liquidation operates to extend, rather than to halt and reverse, the swing of business. And similar considerations apply to expansions. The lag of inventory investment thus helps to account for a notable feature of expansions and contractions: business usually continues to move in the same direction for many months after its pace has begun to slacken. By the same token, it helps account for the fact that cyclical phases usually last two years and often longer during which inventory investment (or liquidation), despite its tendency to lag, reaches high levels. On the other hand, since phases rarely exceed three years, their length does not usually act as a drag, bringing the share of inventory investment in changes in gross national product to a low level.

There are indeed good reasons for believing that the relation between the length of expansions or contractions and the share of inventory investment in changes in gross national product must be inverse. For, as we have seen, if changes in output per unit of time are constant during a phase and changes in inventory are proportionate, an inverse relation is inevitable. This would not be true if we assumed that the rate of change in output increased sufficiently rapidly during a phase. But the assumption would be unrealistic (Ch. 16).

Must the relation be inverse if we make the realistic assumption that inventory movements lag behind those in output at the trough (peak) of business and increase (decline) steadily until the peak (trough)? It must, provided certain restrictions on the variation of inventory-output ratios are accepted. Consider an hypothetical expansion from a trough in an imaginary Year O.

CASE 1

		Y E A R				
		0	*1*	*2*	*3*	*4*
1	Gross national product	100	110	120	130	140
2	Change in GNP between Year O & given year	..	10	20	30	40
3	Inventories (end of year)	40	40	43.2	46.8	50.4
4	Inventory investment	−4.0	0	+3.2	+3.6	+3.8
5	Change in inventory investment between Year O & given year	..	+4.0	+7.2	+7.6	+7.8
6	Ratio: line 5 ÷ line 2	..	.40	.36	.25	.195
7	Inventory - output ratio: line 3 ÷ line 1	.40	.36	.36	.36	.36

The special assumptions of Case 1 are:
a) Inventory investment in the trough year equals 40 percent of the annual change in output assumed. This is reasonable in the last year of a phase in view of the over-all inventory-output ratio in this country.
b) The annual increases in output are constant. The trend of the figures in line 6 would be still more strongly downward if we assumed that output increased at a declining rate. It would not necessarily be downward if the rate of growth in output increased rapidly enough. But, as stated, to assume increasing rates of growth throughout a phase is unrealistic.
c) Inventories do not show any net change during the first year

of expansion. This corresponds approximately with the facts and reflects the long lag of stocks behind output.

d)   The inventory-output ratio falls in the first year, reflecting the lag of stocks behind output, then remains constant. The trend in line 6 would be still more strongly downward if we assumed, in accordance with the evidence (Ch. 6), that the inventory-output ratio continues to decline at least slowly until near the peak of business. But the ratio of the change in inventory investment to that in gross national product need not decline as the expansion lengthens if the inventory-output ratio is allowed to increase.

Case 2 illustrates a situation in which the share of inventory investment in the cyclical rise of gross national product remains constant. But the implications are such as to make this situation unlikely in the real world. The inventory-output ratio rises 28 percent from the first year of expansion to the fourth, the rate of rise accelerating each year. This, moreover, is the ratio of aggregate stocks to aggregate output. Since many categories of stocks lag behind output by more than a year or vary inversely, inventory-output ratios for other categories must rise even more swiftly. A tendency for inventories to increase so much more rapidly than sales would probably be checked by a reduction in inventory accumulation. A stable ratio of change in inventory investment to that in gross national product could be consistent with a stable inventory-output ratio only if output increased at an ever faster pace. And the acceleration in output growth would need to be still more rapid if the inventory-output ratio were to decline during expansions and rise during contractions, as it appears to have done. In

Case 2

		Y E A R				
		0	1	2	3	4
1	Gross national product	100	110	120	130	140
2	Change in GNP between Year O & given year	..	10	20	30	40
3	Inventories (end of year)	40	40	44	52	64
4	Inventory investment	−4	0	+4	+8	+12
5	Change in inventory investment between Year O & given year	..	+4	+8	+12	+16
6	Ratio: line 5 ÷ line 2	..	.40	.40	.40	.40
7	Inventory - output ratio: line 3 ÷ line 1	.40	.36	.37	.40	.46

the light of experience, however, continued acceleration in output growth or decline is an inadmissible assumption.

The tendency for the share of change in gross national product that takes the form of a change in inventory investment to be smaller the longer the phase rests, it appears, on two circumstances: (a) the tendency for the inventory-output ratio to vary inversely to output; (b) the fact that the rate of change in output does not continue to accelerate during expansions and contractions. The inverse movement of the inventory-output ratio may be traced to the conglomeration of factors that together control the volume of stocks—the desire of businessmen to keep stocks of most kinds in line with output or sales; the obstacles to prompt adjustment of stocks to changes in sales, especially the time required for purchasing, production, and transportation, and the difficulties of forecasting; finally, the fact that some kinds of stocks are used as buffers to cyclical changes in demand. The cyclical pattern of changes in output, however, raises problems far beyond the scope of this book. For present purposes, we must accept it as a fact, established empirically and to be explained only by a more comprehensive investigation of business cycles.

3 Short Cycles, Minor Cycles, and Inventory Cycles

The analysis in preceding sections shows that changes in inventory investment are significant in short expansions and contractions. But the longer the phase, the smaller the contribution of inventory investment to the further advance or decline of business. Conversely, the longer the phase, the more it must depend upon consumers' expenditures or business investment in plant and durable equipment for its motive force. In this significant but limited sense, it seems appropriate to think of short cycles as inventory cycles while longer movements are identified with other categories of demand. Short expansions or contractions would be far milder than those we have experienced were it not for the action of inventory investment. Longer phases, say of 3 years or more, could not have occurred without the increasing intervention of changes in consumer or business expenditure that are independent of inventory movements. For after that interval further change in inventory investment, if there is any, is likely to be quite small.

While this aspect of the role of inventories in fluctuations of different length should be recognized, it leaves open another vital question: why do some movements end after 12 or 15 months while others last 4 or 5 years? The outcome may turn on the entire assemblage of forces controlling expenditures on producer durable and consumer goods. These may at times make for a strong sustained increase in demand while at other times their strength is quickly exhausted and a decline ensues. If this is the case, there is nothing to add to what was said in the preceding paragraph.

Several writers, however, have developed a more systematic conception of the relation between short and long cycles in business. Professor Hansen, for example, following the lead of Professor Schumpeter, distinguishes 50 year "long waves", 8 year "major" cycles, and 3 or 4 year "minor" cycles.[8] The long waves and major cycles he attributes to innovations, that is, to investment in construction work and durable equipment associated with the business exploitation of significant developments in technology, business organization, the geography of markets, and the like. The minor cycles he believes are caused "not infrequently" by fluctuations in inventory investment.

The general thesis that business cycles may be arranged in sets of 2 or 3 that together constitute a cycle of a higher order—minor cycles, in Hansen's terminology, combining to make major cycles —is too broad to be examined here. Some preliminary tests by Burns and Mitchell repay study.[9] Here we are especially interested in the possibility that the minor cycles in Hansen's multi-cycle theory are, in some significant sense, inventory cycles.

With respect to this question, Hansen's ideas appear to rest upon his analysis of 1921-32. He observed that the business contractions of 1923-24 and 1926-27 were especially mild. Annual estimates of gross national product in constant prices did not decline, and several important categories of output skipped one or both contractions. He therefore regards 1921-29 as a single major expansion interrupted by two minor recessions. Together with the long and severe contraction of 1929-32, it makes up a major cycle. Hansen points out (Ch. 2) that if we treat this period as a major

[8] Op. cit., Ch. 1.
[9] *Measuring Business Cycles,* Ch. 11.

cycle: "Unlike investment in plant and equipment . . . inventory investment does not progressively sustain the recovery during an entire major upswing. On the contrary, the upswing is checked, at intervals of three to four years, by disinvestment in inventories, or a decline in the rate of accumulation. It is this ebb and flow of inventories which apparently dominates the minor cycle." In the terminology of preceding sections, Hansen finds that the portion of the change in gross national product taking the form of a change in inventory investment was much smaller in the major upswing 1921-29 than in the minor fluctuations within that period.[10] The validity of this observation may be seen in Table 87 which analyzes the major cycle 1921-32 in the same form as the business cycles identified by the National Bureau are analyzed in Table 84. The share of inventory investment was drastically lower in the long cycle 1921-32 than in the five shorter cycles of the interwar period. The difference is especially marked in comparisons between the long expansion 1921-29 and the short expansions. The share of inventory investment in the expansion of gross national product between 1921 and 1929 was only 7.3 percent; excluding farmers, it was 5.8 percent; for manufacturers alone it was 3.3 percent. In the short expansion 1921-23, when inventories were less important than in any other short expansion of the period, the comparable figures were 19.2, 15.8, and 9.6 percent. The difference between the share of inventory investment in the long expansion 1921-29 and its average share in the five shorter expansions was still more marked. A similarly drastic shift appears in the relative size of inventory investment and other elements of private investment. In the shorter expansions the portion of the change in total output that took the form of a change in the rate of accumulation of stocks was regularly larger than that which took the form of an increase in the output of producer durables, consumer durables, or construction. The share of inventory investment by manufacturers alone sometimes exceeded that of the various elements of durable goods output or construction and it was always larger than half the share of each of the other categories. In the 1921-29 expansion, however, total inventory investment increased less than any of

[10] To the writer's knowledge, the first investigator to make this observation was Simon Kuznets (NBER *Bulletin 74*).

TABLE 87

Gross National Product and Its Main Components
Changes during the Major Fluctuation, 1921-29-32

	AV. AN. VALUE, $ BILLION, 1929 PRICES	CHANGE, $ BILLION, 1929 PRICES			CHANGE AS % OF CHANGE IN GNP		
		Exp.	Contr.	Cycle	Exp.	Contr.	Cycle
	(1)	(2)	(3)	(4)	(5)	(6)	(7)
1 Gross national product	82.7	32.9	—32.0	64.9	100.0	100.0	100.0
2 Flow of goods to consumers	67.7	22.6	—15.2	37.8	68.7	47.5	58.2
a Durables	7.0	4.8	—4.5	9.3	14.6	14.1	14.3
b Nondurables	35.8	10.2	—4.4	14.6	31.0	13.8	22.5
c Services	24.7	7.7	—6.2	13.9	23.4	19.4	21.4
3 Capital formation	15.2	10.1	—16.7	26.8	30.7	52.2	41.3
a Construction	8.9	4.7	—5.8	10.5	14.3	18.1	16.2
1) Public	2.1	0.9	—0.2	1.1	2.7	0.6	1.7
2) Business	3.3	2.0	—2.9	4.9	6.1	9.1	7.6
3) Residential	3.5	1.8	—2.7	4.5	5.5	8.4	6.9
b Prod. durable equip.	5.6	3.9	—5.0	8.9	11.9	15.6	13.7
c Net changes in claims against foreign countries	0.44	—0.9	—0.4	—0.5	—2.7	1.2	—0.8
d Net changes in inventories (inventory investment)							
1) Total	0.30	2.4	—5.6	8.0	7.3	17.5	12.3
2) Total, excl. farmers	0.37	1.9	—6.1	8.0	5.8	19.1	12.3
3) Mfr. inventories	0.36	1.1	—2.4	3.5	3.3	7.5	5.4

these other categories of capital formation, and the gain in investment by manufacturers alone was less than half the increase in any of them.

The long contraction 1929-32 was marked by a similar shift in the proportion of the total change in output accounted for by inventory investment. The share of total inventory investment in the decline of output was only 17.5 percent while the average for the 5 contractions was 47.5 percent; the share of total investment excluding that by farmers was 19.1 percent and the five-cycle average, 42.8 percent; for manufacturing alone, the comparable figures were 7.5 and 24.9 percent. The share of all three was much smaller than in any of the shorter contractions.

Hansen offers the following explanation of the role of inventory investment in minor cycles (p. 17):

"When an upsurge in real investment occurs, it is not unusual for the spurt in inventory accumulation to run ahead of the normal requirements indicated by the rising trend. When this is the case, sooner or later a temporary saturation in inventory accumulation develops, leading to an inventory recession. Not infrequently the minor setbacks experienced in the major upswings may be characterized as inventory recessions. But sometimes other situations may initiate or aggravate these minor recessions. Thus, for example, in the beginning of the major upswing it may be that large investment in improved machinery occurs and that after a time a temporary saturation is reached in this type of investment leading to a recession. The general buoyancy of the upswing, however, soon starts the economy upward again with a further burst of real investment after the temporary setback thus sustained. Sometimes special situations are partly responsible for minor recessions, such as critical international developments, labor disturbances, or even special factors having to do with major industries, such as the Ford shutdown in 1927. Regularly, however, inventory movements play an important role."

The prominence of inventory investment as an aggravating agent in short cycles, asserted in Hansen's last sentence, may be considered as established (see Sec. 2 above). The issue, however, is precisely whether the shorter declines of business are initiated by the appearance of saturation in the demand for additional inventories or by a failure of demand for other kinds of goods. Unfortunately, with the evidence now available this issue cannot be brought to a decisive test.

Hansen's statements—"it is not unusual for the spurt in inventory accumulation to run ahead of the normal requirements indicated by the rising trend" and "When this is the case, sooner or later a temporary saturation in inventory accumulation develops, leading to an inventory recession"—leave open the question of the forces that cause inventory investment at first to rise too rapidly, then to fall off. The cause suggested by the analysis in preceding chapters of this study is that output at first rises rapidly but later more slowly and that inventory investment follows the pattern of the rate of change in output. Sooner or later inventory investment would diminish. However, investment in major categories of stocks —raw materials held by manufacturers and stocks of wholesalers and retailers—tends to lag behind the rate of change in output. There is also some evidence that toward the end of expansions, investment in finished goods held by manufacturers tends to rise. It may be questioned, therefore, whether the downturn in inventory investment that the retarded growth in output would eventually bring about actually occurs before the demand for producer durables and other categories of commodities begins to fall. Were adequate monthly data available, this issue could be settled; but, as pointed out above, in their absence the facts remain in doubt (Ch. 14).

Mere retardation in the growth of output is not the sole agency able to cause a decline in inventory investment that may precipitate a business recession. Lloyd Metzler has described another process the outlines of which are plausible (cf. Ch. 1). He calls attention to the fact that when business revives, manufacturers and dealers have difficulty in effecting an appropriate increase in their stocks. Indeed, the first effect of an increase in business is to cause stocks to fall temporarily, leading to a sharp drop in inventory-output and inventory-sales ratios. In subsequent periods businessmen attempt not merely to increase inventories in proportion to increases in output and sales but also to accumulate enough goods in addition to restore inventory-output ratios to desired levels. The process of bringing inventories once more into line with the level of output and sales takes some time, but when it has been accomplished, an important source of demand for additional goods disappears and inventory investment tends to fall.

Forces of this type undoubtedly influence the behavior of some leading categories of stocks. But whether, in the face of the obstacles to the prompt adjustment of stocks to sales and output, they operate sufficiently rapidly is again not clear. Indexes of inventory-sales and inventory-output ratios for all manufacturers suggest that there is no pronounced rise before the peak in business. If this were true for all important inventory categories it would count heavily against Metzler's thesis. But whether or not it is true will be known only when long series of inventory data are available for the components of manufacturers' stocks and of stocks held by other industrial divisions.

A decline in inventory investment may be precipitated by still other causes. Price speculation may occur from time to time leading to periods of rapid accumulation followed by attempted liquidation when price expectations change. Widespread alternations in the degree of optimism with respect to the demand for goods may have the same results. But again there is no evidence that these forces regularly exert a powerful influence on the behavior of stocks.

Finally, there is no presumption in favor of the idea that the role of inventory investment is the same in every short cycle. It may, as Hansen suggests, act as the precipitating agent of some recessions and merely as an aggravating agent in others. The outcome may turn on how soon after the onset of business revival the rate of growth of output begins to decline and on the degree of retardation. If the rate of growth starts to fall relatively early, inventory investment is more likely to reach a peak earlier than other types of expenditure. And if retardation is very marked, the concomitant decline in inventory investment is more likely to be sufficient to precipitate a business recession despite the continued rise in other categories of output. If the retardation occurs relatively late and is relatively mild, the recession in business may be set off by a failure in other types of demand. That the precise order of events does not repeat itself from cycle to cycle is, of course, highly plausible. But future studies must still try to determine the relative frequency with which inventory investment initiates the upturns and downturns of business.

This is an important problem in the mechanism of business cycles quite apart from the Schumpeter-Hansen multi-cycle theory which has given it prominence. If it proves impossible to identify an 8 or 10 year cycle in expenditures for construction and equipment, we shall still want to know how often and under what circumstances upturns and downturns are precipitated by inventory investment. If the existence of a major cycle can be established, the multi-cycle theory will stand whether or not inventory investment turns out to be a regular precipitant of the minor fluctuations it envisages. It would be extremely interesting if one could resolve these questions now, but they must await additional work and better evidence.

Sources and Methods Used to Estimate Manufacturers' Inventories Based on Company Accounts

1 Estimates in Book Values

A KUZNETS' ESTIMATES

These data for total manufacturing inventories are based on estimates of the value of holdings in ten major manufacturing groups on December 31 of each year 1918-41.[1] First, inventories held by corporations were estimated, then holdings of unincorporated business were allowed for.

1) Inventories held by corporations

The sources and methods are best described in four periods.

1926-1939

From 1926 to 1939 the data are based on the inventories reported by corporations submitting balance sheets for income tax purposes and published in *Statistics of Income,* classified in ten manufacturing groups. To render the reported figures representative of all corporations in these branches, they were raised to allow for corporations not submitting balance sheets. The adjustment, based on the ratio of the cost of goods sold by all corporations to that by corporations submitting balance sheets (both from *Statistics of In-*

[1] The series are presented in Appendix F.

The figures I attribute to Kuznets are the ones published in his *Commodity Flow and Capital Formation,* Part VII, for ends of years 1918-33, and later extended by him through 1938. I have revised these estimates in two major respects: (1) I computed separate adjustment factors for noncorporate holdings in 4 manufacturing groups (foods, textiles, leather, and stone, clay and glass products). (2) Using later issues of *Statistics of Income* not available to him, I revised his 1936-38 figures and computed additional ones through December 31, 1941.

come), is minor, less than 3 percent for all groups except miscellaneous manufacturing (3.15 percent) in 1931. For the years before 1931, the 1931 ratios were used. After 1931, ratios for each year were available.

1924-1925

For 1923 and 1924 all corporations reported inventories to the Bureau of Internal Revenue for purposes of the capital gains tax; the figures are published in *Statistics of Income*. As the groupings did not seem comparable with those beginning with 1926, figures for total corporate manufacturing alone were used.

To distribute the totals among the component groups, a sample of 2,046 identical manufacturing corporations was regrouped to be comparable with the manufacturing subgroups in *Statistics of Income* (Table 88).[2] For each group sales and inventories were added and inventory-sales ratios computed for 1924, 1925, and 1926. The ratios were adjusted in accordance with the relation in 1926 between Epstein's figures and inventory-gross income ratios

TABLE 88

Gross Sales, All Corporations and Epstein's Sample of Manufacturing Firms, 1926

	EPSTEIN SAMPLE[a]	ALL CORPORATIONS[b]	% EPSTEIN SAMPLE IS OF ALL CORPORATIONS
	(millions of dollars)		
Total manufacturing	27309	59863	45.6
Food, beverages & tobacco	6400	13199	48.5
Textiles & textile products	1457	7593	19.2
Leather & leather products	369	1630	22.6
Rubber & related products	1035	1534	67.5
Lumber & wood products	537	2938	18.3
Paper, printing & publishing	885	3620	24.4
Chemicals & allied products	4478	7333	61.1
Stone, clay & glass products	570	1619	35.2
Metals & metal products	11065	17970	61.6
Miscellaneous	513	2428	21.1

[a] *Source Book for the Study of Industrial Profits,* Table 1, p. 8.
[b] *Statistics of Income, 1926.*

[2] Ralph C. Epstein, *Source Book for the Study of Industrial Profits* (Department of Commerce, 1932), Table 7, p. 14. Epstein's minor groups combined to form groups comparable with the *Statistics of Income* groups are given in *Commodity Flow and Capital Formation,* Table VII-1, Note B, p. 413.

derived from *Statistics of Income*. The 1924 and 1925 adjusted ratios were then applied to gross income as given in *Statistics of Income*.[3]

1918-1923

For the years before 1924 the manufacturing series depends (as do those for mining and corporate trade) upon a sample of corporate reports compiled by the National Bureau of Economic Research from Moody's Industrials. To avoid the difficulties engendered by mergers, Kuznets constructed an index of inventory-sales ratios. In order to include as many firms as possible, he used an index of linked relatives. All corporations were included that reported for at least two years both inventories and sales (or gross income or gross revenue). Inventory-sales ratios were computed for each industrial branch, and an index was constructed to extrapolate the final inventory-sales ratio for 1924. The resultant ratios were then applied to the gross income of the various branches as shown annually in *Statistics of Income*.[4]

The proportion of total business in each branch done by corporations in the sample varies widely among the groups (Table 89).

2) Noncorporate inventories

The estimates of inventories held by corporations were raised to allow for those held by unincorporated firms on the basis of the relation between their respective values of product in the 1919 and 1929 Censuses of Manufactures (Table 90). Ratios for the years between 1919 and 1929 were obtained by straight-line interpolation and the 1929 ratio was used for subsequent years.

---

[3] A final minor adjustment was necessary. When the 1924 estimates for the various groups and those for corporate trade derived in the same fashion were totaled, the sum was found to exceed the comparable figure from the capital stock returns in the ratio 1: .98906. The estimates for the various manufacturing groups were, therefore, reduced to accord with this ratio. The geometric mean between the latter and a ratio of 1.000 (assumed for 1926, since the data for that year were taken directly from *Statistics of Income*) was used to adjust the estimates for 1925.

[4] A final adjustment of less than 1 percent was again made to equate the resulting estimates with the total shown in the capital stock tax returns for 1923. The years before 1923 were adjusted by the geometric mean of the 1923 and 1924 adjustment ratios: .99161 and .98906.

TABLE 89

Coverage of NBER Inventory Sample

	NO. OF FIRMS	AV. TOTAL SALES ($ MIL.)	SALES AS % OF GROSS INCOME, ALL CORPORATIONS
Food, beverages & tobacco, 1923-24	43	1510.5	13.8
Textiles & textile products, 1923-24	39	351.0	4.7
Leather & leather products, 1920-21	10	234.7	14.2
Rubber & related products, 1923-24	14	633.0	57.5
Lumber & wood products, 1918-19	5	23.9	1.1
Paper, printing & publishing, 1918-19	10	56.1	2.5
Chemicals & allied products, 1918-19	19	830.8	19.2
Stone, clay & glass products, 1921-22	11	80.1	7.5
Metals & metal products, 1923-24	101	3904.2	24.0
Miscellaneous manufacturing, 1918-19	3	19.8	0.6

Commodity Flow and Capital Formation, Table VII-1, Note C, p. 415.

In only one industry, lumber, is the change between 1919 and 1929 more than 10 percentage points. Since these amounts are spread over a decade, the annual adjustments on this account are very small. If straight-line interpolation gives even a first approximation to the desired allowance, the errors due to this method cannot be serious. Census figures for 1939, which became available after our estimates had been made, indicate that in four industry groups the trend toward incorporation continued during the 'thirties. In two others, the trend was reversed. The changes between 1929 and 1939, however, were smaller than in the preceding decade, and our failure to take them into account cannot affect our cyclical measures significantly.

TABLE 90

Ratio of Value of Product of Unincorporated to Incorporated Firms

	1919	1929	1939[a]
		(percentages)	
Food, beverages & tobacco	19.4	12.1	13.6
Textiles & textile products	31.3	23.7	16.8
Leather & leather products	18.3	9.0	6.8
Lumber & wood products	28.2	14.5	21.5
Paper, printing & publishing	16.6	10.2	8.3
Chemicals & allied products	2.5	2.6	2.4
Stone, clay & glass products	15.9	11.4	6.3
Metals & metal products	4.9	2.3	2.4
Miscellaneous manufacturing	16.9	13.4	..

Inventories held by unincorporated rubber and related products concerns were not estimated because of the extremely small proportion of business done by them.

[a] Ratios suggested by the 1939 Census of Manufactures, not available when Kuznets made his estimates, are included here for purposes of comparison.

B   SIGNIFICANCE AND RELIABILITY OF KUZNETS' ESTIMATES IN
BOOK VALUES

1) The reporting date

The data in *Statistics of Income* are conventionally referred to as 'inventories as of December 31'. Corporations are permitted, however, to keep their accounts and to report their income on the basis of a fiscal year other than the calendar year. In 1928 only about 14 percent of the gross income earned by all corporations was reported on a noncalendar year basis.[5] For several groups the figure was much higher (Table 91).

TABLE 91

Manufacturing Industries: Percentage of Gross Income
Reported on a Noncalendar Year Basis, 1928

Total manufacturing	14.3
Food, beverages & tobacco	16.2
Textiles & textile products	26.4
Leather & leather products	42.0
Rubber & related products	16.4
Lumber & wood products	13.9
Paper & pulp	19.3
Printing & publishing	9.7
Chemicals & allied products	10.4
Stone, clay & glass products	10.9
Metals & metal products	10.8

See note 5.

These differences in practice with respect to the reporting basis raise a problem of some importance. First, the inventory data from *Statistics of Income* are weighted fiscal year averages in which dominant weight is given to standings on December 31 and minor weights to standings as much as 5 months earlier and 6 months later. Thus the change in inventories from one year end to the next is not simply due to forces acting during the calendar year in question. It is due also in some degree to the events of a period beginning 6 months earlier and ending 6 months later.

[5] Adapted from *Statistics of Income, 1928*. The published figures show the percentage of net income and net deficit reported on a noncalendar year basis in each industry. In calculating the estimate in the text, these percentages were averaged, weighted in each case by the gross income of all firms reporting net incomes and net deficits, respectively. This procedure implicitly assumes that the relation of gross income to net income or net deficit is the same for firms reporting on a noncalendar and on a calendar year basis.

A difficulty stemming from this situation arises when comparisons are attempted among the inventory groups or between any of them and other bodies of data. In comparisons among the inventory groups some small part of any differences in the behavior of inventories will be due to the fact that the various series are for somewhat different periods rather than to real differences. In comparisons between the inventory and price or production series, the correct figure would be a weighted fiscal year average of exactly the same type as that involved in the inventories series. Unfortunately, the distribution of reports by months is known only for the grand total of all corporations including nonmanufacturing; it is, therefore, necessary to make direct comparisons with December figures.[6]

How serious are the errors thus engendered likely to be? In nine of the ten groups the weight given the December figure is so heavy that there will be no substantial error in treating the reports as if they were unqualifiedly returns as of December 31. In eight, December accounts for over four-fifths of the returns; in a ninth, for nearly three-quarters. In other words, in the least favorable case, the reported figure for the companies operating on a noncalendar year basis must differ from their true December 31 figure by 4 percent in order to cause an error of as much as 1 percent in the group total. And since the reports not on a calendar year basis are scattered on both sides of December 31, considerable opportunity exists for differences between the actual fiscal year returns and those which would have been made had these firms reported on a calendar year basis to offset one another.

Related to this difficulty is one that arises in the process of deflation. Here again we must use an index that would be strictly correct only if the inventory series were really a series of December 31 figures. This source of error is as serious as that involved in the inventory data themselves. But whether errors from the second source offset or aggravate errors from the first cannot be said.

---

[6] For all corporations in manufacturing and other groups taken together we can, however, estimate the distribution of reports by months by methods similar to those described in note 5:

> Percentage of total gross income reported for
> 1928 on a noncalendar year basis, 12.20
> Years ending July to November 1928, 4.92
> Years ending January to June 1929, 7.28

2) Difficulties due to incompleteness of tabulation

J. Franklin Ebersole, Susan S. Burr, and George M. Peterson contend that serious shortages of a mechanical sort are present in certain years in the *Statistics of Income* data before 1926.[7] Of the years of interest to us, 1918-25, the authors contend that a significant shortage appeared only in 1919, when by the test on which they rely most, it was about 16 percent for all industrial divisions. In all later years except 1923 the difference between the apparent figure and the authors' estimate of a true figure was less than 1 percent.

The authors believe that the apparent shortage may be due to any of several imperfections in the tabulation procedure: failure to send returns through the statistical section (presumably due to delinquency in reporting), imperfect tabulation of returns sent through the statistical section, incompletely made-up returns requiring audit to obtain the necessary information.

The evidence on which shortage is estimated, however, is inconclusive in many particulars. The authors' test entails the addition of four expense items believed to be largely constant with respect to short-term variations in output: compensation paid officers, interest payments, domestic taxes paid other than federal income and profit taxes, and depreciation and depletion charges. The sum of these items, it is assumed, would move in a smooth linear trend unless mechanical errors were made in the tabulation.[8] It is such a trend, calculated from the data and based on 1927, that indicates a shortage in 1919.

One objection to the procedure is that the sum of the four fixed

---

[7] Income Forecasting by the Use of Statistics of Income Data, *Review of Economic Statistics,* XI (1929), 171 ff. The authors were at the time of writing employed in the Treasury Department. Their discussion of the overlapping of the various industrial divisions and groups and of the shifting of constituent firms among them is considered in the next section.

[8] Reliance is placed also on a comparison of total returns tabulated in any given year with the trend value calculated for that year. But on this basis, the shortage in 1919 is only some 3 percent, a discrepancy easily accounted for, even if one accepted the assumption that the true value and the calculated trend value were identical, by the fact that the clause with respect to consolidated returns went into effect in 1918. Further consolidations and, therefore, consolidated returns to the number in question would not be surprising.

expense items probably does not move along a smooth linear trend. Indeed, inspection of the figures suggests a tendency towards positive cyclical conformity, which is consistent with the low figures for 1919. Aside from this, however, one would hardly be surprised to find an abnormal movement in an economic series of this sort in the year following the Armistice.

Moreover, a shortage in tabulation is not the only possible explanation of an apparent divergence of the figures from the calculated normal. Ebersole, Burr, and Peterson point out that part of these expenses may have been included in 1919 among 'miscellaneous expenses', a category that grew in 1919 by a larger absolute amount than the four 'fixed costs' fell and by 43 percent of its own 1918 value.[9]

Finally, it is impossible to identify the shortage in manufacturing, the division of special interest to us. A linear trend for manufacturing alone drawn free hand and based on 1927 would show that the 1919 figure is close to its trend value.[10]

One may conclude that, while the opinion of these Treasury experts is not to be lightly discarded, the evidence of shortage in tabulation they are able to adduce does not cast serious doubt on the 1919 estimates of manufacturers' inventories.

3) The classification procedure

a) Industrial overlapping

The basic unit of reporting for tax purposes is a corporation or, before 1934, a group of corporations owned in common and filing a consolidated return. Such firms often engage in a variety of manufacturing activities which, if separable, would be appropriately classified in different industries. Because the activities of a corporation (or group of corporations filing a consolidated return) are not separable, the industrial classification used by the Income Tax Bureau is based on the "main income-producing ac-

---

[9] Op. cit., p. 174.

[10] There may, of course, have been a shift of corporations into manufacturing in 1919 which would hide a real discrepancy. But such evidence as Ebersole, Burr, and Peterson could gather was insufficient to lead them to suppose that this was so.

tivity" of a firm in a given year.[11] This means that, as far as activities properly falling in different classifications are carried on in combination, inventories and sales properly belonging in a certain group will often be placed in other groups and that any given group will include the records of activity that should properly be classed elsewhere. The amount of such overlapping is undoubtedly large in data from *Statistics of Income* relative to the amount to be found in census data which are based on an establishment, rather than a company, as the reporting unit.

Overlapping of this sort renders the definition of industry groups within manufacturing somewhat hazy; more important, it reduces the sharpness of the distinction between manufacturing and other industrial divisions. The chief difficulties arise from firms that carry on both manufacturing and mining operations and both manufacturing and trade.

T. C. Atkeson of the BIR wrote the National Bureau of Economic Research, May 25, 1939:

"If a return, whether or not consolidated, is engaged in a combination of mining a raw material and of converting this raw material into a manufactured product, it is placed in the correct industry group under manufacturing. Even with the discontinuance of the privilege of filing consolidated returns, except by railroads, the inventories of certain mines and quarries are included in the data for manufacturing. This is especially true of certain large oil companies which are engaged in both the extracting of crude oil and the refining of petroleum."

Similar difficulties are involved at the margin between manufacturing and trade. For example, manufacturers' sales branches, which might be thought to resemble wholesaling rather than manufacturing establishments (the census, for example, treats them as distributors), are treated as manufacturers in *Statistics of Income* provided they are operated by a manufacturing company under a single corporate charter. They would presumably be

---

[11] W. L. Crum writes: "A specific inquiry on the blank for corporate income tax returns calls for this information. The wording clearly suggests that production of income should be the criterion for classification, but there is good reason to doubt if this effectively is the case." *Corporate Size and Earning Power* (Harvard University Press, 1939), p. 22, note 2.

grouped with other trading firms if, as sometimes happens, they operate under separate charter.

b) Reconciliation of the census and Kuznets' estimates of manufacturers' inventories

To get some notion of the quantitative importance of these difficulties of classification as far as they affect the relations between manufacturing and other industrial divisions, we attempted to account for the difference between Kuznets' estimates of manufacturers' inventories, based on *Statistics of Income* (company) data, and the census estimates, based on establishment data. For December 31, 1936 the census reported manufacturers' holdings of $8,951 million after adjustments for underreporting of inventories within the industries covered.[12] Kuznets' estimate, corrected for underreporting and raised to allow for unincorporated firms, was $11,171 million.

Part of the difference, $2,220 million, can be accounted for by identifiable shortages in the census coverage of manufacturing establishments or of borderline manufacturing establishments. The census inventory survey did not cover most printing, publishing, and allied industries. If we substitute Kuznets' estimate of inventories in the paper, printing and publishing industry for the census estimate of inventories in the paper industry, the census total is raised about $233 million.

A second adjustment of a more doubtful character is required in tobacco. The census treats warehousing, assembling, and processing of leaf tobacco, even though carried on in connection with manufacturing, as part of distribution rather than of manufacturing. For December 31, 1938 the inventories of such establishments controlled by tobacco manufacturers was estimated to be worth $367 million.

The census treats manufacturers' sales branches as establishments engaged in trade. *Statistics of Income,* and consequently Kuznets' estimate, excludes them from manufacturing only if they are conducted under a separate corporate charter. We estimate that they held some $829 million worth of inventories at the end of

---

[12] In the Census of Manufactures, 1939, establishments accounting for 94.6 percent of the value of product in manufacturing replied satisfactorily to the question about inventories.

1936. But we do not know what proportion operated under separate charter and were, therefore, excluded from manufacturing by *Statistics of Income* and by the census.

Similar to manufacturers' sales branches generally are various establishments engaged in the distribution of petroleum products —largely bulk tank stations. The Department of Commerce estimated that inventories of such establishments owned and operated by refining companies but not reported in the Census of Manufactures were $233 million on December 31, 1938. Again we do not know how many were included in manufacturing by *Statistics of Income*.

The maximum overstatement in Kuznets' estimate, of $1.4 billion or nearly 14 percent above the adjusted census figure, is clearly excessive. The difficulties are both statistical and conceptual. In the reconciliation attempted in Table 92, many shortages in census coverage were not allowed for explicitly. They may amount to $250 million, or just over 2.5 percent of the adjusted census figure in line 5.

The conceptual difficulty concerns the definition of manufacturing. All manufacturing establishments carry on distribution functions of greater or less complexity. To exclude the distributive activities of fabricating companies simply because they are carried on in separate establishments is quite arbitrary. Similarly, almost all mining establishments manipulate their crude products to some degree—by cleaning, crushing, concentrating, and so on. The line between mining and manufacturing is itself vague. A logical criterion would be to include in manufacturing any extractive or distributive function carried on by a manufacturing company and exclusively devoted to providing the raw materials or distributing its products. Extractive and distributive activities not carried on in support of the fabricating activities of a given company ought logically to be excluded. From this standpoint, the census estimate, based as it is on the individual establishment (plant or unified set of works), tends to be low: it excludes nonmanufacturing activities not devoted to the support of the fabrication work of a given company but does not include many nonmanufacturing activities that are so devoted. Kuznets' estimate, based on *Statistics of Income* tends to err in the opposite direction because the reporting

TABLE 92

Manufacturers' Inventories, December 31, 1936: Reconciliation of
Census and Kuznets' Estimates

(millions of dollars)

1) Census figures adj. for underreporting in lines canvassed	8951	
2) Adjustment for printing, publishing, & allied industries	233	
3) Adjustment for undercoverage in tobacco industry[b]	367	
4) Adjustment for distributing establishments owned by petroleum refining companies[c]	233	
5) Census total adjusted		9784
6) Kuznets' estimate		11171
7) Maximum overstatement of manufacturers' inventories by Kuznets		1387
8) Area of doubt		
a) Manufacturers' sales branches,[d] roughly	829	
b) Mining establishments owned by mfg. companies,[e] roughly	200	
c) Census shortages & other unexplained differences[f]	358	
d) Total		1387

[a] Kuznets' estimate for pulp, paper, printing and publishing minus census estimate for paper and allied industries adjusted for underreporting.

[b] Department of Commerce estimate of required adjustment for December 31, 1938 is applied here to December 31, 1936.

[c] Department of Commerce estimate for December 31, 1938. Overstates the value of such inventories included in Kuznets' estimates to the extent that distributing establishments owned by petroleum refining companies operated under separate corporate charter.

[d] The sum of estimates for lines canvassed and not canvassed in *Census Survey of Business: 1937-38, Wholesale Distribution.* U. S. Summary (1938).

1) Lines canvassed, $757,399,000

Estimate equals the figure reported for December 31, 1936 for manufacturers' sales branches in lines canvassed divided by the percentage that inventories held in 1935 by firms reporting in 1936 were of all inventories held by manufacturers' sales branches in 1935.

2) Lines not canvassed, $71,374,000

This estimate was derived as follows:

a) Total inventories of wholesalers in 1936 were calculated by dividing the reported inventories in 1935 by the relation between inventories held in 1935 by firms reporting in 1936 to inventories held by these firms in 1936.

b) Inventories in lines not canvassed in 1936 were calculated by dividing total 1936 inventories from (a) by the relation between total inventories held in 1935 and inventories held in 1935 by lines not canvassed in 1936.

c) Inventories held by manufacturers' sales branches in 1936 were estimated by multiplying total inventories in lines not canvassed in 1936 from (b) by the relation between inventories held in 1935 by manufacturers' sales branches in these lines to total inventories held in 1935 by the same lines.

Notes to Table 92 concluded:
    This procedure yielded $828,773,000 for inventories held by manufacturers' sales branches in 1936.

Since manufacturers' sales branches operated under separate corporate charter would not have been assigned to manufacturing in *Statistics of Income*, the total overstates the value of such inventories included in Kuznets' estimates.

^e Unpublished estimate by George Terborgh.

^f A balancing item. To the extent that items 8a and b overstate the value of inventories included in Kuznets' estimates under those heads, 8d would be larger.

unit, the company operating under separate charter, lumps together all establishments owned by the company and, if the dominant activity is manufacturing, places all in that division.

A valid figure for manufacturers' stocks would seem to lie between the census and Kuznets' figures. In Chapter 2 we put the exaggeration in Kuznets' estimate at half the 'maximum overstatement', $1.4 billion, or roughly $700 million.

c) Consolidated returns

Related to these difficulties and enhancing their importance is the practice with respect to consolidated returns. This form of return, at first compulsory for an affiliated group of companies, was made optional in 1921 and remained so until the Revenue Act of 1934. In 1932 and 1933, however, corporations filing consolidated returns were subject to income tax at a rate 1.5 percent higher (in absolute terms) than that applying to individual returns. The Revenue Act of 1934 abolished the privilege of filing consolidated returns for all corporations except railroads, for taxable years beginning December 31, 1933.[13]

[13] Under the Revenue Acts of 1924-32 two or more domestic corporations were deemed to be affiliated if one owned at least 95 percent of the voting stock of the other or others or if at least 95 percent of the voting stock of two or more corporations was owned by the same interests.

During the entire period when consolidated returns were optional, statute and Treasury regulations stipulated that when a consolidated return was made for one year, the same form had to be used in subsequent years except in certain cases provided by regulation or when the Commissioner granted permission to change for good cause.

I am indebted to E. G. Keith for a memorandum on these points and those covered in note 14.

The influence of these considerations on the data from *Statistics of Income* is twofold. First, the privilege of making consolidated reports gave rise to many more reports of businesses engaged in a mixture of activities than would otherwise have been included. This fact aggravates the difficulties arising from the unavoidable practice of classifying firms according to their predominant business. Secondly, it means that a break in the series occurs between 1933 and 1934 when the privilege of filing consolidated returns was withdrawn.[14]

Fortunately, from *Statistics of Income, 1934,* we can gauge the effect of consolidated returns on the composition of the various groups before 1934 and of the change that took place when the privilege was withdrawn (Table 93). However, even before 1934, the number of consolidated returns was falling because of the unfavorable differential in tax rates applied in 1932.

TABLE 93

Number of Income Tax Returns Filed, All Corporations
Total and Consolidated

		1931	*1932*	*1933*
1	Total	516404	408636	504080
2	Consolidated*	8495	7426	7101
3	Line 2 as % of 1	1.65	1.46	1.41

* Figures obtained through the courtesy of T. C. Atkeson of the Bureau of Internal Revenue.

Unfortunately, Tables 93 and 94 show only the net changes consequent upon the withdrawal of the consolidation privilege. The loss of inventories to manufacturing as a whole was some 3.4 percent, and among the component groups chemicals alone suffered considerably larger percentage changes. However, we are still left wondering how much shuffling about among the manufacturing groups accompanied the reclassification of corporations. Fundamental changes in the composition of the various divisions are consistent with small net changes in the size of inventories.

[14] Since the privilege was abolished for taxable years beginning after December 31, 1933, most of the returns reported in *Statistics of Income, 1934* were subject to the new provision with respect to consolidated returns. The exceptions consist only of affiliated groups whose taxable years began after June 30, 1933 and before January 1, 1934, which are, therefore, included with the 1934 returns although not subject to the new provisions.

TABLE 94

Corporate Inventories for 1934 Classified on 1933 and 1934 Bases

	ALL CORPORATIONS		% CHANGE
	1933 basis	1934 basis	1934 FROM
	(millions of dollars)		1933 BASIS
Total manufacturing	8611.9	8319.2	−3.4
Food, bev. & tobacco	1628.4	1568.2	−3.7
Textiles	1065.7	1071.5	+0.5
Leather	246.5	234.2	−5.0
Rubber	206.7	197.1	−4.6
Forest products	342.5	338.8	−1.1
Paper & printing	383.0	376.4	−1.7
Chemicals	1430.4	1289.0	−9.9
Stone, clay & glass	214.9	218.9	+1.9
Metals	2793.2	2722.1	−2.5
Manufactures n.e.c.	300.5	302.9	+0.8

4) Biased reporting for tax purposes

It is impossible to say anything in detail about this question which affects Kuznets' estimates for the years since 1926. The fact that inventories are an element in the determination of net income for tax purposes undoubtedly influences the value put on them. *A priori*, it would seem likely that this leads to a low valuation of stocks in good years and a high valuation in bad years (the latter in order to keep the reported value from getting too far out of line with reality). Beyond this, one can say merely that there would probably be little room for such biases in the case of raw materials whose purchase price can readily be determined; and probably incorrect valuations are relatively insignificant in the case of other staple goods whose production costs are computed in some regular fashion. But whenever cost is difficult to figure and market value can be influenced by physical deterioration or by changes in style, there will be opportunity for company treasurers to value their inventories according to the dictates of tax convenience.

5) Influence of the large corporation sample

From 1918 to 1922 and again in 1925 Kuznets' estimates for manufacturers' total stocks depend upon inventory-gross income ratios estimated from samples of large corporations. In 1923 and 1924 the distribution of the total by major industry groups, though not the total itself, rests upon the same method. How nearly accurate can we assume this method was? Errors arise from two sources:

sampling and bias due to overweighting large corporations. The experiment described below suggests the importance of the second but not the first.

Since 1931 *Statistics of Income* has published information on sales and inventories of manufacturing corporations by size of assets. Table 95 applies for the most part to 1931-35, although information with respect to the asset class required was not available for four of the industry groups for all years.

TABLE 95

Comparison of Kuznets' Samples and All Corporations in Selected Asset Classes

	RANGE OF AV. SALES KUZNETS' SAMPLE 1918-24	CORP. REPORT, BALANCE SHEETS *Statistics of Income* Size group used in test	*Statistics of Income* Range of av. sales 1931-35	Kuznets' samples as % of gross income of all report. corp.	TOTAL SALES OF CORP. IN Selected asset classes as % of gross sales of all report. corp.
	(millions of dollars)				
Foods, bev. & tob.	35-80	3 & over	27-37	16.0	66.2
Textiles & textile prod.	8-16	5 & over	8-10	5.5	23.5
Leather & leather prod.	23-44	5 & over	12-13	19.2	30.6
Rubber & related prod.	42-62	5 & over	22-28	64.3	74.8
Lumber & wood prod.	6-9	5 & over	2-3	3.0	18.5
Paper, print. & pub.	6-8	5 & over	5-9	2.9	35.7
Chemicals & allied prod.	42-59	10 & over	38-44	29.4	72.7
Stone, clay & glass prod.	7-12	5 & over	5-8	8.7	48.9
Metals & metal prod.	20-41	5 & over	16-23	25.0	67.1
Misc. mfg.	7-8	1 & over	2-3	1-6	53.0

Our procedure involved the following steps:

1) Average sales per firm were computed for the various asset classes in *Statistics of Income,* 1931-35.

2) These figures were then compared with the average sales per firm enjoyed by the firms in Kuznets' samples (*Commodity Flow and Capital Formation,* Table VII-1, Note C, p. 415) and such asset classes from *Statistics of Income* selected for the test whose sales per firm were as nearly similar to the sales per firm in Kuznets' samples as possible. Changes in prices between the two periods were roughly allowed for.

3) The inventory-sales ratios for all incorporated firms in industries submitting balance sheets were extrapolated by indexes of inventory-sales ratios computed for firms in the selected asset classes in each industry.

4) Applying these inventory-sales ratios as calculated in (3) to the gross sales of all corporations yielded estimates of inventories that rest upon the methods Kuznets used earlier, and these may be compared with actual inventories of all corporations. To this statement, however, there is the important exception already noted: Kuznets' information was drawn from samples of large corporations. Our test estimates are based upon the experience of all corporations of about the same average size as those in Kuznets' samples. The significance of this can be judged by comparing the last two columns of Table 95.

Table 96 shows the actual inventories of all corporations reporting balance sheets and inventories as estimated. The movements of both the inventories themselves and of the first differences were compared. In 6 of the 10 manufacturing groups both series moved in the same direction in all four years. In paper and printing there was disagreement in two years. Taking all groups together, there were 27 agreements in 33 comparisons. First differences showed complete agreement in all years in 6 series. In every series there were more agreements than disagreements. For all 10 series, there were 19 agreements in 23 movements.

TABLE 96

Actual Inventories of All Corporations Reporting Balance Sheets and Estimates Based on Inventory-Sales Ratios of Large Corporations

(MILLIONS OF DOLLARS)

		1931	1932	1933	1934	1935
Foods, beverages & tobacco	A	1371	1185	1405		
	E	1371	1208	1479		
Textiles & textile products	A	982	781	1086	1072	1122
	E	982	793	1106	1146	1127
Leather & leather products	A	280	208	255	234	
	E	280	188	240	244	
Rubber & related products	A	163		160	197	186
	E	163		166	219	199
Paper, printing & publishing	A	436	347	370	376	401
	E	436	377	375	363	386
Lumber & wood products	A	448		357	339	352
	E	448		349	348	381
Stone, clay & glass products	A	269	222	215	219	235
	E	269	212	194	214	226
Metals & metal products	A	3045	2447	2583	2722	2967
	E	3045	2570	2607	2790	3037
Chemicals & allied products	A	1643	1347	1352	1289	1282
	E	1643	1299	1312	1286	1240
Misc. mfg.	A	367	302	301	303	314
	E	367	375	307	321	336

A: actual; E: estimated.

C OTHER ESTIMATES FROM BALANCE SHEET SOURCES

In Chapter 4 we noted five sets of estimates based on the annual balance sheets of samples of large corporations chiefly in order to check Kuznets' results for 1918-22, when his figures also depend upon large company samples, and during 1923-25 when his figures, though derived from large corporation samples, were adjusted to comprehensive data from capital stock tax returns. From 1926 forward, as indicated above, Kuznets' estimates are based upon the comprehensive corporation income tax data in *Statistics of Income*. This section describes the methods and sources used to get the alternative estimates for the early period.

1) Dun and Bradstreet's estimates

These figures are based "on an examination of the balance sheet records of 111 large corporations, as reported in Moody's Manuals, for the ends of the years 1913 through 1922. Only those companies were included where a consistent record of inventories could be obtained for the entire period. Where an important merger was involved, the company was included only if data were available for the earlier component firms. The 106 corporations, which are manufacturing and mining enterprises, are estimated to represent between 20 and 25 percent of the total manufacturing picture, so the sample is extremely significant."[15]

The authors doubt that such a group of large corporations can be regarded as typical of all enterprise, but they justly claim that the sample is significant in its own right, that is, is representative of larger companies.[16]

To obtain a general index for manufacturing, the companies were divided into 15 groups. Group indexes, combined on both a

[15] Five companies engaged in distribution are included in the group of 111 corporations but omitted from the index of manufacturers' inventories. The latter, however, includes a few concerns engaged in mining. *Dun's Review*, Feb. 1940, pp. 17, 19.

[16] The representativeness of these series is further restricted because of the apparent omission of leather tanning and lumbering companies except as far as they may be represented in the Dun & Bradstreet building materials group. In addition, it seems doubtful that the 10 companies in 'Consumer Goods, Miscellaneous' adequately represent all textile, clothing, and shoe manufacture.

weighted and an unweighted basis, were remarkably alike, the difference in no year exceeding 2 percent. The weights were based on 1937 Census inventory figures with allowance for differences in the rates of growth of the industries.

The authors' discussion of their results contains an interesting note on both their indexes and Kuznets' estimates (p. 19, note 1):

"His [Kuznets'] estimates [for 1918-23] are based on samples taken from Moody's Manuals, for which he could get both sales and inventory figures for pairs of years. Ratios of inventories to sales were developed for ten manufacturing groups and applied to estimates of total sales to obtain estimates for total inventories.

The principal differences in results are that the main increase from 1918 to 1920 is placed by Kuznets in the first of the two years, and by the Dun and Bradstreet index in the latter year; and that the Kuznets' estimates show a large increase in 1922, while the new index shows little change.

A considerable part of the difference is in the greater weight given to textiles in the Kuznets' sample, coupled with the fact that his estimates for textiles declined in 1920 and then went on to new highs in 1921 and 1922. However, even within the groups which should be fairly comparable, rubber and chemicals, for example, it is clear that quite different results are obtained by applying turnover figures of a sample to known sales figures."

2) NBER Financial Research Program estimates (Schmidt-Young sample)

In connection with its studies in business financing, the Financial Research Program of the National Bureau of Economic Research gathered a sample of balance sheets of large corporations for 1914-22.[17] The estimates are based on reports of 81 large manufacturing companies in Moody's Manuals, supplemented by annual reports to stockholders. The estimates for total manufacturing are simple aggregates of the values in the individual balance sheets. Minor adjustments were made in 1914-17 to allow for a few corporations whose reports were later available but that were either not in existence or not reported in one or more of these years. The sample is confined to companies in agricultural machinery, automobiles and trucks, building materials, chemicals, food (other than meat

[17] See NBER *Occasional Paper 10*, pp. 31 ff. and App. A.

packing), iron and steel, meat packing, petroleum, textiles, tobacco, and transportation equipment. During 1918-22, when the
sample overlaps with Kuznets' estimates of all manufacturers'
stocks, it covers about 18 percent of the total.

3) George Terborgh's estimates

By somewhat different methods and based upon a larger sample,
George Terborgh prepared an index of all manufacturers' stocks
for year ends 1915-23. The sample "covers, for each year of the
period 1916-23, nearly all of the manufacturing concerns for
which both the opening and the closing inventories are reported in
Moody's Manuals. The percentage of the total manufacturing inventory held by these companies ranges from roughly 25 in 1916
to 40 in 1923."[18]

To derive his index for total manufacturing, Terborgh first classified his sample corporations into 19 industry groups, then divided
the companies in each group into 'large' and 'small' on the basis of
their inventories, and derived separate indexes for the large and
small corporations in each industry. Since the sample changes from
year to year, but contains opening and closing inventories for the
same companies in each year, the indexes are constructed by means
of link relatives. Terborgh points out that this form of index may
produce a slight downward bias in the estimates since the number
of companies increased between 1916 and 1923. Indexes for total
holdings by corporations in each industry were constructed by
weighting the size group indexes according to their importance as
inventory holders in 1923. Terborgh assumed that his sample for
1923 included all 'large' corporations, and that the difference between the inventory tabulated for these concerns and the estimated
totals for their industries consisted of small company inventory. The
indexes for the various industries were then combined by means of
1923 weights to yield indexes for durable goods industries, nondurable goods industries, and total manufacturing. At this point, however, allowance was made for unincorporated firms.[19]

---

[18] *Federal Reserve Bulletin,* July 1941, p. 613.

[19] Terborgh and Kuznets treated unincorporated business differently. As Terborgh points out, unincorporated firms are generally small, and "since there
appears a clear tendency for small concerns to have lower inventories *relative*

4) Lauchlin Currie's sample

This estimate, which gives annual (Dec. 31) figures 1922-28, is based on "the results of a study of the annual statements [from Poor's and Moody's Manuals] of 729 companies divided into 30 groups.[20] The basis of selection was availability, all companies being included for which continuous reports, in sufficiently detailed form, were given for approximately the same dates. The great majority of the reports are as of December 31. Although care was taken to include the available reports of all the smaller companies and also of companies in depressed industries, the series as a whole is mainly representative of the larger and more successful companies, owing to the greater availability of their financial statements."

Currie's companies held inventories valued at $5,053 million in 1928 when manufacturers' total inventories are estimated to be worth $13,359 million. A few of Currie's companies were not engaged in manufacturing.

5) NBER Financial Research Program estimates (Koch sample)

Data for a sample of large corporations 1920-39 were gathered by Albert R. Koch in connection with the Financial Research Program of the National Bureau of Economic Research.[21] For most of the period balance sheets were available for 84 corporations. For 1920, however, reports for 15 companies were missing; for 1921, reports for 6 companies were missing. We therefore use

---

to sales than large corporations in the same line of business, we may infer that the ratio of noncorporate to total value of product overstates the relative importance of noncorporate inventory." He assumes that the relative share of unincorporated concerns in the total inventory of their industry is two-thirds their proportion of the value of product.

[20] This estimate originally appeared in Mr. Currie's Note in the *Quarterly Journal of Economics*, Aug. 1931, p. 699.

The 729 companies include 23 chain stores, 23 wholesalers, 11 department stores, and 16 amusement firms. Although they cannot be eliminated, the group as a whole may still be regarded as a sample of manufacturing firms.

Data from the financial manuals on cotton textile companies were supplemented by data from the credit files of the Federal Reserve Bank of Boston.

[21] See *Financing of Large Corporations* (1943); also Corporate Financial Data for Studies in Business Finance (preliminary unpublished draft, 1945), pp. 2-5 and Table A-2.

Koch's estimates only since 1922, although three company reports were missing for that year, and one for 1923-25. As Kuznets' estimates yield annual data based on full *Statistics of Income* figures since 1926, we did not use Koch's estimates after 1929.

Koch's estimates are simple aggregates of the year end inventory values shown by the balance sheets of his sample companies producing automobiles and trucks, building materials and equipment, chemicals, food (other than meat packing), iron and steel, machinery, meat packing, petroleum, rubber, textiles, tobacco. During 1922-29 the companies held about 22 percent of all manufacturers' stocks, according to Kuznets.

D   VALUE OF MANUFACTURERS' INVENTORIES, MONTHLY ESTIMATES

All the estimates described above are for the end of calendar years. Two recently compiled samples furnish monthly information.

1) National Industrial Conference Board indexes

These estimates are designed to represent total manufacturing and two components, durable and nondurable goods industries. Available monthly since January 1929, they are based on the reports of a large number of companies, large and small. The sample does not include companies manufacturing food products, tobacco, liquors, petroleum, and certain lumber products "because these industries are so closely tied up with agriculture or with the extractive industries" and "do not represent the more active sector of industry, in which the individual decisions of industrial management have greatest effect on business activity".[22] In 1940 roughly one-sixth of total manufacturing was covered; in earlier years the coverage was less adequate.

The companies were grouped into 19 industries plus a miscellaneous group.[23] Chain indexes on a 1936 base were computed for

[22] *Economic Record,* II, Supplement, Dec. 26, 1940: Inventories, Shipments, Orders, 1929-40, p. 2.

[23] Durable goods: automobile equipment, building equipment, cement, electrical equipment, glass, iron and steel, machinery, nonferrous metals, office equipment, railroad equipment, house furnishings (since Jan. 1935), metal products.

each industry and corrected for seasonal variations. At this point, the base was shifted to make the 1935-39 average equal 100. The corrected indexes were finally combined into an index for the total and for the two durability groups by means of census weights adjusted for the change in the indexes between 1936 and 1937.[24]

2) Department of Commerce series[25]

These data, covering total inventories held in manufacturing since December 1938, are based upon reports from a sample of manufacturing firms that held nearly 40 percent of all manufacturers' stocks in June 1940 and 36 percent in June 1942. All establishments of the cooperating companies are included in the reports.

The sample is less than completely adequate. First, it is somewhat biased in favor of larger manufacturing firms. The Department of Commerce accepted this deficiency in order to avoid the cost of getting a fair representation for firms with assets under $500,000. It estimates, however, that although 89 percent of all United States manufacturing corporations have assets of less $500,000, they hold only 12.5 percent of all inventories.

The second difficulty lies in the inadequate sample obtained in certain industries where most of the business is handled by very small firms. For example, only 16 apparel manufacturers reported in June 1940. They must have accounted for only a small fraction of inventories in this industry. The Department of Commerce has attempted to remedy this difficulty and reports some progress in improving its samples.[26]

Companies report the value of their inventories for the current and preceding month, and for the corresponding month of the preceding year. Data are compiled for 11 major industry groups

---

Note 23 concluded:

Nondurable goods: boots and shoes, chemicals and drugs, clothing (since Jan. 1932), leather, paper manufactures, rubber goods, and textiles. The miscellaneous industries group is included in the total but not in the two components.

[24] The miscellaneous group was given the relative weight indicated by the ratio of their inventories to all inventories in the sample in 1936.

[25] *Survey of Current Business,* Sept. 1940, pp. 7 ff.; Jan. 1942, p. 22, and June 1942, pp. 6 ff.

[26] Ibid., Jan. 1940, p. 22.

and for two groups of miscellaneous industries, one producing durable goods, the other nondurable. These aggregates are used to construct chain indexes for the 13 industry groups.

Series representing the dollar value of inventories held by all manufacturing firms, durable and nondurable goods industries, are constructed by using the indexes just described to extrapolate the value of inventories for each group as reported to the Census of Manufactures, 1939, for December 31, 1938 and 1939. The census data were first adjusted to allow for establishments that did not report inventories and to get broader coverage in petroleum refining, tobacco, and printing and publishing.

The value of inventories thus established is further divided into holdings of finished goods, goods in process, and raw materials. Firms holding 28 percent of all manufacturers' stocks reported their finished goods and all other inventories in June 1942. Firms holding 24 percent of manufacturers' stocks divided their reports into finished goods, goods in process, and raw materials.

Indexes of finished goods inventories, computed by industries, were used to extrapolate the values reported to the Census of Manufactures for December 31, 1938 and 1939. The aggregate value of finished goods inventories for all manufacturers was then subtracted from the value of total inventories and the remainder split between goods in process and raw materials on the basis of the proportions suggested by the entire sample of reporting firms.

2 Adjustment for Changes in Prices

The series described above yield estimates of inventories in terms of changing book values. They can, no doubt, serve also as first approximations to indexes of physical volume. But an adjustment to take account of changing valuation factors is desirable, the more so as we are interested in studying the value of the physical changes in stocks, which would be seriously distorted if represented by the simple changes in book values. Kuznets' estimates of manufacturers' inventories in current prices were therefore divided by indexes of prices that represent unit values of commodities held in stock.

As the procedures are unavoidably complicated, we begin by setting forth the chief problems encountered in constructing deflaing indexes. We then describe the methods adopted and indicate the degree to which the problems were overcome.

A   MAJOR PROBLEMS IN ADJUSTING INVENTORY VALUES FOR PRICE
    CHANGES

To construct a satisfactory index for a group of manufacturers holding several commodities, account must be taken of many matters that make the problem of inventory deflation somewhat different from the more usual problem of correcting dollar sales or value of output figures for changes in prices.

1) The weights by which price relatives are combined ought to be based on representative values of inventory held—constants more difficult to determine than values of product.

2) All inventories are not valued in the same way. Inventories of purchased materials (in this connection we shall call them raw materials) are usually valued at their purchase cost. If processed by their owners they are valued at the purchase cost plus an allowance for the cost of labor directly employed in processing plus an allowance for overhead expenditures. The allowance for overhead is seldom clearly defined, varies in detail from industry to industry and often from firm to firm. When, therefore, the inventories to be deflated consist in part of goods processed by firms that own them, our series of price relatives should be of three types: prices of raw materials, costs per unit of goods in process, and costs per unit of finished goods. The second and third types should be built by adding allowances for processing costs to the purchase costs of the raw materials in a fashion that takes into account the relative importance of raw materials, direct labor, and overhead costs in the total costs per unit of each type.[27]

3) The cost at which inventories are valued is usually cost at some earlier time, determined by the system of inventory accounting. The most common methods and, until recently, the only ones approved by the Treasury, are the so-called first-in, first-out and the actual cost of specific lots methods.

The first-in, first-out method is perhaps most popular in manu-

---

[27] These categories should, of course, be combined by means of weights proportionate to the value of inventory of each class of goods held. Ideally several classes of goods in process would be recognized.

facturing where inventory items are often so intermingled that it is impossible to determine the invoice or work tag covering the cost of individual lots. The method approximates the desired end by assuming that the goods in stock are those most recently purchased or processed. The costs of the various lots are, therefore, ascertained from the invoices or work tags of most recent date, enough of each being taken into account to cover the number of units in the stock. The problem in such cases, therefore, is to determine the periods to which the invoices or work tags refer.

Accounting by the actual cost of specific lots method is self-explanatory. The average age of the invoices which, under this scheme, determine the value of the goods held at the end of the year depends upon the actual order in which goods are utilized or sold.

4) While inventories are usually valued at cost at some preceding time, the values more often than not are marked down to year end replacement values when the latter are below ordinary accounting cost. The ideal method would be to combine two indexes for each industry, one constituted on the assumption that inventories are always valued at original accounting cost, the other on the assumption that inventories are always valued at the lower of original or replacement cost, weighting each by its relative prevalence. There is, however, little satisfactory evidence on the prevalence of markdowns to replacement values in manufacturing industries.

According to an NICB study of 800 firms about one-half of all inventories are subject to markdowns (Table 97).[28] Markdowns

TABLE 97

Practices in Inventory Valuation

Method of Valuation	Raw Materials	Goods in Process	Finished Goods
	PERCENTAGE OF COMPANIES REPLYING		
A Lower of cost or market	63	37	40
B Actual cost of specific lots	14	19	15
C Average cost	15	18	17
D Standard cost	6	19	20
E Basic or normal cost	1	4	4
F Some other basis	1	3	4
Total	100	100	100

[28] Prevailing Practices in Inventory Valuation, *Studies in Administrative Control*, No. 1, Feb. 1938.

have a clear majority in the case of raw materials and a substantial plurality in goods in process and finished goods.

The meaning of Table 97 for our purposes, however, is difficult to assess. With respect to raw materials, 23 percent of the companies reported valuation methods for general balance sheet purposes that are not approved by the Treasury (methods C to F). Similar figures for goods in process and finished goods were 44 and 45 percent, respectively. It is not clear what methods firms employed for tax purposes. The meaning of method A also is ambiguous. If it is the lower of first-in, first-out cost or market, it is an approved method. But if so, how would a firm that used the lower of actual cost of specific lots or market have answered? In short, did all firms that applied markdowns to market prices answer in category A no matter what measure of cost they employed? How would a company have answered if it used first-in, first-out cost but did not mark its goods down at the end of the year?

Additional information regarding finished goods inventory practices is provided by a report by the National Association of Cost Accountants.[29] Of 156 classifiable replies from firms using actual, as distinguished from standard, costs, 84 reported values at the lower of cost or market and 4 valued the raw material component alone by this method; 75 valued at cost alone. Replies were received also from 131 companies valuing finished goods at standard costs, but how these companies kept their accounts for tax purposes is not known.

Direct quantitative evidence on the practices of manufacturers reporting to the Treasury for tax purposes—for most years the relevant question—does not exist. George Terborgh records the impressions of Treasury officials whom he consulted in preparing a memorandum for the Board of Governors of the Federal Reserve System. In their opinion, markdowns to market value when replacement prices are below cost are "overwhelmingly the more important" in the case of raw materials. For finished goods, markdowns are less prevalent but are used by a majority of firms. For goods in process, the predominance of markdowns was considered

[29] Finished Goods Inventory Practice, NACA Bulletin XXI, No. 14, Sec. III, March 15, 1940.

intermediate between that prevailing for raw materials and for finished goods.

This summary impression of practices should perhaps be qualified for goods in process and finished goods. Terborgh asserts that the practice of the Treasury is to allow writedowns of goods in process only in consequence of price declines in raw materials which accounts for at least 70 percent of their cost. And with respect to finished goods he writes: "The regulations appear to contemplate write-downs whenever the *current replacement market* for the elements of cost embodied in a manufacturers' finished inventory (material, labor and burden) is below the cost valuations at which they are carried on the books. (See *Regulations 101,* Article 22(c)-4, p. 46.) I am informed that in practice writedowns are not permitted on such inventory unless the *selling* price of the goods falls below their inventory valuation at cost."

The validity of Terborgh's last point seems questionable. If his impression is correct, it would indicate a practice in direct contravention of clear statements continually published in the Treasury regulations. Moreover, accountants of wide experience whom I have consulted do not confirm Terborgh's interpretation.

The surveys of practice cited above make it seem likely that markdowns to market values when the latter are below cost are probably made by at least a small majority of firms. In consequence, we consider that our estimates corrected on the assumption that this is always done are preferable.[30] The material in the text proceeds on this assumption. To test the possible range of errors, price corrections were made on both bases (Sec. D).

B CONSTRUCTION OF THE INDEXES

Kuznets and his staff, in connection with their estimates of capital formation, adjusted the estimates for changes in prices (*Commodity Flow and Capital Formation,* Part VII, Sec. 4, and Tables VII-7 to 10). Subsequently it was possible to improve Kuznets' procedure for at least some industry groups.

---

[30] It would have been better to combine indexes made on each assumption weighted by some approximation to the relative prevalence of each practice. But our information about practice in particular industries was too scanty.

1) Kuznets' method

Kuznets' procedures remain applicable to all manufacturing groups 1918-25 and to the metals and machinery, stone, clay and glass, and miscellaneous groups for all years covered. Since he describes his indexes in detail in Table VII-7, Note A, I content myself with describing the general character of his method briefly.

Kuznets' index for each industry group is simply an average of price relatives representative of the wholesale selling prices of the goods held. The component series are combined by means of BLS, that is, value of product, weights. To construct indexes of cost, price relatives for several months, usually in the latter half of a calendar year, are averaged. To construct indexes of replacement market values on December 31, relatives for December and the succeeding January are averaged.

The indexes have many defects. Foremost is the use of value of product instead of value of inventory weights. For the groups and periods in question, this unsatisfactory choice was, of course, dictated by the absence of a reliable method of determining value of inventory weights.

Secondly, the component price series do not accurately represent the cost of inventories because the part consisting of goods processed by their owners is valued not at any commercial selling price but at a figure compounded of the purchase cost of materials, direct labor, and an allowance for some portion of overhead expenses.

A third, but minor, defect inheres in the number of months chosen to represent the period during which goods in stock at the end of the year were accumulated. I shall argue below that a number of months equal to one and one-half times the usual turnover period is probably the best approximation to the correct period that can be made. Kuznets consistently chose a somewhat larger number of months. This, however, is unlikely to have been of substantial importance. Experiment with varying numbers of months yielded substantially the same results (see Sec. C below).

In view of these defects, the accuracy attaching to the deflated figures is due largely to the general family resemblance of price series of many sorts. Even though inaccurate weighting systems are applied to price series that do not themselves strictly represent the movement of the valuation factors for which they stand, the substantial resemblance of the behavior of prices of similar goods at fabrication stages not too far apart is some assurance that the results are not wholly untrustworthy.

2) The revised inventory value deflators

From the 1937 Census of Manufactures with its detailed classification of inventories by minor industry groups we derived inventory weights for constructing indexes to be applied to the manufacturing groups. Seven of the ten manufacturing groups were, therefore, treated more elaborately but only for the period since 1926 because our data in current prices before this date, based upon samples of large corporations, were deemed too crude to justify the labor of refining the deflating indexes.[31]

The solution of our problems in the groups for which a revised index was used calls for some detailed explanation.

The *Statistics of Income* data, which we must deflate, are classified by industry and do not distinguish raw materials, goods in process, and finished goods. Ideally an index is needed for each; and to deflate data that lump together the three categories, the three indexes must be weighted by the relative importance of each in each industry. Given sufficient data, our index for each category of inventory would be based upon three series:

1 Raw materials: raw materials prices
2 Goods in process: raw materials prices, direct labor, and overhead costs per unit, each element weighted by its relative importance in manufacturing costs per unit of goods in process
3 Finished goods: same three classes of cost series, each weighted by the relative importance of its class in manufacturing costs per unit of finished goods

---

[31] More refined indexes were not constructed for the metal products and processes group because its high degree of integration made it unlikely that published commercial prices would reflect accurately the inter-company transfer prices which determined inventory cost even after 1933 when the privilege of presenting consolidated tax returns was withdrawn. The simpler form of index was continued also for stone, clay and glass and miscellaneous industries since it was impossible to get price series sufficiently representative of the raw materials used, in contradistinction to the finished goods produced, by these industries.

The three indexes would be combined, weighted by the relative importance in each industry of inventories of raw materials, goods in process, and finished goods.

The data available make possible a good but by no means perfect approximation to this procedure. To weight the various classes of inventories correctly, we must depend upon the 1937 Census of Manufactures. Establishments in each industry were requested to state the value of inventories held at the beginning and end of 1937 in (a) raw materials and goods in process, and (b) finished goods. As we cannot separate raw materials from goods in process we throw the entire weight of goods in process upon the price of raw materials. This is less serious than may at first seem since, as we shall see, a very large proportion of the total cost of goods in process is composed of the price of raw materials.

In constructing indexes of costs of finished goods in the various industries, difficulties were encountered because of lack of data. No practicable method of measuring the movement of overhead costs per unit of product could be devised and this element does not appear explicitly in any of our indexes; and in five groups labor costs per unit of product do not appear. In two others, however, an index of labor costs per unit of product was constructed by dividing an index based on the sum of wages and salaries of the industries comprising the *Statistics of Income* group by a comparable index of physical output derived from figures presented by Solomon Fabricant in the *Output of Manufacturing Industries, 1899-1937* (NBER, 1940). Monthly movements were based upon either BLS or NICB data on hourly earnings and adjusted to the biennial index just described.

The departures of our methods from those described above as ideal are briefly: non-raw materials elements are not included in any of our indexes of costs of goods in process and in few of our indexes of costs of finished goods; nor are overhead costs in any of the indexes of cost of finished goods; we constructed indexes of labor costs per unit for only two of the seven groups. Finally, the indexes of labor costs per unit cannot be considered better than a crude approximation.

Because of the absence of non-raw materials cost elements from five groups and the heavy weight given raw materials prices in two, our revised indexes may be described as averages of relatives of prices of raw materials or of materials into which they entered. Some idea of the seriousness of the distortions likely to arise may be gained by inspecting Table 98 and the calculation based upon it.

TABLE 98

All Manufactured Goods: Cost of Raw Materials and
Total Costs (Plus Profits)

	1927	1929	1935
Value of raw materials & containers ($ mil.)[a]	32173	35608	24889
Value of product ($ mil.)[b]	60335	67994	44994
Raw materials as % of value of product	53.3	52.4	55.3
Raw materials as % of cost of goods in process[c]	69.6	68.7	71.2

[a] As revised data for 1927 and 1929 in the Census of Manufactures, 1939, do not exclude fuel and purchased electrical energy, the data were adjusted by the ratio of the value of raw materials and containers to total value including fuel and purchased electrical energy (unrevised figures in Census of Manufactures, 1929). For 1927 this ratio is 94.6; for 1929, 95.2.

The 1935 figure, excluding fuel and purchased electrical energy, is from the Census of Manufactures, 1937.

[b] Census of Manufactures, 1939.

[c] Computed upon the assumption that goods in process are, on the average, half-finished and have, therefore, accumulated costs comprising cost of raw materials plus one-half of all additional costs.

These figures are not quite suitable for our purpose in two countervailing ways. The significance of raw materials is exaggerated by an amount equal to the value of the containers used. On the other hand, non-raw materials costs are overstated and raw materials understated by the presence of profits, interest, and selling and general administrative expenses in the value of product.[32] Taking the figures as they stand, however, raw materials account, on the average, for about 54 percent of the costs of finished goods and for about 70 percent of the costs of goods in process. (We assume that goods in process are on the average half-finished and, therefore, that they have accumulated costs equal to the cost of raw materials plus one-half all additional costs.)

Our assumptions about the percentage distribution of inventories by stages of fabrication (Ch. 7) place us in a position to estimate the weights that ought ideally to be attached to raw materials

[32] Non-raw materials costs are further exaggerated to the extent that other elements of overhead cost are not counted as costs of inventory; see below.

prices on the one hand and non-raw materials elements on the other for manufacturing industries taken together.

INDEX OF RAW MATERIALS PRICES, .750				INDEX OF NON-RAW MATERIALS ELEMENTS, .250			
			WEIGHT				WEIGHT
Raw materials	.400 ×	1.00 =	.400	Goods in proc.	.200 ×	.31 =	.062
Goods in proc.	.200 ×	.69 =	.138	Finished goods	.400 ×	.47 =	.188
Finished goods	.400 ×	.53 =	.212				

On the average, a maximum of about one-fourth of the total cost of inventory elements are incorrectly represented in our indexes either because their weight was shifted to raw materials prices or because poor indexes were used to represent them. The distortion may actually be much less, however, for the calculation assumed that all value added entered into the cost of inventory. But profits, general office and selling expenses certainly never enter and other portions of overhead often do not. According to Terborgh's unpublished memorandum for the Board of Governors of the Federal Reserve System, a large portion of overhead is, in fact, neglected in inventory accounting. Tabulating the reports of 446 large manufacturing corporations as shown in the SEC's *Survey of Listed Corporations,* Terborgh found that substantial amounts of three important overhead items were not accounted as 'cost of goods sold'.

	OVERHEAD ITEMS IN COST OF GOODS SOLD	
	Included	Not included
	(millions of dollars)	
Depreciation, depletion, & amortization	319	685
Taxes (other than income & excess profit)	358	381
Rents & royalties	84	73
Total	761	1139

In the absence of special adjustments of the inventory account, costs not included under costs of goods sold would not affect the value of inventories. Such adjustments, if made, would appear in the reports filed with the Treasury in the form of a discrepancy between the inventory value reported on the balance sheet schedule of the corporate income tax return and the value entered on the face of the return for computing the cost of goods sold. Concerning this point, Terborgh writes:

"The Treasury has never tabulated inventory values from the face of the returns for comparison with the tabulations from schedule N (balance sheet schedule); hence no conclusive measure of the disparity, if any, is available. I have consulted several officials of the Bureau of Internal Revenue on the matter, and they are unanimous in the opinion that in the overwhelming majority of the cases there is no disparity. One official was good enough to run over a stack of returns to check the point, and found not a single case in which the two valuations did not agree."

In the light of this evidence it seems likely that many companies omit a substantial fraction of overhead in valuing finished and process inventories. If we assumed that only raw materials, labor, and other direct costs figure as costs of inventory, we would have a counterpoise to our calculation which assumes that all overhead plus interest, profits, and selling expenses (the last three never enter into the inventory value) are counted in the cost of inventory. The two classes of index from which our deflations would then be derived would be indexes of raw materials prices and of labor costs per unit, which would on the average be weighted .818 and .182, respectively. The weight that would fall on non-raw materials cost elements would be substantially less than that indicated above. It is perhaps fair to say that elements not accurately represented in our indexes have a weight, on the average, of 18-25 percent, a range whose lower limit is bound to underestimate and whose upper limit is bound to exaggerate the true figure.

Index of Raw Materials Prices, .818		Index of Labor Costs per Unit, .182	
WEIGHT		WEIGHT	
Raw materials	.400	Goods in process	.042
Goods in process	.158	Finished goods	.140
Finished goods	.260		

Price indexes representative of raw materials costs were selected in the following manner. For each census minor industry in each *Statistics of Income* group, the chief raw materials used were determined from census and other representative sources. Price indexes representing these materials were then selected from the BLS collection and combined by means of weights based on the relative importance of the various materials in the total value of raw materials consumed in each minor industry. When raw materials prices were the only series used, the indexes for each minor industry were combined by means of weights based upon the relative importance of the value of inventories held by each minor industry in the total value held by all minor industries in each *Statistics of Income* manufacturing group. When indexes of labor cost per unit were used, the weight attached to the inventories held by each minor industry was distributed between raw materials prices and labor costs per unit in proportion to the relative importance of each in total costs excluding overhead.

After selecting indexes of prices or unit costs to represent various elements of the cost of different categories of stocks and after choosing a weighting scheme, we had to select the precise months whose standings should be averaged for an index of the cost of goods held in stock.[33] As explained above, the ideal procedure requires a knowledge of the inventory accounting methods in each industry and the rate of purchase of goods toward the end of the year. The methods approved by the Treasury during the period covered by our estimates were the so-called actual cost of specific lots method and the first-in, first-out method.[34]

Properly to deflate year end inventories valued at the actual cost of specific lots, an estimate of the age distribution of the specific lots of goods in stock is essential. In the deflator one could then include prices ruling at each date at which goods represented in the stock were purchased by the industry. Prices ruling at each date would be weighted by the importance of inventories bought on that date.

For inventories valued by the first-in, first-out method, however, what is necessary are the prices prevailing during a period long enough before December 31 for a quantity of goods to have been bought equal in volume to the stock at the end of the year whether or not the latter was bought during the specific period. Prices ruling within the period would be weighted by the rate of purchases at each date.

[33] The index of market, i.e., replacement cost, prices as of December 31 for use whenever they were below cost was uniformly computed by averaging standings for December and the following January.

[34] In 1938 the Treasury sanctioned last-in, first-out accounting for the leather tanning and nonferrous metals industries and has since approved it for other industries.

As neither procedure could be followed very closely, we included a number of months equal to one and one-half times a turnover period, as determined by the quotient of inventories divided by the cost of goods sold in each industry. This decision rests upon the following considerations. For companies charging inventory to process or sales by the first-in, first-out method, the average 'age' of inventory (that is, of the invoices that determine the value of the inventory) would be one-half a turnover period, provided goods were acquired at an even rate during a period equal to the turnover period. Thus for an industry whose turnover period was four months, the cost of inventory would be best represented by an average of the last four months of the year. Although it would be incorrect for any particular year, this figure would probably be the best if all inventories were accounted for on a first-in, first-out basis and if purchase and delivery dates were identical. Accounting by the other Treasury-approved method, actual cost of specific lots, and an interval between purchase and delivery tend to raise the relevant average age.

Accounting by the actual cost of specific lots produces an average 'age' which, of course, depends upon the order of utilization. Perishable goods (in this context 'perishability' is to be understood as a tendency to lose value with time, not through use) are probably used in the order of seniority (any departure from this order would raise the average age somewhat). Many goods that are durable and semidurable as far as their material is concerned are nevertheless to be included in this perishable class because of style characteristics.

If a good is highly durable the order of utilization may reasonably be expected to be random. That is, on the average, the goods used each month would have an average age equal to the average age of the supply of goods available during the month (opening inventory plus purchases). Experiment with arithmetical examples based upon the assumption that the goods used each month have an average age equal to the average of the supply available at the beginning of the month indicates that, on the average, actual cost of specific lots accounting will produce an age distribution of inventory such that the percentage bought in any given month decreases rapidly as one goes backward from the reporting date.

Hence the bulk of the stock is likely to date from the last few months of the year although an infinitesimal fraction is indefinitely old.

In view of these considerations and of another discussed below, we took an average of prices in a number of months equal to one and one-half times a turnover period to represent cost. The average outcome of the assumption of actual cost of specific lots accounting will always be that the bulk of inventory was purchased within such a period. For example, if we assume a turnover period of 4 months, so that we take an average of the last 6 months to represent cost, some 74 percent of total inventory accounted for in this fashion will have been purchased in this period, provided goods are used in the manner described above. If the turnover rate assumed is 12, so that we take an average of the last 2 months ($1\frac{1}{2}$ months rounded to the next higher figure), just 75 percent will have been purchased in the period.

A simple average, which weights each month equally, evidently underweights the most recent months and overweights the more distant months as far as the goods purchased are concerned. But since about a quarter of the goods will have been purchased in still more distant months, the method seems justified.

Finally, if purchase and delivery are not simultaneous, the average 'age' of goods will be increased, for in general the prices applying to a contract are those ruling at the time of sale, not at the time of delivery. It is probably also true that the time required for delivery reduces the variations in the age of inventory about its general average age because of an offsetting tendency in variations of turnover and of delivery periods, respectively. In poor years when deliveries are relatively prompt, turnover periods tend to be relatively long; and in good years, they tend to be relatively short and deliveries slow.

The age of inventory, however, is not a vital question. Experiment indicates that rather large variations in the number of months included in our average cost of inventories produce very small differences in the deflating index.

The methods described above were applied to the following *Statistics of Income* groups: food, beverages and tobacco; chemicals and allied products; textiles and textile products; rubber and related products; leather and leather products; lumber and wood products; paper and products.

Our inability to find price series representative of raw materials used prevented the application of the technique to stone, clay and glass, and miscellaneous industries. And doubts about the values at which raw materials were priced in the integrated blast furnace and rolling mills industry as well as the importance of labor and overhead cost made it unlikely that we could improve the deflation of the metals and machinery group. The way our procedures were applied to the groups for which revised indexes could be calculated is described in the following sections.

Leather and leather products

The minor industries in this group were readily divided into two categories: those whose chief raw materials are (a) hides and skins, (b) leather. The BLS raw materials indexes selected to represent these two materials were combined, weighting by total inventories held at the end of 1936 and 1937 by leather manufacturers and leather products manufacturers, respectively. Hides and skins were weighted by .43 and leather by .57. The months included were September-December.

Non-raw materials cost elements were thus neglected, but extensive tests indicated that the inclusion of an index of direct labor costs or of total non-raw materials elements (when represented by the prices of leather and leather products) would not alter the index materially (see note on experiments in deflating inventories in the leather group). The weight attributable to non-raw materials elements because of inventories of finished goods was 15.5 percent, estimated on the overly conservative assumption that all overhead costs plus profits figure in cost inventory.

Food, beverages and tobacco

Price series for inclusion in this index were obtained by the following procedure. The main raw material (or materials) consumed in each minor industry in the *Census of Manufactures, 1937* were assigned weights determined by computing for each raw material the factor:

$$\text{Weight } a = \frac{I_1}{I} \times \frac{C_{a1}}{C_1} + \frac{I_2}{I} \times \frac{C_{a2}}{C_2} + \cdots \frac{I_n}{I} \times \frac{C_{an}}{C_n}$$

where

$I_1, I_2 \cdots I_n =$ value of inventories (average of Dec. 31, 1936 and 1937) held in census minor industries 1 to n using commodity A as a raw material

$C_{a1}, C_{a2} \cdots C_{an} =$ value of commodity A consumed in industries 1 to n in 1937

$C_1, C_2 \cdots C_n =$ total value of materials included in the index consumed in industries 1 to n.

Shortenings and cocoa beans were excluded when it was found that the weight attributable to each was less than 1 percent. Ten commodities were included with weights adjusted and rounded so that their sum came to 1: granulated sugar, New York, .04; raw sugar, 96°, New York, .09; cottonseed oil, New York, .04; fruits and vegetables index, .17; wheat, no. 2, hard, Kansas City, .09; wheat flour, standard patents, Minneapolis, .03; corn, no. 3, yellow, Chicago, .19; milk, fluid, Chicago, .05; livestock and poultry index, .17; tobacco, leaf, warehouse sales, average for preceding 12 months, .13.

The weight of an index representing non-raw materials elements in cost, if available, would have been .154.

Before weighting, price relatives were converted to the base: average of last four months in 1936 and 1937 = 100.

The months included in the index of cost were September-December.

Paper and pulp products

Three types of industry are included in this group: pulp, paper, and paper products. The group index was, therefore, constructed by combining indexes representative of the raw materials used by each. The weights were the values of inventories held by the minor industries in each group (Census of Manufactures, 1937).

The price index for each group is a weighted average of the prices of raw materials used at each level. The weights for pulp and paper were values of materials consumed. The weights for the two prices combined to yield an index for paper products were obtained by apportioning total 1937 consumption of paper in the manufacture of converted paper products according to whether the final products of the various minor industries were paper or paper board.

Lumber instead of log prices were used in the pulp branch.

COMMODITIES AND BLS PRICE SERIES	WEIGHT
A Pulp	
Spruce, Eastern, Boston	.06
Yellow, mill, Ponderosa, common	.03
Hemlock, Northern, No. 1, Chicago	.03
B Paper	
Wood pulp, domestic, mill, Mechanical, No. 1	.07
Wood pulp, domestic, mill, Sulphite, news grade unbleached	.21
Wood pulp, domestic, mill, Kraft, No. 1	.17
Wood pulp, domestic, mill, Soda, bleached	.04
C Paper products	
Book paper	.18
Paper board, 85 lb. best linen	.21
Total	1.00

A weight of 16 percent would have been attributed to an index of non-raw materials cost elements in this group had the requisite data been available. The months included in the index of cost were September-December.

Rubber and related products

This group consists exclusively of manufacturers who make products from crude rubber.

The index was constructed by combining the BLS price index of crude rubber, weighted by .8, with that of auto tires and tubes, weighted by .2. The weight relevant to inventories of raw materials and goods in process was assigned to the index of crude rubber prices. The weight attributable to inventories of finished goods was distributed between the two component indexes on the basis of the relative importance of raw materials and other direct costs in the total direct costs of producing rubber products as determined from 1937 Census data.

The months included in the index of cost were September-December.

Chemicals and allied products

The index for this group consists entirely of prices representing the chief raw materials used by the various census minor industries in the *Statistics of Income* chemicals group. Had indexes representative of non-raw materials cost elements been included, their weight would have been 25.5 percent.

The chief raw materials, determined from census and other sources, were combined by a process similar to that used in the food, beverages and tobacco group.

The months included in the index of cost were August-December.

BLS PRICE SERIES	BLS NO.	WEIGHT
Flaxseed	49	.0131
Coconut oils	183	.0175
Bituminous coal	346	.0365
Natural gasoline	357	.0204
Crude petroleum	365	.3768
White lead	548	.0319
Lithopone	550	.0154
China wood oil	551	.0210
Linseed oil	552	.0340
Asphalt	559	.0144
Nitric acid	587	.0113
Sulphuric acid	592	.0268
Ammonia	596	.0348
Salt	623	.0984
Soda ash	625	.0313
Caustic soda	627	.0221
Sulphur	630	.0270
Tallow	631	.0498
Wood pulp	748	.0127
Fertilizer materials	Index	.0411
Miscellaneous		.0332
FROM AGRICULTURAL STATISTICS		
Cotton seed		.0268
Soybeans		.0037
Total		1.0000

Textiles and textile products

Minor industries constituting this group were first placed in one of three subgroups: industries consuming fibers, yarns, or cloth. Indexes for each subgroup were weighted by the value of inventories held by minor industries in each group. Prices of the various fibers and yarns consumed in the first two subgroups were weighted by factors computed in a fashion similar to that used for foods, beverages and tobacco. Since in the third subgroup the raw materials used could not be allocated easily among the various types of cloth, prices representative of the chief types were weighted by the value of fibers consumed in the country.

BLS PRICE SERIES	WEIGHT
Cotton, middling	19.7
Wool, medium grades	4.7
Rayon, 150, 2d quality[a]	0.9
Raw silk, double extra, crack, 13-15, 78%	3.6
Cotton yarn, carded, mill, 22/1, cones	9.9
Wool yarn, mill, 2/40's, half-blood, weaving	19.8
Rayon yarn, 150, 2d quality	6.9
Silk yarn, domestic, mill, 60/2	4.2
Cotton cloth index[b]	11.8
Wool goods index[c]	9.8
Rayon and silk goods index[d]	7.8
Jute, raw, medium grades, N.Y.[e]	0.9
Total	100.0

[a] Yarn price used to represent unspun rayon.
[b] Computed by NBER by excluding yarn prices from the BLS index of cotton goods.
[c] Computed by NBER by excluding yarns from the BLS index of woolen and worsted goods.
[d] BLS index used to represent cloths made of rayon and silk.
[e] Used to represent jute cloth.

Had an index of non-raw materials costs been included, it would have borne about 16 percent of the total weight. The months included in the index of cost were August-December.

Lumber and wood products

The final index for this group is a combination of two indexes: one designed to represent the unit value of inventories of industries drawing their raw materials directly from the forests, the other of industries drawing their raw materials from the first group. The two indexes were combined by weighting by the total inventories held by each group.

The first group (lumber and timber, excelsior, turpentine, and rosin) is dominated by the lumber and timber industry which held almost 99 percent of the total inventories held by the three industries. An index for lumber and timber was, therefore, deemed representative of the first group.

The index for the lumber and timber, excelsior, and turpentine industries is a combination of an index of labor costs per unit (computed by adjusting the NICB index of hourly earnings in the lumber and millwork industry to biennial census levels for wages and salaries per unit of output) and the BLS index of lumber prices. Labor costs per unit were weighted by the value of inventories of raw materials and by the portion of the inventories of finished goods equal to the percentage that cost of raw materials consumed in the industry bore to the value of the product. The lumber price index was weighted by the portion of the value of finished goods that was equal to the value added divided by the value of product of the three industries. The index for the other industries in the forest products group was the BLS index of lumber prices. The two indexes were combined by weighting by inventories held in the three basic industries and in other industries, respectively. For the group as a whole labor costs per unit were weighted by .54 and lumber prices by .46.

Other non-raw material cost elements in the woodworking industries would have received 10.4 percent of the total weight had an index representative of the behavior of these costs been available. The months included in the index of cost were September-December.

C   ALTERNATIVE DEFLATORS OF INVENTORY VALUES IN THE LEATHER AND LEATHER PRODUCTS INDUSTRY

Before revising Kuznets' inventory value deflators for manufacturing groups generally, we constructed several other indexes for the leather and leather products group. The original index used in *Commodity Flow and Capital Formation* is the BLS price index of hides and leather products, a combination of indexes of hides and skins, leather, shoes (factory), and other leather products. Each in turn is a combination of several price series. The weights throughout are census values of product. The figure taken to represent the cost of inventories held at the year end is an average of the annual average, weighted one-third, and that for October, weighted two-thirds.

Our other indexes were designed to see what differences would be caused by:

1) Weighting the same indexes by values of inventories and allowing for the importance of the cost of hides and skins in the cost of leather and of the cost of leather in the value of shoes and other leather products. The indexes for hides and skins and leather were taken to be representative of raw materials costs at the two stages of fabrication. The indexes for leather and those for shoes and other leather products were taken to be representative of non-raw materials costs at the two stages. The weights for the four indexes were, therefore:

Hides and skins: $\dfrac{I_{a}'}{I} + \left[\dfrac{I_{a}''}{I} \times \dfrac{R_a}{C_a}\right]$

Leather: $\left[\dfrac{I_{a}''}{I} \times \dfrac{W_a}{C_a}\right] + \dfrac{I_{b}'}{I} + \left[\dfrac{I_{b}''}{I} \times \dfrac{R_b}{C_b}\right] + \dfrac{I_{c}'}{I} + \left[\dfrac{I_{c}''}{I} \times \dfrac{R_c}{C_c}\right]$

Shoes: $\dfrac{I_{b}''}{I} \times \dfrac{W_b}{C_b}$

Other leather products: $\dfrac{I_{c}''}{I} \times \dfrac{W_c}{C_c}$

Symbols:
I = Total value of inventories held by the leather and leather products group

I_{a}' = Inventories of raw materials and goods in process held by leather manufacturers

I_{a}'' = Finished goods held by leather manufacturers

R_a = Value of raw materials consumed by leather manufacturers

W_a = Wages and salaries paid by leather manufacturers

C_a = Cost of raw materials plus wages and salaries paid by leather manufacturers

Same symbols with subscripts b and c refer to inventories and costs of manufacturers of shoes and other leather products, respectively.

2) Using inventory weights, but substituting indexes of labor cost per unit of product for indexes of prices of finished products to

represent non-raw materials cost elements in the value of inventories of finished goods. The weights were computed on the same principle as in (1). The weight attaching to inventories of finished goods was distributed among the relevant raw materials prices and the index of labor costs on the basis of the importance of raw materials and other direct costs respectively.

The labor cost indexes were computed by adjusting the movement of NICB indexes of hourly earnings in the leather tanning and finishing industry and in the boot and shoe industry to biennial data on labor costs per unit of product. The biennial index was constructed by dividing an index of wages and salaries based on Census of Manufactures figures in these industries by Fabricant's indexes of physical output.

3) Using a weighting scheme as in (2), but other indexes of labor costs per unit. Labor costs per unit were estimated by dividing BLS indexes of payrolls in the leather tanning and boot and shoe industries by FRB indexes of production in these industries, the latter adjusted to biennial census data.

4) Weighting raw materials prices in the leather industry (hides and skins) and in the leather products industry (leather) by the total value of inventories held by the two sets of manufacturers.

The details of the construction of these deflators are given in Table 99.

TABLE 99

Construction of Deflators for the Leather and Leather Products Industry

VARIANT 1	WEIGHT	VARIANT 2	WEIGHT
BLS Price Indexes		BLS hides and skins	.398
Hides and skins	.398	Labor costs in leather mfg.	
Leather	.034[a]	(based on hourly earn-	
Leather	.483[b]	ings)	.034
Boots and shoes	.069	BLS leather prices	.483
Other leather products	.016	Labor costs in leather	
		products mfg. (based on	
VARIANT 3		hourly earnings)	.084
Same as 2 except that labor			
cost indexes were com-		VARIANT 4	
puted by dividing in-		*BLS Price Indexes*	
dexes of payrolls by in-		Hides and skins	.43
dexes of physical output.		Leather prices	.57

[a] In leather group.
[b] In leather products group.

For purposes of comparison, the make-up of Kuznets' deflator and that of Variant 1, which uses the same price series but assigns them inventory rather than value of product weights, are given in Table 100.

TABLE 100

Kuznets' and Variant 1 Weights

	KUZNETS'	VARIANT 1
Hides and skins	.2080	.398
Leather	.2236	.517
Boots and shoes	.4749	.069
Other leather products	.0935	.016

The shift in the basis of weighting roughly doubles the weight allotted to hides and skins and leather and makes the other two series about one-eighth as important as in Kuznets' index.

The computations indicated that the months chosen for the averages had negligible effect on the outcome. Differences traceable to the selection of price series and to the relative weights were more noteworthy. Table 101 shows the value of corporate inventories in the leather and leather products groups 1925-35 when corrected by Kuznets' deflator and by deflators 1 to 4 assuming that inventories are valued at cost or market, whichever is lower. The index of cost is constructed in each case by computing an average of prices in October, weighted two-thirds, plus the annual average, weighted one-third.

TABLE 101

Leather and Leather Products Industry
Corporate Inventories, 1929 Prices

	KUZNETS	VARIANT 1	VARIANT 2	VARIANT 3	VARIANT 4
1925	390.8	392.1	384.7	383.1	392.9
1926	443.5	453.3	445.4	445.9	455.3
1927	426.0	413.8	412.6	414.5	411.4
1928	428.8	414.9	416.5	412.7	412.7
1929	426.1	432.8	431.0	425.7	434.1
1930	444.4	501.5	496.7	586.9	513.4
1931	394.7	478.6	470.8	464.7	496.7
1932	331.7	437.2	440.0	434.5	463.2
1933	325.3	376.7	378.4	380.1	386.9
1934	323.8	401.4	403.4	403.4	417.4
1935	336.2	367.0	372.8	373.7	372.8

Data for 1935 adjusted to 1933 basis of classification by means of ratio of data for 1934, computed on 1933 basis of classification, to data for the same year computed on revised basis of classification: 105.3.

D   ERRORS INVOLVED IN THE ASSUMPTION ABOUT PREVALENCE OF
     MARKDOWNS

In Section 2, A, above, I discussed the prevalence of markdowns
of inventory values to replacement costs when these stand at a
level lower than accounting costs at year ends. I there set forth
the grounds for my opinion that markdowns are taken for tax purposes by at least a small majority of manufacturing firms—perhaps
by a substantial majority. The measures in the text are based exclusively upon inventory series corrected for changes in prices
upon the assumption that markdowns are always made when replacement values are below cost. How serious are the errors engendered by this assumption?

Since at least half of all inventories held by manufacturers appear to have been subject to markdown, the extreme limit of the
errors can be tested by comparing inventories deflated upon the
assumption that markdowns are universal with inventories deflated upon the assumption that they are applied to only half the
value of stocks in each industry. We first compare inventory values
themselves, then net changes (first differences) in them.

1   Comparison of inventory series

Inventories of all manufacturers in 1929 prices as revealed by price
corrections carried out upon the two extreme assumptions described above resemble each other very closely. The one serious
divergence, in 1920 when prices changed rapidly, caused the direction of change in inventories to differ in 1920-21.

The percentage that disagreements in direction of change were
of the total number of comparisons is slightly under 5 for total
manufacturing, and about the same for individual groups taken
together (Table 102). In no groups were there disagreements
in as many as 15 percent of the comparisons.

2   Comparison of net changes in inventories

When we compare net changes in inventories, the situation is
somewhat less favorable. For total manufacturing, the values for
individual years often diverge widely. The two series, however,
moved in different directions only three times in 20 comparisons.
The cyclical conformity, moreover, is almost perfect after the

TABLE 102

Manufacturers' Inventories Corrected for Price Changes upon
Different Assumptions about the Prevalence of Markdowns

	NO. OF COMPARISONS OF DIRECTION OF CHANGE	NO. OF DISAGREEMENTS	DISAGREEMENTS AS % OF TOTAL COMPARISONS
INVENTORIES			
Total manufacturing	21	1	4.8
Foods, beverages & tobacco	21	1	4.8
Textiles & textile products	21	2	9.5
Leather & leather products	21	1	4.8
Rubber & related products	21	0	0
Lumber & wood products	21	0	0
Paper, printing & publishing	21	3	14.3
Chemicals & allied products	21	1	4.8
Stone, clay & glass products	21	0	0
Metals & metal products	21	0	0
Miscellaneous	19	2	10.5
Sum of 10 groups	208	10	4.8
NET CHANGES			
Total manufacturing	20	3	15.0
Foods, beverages & tobacco	20	3	15.0
Textiles & textiles products	20	3.5[a]	17.5
Leather & leather products	20	1	5.0
Rubber & related products	20	0	0
Lumber & wood products	20	1	5.0
Paper, printing & publishing	20	2.5[a]	12.5
Chemicals & allied products	20	1	5.0
Stone, clay & glass products	20	0	0
Metals & metal products	20	1	5.0
Miscellaneous	18	0	0
Sum of 10 groups	198	13	6.6

[a] When one series does not change between one year end and the next while
the other does, the disagreement is counted as one-half.

period of extreme price disturbance, 1918-23, except in 1932-33.
And the differences in the timing at the trough in 1932-33 and at
the peak in 1936-37 offset each other.

Disagreements appeared in more than 15 percent of the comparisons only in textiles, and the total number of disagreements for all ten groups together was only 6.6 percent of total comparisons. The possibility of serious error from this source is small in the inventories series and not much greater in the case of net changes.

Determination of Reference Dates for Annual Series
with Various Timing Characteristics

REFERENCE DATES FOR CALENDAR YEAR SERIES (TABLE 15, UPPER HALF)

For the purpose of measuring conformity a series whose cycles tend to turn synchronously with business cycles would be expected to reach calendar year peaks and troughs in the same years as business in general. A series that tends to lag 12 months should reach its peaks and troughs in the years following annual reference cycle turns and one that tends to lead 12 months should reach its peaks and troughs in the years preceding.

Similarly, a calendar year series whose monthly analogue lags 6 months behind business at large should reach its peaks and troughs in the calendar years following the fiscal years (years ending June 30) when business cycle peaks and troughs are recorded. And a calendar year series whose monthly analogue leads by 6 months should reach its peaks and troughs one year earlier. If the fiscal year 1927 is a business cycle peak, a series that lags 6 months should reach its calendar year peak in the calendar year 1927. A series that leads by 6 months should reach its peak in the calendar year 1926.

In the same way a series that lags 3 months behind business cycles should reach its calendar year peaks and troughs in the calendar years following the October-September years when business in general reached high and low levels. Series that lead by 9 months should reach their calendar year peaks and troughs in the calendar years preceding. Thus if the year ending September 1928 is a reference trough for years running from October through September, a series that lags 3 months should reach its trough in the calendar year 1928, while one that leads by 9 months should be at a trough in the calendar year 1927.

Finally, an annual chronology of business cycle turns for years running from April to March provides us with reference dates for calendar year series with turns that lag 9 months behind those of business or that lead by 3. If business is at peak levels, say, in the year ending March 1930, a series that lags 9 months should reach a calendar year peak in the calendar year 1930, and one that leads by 3 months should reach a peak in the calendar year 1929.

Following this plan we take our reference chronology for series that are assumed to run synchronously (Table 15, col. 5) from the National Bureau standard calendar year reference cycle chronology (cf. Table 4). From these dates we derive also our reference chronology for series that lead or lag one year (Table 15, col. 1 and 9). From the reference dates in the National Bureau fiscal year reference chronology we derive the dates for series that lag 6 months (Table 15, col. 7) and for series that lead by 6 months (Table 15, col. 3).

Reference peaks and troughs for the remaining timing categories were chosen according to the turns in the FRB index of industrial production since 1919, and according to those in the American Telephone and Telegraph Company index of business activity for years before 1919. Neither series was adjusted for trend. Annual averages were computed from the monthly data of these two reference series for years ending in March and September. The peaks and troughs of these series provided the reference chronologies for series lagging 9 and 3 months, respectively (Table 15, col. 8 and 6) and from these we derived the reference dates for series that lead by 3 and 9 months (Table 15, col. 4 and 2).

Two figures appear in Table 15, columns 4 and 8, in connection with one trough and one peak because the annual reference series for years ending March declines steadily and at an increasing rate from a peak in the year ending March 1918 to a trough in the year ending 1921. To maintain symmetry with the other timing categories, a trough is assumed in either 1918 or 1919 and a peak in either 1919 or 1920 in column 4 and a trough and a peak one year later in column 8.

REFERENCE DATES FOR END OF YEAR SERIES (TABLE 15, LOWER HALF)

The procedure for deriving reference dates for December 31 series is analogous to that for calendar year series. Again the reference series used are the FRB index of industrial production since 1919 and the A. T. and T. index before that year. The conformity of year end series that run synchronously must be measured in conjunction with reference dates that show the year ends when business was at peak and trough levels. The conformity of year end series whose monthly analogues lag 3 months must be measured in conjunction with reference dates that show the September 30's when business reached peaks and troughs. And so on.

A complete scheme by 3-month intervals follows. Only the first four of the nine sets of dates are independent; the others are derived from these four by predating or postdating one year.

Timing Category of Series	Reference dates derived from peaks and troughs of business recorded annually at:
Synchronous	December 31
Lags 3 months	September 30
Lags 6 months	June 30
Lags 9 months	March 31
Lags 12 months	December 31, postdated one year
Leads 3 months	March 31, predated one year
Leads 6 months	June 30, predated one year
Leads 9 months	September 30, predated one year
Leads 12 months	December 31, predated one year

The process of selecting turning dates was simple in almost every instance. The first step was to chart four annual series, one of December 31 standings (average of December and the following January), the second, of September 30 standings, and so on. The peaks and troughs in these series represented the reference dates required.

Some exceptional instances remain to be noted.

1) The June 30 and September 30 series reached a peak in 1933 and a trough in 1934. As this contraction is not recognized in the National Bureau standard set of reference dates, it was disregarded in our chronology.

2) The December 31 series derived from the FRB index of industrial production does not show a decline in 1923-24 corresponding to the contraction recognized by the National Bureau. A contrac-

tion is nevertheless entered in our chronology to correspond with the contraction recognized in the National Bureau standard chronology and dated in the light of the pronounced decline in the rate of growth of this series which began on December 31, 1922 and ended a year later.

3) In the same way a contraction in the June 30 FRB series was considered to begin in 1926 and end in 1927 although the series shows merely a decline in its rate of growth.

4) A somewhat different source of trouble was found in dating the peaks in general business near the end of 1917. Reading the turning dates directly from the charts we would have to accept for synchronous series, the end of 1916; for series lagging 3 months, the end of 1917; for series lagging 6 months, the end of 1918; for series lagging 9 months, the end of 1918; for series lagging 12 months, the end of 1917.

Chart 102
American Telephone and Telegraph Index
End of Year Standings for Years Ending on Various Dates

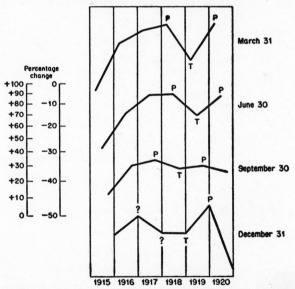

Data are based on the American Telephone and Telegraph index as revised in 1932. Revisions in 1944 altered the composition and method of computing the index. The new data indicate a peak in 1918 and a trough in 1919 for series lagging 3 months, instead of 1917 and 1918 respectively. In view of the uncertainty of conditions during this period it was decided not to alter the reference chronology based on the original series.

If this schedule were accepted at face value we would have to say that series lagging 12 months are expected to turn before those lagging 6 months. The trouble arises because of a sharp random decline in the A. T. & T. index at the end of 1917 which causes the peak in the December 31 series to shift back to the end of 1916. But the September 30 (+3) series has its peak in 1917 and the others in 1918 (Chart 102).

We decided to take the peak in the synchronous series at the end of 1917 in accordance with the evidence of the National Bureau standard set of fiscal and calendar year reference dates (Table 15). The calendar year peak is placed in 1918 and the fiscal year peak in the fiscal year 1918 (July 1917 to June 1918). Thus, the set of peaks for end of year series as finally selected falls within the period straddled by the fiscal and calendar year peaks as selected by the National Bureau on the basis of more comprehensive evidence. A peak at the end of 1916 would fall well outside this period.

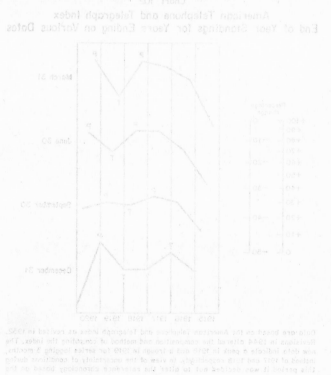

APPENDIX C

Relative Importance of Goods in Process Based on Federal Trade Commission and Securities and Exchange Commission Reports

The *Industrial Corporation Reports* present balance sheets showing year end inventories and stocks of goods in process for 38 industries in 1939 and 16 in 1938.[1] For 1939 the FTC compiled the information from reports submitted directly by selected corporations. For 1938 the data were taken from annual reports to the SEC and from supplementary information submitted at the request of the FTC.

The sample of reporting firms was usually obtained by selecting in each industry some "of the most important concerns . . . from the standpoint of investment and value of goods sold". The sales reported by the sample in 1939 range from 12.5 to 97 percent of the Bureau of Census value of product for corresponding groups (excluding a few cases where the census data were exceeded by the sample figures).[2] In most groups the sample accounted for over half the activity reported to the census. The number of firms reporting in each industry ranged from 4 to 34, but usually from 4 to 9. The over-all coverage of the sample firms compared with

[1] In general, the reports are for the end of the calendar year, but in some cases cover fiscal years ending nearest the end of the calendar year to which the reports are attributed.

[2] These cases are attributed largely to the classification of certain plants of these corporations under other industries by the Bureau of Census, and also to the fact that the census does not cover foreign establishments, while the FTC data cover the consolidated operations of the corporations.

TABLE 103

Sample of Goods in Process Obtained from Federal Trade and Securities and Exchange Commission Reports

Relative Importance of Firms and Industries in Sample

INDUSTRY (1)	TOTAL STOCKS OF FIRMS IN SAMPLE $ MIL. (2)	1 9 3 8 PERCENTAGE RATIO			TOTAL STOCKS OF FIRMS IN SAMPLE $ MIL. (6)	1 9 3 9 PERCENTAGE RATIO		
		Goods in process in sample to total (3)	Total stocks in sample to total stocks in ind. (4)	Total stocks in ind. to total stocks in all mfg. ($8,926 mil.) (5)		Goods in process in sample to total (7)	Total stocks in sample to total stocks in ind. (8)	Total stocks in ind. to total stocks in all mfg. ($9,652 mil.) (9)
			FEDERAL TRADE COMMISSION					
Aircraft	57	69.1	93.4	0.7	92	70.1	93.9	1.0
Auto parts & accessories	90	31.8	68.2	1.5	109	32.5	68.1	1.7
Beet sugar	63	0.8	71.6	1.0	59	0.8	69.4	0.9
Biscuits & crackers					17	0.5	121.4	0.1
Cane sugar					44	1.6	78.6	0.6
Chemicals (ind.)					190	15.8	105.6	1.9
Cigarettes & tob. prod.					536	0.2	291.3	1.9
Clay (other than pottery)	10	8.5	76.9	0.1	11	11.0	84.6	0.1
Confectionery					39	10.3	134.5	0.3
Cotton textiles					120	21.9	43.3	2.9
Domestic laundry equip.	5	29.0	25.6	0.1	6	29.3	60.0	0.1
Eng., turb., waterwheels & windmills	16	42.0	36.4	0.5	17	47.3	35.4	0.5
Firearms & ammunition					12	46.5	63.2	0.2
Furniture					18	23.1	131.4	1.4
Glass & glassware	50	6.9	72.5	0.8	52	8.0	88.1	0.6
Gray-iron & malleable iron castings	8	13.4	26.7	0.3	11	13.5	30.6	0.4
Gypsum & asbestos prod. & roof coating (excl. paint)					53	13.0	171.0	0.3
Hardware					32	35.2	76.2	0.4
Heat. & cook. apparatus (excl. electric)					39	17.0	37.9	1.1
Knitgoods (incl. hosiery)					31	31.3	25.8	1.2
Leather boots & shoes					88	12.1	90.7	1.0

(1)	(2)	(3)	(4)	(5)	(6)	(7)	(8)	(9)
Lumber & timber					39	1.7	20.3	2.0
Machine tool acc. & mach. precision tools					13	39.2	54.2	0.2
Machine tools					24	51.2	34.8	0.7
Matches	14	29.4	280.0	0.1	14	36.0	233.3	0.1
Pumps, pumping equip. & air compressors	11	22.9	20.4	0.6	12	24.1	21.1	0.6
Rayons & allied prod.	29	11.1	87.9	0.4	19	28.9	86.4	0.2
Rubber prod.	195	6.7	132.7	1.6	210	7.4	123.5	1.8
Saws, files & hand tools	11	29.0	33.3	0.4	11	31.9	32.4	0.4
Ships	14	67.7	42.4	0.4	17	69.4	40.5	0.4
Silk	8	20.9	50.0	0.2	9	21.8	47.4	0.2
Silverware & plated ware					12	39.0	80.0	0.2
Soap, cottonseed oil prod. & cooking fats					109	20.3	74.1	1.5
Steel castings					16	26.9	66.7	0.2
Textile dyeing & finishing (excl. woolens)					15	12.2	44.1	0.4
Textile machinery & sewing machines					47	24.4	99.8	0.5
Wool carpets & rugs	30	32.6	68.2	0.5	36	30.7	67.9	0.6
Woolens & worsteds					84	35.1	51.9	1.7
SECURITIES AND EXCHANGE COMMISSION								
Automobiles[a]	279[a]	33.3[a]	82.5	3.8	279[a]	33.3[a]	68.0	4.3
Canning	25	2.1	13.1	2.1	24	2.9	12.2	2.0
Distilled liquors	30	1.7	16.8	2.0	32	1.6	17.8	1.9
Misc. foods: baking powder	21	2.4	84.0	0.3	22	1.7	84.6	0.3
Corn prod.	9	8.2	52.9	0.2	9	7.8	45.0	0.2
Petroleum	41	12.8	9.7	4.7	43	12.7	10.3	4.3
Portland cement	3	10.8	6.7	0.5	3	10.9	6.5	0.5
Steel	530	21.1	72.3	8.2	635	23.5	81.0	8.1
Total	1549	19.1	56.1	30.9	3310	28.6	66.3	51.9
% inv. of sample firms are of total mfr. inventories				*1938* 17.4		*1939* 34.4		

[a] 1937 data. Classification not available for 1938 or 1939.

all manufacturing is far less adequate, since some leading industries are not represented at all; for example, the sales of the sample firms reporting an inventory were only 15 percent of the total census value of product in 1939; the coverage was even smaller in 1938.

To help offset these inadequacies, the National Bureau of Economic Research collected additional information for some of the more important industry groups omitted from the FTC sample. The data were obtained from annual reports to the SEC by corporations listed on the New York Stock Exchange. The industries represented in the augmented sample held stocks amounting to 30.9 percent of manufacturers' total holdings in 1938 and to 51.9 percent in 1939 (Table 103); the sample firms held a smaller portion: 17.4 percent in 1938 and 34.4 percent in 1939.

An over-all ratio of goods in process to total stocks was computed by weighting the ratio of goods in process to total stocks in each industry by the census value of inventories held in that industry at the end of 1938 and of 1939. The result is unsatisfactory partly because of inadequate coverage of many industries and partly because certain groups, notably foods, beverages, paper, printing and publishing, nonferrous metals, and leather, were not represented.

APPENDIX D

Calculation of Value of Goods in Process Held in
Continuous, Discontinuous, and Mixed Industries, 1939

The calculation was in three steps:

1) To compute average ratios of goods in process to total stocks
in the three categories, each industry in the augmented FTC
sample (App. C) was assigned to one of the three categories. Decisions were based on our opinion of the dominant characteristics
of firms in each industry. Ratios of goods in process to total stocks
for the various industries in each category (see Table 103) were
weighted by the census values of total stocks to obtain a weighted
average ratio for each category (Table 104).

2) To compute the value of aggregate inventories in the three
categories, each census minor industry was similarly assigned to a
category. The value of total stocks for each minor industry on December 31, 1939 was taken from the Census of Manufactures,
1939. No adjustment was made for the slight degree of underreporting in most industries (Table 105).

3) To estimate the value of goods in process in each category, the
ratios in Table 104, last line, were applied to the census values of
total stocks in each category as shown in Table 105, line 11. The
results appear in Table 41.

TABLE 104

Computation of Average Ratios of Goods in Process to Total Manufacturers' Inventories for Continuous, Discontinuous, and Mixed Industries, December 31, 1939

	CONTINUOUS		DISCONTINUOUS		MIXED	
INDUSTRY	Ratio of goods in process to total stocks in sample (%)	Census value of total stocks in ind. ($ mil.)	Ratio of goods in process to total stocks in sample (%)	Census value of total stocks in ind. ($ mil.)	Ratio of goods in process to total stocks in sample (%)	Census value of total stocks in ind. ($ mil.)
(1)	(2)	(3)	(4)	(5)	(6)	(7)
Food, beverages & tob.						
Baking powder	1.7	26				
Beet sugar	0.8	85				
Biscuits & crackers	0.5	14				
Cigarettes & tob. prod.			0.2	184		
Cane sugar	1.6	56				
Canning	2.9	197				
Confectionery	10.3	29				
Corn products	7.8	20				
Distilled liquors	1.6	180				
Textiles & textile prod.						
Cotton textiles					21.9	277
Dyeing & finishing (excl. woolens)	12.2	34				
Knitgoods (incl. hosiery)					31.3	120
Silk					21.8	19
Wool carpets & rugs					30.7	53
Woolens & worsteds					35.1	162
Leather & leather prod.						
Leather boots & shoes	12.1	97				
Rubber & related prod.						
Rubber prod.	7.4	170				
Lumber & wood prod.						
Furniture			23.1	137		
Lumber & timber					1.7	192
Matches	36.0	6				
Chemicals & allied prod.						
Chemicals (ind.)	15.8	180				
Petroleum	12.7	418				
Rayon & allied prod.	28.9	22				
Soap, cottonseed oil prod. & cooking fats	20.3	147				
Stone, clay & glass prod.						
Clay (other than pottery)			11.0	13		
Glass & glassware			8.0	59		
Gypsum & asbestos prod. & roof coating (excl. paint)			13.0	31		
Portland cement			10.9	46		

	CONTINUOUS		DISCONTINUOUS		MIXED	
INDUSTRY	Ratio of goods in process to total stocks in sample (%)	Census value of total stocks in ind. ($ mil.)	Ratio of goods in process to total stocks in sample (%)	Census value of total stocks in ind. ($ mil.)	Ratio of goods in process to total stocks in sample (%)	Census value of total stocks in ind. ($ mil.)
(1)	(2)	(3)	(4)	(5)	(6)	(7)
Metals & metal prod.						
Iron & steel						
Blast furnaces & steel rolling mill prod.	23.5	784				
Firearms & ammunition			46.5	19		
Gray-iron & malleable iron castings	13.5	36				
Hardware					35.2	42
Heating & cooking apparatus (excl. electric)			17.0	103		
Saws, files & tools			31.9	34		
Steel castings	26.9	24				
Machinery						
Domestic laundry equip.			29.3	10		
Engines, turbines, waterwheels & windmills			47.3	48		
Machine tool accessories & machinists' precision tools					39.2	24
Machine tools	51.2	69				
Pumps, pumping equip. & air compressors					34.1	57
Textile machinery & sewing machines					24.4	47
Nonferrous metals						
Silverware & plated ware			39.0	15		
Transp. equip.						
Aircraft			70.1	98		
Auto parts & accessories			32.5	160		
Automobiles			33.3	410		
Ships	69.4	42				
S U M M A R Y						
Census value of total stocks held by industries in sample ($ mil.)		2636		1367		993
% distribution of above		52.7		27.4		19.9
Weighted av. ratio (%): goods in process to total stocks		16.1		27.3		23.6

TABLE 105

Manufacturers' Total Stocks by Major Industries
and by Type of Production Process, December 31, 1939
(millions of dollars)

	VALUE OF STOCKS BY PRODUCTION PROCESSES OF MINOR INDUSTRIES			
	Con-tinuous	Discon-tinuous	Mixed	Total
1 Food, beverages & tobacco				
Food & kindred products	1362			1362
Tobacco manufactures		184		184
2 Textiles & textile products	422	18	736	1176
3 Leather & leather products	149	114		263
4 Rubber products	170			170
5 Lumber & wood products	103	226	196	525
6 Paper, printing & publishing				
Paper & allied products	218		80	298
Printing & publishing		not given		
7 Chemicals & allied products				
Chemicals	714			714
Products of petroleum & coal	479			479
8 Stone, clay & glass products	40	101	125	266
9 Metals & metal products				
Iron & steel & products				
(excl. mach.)	855	140	488	1483
Nonferrous metals & their products		439		439
Machinery (incl. electrical)	69	874	468	1411
Transp. equip. (incl. automobiles)	104	521		625
10 Miscellaneous	36	55	146	237
11 Total	4721	2672	2239	9632
12 % of total	49.1	27.7	23.2	100.0

APPENDIX E

Classification of Stocks of Finished Goods
According to Character and Source of Raw Materials

To judge the relative importance of the various categories of finished goods stocks distinguished in Chapters 11 and 12, census
values of stocks in each minor industry as of December 31, 1939
were classified according to the source of their raw materials—
agricultural or nonagricultural—and according to their character
—perishable or durable and staple. In many cases all the inven-

tories of an industry group could, for the purpose of this rough estimate, be assigned to one of the four classes (Table 106). When a division seemed necessary, it was based upon our judgment of the relative importance of goods of different types in the output of each minor industry, allowance being made for the fact that, relative to sales, smaller quantities of perishable than durable goods are kept in stock.

TABLE 106

Inventories of Finished Goods Classified by Character of Product and Source of Raw Materials, December 31, 1939
(millions of dollars)

NO.	MAJOR INDUSTRIAL DIVISION	TOTAL FINISHED GOODS	PERISHABLE GOODS MADE FROM Nonfarm materials	Farm materials	DURABLE & STAPLE GOODS MADE FROM Nonfarm materials	Farm materials
1	Food & kindred products	784		213		571
2	Tobacco manufacturers	24				24
3	Textile-mill products & other fiber mfr.	289			35	253
4	Apparel & other finished prod. made from fabrics & similar materials	144	11	24		109
5	Lumber & timber basic products	177			177	
6	Furniture & finished lumber products	91	7		83	
7	Paper & allied products	90			90	
8	Printing, publishing & allied industries			not given		
9	Chemicals & allied products	293			293	
10	Products of petroleum & coal	285			285	
11	Rubber products	82				82
12	Leather & leather products	92		18		74
13	Stone, clay & glass products	145			145	
14	Iron & steel & products (excl. machinery)	476			476	
15	Nonferrous metals & prod.	148			148	
16	Electrical machinery	155			155	
17	Machinery (excl. electrical)	428			428	
18	Automobiles & auto. equip.	101	51		51	
19	Transp. equip. (excl. automobiles)	14			14	
20	Miscellaneous industries	85	4		81	
	All industries, total	3903	73	256	2461	1113

Census of Manufactures, 1939, II, Parts 1 and 2.
Totals are the sums, to the nearest million, of the individual items originally expressed in units. For this reason, some totals differ slightly from the sum of the items given here in millions.

APPENDIX F

Comprehensive Data on Inventories, Inventory Investment, Inventory-Sales and Inventory-Output Ratios

The tables in this appendix present the basic series used in Chapters 4, 5, 6, 15, and 21.

Estimates of manufacturers' stocks by industry groups in current prices are shown in Table 107, those in 1929 prices in Table 108, and estimates of inventory investment in Table 109. The underlying sources and methods are described in Appendix A.

Tables 110-2 present similar estimates for 5 major industrial divisions. Sources and methods are described in Chapter 4.

Tables 113-6 present manufacturers' sales, output, and inventory-sales and inventory-output ratios studied in Chapter 6. Annual sales by manufacturers (Table 113) are based upon reports of gross sales by manufacturing corporations published in *Statistics of Income* for the years beginning 1922. Before 1922 gross sales of corporations are derived from data on gross income in *Statistics of Income*. These were converted to gross sales by applying the gross sales-gross income ratio in 1922. Total sales by manufacturers were estimated from sales by corporations by calculating the ratio of the value of product of corporations in each manufacturing group to the value of product of all manufacturing establishments. When our estimates were made such figures were available from census data in 1919 and 1929. The 1919 ratios were used for 1918. Between 1919 and 1929 ratios were calculated for each year by straight line interpolation between the 1919 and 1929 figures. After 1929 the ratios for 1929 were applied.

The inventory-sales ratios in Table 114 are based on the inventory estimates in Table 107 and the sales estimates in Table 113. To compute ratios for calendar years, the inventory figure for the end of a given year was averaged with the figure for the end of the preceding year and the result divided by the sales estimate for the given year.

End of year indexes of manufacturing output (Table 115) were compiled by combining FRB indexes for the industries included in the major manufacturing groups used in this study. To get end of year figures, indexes for December and the succeeding January were averaged.

End of year inventory-output ratios in manufacturing (Table 116) were based on manufacturers' inventories in 1929 prices (Table 108), converted into indexes on average 1935-39 = 100. For this purpose, the estimates based on the assumption that stocks were valued at the lower of cost or market were used. The resulting indexes were then divided by the indexes of output from Table 115.

TABLE 107

Inventories in Current Prices, Total Manufacturing
and Major Groups
(millions of dollars)

Dec. 31	TOTAL MFG.	FOOD, BEV. & TOB.	TEXTILES & TEXTILE PROD.	LEATHER & LEATHER PROD.	RUBBER & REL. PROD.	LUMBER & WOOD PROD.	PAPER, PRINT. & PUB.	CHEMICALS & ALLIED PROD.	STONE, CLAY & GLASS PROD.	METALS & METAL PROD.	MISC.
1918	10290	1492	1820	611	240	637	415	923	179	2915	1058
1919	12864	2354	2090	818	294	799	429	1137	213	3367	1363
1920	13462	1791	1951	715	320	991	643	1423	321	3901	1406
1921	10680	1132	2126	596	170	656	588	1047	279	3092	994
1922	12099	1276	2526	582	206	684	594	1622	278	2918	1413
1923	13714	1399	2598	547	228	783	548	1638	293	4045	1635
1924	13277	1666	2586	452	220	813	595	1472	295	4358	820
1925	14015	1827	2581	417	320	859	550	1725	312	4733	691
1926	13734	1974	2270	457	344	935	573	1922	358	4192	709
1927	13284	2095	2381	480	333	888	587	1522	366	4028	604
1928	13359	2152	2367	495	297	838	576	1697	358	3931	648
1929	13917	2205	2276	452	285	826	611	1911	375	4323	653
1930	12258	1926	1703	400	232	748	571	1894	375	3853	556
1931	9856	1556	1242	314	164	524	489	1700	305	3136	426
1932	7944	1338	976	229	132	390	388	1386	250	2512	343
1933	8846	1588	1356	281	161	412	413	1399	241	2650	345
1934	9468	1845	1337	274	207	396	431	1517	243	2874	344
1935[a]	9870	1862	1396	310	195	413	455	1474	260	3131	363
1936[a]	11551	2242	1554	336	232	457	505	1740	287	3778	412
1937[a]	12980	2367	1581	345	274	515	599	1962	331	4526	475
1938[a]	11545[b]	2282	1313	289	216	539	504	1855	297	3835	
1939[a]	12547[b]	2395	1472	310	234	567	541	1954	310	4308	
1940[a]	14021[b]	2484	1596	316	275	590	593	2080	337	5233	
1941[a]	18440[b]	3143	2111	404	318	680	723	2695	400	7284	
1934 Adj. ratio[a]	103.4	103.8	99.4	105.4	104.5	101.0	101.7	111.0	98.4	102.6	99.1

[a] In the source data before and after 1934 are not comparable because of a change in the classification in *Statistics of Income*. The segment beginning in 1935 has been raised to the level of the earlier years by means of a ratio obtained from overlapping figures available for 1934.

[b] Estimated by raising total of nine industries by an amount corresponding to the average proportion of miscellaneous manufacturing to total manufacturing, 1935-37 (3.8%).

Table 108

Inventories in 1929 Prices, Total Manufacturing and Major Groups
(millions of dollars)

C or M	1918	1919	1920	1921	1922	1923	1924	1925	1926	1927	1928	1929	1930	1931	1932	1933	1934	1935[a]	1936[a]	1937[a]	1938[a]	1939[a]	1934 ADJ. RATIO[a]
TOTAL MANUFACTURING																							
C or M	7714	8905	10455	10414	11262	12650	12426	13123	13473	13083	13286	14344	15589	14953	13622	12269	12146	12392	13640	15583	14798[b]	15259[b]	103.3
C	7507	8804	8591	10002	11143	12418	12307	12815	13119	13000	13265	13949	14791	14425	12997	12262	12075	12288	13658	14969	14662[b]	15219[b]	103.4
FOOD, BEVERAGES AND TOBACCO																							
C or M	1183	1787	1665	1298	1386	1538	1691	1760	2004	1906	2040	2264	2575	2809	3027	2638	2318	2360	2382	3100	3320	3510	103.9
C	1147	1759	1442	1314	1408	1500	1712	1764	2004	1906	2040	2181	2349	2611	2877	2638	2318	2245	2382	2827	3320	3473	103.9
TEXTILES AND TEXTILE PRODUCTS																							
C or M	1231	1212	1893	2133	2191	1961	2153	2321	2350	2272	2239	2442	2580	2398	2228	2055	2096	2108	2271	2694	2358	2175	99.4
C	1087	1199	1252	2011	2168	1941	2041	2109	2217	2221	2239	2344	2461	2287	2099	2055	2096	2108	2271	2522	2341	2175	99.4
LEATHER AND LEATHER PRODUCTS																							
C or M	520	467	646	626	600	607	492	446	513	440	454	472	554	498	404	457	457	394	409	396	394	354	105.3
C	522	469	515	620	603	599	494	446	518	440	442	451	506	463	400	457	457	394	409	396	392	352	105.8
RUBBER AND RELATED PRODUCTS																							
C or M	43	60	70	60	84	98	96	81	193	197	319	355	450	503	455	342	307	296	264	345	254	289	104.4
C	38	56	56	42	77	81	89	75	182	197	319	314	465	437	437	342	294	297	265	326	252	225	104.6
LUMBER AND WOOD PRODUCTS																							
C or M	701	642	770	647	618	718	771	813	904	941	848	841	899	751	643	474	473	482	497	538	568	564	101.1
C	701	642	591	631	618	673	771	813	889	920	847	828	867	732	643	474	464	482	497	518	568	564	101.1
PAPER, PRINTING AND PUBLISHING																							
C or M	295	302	339	563	510	467	496	451	525	548	573	616	642	659	600	481	521	568	603	619	630	630	101.8
C	295	302	261	536	510	454	496	447	525	546	565	614	637	608	576	481	505	566	603	573	667	630	101.8
CHEMICALS AND ALLIED PRODUCTS																							
C or M	526	698	787	844	1460	1660	1458	1501	1646	1534	1753	1864	2434	2549	2197	1943	1928	1817	2038	2226	2324	2398	111.0
C	514	690	647	834	1359	1641	1441	1484	1540	1531	1753	1839	2192	2549	1997	1943	1928	1817	2038	2202	2248	2398	111.0
STONE, CLAY AND GLASS PRODUCTS																							
C or M	215	219	266	283	270	284	292	315	369	393	354	381	391	363	294	264	276	296	325	369	352	352	98.2
C	215	219	266	274	270	280	286	313	366	393	354	381	383	349	294	261	276	296	325	366	334	352	98.2
METALS AND METAL PRODUCTS																							
C or M	2136	2543	2994	2999	2847	3816	4198	4771	4269	4227	4044	4443	4428	3843	3204	3251	3365	3637	4368	4729	4080	4544	102.6
C	2081	2543	2663	2811	2839	3787	4198	4700	4192	4227	4044	4345	4384	3778	3144	3251	3338	3637	4368	4729	4041	4544	102.6
MISCELLANEOUS																							
C or M	914	1025	1075	961	1296	1506	779	664	700	625	662	666	636	544	476	417	405	425	474	496			99.3
C	907	1025	898	929	1296	1462	779	664	691	619	662	652	617	531	467	417	399		474	487			99.3

C: cost; M: market.

The data represent the value in 1929 prices of inventories as of December 31 of each year. The figures given under 'cost or market' are calculated on the assumption that inventories are valued at cost or market price (whichever is lower); those under 'cost' assume that inventories are valued at cost only.

[a] See Table 107, note a.

[b] Estimated by raising total of nine industries by an amount corresponding to the average proportion of miscellaneous manufacturing to total manufacturing, 1925...

TABLE 109

Inventory Investment in 1929 Prices, Total Manufacturing and Major Groups
(millions of dollars)

	1919	1920	1921	1922	1923	1924	1925	1926	1927	1928	1929	1930	1931	1932	1933	1934	1935	1936	1937	1938	1939
TOTAL MANUFACTURING																					
C or M	+1191	+1550	−41	+848	+1388	−224	+697	+850	−390	+203	+1058	+1245	−636	−1331	−1353	−123	+246	+1248	+1943	−785	+461
C	+1397	−313	+1411	+1141	+1275	−111	+508	+304	−119	+265	+684	+842	−366	−1428	−735	−187	+213	+1365	+1816	−307	+557
FOOD, BEVERAGES AND TOBACCO																					
C or M	+604	−72	−367	+88	+152	+153	+69	+244	−98	+134	+224	+311	+234	+218	+389	+320	+42	+22	+718	+220	+190
C	+612	−317	−128	+89	+97	+212	+52	+240	−98	+134	+141	+168	+262	+266	−239	−320	−73	+137	+445	+493	+153
TEXTILES AND TEXTILE PRODUCTS																					
C or M	−19	+681	+240	+58	+230	+192	+168	+29	−78	−83	+203	+138	+182	+170	+173	+41	+12	+163	+423	+336	+183
C	+112	+53	+759	+157	+227	+100	+68	+108	+4	+18	+105	+117	+174	+188	−44	+41	+12	+163	+251	+181	+166
LEATHER AND LEATHER PRODUCTS																					
C or M	−53	+179	−20	−26	+7	−115	−46	+67	−73	+14	+18	+82	−20	−36	−94	+53	−63	+15	+45	−60	−40
C	−53	+46	+105	−17	−4	−105	−48	+67	−73	+2	+9	+55	+9	−52	−63	+57	−63	+15	−13	+4	+40
RUBBER AND RELATED PRODUCTS																					
C or M	+17	+10	−10	+24	+9	+3	−15	+112	+4	+122	+36	+95	+53	−48	−113	−35	−11	−32	+81	−91	−15
C	+18	0	−14	+35	+4	+8	−14	+107	+15	+122	−5	+131	+20	−28	−95	−48	+3	−32	+61	−74	−27
LUMBER AND WOOD PRODUCTS																					
C or M	−59	+128	−123	−29	+100	+53	+42	+91	+87	−93	−7	+58	−148	−108	−169	−1	+9	+15	+41	+30	−4
C	−59	−51	+40	−13	+55	+98	+42	+76	+31	−73	−19	+39	−135	−89	−169	−10	+18	+15	+21	+50	−4
PAPER, PRINTING AND PUBLISHING																					
C or M	+7	+87	+224	−53	−43	+29	−45	+74	+23	+25	+43	+26	+17	−59	−119	+40	+47	+35	+16	+60	−49
C	+7	−41	+275	−26	−56	+42	−49	+78	+21	+19	+49	+23	−29	−32	−95	+24	+61	+37	+30	+94	+37
CHEMICALS AND ALLIED PRODUCTS																					
C or M	+172	+39	+107	+616	+200	−202	+43	+145	−112	+219	+111	+570	+115	−352	−254	−15	−111	+221	+188	+98	+74
C	+176	−43	+187	+525	+282	−200	+43	+56	−9	+222	+86	+353	+357	−552	−54	−15	−111	+221	+164	+46	+150
STONE, CLAY AND GLASS PRODUCTS																					
C or M	+4	+47	+17	−13	+14	+8	+23	+54	+24	−39	+27	+10	−28	−69	−30	+12	+20	+29	+44	−35	+18
C	+4	+47	+8	−4	+10	+6	+27	+53	+27	−39	+27	+2	−34	−55	−33	+15	+20	+29	+41	−32	+18
METALS AND METAL PRODUCTS																					
C or M	+407	+451	+5	−152	+969	+382	+573	+502	−42	−183	+399	−15	−585	−639	+47	+114	+272	+731	+361	−649	+464
C	+462	+120	+148	+28	+948	+411	+502	+508	−185	−183	+301	−11	−556	−634	+107	+87	+299	+731	+361	−688	+503
MISCELLANEOUS																					
C or M	+111	+50	−114	+335	+210	−727	−115	+36	−75	+87	+4	−30	−92	−68	−59	−12	+20	+49	+22		
C	+118	−127	+81	+367	+166	−683	−115	+27	−72	+43	−10	−35	−86	−64	−50	−18	+26	+49	+13		

C: cost; M: market.
The data represent year to year changes in the inventories in 1929 prices shown in Table 108.

TABLE 110

Inventories in Current Prices, Five Major Industrial Divisions
(millions of dollars)

	MFG.ᵃ (1)	TRADEᵃ (2)	TRANSP. & OTHER PUB. UT.ᵇ (3)	MINING & QUARRYINGᵃ (4)	AGR. (5)
1918	10290	10684	775	549	6991
1919	12864	13385	741	1017	6844
1920	13462	13681	1147	1100	4922
1921	10680	11005	1019	761	3070
1922	12099	11474	869	607	3814
1923	13714	12603	1081	731	3720
1924	13277	12528	939	807	3946
1925	14015	12989	906	749	4209
1926	13734	12926	950	691	3858
1927	13284	12612	1033	740	4177
1928	13359	12867	1008	561	4544
1929	13917	13229	1129	754	4340
1930	12258	11021	982	483	3107
1931	9856	9043	897	515	2123
1932	7944	7151	749	422	1578
1933	8846	7584	779	445	1928
1934	9468	7924	738	466	2106
1935ᶜ	9870	8244	732	399	3033
1936ᶜ	11551	8892	811	358	3029
1937ᶜ	12980	9438	964	431	3116
1938ᶜ	11545	8782	810	434	3168
1934 ratio	103.4	100.0	116.0	107.1	100.0

ᵃ Corporate and noncorporate business combined.

ᵇ Corporate business only.

ᶜ See Table 107, note a. The data for trade are not affected by the change in the classification beginning with 1934 since they are not based on *Statistics of Income*, nor are those for agriculture, which are derived from commodity stocks.

TABLE 111

Inventories in 1929 Prices[a], Five Major Industrial Divisions
(millions of dollars)

	MFG.[b] (1)	TRADE[b] (2)	TRANSP. & OTHER PUB. UT.[c] (3)	MINING & QUARRYING[b] (4)	AGR. (5)
1918	7714	7664	630	469[e]	5085
1919	8905	8928	589	886[e]	5123
1920	10455	10331	895	847[e]	5957
1921	10414	10611	1029	828[e]	5267
1922	11262	10714	893	561[e]	5104
1923	12650	11777	1057	717[e]	5064
1924	12426	11599	961	798[e]	4347
1925	13123	11737	945	703[e]	4926
1926	13473	12535	952	636	4439
1927	13083	12414	1078	772	4472
1928	13286	12815	1028	571	4629
1929	14344	13521	1154	752	4550
1930	15589	13156	1124	582	4451
1931	14953	12555	1110	673	4996
1932	13622	10912	973	574	5391
1933	12269	9949	936	532	4925
1934	12146	9955	853	544	3833
1935[d]	12392	9921	840	465	4591
1936[d]	13640	10662	918	406	3873
1937[d]	15583	11064	1004	472	4808
1938[d]	14798	10829	862	501	5105
1934 ratio	103.3	100.0	116.1	107.1	100.0

[a] Columns 1-4 represent the value in 1929 prices of inventories as of December 31 of each year, calculated on the assumption that inventories are valued at the lower of cost or market. The data for agriculture are the year end values of physical quantities of stocks valued at the prices ruling at the end of 1929.

[b] Corporate and noncorporate business combined.

[c] Corporate business only.

[d] See Tables 107, note a, and 110, note c.

[e] The data for 1918-25 are based on Kuznets' deflating indexes; from 1926 on the deflating indexes were constructed by me. The data for the early segment were adjusted to the 1926 level by means of a ratio based on figures deflated both ways for that year.

TABLE 112

Inventory Investment in 1929 Prices, Five Major Industrial Divisions
(millions of dollars)

	MFG. (1)	TRADE (2)	TRANSP. & OTHER PUB. UT. (3)	MINING & QUARRYING (4)	AGR. (5)
1919	+1191	+1264	−41	+417	+38
1920	+1550	+1403	+306	−39	+834
1921	−41	+280	+134	−19	−690
1922	+848	+103	−136	−267	−163
1923	+1388	+1063	+164	+156	−40
1924	−224	−178	−96	+81	−717
1925	+697	+138	−16	−95	+579
1926	+350	+798	+7	−67	−487
1927	−390	−121	+126	+136	+33
1928	+203	+401	−50	−201	+157
1929	+1058	+706	+126	+181	−79
1930	+1245	−365	−30	−170	−99
1931	−636	−601	−14	+91	+545
1932	−1331	−1643	−137	−99	+395
1933	−1353	−963	−37	−42	−466
1934	−123	+6	−83	+12	−1092
1935	+246	−34	−13	−79	+758
1936	+1248	+741	+78	−59	−718
1937	+1943	+402	+86	+66	+935
1938	−785	−235	−142	+29	+297

The data represent year to year changes in the inventories in 1929 prices
shown in Table 111.

TABLE 113

Sales in Current Prices, Total Manufacturing and Major Groups
(millions of dollars)

	TOTAL MFG.	FOOD, BEV. & TOB.	TEXTILES & TEXTILE PROD.	LEATHER & LEATHER PROD.	RUBBER & REL. PROD.	LUMBER & WOOD PROD.	PAPER, PRINT. & PUB.	CHEMICALS & ALLIED PROD.	STONE, CLAY & GLASS PROD.	METALS & METAL PROD.	MISC.
1918	48484	10954	8685	1997	1027	2460	2020	3912	777	13153	3499
1919	57740	16316	9170	2545	1142	3043	2516	4371	943	13306	4388
1920	62052	14193	10479	2175	1016	4032	3606	5328	1476	14844	4903
1921	41877	9490	7223	1616	624	2225	2724	3710	1065	9627	3573
1922	48430	10112	8578	1654	923	2862	2990	5452	1304	9775	4780
1923	60518	11448	9888	1792	1061	3514	3319	5864	1516	16474	5642
1924	57562	13272	8939	1682	1104	3307	3382	5583	1532	15829	2932
1925	63459	15096	9468	1657	1423	3364	3574	6637	1649	17981	2610
1926	66205	15073	9567	1822	1534	3484	4045	7568	1825	18473	2814
1927	67018	15450	9568	1878	1414	3161	4160	8277	1750	18890	2470
1928	70328	15741	9555	1855	1350	3165	4568	8876	1794	20752	2672
1929	75165	16225	9991	1863	1384	3073	4817	9454	1796	23909	2653
1930	61141	14489	7788	1486	1059	2187	4442	9080	1532	16933	2145
1931	45820	11583	6424	1187	785	1471	3723	6785	1124	11158	1580
1932	31987	9005	4667	899	606	909	2139	5866	717	6115	1064
1933	35639	9546	5594	1058	690	1066	2179	5766	770	7858	1112
1934	46370	12350	6283	1197	868	1254	3353	7076	945	11712	1332
1935	53962	13864	7070	1348	942	1513	3717	7810	1141	14966	1591
1936	64377	15665	8121	1485	1154	2009	4149	9009	1554	19405	1826
1937	70483	16523	8109	1544	1315	2225	4538	10032	1732	22424	2041
1938	57410	15117	6338	1308	1023	2062	3910	9311	1382	15341	
1939	65699	15553	7419	1435	1295	2497	4230	10337	1707	19374	
1940	75784	16427	8074	1499	1393	2882	4781	11152	1941	25499	
1941	105168	20599	11337	2065	2037	3857	5773	14181	2626	39729	

TABLE 114

Inventory-Sales Ratios in Current Prices
Total Manufacturing and Major Groups
(percentages)

	TOTAL MFG.	FOOD, BEV. & TOB.	TEXTILES & TEXTILE PROD.	LEATHER & LEATHER PROD.	RUBBER & REL. PROD.	LUMBER & WOOD PROD.	PAPER, PRINT. & PUB.	CHEMICALS & ALLIED PROD.	STONE, CLAY & GLASS PROD.	METALS & METAL PROD.	MISC.
1919	20.1	11.8	21.3	28.1	23.4	23.6	16.8	23.6	20.8	23.6	27.6
1920	21.2	14.6	19.3	35.2	30.2	22.2	14.9	24.0	18.1	24.5	28.2
1921	28.8	15.4	28.2	40.6	39.3	37.0	22.6	33.3	28.2	36.3	33.6
1922	23.5	11.9	27.1	35.6	20.4	23.4	19.8	24.5	21.4	30.7	25.2
1923	21.3	11.7	25.9	31.5	20.5	20.9	17.2	27.8	18.8	21.1	27.0
1924	23.4	11.5	29.0	29.7	20.3	24.1	16.9	27.9	19.2	26.5	41.9
1925	21.5	11.6	27.3	26.2	19.0	24.9	16.0	24.1	18.4	25.3	28.9
1926	21.0	12.6	25.4	24.0	21.6	25.7	13.9	24.1	18.4	24.2	24.9
1927	20.2	13.2	24.3	24.9	23.9	28.8	13.9	20.8	20.7	21.8	26.6
1928	18.9	13.5	24.8	26.3	23.3	27.3	12.7	18.1	20.2	19.2	23.4
1929	18.1	13.4	23.2	25.4	21.0	27.1	12.3	19.1	20.4	17.3	24.5
1930	21.4	14.3	25.5	28.7	24.4	36.0	13.3	21.0	24.5	24.1	28.2
1931	24.1	15.0	22.9	30.1	25.2	43.2	14.2	26.5	30.2	31.3	31.1
1932	27.8	16.1	23.8	30.2	24.4	50.3	20.5	26.3	38.7	46.2	36.1
1933	23.6	15.3	20.8	24.1	21.2	37.6	18.4	24.2	31.9	32.8	30.9
1934	19.7	13.9	21.4	23.2	21.2	32.2	12.6	20.6	25.6	23.6	25.9
1935	17.9	13.4	19.3	21.7	21.3	26.7	11.9	19.1	22.0	20.1	22.2
1936	16.6	13.1	18.2	21.8	18.5	21.7	11.6	17.8	17.6	17.8	21.2
1937	17.4	13.9	19.3	22.1	19.2	21.8	12.2	18.5	17.8	18.5	21.7
1938	21.3	15.4	22.8	24.2	23.9	25.6	14.1	20.5	22.7	27.3	
1939	18.3	15.0	18.8	20.9	17.4	22.1	12.4	18.4	17.8	21.0	
1940	17.5	14.9	19.0	20.9	18.3	20.1	11.9	18.1	16.7	18.7	
1941	15.4	13.7	16.3	17.4	14.6	16.5	11.4	16.8	14.0	15.8	

TABLE 115

Federal Reserve Board Indexes of Manufacturing Production,
Year Ends
(monthly average 1935-39: 100)

	TOTAL MFG.	FOOD, BEV. & TOB.	TEXTILES & TEXTILE PROD.	LEATHER & LEATHER PROD.	RUBBER & REL. PROD.	LUMBER & WOOD PROD.	PAPER, PRINT. & PUB.	CHEMICALS & ALLIED PROD.	STONE, CLAY & GLASS PROD.	METALS & METAL PROD.
1919	78.5	76.0	82.5	101.5		133.0	57.5	37.5	61.5	76.5
1920	56.5	61.5	45.5	62.5	14.0	87.5	52.5	45.0	51.0	60.0
1921	61.0	67.5	77.0	92.5	45.5	120.0	56.0	40.0	55.5	44.0
1922	84.0	78.5	86.0	102.5	68.5	134.5	66.5	54.5	86.5	94.5
1923	83.5	81.0	73.5	89.5	67.0	140.5	68.5	56.5	90.5	97.0
1924	87.0	81.5	83.5	89.0	75.5	147.0	75.5	59.5	94.0	95.5
1925	95.5	85.0	85.0	89.0	85.0	150.5	82.0	69.5	101.0	112.5
1926	95.0	84.5	88.5	92.5	81.0	144.0	87.5	74.0	104.5	104.5
1927	93.0	87.0	86.5	94.5	87.0	142.5	87.5	74.5	107.5	99.5
1928	108.0	95.5	93.0	92.5	106.0	151.0	94.0	87.0	118.0	128.0
1929	99.5	99.0	82.0	94.0	83.0	130.5	98.5	92.0	102.5	110.0
1930	78.0	92.0	71.5	74.0	69.0	84.5	84.0	79.5	78.5	75.0
1931	63.5	80.5	71.0	75.0	69.0	56.5	77.5	73.5	62.5	50.5
1932	56.5	78.0	79.5	78.0	53.0	48.0	66.5	69.0	48.0	36.5
1933	69.0	83.0	74.5	87.0	80.5	66.0	75.0	80.0	59.5	56.0
1934	79.5	87.0	90.0	92.0	94.5	66.0	83.5	84.0	66.5	71.5
1935	95.0	93.0	100.5	103.5	101.0	100.5	92.5	93.0	83.5	95.0
1936	118.0	104.5	121.5	116.0	117.5	112.5	112.0	107.0	113.5	128.0
1937	83.0	99.0	65.5	75.5	67.5	83.0	92.0	100.0	86.5	75.5
1938	100.5	104.5	106.5	106.5	110.5	102.5	101.5	101.0	106.0	94.0
1939	124.5	108.0	121.5	104.5	123.5	114.5	119.0	114.5	121.0	138.0

TABLE 116

Indexes of Inventory-Output Ratios, Total Manufacturing and Major Groups, Year Ends

(percentages)

	TOTAL MFG.	FOOD, BEV. & TOB.	TEXTILES & TEXTILE PROD.	LEATHER & LEATHER PROD.	RUBBER & REL. PROD.	LUMBER & WOOD PROD.	PAPER, PRINT. & PUB.	CHEMICALS & ALLIED PROD.	STONE, CLAY & GLASS PROD.	METALS & METAL PROD.
1919	79.1	77.9	63.3	114.8		91.1	84.7	86.1	106.2	77.8
1920	129.0	92.2	179.3	257.8	178.6	166.1	104.2	75.8	155.7	116.8
1921	119.2	65.5	119.4	168.8	47.3	101.8	162.1	97.8	152.1	159.5
1922	93.6	60.1	109.8	146.0	43.8	86.7	123.8	124.0	93.1	70.5
1923	105.6	64.7	115.0	169.2	49.7	96.4	109.9	135.9	93.6	92.1
1924	99.7	70.7	111.1	137.9	45.4	99.0	106.0	113.4	92.7	102.9
1925	95.8	70.6	117.6	124.9	34.1	102.0	88.8	100.0	93.1	99.3
1926	98.9	80.8	114.4	138.3	85.2	118.5	96.8	103.0	105.4	95.6
1927	98.2	74.7	113.2	116.1	81.0	124.6	101.0	95.3	109.0	99.5
1928	85.8	72.8	103.8	122.4	107.6	106.0	98.3	93.2	89.5	74.0
1929	100.6	78.0	128.3	125.2	153.0	121.6	100.9	93.8	110.9	94.5
1930	139.5	95.4	155.4	186.8	233.2	200.8	123.3	141.8	148.5	138.3
1931	164.3	118.9	145.5	177.6	260.7	251.0	137.2	160.5	173.3	178.2
1932	168.1	132.3	120.8	159.2	307.0	252.9	145.6	147.4	182.7	205.5
1933	124.1	108.3	118.8	115.7	151.9	135.6	103.5	112.4	132.4	135.9
1934	106.5	90.8	100.3	123.9	116.2	135.3	100.7	106.2	125.8	110.2
1935	90.9	86.5	90.3	95.0	104.9	90.5	99.0	90.4	105.7	89.6
1936	80.7	77.7	80.5	87.9	80.3	83.4	86.9	88.1	85.5	79.9
1937	131.0	106.7	177.3	149.9	182.8	122.3	108.6	103.0	127.3	146.6
1938	102.7	108.2	95.4	92.3	82.2	104.6	108.0	106.5	94.0	101.6
1939	85.5	110.7	77.1	84.5	69.2	93.0	85.4	96.9	86.8	77.1

APPENDIX G

Catalogue and Description of Statistical Series

The series used in this study are listed in this Appendix by the chapters in which they appear. Immediately following the name of the series is a reference to the tables or charts in which it figures (unless it is referred to only in the text) together with notes describing the source, composition, and coverage of the data. When a series is cited more than once, the reader is referred to the chapter in which its descriptive note appears.

Chapter 1

1 Gross national product and its main components, average changes during 5 business cycles, 1918-38 (Table 1). See notes to Table 1.

Chapter 2

1 Value of inventories by major industrial divisions (Table 3)
   a Kuznets' estimates, 1918-33
   b Department of Commerce estimates, modified by the National Bureau of Economic Research, 1928-39
Kuznets' estimates of the value of manufacturers' inventories described briefly in Ch. 3 and in detail in App. A. Department of Commerce estimates described more briefly in Ch. 3 and App. A. Further references to sources of Kuznets' estimates of inventories held by other divisions may be found in App. F.

Chapter 3

1 Coke production (Tables 5-13; Charts 1-2)
2 Railroad bond yields (Tables 14, 16-19)
3 Deflated clearings (Tables 16-19)
4 Pig iron production (Tables 16-19)
5 Railroad stock prices (Tables 16-19)
6 Shares traded (Tables 16-19)
7 Call money rates (Tables 16-19)
These series, illustrating and testing NBER methods of computing cycle measures, described in *Measuring Business Cycles*, p. 25, note to Table 4, and p. 210, note 7.

CHAPTER 4

1   Manufacturers' inventories, current prices, total and ten groups
    a Kuznets (Tables 20-21; Charts 3-4)
    b Dun and Bradstreet (Chart 3)
    c Schmidt-Young (Chart 3)
    d Terborgh (Chart 3)
    e Currie (Chart 3)
    f National Industrial Conference Board index (Chart 3)
    g Department of Commerce (Chart 3)
    These series described briefly in text; for detailed descriptions see
    App. A. Kuznets' figures are given in Table 107.
2   Manufacturers' inventories, constant prices, total and ten groups
    a Kuznets (Tables 22-23; Charts 5-6)
    The method by which estimates in current prices are adjusted for
    changes in prices described in text; for detailed description see
    App. A, Sec. 2. The figures are given in Table 108.
    b Terborgh (Chart 5)
    See *Federal Reserve Bulletin*, July 1941, pp. 613-7, also references
    under series 1d above
3   Inventories, current prices, 5 major industrial divisions: manufactur-
    ing, trade, transportation and other public utilities, agriculture, and
    mining
    Kuznets' estimates (Tables 24-25; Chart 7)
    For 1918-33, data are from *Commodity Flow and Capital Formation*,
    Part VII, where the methods of estimation are described fully. The
    series extended to later years by me with help of data provided
    by Kuznets. Estimates of inventory investments derived from these
    figures are described by Kuznets in NBER *Bulletin 74* and in *National
    Product since 1869*. Certain revisions of Kuznets' series are described
    in notes to Table 3. For detailed information on manufacturers' in-
    ventories see App. A. Figures are given in Table 110.
4   Inventories, constant prices, 5 major industrial divisions (Tables 24-
    25; Chart 8)
    See series 3 above. Figures are given in Table 111.

CHAPTER 5

1   Manufacturers' inventories, current prices, Kuznets' estimates (Tables
    26-27; Chart 9)
    See Ch. 4, series 1a
2   Manufacturers' gross sales, current prices (Tables 26-27; Chart 9)
    See Ch. 6, series 2. Figures are given in Table 113.
3   National Industrial Conference Board indexes of manufacturers' in-
    ventories and of shipments (Chart 10)
    See Ch. 4, series 1f. NICB indexes of shipments, derived by essentially
    similar methods, described in the same source.

4 Manufacturers' inventories, constant prices, Kuznets' estimates (Tables 28-29; Chart 11)
See Ch. 4, series 2a

5 Federal Reserve Board indexes of manufacturing output at year ends: total and 10 manufacturing groups (Tables 28-29; Chart 11)
The basic data for these series are the indexes computed by FRB and published in *Federal Reserve Index of Industrial Production, October 1943* (Washington, D. C., Board of Governors of Federal Reserve System). The FRB indexes were combined into industry groups comparable with those to which our inventory data refer; end of year indexes are averages of December and January. These procedures are described in the text, Ch. 5, note 9. The resulting year end series are given in Table 115.

CHAPTER 6

1 Manufacturers' inventories, current prices, Kuznets' estimates (Tables 36-37; Chart 12)
See Ch. 4, series 1a

2 Manufacturers' gross sales, current prices (Tables 31-32, 36-37; Chart 12)
See Ch. 5, series 2

3 Inventory-sales ratios, manufacturing (Tables 30-32; Chart 12)
Computed from series 1 and 2 above. Series for calendar years computed by method described in note to Table 30. Series for year ends are averages of sales for pairs of adjoining years. Resulting sales figures were then divided into year end inventory figures. Ratios are given in Table 114.

4 NICB indexes of manufacturers' inventories and shipments (Chart 13)
See Ch. 5, series 3, and Ch. 4, series 1f

5 NICB indexes of manufacturers' inventory-shipments ratios (Table 33; Chart 13)
Computed from NICB inventory and shipments indexes described above.

6 Manufacturers' inventories, constant prices, Kuznets' estimates (Tables 36-37; Chart 14)
See Ch. 4, series 2a

7 FRB indexes of manufacturing output at year ends (Tables 34-37; Chart 14)
See Ch. 5, series 5

8 Indexes of manufacturers' inventory-output ratios (Table 34; Chart 14)
Computed from manufacturers' inventories in constant prices and FRB year end indexes of manufacturers' output. Resulting indexes are given in Table 116.

CHAPTER 7

1 Manufacturers' inventories, percentage distribution by stage of fabrication (Table 38; Chart 15)
   a Relative importance of finished goods in total inventories on
     December 31, 1936 and 1937
   b Relative importance of raw materials, goods in process, and fin-
     ished goods on December 31, 1938 and 1939, and annual averages
     of monthly standings, 1939-45
     The sample reporting at monthly intervals to Department of Com-
     merce is described in App. A.
2 Finished goods and all other manufacturers' stocks, average values as
   percentage of total stocks at year ends, 1936-39; total and 10 manufacturing groups (Table 39)
   The figures, from Census of Manufactures, 1937, and 1939, are not
   adjusted for underreporting. They include returns by establishments
   representing 94.6 percent of the total value of products in 1937 and
   96.4 percent in 1939.
3 Ratio of goods in process to total manufacturers' inventories on
   December 31, 1938 and 1939 (Table 40)
   Based on returns from corporations reporting to Federal Trade Commission. The character of sample and method used to calculate the
   importance of goods in process described in Ch. 7 and in App. C.

CHAPTER 9

The time series studied in Chapter 9 are all described in the statistical
notes to Chapter 10. References to series numbers below indicate the appropriate notes to Chapter 10.

RAW COTTON

1 Stocks at mills (Tables 43-44), series 4
2 Consumption (Tables 43-44), series 6

RAW SILK

3 Stocks at manufacturers (Tables 43-44), series 10
4 Deliveries to mills (Tables 43-44), series 12

RAW CATTLE HIDES

5 Stocks in tanners' hands (Tables 43-44), series 16
6 Wettings (Tables 43-44), series 18

CRUDE RUBBER AND RELATED SERIES

7 Stocks in and afloat for United States (Tables 43-44), series 22
8 Automobile tire, pneumatic casings, production (Tables 43-44),
   series 29

COTTONSEED

9 Stocks at mills, series 30

RAW SUGAR

10   Stocks at ports (Tables 43-44), series 33
11   Meltings at ports (Tables 43-44), series 34

CRUDE PETROLEUM

12   Refinable petroleum in pipelines and at tank farms and refineries (Tables 43-44), series 36
13   Consumption (Tables 43-44), series 37

NEWSPRINT

14   Stocks at and in transit to publishers (Tables 43-44), series 39
15   Consumption (Tables 43-44), series 40

IRON ORE

16   Stocks at furnaces, Lake Superior region, series 41

LEAD

17   Stocks at warehouses (Tables 43-44), series 47
18   Imports (Tables 43-44), series 48

CHAPTER 10

RAW COTTON

1   Total stocks, 1912-44, (a) annual, July 31 (Chart 16); (b) average monthly standings during crop years (Chart 17)
Unit: running bale
Sources and Coverage: 1912-22, N. Y. Cotton Exchange Service; 1923-44, Bureau of Census in accordance with Acts of Congress approved 1912, 1924, and 1938. Data published in Department of Agriculture, *Agricultural Statistics, 1939*, p. 108, and *1945*, p. 76. All holders July 31st of each year.

The total figures include stocks on farms and in transit, in warehouses and at mills. As of July 31st about 75 percent of total stocks are in warehouses; stocks on farms and in transit, taken together, are at their lowest point for the year on this date. Running bales vary in weight according to locality, market price of cotton, and weather and crop conditions. Round bales counted as half bales. Linters (short staple fibers adhering to cottonseed after ginning) excluded.

2   Stocks in public storage and at compresses (warehouse stocks), 1912-42: (a) end of crop year (Chart 16); (b) average monthly standings (Charts 17-18)
Unit: running bale
Source and Coverage: Cotton Production and Distribution, Bureau of Census *Bulletin 135*, pp. 57-8, and subsequent bulletins. Cotton in independent warehouses and other public storage places and at compresses comprise all cotton held in such establishments regardless of ownership. Certain port stocks included. Foreign cotton on

hand included with domestic. Round bales counted as half bales; foreign cotton computed in equivalent 500 pound bales. Linters excluded.

3   Visible supply, 1869-1940 (a) end of crop year (Chart 16); (b) average monthly standings (Chart 17)
Unit: running bale
Source and Coverage: *Commercial and Financial Chronicle*; all stocks in public warehouses in principal ports and interior towns at which raw cotton is held as well as cotton on shipboard but not yet cleared. Total visible supply derived by NBER by adding stocks at United States ports and at interior towns. Because published figures are based on a changing list of ports and towns, the series was divided into overlapping segments. The list of ports and towns changes slightly within each segment but relative effect negligible.

4   Stocks at mills (consuming establishments), monthly 1912-42 (Chart 18)
Unit: running bale
Source and Coverage: See series 2 above; all consuming establishments, as required by Acts of Congress approved 1912, 1924, and 1938.

5   Consumption, annual (years beginning September 1, 1904-13; years beginning August 1, after 1913), 1904-44
Unit: equivalent bale of 500 lbs., gross weight.
Source and Coverage: Cotton Production and Distribution, Bureau of Census *Bulletin 182*, p. 52. All consuming establishments covered. Bales are considered consumed when opened at mill. Linters excluded in 1908 and following years. Separate figures not obtainable prior to that date. Original data in running bales converted by NBER to equivalent 500 pound bales, gross weight, by using average net weight of running bales reported to the census. Net weight of 478 pounds treated as equivalent of 500 pounds, gross weight.

6   Consumption, monthly, 1912-40 (Chart 18)
Unit: running bale
Source and Coverage: Bureau of Census *Bulletin 135*, pp. 57-8, and subsequent bulletins.
See series 5 above.

7   Production (crop), annual, 1866-1944 (Chart 29)
Unit: equivalent bale of 500 lbs., gross weight
Sources and Coverage: 1866-98, Department of Agriculture; Cotton Crop of the United States, 1790-1911, Bureau of Statistics *Circular 32*, Aug. 1912. 1866-68, 1870-78, and 1880-83, figures are for commercial crop as estimated annually by Latham, Alexander & Co. in *Cotton Movement and Fluctuations*. 1884-88 and 1890-98, Department of Agriculture estimates based upon data furnished by officials of rail

and water lines, of mills, and by special agents of the Department at southern ports and important receiving points in the interior. 1869, 1879, and 1889, figures compiled from census returns. 1899-1944, *Agricultural Statistics, 1939*, pp. 102-3, and *1945*, p. 70.

Circular 32 rather than *Agricultural Statistics* was used through 1898 since data for this period had been already converted to 500 pound bales. Comparison of running bales data in *Circular 32* before conversion with those in *Agricultural Statistics, 1939*, shows only minor revisions. Linters excluded after 1898. Separate figures for linters unavailable prior to 1899.

8   Exports, annual, 1866-1944
Unit: see series 7 above
Source and Coverage: *Agricultural Statistics, 1941*, pp. 116-7, and *1946*, p. 72, derived from data furnished by Department of Commerce. Linters excluded after 1913. Separate figures for linters unavailable prior to 1914.

RAW SILK

9   Stocks at warehouses, monthly, 1920-41 (Chart 19)
Unit: picul bale, approximately 132¼ lbs.
Sources: 1920-30, Silk Association of America, *Silkworm*. 1931-41, Commodity Exchange, Inc., New York; published in its *Daily Market Report, Monthly Statistical Supplement: Raw Silk*, July 1933, and subsequent issues.
Coverage: Main warehouses in New York and Hoboken. Data include Commodity Exchange certified stocks and stocks at terminals. The Silk Association (*Mid-Year Report, 1929*, p. 13) indicates that relatively small stocks, about 2 percent of the total, are held at railroad terminals in some years.

10   Stocks at manufacturers, monthly, 1921-34 (Chart 19)
Unit: see series 9 above
Sources and Coverage: Silk Association of America; 1921-29, data published in *Survey of Current Business*, March 1925, p. 27, and 1932 Supplement; 1930-34, see series 9 above. 35-60 percent of all silk manufacturers and throwsters covered, averaging about 45 percent for most of the year 1924. Information for later years unavailable. Hosiery manufacturers not included. The *Survey of Current Business* states that, owing to varying number of mills reporting, original figures were prorated up to 100 percent by dividing stocks reported by percentage of trade they are estimated to represent. Maximum reporting capacity (60 percent in April and May 1923), coming immediately after a month of minimum reporting capacity (35 percent in March 1923), indicates by the close correspondence of these prorated totals that the prorating represents the situation quite accurately.

11   Total visible stocks, monthly, 1923-36; 1930-41
     Unit: see series 9 above
     Source and Coverage: Commodity Exchange, Inc., N. Y.; 1923-36,
     data published in *Survey of Current Business,* July 1936, p. 20, and
     Dec. 1936, p. 57; 1930-41, Feb. 1937, p. 20, and subsequent issues.
     First segment represents stocks of raw silk held in New York ware-
     houses, in Japanese ports, and the estimated amount in transit be-
     tween Japan and United States at end of month. Second segment is
     the series of the first segment revised to include stocks weighed and
     awaiting shipment in the ports of Yokohama and Kobe, Japan. For
     all practical purposes the second segment may be treated as continu-
     ous with the first; the two segments were spliced at July 1930.
12   Deliveries to mills, monthly, 1920-41 (Chart 19)
     Unit: see series 9 above
     Sources: 1920-June 1929, Silk Association of America; thereafter,
     Commodity Exchange, Inc., N. Y. 1920-June 1929, data published
     in Textile Economics Bureau, Inc., *Rayon Organon,* Jan. 1940, spe-
     cial supplement, p. 26. July 1929-41, see series 9 above.
     Coverage: Deliveries to mills were obtained by adding to or sub-
     tracting from imports during a given month the difference in United
     States stock position at beginning and end of month. Reexports in-
     cluded. Imports are based on ships' manifests; time allowed for im-
     ports received at Pacific ports to reach New York overland. Ware-
     house stocks, reported by main warehouses in New York and
     Hoboken, include Commodity Exchange certified stocks and stocks
     at terminals. See also description of warehouse stocks, series 9 above,
     and of imports, series 13 below.
13   Imports, monthly, 1867-86; 1882-1924; 1919-38
     Unit: pound
     Sources and Coverage: Through June 1914, derived from publica-
     tions of Bureau of Foreign and Domestic Commerce (or predecessor
     agencies) ; thereafter, *Monthly Summary of Foreign Commerce of
     the United States.* 1867-86 segment excludes waste raw silk, data for
     which are unavailable prior to 1882. Total imports included in the
     first two segments, but for 1919-38 data are for net imports, i.e., total
     imports minus reexports as computed by NBER. Cocoons excluded
     throughout except from July 1930 to August 1936 when not sep-
     arable from waste raw silk. They are relatively unimportant in other
     years. Beginning with 1934, imports are for consumption instead of
     general imports, but data are treated as continuous. Imports for
     consumption consist of goods entered for immediate consumption
     and withdrawals from warehouses for consumption. Prior to 1934
     published data were based on imported merchandise entered for
     immediate consumption and merchandise entered for storage in
     bonded warehouses.

RAW CATTLE HIDES AND RELATED SERIES

14 Stocks in all hands, monthly, 1920-43 (Chart 23)
    Unit: one hide
    Sources and Coverage: Through April 1932, Bureau of Census,
    Monthly Report on Hides, Skins and Leather; thereafter, reports of
    Tanners' Council of America. Through May 1932, data were col-
    lected by Bureau of Census from all holders: packers, butchers, deal-
    ers, importers, and tanners. Beginning June 1932, changes in stocks
    are computed by Tanners' Council from wettings of cattle hides and
    movement into sight of cattle hides. Since the latter do not reflect
    fluctuations in holdings by dealers of 'country hides', the computed
    stocks series does not represent total raw hide stocks accurately. See
    series 17 and 18 below. Kip sides excluded.

15 Stocks in dealers' and importers' hands, monthly, 1922-39 (Chart 23)
    Unit: one hide
    Source and Coverage: NBER computations from raw cattle hide
    stocks in all hands and stocks in hands of tanners. See series 14 above
    and 16 below. Represented are all stocks other than those held by
    tanners, subject to limitations of series 14 with respect to omission
    of hides from uninspected slaughter in hands of dealers.

16 Stocks in tanners' hands, monthly, 1920-41 (Chart 23)
    Unit: one hide
    Source and Coverage: Tanners' Council. Includes practically all tan-
    ners (98 percent of industry's output although less by number of
    establishments).

17 Total movement into sight, monthly, 1921-41 (Chart 22)
    Unit: one hide
    Sources: 1921-34, Tanners' Council; 1935-41, Commodity Exchange,
    Inc., N. Y., *Daily Market Report, Monthly Statistical Supplement:
    Hides,* July 11, 1941.
    Coverage: Before May 1932, data derived by Tanners' Council from
    raw stocks in all hands and cattle hide wettings, the sum of
    wettings and the change in raw stocks being taken to represent
    movement into sight. As raw stocks were reported to the census,
    the derived series on movement into sight is considered reliable.
    Beginning May 1932, movement into sight series was estimated by
    adding federally inspected slaughter, net imports, and tanners' re-
    ceipts of country hides, that is, hides other than those from federally
    inspected slaughter (by farmers, local butchers, or farm death of
    animals not slaughtered). Since country hides are also received and
    held by many intermediaries before they reach tanners, the esti-
    mate of movement into sight is deficient with respect to changes in
    these holdings. This class of stocks amounted to about 10 percent
    of total raw stocks during census period. The implicit assumption
    that such stocks remain constant means that whenever they increase,

both movement into sight and raw stocks will be somewhat lower than they should be. The reverse is true when dealers' stocks of raw hides from uninspected slaughter decrease.

Data are for cattle hides only, since kip sides are not distinguished from calf skins in basic series.

18 Wettings, monthly, 1921-44 (Charts 20, 22-23)
Unit: one hide
Sources: 1921, computed by NBER from data supplied by Tanners' Council; 1922-34 and 1941-44, Tanners' Council; 1935-40, see series 17 above.
Coverage: Before April 1927, Tanners' Council computed the series by determining the sum of the change in stocks in process and production of all cattle hide leathers, both reported to Bureau of Census. To eliminate kip sides wettings, 10 percent was deducted from total wettings (the average relation of reported wettings of kips to total wettings as reported to the census in 1928-30). Data for 1921 computed by NBER by deducting 10 percent from Tanners' Council figures for 'all wettings'. April 1927-32, series compiled by census from reports from the whole industry. Since 1932, wettings collected by the Council from almost all tanners raised by industry total.

19 Net imports, monthly, 1919-41 (Chart 21)
Unit: one hide
Source and Coverage: Tanners' Council; data compiled from reports of Department of Commerce. Prior to 1934, net imports equal total imports minus exports and reexports; beginning 1934, net imports equal imports for consumption only (excluding hides earmarked for reexport), minus exports.

20 Wholesale price of hides, packers, heavy native steers, Chicago, monthly, 1890-1939 (Chart 21)
Unit: cents per lb.
Source: Department of Labor, Bureau of Labor Statistics: through 1931, published in Wholesale Prices, 1931, BLS *Bulletin 572,* p. 34, and previous bulletins on wholesale prices; beginning January 1932, monthly bulletins.
Coverage: Data indicate the price of green, salted, packers', heavy native steer hides, f.o.b. Chicago. Quotations are from *Shoe and Leather Reporter* for first of the month, 1890-96; average monthly price, 1897-1908; first of the month, 1909-13; first Wednesday in month, 1914-17; beginning 1918, monthly average.

21 Cattle slaughtered under federal inspection, monthly, 1907-42 (Chart 20)
Unit: one head
Source and Coverage: Department of Agriculture, Bureau of Agricultural Economics; published in Production and Marketing Admin-

istration, *Livestock Market News Statistics and Related Data, 1947*, p. 34. Data cover number of animals slaughtered under federal inspection, including rejected carcasses. In 1940 such slaughter accounted for about 65 percent of all cattle slaughtered (see figures for federally inspected and total slaughter in source given above).

Retail butchers, dealers, farmers, and establishments whose products are produced and distributed within the state in which they are located are not subject to federal inspection. Government relief slaughter (June 1934-February 1935 and August-September 1936) excluded.

CRUDE RUBBER AND RELATED SERIES

22 Stocks in and afloat for United States, monthly, 1923-40 (Charts 24 and 28)
Unit: long ton
Source and Coverage: Data computed by NBER by adding stocks in and afloat for the United States as published in *Survey of Current Business*, 1932 Supplement, pp. 248-9, and subsequent issues.
a) Stocks in the United States: 1923-26, data compiled by Rubber Manufacturers' Association, quarterly data through third quarter 1924 interpolated monthly by NBER; 1927-40, data derived from end of year stocks shown by surveys of Bureau of Foreign and Domestic Commerce, Leather and Rubber Division, for each year except 1927-29 when a year end stock figure for 1930 was used. To year end stocks are added Department of Commerce figures for total imports. From this total the Rubber Manufacturers' Association consumption figures raised to 100 percent plus reexports are deducted to obtain month end stock figures. Relatively small revisions were required to reconcile estimated monthly stocks with year end surveys.
b) Stocks afloat for the United States: prior to 1926 and beginning September 1930, compiled by Rubber Manufacturers' Association; January 1926-August 1930, compiled by Bureau of Foreign and Domestic Commerce. Stocks afloat for the United States government are included. For January 1926-August 1930 the figures are practically complete; prior to and since that period coverage at least 75 percent complete.

23 World stocks, annual, 1923-27 (Charts 27-28)
Unit: long ton
Source: George Rae, *Journal of the Royal Statistical Society*, New Series, CI, Part II, 1938, Table XV, p. 347.

24 Consumption, United States, annual, 1919-37 (Chart 25)
Unit: long ton
Sources and Coverage: Estimates of Department of Commerce and Rubber Manufacturers' Association; published in *Survey of Current*

Business, 1942 Supplement, p. 160. The Association reports consumption (annually through 1923, monthly beginning 1924) on basis of reports from both member and nonmember companies. The reported figures were raised to industry totals as indicated by data from Census of Manufactures prior to 1926 and thereafter by annual surveys of the rubber industry by Bureau of Foreign and Domestic Commerce. Included in total rubber consumption are all grades of rubber.

25 Consumption, world, annual, 1919-37 (Charts 25 and 27)
    Unit: long ton
    Source and Coverage: See series 23 above, ibid., Table VII, p. 338. Estimated on the basis of net imports into manufacturing countries, adjusted for changes in stocks in those countries where data are available except in the cases of the United States for which available consumption data were used from 1920 on (see series 24 above) and the United Kingdom for which consumption data are available beginning 1935.

26 Prices, London, annual, 1920-36 (Chart 26)
    Unit: pence per pound
    Source: see series 23 above, ibid., Table II, p. 320

27 Acreage yielding rubber, annual, 1927-36 (Chart 26)
    Unit: acre
    Source: Estimated by NBER from Rae, op. cit. (see series 23 above). Annual increments to planted acreage were added to acreage in 1927, allowing for an 8-year lag between planting and maturity.

28 Increment to acreage, annual, 1920-36 (Chart 26)
    Unit: acre
    Source: see series 23 above, ibid., Table II, p. 320

29 Automobile tire, pneumatic casings, production, monthly, 1921-41 (Chart 24)
    Unit: one pneumatic casing
    Source and Coverage: Rubber Manufacturers' Association; data published in *Survey of Current Business,* May 1939, p. 16, and subsequent issues. Coverage of figures from 75-80 percent during 1921-28 to 97 percent 1934-July 1935, and a slightly lower percentage thereafter, according to *Survey of Current Business,* 1942 Supplement, note 1 to p. 161. Data raised by Association to represent industry totals on basis of biennial Censuses of Manufactures.

COTTONSEED

30 Stocks at mills, monthly, 1916-41 (Charts 29-30)
    Unit: short ton
    Source and Coverage: Bureau of Census *Bulletin 135,* p. 95, and subsequent bulletins. All cottonseed mills in conformity with Act of Congress, August 7, 1916.

31 Crude cottonseed oil production, monthly, 1916-41 (Charts 29-30)
Unit: pound
Source and Coverage: Bureau of Census *Bulletin 135*, p. 95, and subsequent bulletins. Data in source, cumulative from August ١ to July 31 of following year, were converted by NBER into regular monthly production data.

32 Cotton crop (Chart 29)
See series 7 above

RAW CANE SUGAR

33 Stocks at ports, monthly, 1890-1940; 1920-44 (Chart 31)
Unit: long ton
Source: Willett and Gray, Inc., *Weekly Statistical Sugar Trade Journal,* January review issues for first segment; weekly issues for second segment.
Coverage: Stocks held by both importers and refiners, but bulk of stock is held by refiners. Includes all sugar after arrival in port and before melting. Sugar purchased but not yet arrived is excluded. The original data were compiled in two overlapping segments: 1890-1940 and 1920-44. The first segment includes stocks at New York, Boston, and Philadelphia, 1890-February 1922. An inconsequential quantity is reported at Baltimore also before 1903. Beginning March 1922, Baltimore is again reported reflecting the establishment of a refinery. The second segment includes cities previously mentioned plus Savannah, New Orleans, Galveston, and San Francisco, and, beginning April 1929, Norfolk.

The original data are for given weekdays nearest the ends of months. The days differ for cities in the first and second segments and change from time to time. Combinations were made to reflect the situation as near end of month as possible.

34 Meltings at ports, monthly, 1890-1930; 1920-40 (Chart 31)
Unit: long ton
Source: 1890-1930, see series 33 above. 1920-40, *Survey of Current Business,* Oct. 1937, p. 17, and subsequent issues.
Coverage: Refineries at four ports, New York, Boston, Philadelphia, and Baltimore; then at eight ports, the foregoing plus New Orleans, Savannah, Galveston, and San Francisco. Monthly totals computed from weekly reports by prorating data for overlapping weeks. Figures for New Orleans are partly estimated.

35 Total supply, annual (year beginning July), 1899-1939
Unit: short ton
Sources and Coverage: Computed by NBER from series compiled by Bureaus of Agricultural Economics and of Foreign and Domestic Commerce; published in *Agricultural Yearbook, 1924,* p. 801, and *Agricultural Statistics, 1940,* p. 143, and subsequent issues.

Series consists of: (a) Cane sugar produced in continental United States

b) Raw sugar brought in duty free from insular possessions: Hawaii, Puerto Rico, and the Philippine Islands; Virgin Islands included beginning 1917

c) Imports: data are for general imports minus reexports through 1932; thereafter imports for consumption; Virgin Islands excluded beginning 1917

CRUDE PETROLEUM

36 Stocks, 1918-41, monthly (Chart 32)

Unit: barrel of 42 U.S. gallons

Sources: Department of the Interior (or predecessor agencies), Bureau of Mines: 1918-30, Petroleum Refinery Statistics, *Bulletins 339 and 367*; 1931-34, *Statistical Appendices to Minerals Yearbook, 1932-33, 1934*, and *1935*; 1935-38, Petroleum Statistics, 1935-1938, *Economic Paper 20*; 1939-41, *Minerals Yearbook, 1940*, and subsequent issues.

Coverage: All crude oil held in United States whether of domestic or foreign origin; basic sediment and water mixed with the oil excluded. Stocks include holdings at refineries, in pipelines, and at tank farms as well as on petroleum producing properties. Except for the fourth category, the data represent exclusively manufacturers' stocks of raw materials held for fabrication. Stocks on producing properties are, however, relatively unimportant. Since petroleum commonly passes into ownership of refining companies when it leaves producing property, pipeline and tank farm stocks are properly included.

A considerable quantity of heavy crude oil in California is included, and from 1924 to 1929 also residual and distillate fuel oil in California. Since then residual but not distillate fuel oil has been included. These are defects in the series since heavy crude in California is not commonly refined while the fuel oils are already refined products. At a late stage in this study, data eliminating these categories were secured. The total series including and excluding California heavy crude and fuel oils are so nearly alike in behavior that revision was not considered worth while. A division of the data at three dates indicates the relative importance of stocks in different categories.

37 Consumption (runs to stills), monthly, 1917-42 (Chart 32)

Unit: barrel of 42 U.S. gallons

Sources: Bureau of Mines: 1917-30, Petroleum Refinery Statistics, *Bulletins 280, 289, 297, 318, 339*, and *367*; beginning 1931, see series 36 above.

Coverage: Both domestic and foreign crude oil but not reruns of

CRUDE PETROLEUM STOCKS IN VARIOUS CATEGORIES, DECEMBER 31
(thousands of barrels)

	1922	1927	1935
East of California			
At refineries	30,671	39,317	50,704[c]
In pipelines & at tank farms	199,038	312,637	218,077
Producers' stocks	8,428	7,536	7,130
Foreign crude held by importers	5,062	84	c
Total	243,199	359,574	275,911
California			
Light	a	20,086	38,944
Heavy crude & fuel oils	a	93,719[b]	61,227[d]
Total	52,509	113,805	100,171
Total Stocks in U. S.	295,708	473,379	376,082

From time to time it was necessary to revise or reclassify crude oil stocks. When the amounts were substantial, two December 31 figures were shown, one comparable with data for the given year and one for the following year. In such cases the NBER distributed the differences between old and revised figures equally over the 12 months of the given year.

[a] California stocks not differentiated before 1923; fuel oils not included until 1924

[b] Includes both distillate and residual fuel oils

[c] Foreign crude oil held by importers included with refinery stocks since 1929

[d] Includes residual fuel oils but excludes distillate fuel oils since 1929

unfinished oils and unfinished gasoline, or consumption of heavy crude and fuel oil.

38 Production, total, monthly, 1913-40
   Unit: barrel of 42 U.S. gallons
   Sources: 1913-15, Elizabeth Boody, Cyclical Fluctuations in the Volume of Mining, 1913-23, *Review of Economic Statistics*, April 1924, p. 88; 1916-17, Geological Survey, *Mineral Resources of the United States*, II, 1917 and 1918; 1918-40, see series 36 above. 1913-15, figures estimated from data compiled by Department of Interior, Geological Survey. Monthly figures for the Appalachian, Lima-Indiana, Illinois, Mid-continent, and Gulf fields, when added, constituted 59.6 percent of annual United States production in 1913, 61.0 percent in 1914, and 67.6 percent in 1915. On the basis of these figures monthly output in the five fields was prorated up to 100 percent of the total United States output of these three years.
   Coverage: Through 1918, figures represent marketed production, i.e., the quantity transported from producing properties, excluding petroleum consumed on the leases, usually about 1 percent of the petroleum brought to the surface. Beginning 1919, figures obtained by combining monthly and annual reports to Geological Survey and

later to Bureau of Mines. Monthly reports of pipeline and other companies, which give quantity of petroleum transported from producing properties, constitute preliminary data. To these figures were added the quantity of petroleum consumed as fuel on the leases and the net change in stocks held on producing properties on the first and last days of the year. Prior to 1919, producers' stocks were not taken into account.

NEWSPRINT

39 Stocks at and in transit to publishers, monthly, 1919-44 (Chart 33)
    Unit: short ton
    Sources and Coverage: 1919-May 1923, Federal Trade Commission; published in *Newsprint Paper Review*, Jan. 1922, and subsequent issues. June 1923-44, American Newspaper Publishers' Association; published in *Survey of Current Business*, Sept. 1938, p. 20, and subsequent issues.

Figures for stocks at publishers were added to stocks in transit to publishers by NBER throughout the period and adjusted as follows:

Farm magazine newsprint data, excluded beginning June 1923, were also deducted from FTC figures, 1919-May 1923; for January-May 1919, lacking separate data on farm magazine newsprint, such figures were estimated on the basis of their relation to the total during June-December 1919. The resulting series for 1919-May 1923 was then multiplied by the ratio $\dfrac{134,576}{176,347 - 2,406} = .77369$ to reduce the FTC figures to the level of stocks reported to the American Newspaper Publishers' Association. The numerator of the fraction is the number of short tons of newsprint held on May 31, 1923 by the 422 publishers reporting to that organization; the denominator represents stocks held on the same date by publishers reporting to the FTC exclusive of farm magazine newsprint.

For June 1923-44, owing to changes in the number of publishers reporting to American Newspaper Publishers' Association, the reported figures were adjusted by NBER to the total of 422 publishers throughout by the use of year to year link relatives for identical publishers. Data for overlapping years were obtained directly from the Association. The reporting publishers accounted for 77 percent of all newsprint consumed beginning in 1937; 80 percent, 1927-36; and 60 percent in earlier years.

40 Consumption by publishers, monthly, 1919-39 (Chart 33)
    See series 39 above

IRON ORE

41 Stocks at furnaces, Lake Superior region, monthly, 1918-41 (Tables 45-48; Charts 34-36)
    Unit: long ton

Sources: Lake Superior Iron Ore Association; published in Bureau of Census, *Record Book of Business Statistics,* Part II, p. 13, and *Survey of Current Business,* 1932 Supplement, pp. 198-9, and subsequent issues.

Coverage: Lake Superior ore, i.e., ore mined in Minnesota, Wisconsin, and Michigan. The inclusion of rail and Canadian furnaces beginning June 1922 affects comparability only slightly. The number of furnaces varies from 341 to 189. The large reduction is due to dismantling of furnaces and elimination of furnaces which no longer use Lake ore.

42 Stocks on Lake Erie docks, monthly, 1918-41 (Tables 45-47; Chart 34)
Unit: long ton
Source: see series 41 above
Coverage: Lake Superior ore only

43 Stocks on Lake Erie docks at opening and closing of navigation, 1887-1945
Unit: long ton
Sources: Through 1928, compiled by *Marine Review* and *Iron Trade Review;* thereafter, by Lake Superior Iron Ore Association. Published in successive annual issues of *Mineral Resources* through 1931, and *Minerals Yearbook, 1932-33,* and subsequent issues.
Coverage: Data are for stocks at opening and closing of navigation, approximately May 1 and December 1.

44 Stocks at furnaces and Lake Erie docks, monthly, 1918-41 (Tables 46-47; Chart 34)
Unit: long ton
Sources: Obtained by NBER by adding series 41 and 42 above

45 Stocks at mines, annual (December 31), 1920-37 (Table 45)
Unit: long ton
Source: see series 43 above
Coverage: Lake Superior ore mined in Minnesota, Wisconsin, and Michigan.

46 Consumption by furnaces, Lake Superior ore, monthly, 1918-40 (Tables 45 and 48; Charts 35-36)
Unit: long ton
Sources: 1918-22, Lake Superior Iron Ore Association, *Lake Superior Iron Ores, 1938,* p. 330. 1923-40, *Survey of Current Business,* 1932 Supplement, and subsequent issues.
Coverage: see series 41 above

LEAD

47 Stocks at warehouses, monthly, 1894-1922, 1924-30 (Chart 37)
Unit: short ton
Sources: see series 13 above
Coverage: Bonded custom warehouses covered. Because data after

1919 are inaccurate, they were not analyzed. The inventory of lead in bonded warehouses, submitted by customs collectors in accordance with a new tariff, revealed that for many years collectors had omitted certain withdrawal data but recorded entries into warehouses. Data from 1919 to July 1930, therefore, do not show the correct movement of inventories. These discrepancies could not be adjusted because complete records are lacking.

48 Imports, monthly, 1894-1933 (Chart 37)
    Unit: pound
    Sources: see series 13 above
    Coverage: March 1894-June 1897, pigs, bars, old, and other in ore. July 1897-June 1900, lead in ore, etc. July 1900-June 1909, lead ore and base bullion. July 1909-September 1922, lead ore, bullion, and base bullion. October 1922-December 1933, lead ore, matte, bullion, and base bullion.

    A major change in coverage occurred in 1897; other changes affect terminology primarily. In 1897 the series pigs, bars, old, and other in ore was split into two series, lead in ore, etc., and pigs, bars, and old. The latter represented only 1 percent of total imports of lead July 1897-June 1899; consequently the lead in ore series is treated as continuous from 1894. The data represent general imports, that is, merchandise entered for immediate consumption and merchandise entered for storage in bonded warehouses.

CHAPTER 11

STEEL SHEETS

1 Stocks made to stock, monthly, 1919-36 (Tables 49-50; Chart 38)
   Unit: short ton
   Sources and Coverage: National Association of Flat Rolled Steel Manufacturers; published in *Record Book of Business Statistics*, Part II, p. 24, and in *Survey of Current Business*, 1932 Supplement, pp. 216-7, and subsequent issues. The Association represents almost all independent manufacturers of black, blue, galvanized, and full finished steel sheets. The reported figures are estimated to represent 60 percent of hot mill capacity of United States in 1919-21, 75 percent in 1925-26, and 59 percent in 1935. No adjustment made for complete coverage.

2 Stocks made to order, monthly, 1919-36 (Chart 38)
   Unit: short ton
   Sources and Coverage: Derived by NBER from total stocks of steel sheets and stocks of steel sheets made to stock; see series 1 above

3 Shipments, monthly, 1919-36 (Table 49; Charts 38-39)
   See series 1 above

4 Production, monthly, 1919-36; quarterly, 1932-43 (Chart 39)
   Unit: short ton

Sources and Coverage: For monthly segment, 1919-36, see series 1 above; annual production for 1933 and quarterly data beginning 1934 compiled by American Iron and Steel Institute, and published in *Survey of Current Business*, Nov. 1940, p. 14, and subsequent issues. Figures for the second segment compiled from reports of firms representing more than 95 percent of the industry's capacity and production. Sheets include hot rolled, hot rolled annealed, galvanized, cold rolled, and all other. The industry includes only processors who are also primary producers of steel. Sales to members of the industry for further conversion are excluded.

The Association's monthly series differs from the Institute's quarterly series chiefly in that it excludes U. S. Steel Corporation and covers fewer independent producers.

The NBER raised quarterly totals obtained from the monthly series for 1932 and 1933 to level of second segment by using the ratio of the 1933 annual total for steel sheet production for sale to the 1933 annual total for steel sheet production (2.2325).

PAPER, ALL GRADES

5 Stocks at mills, monthly, 1918-33 (Tables 49-50)
Unit: short ton
Sources and Coverage: Through May 1923, FTC; thereafter, American Paper and Pulp Association. 1918-22, data published in FTC *Statistical Summary of the Paper Industry*, Jan. 1922, and subsequent issues; 1923-32, *Survey of Current Business*, 1932 Supplement, pp. 238-9, and subsequent issues; 1933 data furnished by *Survey of Current Business;* compilation of series discontinued 1934. Through 1923, FTC data represent practically complete coverage. Thereafter, the figures were prorated to represent complete coverage on the basis of data from Census of Manufactures. The series includes figures on newsprint as compiled by Newsprint Service Bureau, on boxboard as compiled by Bureau of Census, as well as book paper, writing, wrapping, and all other grades of paper. Stocks represent paper at mills only, excluding stocks at terminal and delivery points.

6 Production, monthly, 1918-41 (Table 49)
Unit: short ton
Sources and Coverage: 1918-20, see series 5 above; 1921-33, unpublished data from files of *Survey of Current Business;* 1934-41, *Survey of Current Business*, Nov. 1940, pp. 12-3, and subsequent issues. FTC series, compiled by that agency through May 1923, represents complete coverage of industry. Data obtained from *Survey of Current Business* are based on that series prior to June 1923, and thereafter, on compilations by American Paper and Pulp Association; they have been adjusted to industry totals by distributing Bureau of Census

production figures on a monthly basis in accordance with the movement of the sample data.

Revised segment after 1933 was compiled by Department of Commerce by adding to total paper production excluding newsprint and paperboard, compiled by American Paper and Pulp Association, newsprint production data furnished by Newsprint Service Bureau and paperboard production compiled by Bureau of Census. The revision removed duplication arising from inclusion of kraft board in the data compiled by both the Association and Bureau of Census. Also eliminated were all four- and five-week monthly totals in the case of data obtained from weekly reports, by prorating data for weeks falling in two months. The NBER further adjusted 1934-41 data by raising their level to agree with the totals for census years and with the Census of Forest Products for intercensal years.

NEWSPRINT

7 Stocks at mills, United States and Canada, monthly, 1918-37; 1936-46 (Tables 49-50)
Unit: short ton
Sources: United States figures through May 1923 compiled by FTC; Newsprint Service Bureau for all other. United States data 1918-19, see series 5 above; all other including unpublished revisions furnished by Newsprint Service Bureau.
Coverage: The second segment, 1936-46, includes stocks owned by mills but stored in warehouses. These figures are not separable from stocks at mills. For certain years NBER obtained total stocks by adding United States and Canadian figures. United States and Canadian statistics cover practically the entire industry (see also *Survey of Current Business*, 1947 Supplement, note 3 to p. 160).

8 Shipments from mills, United States and Canada, monthly, 1919-45 (Table 49)
Unit: short ton
Sources: See series 7 above. United States data 1919-21, published in FTC *Statistical Summary of the Paper Industry*, Jan. 1922, and subsequent issues; United States and Canadian, 1938-45, in *Survey of Current Business*, 1940 Supplement, pp. 145-6, and subsequent issues; all other United States and Canadian including unpublished revisions furnished by Newsprint Service Bureau, except revised United States figures for 1922-24 and 1926, furnished by American Paper and Pulp Association. United States and Canadian figures combined into totals by NBER throughout the period.
Coverage: Entire industry is covered by the series.

SOUTHERN PINE LUMBER

9 Stocks, monthly, 1916-29; 1929-40 (Tables 49-50)
Unit: board feet

Source: Southern Pine Association; data for 1916-April 1929 (first segment) and 1929-33 (second segment), direct from the Southern Pine Association; May-December 1929 (first segment) and 1934-40 (second segment) published in the *Survey of Current Business*, 1931 Supplement, p. 63, 1938 Supplement, p. 128, and subsequent issues. Through 1927, stock figures reported direct; thereafter, computed from the movement of production, shipments, and previous stocks. *Coverage*: For 1916-29, figures adjusted by the Association to a constant sample of 192 mills by applying the ratio of actual to 'normal' stocks of the mills reporting in any given month to 'normal' stocks of 192 mills originally reporting. 'Normal' represents the average of stocks during 16 months ending April 1916. A new series beginning in 1929 is based on estimated industry totals (see series 10 and 11 below for description of components). NBER reduced these totals to level of the 1916-29 data on basis of the average monthly relationship of the two segments in 1929, the ratio being 0.3563; 1916-28 of earlier segment combined with second segment beginning 1929 into a continuous series.

10 Shipments, monthly, 1916-40 (Tables 49 and 54; Chart 39)
Unit: board feet
Source: see series 9 above
Coverage: First segment data represent 192 mills as described in series 9 above except that average shipments in the first four months of 1916 are considered 'normal'. Reported figures for the second segment are adjusted by the Southern Pine Association to correspond to estimated production totals (see series 11 below). The NBER reduced these totals to the level of the 1916-29 data on the basis of the average monthly relationship of the two segments in 1929, the ratio being 0.3944; 1916-28 of earlier segment was combined with second segment beginning 1929 into a continuous series.

11 Production, monthly, 1916-40 (Table 54; Chart 39)
Unit: board feet
Source: see series 9 above
Coverage: First segment data represent 192 mills as described in series 9 above except that average production in first four months of 1916 is considered 'normal'. Data for the second segment are estimated industry totals based on reports from mills representing 25-40 percent of total production from 1929 to mid-1933, 60-90 percent from mid-1933 to March 1935, 30-40 percent from April 1935 to the end of 1937, and roughly 30 percent since then (see *Survey of Current Business*, 1942 Supplement, note 1 to p. 134). The source adjusted the reported figures to total annual production reported by the Bureau of Census. The NBER reduced these figures to the level of the 1916-29 data on the basis of the average monthly relationship

of the two segments in 1929, the ratio being 0.3941; 1916-28 of earlier segment was combined with second segment beginning 1929 into a continuous series.

OAK FLOORING AND RELATED SERIES

12 Stocks, monthly, 1912-43 (Tables 49-50)
   Unit: board feet
   Source and Coverage: National Oak Flooring Manufacturers' Association, Inc.; published in *Survey of Current Business*, May 1924, pp. 36-7, 1932 Supplement, pp. 188-9, and subsequent supplements. Prior to 1929 coverage is uncertain but is believed to be 90 percent of total oak flooring industry. 1929-33, reporting firms represent 90-95 percent of total production; the rest was estimated. 1934, coverage is complete, and for subsequent years 75-80 percent of the industry was covered by actual reports, the balance being estimated.

13 Shipments, monthly, 1912-43 (Tables 49 and 54; Chart 39)
   Unit: board feet
   Source and Coverage: See series 12 above; revisions made by the National Oak Flooring Manufacturers' Association beginning 1934 could not be incorporated in the figures for earlier years.

14 Production, monthly, 1912-42 (Table 54; Chart 39)
   See series 12 and 13 above

15 Total hardwood stocks, monthly, 1924-40 (Table 50)
   Unit: board feet
   Sources and Coverage: 1924-33, Hardwood Manufacturers' Institute; 1934-40, National Lumber Manufacturers' Association. Published in *Survey of Current Business*, 1932 Supplement, pp. 190-1, and subsequent supplements. 1924-33, data from reporting mills in Southern and Appalachian District adjusted to cover the entire country. This district accounted for about 84 percent of total hardwoods produced in 1929. 1934-40, data based on reports from regional associations were corrected to the trend shown by annual production figures in the Censuses of Forest Products and of Manufactures (except for 1932 and 1933 when census coverage was not considered complete, see *Survey of Current Business*, 1942 Supplement, note 2 to p. 132). According to that source, coverage within the regions varies from 30 to 90 percent, but actual figures from producers for the country as a whole covered 80-90 percent of the total cut during 1934, 70-80 percent in 1935, 50-65 percent in 1936-37, and 50-60 percent in 1938-40. The NBER raised the data for 1924-33 to the level of total hardwood stocks on the basis of the average relation between the two series in 1934, 112.2. While monthly figures for the second segment begin only in 1934, quarterly figures are available for 1929-33, and comparison of the two series shows that they behaved in strikingly similar fashion during the overlapping period.

PORTLAND CEMENT

16 Stocks, monthly, 1911-41 (Tables 49-50)
    Unit: barrel of 376 lbs., net weight, or 380 lbs., gross weight
    Sources and Coverage: 1911-19, Portland Cement Association; 1920-41, Geological Survey and Bureau of Mines. 1911-20, data compiled by E. F. Burchard of the Geological Survey; published in the *Problem of Business Forecasting*, Warren M. Persons and others, editors (Boston: Houghton Mifflin Co., 1924), pp. 160-1. 1921-41, published in *Survey of Current Business*, Sept. 1923, p. 47, 1932 Supplement, pp. 256-7, and subsequent issues. Data through 1920 represent companies with 85-95 percent of total output. Data after 1920 based mainly on reports of producers of Portland cement but in part on estimates. Monthly figures reflect practically complete coverage, according to final annual reports of the producers. Beginning January 1940, data for one plant in Puerto Rico included. Stocks are those of finished cement rather than of clinker.

17 Shipments, monthly, 1911-41 (Tables 49 and 54; Chart 39)
    See series 16 above; data through 1920 adjusted to equal the total for the year as ascertained by the annual statistical canvass by the Geological Survey.

18 Production, monthly, 1911-42 (Table 54; Chart 39)
    See series 16 and 17 above

BATHTUBS

19 Stocks, monthly, 1919-31 (Tables 49-50)
    Unit: one piece
    Sources and Coverage: Bureau of Census: prior to 1928, compiled from reports to the Enameled Sanitary Ware Manufacturers' Association; thereafter, from reports to Bureau of Census. Believed to represent almost the entire industry. Data published in *Record Book of Business Statistics*, Part II, pp. 36 ff., and *Survey of Current Business*, 1932 Supplement, pp. 206 ff. Discontinued after 1931.

20 Shipments, monthly, 1917-31 (Table 49)
    See series 19 above

LAVATORIES

21 Stocks, monthly, 1919-31 (Tables 49-50)
    See series 19 above

22 Shipments, monthly, 1917-31 (Table 49)
    See series 19 above

KITCHEN SINKS

23 Stocks, monthly, 1919-31 (Tables 49-50)
    See series 19 above

24 Shipments, monthly, 1917-31 (Table 49)
    See series 19 above

MISCELLANEOUS ENAMELED SANITARY WARE

25 Stocks, monthly, 1919-31 (Tables 49-50)
    See series 19 above

26 Shipments, monthly, 1917-31 (Table 49)
    See series 19 above

GASOLINE

27 Stocks at refineries, monthly, 1917-40; 1932-40 (Tables 49-50)
    Unit and Sources: see Ch. 10, series 36 and 37
    Coverage: 1917-May 1923, stocks at all refineries. June 1923-31,
    stocks at all refineries east of California plus refiners' and marketers'
    stocks on the Pacific Coast, excluding negligible quantities of nat-
    ural gasoline. Overlapping data for June 1923-December 1924 per-
    mitted a splicing of this segment with earlier data. The earlier seg-
    ment was 92.1 percent of the later in the period common to both.
    1932-40, stocks at refineries and bulk terminals and, from 1933, stocks
    in pipelines and in transit. The NBER made minor revisions in
    1932-34 to take account of year end adjustments in the source.

28 Refinery production, monthly, 1917-40 (Table 49)
    Unit and Sources: see Ch. 10, series 36 and 37
    Coverage: Complete output of refineries in operation. The output
    of natural gasoline, though partly blended to make it stable, is in-
    cluded with straight run gasoline. Although gasoline is produced
    by three methods, 'straight run', 'cracked', and 'natural gasoline
    blended', the final product is generally a blend of any two or all
    three types.

LUBRICANTS

29 Stocks at refineries, monthly, 1917-27; 1921-43 (Tables 49-50)
    Unit and Sources: see Ch. 10, series 36 and 37
    Coverage: Beginning June 1923, figures for California include mar-
    keters' and some previously unreported refinery stocks. In December
    1923 these amounted to 360,000 out of a total of 710,000 barrels of
    California stock. Applying this ratio, California marketers' stocks
    were estimated for each month, June 1923-27, and subtracted from
    the total for United States; the result yielded information for the
    first segment through 1927. The second segment was then extra-
    polated to 1921, using the ratio of overlapping data for June 1923-
    May 1924.

30 Production, monthly, 1917-40 (Table 49)
    Unit and Sources: see Ch. 10, series 36 and 37
    Coverage: Entire output of refineries in operation

PIG IRON

31 Stocks at merchant furnaces, monthly, 1919-26 (Tables 49-50)
    Unit: long ton

Source and Coverage: American Pig Iron Association; published in the *Record Book of Business Statistics,* Part II. Monthly reports from 94 to 131 stacks which represent the following percentages of total merchant pig iron production, as compiled by *Iron Age*:

| 1919 | 77 | 1921 | 68 | 1923 | 51 | 1925 | 55 |
| 1920 | 71 | 1922 | 57 | 1924 | 58 | 1926 | 53 |

The reporting plants are said to account for about 90 percent of production in strictly merchant furnaces, that is, those making iron for sale instead of for further use in their own plants. American Pig Iron Association discontinued its statistical services after 1926, when many merchant furnaces closed and many steel plants engaged in the sale of merchant pig iron.

32 Shipments from merchant furnaces, monthly, 1919-26 (Tables 49 and 54; Chart 39)
See series 31 above

33 Production at merchant furnaces, monthly, 1919-26 (Table 54; Chart 39)
See series 31 above

REFINED COPPER

34 Stocks, United States, monthly, 1909-14; North and South America, monthly, 1919-38 (Tables 49-50)
Unit: short ton
Sources: 1909-June 1914, American Copper Producers' Association; July 1914-December 1914, American Metal Market; 1919-23, Copper Export Association; 1924-38, American Bureau of Metal Statistics. Data prior to 1926 published in *Record Book of Business Statistics,* Part II, pp. 47 and 49; 1926, American Metal Market, *Metal Statistics, 1936,* pp. 248 ff.; beginning 1927, American Bureau of Metal Statistics, *Yearbook, 1927,* p. 10, and subsequent issues.
Coverage: 1909-14, only domestic stocks of refined copper covered; discontinued during World War I. 1919-38, stocks in North and South America.

35 Shipments, North and South America, monthly, 1919-38 (Tables 49 and 54; Chart 39)
Unit: short ton
Sources and Coverage: Through 1923, data compiled by Copper Export Association; thereafter, by American Bureau of Metal Statistics. Data for 1919-25 obtained from American Bureau of Metal Statistics; thereafter, see series 34 above. Exports as well as domestic shipments covered. 1919-23 data converted by NBER from pounds to short tons.

36 Production, North and South America, monthly, 1919-38 (Table 54; Chart 39)

Unit and Source: see series 34 above

Coverage: Total output of primary refined copper. American Bureau of Metal Statistics claims practically 100 percent coverage of copper refineries in North and South America; only one small concern fails to report regularly. Its occasional reports are used as basis for estimating the total.

Areas covered include the United States and Chile through 1925; Canada was added, 1926-38. United States not available separately. Ingot copper produced by concerns that treat only secondary material was omitted, but copper derived from secondary material that passes through the primary refineries along with copper derived from ore was included. Copper produced directly of sufficient purity for market is considered to be refined copper, and included.

REFINED LEAD

37   Stocks at smelters and refineries, monthly, 1924-30; 1930-39 (Tables 49-50)

Unit: short ton

Source and Coverage: Furnished by American Bureau of Metal Statistics; data for second segment published in American Metal Market, *Metal Statistics,* annual issues. 1924-30, all refineries except 3 in United States and Mexico; 1930-39, United States refineries only. First segment was lowered to level of second by .728, the average ratio between the two series in January-March 1930. Stocks include refined pig lead and antimonial lead, which are finished products, and also lead in ore and in process of smelting and refining. During 1930-40, about two-thirds of total stocks were finished products.

38   Ore receipts, domestic, monthly, 1921-40 (Table 49)

Unit: short ton

Source and Coverage: American Bureau of Metal Statistics: 1921-22, published in *Record Book of Business Statistics,* Part II, p. 56; 1923-40, in *Survey of Current Business,* 1932 Supplement, pp. 226-7, and subsequent issues. 1921-22, estimates by Bureau of Census based on figures made available by American Bureau of Metal Statistics. These figures are believed to represent conditions approximately. They were raised to include data for two nonreporting smelters producing pig lead for their own consumption. Since receipts at these two smelters constituted about 18 percent of total receipts in 1923, a corresponding percentage was added to reported figures for 1921-22 to obtain estimated totals. The statistics representing lead content of domestic ore received by United States smelters were based on estimated recoverable lead. According to the reporting source the monthly totals probably understate actual production of pig lead because some lead receipts may have been omitted.

39   Production from domestic ore, monthly, 1929-41 (Table 54; Chart 39)

Unit: short ton

Source: American Bureau of Metal Statistics; published in *Survey of Current Business*, 1932 Supplement, p. 227, and subsequent issues.

Coverage: Total refined lead produced from domestic ore, as reported by primary refiners, plus some production from secondary material passing through primary smelters.

40 Shipments, monthly, 1928-41 (Table 54; Chart 39)

Unit and Source: see series 39 above

Coverage: Total reported shipments of domestically refined lead, including antimonial, for consumption in United States, excluding lead for domestic consumption supplied from stocks of imported refined lead, which have grown significantly since the middle of 1940.

SLAB ZINC

41 Stocks at refineries, monthly, 1920-40 (Tables 49-50)

Unit: short ton

Source: American Zinc Institute; published in *Record Book of Business Statistics*, Part II, p. 52, and in *Survey of Current Business*, 1932 Supplement, pp. 228-9, and subsequent issues.

Coverage: Complete refinery stocks of primary zinc from domestic and foreign ore through September 1929; thereafter, of primary and secondary zinc at primary smelters from domestic ore. The differences are negligible, and figures were used in one continuous series.

42 Shipments, monthly, 1920-41 (Tables 49 and 54; Chart 39)

Unit: short ton

Sources and Coverage: American Zinc Institute: 1920-22, data published in American Metal Market, *Metal Statistics, 1920*, p. 409; thereafter, in *Survey of Current Business*, 1932 Supplement, pp. 228-9, and subsequent issues. Revised data for 1927, 1928, and 1930 furnished by *Survey of Current Business*. Total shipments of slab zinc include domestic deliveries and shipments for export.

43 Production, monthly, 1917-18; 1920-39 (Tables 49 and 54; Chart 39)

Unit: short ton

Sources: 1917-18, Department of Interior, Geological Survey; beginning with 1920, American Zinc Institute. Published in *Record Book of Business Statistics*, Part II, p. 52, and in *Survey of Current Business*, 1932 Supplement, pp. 228-9, and subsequent issues. No monthly data available for 1919.

Coverage: see series 41 above

AUTOMOBILE TIRES

44 Pneumatic casings, stocks, monthly, 1921-41 (Tables 49-50)

Unit: one pneumatic casing

Source and Coverage: Rubber Manufacturers' Association; published in *Survey of Current Business*, May 1939, and subsequent issues.

Coverage of figures from 75-80 percent during 1921-28 to 97 percent 1934-July 1935, and a slightly lower percentage thereafter (see *Survey of Current Business,* 1942 Supplement, note 1 to p. 161). Data raised by Association to represent industry totals on basis of biennial Censuses of Manufactures.

Items forwarded to warehouses, branches, or on consignment basis included, together with stocks in hands of manufacturers, that is, items owned by manufacturers held in the domestic market are considered manufacturers' stocks.

45 Pneumatic casings, shipments, monthly, 1921-40 (Table 49; Chart 39)
Unit: one pneumatic casing
Source and Coverage: See series 44 above; data represent only shipments forwarded to purchasers.

46 Pneumatic casings, production, monthly, 1921-41 (Chart 39)
See Ch. 10, series 29

INNER TUBES

47 Stocks, monthly, 1921-41 (Tables 49-50)
Unit: one inner tube
Source and Coverage: see series 44 above

48 Shipments, monthly, 1921-40 (Table 49; Chart 39)
Unit: one inner tube
Source and Coverage: see series 44 above; data represent only shipments forwarded to purchasers.

49 Production, monthly, 1921-41 (Chart 39)
See Ch. 10, series 29

CHAPTER 12
CRUDE COTTONSEED OIL

1 Stocks, monthly, 1917-40 (Tables 55-56; Charts 40 and 43)
Unit: pound
Source: Bureau of Census *Bulletin 135,* p. 100, and subsequent bulletins.
Coverage: Complete coverage for stocks at mills, refineries, consuming establishments, and in transit to refiners and consumers. The Bureau of Census could not estimate the typical percentage distribution between stocks at refineries and at consuming establishments since the majority of refineries are also consumers. For the few refineries not consumers, data on month end stocks were not compiled separately.

2 Production, monthly, 1916-41 (Tables 55-56; Charts 40-41, and 43)
See Ch. 10, series 31

REFINED COTTONSEED OIL

3 Stocks, monthly, 1917-42 (Tables 55-56; Charts 40 and 43)
Unit and Source: see series 1 above

Coverage: Stocks at refineries and consuming establishments, in warehouses, or in transit to refiners and consumers covered. Excluded are quantities held by small occasional users, accounting for a minor part of total stocks.

4 Production, monthly, 1916-41 (Table 56; Charts 40-41, and 43)
Unit: pound
Source and Coverage: Cotton Production and Distribution, Bureau of Census *Bulletin 140*, p. 91; *156*, p. 60, and *Survey of Current Business,* 1932 Supplement, pp. 136-7, and subsequent issues. Coverage complete for cottonseed oil refineries. Original data, cumulative from August 1 until July 31 of the following year, were converted by NBER into monthly data through 1922.

5 Cotton crop, annual, 1866-1940 (Chart 41)
See Ch. 10, series 7

PORK, LARD, AND BEEF

6 Cold storage holdings of pork, monthly, 1916-40 (Tables 55-56; Chart 44)
Unit: pound
Source: Department of Agriculture; published in War Food Administration, *Livestock, Meats, and Wool Market Statistics and Related Data, 1943,* pp. 51 f.
Coverage: 98 percent complete; stocks of meat purchased for government account under the emergency hog control program in certain months of 1933, 1934, and 1935 excluded. Pork includes frozen, dry salt, pickled, and cured pork, and pork in process of cure, in public warehouses and in packing plants.

7 Cold storage holdings of lard, monthly, 1916-40 (Tables 55-56; Chart 44)
Unit and Source: see series 6 above
Coverage: Lard includes all prime steam, kettle rendered, neutral, other pure lards, and rendered pork fat, in public warehouses and in packing plants; lard substitutes or lard compounds excluded.

8 Cold storage holdings of beef and veal, monthly, 1916-43 (Tables 55-56; Chart 44)
Unit and Source: see series 6 above
Coverage: Beef includes beef and veal frozen, cured, and in process of cure in public warehouses and packing plants. Stocks of meat from drought-stricken livestock purchased for government account in certain months of 1934 and 1935 excluded.

9 Pork, frozen or placed in cure in meat packing establishments, monthly, 1919-36 (Tables 56-58; Charts 44-46)
Unit: pound
Source: Bureau of Agricultural Economics; data for 1919-33 published in Cold Storage Holdings, Department of Agriculture *Statis-*

tical Bulletin 48, pp. 22-4; 1934-36, *Crops and Markets*. Includes frozen, dry salt placed in cure, and pickled placed in cure at packing plants; data totaled by NBER.

10   Beef, frozen or placed in cure in meat packing establishments, monthly, 1919-36 (Tables 56-58; Charts 44-46)
Unit and Source: See series 9 above, *Statistical Bulletin 48*, pp. 19-20.
Coverage: Series for frozen beef and beef placed in cure at packing plants totaled by NBER.

11   Lard production from federally inspected slaughter, monthly, 1919-24; 1921-40 (Tables 56-58; Charts 44-46)
Unit: pound
Sources and Coverage: Department of Agriculture: 1919-24, published in *Survey of Current Business*, March 1924, p. 54, and Feb. 1925, p. 99; 1921-40, Agricultural Marketing Service, *Livestock, Meats, and Wool Market Statistics and Related Data, 1939*, p. 95, and *Survey of Current Business*, Oct. 1940, p. 44. 1919-24, data represent production of identical firms which in 1921 produced about 79 percent of total lard production as estimated by the Bureau of Agricultural Economics and which, on the average, accounted for about 68 percent of total production during that period. 1921-40, data represent the estimated production of lard obtained by applying the average yield per hog at plants that regularly report their production to Agricultural Marketing Service to the number of animals passed for food. Figures are on the average 66 percent of total estimated production, rising to 72 percent of the total in 1923, 1928, and 1929, and falling to 52 percent in 1935 (see *Agricultural Statistics, 1942*, Table 530, p. 409).

12   Hogs slaughtered, monthly, commercial, 1879-1906; under federal inspection, 1907-43 (Table 57; Chart 45)
Unit: one hog
Source and Coverage: Department of Agriculture; data published by War Food Administration in *Livestock, Meats, and Wool Market Statistics and Related Data, 1943*, p. 32. Prior to 1907, commercial annual slaughter estimated by Bureau of Agricultural Economics on the basis of total eastern and western slaughter. These data were interpolated monthly on the basis of monthly western slaughter and records of receipts at eastern seaboard markets. Federally inspected slaughter averages approximately 62 percent of total slaughter, which includes noninspected wholesale, retail, and farm slaughter. Purchases under the government emergency hog production control program between August 22 and October 7, 1933 were added to the number slaughtered in September 1933 by NBER. This figure is available in *Agricultural Statistics, 1942*, p. 404.

13 Cattle slaughtered under federal inspection, monthly, 1907-43 (Table 57; Charts 45 and 47)
See Ch. 10, series 21

INEDIBLE TALLOW

14 Stocks at factories and warehouses, quarterly, 1919-44 (Tables 55-56; Chart 50)
Unit: pound
Source: Bureau of Census, *Animal and Vegetable Fats and Oils: Calendar Years 1919 to 1923*, p. 16, and subsequent issues.
Coverage: Practically complete; stocks are quantities held by producers, by factory consumers, and in public storage at the end of each quarter.

15 Production, quarterly, 1919-44 (Tables 56 and 59; Charts 47, 49-50)
Unit and Source: see series 14 above, ibid., p. 8
Coverage: Factory production only

16 Production by meat packers, annual, 1914-27 (Table 59)
Unit: pound
Source: L. B. Zapoleon, *Fats and Oils Studies, 3* (Stanford University, Food Research Institute, Dec. 1929), p. 107.

17 Production by other producers, annual, 1914-27 (Table 59)
See series 16 above

18 Wholesale price, monthly, 1918-41 (Chart 48)
Unit: cents per pound
Source: BLS bulletins on wholesale prices; see Ch. 10, series 20.
Coverage: 1918-October 1923, the average of the range of prices on Fridays of a month; thereafter, average range of prices on Tuesdays of a month. Quotations refer to 'packer's prime', f. o. b. Chicago.

19 Ratio of inedible tallow to meat production, annual, 1918-40 (Chart 48)
Unit: percent
Source and Coverage: Computed by NBER from series on inedible tallow and meat production. For tallow, see series 14 and 15 above. Meat production was obtained by NBER by combining the series on beef, veal, and lamb and mutton production estimated by Bureau of Agricultural Economics from its estimates of total slaughter of cattle, calves, sheep and lambs (see *Agricultural Statistics, 1942*, p. 444). Animals slaughtered under the emergency government relief purchase program in 1934 and 1935 excluded.

LINSEED OIL

20 Stocks at factories and warehouses, quarterly, 1919-42 (Tables 55-56; Charts 54-56)
Unit and Source: see series 14 above
Coverage: Practically complete; stocks are quantities held at factories

and in public storage, factory holdings accounting for the majority
of stocks. The data may in some instances include imports not withdrawn from bonded warehouses during the quarter.

21 Shipments, quarterly, 1919-42 (Charts 52-53, and 55)
    Unit: pound
    Source and Coverage: Computed by NBER so that shipments equal
    production (see series 22 below) minus change in stocks (see series
    20 above).

22 Production, quarterly, 1918-42 (Table 56; Charts 51-54)
    Unit: pound
    Sources: 1918, United States Food Administration: published in
    Production and Conservation of Fats and Oils in the United States,
    Department of Agriculture *Bulletin 769*, supplement, p. 4; 1919-42,
    see series 14 above.
    Coverage: Beginning 1919, practically complete; data represent only
    factory production.

23 Production from domestic materials, annual, 1923-30 (Chart 51)
    Unit: pound
    Source: Tariff Commission, Report to Congress on Certain Vegetable
    Oils, Whale Oil, and Copra, *Report 41*, 2d series, 1932, pp. 73-4.
    Estimated as follows: from domestic flaxseed output for the cal-
    endar year the estimated amount of seed retained for planting in
    the following year was deducted. The resulting figure was con-
    verted into equivalent pounds of oil at the rate of 33.5 percent oil
    yield. Linseed oil shown for any given calendar year, however, is
    not all produced in that year; part of the seed is carried over and
    crushed the following year.

24 Production from foreign materials, annual, 1923-30 (Chart 51)
    See series 23 above

25 Flaxseed production, annual, 1918-39 (Chart 51)
    Unit: bushel of approximately 56 lbs. net
    Source: *Agricultural Statistics, 1942*, p. 173; data are for years start-
    ing July, the opening of the crop year for flaxseed.

FINISHED CATTLE HIDE LEATHER

26 Stocks in tanners' hands, monthly, 1921-41 (Charts 58-59)
    Unit: one hide
    Source and Coverage: 1921-41, Tanners' Council. The Council re-
    ceived reports from nearly all tanners except in 1921 when data
    were raised by NBER to census levels.

27 Stocks in all hands, monthly, 1920-41 (Tables 55-56)
    Unit: one hide
    Sources and Coverage: 1920-April 1932, Bureau of Census; there-
    after, Tanners' Council. 1920-31 and 1941, compiled from data fur-
    nished by the Council; 1932-40, published in Commodity Exchange,

Inc., N. Y., *Daily Market Report, Monthly Statistical Supplement: Hides,* Jan. 1935, and subsequent issues. Before May 1932, Bureau of Census compiled this series from reports by tanners and manufacturers of leather products. Tanners' Council converted the data into equivalent hides when census data varied as to unit, i.e., piece, pounds, backs, sides, and bends. Beginning May 1932, the series has been compiled by the Council from reports by tanners of stocks of finished leather on hand plus estimates of stocks held by manufacturers of leather products. According to *Survey of Current Business,* 1942 Supplement (note 4 to p. 130), figures reported to the Council by practically the entire industry and adjusted by the Council to an industry basis to make them comparable with the census figures of packers, tanners, dealers, importers, and manufacturers; finished stocks include all finished leather held by tanners, shoe manufacturers, glove manufacturers, belting manufacturers, etc. Data include leather made from kip sides.

28 All cattle hide and kip leather production, monthly, 1921-41 (Table 56; Charts 57-59)
Unit: one hide
Sources and Coverage: 1920-April 1932, Bureau of Census; thereafter, Tanners' Council. 1921-34, data direct to NBER from the Council; thereafter, data published in *Survey of Current Business,* 1938 Supplement, p. 124, and subsequent supplements. Census data represent the entire industry; Tanners' Council data are based on reports from almost the entire industry and adjusted to an industry basis.

29 Total shoe production, monthly, November 1921-43 (Charts 57-59)
Unit: one pair
Source and Coverage: Bureau of Census, *Production of Boots, Shoes, and Slippers Other than Rubber in the United States* (monthly). 1922-29, reports of manufacturers represent approximately 95 percent of total United States production; 1930-33, 98 percent; 1934-36, 99 percent; 1937-42, 98 percent. Excluded are rubber soled footwear with canvas and other textile uppers; included are slippers for house wear, barefoot sandals, play shoes, moccasins, and all other not specified above.

EVAPORATED MILK

30 Case goods, stocks at manufacturers, monthly, 1920-43 (Tables 55-56; Chart 60)
Unit: pound
Sources: Department of Agriculture, Bureaus of Markets and of Agricultural Economics. Through November 1920, data published in the *Market Reporter,* June 4, 1921, p. 358, and subsequent issues; December 1920-April 1922, *Weather, Crops and Markets,* Feb. 4,

1922, p. 95, and subsequent issues; thereafter, in *Survey of Current Business,* Aug. 1925, p. 86, 1932 Supplement, pp. 148-9, and subsequent supplements.

Coverage: Figures are based on monthly market reports and apply to all stocks held by manufacturers whether their own or belonging to others; whether on their own premises, in storage, or in transit (unsold) for warehouse consignments; and whether sold or contracted for and not delivered. Data cover unsweetened, unskimmed milk, and represent practically the entire industry.

31 Case goods, production, monthly, 1918-42 (Table 56; Charts 60-61)
Unit: pound
Source and Coverage: Bureau of Agricultural Economics: 1918, published in Dairy Statistics, Department of Agriculture *Statistical Bulletin 25,* p. 159; 1919-37, Edmund E. Vial, Production and Consumption of Manufactured Dairy Products, *Technical Bulletin 722;* 1938-42, *Survey of Current Business,* 1942 Supplement, p. 116, and subsequent issues. Monthly figures for 1918 are incomplete and were raised by NBER by the ratio of the complete to the incomplete annual total, 1.0945. Otherwise the series covers almost complete production of unsweetened, unskimmed evaporated milk in cans sold in cases.

32 Milk production on farms, annual, 1924-40 (Chart 61)
Unit: pound
Source and Coverage: Bureau of Agricultural Economics; published in *Agricultural Statistics, 1942,* p. 462. Data represent estimated total production of milk on farms based on daily average milk production per cow exclusive of milk sucked by calves, and the estimated number of cows on farms in about 22,000 herds kept by crop correspondents.

SHORTENINGS

33 Lard compounds and other lard substitutes, stocks at factories and warehouses, quarterly, 1922-42 (Tables 55-56; Chart 62)
Unit and Source: see series 14 above
Coverage: Practically complete stocks at factories and warehouses, stocks in hands of households, local tradesmen, retailers, wholesalers, or jobbers. Included are the quantities held in public warehouses and some imports not yet withdrawn from bonded warehouses. Importers and exporters sometimes hold considerable quantities of these commodities.

34 Lard compounds and other lard substitutes, production, quarterly, 1922-42 (Table 56; Chart 62)
Unit and Source: see series 14 above
Coverage: Practically complete factory production; considerable quantities of lard, tallow, and grease produced in households, on

farms, and by small local butchers and meat markets excluded. Shortenings are produced mainly from vegetable oils with cottonseed oil predominating.

CHAPTER 14

1 Manufacturers' inventory investment, constant prices, total and 10 groups, Kuznets' estimates, annual, 1919-39 (Tables 61-63; Charts 63-65)
Derived from series 2, Ch. 4. The figures are given in Table 109.

2 Manufacturers' inventory investment, current prices, total, Kuznets' estimates, annual, 1919-38 (Chart 64)
Figures in constant prices (series 1) converted to current prices by use of price indexes from *Commodity Flow and Capital Formation* as revised and extended by NBER. See App. A for description of revised price indexes.

3 Inventory investment in 5 major industrial divisions, constant prices, annual, 1919-39 (Table 63; Chart 65)
Derived from series 4, Ch. 4. Figures are given in Table 112.

4 Total inventory investment and total nonfarm inventory investment, current and constant prices, annual, 1919-38 (Chart 66)
From Kuznets' *National Product since 1869*, Table I 11.

CHAPTER 15

The series studied in this chapter are for aggregate output and manufacturing production. The latter fall into 3 groups: (A) general indexes; (B) indexes of production in 14 groups of manufacturing industries; (C) 57 series representing production by individual industries or of individual commodities.

AGGREGATE OUTPUT

1a Barger, outlay, quarterly, 1921-38 (Table 64; Chart 67)
1b Barger, national income, quarterly, 1921-38 (Table 64; Chart 67)
Unit (1a and 1b): dollar
Source (1a and 1b): Estimates by Harold Barger in *Outlay and Income in the United States, 1921-1938,* Table 11, pp. 114-9, and Table 18, pp. 178-83.

2 Bank clearings outside N. Y. C., monthly, 1919-38 (Table 64; Chart 67)
Unit: dollar
Source: Compiled by NBER from *Commercial and Financial Chronicle*

3 Industrial production index, FRB, monthly, 1919-38 (Table 64; Chart 67)
Base: 1935-39:100
Source: *Federal Reserve Index of Industrial Production, October 1943,* p. 45

MANUFACTURING PRODUCTION

A   General Indexes (Tables 65, 69, and 71; Charts 68-71)

1   Manufactures, total, FRB, monthly, 1919-40
    Base: 1935-39:100
    Source: *Federal Reserve Bulletin*, Aug. 1940, pp. 764-5; April 1941,
    p. 344 (for revised data see *Federal Reserve Index of Industrial Pro-
    duction, October 1943*)

2   Manufactures, total, Y. S. Leong, monthly, 1919-39
    Base: 1923-25:100
    Source: Through 1933, data furnished by Y. S. Leong, National Re-
    covery Administration, Division of Research and Planning (also
    published in *Journal of the American Statistical Association*, Vol. 30,
    June 1935, pp. 370-1); thereafter, by George W. Hervey, Agricultural
    Adjustment Administration, Consumers' Counsel Division.

3   Basic materials, Harvard Economic Service, monthly, 1919-31
    Base: Normal:100
    Source: Through 1928, *Review of Economic Statistics*, Aug. 1929, pp.
    137-9; 1929-31, Harvard Economic Service, *Weekly Letters*, Jan.
    1931, p. 16, and subsequent issues.

4   Durable goods, Federal Reserve Bank of N. Y., monthly, 1919-43
    Base: estimated long term trend:100
    Source: Through 1941, data furnished by FRB of N. Y.; 1942-43,
    published in its *Monthly Review of Credit and Business Conditions*

5   Durable goods, Leong, monthly, 1919-39; same as 2 above

6   Durable manufactures, FRB, monthly, 1919-40; same as 1 above

7   Producer durable goods, FRB of N. Y., monthly, 1919-43; same as
    4 above

8   Consumer durable goods, FRB of N. Y., monthly, 1919-43; same as
    4 above

9   Nondurable goods, FRB of N. Y., monthly, 1919-43; same as 4 above

10 Transient goods, Leong, monthly, 1919-39; same as 2 above

11 Nondurable manufactures, FRB, monthly, 1919-40; same as 1 above

12 Producer nondurable goods, FRB of N. Y., monthly, 1919-43; same
    as 4 above

13 Consumer nondurable goods, FRB of N. Y., monthly, 1919-43; same
    as 4 above

14 Producer goods, FRB of N. Y., monthly, 1919-43; same as 4 above

15 Producer goods, Leong, monthly, 1919-39; same as 2 above

16 Consumer goods, FRB of N. Y., monthly, 1919-43; same as 4 above

17 Consumer goods, Leong, monthly, 1919-39; same as 2 above

18 Consumer goods, excluding automobiles, Leong, monthly, 1919-39;
    same as 2 above

B   Fourteen Industry Groups (Tables 66, 70, and 72)

1   Production of manufactured food products index, monthly, 1919-44

Base: 1935-39:100
Sources: 1919-22, NBER; thereafter, Board of Governors of the FRB. 1919-22, data are based on 15 seasonally adjusted FRB indexes of manufactured food products and lowered to the level of the total FRB index of manufactured food products by using the January 1923 ratio of the FRB to the NBER index, 0.671. 1923-45, *Federal Reserve Index of Industrial Production, October 1943*, and *Federal Reserve Bulletin*, March 1944, and subsequent issues.

2 Production of textiles index, monthly, 1919-43
Base: 1935-39:100
Source: *Federal Reserve Index of Industrial Production, October 1943*, and *Federal Reserve Bulletin*, March 1944: tables on indexes by groups and industries.

3 Production of leather and leather products index, monthly, 1919-43
See series 2 above

4 Paper and pulp production index, monthly, 1919-43
See series 2 above

5 Printing index, monthly, 1919-33
Source: NBER; average computed from reference cycle rates of change of two series: newsprint consumption by publishers and book paper production. For newsprint consumption see Ch. 10, series 39. Book paper production for 1918-20 and 1922-24 furnished by *Survey of Current Business;* 1921 and 1925-33, published in *Survey of Current Business,* Dec. 1933, p. 19.

6 Crude rubber consumption, monthly, 1924-41
Unit: long ton
Source: 1924-33, furnished by *Survey of Current Business;* 1934-41, *Survey of Current Business,* 1938 Supplement, p. 148, and subsequent supplements. See also Ch. 10, series 24.

7 Crude petroleum consumption, monthly, 1917-42
See Ch. 10, series 37

8 Production of metal products index, monthly, 1919-24; 1923-43
Bases: 1923-25:100 (1st segment); 1935-39:100 (2d segment)
Sources: Indexes for first segment furnished by FRB; for second segment, see series 2 above. Data computed by NBER by averaging two FRB indexes: production of iron and steel and of nonferrous metal products, weighted by value added.

9 Lumber production index, monthly, 1919-43
See series 2 above

10 Production of furniture index, monthly, 1923-43
See series 2 above

11 Production of stone, clay and glass products index, monthly, 1919-43
See series 2 above

12 Production of transportation equipment index, monthly, 1919-38
Source: NBER; the weighted average, computed from reference

cycle rates of change, of 7 series; see Sec. C, series 48-54, below.

13 Production of machinery index, monthly, 1923-43
See series 2 above

14 Production of chemical products index, monthly, 1923-39; 1939-43
See series 2 above

C   *Fifty-seven Industries and Commodities* (Tables 67-68, 70, 73-75; Chart 82)

FOODS, BEVERAGES AND TOBACCO

1 Animals slaughtered under federal inspection index, monthly, 1907-38
Base: 1919-21:100
Source and Coverage: See Ch. 10, series 21, ibid., pp. 33-6. Computed by NBER, this index is based on 4 series of slaughter under federal inspection, weighted by their relative importance as indicated by the average value of the animals of each type slaughtered, according to successive Censuses of Manufactures, 1909 through 1929. Weights: cattle, 52 percent; calves, 6 percent; hogs, 33 percent; sheep and lambs, 9 percent.

2 Volume of milk used in factory production of principal dairy products, monthly, 1919-43
Unit: pound
Source and Coverage: Bureau of Agricultural Economics: 1919, computed by NBER; 1920-43, furnished by *Survey of Current Business*. Figures for 1919 derived from the production series published in Department of Agriculture *Technical Bulletin 722*, pp. 63-71; Bureau of Agricultural Economics conversion factors used to convert the various dairy products into equivalent quantities of milk. The series represents consumption of milk in creamery butter, cheese produced from whole milk, condensed and evaporated milk (bulk and case goods), and unskimmed and dried whole milk.

3 Wheat flour production, monthly, 1914-26; 1923-42
Unit: barrel of approximately 196 lbs. net
Sources and Coverage: 1914-26, A. L. Russell; 1923-42, Food Research Institute, Stanford University, California. 1914-26, published in *Survey of Current Business*, Oct. 1922, p. 47; Nov. 1924, p. 121; 1932 Supplement, p. 158. 1923-31, Food Research Institute, *Wheat Studies*, IX, 3, p. 130; X, 4, p. 179; X, 7, p. 285. 1932-42, ibid., XIV, 1, p. 33; XVI, 1, p. 35; XVII, 1, p. 34; XVII, 8, p. 416; XVIII, 5, p. 224; XVIII, 8, p. 364.

1914-June 1920, compiled from records of U. S. Food Administration Grain Corp. and of U. S. Grain Corp.: 1914-16, adjusted to census total of 1914; 1917-20, adjusted to cover 100 percent of rated capacity of the industry. July 1920-26, compiled by *Russell's Commercial News*, prorated to represent total industry "from representative current data". 1923-42, total production estimated by Food Research Institute to represent output of commercial mills included in biennial censuses plus an allowance for 100,000 barrels per month for custom mills and very small commercial mills.

4 Sugar meltings, monthly, 1890-1930; September 1920-41
See Ch. 10, series 34

5 Shortenings (lard compounds and other lard substitutes) production, quarterly, 1922-42
See Ch. 12, series 14 and 34

6 Tobacco consumption, small cigarettes, monthly, 1915-42
Unit: number of cigarettes
Source and Coverage: Treasury Department, Bureau of Internal Revenue: 1915-19, published in Standard Statistics Co., Inc., Standard Trade and Securities, *Standard Statistical Bulletin, Base Book,* Jan. 1932, p. 321; 1920-42, *Survey of Current Business,* May 1922, p. 103; Aug. 1924, p. 161; 1932 Supplement, pp. 170-1, and subsequent supplements. Data represent withdrawals from bonded warehouses upon payment of tax for domestic consumption. Small cigarettes are those weighing 3 pounds per 1,000 or less. The figures cover the entire output of that class of cigarettes; up to 1933, small cigarettes were about 90 percent of total cigarette production; from 1934, they represent 99 percent of total cigarette production.

TEXTILES

7 Cotton consumption, monthly, September 1912-40
See Ch. 10, series 5 and 6

8 Total wool consumption, scoured basis, monthly, 1918-40
Unit: pound
Source and Coverage: Bureau of Census: 1918-19, data obtained by NBER by adding series on apparel class wool and carpet class wool from Bureau of Census, *Raw Wool Consumption Report,* March and Sept. 1935 Supplements; 1920-40, *Rayon Organon,* Special Supplement, Jan. 21, 1941, p. 27. Beginning July 1934 census data, reported on a weekly basis, were converted to a calendar month basis by the Textile Economics Bureau, Inc. These figures are considered almost complete through September 1920 and complete thereafter, when allowance was made for consumption by the few manufacturers from whom no schedules were received.

9 Raw silk deliveries to mills, monthly, 1920-July 1941
See Ch. 10, series 12

10 Rayon deliveries index, monthly, 1923-43
Base: 1935-39:100
Source and Coverage: *Federal Reserve Index of Industrial Production, October 1943,* pp. 31 and 63, and *Federal Reserve Bulletin,* March 1944, p. 272. The index, based on data compiled by the

Textile Economics Bureau, Inc., represents seasonally adjusted 3-month moving averages placed at the last month. Its components are weighted averages of rayon filament yarn and staple fiber deliveries (gross) plus imports for consumption (the latter through September 1941). Deliveries are those made by American producers to domestic mills exclusive of adjustments for returns and include all processes: viscose and acetate (the latter partially estimated), cuprammonium, and nitrocellulose (the last discontinued in 1934).

11   Factory employment index, fabrics, BLS, monthly, 1919-September 1942
Base: 1923-25:100
Source and Coverage: BLS: 1919-22 and 1933-39, obtained from FRB; 1923-32 and 1940-42, published in *Federal Reserve Bulletin*, Oct. 1938, pp. 855-6, April 1941, p. 348, and subsequent issues. This index is a composite of indexes of employment in the manufacture of the following textile products: carpets and rugs, cotton goods, cotton small wares, dyeing and finishing textiles, fur and felt hats, silk and rayon goods, woolen and worsted goods, and knit goods. These series have been weighted by the annual average number of wage earners in the respective industries as shown by Census of Manufactures, 1929, and were adjusted to conform with levels of employment indicated by successive censuses through 1939.

12   Factory employment index, wearing apparel, monthly, 1919-September 1942
Base: 1923-25:100
Source and Coverage: BLS: prior to 1923, see series 11 above; 1923-42, published in *Federal Reserve Bulletin*, Oct. 1938, pp. 858-60, Oct. 1939, p. 885, Nov. 1940, p. 1216, and subsequent issues. Method of compilation same as series 11. This index covers men's clothing, women's clothing, corsets and allied garments, men's furnishings, millinery, shirts, and collars.

HIDES, LEATHER, AND SHOES

13   Cattle hide and kip leather, production, monthly, 1920-41
See Ch. 12, series 28
14   Total shoe production, monthly, November 1921-43
See Ch. 12, series 29

PULP, PAPER, AND PRINTING

15   Fine paper production, monthly, 1918-33; 1932-43
Unit: short ton
Sources and Coverage: Through May 1923, FTC; June 1923-43, American Paper and Pulp Association. 1918-20 and 1922-24, data furnished by *Survey of Current Business;* 1921 and 1923-33, published in *Survey of Current Business*, Dec. 1933, p. 19, and 1936

Supplement, p. 128. 1934-43, furnished by American Paper and Pulp Association. The first segment, ending 1933, includes only writing paper; the second segment includes also cover and bristol papers. The figures were raised to levels indicated by Census of Manufactures for the corresponding types of paper.

16 Wrapping paper production index, monthly, 1923-40
Base: 1935-39:100
Sources and Coverage: Through May 1923, FTC; June 1923-40, American Paper and Pulp Association. Data published in *Federal Reserve Bulletin*, Aug. 1940, p. 867, and Dec. 1940, pp. 1309-11. June 1923-33, figures based on a sample of identical mills; thereafter, on a changing sample of mills. Index compiled by FRB as a continuous series adjusted to conform with annual totals of wrapping paper production published by Bureau of Census.

17 Newsprint shipments from mills, United States and Canada, monthly, 1919-45
See Ch. 11, series 8

18 Book paper production, monthly, 1918-33
Unit: short ton
Sources and Coverage: Through May 1923, FTC; June 1923-33, American Paper and Pulp Association. 1918-20 and 1922-24, furnished by *Survey of Current Business;* 1921 and 1925-33, published in *Survey of Current Business*, Dec. 1933, p. 19, and March 1934, p. 50. Data adjusted to census totals to cover entire industry. Figures not carried beyond the end of 1933 because of changes in classification affecting the comparability of the series.

19 Factory employment index, paper boxes, BLS, monthly, 1919-September 1942
Base: 1923-25:100
Source and Coverage: BLS: data for 1919-30 published in Revised Indexes of Factory Employment and Pay Rolls, 1919 to 1933, BLS *Bulletin 610*, pp. 106, 78-9; 1931-34 and 1935-39, BLS releases *6609*, Sept. 1938, and *9173*, May 1940; 1940-August 1942, *Monthly Labor Review*, June 1940, p. 1508, and subsequent issues; September 1942, *Federal Reserve Bulletin*, Nov. 1942, p. 1141.

20 Newsprint consumption by publishers, monthly, 1919-39
See Ch. 10, series 39 and 40

RUBBER PRODUCTS

21 Automobile tire, inner tubes, production, monthly, 1921-41
See Ch. 10, series 29

22 Automobile tire, pneumatic casings, production, monthly, 1921-41
See Ch. 10, series 29

CHEMICALS

23 Ethyl alcohol production, monthly, 1920-41

Unit: one proof gallon

Source and Coverage: Treasury Department, Bureau of Internal Revenue; published in *Survey of Current Business,* April 1925, p. 27; 1932 Supplement, pp. 124-5, and subsequent supplements. Data represent complete coverage of the industry, including operations in Hawaii and Puerto Rico.

24 Fertilizer consumption, quarterly, 1922-June 1941

Unit: short ton

Source and Coverage: National Fertilizer Association; published in *Survey of Current Business,* Jan. 1934, p. 19, 1936 Supplement, p. 78, and subsequent supplements. Compiled from tax tag sales reports of the Commissioners of Agriculture in 11 southern states. These tags, which must be attached to fertilizer bags sold, represent an equivalent number of short tons of fertilizer. Such tag sales as recorded by state officials may be larger or smaller than actual fertilizer sales. Monthly figures are available in the source.

25 Inedible tallow production, quarterly, 1919-42

See Ch. 12, series 14 and 15

26 Explosives, shipments, monthly, 1920-43

Unit: pound

Source and Coverage: 1920-June 1933, Bureau of Mines; July 1933-August 1943, Institute of Makers of Explosives. Published in *Survey of Current Business,* Jan. 1934, p. 19, 1936 Supplement, p. 76, and subsequent supplements. Data cover sales for domestic consumption of black blasting powder, permissibles, and other high explosives, excluding ammunition, fireworks, and nitroglycerin. Believed to represent total manufacture of black blasting powder and permissible explosives, and about 96 percent of industry making high explosives other than permissibles. Monthly data prior to 1926 are not entirely comparable data for 1926 and later years because of varying coverage. However, the entire series was treated as continuous.

27 Linseed oil production, quarterly, 1918-42

See Ch. 12, series 22

28 Refined cottonseed oil production, monthly, 1916-41

See Ch. 12, series 4

PETROLEUM PRODUCTS

29 Gasoline refinery production, monthly, 1917-40

Unit and Source: see Ch. 10, series 36 and 37

Coverage: see Ch. 11, series 28

30 Lubricants, production, monthly, 1917-41

Unit and Source: see Ch. 10, series 36 and 37

Coverage: Total refinery production

METALS

31 Pig iron production, monthly, 1877-1942
Unit: long ton
Sources and Coverage: 1877-1921, F. R. Macaulay, *Movements of Interest Rates, Bond Yields and Stock Prices in the United States Since 1856* (NBER, 1938), Table 27. 1922-42, *Iron Age*, 1st or 2d issue in month. The series represents daily averages obtained by dividing by the number of calendar days in the month. Charcoal pig iron and pig iron made in electric furnaces not included.

32 Steel ingot production, monthly, 1899-1939
Unit: long ton
Source and Coverage: 1899-June 1917, *Iron Age;* July 1917-39, American Iron and Steel Institute; data published in *Iron Age*, 1st or 2d issue in month. The series represents average production per working day (calendar days in month minus Sundays, Independence Day, and Christmas) and includes production of open hearth, bessemer, crucible, and electric ingots.

33 Refined copper production, North and South America, monthly, 1919-38
Unit and Sources: see Ch. 11, series 34
Coverage: see Ch. 11, series 36

34 Steel sheet production, monthly, 1919-36; quarterly, 1932-43
See Ch. 11, series 4

35 Lead ore shipments, Joplin district, monthly, 1895-1928; 1923-41
Unit: short ton
Sources and Coverage: 1895-1903, *Engineering and Mining Journal;* 1904-October 1928, New York Metal Exchange, *Official Daily, Market Report;* 1923-41, compiled by *Joplin Globe,* and published in *Survey of Current Business,* 1932 Supplement, pp. 226-7, and subsequent supplements. Data represent weekly average carloadings of concentrates (about 80 percent lead content) for shipment from mines to smelters in the Joplin district.

36 Slab zinc production, monthly, 1917-18; 1920-39
Unit and Source: see Ch. 11, series 43
Coverage: see Ch. 11, series 41

37 Tin and terne plate production, monthly, 1922-34; quarterly, 1932-41
Unit: long ton
Sources and Coverage: 1922-34, American Bureau of Metal Statistics; 1934-41, American Iron and Steel Institute, 1922-34, published in *Survey of Current Business,* Dec. 1932, p. 20, and subsequent issues; 1934-41, Nov. 1940, p. 14, and subsequent issues. First segment covers approximately entire output of tin and terne plate in United States. Second segment covers only tin plate and represents production for sale outside the industry as reported by more than 95 percent of its members; production for sale to members of the industry

for further conversion is excluded. The ratio of tin plate production to tin and terne plate production in 1933 was 0.934.

38 Enameled sanitary ware shipments, monthly, 1917-31
    See Ch. 11, series 19. Figures used are an average of four series: bathtubs, lavatories, kitchen sinks, and miscellaneous enameled sanitary ware (see Ch. 11, series 20, 22, 24, and 26).

LUMBER AND PRODUCTS

39 Douglas fir production, monthly, 1917-35
    Unit: board feet
    Source and Coverage: West Coast Lumbermen's Association: published in *Survey of Current Business*, Dec. 1922, p. 49; Aug. 1924, p. 119; 1932 Supplement, pp. 192-3, and subsequent issues. Data adjusted to the level of actual production of 124 reporting mills for May 1920.

40 Southern pine production, monthly, 1916-40
    Unit and Source: see Ch. 11, series 9
    Coverage: see Ch. 11, series 11

41 Oak flooring production, monthly, 1912-42
    See Ch. 11, series 12 and 13

42 Production of furniture index, monthly, 1923-43
    Base: 1935-39:100
    Sources and Coverage: *Federal Reserve Index of Industrial Production, October 1943*, pp. 29 and 58; *Federal Reserve Bulletin*, March 1944, p. 272. Based on manhour data for furniture industry; adjusted for estimated changes in output per manhour.

STONE, CLAY, GLASS, AND OTHER CONSTRUCTION MATERIALS

43 Portland cement production, monthly, 1911-42
    See Ch. 11, series 16 and 17

44 Polished plate glass production, monthly, 1923-43
    Unit: square foot
    Source and Coverage: Plate Glass Manufacturers of America: 1925-27, revised figures from Plate Glass Manufacturers of America; 1923-24 and 1928-43, published in *Survey of Current Business*, 1932 Supplement, pp. 258-9, and subsequent supplements. Data comprise practically the entire industry.

45 Face brick production, monthly, 1919-25; 1923-36
    Unit: number of bricks
    Source and Coverage: American Face Brick Association: 1919-25, published in *Survey of Current Business*, April 1923, p. 53, and subsequent issues; 1923-28, 1932 Supplement, pp. 256-7; 1929-36, June 1933, p. 20, and subsequent issues. 1919-25, data are for monthly production of 32 identical firms. 1923-36, data are for average monthly output of 54 identical firms except for 1923-27 when a

varying number of firms, 20 to 30, reported. For these years average output was adjusted to the 54 plant level. Beginning 1929, adjustments were required to allow for discrepancies between machine production of bricks (i.e., the output of bricks prior to burning) and the number drawn from the kilns.

46 Prepared roofing shipments, monthly, 1919-September 1928; 1928-34; 1932-43

Unit: one roof square (equivalent to amount of roofing needed to cover 100 sq. ft.)

Sources and Coverage: 1919-28, Asphalt Shingle and Roofing Association (prior to 1926, Prepared Roofing Manufacturers' Association); 1928-43, Bureau of Census. 1919-28, published in *Survey of Current Business*, Sept. 1923, p. 55, and subsequent issues; 1928-43, Bureau of Census, *Asphalt Prepared Roofing Shipments;* 1932 of last segment, from *Survey of Current Business*, 1936 Supplement, p. 84.

1919-28, data compiled "from reports of 60 to 90 percent of total machine capacity" and adjusted to 100 percent of the industry. 1928-34, compiled from reports of 40 plants "comprising practically the entire industry". 1932-43 segment covers reports ranging from 23 companies in April 1932 to 33 in 1943. The coverage has varied somewhat from over 90 percent in 1929-31 to a low of approximately 85 percent in 1935, and up to about 96 percent in 1941. The differences between this series and the one published for 40 plants are relatively slight.

47 Asphalt production, monthly, 1917-44

Unit: short ton

Sources: see Ch. 10, series 36 and 37

Coverage: Data are for asphalt derived as a byproduct from domestic and foreign petroleum, the larger proportion derived from the latter. Native asphalt is thus excluded.

TRANSPORTATION EQUIPMENT

48 Automobile production, passenger car, monthly, 1913-March 1942

Unit: number of cars

Sources and Coverage: 1913-June 1921, National Automobile Chamber of Commerce; beginning July 1921, Bureau of Census. 1913-June 1921, data published in *Survey of Current Business*, June 1927, p. 22; beginning July 21, Bureau of Census, *Automobiles*. 1913-June 1921, estimated industry totals based on returns from companies accounting for 90 percent of the output; beginning July 1921, reports received from practically the entire industry. Data are for domestic factory sales including units assembled in foreign countries from parts made in United States. Taxicabs are included, but are a negligible part of the total.

49   Automobile production, truck, monthly, 1913-March 1942
     Unit: number of trucks
     Sources: see series 48 above
     Coverage: Trucks include commercial cars, road tractors, ambul-
     ances, funeral cars, fire apparatus, street sweepers, buses, and other
     special purpose vehicles.

50   Automobile accessories and parts shipments index, monthly, 1925-41
     Base: January 1925:100
     Source and Coverage: Motor and Equipment Manufacturers' Asso-
     ciation: 1925-32, published in *Survey of Current Business*, Feb. 1934,
     p. 20; 1933-41, 1936 Supplement, p. 147, and subsequent issues.
     Data represent a combined index based upon the value of sales of
     accessories and parts (original equipment) to vehicle manufac-
     turers and wholesalers, replacement parts to wholesalers and re-
     tailers, and service equipment to wholesalers.

51   Vessels under construction, quarterly, 1910-14; 1918-39
     Unit: gross ton
     Source and Coverage: Lloyd's Register of Shipping; published in
     Lloyd's Register Shipbuilding Returns. Only vessels of 100 tons gross
     and upwards, construction of which has actually commenced, are
     included; vessels for other than mercantile purposes excluded. Series
     represents sum of figures for the four regions, Atlantic Coast, Gulf
     Ports, Pacific Coast, and the Great Lakes.

52   Freight car shipments, monthly, 1919-43
     Unit: number of cars
     Source and Coverage: American Railway Car Institute; published in
     Survey of Current Business, March 1940, p. 16; 1942 Supplement, p.
     172, and subsequent issues.
         "Reported by members of the American Railway Car Institute and
     cover all car builders in the United States. The figures do not in-
     clude shipments (installations) of cars built in railroad shops nor
     for the Pullman Company." (*Survey of Current Business*, 1942 Sup-
     plement, note 1 to p. 172).

53   Railroad passenger car shipments, monthly, 1919-43
     See series 52 above

54   Railroad locomotive shipments, monthly, 1918-41
     Unit: number of locomotives
     Sources and Coverage: 1918-19, U. S. Railroad Administration; 1920-
     41, Bureau of Census. 1918-19, published in *Federal Reserve Bul-
     letin*, Feb. 1919, p. 162, and Feb. 1920, p. 183; 1920-41, Bureau of
     Census, *Railroad Locomotives*, Dec. 1931 and subsequent December
     releases through 1937, monthly thereafter. Data are for steam loco-
     motives through 1919; steam and electric thereafter. Exports and
     locomotives produced in the railroads' own shops excluded.

MACHINERY

55 Machine tool shipments index, monthly, 1925-34
    Base: 1922-24:100
    Source and Coverage: National Machine Tool Builders' Association;
    published in *Survey of Current Business,* 1932 Supplement, pp.
    220-1, and subsequent issues. Data cover the dollar value of ship-
    ments, based on returns of 50-60 firms representing one-third of the
    industry.

56 Industrial pumps (steam, power, and centrifugal), shipments,
    monthly, 1919-33
    Unit: value in dollars
    Source and Coverage: Hydraulic Society; published in *Survey of
    Current Business,* Feb. 1927, p. 24, 1932 Supplement, p. 222, and
    subsequent issues. Data are believed to represent about two-thirds of
    the industry.

57 Woodworking machinery, shipments, monthly, 1919-40
    Unit: value in dollars
    Source and Coverage: Association of Manufacturers of Woodwork-
    ing Machinery: published in *Record Book of Business Statistics,* II,
    p. 41; *Survey of Current Business,* 1932 Supplement, pp. 222-3, and
    subsequent issues. Data are compiled from reports covering about
    50 percent of the total industry. About 27 products are included.

CHAPTER 17

Series numbers refer to the notes to Chapter 10 in this Appendix

RAW COTTON

1 Stocks at mills (Table 76; Chart 72), series 4
2 Consumption (Table 76; Chart 72), series 6

RAW SILK

3 Stocks at manufacturers (Table 76; Chart 73), series 10
4 Deliveries to mills (Table 76; Chart 73), series 12

RAW CATTLE HIDES

5 Stocks in tanners' hands (Table 76; Chart 74), series 16
6 Wettings (Table 76; Chart 74), series 18

LEAD

7 Stocks at warehouses (Chart 75), series 47
8 Imports (Chart 75), series 48

CRUDE RUBBER AND RELATED SERIES

9   Stocks in and afloat for United States (Chart 75), series 22
10 Automobile tire, pneumatic casings, production (Chart 75), series 29

NEWSPRINT

11 Stocks at and in transit to publishers (Chart 75), series 39
12 Consumption (Chart 75), series 40

CRUDE PETROLEUM

13 Stocks (Chart 75), series 36
14 Consumption (Chart 75), series 37

RAW SUGAR

15 Stocks at ports (Chart 75), series 33
16 Meltings (Chart 75), series 34

CHAPTER 18

Series numbers refer to the notes to Chapter 11 in this Appendix

PAPER, ALL GRADES

1 Stocks at mills (Tables 77-81; Charts 77-81), series 5
2 Production (Tables 77-79; Charts 77-80), series 6

NEWSPRINT

3 Stocks at mills, United States and Canada (Tables 77-81; **Charts** 77-81), series 7
4 Shipments from mills, United States and Canada (Tables 77-79; Charts 77-80), series 8

SOUTHERN PINE LUMBER

5 Stocks (Tables 71-81; Charts 77-81), series 9
6 Shipments (Tables 77-79; Charts 77-80), series 10

OAK FLOORING

7 Stocks (Tables 77-81; Charts 77-81), series 12
8 Shipments (Tables 77-79; Charts 77-80), series 13

PORTLAND CEMENT

9 Stocks (Tables 77-81; Charts 77-81), series 16
10 Shipments (Tables 77-79; Charts 77-80), series 17

BATHTUBS

11 Stocks (Tables 77-81; Charts 77-81), series 19
12 Shipments (Tables 77-79; Charts 77-80), series 20

LAVATORIES

13 Stocks (Tables 77-81; Charts 77-81), series 21
14 Shipments (Tables 77-79; Charts 77-80), series 22

KITCHEN SINKS

15 Stocks (Tables 77-81; Charts 77-81), series 23
16 Shipments (Tables 77-79; Charts 77-80), series 24

MISCELLANEOUS ENAMELED SANITARY WARE

17 Stocks (Tables 77-81; Charts 71-81), series 25
18 Shipments (Tables 77-79; Charts 77-80), series 26

GASOLINE

19 Stocks at refineries (Tables 77-81; Charts 77-81), series 27
20 Refinery production (Tables 77-79; Charts 77-80), series 28

LUBRICANTS

21 Stocks at refineries (Tables 77-81; Charts 77-81), series 29
22 Production (Tables 77-79; Charts 77-80), series 30

PIG IRON

23 Stocks at merchant furnaces (Tables 77-81; Charts 77-81), series 31
24 Shipments from merchant furnaces (Tables 77-79; Charts 77-80), series 32

STEEL SHEETS

25 Stocks made to stock (Tables 77-81; Charts 76-81), series 1
26 Stocks made to order (Chart 76), series 2
27 Shipments (Tables 77-79; Charts 76-80), series 3

REFINED COPPER

28 Stocks, United States; North and South America (Tables 77-79; Charts 77-81), series 34
29 Shipments, North and South America (Tables 77-79; Charts 77-80), series 35

LEAD

30 Stocks at smelters and refineries (Tables 77-81; Charts 77-81), series 37
31 Ore receipts, domestic (Tables 77-79; Charts 77-80), series 38

SLAB ZINC

32 Stocks at refineries (Tables 77-81; Charts 77-81), series 41
33 Shipments (Tables 77-79; Charts 77-80), series 42

AUTOMOBILE TIRES

34 Pneumatic casings, stocks (Tables 77-81; Charts 77-81), series 44
35 Pneumatic casings, shipments (Tables 77-79; Charts 77-80) , series 45

INNER TUBES

36 Stocks (Tables 77-81; Charts 77-81), series 47
37 Shipments (Tables 77-79; Charts 77-80), series 48

38 Fifty-seven production series (Tables 82; Chart 82)
See Ch. 16, Sec. C

CHAPTER 19

Series numbers refer to the notes to Chapter 12 in this Appendix,
except when otherwise indicated

PORK, LARD, AND BEEF

1   Cold storage holdings of pork (Charts 83 and 86), series 6
2   Cold storage holdings of lard (Charts 84 and 87), series 7
3   Cold storage holdings of beef and veal (Charts 85 and 88), series 8
4   Pork, frozen or placed in cure in meat packing establishments (**Charts** 83 and 86), series 9
5   Beef, frozen or placed in cure in meat packing establishments (Charts 85 and 88), series 10
6   Lard production from federally inspected slaughter (Charts 84 **and** 87), series 11
7   Hogs slaughtered, commercial; under federal inspection, series 12
8   Cattle slaughtered under federal inspection, Ch. 10, series 21

CRUDE AND REFINED COTTONSEED OIL

9   Crude cottonseed oil stocks (Charts 89 and 91), series 1
10   Refined cottonseed oil stocks (Charts 90, 92-93), series 3
11   Crude cottonseed oil production (Charts 89 and 91), Ch. 10, series 31
12   Refined cottonseed oil production (Charts 90 and 93), series 4
13   Shortenings (lard compounds and other lard substitutes), production, series 34

EVAPORATED MILK

14   Case goods, stocks at manufacturers (Charts 94-95), series 30
15   Case goods, production (Charts 94-95), series 31

LINSEED OIL

16   Stocks at factories and warehouses (Charts 96-98), series 20
17   Production (Charts 96 and 98), series 22
18   Shipments (Charts 97-98), series 21

FINISHED CATTLE HIDE LEATHER

19   Stocks in tanners' hands (Charts 99-101), series 26
20   All cattle hide and kip leather production (Chart 99), series 28
21   Total shoe production (Chart 100), series 29

CHAPTER 21

1   Gross national product and its components, 1919-38 (Tables 84-87) See notes to Table 1

Index

NATIONAL BUREAU PUBLICATIONS ON
BUSINESS CYCLES

I Books on Business Cycles

Business Cycles and Unemployment (1923)   448 pp., $4.10
Committee on Unemployment and Business Cycles of the
President's Conference on Unemployment, and a Special
Staff of the National Bureau

*Employment, Hours and Earnings in Prosperity and De-
pression, United States, 1920-1922* (1923)   150 pp., 3.10
W. I. King

Business Annals (1926)   382 pp., 2.50
W. L. Thorp, with an introductory chapter, Business Cycles
as Revealed by Business Annals, by Wesley C. Mitchell

Migration and Business Cycles (1926)   258 pp., 2.50
Harry Jerome

Business Cycles: The Problem and Its Setting (1927)   514 pp., 5.00
Wesley C. Mitchell

Planning and Control of Public Works (1930)   292 pp., 2.50
Leo Wolman

The Smoothing of Time Series (1931)   174 pp., 2.00
F. R. Macaulay

Strategic Factors in Business Cycles (1934)   256 pp., 1.50
J. M. Clark

German Business Cycles, 1924-1933 (1934)   308 pp., 2.50
C. T. Schmidt

Public Works in Prosperity and Depression (1935)   482 pp., 3.00
A. D. Gayer

Prices in Recession and Recovery (1936)   602 pp., 4.00
Frederick C. Mills

*Some Theoretical Problems Suggested by the Movements of
Interest Rates, Bond Yields and Stock Prices in the United
States since 1856* (1938)   612 pp., 5.00
F. R. Macaulay

Consumer Instalment Credit and Economic Fluctuations
(1942)   262 pp., 2.50
Gottfried Haberler

Measuring Business Cycles (1946)   592 pp., 5.00
A. F. Burns and Wesley C. Mitchell

Price-Quantity Interactions in Business Cycles (1946)
Frederick C. Mills
158 pp., 1.50

Changes in Income Distribution During the Great Depression (1946)
Horst Mendershausen
192 pp., 2.50

American Transportation in Prosperity and Depression (1948)
Thor Hultgren
432 pp., 5.00

Inventories and Business Cycles, with Special Reference to Manufacturers' Inventories (1950)
Moses Abramovitz
672 pp., 6.00

What Happens during Business Cycles—A Progress Report (1950)
Wesley C. Mitchell
304 pp., 3.50

II Books Partly Concerned with Business Cycles

The Behavior of Prices (1927)
Frederick C. Mills
598 pp., 7.00

Recent Economic Changes in the United States (1929)
Committee on Recent Economic Changes of the President's Conference on Unemployment, and a Special Staff of the National Bureau
2 vol., 990 pp., 7.50

Seasonal Variations in Industry and Trade (1933)
Simon Kuznets
480 pp., 4.00

Production Trends in the United States since 1870 (1934)
A. F. Burns
396 pp., 3.50

Industrial Profits in the United States (1934)
R. C. Epstein
692 pp., 5.00

Ebb and Flow in Trade Unionism (1936)
Leo Wolman
272 pp., 2.50

The International Gold Standard Reinterpreted, 1914-1934 (1940)
William Adams Brown, Jr.
2 vol., 1474 pp., 12.00

National Income and Its Composition, 1919-1938 (1941)
Simon Kuznets
1012 pp., 5.00

Financing Small Corporations in Five Manufacturing Industries, 1926-36 (1942)
C. L. Merwin
192 pp., 1.50

The Financing of Large Corporations, 1920-39 (1943)
Albert R. Koch
160 pp., 1.50

Corporate Cash Balances, 1914-43: Manufacturing and Trade (1945)
Friedrich A. Lutz
148 pp., 2.00

National Income: A Summary of Findings (1946)
Simon Kuznets
160 pp., 1.50

Value of Commodity Output since 1869 (1947)
W. H. Shaw
320 pp., 4.00

Business Incorporations in the United States, 1800-1943 (1948)   196 pp., 6.00
G. Heberton Evans, Jr.

III Papers on Business Cycles

*Testing Business Cycles (Bulletin 31, March 1, 1929)
Wesley C. Mitchell

*The Depression as Depicted by Business Annals (Bulletin 43, September 19, 1932)
Willard L. Thorp

*Gross Capital Formation, 1919-1933 (Bulletin 52, November 15, 1934)   .50
Simon Kuznets

*The National Bureau's Measures of Cyclical Behavior (Bulletin 57, July 1, 1935)   .50
Wesley C. Mitchell and Arthur F. Burns

*Production during the American Business Cycle of 1927-1933 (Bulletin 61, November 9, 1936)   .50
Wesley C. Mitchell and Arthur F. Burns

Technical Progress and Agricultural Depression (Bulletin 67, November 29, 1937)   .50
Eugen Altschul and Frederick Strauss

Statistical Indicators of Cyclical Revivals (Bulletin 69, May 28, 1938)   .50
Wesley C. Mitchell and Arthur F. Burns

Commodity Flow and Capital Formation in the Recent Recovery and Decline, 1932-1938 (Bulletin 74, June 25, 1939)   .25
Simon Kuznets

*A Significance Test for Time Series and Other Ordered Observations (Technical Paper 1, September 1941)   .50
W. Allen Wallis and Geoffrey H. Moore

Railway Freight Traffic in Prosperity and Depression (Occasional Paper 5, February 1942)   .25
Thor Hultgren

*Wartime 'Prosperity' and the Future (Occasional Paper 9, March 1943)   .35
Wesley C. Mitchell

Railroad Travel and the State of Business (Occasional Paper 13, December 1943)   .35
Thor Hultgren

Railway Traffic Expansion and Use of Resources in World War II (Occasional Paper 15, February 1944)   .35
Thor Hultgren

*Economic Research and the Keynesian Thinking of Our Times (Twenty-sixth Annual Report, June 1946)
Arthur F. Burns

The Role of Inventories in Business Cycles (Occasional Paper 26, May 1948)   .50
Moses Abramovitz

The Structure of Postwar Prices (Occasional Paper 27, July 1948)   .75
Frederick C. Mills

Out of print.